1983

GHANA'S FOREIGN POLICY, 1957-1966

GHANA'S FOREIGN POLICY

1957-1966

Diplomacy, Ideology, and the New State

BY W. SCOTT THOMPSON

Princeton University Press, Princeton, New Jersey, 1969

For Francis and Loretta Thompson

ACKNOWLEDGMENTS

SINCE THOSE who have assisted him have done so on faith, a young author has far greater debts to record after completing his first study than does the experienced scholar.

No group of people were more helpful than the foreign service officers and civil servants of Ghana. It is a tribute to the high standard of professional ethics and clear sense of the "dignity of the calling" among them that they would prefer that I not mention them by name. Courageous and skillful diplomats like Frank Boaten and Ambassadors K. B. Asante and Major Seth Anthony, however, were the unsung heroes of Ghana's foreign policy, and I do wish to acknowledge with gratitude the interest they and others took in my research. Doubtless many of these will disagree with my conclusions, and will find errors and omissions; hopefully, this book will encourage them to write, in due course, their own judgments of the period, and, more immediately, to set the record straight where it runs askew herein.

The financial support that made this book possible came from three sources: Brigadier E. T. Williams, Secretary of the Rhodes Trust, is twice thanked, first for making special provisions so that I could go to Ghana while still under the Trust's auspices and, second, for taunting me with his judgment that its issue would be the book of a war correspondent and not Oxford's D. Phil. degree. That he was proved wrong on the second count is due in part to that special brand of encouragement he gave. The Graduate Fellowship program of the Danforth Foundation generously financed the second half of my research and writing. The Fletcher School of Law and Diplomacy and, more particularly, my chief, Robert West, Director of International Development Studies, allowed me the time and provided every imaginable assistance to carry out the extensive revisions of my Oxford study. Mrs. Mortimer Parker, my godmother, is also thanked for her innumerable kindnesses.

Three men who held the foreign affairs portfolio during the Nkrumah period graciously and patiently answered hundreds of questions during many long (and usually lively) interviews: Ako Adjei, Kojo Botsio, and Alex Quaison-Sackey. Other Ghanaians who aided me throughout 1966 were Modesto Apaloo and Richard Quarshie; S.I.A. Kotei and his staff at the Padmore Library (as

vii

it was then known); Professor K.A.B. Jones-Quartey; Isaac Bissue, B.F.D. Folson, and A.S.Y. Andoh of the University of Ghana (my home for a year); and Commissioner Anthony Deku, C.I.D., who showed me an important aspect of Ghanaian life.

Many diplomats and officials of other governments and institutions in Accra gave assistance which I wish I could acknowledge more personally. The same is true for those who granted me interviews at the Commonwealth Office, the Foreign Office, the Quai d'Orsay, the United Nations, and the U.S. Department of State. Beyond these, I particularly wish to thank for their assistance Colin Legum, A. L. Adu, Commander Sir Robert Jackson, Governor G. Mennen Williams, David Williams, Dr. Lawrence Fabunmi, the late High Commissioner Isa Wali, and Nana Mahomo.

In both Ghana and Britain many friends sustained my efforts: Patsie and Nigel Fisher, Rup Anand, Erwin Baumgarten, May Beck, Harriet Berry, James Douglas-Hamilton, Captain Tom Foden, Lord and Lady Hartwell, John Heilpern, Ambassador Guy de Keller, Myna Mahendren, and Barry Price.

Many colleagues aided me in interpreting my material and improving my manuscript. Dame Margery Perham suggested the topic in the first instance. The debt owed to my friend and colleague Robert Legvold would be embarrassing to reveal and impossible to discharge. Catherine Hoskyns and Jon Kraus generously shared their own material and ideas with me. Any infelicitous English and logical inconsistencies found in the book appear in spite of the efforts of Frederick Hohler, who labored through the manuscript at its primitive stage, and of Jonathan Small and William Zartman, who did the same at later stages. Zdanek Cervenka, Robert Meagher, Cornelia Mendenhall, Desaix Myers III, William Nitze, Joseph Nye, Uri Ra'anan, Jaime Reis, Nathan Shamuyarira, and Robert West each gave time-consuming and thoughtful advice in the re-working of the original Oxford draft. William McClung, of Princeton University Press, is thanked for his encouragement and, more pertinently, his patience. Mrs. Stanley Krauz typed the entire manuscript, and Gladys Manley and Barbara Fennessy gave additional assistance.

I also wish to thank Dennis Austin, whose own definitive study of Ghanaian politics clearly influenced my book, and J. A. Gallagher, my supervisor at Oxford, both of whom gave me the benefit of their time throughout my days in England. James Watkins sparked my interest in international politics and pointed the way to the academic world. However, it must still be said that no matter how much help he has received, the scholar's first book may well be more truly his own in the final analysis than any future studies. He has walked a hazardous, lonely, but sometimes exciting path, without assistance from secretaries or research assistants until the last stage. In my case, I experienced more harassment than seemed possible and more luck than anyone could take advantage of. But of these three last-named individuals, it is appropriate to paraphrase Dr. Johnson; the notice they took of my labors was early, and therefore kind. Without their encouragement, this book would not have been written.

W. SCOTT THOMPSON

Balliol College, Oxford
August 1967

International Development Studies Program
The Fletcher School of Law and Diplomacy
Medford, Mass., June 1968

PREFACE

THE ACQUISITION of nuclear weapons by the great powers and the independence of some fifty territories which have become minor but sovereign actors in world politics has transformed the character of the international system in the course of the past quarter century. This book examines some of the phenomena accompanying the second development, through a case study of the foreign policy of Ghana—a small, determined state which attempted to enlarge its influence and increase its power.

The widening economic disparity between the northern and southern hemispheres has stimulated much discussion and some action. But the perception that disparities of power in the political kingdom have not been mitigated has been vital to leaders of some of the new states. Possessing no power, several of them, in the first years after independence, became convinced that power could be eliminated as the currency of international politics and that a new pattern of international relations would emerge in Africa or Asia. In 1958 Kwame Nkrumah said that "Force alone is no longer a decisive factor in world affairs," and visualized "a distinctive African contribution to international discussions and the achievement of world peace."

A new, imponderable, "moral" factor had in fact acquired importance. Herbert Butterfield writes that "In this new kind of world the Egyptians can secure a victory, and they can proceed to make changes in the status quo which the West may fail to check, or can only check if they enlist the aid of the moral factor themselves." The game of international politics had not changed: but states previously not entitled to exercise power suddenly did have an important card to play, if they understood it was a card, not a new game. This was particularly true for such small states as Ghana, which did not possess the strategic significance for the great powers that Egypt, for example, had in the Suez Canal, and which enabled that state, as much as the "moral factor," to attain its victory. Those who thought a new game was being played filled the void created by the absence of power with an ideological persuasion which, as William Zartman describes it, "depends on the creation and acceptance of a system of values that denigrates power, inhibits its use, and establishes rights. Because the existence of power, influence, and even domination cannot be denied, it must be disarmed, and the prohibition and rights must be codified into an accepted value construct that can govern action and explain events. This is the role of ideology."

Many of the new states went on to develop formidable diplomatic and military instruments, and became more realistic about the nature of the international system. They came to realize that every state seeks to widen its influence, and they also perceived the distinction between influence and power that Arnold Wolfers makes in his essay "Power and Influence." They sensed that a measure of power, obtained through regional organization, the construction of a bloc of states in world affairs, or the threat of a shift in alignments would be necessary for achieving their ends. Left over from the earlier era, and as a function of continuing aspirations outrunning capacities, was the ideological impulse. In their quest for power, for security, for the confirmation of their sovereignty, and for economic aid, several began practicing what Roger Hilsman, in *To Move a Nation*, has called "troublesome diplomacy." To the West, such ideological clamor from those who formerly had no voice at all has proved irritating. Hilsman writes that "their demands are strident . . . and their methods reckless. Sukarno . . . once argued that reckless measures are the only means that a new and weak nation has for attracting the attention of the great powers and making its needs and demands felt, and there is a point to his argument."

The number of states that practiced such diplomacy is small: Indonesia, the U.A.R., Ghana, Guinea, Algeria, and, perhaps, a few others at different times. Are we talking of policy aims or diplomatic style—and how are we to discriminate between them? The two cannot be wholly separated but, to the extent that they can, it may be observed that the fundamental aims of a great number of the Afro-Asian states, especially those of the five named above, were essentially similar in the past decade and may well continue to be so. Between 1958 and 1968, Ethiopia and Guinea, however different internally, shared basically similar foreign policy objectives. Both sought to broaden their contacts among the great powers in order to reduce their dependence on any one; to increase the opportunity of obtaining economic assistance; to use diplomacy to increase their influence in their regional system; to gain prestige with other Afro-Asian states and, when successful, to maximize the advantages obtained. Indeed, the similarity of their aims was so great that it enabled them to share in the leadership of the most important diplomatic initiative taken during these years—the formation of the Organisation of African Unity.

Ethiopia was most successful in accomplishing its ends. Its foreign policy succeeded in putting Addis Ababa at the crossroads of Africa, increased its influence at the United Nations and its standing among all great powers, and won substantial amounts of aid from several of these powers. A very modest use of ideology in giving voice to African aspirations and a clear sense of the changing patterns of world politics made the Emperor's statecraft brilliantly successful. Ethiopia, however, is not a new state. Well-schooled in the art of survival, Haile Selassie had given careful thought to the interests of the nation as well as of his own regime, and he geared his foreign policy to support them in a style guaranteeing its success.

Elsewhere in Africa, in Guinea, for example, national interests were less well-defined. As a perceptive foreign service officer once observed, when his fellow African diplomats justified a policy by saying it was in their country's "national interest," they were in fact only covering a whim of their leader. This raises another, much debated and important question: to what extent do diplomatic patterns emerge from the nature of the state's internal system? How indeed could an avowedly Marxist-populist revolutionary leader like Sékou Touré espouse in substance the same policies as the Emperor of Ethiopia? The importance of the connection between internal and external politics is not in question; as Wolfram Hanreider states, in his article "International Comparative Politics," to talk about it "means to talk about all the major elements that form the patterns of power and purpose in the domestic as well as the international systems." It does not necessarily follow, however, that the relationship between internal and external politics is fundamental to an understanding of every foreign policy. In the case of Guinea, such an understanding can probably only flow from knowledge of the domestic political structures. Sékou Touré, like the Ethiopian Emperor, possessed an intuitive grasp of what was possible in the Africa of his day and was able to work with him toward the realization of an old ideal, during a time of easing domestic difficulties. Yet on many other occasions, Touré's foreign policy was disastrous, which may have been due to economic and political problems within Guinea. In the case of Ghana, on the other hand, it might be concluded that Nkrumah's foreign policy affected the Ghanaian domestic scene more deeply than the domestic scene affected foreign policy. True, one of the determinants of Ghana's foreign policy was a struggle for power which helped to determine Nkrumah's options, and due note is taken of this struggle—although its origins are not properly at the center of a foreign policy study, particularly in this case.

Accepting the importance of the linkages between power patterns in the domestic and foreign policy field does not logically lead to what has sometimes been considered the corollary, namely that the quality of a state's diplomacy and the nature of its goals are basically determined by the character of a regime, which, as Kenneth Waltz has argued (in *Man, the State, and War*), is a dubious proposition. Ghanaians frequently said that their foreign policy reflected domestic policy, but it will be seen, at least in this case, that the relationship is more complex. It is possible to argue that the quality of Russian diplomacy, from Tashkent in 1965 up to the 1968 Czech invasion, surpassed that of America's and this conclusion would be reached from a judgment of the extent to which each power matched her goals to her capacity, to her will, and to the realities of the context in which her policy operated. But it would be hard to argue that domestic political structures accounted for the difference in the effectiveness of the two policies. Conversely, and more pertinently, Presidents Houphouet-Boigny and Nkrumah did run states of similar size in a manner similar in its autocracy if not in ideology: but the difference in the quality of the Ivory Coast's and Ghana's diplomacy was marked.

Is "quality" as used here a subjective term, and one dependent on a policy's success? If not, how do we determine it? Success and quality, in the first place, are not interchangeable terms. Success is usually an attribute of a diplomacy of high quality but the opposite does not necessarily follow, since international events may fortuitously conspire in favor of or against a particular country. Had the world price of cocoa, for example, risen in the mid-1960's to its level of the mid-1950's, greater success might have attended Ghana's foreign policy; the state could, in that case, have afforded the expansive (and expensive) programs it sought to implement; whereas the known disparity between its domestic economic needs and the extravagance of its policy lowered Ghana's prestige in Africa and among the great powers. The quality of a state's diplomacy and of its foreign policy can be determined by two factors that may be judged with some detachment, namely flexibility in determining strategy—and, ultimately, the goals—in light of the international context, and discrimination in choice of instruments for implementing strategy and attaining goals.

1. The international system is dynamic, so foreign policy formulation is by nature a dynamic process. A regime might advance its own interests, those of the state, and of all those whose cause it espouses, by discarding objectives, as it indeed must if the international context alters significantly or develops differently from what the formulators originally envisaged. In the first instance, then, the quality will be affected by the discrimination with which its authors constantly reformulate their objectives in light of the changing currents of the international system and of the state's capacities for affecting world politics. This depends on their ability to perceive objectively the context in which their policies are to be implemented and the limits of their influence. Professor and Mrs. Sprout make a similar distinction between the "psychological" environment of the decision-maker and the "operational" environment in which his decisions will be implemented.

2. For a foreign policy of high quality it is a necessary (though not sufficient) condition that its draftsmen grasp what is possible; in addition they must be able to implement it. Statecraft is made up of different instruments, and the use of one and not another may prove discordant. In this book, careful attention has been paid to the development and the use made of Ghana's diplomatic service and to the diplomatic coordinating mechanism that must exist somewhere—usually, though not in the case of Ghana, in the foreign ministry. Public speeches and the articulation of a people's aspirations can be a significant diplomatic instrument, but can be self-defeating unless construed as such and thus backed and followed up by organization and coherent policy.

Ideology—the attempt to harness a coherent doctrine to the power of a state—is a double-edged and even more delicate instrument. In the context of diplomacy, ideology may come to be seen as an end in itself, particularly in an area such as West Africa where competition for ideological leadership has characterized the struggle for mastery itself. Yet it is difficult, as this book suggests, to separate an ideology from the power and success of the state-sponsor itself. The other danger lies in the very nature of ideology, which Zartman, in *International Relations in the New Africa*, describes as "a system of internal logic derived from premises which bear a selective, not a rigorous, relation to reality." Marxism-Leninism, the most inherently rigorous ideology still alive, has proved a difficult enough directive for action; ideologies that were expounded in the West Africa of the 1950's and 1960's were arrived at with very litle external rigor. Thus, it was only the aspiration to possess a distinctive ideology that characterized the radical states in this period. As such, "ideology" proved the more confusing in the exercise of statecraft and will be seen here as a clear counterpoise to diplomacy.

We are suggesting that evaluation of the quality of a state's diplomacy and, ultimately, of its foreign policy, may be made without passing judgment on the merits—as distinct from the realism—of the state's specific goal. If such objectives develop a regional following and elicit international respect for the success of their implementation, however controversial they may be, then they will elicit careful attention from the scholar whose only business is to judge whether an ideology, a policy, or a goal is realistic, and does not work against national or regional interests. It is, in any case, the style of the diplomacy and the nature of the foreign policy that interests us, for it is in the examination of these, not in the goals, that we see why some states have had some success and others, possessing the same goals as did most of the new states, had less.

It is now commonplace to ask, as F. A. Sondermann does, whether, at the present stage of the evolution of the discipline of international relations, "we need more data from which to construct theories, or whether, instead, we need more and better hypotheses to guide our search for additional data." Despite the rhetorical nature of the question, it is not self-evident that the types of data we now possess on the behavior of the new states in the international system are adequate for the formulation of hypotheses of much relevance. Speeches, policy statements, and the UN votes, which new methods of data generation and content analysis use, only take us a short way along the path of understanding the decision-making process and the behavior of the new states. Nor is it self-evident that the data we possess on the behavior of older states can lead us to hypotheses that can guide our study of the new members in the international system. When this book was undertaken, no major study of African foreign policies had been published; in particular, we knew little about Ghana's foreign policy despite the manifold references in many studies to its aspirations, and despite the very extensive literature on Ghanaian domestic politics. It seemed important that we have some micro-studies of the behavior of such states as Ghana—in the areas that interested them, rather than in the broader arenas of world politics or in the international conflicts involving these states which interested Paris, Washington, or various research centers. What we need to know is, how, in practice, do these states behave; what does motivate them; how is their foreign policy framed.

This book begins with acceptance of the modest hypothesis that foreign policy-making and implementation are intricate systems composed of many subsystems which are unlikely to serve the interests of the state when they are uncoordinated; that is to say, we are asking how successes and failures in one area of concern affect other concerns. The subject is approached historically, in terms of the state's interaction with its neighbors and its continental aspirations, as well as in its attempts to obtain influence with the great powers or to aid one or more of them. This approach is not meant to suggest an indifference to theory; on the contrary, the objectives in writing this book will be fulfilled if students are better able to undertake theoretical examinations of those aspects of the international system affected by the new states, or better able to construct meaningful theories of the behavior of this new component of the world system.

Beyond this, Ghana's foreign policy is intrinsically important during the years covered. This state, the first sub-Saharan colony to gain its independence, played a larger role in African and international affairs in its first nine years than might be expected from a country of seven million people. Excluding India, none of the successor states in the post-colonial era aroused so many hopes as Ghana, and none came to independence with so extensive a commitment to the development of a forceful foreign policy. On attaining independence, Ghana's leaders pledged to work toward the liberation of the rest of the continent, accumulating immense political capital in making their state the Mecca of African nationalism. Thus pan-Africanism, an historical movement championing the cause of black people, was brought to African soil for the first time.

The movement was brought to a state well-endowed with natural and human wealth. Ghana supplied one-third of the world's cocoa and was its fifth exporter of gold. Its external reserves in 1957 were over half a billion dollars, more than India had at the time; this degree of wealth meant that the government had no pressing need to seek aid anywhere. Ghana also possessed the best civil service in black Africa, with much more than a hard core of talented and well-educated officials. Nkrumah, who had dominated the nationalist movement in the Gold Coast and had worked closely with the British to achieve independence, was the foremost African in a period when the continent was ripe for leadership. No wonder, then, that the Gold Coast had been the "model colony," and that expectations for it were so high throughout Africa as well as Europe.

These were the reasons that Ghana, even as a small state, should have had a considerable impact on world politics—it was, for one thing, a period when the great powers were vying for the favor of the small new states. It also had the framework of the Commonwealth through which to wield influence and, certainly, at the time Ghana obtained independence the Commonwealth was still important. Moreover, as Thomas Hodgkin wrote in 1957, a small state can count in the world "if it represents some principle . . . which is inadequately, or not at all, represented by the 'Great Powers' as conventionally understood. . . . Ghana's foreign policy will be judged, very largely, on the extent to which its leaders and representatives succeed in identifying themselves with the principle of Negro-African liberty. This is less a matter of speeches than of policies." But he warned that to make the foreign policy successful in these terms was likely to be more difficult than it had been to win the struggle for independence. To make the policy successful in any terms came to be seen as more difficult than the leaders had envisaged, and in the ensuing years Ghana became a model of a different sort—for underlining the limits of the influence of a small state, for demonstrating the difficulty of forcing novel ideologies to take root overnight, and for testifying to the risks in pressing friendships upon states with which few links exist.

SOME OF THE ACTORS

Alhaji Sir Abubakar Tafawa Balewa: Prime Minister of Nigeria, 1957-66

Tawia Adamafio: Member, opposition Ghana Congress Party, until 1954; General Secretary, CPP, 1960; Minister of Information, 1960-62

Ako Adjei: Minister of External Affairs, April 1959-May 1961; Resident Minister of Ghana in Guinea, February-September 1959; Foreign Minister, May 1961-August 1962

A. L. Adu: Principal Secretary, Ministry of External Affairs, 1957-59; Secretary to the Cabinet, 1959-60; Deputy Secretary-General, Commonwealth Secretariat, the Commonwealth of Nations, London, 1965

Major-General H. T. Alexander: Chief of Staff, Ghana Armed Forces, 1960-61

H. R. Amonoo: Ghanaian Foreign Service, member of first group; Principal Secretary, M.F.A., for Eastern European and Chinese Affairs, 1962-63; Principal Secretary, African Affairs Secretariat, 1963-66; Ambassador to Ethiopia, 1968

F. S. Arkhurst: Ghanaian Foreign Service, member of first group; Principal Secretary, M.F.A., 1962-65; Permanent Representative, with rank of Ambassador, at the UN, 1965-67

Kwesi Armah: High Commissioner of Ghana in Britain, 1961-65; Minister of Trade, 1965-66.

K. B. Asante: Ghanaian Foreign Service; Principal Secretary, African Affairs Secretariat, 1962-66; OAU Secretariat, 1966-67; Ambassador to Switzerland, 1967—

Ehud Avriel: Ambassador of Israel to Ghana, 1957-60; Ambassador of Israel to the Congo, 1960-61

Nnamdi Azikiwe: Prime Minister, Eastern Region, Nigeria, 1954-59; Governor General, Nigeria, 1960-63; President of the Republic of Nigeria, 1963-66

A. K. Barden: Secretary, Bureau of African Affairs, 1959-60; Director, Bureau of African Affairs, 1960-65

Geoffrey Bing: British lawyer and former MP; Attorney-General of Ghana, 1957-61; Adviser to the President of Ghana, 1961-66

F. E. Boaten: Ghanaian Foreign Service, member of first group; opened

xix

Ghanaian embassy in Moscow, 1960; Director, the Accra Assembly, 1962-66; Senior Principal Secretary, M.E.A., 1966—

Kojo Botsio: Minister of External Affairs, November 1958-April 1959; Minister of State, 1959-61; Foreign Minister, March 1963-June 1965; Chairman, State Planning Commission, June 1965-February 1966

Michael Dei-Anang: Secretary to the Governor-General of Ghana, 1957-59; Principal Secretary, Ministry of External Affairs, 1959-61; Ambassador, Special Duties and Head, African Affairs Secretariat, 1961-66

Hamani Diori: President of Niger, 1960—

Andrew Djin: Treasurer, Convention Peoples Party; Ambassador of Ghana to the Congo, July-September 1960

The Rev. Stephan Dzirasa: Parliamentary Secretary to the Prime Minister and Minister of External Affairs, 1957-60; Resident Minister of Ghana in Guinea, 1960-62; Deputy Foreign Minister, 1962-64

John B. Elliot: Ambassador of Ghana to the Soviet Union, 1960-66

Komla Gbedemah: Minister of Finance, 1954-61

Nicholas Grunitzky: Prime Minister of Togoland, 1956-58; President of Togo, 1963-67

Dr. Félix Houphouet-Boigny: Founder, *Rassemblement Democratique Africaine*; Minister, Cabinet rank, Fourth French Republic 1956-59; President of Ivory Coast, 1960—

Samuel G. Ikoku: Nigerian radical leader; member, Action Group; in exile and de facto editor of *Spark* in Ghana, 1962-66; unofficial adviser to the President of Ghana

Commander Sir Robert Jackson: Assistant Secretary-General, UN, 1947; Chairman, Ghanaian Development Commission, 1957-61; Member and Consultant to Volta River Authority, 1962—

Modibo Keita: President of Mali, 1960-68

T. R. Makonnen: Guyanese-born pan-Africanist; Treasurer, Fifth Pan-African Congress, 1945; Director, African Affairs Centre, Accra; Member of the Board, Bureau of African Affairs

Kwame Nkrumah: Founder, Convention Peoples Party; Leader of Government Business, Gold Coast, 1951-52; Prime Minister, 1952-1957; Prime Minister of Ghana, 1957-1960; President of the Republic of Ghana, 1960-66

Enoch Okoh: Secretary to the Cabinet, 1961-66

Sylvanus Olympio: Prime Minister of French Togoland, 1958-60; President of Togo, 1960-63

Eric Otoo: Member, Ghanaian Foreign Service; Director of Presidential Detail Department, 1964-66; Principal Secretary, M.E.A., 1966—

George Padmore: Author, *Pan-Africanism or Communism*; Adviser to the Prime Minister on African Affairs, Ghana, 1957-59

Alexander Quaison-Sackey: Permanent Representative of Ghana to the United Nations, with rank of Ambassador, 1959-65; President, 19th Session of the UN General Assembly; Foreign Minister, June 1965-February 1966

Georgi Rodionov: Ambassador of the Soviet Union to Ghana, 1962-66

Francis Russell: Ambassador of the United States to Ghana, 1961-62

Duncan Sandys: Secretary of State for Commonwealth Affairs, H.M.G., 1960-64

Diallo Telli: Administrative Secretary-General of the Organisation of African Unity, 1964—

Sékou Touré: President of Guinea, 1958—

William V. S. Tubman: President of Liberia, 1944—

Jaja Wachuku: Minister of External Affairs, Nigeria, 1962-65

Alhaji Isa Sulaiman Wali: High Commissioner of Nigeria in Ghana, 1964-66

Nathaniel Welbeck: Resident Minister of Ghana in Guinea, February 1959; *Chargé d'affaires*, Léopoldville, October-December 1960; Executive Secretary, CPP, 1962-66

Maurice Yameogo: President of Upper Volta, 1960-66

Organizational Listing and Abbreviations

INTER-AFRICAN ORGANIZATIONS

African Group: caucus of African representatives at the United Nations; created by a brief from the first IAS conference; served as the IAS's instrument of coordination, and continued to function after the demise of the IAS

Afro-Asian Peoples Solidarity Organization (AAPSO): composed of political parties and movements in Africa and Asia, including the USSR and China; first conference in Cairo December 1957-January 1958; successive meetings in Conakry (April 1960); Moshi, Tanganyika (February 1963); and Winneba, Ghana (May 1965); headquartered in Cairo

All-African Peoples Conference (AAPC): composed of African political parties and movements; first conference in Accra, December 1958; successive meetings in Tunis (January 1960) and Cairo (March 1961); headquarters in Accra

Brazzaville Group: *see* OCAM

Casablanca Group: political grouping of states with radical foreign policy objectives (Algeria, Ghana, Guinea, Mali, Morocco, and U.A.R.); founded in Casablanca, January 1961; successive meetings of heads of state in Cairo (August 1961) and Cairo (June 1962); headquartered in Bamako; dissolved May 1963

Conseil de l'Entente: Formed in 1960 in Abidjan, Ivory Coast, at initiative of President Houphouet-Boigny, bringing together Ivory Coast, Dahomey, Niger, and Upper Volta. Togo became the fifth member, in 1966

Ghana-Guinea Union: *see* UAS

Ghana-Guinea-Mali Union: *see* UAS

Independent African States (IAS): Grouping of African governments; first conference in Accra, April 1958; successive meeting in Addis Ababa (June 1960); no headquarters established

Key: "P.R." refers to publicity releases of the Ministry of Information

"P.S." is principal secretary, the senior civil servant in Ghanaian ministries

"P.A.S." is the principal assistant secretary

Monrovia Group: political grouping of 20 to 22 states with Brazzaville Group as core, and all other non-Casablanca powers with exception of Sudan and Congo-Léopoldville; founded at Monrovia, May 1961; successive conference of heads of state Lagos, January 1962; dissolved May 1963

Organisation Commun d'Afrique et Malgache (OCAM): in December 1960 12 ex-French colonies met in Brazzaville, forming the *Union Afrique et Malgache* (UAM); these twelve, Cameroun, Central African Republic, Congo-Brazzaville, Ivory Coast, Dahomey, Gabon, Upper Volta, Madagascar, Mauritania, Niger, Senegal, and Chad, became known as the *Brazzaville Group*; the group was transformed in Dakar into the *Union Afrique et Malgache pour Co-operation Economique (UAMCE)* in March 1964; and into *OCAM* in Nouakshott, in February 1964

Organisation of African Unity (OAU): organization of all independent African governments; first conference in Addis Ababa, May 1963; successive meetings of heads of state in Cairo (July 1964), Accra (October 1965), Addis Ababa (November 1966), and Kinshasa (September 1967)

Union of African States (UAS): The Ghana-Guinea Union was proclaimed in Accra November 1958; after its de facto dissolution, it was recreated in Conakry in December 1960 with Mali, as the Ghana-Guinea-Mali Union; in April 1961 it was renamed the Union of African States, its charter being made public 1 July 1961; dissolved May 1963

Ghanaian Foreign Policy Structures

African Affairs Centre: residence of most "freedom fighters" working and living in Ghana

African Affairs Secretariat (AAS): created in May 1961 to coordinate all foreign policy/diplomatic matters pertaining to Africa; located within the presidential compound, Flagstaff House; dissolved in 1966

Bureau of African Affairs (BAA): given legal status in 1959 upon the death of George Padmore, until then Adviser to the Prime Minister on African Affairs, and built upon the foundation of his office; the BAA was by statute a nongovernmental organization, designed to coordinate aid to freedom movements in dependent African territories, although it became headquarters for all nondiplomatic Ghanaian involvements in Africa, and a chief instrument of Ghana's Africa policy

Ministry of External Affairs (MEA): the Ministry of Defence and External Affairs, created prior to independence, became the Ministry of External Affairs in July 1958. In May 1961, African affairs was removed from the MEA's jurisdiction upon the creation of the African Affairs Secretariat, whereupon the MEA was renamed the Ministry of Foreign Affairs (MFA). Following the 1966 coup, it reverted to its former name, MEA, and assumed its former jurisdiction over all foreign policy matters. Otherwise unqualified references to "the ministry" refer to the MEA or MFA.

Ministry of Foreign Affairs (MFA): *see* MEA

CONTENTS

XXV

CONTENTS

I

Opportunities

1957–1960

◦ 1 ◦

INTRODUCTORY PREVIEW

AN AFRICAN became a member of the Legislative Council of the Gold Coast colony as early as 1850. By the time of Sir Gordon Guggisberg's governorship in the 1920's there had been considerable African advancement, certainly far more than in any other African colony. The roots of the nationalist movement go back a long way,[1] although the modern phase began in August 1947 when Joseph Danquah, a lawyer and writer, and other nationalist leaders formed the United Gold Coast Convention. On the advice of Ako Adjei, then a young Accra lawyer (graduate of Lincoln and Columbia Universities), the party invited Kwame Nkrumah to come from London to be its general secretary, a post he accepted after some hesitation according to his own account of the event.[2] His arrival in December 1947 coincided with an economic postwar crisis and with the demand (Dennis Austin has pointed this out) for a share of power by those at the bottom of the educational pyramid, the "elementary-school-leavers."[3] The first major crisis came in February 1948 when large-scale rioting broke out, owing primarily to economic grievances. Twenty-eight were killed, and Danquah, Nkrumah, Adjei, and three others were briefly detained.

Nkrumah was clearly different from the professional men who led the Convention; he had wide support of great fervor from young men organized in youth movements which he soon led, whose members pressed him to more radical action. Step by step events led to a rupture between Nkrumah and the party, and to the founding of the Convention Peoples Party in the summer of 1949. In January 1950 a somewhat reluctant Nkrumah led his followers in "Positive Action" against the colonial regime, after which he was sentenced to a prison term of one year. But within that year his colleagues Komla Gbedemah and Kojo Botsio had organized a victory of the party at the polls: he was released, brought

---

[1] For general background, see D. A. Kimble, *A Political History of Ghana: The Rise of Gold Coast Nationalism 1850-1928*, Oxford, 1963.

[2] Kwame Nkrumah, *Ghana, The Autobiography of Kwame Nkrumah*, New York, 1957, pp. 61-62.

[3] Dennis Austin, *Politics in Ghana, 1946-60*, London, 1964, p. 13. In this section, I have drawn liberally on Austin's account of the pre-independence years.

to the castle, and invited by Governor Arden-Clarke to be "leader of government business," and in fact partner (if sometimes a tense one) in a diarchy that lasted six years.

C.L.R. James, a long-time pan-Africanist, wrote that Nkrumah's successful two-year struggle for power "remains the most systematically planned and executed revolutionary struggle" that he had heard of[4]— but luck was there in great quantities. Moreover, the major struggle prior to independence was not that against the British, his partners in power after 1951, but against domestic opposition, a fact which was to have enormous significance for the way he perceived the world in which Ghana's foreign policy was to operate.

Much of the bitterness in the struggle was centered on Nkrumah's person. Those with whom he had broken in 1949 were not innocent of nationalism, nor had their avowed intentions been different from those proclaimed by the CPP in the 1950's. As early as 1942 Dr. Danquah had written to Rita Hinden: "I do not believe that any economic measures for the 'Colonies' mean anything much in happiness, content, as long as the political power is in the hands of vested interests and not in the people's hands."[5] Nkrumah put it more dramatically, "Seek ye first the political kingdom," but it amounted to the same thing. Nkrumah's popularity and prestige were immense, but he conceded nothing to the old elite, and before long had labeled anyone who opposed him a "stooge" or puppet of the imperialists, despite the fact that it was he who supped at the Governor's table throughout the 1950's. True, his differences with the elite were partly ideological, but it can also be said that he felt insecure in the midst of these better educated men. Nor was he possessed of a character willing to share either credit or power.

An example of this bitter quality of Nkrumah's personal relations during the pre-independence period, in terms of his foreign policy, may be useful. Opposition party leaders had not attended a conference of West African nationalists in Kumasi (in December 1953) because they had been invited as individuals, not as a party. "[The CPP's] charge of anti-nationalism, whatever it means, and of stabbing Mr. Nkrumah in the back is therefore preposterous," the opposition paper the *Ashanti Pioneer* wrote. It suggested that delegates would find the Gold Coast "in a state of near-totalitarianism."[6] Nkrumah refused to alter his position; pan-Africanism was to be his exclusive movement, and the opposi-

---

[4] C.L.R. James, "Notes on the Life of George Padmore," unpublished manuscript, p. 39, writer's files.

[5] J. B. Danquah to Rita Hinden, 17 September 1942, in files of Fabian Bureau, London.

[6] Editorial, *Ashanti Pioneer*, 8 December 1953; John Citizen, "Totalitarianism or Democracy," *ibid.*, 4 December 1953.

4

tion could have no part in it. In fact opposition leaders had had significant experience and interest in pan-African affairs themselves. Many had been active in pan-African organizations in London in the late 1940's, had attended conferences and had close friends in other African states.

The federal-unitary dispute between the CPP and its opponents throws additional light on the future foreign policy of the regime. By 1954 the CPP looked successful. Before the leaders lay the "dazzling prospect" of the "new world of international and pan-African relations," Austin wrote. "It was announced that the party would open an office in Accra from which it would 'launch a pan-African Movement,' and bring about 'the federation of nationalist parties decided upon' [at the 1953 Kumasi conference]. . . . A former editor of the *Evening News*, James Markham, was brought from the Anti-Colonial Bureau of the Asian Socialist Conference in Rangoon to be the secretary of the pan-African office; and the *Evening News* announced that the party hoped 'to call a conference of delegates from organizations all over Africa in August 1955.' "[7] But the opposition had been transformed by the creation, in Kumasi, of the "National Liberation Movement," an alliance of cocoa farmers, chiefs, intellectuals, and rank and file Ashanti, which was formed to resist the CPP and to compel the British to concede a federal structure to the new state which they thought would protect their interests. By the end of 1954 the CPP had to take their threat seriously enough to put aside, once again, their pan-African ambitions.

It was a power struggle in which, as Austin suggests, the position on the central question of federalism could as easily have been reversed. But Nkrumah thenceforth equated federalism with feudalism, bourgeois reaction, and tribalism, since the movement had jeopardized an early grant of independence and had made necessary another pre-independence election. Kofi Busia, an opposition leader and scholar, flew to London to try to obtain a postponement of independence at the eleventh hour; Nkrumah, for his part, began to see the fight against the NLM as the paradigm of his pan-African struggle. He looked back to the three years of effort—1948 to 1951—which had brought him domestic power and assumed that he could repeat this process on that broader map of Africa that had always been his focus. But obstacles appeared by 1960, three years after independence, just as obstacles had appeared three years after 1951 in his drive to independence. Thus, it seemed that he later equated obstinate heads of state, who would not surrender their "petty national sovereignty" (as he called it), with Ashanti chiefs, and thus as candidates for destoolment.

---

[7] Austin, *Politics in Ghana*, pp. 283-84.

The African and International Setting

Ghana's foreign policy obviously did not begin in a vacuum in 1957. Beyond those antecedents in the domestic struggle for power, there were more specific ones as a result of the African and international context. The most obvious and available frameworks for pan-African cooperation, through which Ghana could extend its influence, were the inter-territorial British West African boards—the Examination Council, the Cocoa Research Institute and, most crucial, the Currency Board (controlling the common currency of the four territories), the Frontier Force (uniting the officers and soldiers of these territories), and the Airways Corporation. More important in practice, however, were the several strands of pan-Africanism. There was the "back to Africa" movement of Marcus Garvey, the Jamaican whose followers elected him "provisional president of Africa," and whose writings, with those of the Marxists, were probably the strongest influence on Nkrumah as a student.[8] There was the strand derived from the remarkable career of W.E.B. duBois, who helped to found the National Association for the Advancement of Colored People, and died a citizen of Ghana at the time of the 1963 "march on Washington." His career reached its climax in the last of a series of pan-African conferences, in Manchester. This was attended by leaders who were to find positions of influence throughout the English-speaking black world in the future; it was organized by Kwame Nkrumah and his colleague George Padmore.[9]

Nkrumah also organized a "West African National Secretariat" to implement the Manchester resolutions, and the Secretariat held a conference of its own in 1946, attended by French-speaking delegates as well, among whom was a future Dahomean president. There was a "vanguard" group within the Secretariat, "The Circle," whose members are said to have sworn personal allegiance to Nkrumah.[10] The West African Students Union in London also brought together many of the nationalists of West Africa, and Nkrumah and other Ghanaians held office in this as well.

There was also an indigenous movement in the British West African colonies which developed links between the four territories. As early as 1913, J. E. Casely Hayford of the Gold Coast said: "United we stand, divided we fall. . . . United West Africa . . . shall take her true part

8 Nkrumah, *Ghana*, pp. 35-36.

9 For background of the conference, see George Padmore, *Pan-Africanism or Communism, The Coming Struggle*, London, 1956, pp. 154-70. See also Colin Legum, *Pan-Africanism*, London, 1965, pp. 33-35.

10 For background to "the circle," see Colin Legum, "Socialism in Ghana: A Political Interpretation," in William H. Friedland and Carl Rosberg, eds., *African Socialism*, Stanford, 1964, pp. 135ff.

among the nations of the earth."[11] In 1920 he organized a conference in Accra that brought together fifty nationalists, after which the National Congress of British West Africa was formed. It withered after three further conferences, following Casely Hayford's death in 1930. If these men were "middle-class intellectuals,"[12] they were doing what they could within the context of their period, and Nkrumah was to find but never to admit that at several stages he could do little more.

Indeed, Nkrumah's first pan-African conference in the Gold Coast— that in Kumasi in 1953—was not dissimilar. Its most important result was to bring Nkrumah together with his one-time mentor, Azikiwe of Nigeria. The conference did, however, decide that "the political objective of the West African Nationalist Congress is to establish a strong and truly federal state that is capable of protecting its security from outside invasion and to preserve its internal security."[13] It was largely left to the opposition to note the similarities with the conferences of the 1920's.[14] Nor is it clear that the conference had positive results beyond the Gold Coast; a Nigerian delegate later claimed that he and Azikiwe felt that Nkrumah had summoned the conference mainly to dramatize his own stature on the eve of a Ghanaian election.[15]

As a historical movement, pan-Africanism was concerned with black peoples. Thus in the early foreign policy statements of the Ghanaian government there was the expressed intent of aiding, if only by uplifting the dignity of, the black man everywhere. Black men were from Africa, but what was Africa? Was Nkrumah's pan-African movement, launched from Ghanaian soil, to work for the unity of those black peoples among whom there were racial links, common traditions, and historical associations, as Chief Awolowo proposed?[16] Was the concern to be for West Africa as a unit, as it had been for the nationalist fathers for a generation and, indeed, for Nkrumah himself in his institutional efforts? Or was it to be all Africa, including the Arab states, whose ties with Europe were far closer at this time than with black Africa?[17] Finally, what was to be the nature of the links between existing territories? At Manchester, the need to revise these "artificial divisions and territorial boundaries" which cut across tribes and peoples had been emphasized; but what was to be substituted as the irreducible unit in the pan-African search, if not

---

[11] Kimble, *A Political History of Ghana*, p. 375.

[12] Padmore, *Pan-Africanism or Communism*, p. 128.

[13] *Daily Graphic*, 8 December 1953.

[14] *Ashanti Pioneer*, 4 December 1953.

[15] Interview, F. S. McEwen, formerly treasurer of the NCNC.

[16] Obafemi Awolowo, "Foreign Policy for Independent Nigeria," Ibadan, 1958.

[17] See Ali Mazrui, *Towards a Pax Africana*, London, 1966, Chapter III, "On the Concept 'We are all Africans,'" pp. 42-58, for an interesting commentary on this point.

7

the territories as they stood, within which there were elected governments and emerging elites?

Circumstances determined the answer to some of these questions. Concern for the black man outside Africa could not become an operational part of Ghana's foreign policy, for no mechanism existed through which it could work with these peoples. When Nkrumah rode triumphantly through Harlem in 1958, some commentators foresaw a relationship developing of the kind Israel had with the United States. But American Negro leaders were not ready for this, and in actual practice Nkrumah was more concerned with obtaining aid from the United States for the Volta River scheme.

Most of the London based pan-Africanists agreed that a united West Africa was the goal, and that they had to work within the framework of the existing territories. Nkrumah always argued that his colleagues must think in broader terms, and castigated those who did not do so.[18] He foresaw, however, that the French territories were of critical importance to any plans an independent Ghana could have for building West African unity. Thus he visited Paris in 1947, and both the Ivory Coast and Guinea in 1948, less than a year after he had returned to the Gold Coast from London.

Yet, for Nkrumah, even West African nationalism was an expedient. Whereas for George Padmore, his mentor, an "ultimate amalgamation" of a "United States of Africa" was a distant hope,[19] Nkrumah always saw a union of all Africa as imminent, regardless of the obstacles in his path. To the editors of the Ghanaian press, he was "Kwame Nkrumah of Africa," and this is how he had always seen it. This may be demonstrated by his views on the question of the links with the Arabs, one of the most difficult issues for most pan-Africanists. T. R. Makonnen, one of the most important of them in the 1940's, said in 1966: "We knew —and Kwame would be lying if he denied it—that the Egyptians looked down at us because of our color. Look at their historic policy: look at the color of those hauling the stones of the pyramids, and the color of those with the whips. That was the beginning."[20] Botsio, later the Foreign Minister, wrote that "we were prepared to forgive and forget the Arabs' previous attitude of looking down on Black Africa," although the memory was implicitly there.[21] Indeed, since Ghana was seeking support for the liberation of black Africa, it was logical to seek the help of the five independent Arab-African nations who, if nothing else, were members

[18] Interviews: Ako Adjei; Kojo Botsio; F. S. McEwen, December 1965.
[19] Padmore, *Pan-Africanism or Communism*, p. 379.
[20] Interview: T. R. Makonnen, 20 February 1966.
[21] Botsio to author, 15 July 1966.

of the United Nations. But diplomatic links and alliances are one thing. Nkrumah, however, foresaw organic ties with these states, and foresaw the colonial boundaries disappearing from the entire continent. The political map of Africa he had at the back of his mind was the same as that on the cover of *Pan-Africa*, the little magazine published during the London days. It was the whole continent "from Algiers in the north to Cape Town in the south; from Cape Guardafui in the east to Dakar in the west" (as he later put it);[22] it was the "whole of Africa," a mystical One. To be a strong world power, it could afford no divisions. This was taken seriously enough for him to marry an Egyptian woman he had never met when he was 48—and by the accounts of two of those closest to him at the time (though not at the time of interview), to plan to strike an alliance with the *Räis* himself "in order to supplant him."[23]

Nkrumah's pan-African dream was a bold idea, with immense practical difficulties in its path. Pan-Africanism, however, was not a historically developed and rigorous ideology, but a number of ideas of different meaning to different nationalists. Only the desire that the black man should find justice united its adherents. Thus there was to be an obvious dilemma. Would Nkrumah, once he had a territorial base, deal with established leaders in territories, or with opposition leaders who shared his radical pan-African and Marxist views? He was in fact to try to do both, and both were to fail; they were destructive of each other. It was a dilemma the young Soviet state had in its relations with the Comintern, but among the differences between the two situations one is obvious: international Communism, as a movement, could move forward with the immense resources of an enormous power behind it, or it could stand and wait, because its base was a great power. That the most radical and ambitious pan-Africanist should have the Gold Coast as his base was almost as if Béla Kun's revolution had survived in Hungary, rather than Lenin's in Russia.

Beyond the influences that pan-Africanism, as a doctrine, was to have on Ghana's foreign policy from the time of independence, there were the more practical geopolitical dilemmas posed by Ghana's neighbors. "Canada is more important to the United States than any other single country," Ambassador Livingston Merchant once said,[24] and in a smaller setting Ghana's neighbors were to be more important to it than any other countries for exactly the same reasons. A nation's power is often

[22] "Laying of the Foundation Stone of the Kwame Nkrumah Institute, an Address by Osagyefo Dr. Kwame Nkrumah," Accra, 1961, p. 8.

[23] Interview: Ako Adjei, also CF-76.

[24] Quoted by Prime Minister Lester Pearson, "Good Neighborhood," *Foreign Affairs*, 43, No. 2 (January 1965), 251.

exercised, or dissipated, outside its boundaries in inverse ratio to its distance from a second country; hence it is important that Ghana's relations with Togo and the Ivory Coast (and Nigeria, at a later point) be considered as carefully as its relations with greater, more distant powers.

In a sense, no state was to be more important to Ghana than Togo. The Ewe people were split three ways: between the Gold Coast colony, British-administered Togoland, and French-administered Togoland. The unity movement among them almost equaled in intensity Gold Coast nationalism itself in postwar years. To the French, the demand for Ewe unity looked like a British-expansionist bid, particularly as some of the most noted pan-Ewe leaders were from the Gold Coast colony, notably Daniel Chapman, founder of the movement in 1945, who was later Nkrumah's cabinet secretary. Thus the French and British did not agree to the demands of the Ewe leaders, even for closer cooperation between the two segments of the old German trust territory, administered after World War I half from Lomé (by the French), and half from Accra (by the British). Sylvanus Olympio, then a Lomé businessman who had testified frequently and brilliantly at the United Nations, realized this early, so that by 1951, as Claude Welch writes, "the objective of Ewe unification was subordinated to different goals."[25] Olympio's party had changed its aim from Ewe unification to the reconstitution of German Togoland—the British and French administered trust territory; thus Dennis Austin's contention that the Ewe sought a "homeland," not just a "home."[26]

It was natural for Nkrumah and the CPP to campaign for the permanent integration of British-administered Togoland into their state, for the region had been administered from Accra since 1914, when the Royal West African Frontier Force chased out the Germans in one of the opening battles of the great war. In very few cases, in any event, have leaders resisted opportunities to enlarge their territory, particularly leaders who are sensitive about the small size of their own state. But Nkrumah and his colleagues seem to have misconstrued the nature of the transition of 1951, and used the standard of pan-Eweism to support their claims. Governor Arden-Clarke writes of "twitting" his ministers about their "Gold Coast imperialism" (which he encouraged).[27] In practice the policy was just that, and had only incidentally to do with the reuniting of divided tribes.

In a United Nations plebiscite in 1956, voters in British-administered

[25] Claude Welch, *Dream of Unity*, Ithaca, 1966, p. 83.

[26] Dennis Austin, "The Uncertain Frontier: Ghana-Togo," *Journal of Modern African Studies*, 1, No. 2 (June 1963), 141ff.

[27] Sir Charles Arden-Clarke, "Gold Coast into Ghana: Some Problems of Transition," *International Affairs*, 34, No. 1 (January 1958), 54.

Togoland were asked to choose between continued trusteeship and integration into the soon-to-be independent Gold Coast, and they chose integration. The nationalist leaders in Lomé were convinced that the election was rigged and that the question was loaded. Had it been asked if voters wished reunification with their Ewe brothers in French Togoland, there would have been a different result, it was argued; some members of the UN Trusteeship Committee shared their reservations.[28]

This may be so: Politics, however, is the art of the possible, and Nkrumah had won this battle. But having succeeded with this objective, he wished to go further, failing to comprehend that there was no basis for further expansion eastward. After Togo's independence in 1960, it was as logical to ask if Ghana should be integrated into Togo as the reverse, if the realities of size and power were not considered. Ambassador S. W. Kumah, a one-time Ewe nationalist turned CPP leader, advised his diplomatic colleagues at a presidential meeting in 1962 that:

> Olympio . . . hates colonialism. . . . He is accepted by the leading personalities in French Togoland as their emancipator. Such a man would not like to surrender any fraction of his power so soon after independence, no matter how poor the country may be, no matter how much aid we in Ghana gave him during the struggle [for], the first and foremost aim was to project the Republic of Togoland as an independent and sovereign state which can take its rightful place in the Community of Nations. We must not lose sight of the fact that in every country the person who leads the struggle for emancipation is the accepted hero. . . . We in Ghana hail Osagyefo—and this is correct—as Emancipator of Ghana, Messiah of Ghana, etc., etc. But we have to exercise the greatest caution whenever we want to extend this to other territories. . . .[29]

Yet Nkrumah never ceased hoping to absorb Togo, always justifying his hopes (and actions) on the basis that unnatural colonial divisions had to be corrected. His oft-repeated statement to this effect became a stock joke in some capitals, where it was also accepted as a warning of Ghanaian imperialist intention, and a *leitmotif* of new Ghanaian interference. In practice, it was difficult even to digest British Togoland on a permanent basis. Anti-Nkrumah sentiment there was so strong that disturbances were planned to coincide with Ghana's independence celebrations;

[28] See, for example, the comments on behalf of the Trusteeship committee by M. Asha of Syria, when welcoming Ghana to membership in the UN: "We felt that the integration . . . was too complete and too thorough to allow the aspirations of the Trust Territory to have free play." *UNGA*, 668th plen, 8 March 1957, p. 1309 P. 62.

[29] S. W. Kumah, "Ghana-Togo Relations," in *Ministry of Foreign Affairs*, "Conference of Ghana Envoys, January 1962," pp. 135-36.

those who objected to the CPP regime, or who had to escape from it, went to Lomé where, in the manner of the Germans from the eastern territories after World War II, they became a constant source of pressure on Olympio not to accept the 1956 plebiscite.

The challenge in the opposite direction was less entangling, but more formidable. Dr. Félix Houphouet-Boigny, president of the *Rassemblement Democratique Africaine*, the most powerful parliamentary group in French West Africa, and minister of cabinet rank in the French government was the chief power in a state similar to Ghana in size, resources, and, to a certain extent in political background, though far less developed economically.[30] He met Nkrumah in 1947, when his own party was allied with the French Communists, but by the time of Ghana's independence, Houphouet was France's best friend in Africa, with such enormous personal prestige that he saw no need to defer to Nkrumah. He sought not independence for the Ivory Coast, but "partnership" with France; in 1957 he wrote in *Foreign Affairs* that Ghana's example was "very tempting . . . but the exercise of this power in a fashion consonant with national and human dignity is difficult . . . we have won a place in the history of France and of the free world. We do not want to abandon this recent heritage by trying to go back to our origins."[31] It is hard to imagine sentiments more antithetical to those of Marcus Garvey's political heir. Houphouet and his followers not only considered a "monolithic" African state an impossibility, but not even desirable.

Contacts between the Ghanaian and Francophone leaders were few, and channels through which Ghanaian influence could be exerted were nonexistent, but Nkrumah was determined to make the Ghanaian example compelling. Just after independence, he visited Abidjan and Conakry, hoping to stir nationalist sentiment which, by *West Africa*'s account, he indeed did.[32] But the tension between the two most important leaders in West Africa came to a head at an official reception: Houphouet predicted that in ten years Ghana would become economically weak and isolated: "Faisons chacun notre expérience, dans le respect absolu de l'expérience du voisin, et dans dix ans, nous établirons les bilans de la comparaison."[33] Nkrumah accepted the bet, adding that Houphouet had chosen the path of illusion.[34]

Houphouet was swimming against the tide in trying to forestall inde-

[30] See Aristide Zoldberg, *One-Party Government in the Ivory Coast*, Princeton, 1964, an excellent study of Ivorien politics of the period covered in this book.

[31] Félix Houphouet-Boigny, "Black Africa and the French Union," *Foreign Affairs*, 35, No. 34 (July 1957), 599.

[32] *West Africa*, 13 April 1957, p. 338.

[33] Quoted in "Si le Ridicule Tuait. . . ." *Fraternité* (Abidjan), 12 March 1965.

[34] *West Africa*, 13 April 1957, p. 343. See also *Daily Graphic*, 8 April 1957.

pendence, but in those ten years the essential terms of the bet were not to change, for the independence Ivory Coast took in 1960 did not substantially alter the close association with France that was Nkrumah's main target of criticism, and one of the greatest obstacles to his pan-African ambitions. The wager was of great significance, marking out as it did the two paths that every country in the developing world had to choose between for itself.

Finally, Ghana's ties on the eve of independence with countries outside Africa must be considered, in terms of Britain's willingness to grant the colony its independence. Was there any basis for the British to have foreseen that, within five years, the goal of the CPP would be to make Ghana an African bastion of "scientific socialism"? Why were the British prepared to cooperate with an avowed Marxist? There were, after all, about fifty million pounds of British investment there and, according to one student of the period, the British business community "seemed unconvinced of Nkrumah's ability to rein in what they regarded as an incipiently Communist party."[35]

It is the thesis of two American Marxists that independence was part of a cynical *quid pro quo*; in return for political power, the CPP leadership committed itself to the support of the pound sterling, the "anchor" of the Ghanaian pound.[36] Until more evidence than the parliamentary debates offer is produced, less subtle interpretations must be relied upon. David Apter, writing of left-wing influences in the CPP during the pre-independence period, noted that "Mr. N. A. Welbeck, formerly the national propaganda secretary of the CPP, has indicated that the commitment to power comes first, while the commitment to ideologies comes second."[37] Undoubtedly the British saw this to be the case generally. Indeed, circumstances might have kept it so, had external events been different; for the roots of socialism in the Gold Coast were shallow. If traditional Ghanaian society is characterized by strong communal ties, it is more significant that the semimodern and modern sectors are notable for the individualism in their organization. The market mammies, the fishermen, and the petty traders made the country hostile ground for the few Marxist pamphlets that found their way in during the 1930's,[38] and for the views of a handful of radicals in the early 1950's; the reaction to later attempts to institute regimented socialism by a one-party regime revealed the same hostility.

[35] Richard Rathbone to author, 27 June 1967.
[36] Bob Fitch and Mary Oppenheimer, "Ghana: End of an Illusion," *Monthly Review*, 18, No. 3 (July-August 1966).
[37] David Apter, *Ghana in Transition*, New York, 1963, p. 210.
[38] See Kimble, *A Political History of Ghana*, p. 549.

The Marxist handful, to be sure, was determined and well-trained. Kofi Batsaa, for one, went to Prague, took courses in journalism, and on return bided his time as correspondent for the Czech news agency until he became one of the most influential Ghanaians around Nkrumah. These men were, with others, deeply involved in the vanguard cadres of the CPP, particularly the National Association of Socialist Youth (NASSO) which, as Colin Legum points out, owed much to "the circle" in its organization.[39] But Nkrumah, in a period in which the Marxist-influenced government of Cheddi Jagan in British Guiana was deposed, was hardly going to permit Marxism to prevent independence. In the National Assembly on 25 February 1954, he stated that the government's employment of those "who have shown that their first loyalty is to an alien power, or a foreign agency which seeks to bring our country under its domination . . . would be severed."[40] The party's action was equally severe: Batsaa and others had their cards confiscated.

Thus there was little evidence of socialism in Ghana at independence. T. R. Makonnen, the Guyanese pan-Africanist (who stayed in Ghana following the celebrations of March 1957), told of how he and George Padmore brought a nucleus of influential party members together, and invited such people as there were (the Israeli diplomats, for example) to stimulate thinking. "But nobody was asking 'What Is To Be Done'! The difficulty was that everyone in Ghana was a trader, and there were no artisans with which to begin communally owned factories. As for the CPP elite, they did not know the difference between a plantation and a collective farm. We told them a revolution must occur in Ghana; that Chicherin had to rob a train to finance his. They obviously thought Chicherin had put the money to bad use."[41] The nature of the situation, then, and the predisposition of the leaders made a "pro-West" bias for Ghana inevitable at the beginning. They wished to industrialize Ghana, and even a Marxist like George Padmore advocated an "American Marshall Plan for Africa" to accomplish this.[42] From the beginning of the nationalist struggle the leaders made clear that they aspired to membership in the Commonwealth; the club was much smaller and membership in it brought to a state both influence and close ties with strong powers. They wished to retain the monarchy, too, unlike India before

---

[39] "Socialism in Ghana," in Friedland and Rosberg, p. 138.
[40] *Debates*, 25 February 1954, p. 981.
[41] Interview: T. R. Makonnen.
[42] Padmore, *Pan-Africanism or Communism*, p. 375. Marxists like duBois were horrified by this. In a review of Padmore's book, he wrote: "he welcomes British capital for the Volta dam. He thinks the Philippines are free. This seems to me dangerous thinking." Undated clipping from *National Guardian*, Padmore library, Accra. Richard Wright shared these apprehensions about the dam. See *Black Power*, London, 1956, pp. 189, 288.

them. They could announce without fear that their foreign policy would be one of "positive neutralism," because the hard Western attitude towards nonalignment was on the retreat at this time, just after Suez. Perhaps Nkrumah's most famous statement of his intentions, in the period around independence, was a widely read article in *Foreign Affairs*:

> The West has set the pattern of our hopes. . . . We have to modernize. Either we shall do so with the interest and support of the West or we shall be compelled to turn elsewhere. This is not a warning or a threat, but a straight statement of political reality. And I also affirm, for myself and I believe for most of my fellow leaders in Africa, that we want close cooperation with our friends. We know you. History has brought us together. We still have the opportunity to build up a future on the basis of free and equal cooperation. This is our aim. This is our hope.[43]

Could this have possibly been a calculated deception? It seems unlikely, but the events of subsequent years were to make many of his colleagues reexamine his motives of the earlier period.

THE NATIONAL INTEREST

The national interest has always been . . . whatever the policy-makers have at any given moment decided that it should be. . . . It is a Platonic concept.—ALFRED DE GRAZIA[44]

With independence, competing elite groups with different interests could attempt to affect Ghana's foreign policy. For this reason, a survey of the historical background of the policy is inadequate for an understanding of its determinants at independence. De Grazia's argument is only valid at a certain level, but it has increased cogency for the study of a new state, where trade patterns are only beginning to be diversified from restricted colonial patterns, and where traditions in the conduct of foreign policy are still being formed. If the familiar distinction between "absolute" and "competitive" national goals is adopted,[45] we can say that all groups wished to improve the standard of living, and that there was an

---

43 Kwame Nkrumah, "African Prospect," *Foreign Affairs*, 37, No. 1, p. 53. Forecasts that echoed Western optimism are found in D. G. Anglin, "Ghana, the West, and the Soviet Union," *Canadian Journal of Economics and Political Science*, 24, No. 2 (May 1958), 152; also in J. G. Amamoo, "Ghana and the Western Democracies," *African Affairs* (January 1959), 54-60.

44 "Conference Discussion on Objectives," J. C. Charlesworth, ed., *A Design for Political Science: Scope, Objectives, and Methods*, American Academy of Political and Social Science, Philadelphia, December 1966.

45 See A.F.K. Organski, *World Politics*, New York, 1960, pp. 53-55.

obvious and common interest in high world-cocoa prices. There is also no doubt that any leader of Ghana would have adopted competitive national goals, at least within the West African context, given the natural opportunity Ghana held for assuming a position of influence in that area. But what to do with that influence? The contrasting policies of Nkrumah and Houphouet-Boigny were to underline the importance of this question, for on it there was little agreement in Ghana. "From the beginning Nkrumah made the foreign policy," it was said in Flagstaff House.[46] There was much truth in this; but his statecraft was seldom successful, and it will be argued that one reason is that it worked against Ghana's obvious and absolute national interests, and against the interests of some important groups which are discussed here.

Consider, for example, the interests of the "masses." Did they have any interests beyond a gradually rising standard of living? Nkrumah had, after all, made the common man the symbol of the nationalist struggle, for which he had been rewarded with vast popularity. Much was made in later years of the "yearning of the masses for African unity," but was there any truth in this? The Gold Coast had been the model colony, and its citizens knew it. Other West Africans called them flamboyant or arrogant, and resented their early successes. There was enthusiasm for Nkrumah's foreign policies when these meant conferences and parades in Accra for visiting dignitaries. The populace liked being told that Ghana was the leading African state, which is not to say that they wanted to lead other African states. Nkrumah understood this distinction; David Williams tells of a conversation with him in early 1965, when the biggest show of all, the Accra OAU heads of state conference, was threatened because of the bad relations between Ghana and its neighbors. By his own account, he pointed out that the local press had caused the people to expect much from the conference, and that it would be a bad thing for the regime were it not to take place. "Nkrumah replied that he had scheduled the grand opening of the Volta Dam for the same time, so that one way or the other the people would have a show."[47] As this was at a time when the price of bread was sufficiently inflated to cause agitation against the regime, circuses were all the more important as an antidote. As early as 1954, Richard Wright could say that the Gold Coast African "feels that he is at the centre of the universe and a conversation about world affairs is likely to elicit silence. . . ."[48] This did not appear to change in the ensuing decade.

Yet broad and sophisticated pan-African sympathies might have

46 Interview: CF-28.
47 Interview: David Williams, editor, *West Africa*, 31 May 1965.
48 Wright, *Black Power*, p. 188.

16

emerged had the regime, for its part, looked to less exciting responsibilities first. Ghana's population in 1960 was 6,727,000, of which 827,000 were "foreign nationals," whether born in Ghana or outside; 280,600 were Togolese; 194,600 Voltaics; 54,400 Ivoriens; and 190,800 were Nigerians.[49] Thus effective links with other West African states were a vital—an absolute—national interest, attention to which would be the base for the pursuit of competitive goals. But after eight years of Nkrumah's pan-African policy, a CPP parliamentarian noted that it was difficult for his people to attend a family funeral 52 miles away in Togo:

> I . . . tell them that some evil-minded people had been moving in and out of Ghana and because of them we had to restrict movement across the border. I however explained that with the coming of African unity visits to our brothers beyond the boundaries, would be easy. . . .
>
> Many people cannot see our connections with Uganda, Kenya, Southern Rhodesia and the other states far away. They know Bondoukou in the Ivory Coast, Togo, Nigeria, Sierra Leone. . . .
>
> If we tell them that we are going to have African unity with the U.A.R. they ask, "where is it?" . . . If one speaks about East Africa they think that it is a far away place, probably at the end of the world. Some remember that in 1914 there was war in East Africa. That is all they know.[50]

If the masses' interests were inchoate, there were several groups, now considered, with clearly defined goals.

a. *The nationalist elite.* Nkrumah had able associates in the 1950's. Komla Gbedemah was the most conspicuous and probably the ablest, gifted with a sense of timing and a shrewd business instinct. By the late 1930's he had developed varied personal interests, and he made an excellent minister of finance from 1954 until replaced in 1961. Prior to independence he traveled widely encouraging foreign investment, and had also been the Colonial Office's adviser to the British UN delegation on the Fourth Committee.

Kojo Botsio had broader continental concerns than Gbedemah, having had experience in the London pan-African movements of the late 1940's. He also represented the Gold Coast at Bandung in 1955, despite British apprehensions.[51] It was, obviously, an experience that was to be

[49] *Ghana*, 1962 Statistical Year Book, Accra, 1962, p. 25.
[50] *Debates*, 15 February 1965, pp. 1060-61.
[51] By his own account, the British feared that his presence there might indicate British acceptance of resolutions framed by the conference. As a compromise, it was decided that he would go as an "observer."

17

useful during his years as foreign minister. But he too had wide business interests, and his wife was one of the most important traders of Ghana.

Ako Adjei, foreign minister from 1959 until his detention in 1962, was perhaps the most radical (and least influential) of the inner elite. He was responsible for Nkrumah's return to the Gold Coast, but did not join the CPP until 1954.[52] He represented the colony at an I.L.O. conference in Geneva in 1955, and from then was to travel widely on representational missions.

It was this group that, with Nkrumah, formed the Governor's Advisory Committee on Defense and External Affairs, established in June 1954. Its primary concern was independence, and the preparation for the numerous responsibilities that were entailed in such a change in status. The committee was thus in no way parallel (nor was there a Gold Coast parallel) to the working committee of the Congress in India, that argued and took position on international questions prior to independence. The Governor did, however, brief them on international questions that might concern them (and on some that did not), more and more as independence approached.[53]

Among the nationalist elite there existed what Richard Rathbone terms an "embryo foreign policy," that was the sum of its international business experience and its more marginal (but not inconsiderable) experience in dealing with such issues as Togoland at the United Nations. Rathbone suggests that the elite was perhaps attempting to tell the Ghanaian voter "that the old Ghost of British commercial dominance" had been laid to rest.[54] The CPP offered him a new presence, of West Germany, Holland, the United States, and others. Clearly this elite's views on the development of Ghana were most conventional from a Western perspective.[55] St. Clair Drake wrote in 1956 that every member of the cabinet was "pro-West."[56] Their personal interests dictated this, and their view of Ghana's interests followed accordingly. Nkrumah, at this stage, may not have shared their desire to amass wealth; these other CPP leaders were, however, something of a bourgeois lot.

b. *The Foreign Service.* "Other things being equal, the success of a nation's policy will depend on the quality of its diplomatic corps, which

---

[52] His late capitulation to the CPP perhaps explains his relative radicalism.

[53] Interviews: Ako Adjei; Botsio; and Gbedemah.

[54] Richard Rathbone to the author, 27 June 1967.

[55] T. R. Makonnen spoke of warning them against Western investment, and said they were thinking, rather, "of all the cuts they could get. They could not wait." Interview.

[56] St. Clair Drake, "Prospects for Democracy in the Gold Coast," *Annals of the American Academy of Political and Social Science*, 306, July 1956.

must execute it."[57] From the beginning a high standard was set for the foreign service. The Advisory Committee on Defense and External Affairs decided that the nucleus would be chosen from the senior administrative grade of the civil service, and by August 1955 the first selection process had been completed. From over a hundred applications, eight were chosen as a nucleus for the "foreign and commonwealth services of the Gold Coast," and they were among the country's most worldly and sophisticated men.[58] F. S. Arkhurst, then thirty-five years old, had taken a first in economics at Aberdeen and developed a reputation as one of the shrewdest African diplomatists at the United Nations. Major Seth Anthony had been the third Ghanaian admitted to the administrative branch of the civil service, after A. L. Adu and Professor Busia. Alex Quaison-Sackey, then thirty-one, had begun making a name for himself at Oxford, and was later to be president of the General Assembly. They were conspicuous men, and it might have been predicted that if their assumptions about Ghana's interests did not square with Nkrumah's, then Ghana would not have a cohesive foreign policy.

They were sent as a group to London, where they attended a course at the Foreign Office, and at the London School of Economics. In 1956 they were sent to British missions in the field, from Rio de Janeiro to Canberra, for more practical experience, and eventually to the Gold Coast Commission in London itself, until then largely run by expatriates. Nkrumah considered the civil service "absolutely British in substance and nature,"[59] and because of their training these eight were open to still graver charges. For their own part, they disagreed with the assumption that such training prejudiced their view of Ghana's interests. By all accounts, the British did not involve them in their own disputes, and kept the training technical. "But they were good—and we were not to forget this."[60] Thus a subtle influence was inevitable, to which there was no reasonable alternative. The issue symbolized the dilemma of the regime. The diplomats insisted that it was a question of standards, not of ideology, that was at stake—but does the acceptance of certain diplomatic standards inherently restrict the scope of foreign policy goals?

In fact, their view of Ghana's extra-African interests coincided with Nkrumah's during the early period after independence. They too gave priority to the obtaining of foreign investment; Quaison-Sackey, in a paper given at the Institute of Commonwealth Studies, in London, wrote

[57] Gordon A. Craig, *War, Politics, and Diplomacy*, London, 1967, p. 179.
[58] The writer's conclusions about the role of the "eight" are derived, in part, from interviews with seven of them.
[59] Nkrumah, *Africa Must Unite*, London, 1963, p. 87.
[60] Interview: CF-33.

that the government's policies would have to "inspire [that] confidence without which foreign assistance is impossible."[61] Beyond that, they wished to use the Commonwealth mechanism to the fullest but, if anything, were less romantic about that organization than Nkrumah and his ministers, perhaps because they were more perceptive as to its declining importance. Quaison-Sackey's paper went on: "The Gold Coast as a militarily weak country will, no doubt, join the 'glorious' band of small powers, like New Zealand, which look upon themselves as custodians of international morality. In this role she will expect to receive the good will of the rest of the Commonwealth." A recurrent theme in their testimony was the effect of Suez on them, during their training in London. One said that if he had lacked consciousness as an African, or Afro-Asian, before this, he did not after.[62] Another said that "It became clear during Suez that the British would go to any lengths to protect their interests; thus we had to make clear that we would use every weapon we possessed to protect ours."[63]

Over pan-Africanism, however, there was a great cleavage. These men shared nothing of the tradition of Manchester, Marcus Garvey, or George Padmore. Few took Nkrumah's phrase, that Ghana's independence was meaningless until all Africa was free, very seriously. "I doubted that we could do much to free these other territories, other than by an example of good government at home."[64] They did see regional links as a possibility, but were more acutely aware that (as Quaison-Sackey wrote), Ghana would "definitely be jealous of her independence."[65] In his 1956 preview of Ghana's foreign policy, he did not even mention pan-Africanism as such.

These men, then, were heirs to the Western tradition in diplomacy, and had an interest in a rational and gradual development of Ghana's diplomatic network. Indeed, they expected to play a major role, and to be ambassadors within several years. Their first setback came with the announcement in parliament (in 1956) that "Ambassadors are appointed by the party in power and are therefore political appointees."[66] The trainees, then, were to be permanent secretaries to the embassies— but they understood the implications.

c. *Expatriates.* One of Nkrumah's gravest dilemmas at independence was his government's reliance on British civil servants. By 1959, however, the results of Africanization were so impressive that he could him-

---

[61] Alex Quaison-Sackey, "The Foundations of Gold Coast's Foreign Policy: A Study of an Emergent Nation in the International Society," *Institute of Commonwealth Studies,* London, CW/55/8, 1955.
[62] Interview: CF-33.　　　[63] Interview: CF-20.　　　[64] Interview: CF-33.
[65] Quaison-Sackey, *loc.cit.*　　[66] *Debates,* 3 September 1956, p. 532.

self choose whether to renew the contracts of those still present, at which time he kept only those considered trustworthy or indispensable. Thus within two years of independence Ghana was virtually free of the type of *fonctionnaire* that so heavily affected policy in French Africa.[67] Nor is it clear that the expatriate business community actively attempted to influence foreign policy-making. Their reactions to policy were, of course, carefully considered, as the regime wished to attract more investment. But the role of the business community would seem to have been a passive one.

In a different category were the several distinguished advisers that Nkrumah attracted from the West to advise him on Ghana's development. Sir Arthur Lewis spent much time in Ghana during the 1950's, but, by 1959, he felt that his counsel was going unheeded and departed. Commander Sir Robert Jackson, on the other hand, maintained an active interest in all Ghanaian affairs from 1953 onward, and was retained by Nkrumah's successors as an adviser. Jackson, an Australian who maintained an affiliation with the British treasury from 1945, had been an assistant secretary-general of the United Nations and an adviser to both the government of India and Pakistan before coming to Ghana in 1953 to advise Nkrumah on the Volta River Project. From 1956 to 1961, he was chairman of the development commission, but his influence —developed through his and his wife Barbara Ward's close relations with Nkrumah—extended far beyond the commission. Economists have criticized him for giving Nkrumah the economic advice he wished to hear but Jackson, understanding the limits on Nkrumah's willingness to accept advice and knowing how to give it, undoubtedly calculated that it was more important to maintain a position through which influence could be exerted on all issues affecting Ghana's ability to develop the basis of economic independence (and, hence, her relations with the West). He was skillful in the use of his position and, in Ghana's first four years of independence, did much to delay Nkrumah's shift of the orientation of Ghana's foreign policy.

Those who were attracted to a cause, to a country espousing an ideology, must also be carefully considered. These were in the end to be a major factor in Nkrumah's undoing, partly because their interests infrequently coincided with those of the Ghanaian people, and their advice was, therefore, often not what could sustain the regime's popularity. The political refugee-expatriates were the largest group in this category, but as their influence came at a much later stage they will be discussed

---

67 See Nkrumah, *Africa Must Unite*, Chapter II, for his view of the dilemma posed by the civil service. James Moxon was helpful in describing the evolution of the role of the civil service following independence.

in a later chapter. The background and roles of the two foremost ex-patriates, whose shadows were long indeed over Flagstaff House, merit careful attention, however. First, George Padmore. The young Oscar Kambona, then a law student in London, summarized the importance of Padmore's *Pan-Africanism or Communism?* by writing to him in 1957 that his "achievement on writing this book is on the same level as the achievement of Dr. Kwame Nkrumah in bringing his country to inde-pendence."[68] C.L.R. James, the Trotskyite associate of Padmore and Nkrumah, vastly exaggerates the importance of theory to the success of the Gold Coast's "revolution" in his unpublished study of Padmore, but this passage is significant for showing Padmore's channels of thinking:

> . . . one of the great political achievements of our time [is Padmore's] working out of the theory which shaped the revolution in the Gold Coast. . . . We aimed at preserving the Marxist approach, keeping far away from the reformism of the Second International, but at the same time fighting and warning against the Communist International. This determination never to submit himself or his ideas to any European-dominated organization was as usual denounced as black chauvinism. It was in reality George's refusal to be in any way caught by what had happened to him in the Kremlin [with which he had broken in 1935].[69]

By 1955, a duality admittedly existed in Padmore's thinking; he could write of a "libertarian political system" fulfilling the "social-economic mission of Communism."[70] But he remained a Marxist, and encouraged Nkrumah in his resolve to consolidate power and move toward the crea-tion of a one-party socialist state.[71] There was no doubt of his dislike of the Russians, and he was much criticized by his former colleagues for having reacted so strongly against his bitter memories of 1935.[72] Only Nkrumah had a greater hand than Padmore in shaping Ghana's foreign policy during the first two years, so his attitude was important.

For all that, Padmore, like Nkrumah, was looking at Ghana as a stepping-stone. If he possessed the modesty and sense of proportion

[68] Kambona to Padmore, 19 January 1957, in Padmore library, Accra.

[69] C.L.R. James, "Notes on the Life of George Padmore," pp. 37-38.

[70] Padmore, *Pan-Africanism or Communism*, pp. 21-22.

[71] Interviews: CF-27, CF-56, and T. R. Makonnen.

[72] A long-time colleague of Padmore's wrote him as follows: " 'Pan-Africanism' with-out economic content is hollow. You feel it yourself when you write on page 374 [of *Pan-Africanism or Communism*], that 'unless political power is used to liberate the African masses from their state of abject poverty, ignorance and disease, self-govern-ment is meaningless.' But you eschew the conclusions which the reader is vainly waiting for—that is: *how, that economic liberation*? How to go beyond bourgeois nationalism? The answer is *socialism, marxism, communism*, but not the caricature of marxism . . . offered by Stalin and his agents. Why don't you say that clearly?" Daniel Guerin to Padmore, 18 September 1956, in Padmore Library, Accra.

that Nkrumah lacked, and could give rational advice on foreign policy, he could never see Ghana as an end in itself. As such, he was bitterly resented by men like Robert Gardiner, perhaps the most formidable Ghanaian, and many others as well.[73]

There is less to say for Geoffrey Bing, the other preeminent expatriate. After ten years in parliament, he came to Ghana as attorney general, a post he held until 1961. He was a restraining influence on Nkrumah at one level, during these years, and began losing influence when he advised against the excessive use of preventive detention, a draconian instrument for which he had devised the legal basis.[74] He came back to a position of some power during the Congo crisis, and was an almost full-time adviser to Nkrumah during the ensuing five years. In this period it would also appear that he exercised a restraining hand, in the sense that he sought to rationalize the instruments of foreign policy, and to bring order to the decision-making process. Yet at a more important level, he affected policy-making in a different direction. He had little interest in pan-Africanism as such; since from the time of the Spanish Civil War he had been identified with the British left, he could work for the success of a foreign policy the main thrust of which was "union government" because a secondary thrust was "anti-imperialism."

Padmore wanted Ghana to lead (and be totally committed to) a pan-African movement, and posed pan-Africanism as an historic alternative to Communism (telling the West that its own "best guarantee against Communism" was attention to Africa's needs).[75] Bing, if forced to a choice, might have opted for a variation of the alternative, to the extent that Ghana might become a member of a large "socialist commonwealth" of the Eastern European states, China, and the several radical Afro-Asian states. This was particularly true in the last two years of the regime, after the leaders of the Parliamentary Labour Party made clear that Bing would not be welcomed back into their ranks.[76]

d. *Nkrumah.* How Nkrumah saw Ghana's interests is a complex question, best discussed in the context of a brief analysis of those personal traits that probably affected his formulation of policy. The emotion that surrounded any discussion of Nkrumah, in Africa, renders it difficult to relate these traits to aspects of Ghanaian policy; it is one measure of his impact, but only indirectly helpful in an assessment of his motives. Mor-

[73] Gardiner once quoted Dr. Johnson to describe Padmore: "That fellow seems to me to possess but one idea, and that is a wrong one." Interview: CF-56.

[74] Interview: CF-85.

[75] Padmore, *Pan-Africanism or Communism*, p. 21.

[76] Bing hoped for a seat in the 1964 British parliamentary election (which the British High Commissioner in Accra, Sir Geoffrey de Freitas, succeeded in getting) but found no encouragement at any level of the Labour Party.

23

genthau argues that "the knowledge of the statesman's motives may give ... one among many clues as to what the direction of his foreign policy may be" and urges us to pay more attention to the perennial interests of the state.[77]

Yet the traditional rules must be discarded when discussing a new nation, led by a powerful leader sponsoring a transnational ideology. By 1962 Ghana's foreign policy was dominated by Nkrumah's obsession, shared in its particular form by no one of influence in Ghana, to bring "continental union government" to Africa, and to align Ghana with all anti-imperialist groups and countries. Since Nkrumah had dictatorial powers both explicitly and constitutionally, he could set the policy virtually without regard to domestic pressure. Like Endymion's Lord Rushmont, he did not "care a rush whether the revenue increases or declines. He is thinking of real politics: foreign affairs. . . ." He could do so, for the CPP chant, "Kwame Nkrumah is the CPP and the CPP is Ghana," symbolized the power relationships of the time. As elsewhere on the continent, the perennial interests of the state had not been agreed upon in any event, making of Ghana only an extreme example of a general rule in the Africa of this period.[78]

For lack of a definitive biographical study of Nkrumah, it is difficult to explain satisfactorily why his behavior took certain forms. On several essential points, however, the explanation seems obvious. By the time he left the Gold Coast in 1935, he was already the most radical of his contemporaries, and felt acutely the injustices of colonialism. But it was during the ten years he spent in America that a more important and personal dimension was added, as a result of deep scars any sensitive person would have acquired from the racial discrimination to which he was subjected. He had time, too, to read much of Marx, Lenin, and to study "revolutionaries and their methods," namely Hannibal, Cromwell, Napoleon, Lenin, Mazzini, Gandhi, Mussolini, and Hitler, by his own account.[79] Thus he began to patch together serviceable ideas for the future. Professor Jones-Quartey, then his close friend, noted that the entire group at Lincoln University shared his anti-imperialist ideas, but that he was always the most radical: "Although he had these ideas before arriving, his experiences in America sharpened his distress, and while we talked, he laid his plans. All his later foreign policies—anti-Americanism, friendship with the East, the moving of Ghana towards "scientific socialism"—have their origins in his decade in America."[80]

[77] Hans Morgenthau, *Politics among Nations*, New York, 1963, p. 6. Also see James Rosenau, *Intervention, Politics and Foreign Policy*, New York, 1964, p. 143.

[78] See Preface, p. xiii.   [79] Nkrumah, *Ghana*, pp. xiii-xiv.

[80] Interview: Professor K.A.B. Jones-Quartey.

24

Another baffling characteristic perhaps has its origin in the same period. His passion was to make Ghana count, yet he was to rely on non-Ghanaians to bring about the "political kingdom" to a surprising degree. Sophisticated advisers such as Sir Robert Jackson had enormous influence on him.[81] Sukarno was shocked to meet Nkrumah's English secretary[82] (shocked, no doubt, also to meet the British chief of defense staff) in 1961, and it was a constant source of irritation to Ghanaians that Nkrumah preferred the advice of people with "real" (i.e., non-Ghanaian) experience to their own,[83] even when the advisers were such interested businessmen as Sir John Howard, F. J. Pedler (of Unilever), or Edgar Kaiser (the American industrialist). Ghanaian diplomats resented Geoffrey Bing for the same reason. Royal favor, or gestures from the White House, easily influenced Nkrumah, because of his awe for the very Western power he wished to displace.

Related to this attitude was a distrust of Ghanaians at certain levels of his work. There were advantages (to Nkrumah) in the employment of expatriates. They could hold no direct political ambitions in Ghana and were dependent on Nkrumah's goodwill; they were free of the communal Ghanaian society which made keeping government secrets or strategy so difficult. His attitude toward Ghanaians was partly one of arrogance, however. When he returned to the Gold Coast after ten years' education in America, it was, some said, with the assumption that he was the best educated of his generation. But many had in the meantime been to Oxford or Cambridge, whereas Nkrumah's undergraduate degree was little more than the equivalent of that from a good secondary school. After spending so many years abroad, he found it difficult to believe that even Ghana's professional diplomats could know more about diplomacy than he; this was to prove embarrassing at times, particularly when questions of protocol were involved.

Another set of convictions perhaps also developed during these same years in America was a Wilsonian strand of utopianism. It was to help account for a strange duality in his foreign policy toward the end when, though Ghana's major international policies stemmed from his Marxist beliefs, unlimited faith that the United Nations could help reshape the world derived from his early idealism. In a dedication ceremony in 1954, Nkrumah said that the cause of the mistrust and fear in the world was

[81] See interviews: CF-56, CF-85, and CF-60 for comments on Jackson's role.
[82] Interview: CF-14.
[83] This was particularly resented by Ghanaian economists. J. H. Mensah, one-time head of planning, arranged for his re-secondment to the E.C.A. in Addis Ababa as a result of this in 1965, whereupon Nkrumah reportedly commented to him that this was an excellent opportunity to get some "*real* economic experience."

ignorance, from which stemmed the ". . . hate and intolerance which leads to war. When all citizens are able to call upon unbiased information on any subject, world opinion would soon be able to influence governments entangled in armaments races . . . the people of the world will not tolerate the distortion of scientific and engineering skill into the devilish travesty of research into new methods of mass destruction."[84] Thus he proposed a UN Institute of Truth, for bringing world peace. The "characteristic weakness of utopianism," E. H. Carr writes, is that it leads to a "failure to understand existing reality."

The difficulty in detecting how Nkrumah saw Ghana's interests in 1957 is that he was an embodiment of so many contradictions: by 1965, a Marxist living an undisciplined life of ostentation, dedicating his life to the destruction of imperialism while remaining a close friend of Westerners than whom there were no greater imperialists. While Sir Robert Jackson spoke of the "separate sealed compartments" in his mind, to explain this, a British diplomatist described him as a chameleon for the same reason.[85] Both are right, but Jackson's explanation is more profound. Nkrumah had qualities of charm and graciousness that took Western statesmen completely by surprise; but the important duality was not between Nkrumah, charmer of aid-bearing emissaries and Nkrumah, the tireless revolutionary. Some who knew Nkrumah well felt that when he told Western statesmen prior to 1960 that his heart was with the West he for the moment truly believed it, as he likewise believed it when he told Eastern envoys that they should bide their time until he was in a position to declare that his real loyalties were with their cause. The "separate, sealed" Eastern compartment of his mind in the event turned out to be bigger than the Western one.

As with most Marxists-Leninists, he could not foresee a long-term power base in a peasant economy and, like Lenin, looked to electrification to lay the basis of Ghana's industrialization. Thus his fascination with the long-laid plans to develop the Volta River, and thus his need (as Sir Robert Jackson continually reminded him) to have the support of the West. He wished to consolidate his domestic base as quickly as possible without frightening potential investors, and wished to free himself from the dependence on British civil servants. He wished to move into that world of nonalignment whose leaders (like Nehru and Nasser) played a role in international affairs. One close observer (David Williams) reconciled Nkrumah's caution and moderation prior to 1960, with his known Marxist sympathies in this period, as follows. "Nkrumah was convinced he would have to be the perfect 'neo-colonialist' leader to get

84 *Daily Graphic*, 12 May 1954.
85 Interviews: Sir Robert Jackson, and CF-106.

26

Western investment; the West would have to think him one of theirs. And he had an image of exactly how he would have to behave to preserve their support. In fact he was trying too hard, which was to produce its own reaction."[86] Put differently, the Volta River Project and the industrialization of Ghana were, in the first period studied in this book, worth some deference to the West.

[86] Interviews: David Williams, Editor of *West Africa*, December 1966.

27

DIPLOMATIC STIRRINGS

March 1957–October 1958

THE GOLD COAST's independence, "the most important event in the history of modern Africa,"[1] was an auspicious occasion. Fifty-six nations sent delegations: the United States was represented by Richard Nixon, Britain by R. A. Butler (as he then was), Russia by its minister of state farms, Tunisia by Bourguiba himself, and the head of the new state of Ghana, by the Duchess of Kent. "Our country is no stranger to world affairs," Nkrumah said at the state banquet,[2] and this was underlined by the nature of the occasion. He also stressed that the material basis for Ghana's independence existed. "We can stand on our own feet. The foreign policy of Ghana will not, therefore, be dictated by the need for us having to seek assistance from other countries."[3] Indeed, from Nkrumah's point of view, the most significant consequence of independence was that Ghana could now have a foreign policy, which from the first was defined as a dynamic process concerned with broader ends than merely the search for aid.

Ghana was now in the international system. With the sponsorship of its Commonwealth partners, it became the 81st member of the United Nations. It joined the major international institutions one by one, including even the Commission for Technical Co-Operation in Africa South of the Sahara (CCTA), an organization of the colonial powers, South Africa, and Liberia. For all his insistence on Ghana's role as liberator, Nkrumah moved cautiously. He expressed a willingness to establish diplomatic relations with those countries which had "honoured Ghana by sending delegations to the Independence Celebrations."[4] While efforts were made throughout the first year to exchange ambassadors with South Africa, it was to be over two years before a Russian embassy was established in Accra. From the vantage point of the West, Ghana appeared safe; the British and American envoys presented their cre-

---

[1] Aristide Zolberg, *One-Party Government in the Ivory Coast*, Princeton, 1964, p. 219.
[2] Kwame Nkrumah, *I Speak of Freedom*, London, 1962, p. 95.
[3] Nkrumah's address to the last session of the Gold Coast parliament, *ibid.*, p. 99.
[4] "Ghana's Diplomatic Relations," P.R. #344/57, 14 March 1957.

28

dentials first, with the Australians, French, and West Germans not far behind. Even with Cairo (which was not invited to the celebrations),[5] ambassadors were not exchanged for a year, by which time the Israeli ambassador had established himself as the most influential diplomat in Accra.

Like Trotsky in revolutionary Russia, Nkrumah's inclination after independence might have been to issue "a few revolutionary proclamations to the peoples of the world, and then shut up shop," to emphasize that "the center of gravity was not in diplomacy at that time."[6] But in accepting and in working with the British toward an orderly transfer of power, bending his own tendencies to their minimal requirements, Nkrumah necessarily gave priority to diplomacy, foreign office and all, rather than to revolutionary pan-Africanism. Nkrumah himself held the portfolio of Defense and External Affairs (as it was until divided in mid-1958), and had as his principal secretary the ablest Ghanaian there could have been for the post, A. L. Adu. By independence, twelve officers had been trained for the foreign and Commonwealth service, and another group was completing a course in Accra given by a British diplomat.[7] It is well to note, however, that the dichotomy in policy-making that was later to wreck Ghana's policy, between professional diplomats on the one hand and self-styled militant revolutionaries on the other, began (if harmlessly and unavoidably) almost from the start. George Padmore had returned to London in May 1957, but was persuaded to come back in September to take up a post as adviser to the prime minister on African affairs. Adu argued strongly against the appointment, on the grounds that a West Indian could hardly have anything to teach them about Africa.[8] But Padmore came, bringing with him all his immense prestige; if his budget were under Adu's control, his office was next to Nkrumah's. "Once more George sat in an office with adequate resources,

---

[5] Invitations were sent by Britain, which had no diplomatic relations with Egypt. The Egyptian leaders, for their part, may well have wondered how to appraise Ghana's leaders. The confidential report on the Bandung conference of the Arab League termed the Gold Coast "a follower of Great Britain," attaching a significance to this that went beyond the obvious fact that the Gold Coast was a colony of Britain. *League of Arab States*, Report Submitted by Mohamed A. K. Hassouna, Secretary-General, on The First Asian-African Conference, p. 40; writer's files.

[6] Leon Trotsky, *My Life*, London, 1930, p. 293. Quoted in Robert Slusser, "The Role of the Foreign Ministry," in I. J. Lederer, ed., *Russian Foreign Policy*, New Haven, 1962, p. 212.

[7] See F. E. Boaten, "Brief Notes on Administrative Organisation of the Ministry of Foreign Affairs," in *Ministry of Foreign Affairs*, "Conference of Ghana Envoys, January 1962," p. 175.

[8] Interview: CF-28.

29

doing the work he had done in the Kremlin, and in his little London flat."[9]

The domestic scene was unsettled throughout 1957. There were, for example, serious "disturbances" in former British Togoland, where prior to and during the independence celebrations the army itself had to assist the police in quelling armed mobs.[10] This made clear how delicate was the position with respect to French Togoland, with which those demonstrating wished to unite. In Accra itself there were extremely threatening developments during the summer of 1957. The Ga people, indigenous to the city, organized the "Ga Shifimo Kpee" movement—the Ga Standfast Association—to oppose the CPP, and demonstrations and arrests became a pattern for several months.[11] This led to much stronger government by Nkrumah, whose reaction, to some observers, had an ugly look. The *Economist Intelligence Unit* reported that foreign firms in Ghana were postponing decisions about further investment.[12] The British press began criticizing the regime frequently, from the time that Nkrumah moved into the Castle, seat of the Governor-General.[13] Ironically, the Ga movement began just after this symbolic change, by which Nkrumah seemed to have ended the accessibility which had made his leadership so effective.[14] In all, there was little chance to take foreign policy initiatives in 1957. Ghana needed to be "given time to sort herself out," as Nkrumah said.[15]

The second year was to be diplomatically eventful, and would prove extraordinarily successful. At independence itself, Nkrumah had held informal consultations with the African delegations about the possibility of convening a conference of all the African states, including South Africa. The general reaction "was that such a conference was desirable," as Nkrumah wrote to the eight heads of African states and govern-

[9] C.L.R. James, "Notes on the Life of George Padmore," unpublished manuscript, p. 61.

[10] See "Minor Disturbances in the Trans-Volta Region," P.R. #324/57, 10 March 1957; "Use of Military Force in Trans-Volta Togoland," P.R. #330/57, 12 March 1957. By one account, Special Branch was forewarned of the trouble, and was able to move quickly. CF-28.

[11] See Dennis Austin, *Politics in Ghana 1946-1960*, London, 1964, pp. 373-76.

[12] *Economist Intelligence Unit*, West Africa Series, No. 18, 30 May 1957.

[13] The British press considered this an insult to the newly appointed Governor-General. Nkrumah justified the move on the grounds that independence had to be credible to the average Ghanaian, who associated the castle with effective power. See Anthony Sampson's perceptive article "Ghana: The Morning After," *Africa South*, 2, No. 2, January-March 1958.

[14] David Apter wrote that "accessibility" had always been evidence of the CPP's direct control. *Ghana in Transition*, New York, 1963, p. 208.

[15] *Times*, 25 June 1957.

ments six weeks later.[16] The conference took place in April 1958 and, with its success, Nkrumah established himself beyond any further question as "something more than a local leader."[17] Its contrast with Nasser's Afro-Asian Peoples Solidarity Conference of December 1957 (which included Russian and Chinese delegations) was reassuring to the West. By visiting the participating states soon afterward, Nkrumah laid the basis for an effective diplomatic network in independent Africa.

At the first anniversary celebrations of March 1958, nationalists from unliberated territories, moreover, gathered to hear of Nkrumah's and Padmore's plans for a great pan-African conference of all political parties to take place later in the year. Among those present were Nyerere, Mboya, Azikiwe, Murumbi, Apithy, Garba-Jahumpa, and Bakary Djibo.

In 1956 the government had deferred plans for soliciting support for the Volta River Project until after independence. Nkrumah had hoped to secure financing for it during the first year or two, so that he could thenceforth devote his time to African liberation. He had looked to Britain for support, and went to the 1957 Commonwealth conference hoping to find encouragement. But Britain did not have funds of the size required, and thus he had to put his hopes, following the advice of Sir Robert Jackson, his development adviser, on American support. (Indeed, Jackson was given "something of a veto on policy to prevent anything from compromising the possibility of financial support.")[18] His trip to America in 1958 like that to Britain in 1957, was a personal success increasing his international prestige; but as in Britain, there was no rush to build the Volta dam, and thus was it becoming clear that the Volta Project and the industrialization of Ghana were further away than he had hoped.

THE CONFERENCE OF INDEPENDENT AFRICAN STATES

"The time has come for Africa to view the international situation in the light of her own interests."[19]

Alex Quaison-Sackey, in 1957 the second secretary at the high commission in London, later wrote, that despite Western presentiments of failure

16 Nkrumah to heads of independent African states, 16 April 1957, in Ghana, "Confidential Report—Conference of Independent African States" (hereafter referred to as *CIAS Report*), Accra, 1958, p. 681.

17 *Times*, 10 April 1958.

18 Interview: CF-85.

19 "Draft Memorandum—Conference of Independent African States," *CIAS Report*, p. 750. I am grateful to Professor Thomas Hovet for permitting me to see an earlier draft of the memorandum.

31

for the conference of independent African states, "Kwame Nkrumah knew what he was doing. He was aware, most of all, of the need to plan carefully" for its success.[20] This was no exaggeration. More important, at no point did the Ghanaians attempt to monopolize the initiative. At the 1957 Commonwealth conference, Nkrumah arranged for the African ambassadors in London to lay the groundwork for the gathering, a decision complicated only by the fact that the Egyptians could thus not take part, owing to their break with Britain after Suez. It was also clear by this time that the South Africans would not participate at any stage, having—revealingly—made their acceptance contingent on the participation of the colonial powers.[21]

The first ambassadorial meeting finally took place on the 15th of August, at the Embassy of Sudan. It is interesting that the host thought that John Jantuah, the acting Ghanaian high commissioner, should preside, for, as Simpson the Liberian ambassador said, "Ghana initiated the idea of a Conference."[22] It was characteristic of Ghanaian diplomacy in this period that Jantuah not only turned this down, but added that Ghana, in calling for a conference, "was not aiming at forming a political or an ideological bloc, but wanted the States in Africa to know themselves," and to establish personal contacts. He invited them to look upon it "as a joint effort and not as a Ghana affair. . . ."[23] Yet Liberia made clear from the beginning that Ghana's role would be watched. When Ghana made a concession, Liberia asked for another. Thus Ambassador Simpson wondered if invitations could not be issued by a group of states, and he asked whether Ghana had in fact "consulted other Governments before issuing the invitations," a question that was clearly inappropriate in view of Ghana's cautious preparation.[24]

Little planning took place until the third meeting, by which time a Ghanaian draft memorandum on the aims of the conference had arrived. It was the most clearly articulated foreign policy statement ever produced in Ghana: it called for policy coordination (giving concrete reality to Nkrumah's abstraction, the "African personality") and for Africa to view the international situation "in the light of her own interests." It urged that "suggestions . . . be put forward to accelerate" the pace of liberation elsewhere in Africa and, most importantly, concluded with the hope that the conference would result in the "setting up of . . . permanent machinery for co-operation and consultation among the

[20] Alex Quaison-Sackey, *Africa Unbound*, New York, 1963, p. 63.
[21] See *CIAS Report*, p. 680.
[22] *Ibid.*, p. 676.   [23] *Ibid.*, p. 677.   [24] *Ibid.*, p. 681.

states."[25] The Sudanese ambassador, for his part, assumed that such machinery would be in Accra.[26]

The Liberians had a proposed addition to the memorandum: "In view of the tensions which exist in the world today the matter of subversive ideologies or coups d'etat whose designs are to overthrow organised governments should be discountenanced and condemned as subversive and destructive ideologies."[27] Tubman realized that Liberia's most difficult days were to come, and he sought to protect it from the forces that Nkrumah represented, to give it a more casual entry into the modern world. Thus began a dialogue of the deaf that was to last for eight years. At this point, however, the five other delegates went to Ghana's defense. The Libyan ambassador thought the Liberian proposal would be "an interference in the domestic affairs of each country" if accepted, and Taiib Slim, the distinguished Tunisian diplomat, thought that "African Governments must not tie their hands by condemning" ideologies from outside.[28] How was subversion defined, in any case? Simpson was in a corner, and said Liberia was concerned with the "coup d'etat method." He wished it to be on record "that African Leaders would discountenance undemocratic actions in overthrowing governments. He equated undemocratic actions with subversive acts, a point on which the High Commissioner for Ghana begged to differ."[29] At the next meeting, in February, the Liberians produced a much-revised version of their statement, asking the conference to condemn conspiracies aimed at African states—from outside Africa. Their bluff had been called, though this was far from the last word.

These meetings had in large measure been successful, but the shadow of Cairo—which had been receiving copies of the minutes through the Indian High Commission in London—hung over them. Partially as a result, the Ghanaians conducted two other offensives to ensure that nothing was missed by way of preparation. Ako Adjei visited Cairo as early as August 1957, partly to apprise the Egyptians of Accra's hopes; then, early in 1958, Padmore and Adjei toured all seven participating states trying, as Adjei put it, to assure them that Ghana "was not seeking the leadership of Africa. We also wished to anticipate difficult issues on the agenda." They were also learning how necessary such an approach was for, as Adjei added, no state was willing to go nearly so far as Nkrumah wished in the direction of unity.[30] They also learned the extent of

---

[25] *Ibid.*, pp. 749-55. The memorandum was written by A. L. Adu and A.B.B. Kofi.
[26] *Ibid.*, p. 685.   [27] *Ibid.*, p. 754.   [28] *Ibid.*, pp. 694, 696.
[29] *Ibid.*, p. 695.   [30] Interview: Ako Adjei.

Ghana's differences with Cairo on two issues, namely, representation of Algeria at the conference, and the question of Palestine.

There was, finally, a joint secretariat in Accra, which developed from a proposal by Cairo that senior officials should gather to take the preparations a stage further than the ambassadors could themselves. The ambassadors made Adu the conference's secretary-general,[31] and by March 27th officials from most states had arrived to begin the work of the joint secretariat. Padmore had not thought Adu competent to organize the conference (their rivalry was in the open by this time) and so he arranged behind Adu's back for the services of Dr. A. Appadorai, the secretary-general of the Indian Council on Foreign Affairs. To Adu's immense relief, Dr. Appadorai fell ill prior to his departure for Accra. Padmore's reward was that he was left off the official Ghanaian delegation to the conference.[32]

In fact Adu's preparations had been so thorough that there was agreement on all but two questions. The CCTA had agreed to provide interpreters, but the Ghanaians had not considered the security of the sessions, and found they had obtained, amongst others, a South African linguist. When objections were raised, a successful eleventh hour request to the United Nations was made for replacements.[33] In addition, the Arab states wanted Arabic as an official language of the conference, but on this the Ghanaians were not prepared to give way.[34] It was, after all, a major item of Ghanaian policy to induce the Arabs to "think African."

The Proceedings. The Ghanaians were disappointed at first that only one head of state or government had come to Accra for the conference. But there were many compensations: Its entire character would be altered had Nasser, the dominant figure of the continent, attended. The Ghanaians were thus able to influence the outcome far more, and to lay groundwork that might otherwise have been impossible. The Liberians also benefited. They had wanted the conference at ministerial level— as by and large it turned out to be—but as their president was the only head of state present, they affected its issue far more than they might have otherwise.

The discussions are significant, revealing as they do the individual interests of the participants, as well as the limits on Ghana's Africa policy. In later years it was easy to forget how different was the view from Accra at the time of the conference's opening. Accra was not the "diplomatic cockpit of Africa," nor was "African unity" a slogan of the day or even

[31] *CIAS Report*, pp. 762-63.
[32] Interview: CF-28.   [33] *CIAS Report*, pp. 763, 767.   [34] *Ibid.*, pp. 204-13, 720.

of the meeting. True, the Ghanaian delegation underlined its responsibilities to the rest of Africa, but it was with far more restraint than was to be the case ever again. Ghana may have been the first sub-Saharan colony to gain its independence but, from the point of view of the other seven, it was "the last . . . to have achieved independence."[35]

These states were only gradually becoming aware of their common interests, and Ghana, through its caution, made a significant contribution in bringing them together. It wanted an "African personality" to emerge, an aim well expressed by the Tunisian delegate who said the states must "single out the general lines of agreement and co-operation on common problems."[36] This was not to be easy; five of the states were Arab, and the other three had widely separate backgrounds and interests.

The most memorable phrase of the day was Nkrumah's, that the Sahara had been found to unite, not divide Africa. To the extent the cooperation ensued, this was true. But the conference highlighted the differences for what they were, and offered valuable lessons for the future. For it was on the vital issues that the Sahara's division was seen to be relevant. There was a different approach to problems: A new state like Ghana was full of idealism. In a discussion of the means available for liberating the rest of Africa, Nkrumah noted how much he depended on the United Nations, and added: "We may not have arms, but there is something like moral force in the Universe and if that moral force stands behind you, you have all the battalions behind you, and that is the way we are going to face this issue."[37] The U.A.R., on the other hand, possessed the other type of battalions, and had had experience with the UN, and its "helplessness . . . when somebody, supported by powerful influences and forces, says 'no' to [it]."[38] At a time when Ghana was making its international debut, Fawzi, the Egyptian foreign minister, insisted that "we must not just shout from roof tops telling everybody else . . . 'hands off our independence.' We must make this independence so active and robust that nobody can encroach upon it."[39] Indeed, the Egyptians must have appeared to the Ghanaians just as the Ghanaians certainly appeared to their proportionately smaller neighbors after 1960: more experienced, skeptical, and willing to carry the struggle alone.

Then there were expressly divisive issues. From the beginning of the London meetings, Ghana had insisted that there be no observers from dependent territories at the conference, for very good reasons from its point of view. It did not want attention diverted from the pan-African conference planned to come after the IAS conference, at which the focus would be on the unliberated territories. It particularly did not

[35] Ibid., p. 272.   [36] Ibid., p. 246.   [37] Ibid., pp. 309-10.
[38] Ibid., p. 306.   [39] Ibid., p. 378.

wish to share the limelight with Nigeria. Perhaps most important, it did not want North Africa to be the center of the conference which assuredly it would have been had the Algerians been delegates.[40]

Dr. Fawzi insisted that the Algerians be brought to the table, while the Ghanaians would not have them even as observers. After the Ghanaians reluctantly agreed to permit them to testify, Fawzi sardonically noted that Algeria (which, he said, the U.A.R. considered an "independent country") held higher status at Bandung, "and now in Accra, right in the heart of Africa . . . we bow before one difficulty or the other and go backward instead of going forward."[41]

Five days later, when resolutions were being drafted, Ghana tried to prevent the inclusion of a phrase pledging "moral and material" aid to the Algerians, arguing that it was sufficient to say simply that "every possible effort" should be made to help them.[42] The trap was not so easily avoided, and in the confused debate the phrase "moral and material" found its way back. Tubman momentarily saved the Ghanaians by bringing his own opposition to the phrase into the open, and Ghana for once wished "to support what the Liberian Delegation has just said." For "every possible effort" (the conservative phrase that the Ghanaians had conceded support to a few minutes earlier), where there is already a state of war, "might mean the assistance . . . of arms which we do not consider are in the interest of peace." The Ghanaians had twice retreated, and now proposed that the resolution simply pledge all aid "by peaceful means." But the Ghanaians were cornered: when the issue of moral and material aid was pressed by the Arabs, Nkrumah, the Chairman, interceded to try to rid the resolution of the word "material." After all, "We do not have to tell the whole world the form of help it is going to take."[43]

There was, too, a Moroccan proposal that a secretariat be established —in a state neighboring on Algeria—to coordinate efforts to propagate Algeria's cause. Liberia never let the proposal get very far, and the Ghanaians only cautiously supported it after it was evident that the Liberians would never let it be passed, and when the Arabs were on the defensive. (Botsio, much later, made clear that Ghana was against the secretariat.)[44] The final compromise was the decision that delegations

---

40 See ibid., p. 679, and Interview: Botsio.

41 Ibid., p. 223. In fact, Egypt had accorded neither de facto nor de jure recognition to a provisional Algerian government, of which one did not exist at this point. Moreover, Fawzi, who attended Bandung, should have recalled that the Algerians were not delegates there in their own right, but attended as members of the Iraqi delegation. See League of Arab States, p. 199, n.5.

42 CIAS Report, p. 560.

43 Ibid., pp. 561-66.   44 Ibid., pp. 574-88, Interview: Botsio.

should visit capitals of countries whose votes at the UN might be influenced, namely, the Scandinavians and Latin Americans. This effort was to have much success.

When liberation in black Africa was discussed (and here Ghanaian passion matched the Arabs' over Algeria) the roles were reversed, as between Ghana and the U.A.R. Ghana proposed the establishment of a fund "for assisting the Nationalists struggling in the various dependent Territories for their freedom."[45] Dr. Fawzi, on the other hand, said that although the idea initially looked good, "when there is a fund like that everybody will be rather inclined to wait on the others to see how much they contribute and so on. I think it might give us . . . negative instead of positive results." He wanted each state to have individual competence on this matter, adding that, in Cairo "we have had . . . some experience in this respect"; more to the point, the Solidarity Organization in Cairo already had a fund.[46]

The Ghanaians had their revenge in the debate on Palestine, and the Israelis, their reward for a year's intense diplomatic activity in Accra. The most compelling reason for Ghana's position was not its friendship with Israel, however, but its desire to prevent "Africa" from being absorbed in, and from having its energies diverted by, Middle-Eastern problems.

Once again the Liberians saved the Ghanaians from embarrassment, so blunt was their opposition even to a discussion of Palestine. The astute Ghanaian delegation was never forced to argue on Israel's behalf. Fawzi was furious, and in view of the number of times he reopened the question, it seems clear that he had strict instructions to bring results back to Cairo. Liberia at one point suggested that non-African problems should not be brought to the conference "by the back door,"[47] but Fawzi's position was understandable: "part of Africa was attacked a little while ago."[48] Nkrumah found a compromise, during a discussion of "world peace." The conference would support peace everywhere, throughout the world: Kashmir, South Africa—and Palestine. "This will be taking a broad view of the matter," he said.[49]

A decade after the conference, it was easy to see that the most important subject of debate in 1958 was over the establishment of a permanent secretariat. The absence of deeply rooted institutions was a sufficient (if hardly the sole) cause of the schism in Africa between 1960 and 1963: fifteen states became independent in 1960, and there was no

[45] *Ibid.*, p. 368.   [46] *Ibid.*, p. 374.   [47] *Ibid.*, pp. 500-01.
[48] *Ibid.*, p. 497.   [49] *Ibid.*, p. 503.

body strong enough uniting those already independent to prevent some of these from going their separate ways. Adu's joint secretariat had in fact prepared a careful and prophetic working paper on this question, in which the Ghanaian hand was evident. A permanent secretariat with a secretary-general and small body of seconded officials was seen to offer the possibility of coordination on issues of common interest. It was pointed out in the draft that periodic meetings of ministers would not alone be sufficient to keep questions of interest under review. "Possible objections" included the possibility that "if it becomes too effective it may tend to become a supra-national organisation"; it is therefore clear that a body like the Organisation of African Unity, to be created five years later, was in the minds of those who wrote the paper.[50]

Two delegations found this too ambitious, and it was the same two that had caused Ghana the greatest difficulties throughout. The U.A.R., for one, did not like the idea, as dependent peoples in Africa would criticize the body for not doing "the right thing." "Another will say that you did not do enough for us. Then again, we would be perhaps inclined to rely too much on this permanent body, and then we would sit back and see what it will do in order to further the purpose of African independence."[51] In any case, they could all meet at the UN, Fawzi said, hardly expecting that this suggestion would be taken up and formalized. The Egyptians had many reasons for taking this position, the most important being the existence of their own organization, AAPSO. Tubman allied Liberia with them in order to dampen Ghana's initiative and commented: "I did not see Dr. Fawzi last night but I find myself in such . . . agreement with him as to make you suspect that we have consulted. I think that each one of the reasons given are so important and so substantial that I need only say that I agree with them."[52] The debate became sharper two days later. Fawzi now added that a secretariat "would be subject to attack and intrigue from outside and attack and weakening from inside," and that "we would risk withering away and getting weaker." Tubman, slightly more positive, conceded that there should be a mechanism for pursuing the work of the conference, if not any which would "continuously meet to discuss problems and propositions."[53]

Ghana began giving way, and stressed the "*ad hoc* nature of this kind of consultation." It was not asking for a "huge and permanent office," but only a "small Secretariat." Tubman agreed that the time and place of the next meeting should be decided before the conclusion of the conference, but Fawzi did not want even this: "Mr. Chairman, the world is

50 *Ibid.*, pp. 670-75. See also *Guinea Times*, 15 April 1958, in which it is suggested that a secretariat could be in Accra.
51 *CIAS Report*, p. 375.   52 *Ibid.*, p. 376.   53 *Ibid.*, pp. 507-08.

moving so fast. How do we know that at such a time and at such a place we would be all ready to meet?"[54] Bandung, which had established no machinery and had held no further conferences, was on the other delegates' minds. Moreover, the Sudanese, Ethiopians, and Tunisians were pleased with the Accra conference, and so the Sudanese delegate answered Fawzi by simply pointing out that were he to have his way "this will be the first and last Conference of Independent African States."[55] These states now brought together the proposal for the establishment of an office at the United Nations. In view of Fawzi's veto of administrative machinery, and Tubman's probable veto of any machinery established in Accra, it is all that could have been hoped for.

For all that, history had been made in Accra. If, in the *Economist*'s words, it had "just failed to be a big stir" internationally, it was "the start for the young African states as Bandung, more pretentiously, was a start for the Asians: the announcement of a new bloc, perhaps, of a new force, but above all of their own, surprising existence in diplomacy."[56] It had provided a framework within which common views on issues uniting all eight states—antiracialism, anticolonialism—might have stimulated some cooperation in other spheres.

Nkrumah's Diplomacy, and the African Group. Fearing that the good results of the conference would be lost without follow-up, Nkrumah set out five weeks later with two ministers, George Padmore, and A.B.B. Kofi, a diplomat, to visit all seven participating states. It was an ambitious endeavor, a pan-African voyage. Ghana had ambassadors only in Egypt and Liberia, limited contact with the rest, and had realized just how weak the links were between each of these states. As Tubman had been the only head of state to attend the conference, the trip also gave Nkrumah a chance for extended discussions with other leaders, both peers and otherwise, to "feel the pulse"[57] of Africa prior to his American visit. Finally, "it was an African way of saying thank you to the states for coming to our conference," Kofi added.[58]

The reception in Ethiopia was typical of the visits—and extraordinary. It was the first visit of a black African statesman. They agreed to exchange embassies, to negotiate a trade agreement, and to coordinate their foreign policies at the United Nations. For Nkrumah, it was a chance to meet the man whose exile in 1935 had so moved him; throughout the ensuing years the Emperor was to exercise a special influence on him. The Ethiopians, for their part, were only in the process of orienting

---

[54] *Ibid.*, pp. 509-13.   [55] *Ibid.*, p. 514.   [56] *Economist*, 26 April 1958, p. 286.
[57] *Guinea Times*, 11 June 1958.
[58] Interview: A.B.B. Kofi.

their diplomacy to Africa. In 1954, the Americans apparently had refused Ethiopia membership in the Baghdad pact, as Ethiopia "was not a Middle-Eastern country."[59] As it could not go north, it had to go south. Thus the Ethiopians were cautious, and the visit might have made clear the limits to Nkrumah's pan-African plans. Like the Moroccans, they expressed a preference for the Liberian approach to pan-Africanism. The communiqué also "affirmed anew . . . the principle of refraining from interference . . . in the internal affairs of any country,"[60] a clause absent in the Ghana-U.A.R. communiqué.

Ghana's Africa policy appeared to become more flexible in the course of the trip. In the Sudan (which had not joined the Commonwealth) Nkrumah announced that Ghana was free to leave the Commonwealth if it so wished. This was not in question, but in the saying his policy was given a new cast. He also promised that Ghana would abide by any unanimous African decisions with respect to Israel. In Tunis, he had constructive talks with his friend Bourguiba, particularly about the need to establish the UN African Group at an early date, and in Morocco he made a new friend in the Sultan.

The most significant visits were to the two states which posed obstacles to Ghana's leadership in Africa, the U.A.R. and Liberia. Nasser went to some lengths to make the visit a successful one, and Nkrumah extended his stay from five to eight days. But the discussions, in Accra and now in Cairo, made clear where cooperation was and was not possible. On the one hand, they found such broad agreement on issues as "positive neutralism" and French atomic testing in the Sahara that the Western press expressed "fear" that they were growing closer. This feeling was heightened by Nkrumah's announcement in Cairo that Ghana would become a republic, an intention he had always had, but with added significance when announced in that city. On the other hand, there was no agreement on the Palestine question, to which, in the communiqué, they urged a "just solution." Nkrumah did not agree to fill Ghana's seat in the Solidarity Organization. Nothing was said of the African Group to be formed at the United Nations.[61] "The Egyptians did not know which way they would go at that point, Africa or the Middle East," a Ghanaian diplomat said.[62] Yet it was perfectly clear; they would go in both directions, but more in one than in the other. In the ensuing years Ghana and the U.A.R. found a basis for cooperation only on international Afro-Asian radical causes.

Nkrumah's visit to Liberia was important for a different reason. By this time he had circled the continent he sought to lead: 20,000 miles

[59] Interview: CF-63A.
[60] *Guinea Times*, 3 June 1958.
[61] Communiqué, in *Ghana Times*, 23 June 1959.
[62] Interview: CF-109.

and 70 flying hours. There in Liberia, by the account of a distinguished diplomat who knew him well, he realized that a dictatorship could maintain its Western friends and still attract investment. The Ghanaian opposition had slowed his pan-African momentum, he thought, and the trip had made clear how much work remained unfinished. "He thus decided to start running Ghana as Tubman ran Liberia. But there would be a purpose in his own actions, as they would be for the sake of Africa. I kept a checklist of all the new procedures he instituted on his return, in imitation of Tubman's regime. It was incredible."[63]

Nkrumah's trip was not the only follow-up to the April conference. With the establishment of the "informal permanent machinery" of the Independent African States (IAS) at the United Nations, Ghana had an institutional framework for leadership. A Ghanaian diplomat posted at the New York mission, Y. D. Turkson, became the executive secretary of the group; there were Tunisian, Liberian, and Egyptian officers as well. According to Turkson, the emphasis in discussion was put on consensus, not votes; but there was success on both counts. In the 13th and 14th sessions no member of the Group voted against any other member on African issues, however many "solidarity abstentions" there were. "This was the most effective machinery Africa has ever had."[64]

Professor Hovet's studies of these sessions show that Ghana voted more often with the group majority than any other state. While in 1958 Ghana was never in opposition to the vote of the majority of members, "Ethiopia and Liberia opposed the majority . . . in 9 percent of the votes."[65] (By several accounts, it was in fact the Egyptians whose views were the most discordant.) Nonetheless, the supreme opportunity for cooperation was lost. After Guinea's independence in October 1958, the Ghanaian and Liberian representatives were chosen to find the best multilateral means of going to Guinea's aid. Fred Arkhurst, the ranking professional diplomat at Ghana's mission, returned to Accra in November on his own initiative partly because "no one was answering our telegrams regarding aid to Guinea," and to press for recognition of the newly formed Algerian Provisional Government. He was told to wait several days. On November 23rd the Ghana-Guinea union was proclaimed, a unilateral action which apparently shocked the other members of the group. "Had we worked together to help Guinea subsequent African history could have been very different and much happier."[66]

63 Interview: CF-27.
64 Interview: Ambassador Y. D. Turkson.
65 Thomas Hovet, *Africa in the United Nations*, London, 1963, p. 116.
66 Interview: F. S. Arkhurst.

EXTERNAL RELATIONS

Ghana and the West. In his diplomacy with the Western powers, Nkrumah, during the first years of independence, was to their point of view a model nonaligned leader. This was intentional. His purpose was the industrialization of Ghana.

At the 1957 Commonwealth Prime Ministers' Conference, he was an "immediate success," wrote Colin Legum, "not so much by the weight of his contributions, so far, but by his modesty."[67] It appeared that he was unwilling to take a contentious stand on any issue, and it was even reported that he was in harmony with South Africa's foreign minister, Eric Louw, on the question of the "danger of Communism."[68] He also established warm relations with the leaders of the old Commonwealth, far more so than those made with Nehru.

What he did press for was economic help. He asked for a guaranteed cocoa price, and a "Colombo Plan" for Africa, but he found a response to neither. More important, he discovered that the money for the Volta River Project did not exist in Britain.[69]

This was, in a sense, the last meeting of its kind, before the Commonwealth was transformed by new pressures and forces, largely from Africa. Nkrumah, with his low-keyed diplomacy in 1957, deserves part of the credit that the change took place so easily. Yet Nkrumah on the one hand and the leaders of the old Commonwealth on the other probably failed to see the meeting's real importance. For Nkrumah, it was a chance to be received by the Queen, to be entertained by Mountbatten and Home, to drive around at night with Sir Robert Jackson, and to see again and again the fortresses of power that he once had peered at from without. The Commonwealth leaders, for their part, probably failed to see Nkrumah's symbolic significance, portending a doubling of the group. In its final summary of the meeting, the *Times*'s only mention of Ghana was that "one of the most enjoyable aspects of the conference has been the obvious pleasure of the Ghana representatives at being present on equal terms."[70] Menzies promised to send an envoy to Accra, and Diefenbaker warmly urged Nkrumah to visit Canada. This was not the same type of interest, however, that Attlee's government had shown when India joined the Commonwealth, or when the Colombo Plan was begun.

Nkrumah, for all that, thought highly of the Commonwealth connection, as is shown by his diplomatic overtures to South Africa. His ap-

[67] *Observer*, 30 June 1957.
[68] *Scotsman*, 29 June 1957. See also *Hindu*, 28 June 1957.
[69] *Times*, 3 July 1957; *Observer*, 30 June 1957.
[70] *Times*, 6 July 1957.

proach resembled India's, that the Commonwealth was big enough for both Ghana and South Africa, and that the Commonwealth conferences were not the forum to discuss *apartheid*. Rather, the connection could be used to stimulate cooperation that might influence the other party. At the time the South African nationalists were feeling their growing isolation, and the possibility of exchanging ambassadors with Accra was being hotly debated in Cape Town. Louw had stated that diplomatic representation "must come in the future but it cannot be done overhastily," and he had also noted that it would need be done in such a manner that the Africans could "be received . . . and treated with dignity."[71] Nkrumah could not have foreseen that his own efforts were to be rebuffed, even if this were a time when Dr. Azikiwe's Nigerian paper was demanding that South Africa leave the Commonwealth.[72]

As for the Volta Project, it would have to be built with American money, Jackson bluntly informed Nkrumah.[73] The scope of the $600,000,000 scheme, and the relatively small amount of Russian aid distributed by this time (even the Aswan dam had not yet been promised to Nasser) pointed to this same conclusion. Nkrumah was fortunate in his timetable, as his 1958 pan-African tour just preceded his arrival in America. The point was not missed. He came as "the emissary of all Free Africa."[74] His public remarks were calculated to further an appropriate image for the occasion. He thought Nasser should "exercise more restraint" in his dealings with the West;[75] he said Communism was no danger in Ghana ("our better institutions . . . do not allow the ideology to have any fruitful set-up in our country").[76] Even more astonishing, he suggested that "the racial question in the United States had often been exaggerated deliberately by those who hoped to bring the country into disrepute,"[77] this from a man who had suffered ten years discrimination in that country. He promised to enact generous investment laws, and kept his word.

He tried to be helpful in a more concrete way. American interest was in the Middle East, where marines had just landed. Nasser had just returned from Moscow. Nkrumah proposed that a UN force (to which he would contribute three Ghanaian battalions) replace the marines in

[71] *Union of South Africa, Debates*, 10 June 1957, cols. 7670, 7662.
[72] *West African Pilot*, 7 June 1957.
[73] Interview: Sir Robert Jackson, 21 January 1966, 12 January 1967.
[74] *Manchester Guardian*, 8 June 1958. See also *New York Herald Tribune* (European edition), 23 July 1958, *Guinea Times*, 28 May 1958 and 16 June 1958.
[75] *New York Times*, 25 July 1958. See also his similar comments to Kingsley Martin, *New Statesman*, 5 October 1957.
[76] Nkrumah, *I Speak of Freedom*, p. 139.
[77] *Ibid.*

Lebanon, and that the entire Middle East be quarantined, with the borders frozen and guaranteed.[78] He need not have bothered reassuring the Americans that his proposals were not meant to be hostile. They knew that UN troops in Lebanon would accomplish the same purpose as those of the United States, preserving a status quo which Nasser wished changed. No wonder *Time* could say that "seldom was a guest from a small country more welcome. The State Department saw the nationalism of his year-old country and the promise of his African leadership as a possible future counter-balance to rampant nationalism spreading from the Midcast."[79]

Nkrumah had now made every gesture consistent with dignity to lay the groundwork for his request for support of the Volta Project. What were the results? Little attention was paid to his proposals for the Middle East, which underlined how little attention Washington paid to proposals by those with no real weight on international issues. True, in his tour of Harlem he did capture "the somnolent imagination of the American Negroes,"[80] but this was not much help, and was an occasional embarrassment.[81] The main result was that he met Edgar Kaiser, who was to become a close confidant. Probably because of a world surplus of aluminum at the time, America made little further effort to be helpful on the Volta scheme. It did agree to pay half the cost of a reassessment of the project, which gave Kaiser an opening to investigate possibilities.[82]

Nkrumah's expectations had once again been too high. American interest in Africa was growing rapidly, but not enough to bring the Ghanaians what they wanted. The young diplomats in the Washington embassy were seeking levers of influence, but found little beyond fine words. "The tiny Bureau of African Affairs at the State Department tried to be helpful, but was suspicious when we attempted to develop contact in other areas of the department or at the White House."[83]

[78] See *New York Times*, 25 July 1958, and *Ghana Times*, 22 July 1958. More radical proposals are suggested by the *Evening News*, 25 July 1958.

[79] *Time*, 4 August 1958, p. 14.

[80] Patrick O'Donovan, *Observer Foreign News Service*, 31 July 1958.

[81] According to a Ghanaian diplomat then at the Washington embassy, many American Negroes wished to go to Ghana to help "nation-build," but were in little position to be helpful. CF-17.

[82] Gbedemah had been conducting discussions at a lower level with American officials for almost a year, but these made little headway until the famous incident in which he was refused restaurant service, after which he was invited to breakfast at the White House, where he acquainted Eisenhower with the project. See "Edgar Kaiser's Gamble in Africa," *Fortune* (November 1961).

[83] Interview: CF-14.

Nkrumah's diplomacy in the Western capitals contrasted sharply with his attitude towards Western diplomacy in Accra, whose influence he was trying to eliminate step by step. At the April IAS conference and at the pan-African conference at the end of the year, he warned of "new forms of colonialism which are now appearing in the world";[84] it was widely believed that he was pointing toward the East or to Cairo. But the statement was purposely ambiguous, and he very likely intended America to be included. Botsio recalled that Nkrumah was "very concerned about American neo-colonialism at that time."[85] To be sure, this was a different line than had been heard from him in Washington and London, but this contradiction was wholly in character. He had given them their *bon mots*, and it was for them to respond in the way he wished.

Nonetheless, Nkrumah was easy to influence, and what he did depended to a degree on the diplomatic influences brought to bear in Accra. In a small capital a good diplomat can become a man of immense influence, as was shown by the *tour de force* of the Israeli ambassador to Ghana during this period. Western diplomacy was weak, however. The British high commissioner was not prepared to use the influence at his disposal, and the American ambassador was widely considered incapable of wielding much influence in any case.[86] Both envoys were career diplomats not well-suited for their assignment, but it was the fault of their governments for not foreseeing the importance of the post.

In the British case, it is argued that there was a strong desire to "set a good precedent in post-colonial relations for the sake of the colonies that were to follow";[87] it has also been pointed out that the Commonwealth Office was dealing with an independent black African government for the first time. Yet a skillful diplomatist like Cumming-Bruce (briefly the deputy high-commissioner) demonstrated clearly how influence could be wielded without it appearing part of the colonial legacy. Some observers thought the British were unable to see beyond their commercial involvement in Ghana, merely seeking to preserve their commercial superiority in the face of new European and American competition;[88] they did nothing, for example, to stop Ghana's withdrawal from the British West African cooperation boards, which might so easily have been transformed into constructive pan-African concerns. They stood idly by while Nkrumah imprisoned his opponents and oiled the machinery of colonialist autocracy eight years out of use. The West could not see the chain of events which Nkrumah's actions had begun. It was weak diplomacy, and in the American case the failure was inexcusable. Two and a

[84] *CIAS Report*, p. 4.   [85] Interview: Botsio.   [86] Interviews: CF-113, 60, 34.
[87] Interview: CF-106A.   [88] Interview: CF-27.

half years after independence, a Russian ambassador began making the efforts to influence Nkrumah that Wilson Flake, the American envoy, had failed to make.

Ghana, Israel, and "Afro-Asia." In its first five years Ghana did not take an active part in Afro-Asian affairs, insofar as these constituted a political movement. Nkrumah's concern was Africa, and at the IAS conference he even insisted that Bandung be referred to as the "African and Asian" (rather than Afro-Asian) conference[89]—no possible leadership role existed for him in the Afro-Asian movements, and too much involvement in the People's Solidarity Organization (headquartered in Cairo) could only compromise his relations with the West. It was, however, a cardinal objective of Ghanaian policy to draw the Arab-African states into purely African affairs, and from the beginning it was clear that far-reaching cooperation with Nasser was essential if his plans for Africa were to succeed. But Israel became Ghana's closest friend in the early years, which made some wonder whether Nkrumah were not purposely seeking to counter potential Egyptian influence in black Africa.[90] The sequence of events with respect to Israel and the Middle East must be carefully considered before any judgment may be made on Nkrumah's strategy towards the U.A.R. and the Afro-Asian world.

How important was Israel's accomplishment? Accra, Mecca of African nationalism, was seen by every pilgrim—Hastings Banda, Kenneth Kaunda, Julius Nyerere, Tom Mboya—to have warm ties with Jerusalem. After their separate independence celebrations, they all followed Ghana in establishing equally close ties with Israel. Kojo Botsio, who coordinated aid to the nationalists, was known among his friends as "Soleh Boneh" (after the Israeli firm) and was Israel's best friend in Africa.[91] Israel at the time had only twelve full embassies,[92] and had never truly developed the ties in Asia that might have countered its isolation in the Middle East. Through Nkrumah, it achieved a great diplomatic coup, by establishing itself throughout Africa; this in the wake of Suez, and in spite of its conservative UN voting record.

This was possible for several reasons. The British had permitted the

---

[89] *CIAS Report*, p. 627; see also *Daily Graphic*, 6 March 1958.

[90] See, for example, Arnold Rivkin, "Israel and the Afro-Asian World," *Foreign Affairs*, 37, No. 3 (April 1959), 486.

[91] Krobo Edusei gave him this name. It was widely felt that Botsio benefited financially from his connections with Israeli firms. This may well be true. It would not, however, explain the extent of his help to the Israeli cause. By all accounts he returned from a visit to Israel in 1957 incredulous at what he had seen.

[92] Walter Eytan, *The First Ten Years, A Diplomatic History of Israel*, London, 1958, pp. 177-78, 196.

Israelis to establish a consulate in Ghana prior to independence, while Egypt was not even invited to the independence celebrations. The consul, Chanan Yavor, moved quickly and effectively to establish a network of friends. There was luck, too. A group of young CPP radicals coming from a conference in Indonesia stopped for a brief visit in Israel and were sufficiently overwhelmed to remain a few weeks. This story was to be repeated over and over after independence: when John Tettegah (the trade union leader) returned in early 1957 from ten days there he told reporters that he had learned more about trade unionism than he "could have learned in a British university in ten years," and decided to model Ghana's T.U.C. on the Israeli Histadrut.[93] Eight years later when the Israeli cause was no longer a popular one in Accra he was still prepared to stand by his former mentors.

Moreover, Padmore had little use for Nasser, whom he thought was being used by the Russians, and felt profound sympathy for the Jews. "It was a question of 'niggers and Jews' for all of us," Makonnen noted.[94] Nor was Nkrumah's own attitude altogether negative. True, he considered the country as an imperialist enclave, but not an artificially created one, like Rhodesia. He admired what they had accomplished. "Remember too that in those early years his first priority was to develop Ghana, and he thought we could do much to help him. Indeed, his ideas of what we could provide were too grandiose,"[95] an Israeli diplomat noted. But they did much. The partnerships established in shipping and building are well described elsewhere.[96] If they could not grant massive assistance to Ghana, they could give what was within their means (including a $20m credit) without red-tape and long delays. They were quick, efficient, and knew what was needed. There were more subtle benefits, too. Nkrumah could bestow favor on African nationalists by arranging to send them to Israel. This easily fit into his objectives: he would hardly have wished to send someone like Kaunda to East Germany on the one hand, or Britain on the other. He could preserve his anticolonialist stance by sending them to Israel, and Israel, for its part, was not going to object if a nationalist of Kaunda's stature, delivered into their grasp for several weeks by Nkrumah, wished to consider the trip as Nkrumah's gift.

Then, too, there was Nkrumah's ambition of settling the Middle East conflict. This desire was something less than consistent with his efforts to prevent the Arab-Africans from hobbling Africa with their Middle-

[93] Quoted in A. A. Syme, "Ghanaians Salute Israel," Accra, 1958, p. 5. Also Interview: John Tettegah.
[94] Interview: T. R. Makonnen.
[95] Interview: CF-27.
[96] See Arnold Rivkin, *Africa and the West*, London, 1962, pp. 72-76.

47

Eastern concerns; his justification, that a settlement there would enable them to turn their eyes toward Africa, was no more relevant than his desire itself. Only pained interest was taken in his proposals by either side.[97]

In the final analysis, however, Israel's achievement in Ghana was the result of one man's diplomacy. In Nkrumah's nine years, only two ambassadors ever completely dominated the diplomatic scene in Accra, through great influence with him. One was Georgi Rodionov, between 1962 and 1966 the Russian ambassador to Ghana; the other, and first, Ehud Avriel. It was Avriel, according to Christopher Sykes, who broke the arms embargo imposed on Israel during the first Arab-Israeli war, thus succeeding in "perhaps one of the most crucial [missions] in Jewish history."[98] Subsequently he became one of Israel's first diplomats. He soon filled the role of confidant to Nkrumah which Arden-Clarke had played. It was he who introduced Nkrumah to Lumumba; but in diplomatic circles this was considered less remarkable than that at times it was Avriel who had to intercede to arrange an appointment for the American ambassador with Nkrumah.[99] When Nkrumah wished to write a book, it was Avriel who produced the "ghost," who in turn quickly produced a serviceable manuscript.[100] True, Avriel was the beneficiary of weak American and British diplomacy, but his competence and foresight stand out no less for this.

Yet the limit to Israel's influence in Ghana was evident to a perceptive observer. Nkrumah, for example, was extremely cautious in what he himself said about Israel; indeed, at the dedication of a Black Star Line ship built and financed by the Israelis, he pointedly did not thank them. (He did express gratitude the next day in parliament after Avriel had pointed out this omission, however.)[101] Nor did he accept their invitation to visit Israel, although he visited Egypt several times in the first few years.

For over a year, Avriel had a clear field but, apparently sensing that at some point Nkrumah's pan-African ambitions and Israel's diplomatic aims would collide, he ran scared from the first. Unlike the Anglo-Saxons, he made the most of his opportunity, obtaining the substance of what Israel wanted—its entry into Africa. In 1959, he began scaling the

[97] Interviews: CF-27, 96. See also Nkrumah, *I Speak of Freedom*, p. 152.
[98] Christopher Sykes, *Crossroads to Israel*, Cleveland, 1965, p. 339.
[99] Interviews: CF-113, 27, 34.
[100] The writer was Moshe Pearlman, who was later to write the memoirs of (among others) General Dayan. The manuscript was entitled, curiously, "My Task." Although it was never published as such, much of Nkrumah's third book, *Africa Must Unite*, and parts of some of his speeches, were extracted from it. (Writer's files.)
[101] See *Debates*, 19 December 1957, pp. 787-88; also, Interview: CF-27.

conspicuous activity down so as to make their long-range position more tenable. When Nkrumah's ideas for the Black Star Line became extravagant by Israeli standards, the Israelis opted out, before Egyptian pressure might drive them out. The ships were, after all, blacklisted from Suez, and it was a delicate situation which neither Nasser nor Nkrumah wished to put to the test. According to Israeli sources, Nkrumah subsequently asked the Israelis to manage the line for twenty-five years and they, making a virtue of necessity, countered with the more realistic suggestion of five years, making it appear that Israel was not in pursuit of Ghana's grace.[102]

In the meantime, relations with Egypt had grown apace. Ako Adjei became, in effect, the spokesman for pro-Arab sentiment, and the instrument for the development of ties there. He visited Cairo twice prior to the IAS conference, requested assistance of various sorts, and attacked Israel.[103] In December 1957, Nkrumah married an Egyptian Coptic woman, one of the more bizarre alliances caused by his foreign policy.[104] During the IAS conference, he apparently discussed the possibility of military cooperation with Dr. Fawzi, including a joint African high command; which, though the proposal went no further for two years, shows remarkable foresight.[105]

Egypt and Ghana agreed to exchange ambassadors, but the Egyptian did not arrive until mid-1958. Once there, he did not for a time alter the situation because, some said, his diplomatic efforts were counterproductive.[106] His was an essentially negative policy, combatting Israeli influence, trying to get them out. Avriel's was keeping Israel in, a positive policy with its inherent advantage over a negative policy. All this is not to say that the Egyptians came to Accra only in response to the Israelis, but rather that they were forced to define their diplomacy in Accra as one of counteracting Israeli influence;[107] and in fact their diplomacy consisted of a series of reactions to Israeli initiatives.[108]

---

[102] Interview: CF-27.

[103] See *Egyptian Gazette*, 18 August 1957, and *Scotsman*, 6 September 1957. In interviews at a later date, however, Adjei expressed the profoundest admiration for Israel, which was probably part of his general reaction to his past roles after release from four years' detention.

[104] The marriage was to be a continuing embarrassment to Nkrumah, and to his colleagues. He seldom paid any attention to her. At the time of writing, it was reported that she was suing Nkrumah for divorce. See R. W. Howe, "Fortunes Dwindle for Silent Nkrumah," *Sunday Times*, 24 December 1967.

[105] Interview: CF-27, and letter, CFL-P.

[106] Interviews: CF-113, 34.

[107] Interview: CF-96.

[108] Thus, when Israel negotiated a trade agreement with Ghana, Egypt tried to do likewise, but according to Botsio, the size they envisaged for it barely justified his devoting time to it. See Ali Mazrui's article, "Africa and the Egyptian's Four Circles,"

Curiously, the Ghanaian opposition thought Nkrumah was naive with regard to Nasser's aims, believing he was being used. Joe Appiah added in a debate that he had never heard an Arab call himself an African.[109] The opposition correctly guessed that Nkrumah's sympathies would lie ultimately with Nasser, and argued that the government was equivocating on the rightness of Israel's cause. They failed to see that it was only Avriel who had a successful strategy in respect to the Ghana-U.A.R.-Israel triangle. Israel and Egypt fulfilled different functions in Nkrumah's strategies, but there can be no question that Avriel ran diplomatic circles around Nkrumah. Nkrumah could not intend that events develop in this manner, if only because he could not anticipate how effective an ambassador Israel would send to Accra. Avriel had obviously seen the long-term deal in the making: were Nkrumah to involve Ghana in international issues, and were Nasser to involve Egypt in sub-Saharan conflicts, the two would find the sacrifice of Ghana's special relationship with Israel as the basis for a bargain. But Israel in the meantime obtained what it had sought, did much for Ghana, and developed a strong enough position to ride out what was, in the end, only one year of utterly strained relations.

It is with this as background that the alleged "Nasser-Nkrumah rivalry" must be considered. Obviously ambitious statesmen with overlapping interests will see each other in a competitive light but this does not necessarily make their foreign policies competitive. Nkrumah's star was rising but Nasser's had risen, and what was central to Nkrumah was marginal to Nasser. So long as Nasser did not proselytize for allies in West or East Africa, there was nothing to bring conflict between them, and there was nothing at this early stage which Nasser could offer Nkrumah as an alternative to his Israeli ties. That the two held similar outlooks on world problems became obvious during Nkrumah's visit to Cairo in June 1958.

Where tension developed was between the overlapping and competing people's organizations, established in Cairo at the end of 1957 and in Accra a year later. Nkrumah had stayed clear of AAPSO "because of its external involvement,"[110] and because it was not his organization. He had no objection, as such, to the extreme left resolutions passed at the 1957 conference in Cairo, but there was little to be gained by

---

African Affairs, 63, No. 251 (April 1964), in which, by implication, he counters the argument that Egypt was in black Africa merely to combat Israeli influence. In the present writer's study, Egypt's genuine interest in black Africa is not in question. It had simply been outmaneuvered, and was forced to react.

[109] *Debates*, 15 July 1958, pp. 2091-93, 99.

[110] Interview: Botsio.

identifying Ghana with them.[111] The Ghanaians did object, on the other hand, to the attempts by the Egyptians to pack their delegation to the peoples' conference in Accra, but George Padmore made known his objections and frustrated their plans.[112] This Egyptian effort, however, was not evidence of a rivalry between statesmen, but a reflection of the differing interests that states on either side of the Sahara possessed. At the IAS conference, the Egyptians had been outmaneuvered, and wanted as many delegates as possible at the next Accra conference to support the Algerian, and anti-Israeli, cause.

Had Ghana been interested in the Afro-Asian movements, it might also have been expected to develop close ties with India. It did not. The nationalist leaders before independence had looked to India, and Nkrumah had admired Gandhi and Nehru. There had been diplomatic contact with India prior to independence, and afterwards the ministry in Accra took India's foreign policy as a standard for its own in some regards.[113] This did not last long: from their first meeting Nkrumah and Nehru had bad personal relations. At the 1957 Commonwealth conference, Nkrumah had informed Nehru, no doubt enthusiastically, that the Ghanaian parliament was erecting a statue of its leader outside its seat. The Cambridge-educated Brahmin noted that this would not be possible in India until he himself had died, and from then on he considered Nkrumah an opportunist of the Sukarno stamp and of no long-term significance.[114] Nkrumah, in turn, never forgave Nehru.

He still wished to visit India, much the most important nonaligned country. He was received there at the end of 1958 as "Africa's man of destiny,"[115] received great publicity, but overplayed his hand. Cyril Dunn wrote that he seemed "eager to present himself as spokesman, not for Ghana alone, but for the whole African continent, and to be seen standing up alongside Mr. Nehru as another statesman of international significance. There were some in the sophisticated audiences of this city who, while admiring his spirit, doubted his qualifications."[116] Nor did relations develop at other levels. The Ghanaian students sent

---

[111] According to Ambassador Bediaku Poku, in interview, who attended the first AAPSO conference as a Ghanaian delegate. There were others who did not object in Accra. See Volumes 1 and 2 of *The Pan-African Age*, a journal which briefly appeared in Accra in this period.

[112] Interviews: Botsio, Markham, Makonnen.

[113] Interview: CF-28.

[114] Interviews: CF-113, 70.

[115] *Hindu*, 27 December 1958.

[116] *Observer Foreign News Service*, 9 January 1959.

to Indian universities were not the country's best and, in Accra, India was neither the Congress party nor Nehru, but the much disliked Indian trader.[117] Both by design and fortuity, Ghana was by the end of its second year presenting a wholly different image from the existing standard-bearers of nonalignment. Thus was its commitment to African unity reinforced.

Ghana at the UN. Unlike the U.A.R., Ghana had found only success in its previous dealings with the United Nations; at the IAS conference, Nkrumah told his colleagues how British Togoland was obtained:

> . . . with the strength of organisation I had behind me, I was able to tell the British Government to make it quite clear that they would have to relinquish their trust territory. So Britain had to negotiate with the United Nations . . . and we were able to get that territory to our side. . . .
>
> If we can have some sort of pressure brought to bear on the United Nations to act strongly upon their obligations to these trust territories, I am quite sure we would not have such a problem.[118]

Thus, Ghana's commitment to the United Nations can for the most part be explained without reference to the powerful idealism shared by Nkrumah and his diplomats.

The Ghanaian team at the UN nonetheless did credit to its ideals and set a high standard for other newly independent states to follow. Major Seth Anthony who established the mission had general instructions to follow Canada on Western, and India on Eastern, questions,[119] but from the first a tradition of independence developed in the delegation which resulted in a better balanced nonalignment than was evident in Accra during the same period. At the opening of the 13th session, Anthony felt that the Indian position over Hungary as explained by Arthur Lall was not right, so he cast Ghana's vote with the Western majority: "As a nation which has only recently achieved its independence, we have a vested interest in orderly international intercourse and the rule of law, and we would always vehemently protest in any instance in which . . . one country had used its superior military power to crush a movement for freedom in another country."[120] In any event, India was not a model for long. The Ghanaians found Krishna Menon sanctimonious and patronizing.

Gradually the delegation moved away from its initial caution, which

[117] Interview: CF-33.   [118] *CIAS Report*: pp. 320-21.   [119] Interview: CF-28.
[120] *UNGA*, 677th Plen., 13 September 1957, p. 1468, Para. 184-85.

had been the result of inadequate staff and Anthony's own unwillingness to venture into areas where he was not briefed. The permanent
representative, Daniel Chapman, the former cabinet secretary, was conservative, but soon had a group of radical young diplomats under him
who argued for Africa's interests on a number of fronts. In the second
committee F. S. Arkhurst pressed for the creation of an economic commission for Africa, and for the establishment of the Special Fund.[121]
In the fourth committee, another member questioned whether the association of the non-self-governing territories with the European Common Market was "calculated . . . to speed the development of the
'NSGT's' toward economic viability and ultimate political responsibility?"[122] And John Jantuah, a former CPP minister, questioned the
relevance of a Latin American's remark that "newly emerged States
should not criticize the older States that had brought them to nationhood. . . . The sovereignty of a nation had no bearing on the length
of its existence as a state nor upon its size or strength."[123] They also
directly opposed Ghanaian policy on occasion, at one time regretting
"the lack of cooperation on the part of the Israeli Government" with
UN resolutions;[124] this was largely the work of Harry Amonoo, probably the most radical of Ghana's first eight diplomats. They could do
this because Nkrumah did not follow UN affairs; the delegation became a virtually independent subsystem of Ghana's foreign policy, seldom worrying about Accra's reaction to particular votes. When this
became apparent to the foreign missions in Accra, the diplomats there
stopped lobbying on particular votes, and began a similar process in
New York. One of the Ghanaians commented that "everybody seemed
to value our opinion. We consulted freely with the Soviets long before
they had a mission in Accra, and voted for Algerian independence
before Accra had recognized the provisional government. In those days
we were truly non-aligned."[125]

FOREIGN POLICY AND DOMESTIC POLITICS

The first year and a half had been exciting. "Ghana has within a short
time become a household word in all civilized countries," Komla Gbedemah said in parliament, during the July 1958 foreign policy debate.
He was asking for a much increased budget for the Ministry of External
Affairs, one which reflected "the great events of the past year." £35,000
was appropriated for a Telex, and £65,000 for a diplomatic courier

121 *Ibid.*, IInd Comm., 468th meeting, 21 October 1957, pp. 24-27.
122 *Ibid.*, IVth Comm., 28 October 1957, Para. 29.
123 *Ibid.*, Special Pol. Comm., 21 October 1958, pp. 38-39.
124 *Ibid.*, 17 November 1958, pp. 6-9.   125 Interview: CF-20.

service; £172,000 for acquiring new embassies in Bonn, Tel-Aviv, Moscow, Khartoum, and consulates in West Africa.[126]

Yet something was amiss. In its external relations, Ghana had become highly sensitive about criticism in the Western, particularly the British, press, which Nkrumah saw as one unrelenting campaign to bring about the disintegration of the young nation. Yet the government's riposte to its domestic opponents—deportations and arrests—had been enough even to drive Fenner Brockway to plead that Nkrumah not use the excuses of the former imperial authority, security and peace, to suppress liberty.[127] Nkrumah, in turn, justified harsh legislation, such as a preventive detention act that empowered the government to detain who it pleased for five years (in contrast to the 90-day law of the country for which he was trying to set an example) on the grounds that the eyes of the world were on Ghana, that stability was needed if investment were to flow to Ghana. Indeed, in America these sentiments had been applauded.[128] But in Britain, there was an obsession with what happened in Ghana and the attitude was largely critical. The Ghanaian leaders, for their part, seemed unable to distinguish between "critics and enemies" (as Kingsley Martin put it),[129] while Colin Legum wrote that it was "the mild paranoia of nationalism to look for hurt where none exists."[130]

The psychological strains of de-colonization were not the whole story, however. The radical young CPP leaders realized that the British criticism could be turned to their own advantage; John Tettegah, the young trade union leader, used it as an excuse to argue for Ghana's withdrawal from the Commonwealth. It was, obviously, in their interest to rid Ghana of all vestiges of the imperial era, in order to make more easy the removal of the CPP's old guard—with ties with the West. The threat the radicals posed was serious enough to convince Legum, for one, that Ghana's continued membership in the Commonwealth was at stake.[131]

This exaggerated their power at this stage.[132] Nkrumah was in control of his party in 1957, and knew how much he had to gain from cordial relations with Britain: Nkrumah's first enquiry of the new Governor-General, the Earl of Listowel, was about the possibility of a royal visit, which he had calculated would go far to consolidate CPP authority throughout the country.[133]

It was always to be the case that Ghana's relations with states outside

---

126 *Debates*, 15 July 1958.
127 *Ashanti Pioneer*, 19 September 1957.
128 See Nkrumah, *I Speak of Freedom*, p. 139.
129 *New Statesman*, 12 October 1957.
130 Colin Legum, "The Commonwealth as a Factor in Ghana's Internal Politics," Pan-African papers, 1957, Institute of Commonwealth Studies, University of London.
131 See *ibid.*   132 Interviews: CF-34, 45.   133 Interview: CF-70.

Africa were more intricately involved with domestic political developments than were relations with African states, if only because Nkrumah's
pan-African formulations were too inflexible to be affected by anything.
But the ideology of Ghana's governing party was a reflection of the interests of its dominant group; it was in the interests of moderates like
Botsio and Gbedemah to remain close to the West, and since the young
challengers were trying to replace them, it was natural for them to seek
closer ties with the East. Step by step the radical wing was to gain
strength, partly encouraged by Nkrumah, partly on its own, and partly
as a result of the turn of events. It was the failure of Western diplomacy
that the danger posed by these developments was not even seen.

The relationship of domestic affairs and Africa policy was the opposite: if Nkrumah's pan-African ideas were not flexible enough to be
affected by the domestic power struggle, he seemed to change his style
of governing Ghana according to his own perception of the African
scene. It was at a time when he felt he needed to seize the African initiative even more firmly—at the end of this period—that he detained 43
members of the opposition. Shortly thereafter he detained two of the
opposition's most outspoken critics; they were never to be released during the Nkrumah period.[134]

Nor was all that marring his Africa policy. There had, to be sure,
been great accomplishments in African diplomacy. In itself, the Conference of Independent African States had been a tremendous success.
Ghana had a framework for African cooperation, the African Group at
the United Nations, to make the continent felt in the councils of the
world. In parliament, however, Nkrumah correctly noted that this was
not enough, that "the fundamental unity of outlook on foreign policy"
achieved at the IAS conference did not compare in importance to the
functional cooperation at the economic and social level that was a necessary basis of African unity.[135] Yet by his actions he proceeded in the
opposite direction. From a traditional diplomatic point of view Ghana
should have opened a mission in Lagos before anywhere, yet it was
almost two years before Ghana had opened a consulate there—although,
as the opposition *Pioneer* pointed out, embassies had been opened
"around the Mediterranean."[136] Worse, Nkrumah was in the process of
withdrawing from (and thus breaking up) the British West African
boards that for a generation had bound it to its sister colonies in West
Africa. A cabinet official noted that his saddest duty in this period was

---

[134] These were M. K. Apaloo and R. R. Amponsah. The suspicion comes easily that
their real offense had been to make short shrift of Nkrumah's policy in assembly debates.
[135] *Debates*, 15 July 1958, pp. 468-74.
[136] *Ashanti Pioneer*, 11 April 1958.

to tell the Nigerians to "collect their assets" from those organizations headquartered in Ghana.[137] Nkrumah justified his actions by arguing that only by doing this could Ghana be independent of British military and monetary control. Yet Robert Gardiner, the establishment secretary, had drawn up careful plans that gave Ghana complete control over its own reserves while it awaited the independence of its partners; the justification for destroying the Cocoa Research Institute, and the airways, was still more obscure. It was beginning to seem that Nkrumah, for all his ideals and hopes, could not tolerate any organizational ties that restricted his own movement. Indeed, the next period's opening is marked by a most dramatic unilateral move, the announcement of a union with Guinea.

To every criticism, Nkrumah responded that Ghana's enemies were legion, that it must make of itself a secure, independent, and unrestricted bastion of African freedom. Joe Appiah, an articulate opponent (and later a detainee) suggested that it was one thing for a little maiden to overestimate her own importance, but another for the prime minister to say that everybody's eyes were on Ghana "and that great and small Powers are trying to pounce upon little Ghana and destroy her."[138] The difficulty was that the world's eyes *were* on Ghana; Anthony Sampson wrote that it was becoming "impossible to be objective" about that country, which "has become so much a symbol of right or wrong, such a complete guinea-pig in the eyes of the world, that she cannot be recognized and judged for what she is—just another independent country. . . . The world sits watching, deeply prejudiced on one side or the other. . . . [But] there is certainly something going wrong."[139]

[137] Interview: CF-28.
[138] *Debates*, 15 July 1958, p. 480.
[139] "Ghana: The Morning After," *loc.cit.*

◦ 3 ◦

AFRICAN LIBERATION
November 1958–June 1960

ON 23 NOVEMBER 1958, the president of Guinea and prime minister of Ghana announced to the world that, "Inspired by the example of the thirteen American colonies, the tendencies of the countries of Europe, Asia, and the Middle East to organise in a rational manner, and the declaration of the Accra conference, we . . . have agreed to constitute our two States as the nucleus of a Union of West African States." These were bold words, which reflected the early hopes of Ghana's first years when it was able to hold the initiative in Africa both because of its early independence and the caution which it brought to its African policies. The speed with which the new Union was brought into being bore witness to the fact that Nkrumah felt compelled to move quickly in order to continue to play the part of standard bearer of an all-African nationalism. But the Ghana-Guinea Union was to be a false dawn of hope.

The Conference of Independent African States had been held at the governmental level, and with it Nkrumah had hoped to establish a diplomatic network to support his efforts to liberate the rest of the continent. In this second period, his prime concern was the nationalist movements in the unliberated territories. Planning for a great conference of their representatives had been progressing since Ghana's first anniversary celebrations, when a collection of African nationalists had gathered in Accra. But the All-African Peoples Conference held in December 1958, though a remarkable success in itself, did not provide him with the framework for liberation he sought, and, by the end of the period, he had in effect discarded its secretariat as he was to do with all the institutions and bodies he created.

The period between the end of 1958 and the middle of 1960 was also to be more turbulent than was foreseen in Accra, and it drew to a close on the eve of the most eventful of all the post-independence problems in Africa—that of unity and government in the Congo. Ghana was able to take the initiative throughout the continent, but it became clear that its importance was increasingly dimmed by the very significance of the events that Nkrumah wished to affect, namely, the sudden success of

57

independence throughout both French and British Africa. These two years also included the death of George Padmore in September 1959, and thereafter it is difficult to detect any clear plan in Ghana's African policy. "There was an idea—African Unity—but there was very little strategy," Quaison-Sackey said.[1]

On the international front, Nkrumah was to discover that Ghana's standing in Washington and London was unaffected by his initiatives in Africa. The obvious inference, that there were clear limits both to the influence a state of Ghana's size could have on the great capitals and to the interest it could elicit therefrom by its moves, was not drawn in Accra or elsewhere. On the contrary, as time progressed, the attention given Nkrumah and Ghana both by the world press and by African nationalists looking for a Mecca (and money) convinced him there were new areas in which he could wield influence.

New Frameworks for Influence in Africa

The All-African Peoples Conference. In 1958, Nkrumah had progressed from triumph to triumph, none of which was greater than his and Padmore's pan-African gathering at the end of the year, which was sponsored by the thirty-six nationalist organizations that had been invited to Ghana's March 1958 celebrations. The name chosen for the meeting, the All-African Peoples Conference, is itself significant since the conference is considered as a successor to the pan-African meetings of earlier decades, the last of which was held in Manchester in 1945: But Nkrumah insisted—in spite of Padmore's objections—on changing the name from "pan-African" to "All-African" to make it clear that Ghana and Nkrumah had begun a new tradition.[2]

Still, this was to be Padmore's conference, and was "nearer to his heart" than had been the IASC.[3] He wrote to A. L. Adu (there had been a reconciliation between them) that, although the government was not "officially responsible" for it, the preparatory committee appointed in March 1958 "has invited me to serve on it in a purely advisory capacity."[4] But the journalist chosen as secretary-general of the preparatory committee had little influence, and there was no doubt that Padmore was running the affair.

Financial support came in the form of a direct grant from the gov-

[1] Interview: Quaison-Sackey.

[2] Interview: James Markham, Padmore's assistant at this time.

[3] C.L.R. James, "Notes on the Life of George Padmore," unpublished manuscript, p. 61.

[4] Padmore to A. L. Adu, 14 August 1958, CFA-103. See also *Guinea Times*, 13 June 1958.

ernment—£27,710 in the first instance. From the beginning, however, there was tension between the civil servants and the conference organizers, and this symbolized a conflict that was to persist throughout the Nkrumah period. In September, the cabinet decided that the monthly accounts of the committee did not need to be checked by the ministry of finance, on the curious ground that parliament had already approved in principle to help African territories still under colonial rule.[5] The civil servants challenged this. When A. L. Adu asked Andrew Djin, treasurer of the preparatory committee, for financial details about the organization, he received a blunt refusal: "It is not . . . devolved upon me to submit 'detail of approved rates, guest list, etc. for examination purposes' [sic]."[6] The auditor-general then wrote to Adu regarding the lack of vouchers in the organization into which £30,000 had now been poured, and he and the principal secretary at the ministry of finance, Millar-Craig, arranged with Nkrumah that moneys appropriated for "intelligence purposes" would be put under "the personal control" of the principal secretary to the ministry of external affairs (Adu) as "external intelligence."[7] This solved the immediate problem for those whom the politicians considered of a nonrevolutionary mentality. The money would be available, unaudited, to the conference, but under the administration of a civil servant. Padmore now had access to what Makonnen called the "slush fund," similar to the one he had administered in Moscow a generation before.

In addition to the conflict between civil servant and politician, there was the almost total lack of coordination between the ministry and the conference office. Enquiries came from a number of Ghanaian missions abroad seeking information about the conference; as late as October 1958 A.B.B. Kofi, Adu's assistant, had to reply that he could not be of help, but that he had asked the secretary-general of the AAPC "to grant me an interview in order that this Ministry may be brought into the picture."[8] In the end, however, the ministry had to be brought in, if only to save the conference from chaos. In the last few weeks, foreign service officers played a large role in solving the outstanding problems at the secretariat, and the conference went smoothly, despite the absence of adequate translation equipment.

The "Call" that went out before the conference in the summer of 1958 summarized succinctly where its main emphasis was to be placed.

[5] Cabinet Memorandum, 9 September 1958, Item 6, "All-African Peoples Conference," CFA-103.

[6] Djin to Adu, 18 September 1958, CFA-103.

[7] Auditor-general to Adu, 8 October 1958; Millar-Craig to auditor-general, 30 October 1958, CFA-103. Also letter, CFL-A, 5 July 1967.

[8] Kofi to Major Seth Anthony, Ghana/Washington, 8 October 1958, CFA-104.

THIS CONFERENCE WILL FORMULATE AND PROCLAIM THE
PHILOSOPHY OF PAN-AFRICANISM AS THE IDEOLOGY OF THE AFRI-
CAN NON-VIOLENT REVOLUTION.
HENCEFORTH OUR SLOGAN SHALL BE: PEOPLES OF AFRICA UNITE!
YOU HAVE NOTHING TO LOSE BUT YOUR CHAINS!!
YOU HAVE A CONTINENT TO REGAIN!!
YOU HAVE FREEDOM AND HUMAN DIGNITY TO ATTAIN!!
HANDS OFF AFRICA!!
AFRICA MUST BE FREE!!!!![9]

There was surprisingly little protest against the ideas embodied in it
except, as might be expected, from the Liberians. The True Whig
party leaders wrote to the organizing secretariat, in response to the
"Call," that "The 'philosophy of Pan-African Socialism' therein proposed as an ideology of the African Non-Violent Revolution, may
not be one adapted to the African way of life. . . . Each state . . . should
be left free and untrammelled to work out and adopt the ideology best
suited to its particular needs . . . and above all to its own wish and
will."[10]

The "Call's" stress was on nonviolence for several reasons. As Botsio
said, Ghanaians knew that the colonial powers would win if it came to
a war fought with military weapons.[11] Equally important, he added,
Nkrumah wished to keep the war cries of the Middle East over Palestine out of his sphere of influence. There was a continent to regain,
and from the beginning Nkrumah contended that the Arab states had
to be brought into the African vortex.

Nkrumah also disliked any talk of "regionalism" which, according
to Botsio, Adjei, and Markham, became a major issue of contention
during this period. Padmore, for his part, had lost any illusions he
might have had about "continental unity" during his tour around
Africa in February 1958.[12] Thus no Ghanaian except Nkrumah saw
any wisdom in trying to unify the continent, except perhaps in the
very long run. This similarly was the position of the most radical
nationalists, in the French territories as well.[13] Regionalism had the
merit of sensibility and was hardly an imperialist weapon. The "Call,"

[9] "The Call," All-African Peoples Conference, Accra, 1958.
[10] "Statements to AAPC," True Whig Party National Headquarters, Monrovia, 1958,
CFA-6.
[11] Interview: Botsio. The issue of violence figured large in the conference. See
Soviet Survey, No. 28, April-June 1959, p. 44; Legum, *Pan-Africanism*, New York,
1965, p. 43, and G. A. Acquah, "An Epoch of Social Revolution," *Evening News*,
28 March 1959.
[12] Interviews: Ako Adjei, Kojo Botsio, James Markham.
[13] See Albert Tevoedjre, *L'Afrique Revoltée*, Paris, 1958, p. 132.

written by Padmore, actually advocated the "amalgamation or federation of territories on a regional basis," and complex and careful resolutions were drawn up at the conference outlining the plans for regional units in Africa. Nkrumah could not, in this period, have overridden such strong opposition to his own *simpliste* ideas. Instead, both in the "Call," and then in the resolutions of the conference, he made certain that regionalism was specified as an intermediate policy, and that in the end there would be one united Africa, in which colonial frontiers would be redrawn or abolished.

But the euphoria of the conference itself, where Egyptians discovered Congolese nationalists, Kenyan labor organizers discovered their Moroccan counterparts, South African refugees found ears attuned to their needs, was such that Nkrumah's continental approach for once had a certain plausibility. Thus the *Observer* correspondent could write that "This may, in fact, prove to have been the starting point of a move towards a continental unity such as exists nowhere else in the world."[14]

The conference, so widely noted at the time,[15] so thoroughly discussed by Africanists in subsequent years,[16] is important in showing the origin of much of the strength on which Nkrumah was able to draw in later years. He remained within the castle throughout most of the proceedings, consulting, reconciling, advising delegates; he was never too conspicuous. He dominated the conference all the more by such tactics. Thereafter, he had a network of admirers throughout the continent, some of whom, like Kenneth Kaunda, were to remain loyal even after being assailed by Ghanaian organizations, and were to stand by him even after he had been deposed.

Most important, the conference was ideally timed to meet the needs and mood of a rebellious continent. One Congolese delegate, Patrice Lumumba, returned to Léopoldville determined to press for independence, and shortly thereafter sparked the demonstrations which ignited Congolese nationalism. Kanyama Chiume of the Nyasaland-ANC wrote that a new attitude toward African liberation was evolved from the AAPC: "We went back to intensify the struggle for freedom . . . with the conviction, in the light of the Accra spirit, that an independent Nyasaland will, like Ghana, be in a stronger position to help

[14] George Clay, "Accra (2): Africa's Move Towards Unity," *Observer Foreign News Service*, 15 December 1958. See also Tom Mboya, *Freedom and After*, London, 1963, p. 220.

[15] Well that it should have been. Forty international correspondents, from East and West, covered it.

[16] See, in particular, E. S. Munger, "All-African People's Conference: A Report," in *African Field Reports, 1952-1961*, American Universities Field Service, 1962, p. 52.

the liberation of Africa."[17] When the great troubles then erupted throughout the Federation of the Rhodesias and Nyasaland, with co-ordinated mass demonstrations and mass arrests, Prime Minister Roy Welensky blamed Nkrumah and the conference. Nkrumah welcomed the charge, and added that he and his colleagues were "proud to know that Ghana is a symbol of hope and inspiration to Africans."[18]

But there was another view of the conference which was equally perti-nent, namely, that a favorable start does not necessarily presage a favorable conclusion, or, as the *Economist* put it, "At Accra [Dr. Nkru-mah] has thrown a lot of balls in the air; now he has to keep them up."[19] In the event, the conference marks at once the high point of Ghana's influence in Africa, and the turning point in Ghana's foreign policy in the period between independence and the birth of the repub-lic. This critical transition was taking place at several levels; money was slipping into the hands of those who were not using it judiciously, as already foreshadowed, and as will be seen more fully in the discus-sion of the implementation of the conference's plans. Ghana was ven-turing into liberation, and this was a more risky business than the careful diplomacy exercised at the IAS conference earlier in the year. Two further aspects were still more important in the transition, namely, the question of representation at the AAPC and in its ensuing activi-ties, and the very organization of the follow-up activities themselves.

Nkrumah and Padmore hoped that *all* parties in Africa, including those of white South Africa, would participate in the conference. Step by step, however, the AAPC became a more selective organization until, at a much later date, it became the narrow arena of support for splinter groups and dissident factions across the continent.

This was not for lack of effort to make it representative. The Quai d'Orsay, for example, complained that Olympio, Bakary Djibo, Touré, Moumié, and other radical Francophone Africans had been invited, but not Houphouet, Senghor, Keita, or other leaders friendly to France. A Ghanaian diplomat in Paris wrote that they inferred from this that Ghana had only invited persons "whose political views agree with our own and through whom we think we can most successfully give

[17] *Evening News*, 7 September 1959. At the AAPC, all the delegates from the Federation of Rhodesia and Nyasaland signed a pact pledging opposition to the Federation.

[18] *Information Bulletin on African Affairs*, AAPC Steering Committee, 2, No. 8, 20 March 1959.

[19] *Economist*, 20 December 1958, p. 1060.

effect to our designs." He suggested that all be invited, "in order not to give any impression that we are pursuing any policy which may be inimical to any of our neighbouring states."[20] Adu's correspondence with Padmore makes clear what Nkrumah's intentions were: "The PM, with whom I have discussed this message . . . agrees that all leaders of French Africa, including those alleged to have been left out . . . and also all shades of political leaders in French Camerouns should be invited. . . . The PM has instructed me to request you to be good enough to give early attention to this matter."[21] Extensive efforts in fact had been made, though in vain, to induce Houphouet to attend, so as to involve his *Rassemblement Democratique Africaine* in the conference's work.[22]

Nonetheless, mistakes had been made. The thirty-six sponsoring bodies were a fortuitously chosen group, and less than broadly representative. Liberia was represented by the "Pan-Africanist Unificationist Organization," and until a month prior to the conference, the governing True Whigs thought they had not been invited, and protested through the Ghanaian embassy in Monrovia.[23] There was no Egyptian representative, and Senghor's party was the only one from *Afrique Occidental Française*. There were no delegates from the Action Group and the N.P.C. of Nigeria, and Gambia was represented by Garba-Jahumpa's Muslim League, hardly the major force in that colony. True, the difficulties of communication made it necessary to depend on old friends and contacts, rather than try to create new ones when time was short, but many future difficulties might have been avoided had there been greater efforts to obtain a more broadly based sponsoring body.

The greatest trouble lay in the conference organization which followed. Indeed, by the time of the conference it was already suspected that members of the secretariat had helped themselves to the unaudited funds of the preparatory committee, and there was to be much greater suspicion that such malpractices were commonplace.[24]

[20] Richard Quarshie, Ghana/Paris, to H.A.H.S. Grant, M.E.A., 23 July 1958, CFA-105. The French claim was not correct. Senghor's party was a sponsor of the conference, and others had been invited.

[21] Adu to Padmore, 13 August 1958, CFA-105.

[22] See "Nouvelles Assises Panafricaine à Accra," *le Monde*, 9 December 1958. Also interview: Markham.

[23] Debrah, Ghana/Monrovia, to A. L. Adu, 13 November 1958; A.B.B. Kofi to Debrah, 24 November 1958, CFA-9. Kofi's telegram stated, however, that they had been invited, that the invitation was no doubt lost, but that a second had been sent in any event.

[24] Interviews: CF-76, 27.

The preparatory secretariat in Accra New Town became the permanent headquarters, and a clerk with the preparatory committee, Sylvester Paintsil, became its administrative secretary. Paintsil was thought pliant enough to run the office silently, but from the first he sought to frustrate Padmore's attempts to keep the organization solely in Ghanaian hands. It was, after all, an all-African body; Padmore presumably felt it would not flourish unless kept under careful—and radical—Ghanaian guidance.[25] F. S. McEwen, the Nigerian who had been joint secretary of the December sessions and who became a member of the steering committee, said it was immediately apparent that the Ghanaians intended to use it as a front for their own ends; quickly he lost interest—attending none of the steering committee meetings thereafter.[26] Botsio justified the strategy by arguing that the organization would indeed have perished had Ghana not closely managed its affairs.

When the December conference brought so startling a result in the Federation of Rhodesia and Nyasaland, with the emergency, Nkrumah decided to press his advantage and called an emergency meeting of the steering committee to consider the situation, presumably to dramatize it. The flexibility of the mechanism was to have its first test.

The venue was to be Conakry, Guinea's capital, for obvious reasons. Ghana and Guinea had in the meantime declared themselves united, and Padmore and Abdoulaye Diallo, Guinea's resident minister in Ghana, had found they could work together. Padmore had found Paintsil useless, and it was thought that on home ground they could force through the election of Diallo as secretary-general and thus have the organization properly managed under their own control. But there was all manner of opposition to the meeting. The Egyptian ambassador, for instance, wrote Adu of his government's opposition to the meeting, and suggested in a letter to Nkrumah that "there was a danger that the peoples of Africa would lose confidence in the resolutions of their own conference," if gatherings were organized haphazardly. Nkrumah replied, rather frostily, "On the contrary, they feel that if immediate response were not made to the appeal . . . for assistance, before the judicial commission begins its investigations [into the Federation of the Rhodesias and Nyasaland], the peoples of Africa would lose their confidence in the effectiveness of the Steering Committee."[27]

Ghana and Guinea went ahead—although the Ghanaian team had to wait a week before a semblance of a quorum had arrived in Con-

[25] Interviews: Sylvester Paintsil, Kojo Botsio.
[26] Interview: F. S. McEwen.
[27] Nkrumah to Amb. Hamid, UAR/Accra, 11 April 1959, CFA-5.

akry,[28] and even then, the AAPC Chairman, Tom Mboya, was absent.[29] The Nigerians, Egyptians, and Tunisians were other prominent absentees[30] and, as a result, Ghana and Guinea had a majority of the votes of those present: themselves, Togo-Juvento (Amorin), Nyasaland-ANC (Chiume), and Ivory Coast ("represented" by a dissident resident in Conakry). They voted Diallo into his post. The public aim, of focusing attention on the Federation emergency, was at least compromised by their success in accomplishing the more immediate end, however. Nor could there be much doubt that the other founding members of the AAPC were aware of, and unimpressed by, Ghana's stratagem.[31]

Early in May 1959, the first regular meeting of the steering committee was still planned for Cairo but, by mid-May, it was clear that the meeting was to take place in Tunis, presumably because the Egyptians were irritated over the emergency meeting in Conakry, and because the chairman, Mboya, was unable to obtain a visa for the U.A.R.[32] That meeting began on May 26th—without any Ghanaians. When the one resident foreign correspondent wrote (in the *Sunday Times*) that Ghana was boycotting the meeting, he was expelled from Ghana.[33] Tettegah denied the allegation, and claimed that Diallo had canceled the meeting in Tunis, and that Ghana had "not yet been told about the new meeting."[34] Unfortunately, Diallo's story was different; he denied there were contradictions within the AAPC (as the correspondent had argued) and attributed the absences from the Tunis meeting to "a confusion resulting from long distances which had to be covered."[35] In fact Ghana was boycotting the meeting, "to show that Ghana was the most radical" said Paintsil. Shortly thereafter Paintsil's papers were confiscated, he was arrested, and finally let out on bail.[36] Thenceforth the organization was run by Edwin DuPlan,[37] an associ-

[28] *West Africa*, 6 June 1959; Interview: Botsio.

[29] He was then in America, and constitutionally, his presence and the presence of seven others was required.

[30] See Padmore's press statement, *Evening News*, 7 May 1959.

[31] On this conference, see also *Information Bulletin on African Affairs*, 2, Nos. 18, 19; *Manchester Guardian*, 25 April 1959; *NCNA*, 7 April 1959; and *le Monde*, 17-18 April 1959.

[32] British Kenya had no diplomatic relations with Egypt.

[33] See *Sunday Times*, 31 May 1959, 7 and 14 June, 1959. R. W. Howe, the correspondent, claimed to get his information from Paintsil, which Paintsil later denied. Interview: Paintsil.

[34] *West Africa*, 6 June 1959.

[35] *Ghana Times*, 3 June 1959.

[36] By his own account, in interview.

[37] In many circles, DuPlan was not considered reputable and many tales of allegedly illegal activities on his part were told.

ate of Makonnen and Padmore from London days, and Kojo Addison, a Marxist who up to this point had been deliberately held down by Nkrumah.

Under their direction, another steering committee meeting was held in October, safely in Accra. Lumumba (back from Brussels), Joshua Nkomo, of Southern Rhodesia, and Ntsu Mokhehle, of Basutoland, were present. Botsio was elected chairman in the absence of a disgusted Mboya[38] (whose status was demoted at the conference). Thus there was a sufficient "Ghana wing" to avert difficulties and, as more careful preparations had been made, it was possible to obtain recognition of the *fait accompli* of Diallo's election.[39]

Ironically, by this time the working relationship between Ghana and Guinea within the AAPC had become marked with difficulties. Padmore was dead, the AAPC was increasingly a Ghanaian adjunct, and Abdoulaye Diallo was becoming less and less popular in Ghanaian circles. His first responsibility, of course, was as representative of the government of Guinea.

It was in its failure to evolve AAPC channels to support nationalist movements that Ghana set its worst precedent. Within several years, subversion in independent Africa had become a vital part of Ghana's Africa policy, and its roots lay in the method which Ghana devised for such aid in 1959. "Subversion" has a subjective sense, and activities are usually "subversive" only when their ends conflict with those using the term; only those that had colonial interests to defend considered aid to the African nationalists as subversive. Ghana was thus on good ground at first.

In the first year after independence, Nkrumah could not take seriously his own promise to consider Ghana's independence "meaningless" until all Africa was free. Although small quantities of aid were going to a few nationalist leaders there was no mechanism, and funds were too low, for a wide-scale and generous policy. But at the AAPC conference, a "Freedom Fund" was established, on paper, like the one unsuccessfully advocated by the Ghanaians at the IAS conference. From the beginning, the Ghanaians chose not to use the multilateral framework it had established, and it was the presence of the "slush fund" that made this inevitable. Ghana secretly gave Foncha's KNDP in the British Cameroons a substantial sum—probably

---

[38] Nkrumah had named Mboya chairman of the first AAPC. Conflict developed over Mboya's view that trade unions should be permitted to affiliate with international unions, and in November 1959 the dispute became public. It was suggested in various quarters, however, that Nkrumah had become jealous of Mboya much earlier, owing to the publicity he received in his position as chairman at the AAPC.

[39] CFA-7.

£10,000[40]—to organize its campaign for the elections of January 1959, and with his success Nkrumah had an ally, as will be seen, against Nigeria. Even when donations were publicized, they were not channeled through the AAPC; Ghana openly gave Banda's ANC-Nyasaland £10,000 in April 1959.[41] Throughout that year, support to individual nationalist leaders became looser and looser. True, it could not have been extensive, as there was only £100,000 in the contingency fund, already mostly used for the AAPC conference itself and for the establishment of the "research [that is intelligence] office" at the ministry. Funds under Nkrumah's direct control (like the development budget) offered insufficient margin for extensive grants. It is important that money granted was given without guidelines, according to whim, and it was inevitable that this should eventually become merely a reward for doing Ghana's bidding, irrespective of work in and contribution to the nationalist movements. By mid-1959, groups were requesting funds as a matter of course, but in few cases was there action taken. Thus, leaders of the newly formed UNIP in Northern Rhodesia wrote to the AAPC in September that their opponents were unprepared to join a united front (as Nkrumah had sought to arrange during the AAPC conference), that a mass party had to be organized, and thus, "to do all this, much as we know, that it is a race against time and against well founded political opponents, we feel oppressed by circumstances and appeal to you for financial assistance."[42] But the AAPC could do nothing (nor, for that matter, is there evidence that the Ghanaians acted).[43] Prominent Ghanaians, like Botsio, believed that Ghana had financed elections in every African territory. "We had financed every party. Every election. They all looked to us!" Although this may have been a common Ghanaian sentiment, it is not true. By providing aid in a random manner, Ghana had missed the opportunity to establish a systematic network of support such as would be established by the OAU four years later.

The Ghana-Guinea Union. With the independence of Guinea on 2 October 1958, the whole concept of independence in French Africa was at stake. Nkrumah sensed that he had a potential new ally, and almost immediately invited Sékou Touré to Accra. It was always likely that the Guinean leaders, given their radical pan-Africanist background,

---

[40] Interviews: CF-109, 45. Endeley later claimed Nkrumah had given Foncha £25,000, but the lower figure is probably correct.

[41] *Ghana Times*, 8 April 1959.

[42] Pres., Sec.-Gen., and Sec. of UNIP to Ad. Sec., AAPC, cc. to Nkrumah, M.E.A., and Pafmeca, 29 September 1959, CFA-100.

[43] See CFL-A, 5 July 1967, p. 4.

would not remain content with their independence, and indeed later in October President Touré stated that he would seek some form of association with Ghana.[44] There was nowhere else to look, and Guinea was desperate; the budget had never been balanced before without a French subsidy of about £5,000,000.[45] On November 20th, Touré arrived in a Ghanaian chartered plane in Accra, stating that he had come to discuss everything "that can unite our two countries."[46]

Discussions began November 21st. A. L. Adu and Diallo Telli, working through an interpreter, spent the entire day drafting an agreement on cooperation. Adu had anticipated a final session with Nkrumah and Touré from six to nine o'clock in the evening, but Touré did not arrive at the castle until nine, by which time Nkrumah had retired to his apartment, disappointed.[47] As soon as Touré arrived and saw the draft agreement, he began a lengthy polemic in which he insisted on an organic union of the two states. "I give you Ghanaians a blank check to write a constitution for an organic union," Ako Adjei and Makonnen remembered Touré saying.[48] Questions of leadership were waived aside as mere details. Nkrumah (Touré was quoted as saying) was, after all, the elder brother, and would be the leader.[49] Nkrumah was delighted to agree, but the Ghanaian civil servants were suspicious of Touré's intentions. They feared he would exploit such a union just so long as it brought economic benefits, and then find an escape clause—as in fact he did. Adu used the problem of Commonwealth ties as a delaying tactic in order to bring Nkrumah to reality, and asked Nkrumah for just enough time before implementing the union to effect the "necessary" withdrawal from the Commonwealth to become a republic. The strategy worked, and by three-thirty in the morning the declaration of what was in effect an alliance was completed. A loan of £10,000,000 was promised shortly thereafter.[50]

The lack of content to the union has been widely discussed but what explains the motives of the two leaders? Touré's are evident: Guinea was heading for bankruptcy; her relationship with France was as yet undetermined and Touré needed a stronger basis for negotiation with Paris. He was also in competition with Houphouet-Boigny (whose party,

44 *Sunday Times*, 19 October 1958.
45 See *Economist Intelligence Unit*, West Africa Series, No. 24, 30 November 1958. Tubman was quick to cement cordial ties with Touré, but Liberia could hardly help Guinea, and the ideological gulf was wide indeed.
46 *AFP Sp. outre-mer*, No. 3709, 21 November 1959.
47 Interview: CF-28.
48 Interviews: Ako Adjei and T. R. Makonnen.
49 Interview: CF-28.
50 P.R. #1058/58, 1059/58, 24 November 1958.

the RDA, had expelled Touré's Guinean branch from it) for the leadership of French Africa, and the question of those territories seeking independence was at stake. It is doubtful that he saw Nkrumah as more than a peripheral ally in this struggle. In his first public statement after the union, Touré said that Guinea was working toward a United States of Africa, and that Guinea had been placed in the leadership of *"l'émancipation africaine."* There was no mention of Ghana, nor of the Union.[51]

Nkrumah, on the contrary, made as much of the Union as possible. In the Assembly he expressed "a deep sense of pride . . . that I have been an instrument in this move. . . . This new Africa of ours is emerging into a world of great combinations—a world where the weak and the small are pushed aside unless they unite their forces. . . . Our African edifice, though we still have to draw up the plans for it, must have solid foundations . . . whether we like it or not, history has assigned us a great responsibility."[52] There is little doubt that Nkrumah believed the Union to be an organic one, with himself at its head.[53]

The Ghanaian government began mobilizing aid to Guinea, at various levels, almost immediately after the proclamation. At the United Nations, the Ghana mission gave Diallo Telli an office, and paid his hotel bills as well.[54] At a cabinet meeting in Accra just after the announcement of the union, it was decided to establish communications link as a first priority, and correspondence began almost immediately between the two parties. By January 23rd, the army had already "earmarked and partially packed" telegraphic equipment and a 350-watt transmitter.[55] It seems that a large part of the Ghanaian government was engaged in suggesting forms of aid that Ghana could pledge to Guinea.[56]

Reactions in Ghana to the union were interesting. Gbedemah told interviewers that he thought the loan had been granted too quickly,[57] but he broadcast a defense of it. Busia, the leader of the opposition, prophetically noted, however, that "to lend money to a person who

[51] Sékou Touré, *Expérience Guinean et Unité Africaine*, Paris, 1961, p. 307.
[52] *Debates*, 12 December 1958, pp. 388-93.
[53] See CF-70.
[54] Interview: CF-109. Diallo, for his part, telegraphed Nkrumah that he would "not fail to explain to my government the decisive role of your co-operation . . . ," thus indicating that he well understood what Nkrumah was attempting to accomplish. Diallo Telli to Nkrumah, 17 December 1958, CFA-101.
[55] Minutes, "Meeting at Ministry of Interior on Aid to Guinea," 23 January 1959, CFA-101.
[56] Only one example appears of Ghanaian hopes of Guinean aid, Kofi Baako's suggestion that Guinea might help Ghana on French broadcasting, as Guinea no doubt had good contacts in Dakar. It was from such ignorance of Guinea's status in West Africa that part of the tension between the two states derived. CFA-101.
[57] E. S. Munger, "Portrait of Gbedemah," *African Field Reports, 1952-1961*, p. 35; and interview with Gbedemah.

could not possibly repay except in the very distant future is to create a condition not for friendship but for resentment and enmity."[58] Indeed, more than seven years later, it was possible very roughly to gauge contemporary reaction to the loan by the extent to which it appeared as an accusation against the deposed Nkrumah.

The CPP leaders, however, were greatly moved by what had been accomplished, feeling a great sense of satisfaction in helping to save Guinea from collapse.[59] Gbedemah, despite what he said elsewhere, presented a report to the cabinet, in which he wrote: "The long-term prospects of the country's economy are good. . . . There is every prospect that any loan which we make will be repaid. Ten million would be appropriate, two million of which could be paid immediately. Interest rates and other details could be worked out in time: Guinea's survival was now at stake and there was no time to waste."[60]

Guinean reaction at official levels was such as to give the union an ominous beginning. Arthur Lewis stopped in Conakry on return from a CCTA conference in Dakar, and was joined by Gbedemah, Adu, the permanent secretaries of the ministry of finance and trade, and the governor of the Bank of Ghana to discuss the implementation of the loan. They waited two days before the Guineans arranged a formal meeting with them; the Guineans then acted as if they were "bestowing a favour" on Ghana by allowing it to contribute to their treasury.[61] Gbedemah said "I had packed my bags to return to Accra—I couldn't take any more," and it was Adu's particular task to prevent such a move.[62]

Achkar Marof, a Guinean diplomat, advanced one explanation of Guinea's attitude by noting the shock in Conakry at seeing expatriate officials with the Ghana delegation.[63] A more satisfactory explanation is that this reserve was a combination of their real feeling toward Ghana and of their desire to further the reconciliation with the French, who were negotiating in Conakry with the Guineans while Gbedemah waited. Diallo Telli, in London shortly afterward, said that "one does not leave monetary zones as one leaves a house."[64]

For all this, Nkrumah had made a bold move with the Ghana-Guinea union: it was "the first check to the process of disintegration in West Africa which has been going on for years."[65] But he had to make it

[58] *Daily Graphic*, 28 and 29 November 1958.
[59] Interviews: Ako Adjei, Botsio.
[60] Cabinet Minutes, 28 November 1958, CFA-101.
[61] Interview CF-28, and letter, CFL-A, 7 July 1967, p. 2.
[62] Interviews: Gbedemah, and CF-28.
[63] Interview: Amb. Achkar Marof.
[64] *Daily Graphic*, 29 November 1958. Also see *ibid.*, 1 December 1958.
[65] *West Africa*, 29 November 1958.

succeed. Just after the AAPC closed, a parliamentary debate on the union occurred, which brought out the dichotomy in approaches to unity that would exist in Ghana throughout the Nkrumah period; at this time a split between the CPP and the opposition, it later became the conflict between Nkrumah and his civil service advisers; and between his "militant" advisers and the professional Ghanaian diplomatists.

Nkrumah finished his defense of the union by suggesting it could be said, "Well done, Ghana." Joe Appiah urged that a conference of West African leaders be convened, so that other states and territories could join from the beginning, otherwise "Does not national pride itself get hurt?" If it built a community, then it could instead be said, "West African leaders . . . well done!"[66] Braimah, another opposition spokesman, took advantage of the terminological laxity of the CPP to point out the "hollowness" of the union; Nkrumah referred to it in terms of a "United States of Africa" while Kofi Baako had spoken of the common aim of a "Commonwealth of African States." The two were not the same.[67] The CPP responded: "Let us call it a Federation of West African States; let us call it a Commonwealth of West Africa; let us call it anything; but the question is, how do we start the ball rolling?"[68]

Nkrumah himself had "started the ball rolling" that day by announcing the appointment of Nathaniel Welbeck as the first "resident minister" to Guinea. At the end of December Welbeck led a ten-man delegation to Guinea for a seven-day visit, and returned to claim that the union was now "a reality."[69] The resident minister Touré appointed to Accra, Abdoulaye Diallo (a former vice-president of W.F.T.U.), returned Welbeck's preliminary visit, and addressed CPP rallies on his tour around Ghana—a somewhat unusual diplomatic practice.[70]

But the unreal nature of the union was shown by the accord three Guinean ministers signed in Paris on 7 January 1959, by which Guinea undertook to remain in the franc zone, and France undertook—in what was de facto recognition of the regime—to continue to supply teachers. Indeed, problems were already arising in the union, in terms of the implementation of plans already outlined. The radio link, for example, was not installed until May. More important was the appointment of Welbeck. He was one of the few well-known Ghanaians who spoke French, and no doubt this gave Nkrumah a sense of correctness in his choice. Most probably Welbeck was chosen because of his political dependability and loyalty, but his personal habits made him ill-suited

[66] *Debates*, 12 December 1958, pp. 393-95.   [67] *Ibid.*
[68] *Ibid.*, p. 407.
[69] *Daily Graphic*, 5 January 1959.
[70] Although as a minister he was accredited to the government, not to the state.

even for "revolutionary diplomacy." By all accounts, Welbeck left his plane en route to Guinea, in Abidjan, became drunk in the city, and missed his plane to Conakry, where Touré was awaiting him. Touré was livid. On 23 February 1959, shortly after his inauspicious arrival, he was recalled and Ako Adjei, minister of labor and cooperatives, was named the new resident minister—though on a nonresident basis.

There were causes of tension at the other end, too. According to the original agreement, each resident minister was to be a member of the cabinet of the country to which he was accredited. But in 1959, the Ghanaian cabinet was the supreme policy-making body and a well-organized one at that, whereas most Guinean decisions were taken in the party's central committee, of which the Ghanaian resident minister was not a member. The exchange of privileges, therefore, could not be put on a reciprocal basis, in the view of Ghana's cabinet secretariat; Adu did not send Diallo advance papers on the agenda, and Diallo had to surrender his papers when leaving cabinet meetings.[71]

On 23 April 1959, Nkrumah returned Touré's visit and spent three weeks touring Guinea. The upshot was the "Conakry Declaration," in which it was agreed "to seal the Ghana-Guinea Union in practice," and to make this union the nucleus of a "Union of Independent African States," each with a separate army and separate foreign representation.[72] Thus it provided what might have become a flexible framework for a loose association of states. It also made evident that Touré was unwilling to concede anything which touched effective political sovereignty except that of a common monetary zone—which Ghana's financial experts had no intention of conceding. Thus, even on paper, the union had receded since the previous November. In reality, "it had never begun."[73]

The political setting in West Africa had also changed since November 1958. The Mali Federation, composed of Senegal and Soudan, and Houphouet's Entente, composed of the Ivory Coast, Upper Volta, Dahomey and Niger, were now established, and Touré had to take care lest his relations with Ghana prejudice future relations with Mali and the rest of French Africa. Thus, to one reporter, Sékou Touré compared the union to that of the Anglo-American alliance. *West Africa* added, "Equally, M. Sékou Touré, in refusing to tie himself too closely politically or economically to Ghana at this stage has left the door open

[71] Interview: CF-28.

[72] See Legum, *Pan-Africanism*, pp. 178-79. The Guineans were amused to see Nkrumah come with a larger retinue than de Gaulle had brought the preceding September. Interview, Amb. Achkar Marof.

[73] Interview: CF-28.

for Guinea's closer association with the Mali federation which both he and, certainly, the Sudanese wing of Mali, openly envisage."[74]

Upon his return to Accra, Nkrumah showed in his request to the Assembly for ratification of the Conakry Declaration that he was particularly dependent on the existence of the union for visible proof of progress toward African unity: "I am firmly persuaded that unless we work toward a close organic identification within some form of constitutional Union of Africa, our Continent will remain what it is today—a balkanized mass of small individual units, used as a political and economic pawn by those external forces which seek to keep us divided and backward."[75] Yet within a week, the union was to take a still greater step backward.

Tubman, Sanniquellie, and the Union. Apart from Guinea and Ghana, Liberia was the only other independent state in West Africa prior to 1960, and this gave it a right to be heard. We have seen that during the first years of Ghana's independence it played an essentially negative diplomatic role in Africa, but in 1959 it began to offer an alternative to Nkrumah's proposals. Despite its "somewhat chequered history" (Nkrumah's phrase)[76] its leaders had learned the art of survival the hard way. With the wisdom of hindsight various writers have praised Tubman for the "realistic" role he is said to have played in this period, and it is true that Tubman's proclaimed functional approach to African unity was vindicated by the course of events, and that he "correctly assessed the African political horizon" in this period.[77]

Early in 1959 there was broad general agreement, however, between Ghanaian civil servants and politicians that Liberia was the greatest obstacle to Ghana's pan-African drive. This in itself underlines the fact that the officials were by no means conservative and that there was broad agreement on the ends for which Nkrumah strove. A cabinet official said that "We knew we had to counter Tubman at some point. So our policy was to get him to bend, and if he did not, show him for the reactionary that he was. What we did not anticipate was his skill as a politician and diplomat."[78]

When Nkrumah was in India he commented indiscreetly that "It would be in Liberia's interest to join [the Ghana-Guinea Union]."[79] Liberia's ambassdor in Accra protested, noting that his government had

[74] *West Africa*, 9 May 1959.
[75] *Debates*, 10 July 1959, pp. 368-69.
[76] Nkrumah, *Africa Must Unite*, London, 1963, p. 147.
[77] Arnold Rivkin, *The African Presence in World Affairs*, London, 1963, p. 174.
[78] Interview: CF-28.   [79] *Times*, 23 December 1958.

73

never attributed to Ghana's premier "either the ability or the capacity to determine better than the Liberian Government . . . its best interests."[80]

Tubman nevertheless grasped Nkrumah's meaning, and late in January he produced a plan for "The Associated States of Africa," that at least in form was a forerunner of the OAU charter of 1963. On April 7th Tubman wrote to Touré and Nkrumah suggesting a meeting to discuss "matters of interest to our respective countries," and began to take advantage of what were thought to be growing differences between Nkrumah and Touré.[81]

Tubman's conference took place in July, in Sanniquellie, Liberia. The "Community of African States" that was proposed in the communiqué, together with the "Sanniquellie Declaration," had a "decidedly Tubman ring,"[82] and most writers thenceforth considered the results a sweeping Tubman victory. Liberian diplomats delighted in telling how Tubman gained Touré's support for a loose association, and how together they had forced Nkrumah to accept a nonpolitical pan-African framework.[83] Indeed, two Ghanaian officials present said they felt at the time that Nkrumah had not even known what he was doing; that he had not realized that the Sanniquellie Declaration rendered the Conakry Declaration null and void.[84]

But there was another vantage point from which to view the results. Adu, for one, believed that Nkrumah was well aware of Tubman's strategy and told of one meeting in which Tubman and Nkrumah had reached a deadlock. Touré was the *interlocoteur valable* and, according to Adu's recollection, stated, "You two are my seniors. African unity cannot wait on your disagreements."[85] Thus was a compromise found. It was not, then, entirely to save face that Nkrumah, on his return to Accra, said the Declaration was "greater than an atomic bomb" in force.[86] ". . . at Sanniquellie, Nkrumah succeeded in committing Tubman to the idea of African unity, an idea to which he had previously been, to say the least, lukewarm."[87] Nor was it clear that the "Community" agreed to was the lineal descendant of Tubman's own January proposals which (according to the Sanniquellie Declaration) had been the basis—together with the Conakry Declaration—of discussion. Tub-

80 *Liberian Age*, 2 January 1959.
81 This correspondence was published in the *Liberian Gazette*, and is quoted in full in Marinelli, *The New Liberia.*
82 Gus Liebenow, "Which Road to African Unity? The Sanniquellie Conference," in Gwendolyn Carter, *Politics in Africa*, New York, 1966, p. 20.
83 Interview: Amb. George F. Sherman, Liberia/Accra.
84 Interview: CF-109.   85 Interview: A. L. Adu.
86 *Ghana Times*, 23 July 1959.   87 Letter, CFL-A, 5 July 1967, pp. 2-3.

man's proposals had gone little beyond the resolutions of the 1958 IAS conference. Ghanaian delegates also noted that they found, in their discussions with Liberian townspeople, that the idea of African unity had spread from Accra even to the Liberian interior, and that Tubman was being forced by domestic pressure to take this awakening into account.[88]

On paper there was an important distinction to resolve. The three leaders had agreed to call a conference to 1960 of all the independent states together with those, like Nigeria, which had firm dates set for their independence, to form the "Community of African States." Thus Tubman had succeeded in a holding operation until the next year. What would happen in the meantime to the Ghana-Guinea union? Ako Adjei said that the union would remain but that the "general aspect of the Ghana-Guinea declarations is now merged with the new idea of a Community of Independent African States."[89] What did this mean? Cabinet officials said that everyone felt Nkrumah had finally accepted their tenet that political fusion had to come about more gradually, that "the Ghana-Guinea union would survive, but that the Community would be the cadre within which we would bring in the rest of independent Africa—and at some point the two would coalesce."[90] But precisely because Nkrumah did not accept the new thesis, it was impossible to have any coherent strategy. The effect of Tubman's action had been to divide Ghanaian ranks; and by the institution of a new framework of action he had so confused the picture that any future progress was to be that much more difficult.

Nkrumah had no intention of abandoning the Ghana-Guinea union since it remained his only link with French Africa, and Guinea was a state attracting a great deal of attention as a radical, near-revolutionary force. Moreover, it seemed that some of his advisers believed that some substance still existed in the union. Ako Adjei reported that Touré had referred to him as his "Vice-President," and that they traveled together throughout Guinea, Adjei being only too ready to confuse appearances maintained by a clever president with the substance of influence and power.[91]

In September, Adjei was replaced by J. H. Allassani, a minister from the north without experience in diplomacy. A cable which he sent

[88] Interviews: CF-28, 63.
[89] *Ghana Times*, 22 July 1958.
[90] Interview: CF-28.
[91] Interview: Ako Adjei. Touré, like Lumumba the following year, knew what to say when he was certain it would be passed on to Nkrumah.

to Kofi Baako, requesting that Ghana send a cameraman to follow Touré on his 1959 world tour (and make a film therefrom) is interesting: "The more we make the Guineans feel a sense of gratitude and indebtedness towards us by helping them when necessary the better it is for the success of our Union. It is not too late to send a cameraman after him. [He left only two days ago.]"[92]

The strategy which Allassani advised was very much that which was followed: Ghana would help Guinea on small matters. Thus, Nkrumah sent his Dakota to Guinea to bring the party heading for America and Russia to the Pan-American flight (that left from Accra); Touré thus visited Ghana for a day. Embassies on Touré's route were instructed that he was "to be given every facility," but this did not stop Touré from making veiled attacks on Nkrumah in some of his speeches on the tour.[93]

By this time Touré had averted disaster in Guinea, and had also ceased to have hope for reconciliation with France.[94] Furthermore, Guinea was becoming a center in its own right; radicals like Moumié, of the U.P.C., and the leaders of the Angolan M.P.L.A., were finding Conakry ideologically preferable to Accra (though the former still picked up cheques in Ghana). Involvement with the Soviet Union and other Communist countries gave it much attention in the West (and in the Ghanaian Intelligence office, too).[95] But the link with Accra remained important for one paramount reason: no solution had been found for Guinea's monetary predicament. Indeed, from the Conakry Declaration through to the Congo crisis, this problem appeared in every Ghana-Guinea communiqué. The opposition of key civil servants (like Adu) and politicians (like Gbedemah) made a joint currency zone out of the question, however. Gbedemah knew that it would ruin the stability of the Ghanaian pound, which was too great a sacrifice—he felt Ghana had been sufficiently generous, with the £4 m. (of the promised £10 m.) Guinea had already received.

The end to the union, in every meaningful sense, came over the monetary issue shortly after Guinea had finally withdrawn from the franc zone. A twelve-member delegation, led by Gbedemah, left 27 May 1960 for several days' discussion; the joint communiqué noted that "both delegations unanimously recognized the need to establish the Union on a practical basis," and called for quarterly meetings of the

[92] Allassani to Kofi Baako, 26 October 1959, CFA-101.

[93] Dei-Anang to ambassadors in Bonn, New York, London, Washington, 25 October 1959, CFA-102.

[94] Relations froze after Guinea's *de jure* recognition of Algeria in August 1959.

[95] See CFA-101.

Heads of State, trade agreements, postal links, and the like.[96] But Touré made the continuation of the Union contingent on Ghana's declaring a joint currency zone; the decision was left in abeyance for Nkrumah to decide, or, in effect, to veto.[97] There could never be any doubt of its issue: Touré's bluff was now called by Ghana. The Congo crisis intervened, and the question was never again put.

Where the union had developed significance, however, was in the ideological impact Guinea made on Ghana; Guinea's leaders were the first African nationalists more radical than Nkrumah. They could impose their thinking on their state; they could nationalize firms, fraternize with Communist diplomats and, in general, make evident how much more "progressive" they were than Ghana. They could not understand, as Adjei said, why Ghana could not, and would not, withdraw from the Commonwealth and nationalize the large firms. It was a nearly complete gulf, deriving from their very different historical experiences, and, in the ensuing year, the two states would become openly competitive.

THE STRUGGLE FOR INFLUENCE
IN NONINDEPENDENT WEST AFRICA

Nigeria. Some tension was inevitable between a newly independent, small Ghana and a still dependent, but large Nigeria. By the time of Nigeria's independence on 1 October 1960, there had been too many incidents between them for this to explain everything. A Nigerian diplomat suggested that the Ghanaians had two choices: "cooperate with us in West Africa or oppose us. To cooperate entailed playing second fiddle, so they chose to oppose us."[98] The more complex reality was a compound of interparty rivalry within Nigeria, Nkrumah's paternalistic attitude, suspicions of his Nigerian colleagues, and a series of policy decisions by Ghana which created a distrust in Lagos that, with one brief interval, was to increase until 1966.

Until 1959 Chief Awolowo, of the Action Group, and Dr. Azikiwe, of the NCNC, invariably took opposite sides in controversies regarding Ghana. Awolowo's charges against Nkrumah dated back to 1951, but the first major one followed Nkrumah's London visit in 1957, when the Nigerian ministers were simultaneously engaged in constitutional discussions in London. He alleged that Nkrumah cursorily informed him he had only fifteen minutes to spare for talks with him, and accused him

[96] Joint Communiqué Issued by the Ghana-Guinea Conference, P.R. #446/60, 3 June 1960. See also *Ghana Times*, 8 January 1960.
[97] Interview: Gbedemah.
[98] Interview: CF-83E.

of interfering in Nigerian affairs by supporting the NCNC. Awolowo then attacked Ghana, and his riposte used Nigeria's primary advantage —her size—to the fullest. "One of our . . . neighbours . . . chooses to meddle in our internal affairs. A small country, like a small business, is much easier to organize and manage. Nigeria is a colossal venture."[99]

Ghana's independent status did make it difficult for her to treat Nigeria as an equal. Nigeria could not have attended the 1958 IAS conference, but the northerners and Action Group resented the absence of any gesture toward Nigerian involvement. Finally, on the eve of the conference, Nkrumah offered to travel to Nigeria for consultations, in order to be able "to represent their point of view at the conference."[100] Thus was the damage compounded, and Abubakar Tafawa Balewa, the federal prime minister, the Sardauna, prime minister of the north, and Chief Awolowo made clear they would not find it convenient to see Nkrumah on his visit. He canceled the trip, and sent Adjei, Padmore, and Kofi instead—who went only to Enugu to see Azikiwe. "It is an egregious insult for the Prime Minister of a small country like Ghana to essay to be Nigeria's spokesman," Awolowo commented.[101]

Officially, the NCNC saw it all differently. Zik's *West African Pilot* said that Ghana "will at all times be our best friend in the world" in any event:[102] but personal attitudes were different in the party. It was said that Nkrumah did not understand the Nigerian political situation, that in 1957 he tried to convince the NCNC to precipitate a crisis with the British, on the grounds that independence would not otherwise be granted.[103]

As for the northern leaders, Nkrumah found it difficult to veil his suspicions, and probably underestimated their considerable talent for administration. It was difficult to persuade him to give Abubakar a full head-of-government reception on his Ghanaian visits, but it is precisely in these areas of protocol where Nigerian susceptibilities were greatest.

Political jealousies can be forgotten with the turn of events, however, as was to be seen with the Action Group's *volte-face* toward Ghana in 1961. Policies that erode close governmental relationships create problems of a different sort. Thus Ghana's break-up of the British West African boards genuinely shocked Nigerians. Nkrumah's justification, that independent Ghana could not work in a colonial cadre, seemed in-

[99] *Daily Service*, 13 July 1957. See also *ibid.*, 15 July 1957, and Richard Sklar, *Nigerian Political Parties*, Princeton, 1963, p. 144.

[100] *Daily Service*, 2 April 1958.

[101] *Ashanti Pioneer*, 10 April 1958. According to A.B.B. Kofi, the real reason Nkrumah did not himself go to Nigeria was fear for his security.

[102] *West African Pilot*, 22 April 1958.

[103] Interview: F. S. McEwen.

adequate, as civil servants had given much thought to plans that would give Ghana control over its own reserves, as was later to be done, in part, for Tanganyika in East Africa; Awolowo publicly proposed this.[104] Nkrumah's real reason for his action was different. "He feared 'neo-colonialist' influences in Nigeria; he was convinced that British influence among Nigeria's leaders was so great as to expose Ghana to the gravest risks were it to remain within the West African structures."[105] Those who saw only pettiness in Nkrumah's attitude, the desire to prevent Nigerian dominance in West Africa, were thus only partly right.

Ghana also worked against Nigeria on the issue of the Southern Cameroons. Chief Endeley, who in 1957 became that territory's first premier, stood on a platform of remaining within the Nigerian federal structure; Foncha's KNDP, on the other hand, campaigned for union with French East Cameroun. Interestingly, it was Endeley who, according to Ardener, spoke "the language of anti-imperialism," and it was Endeley who had attended the AAPC, while Foncha's KNDP was "highly traditionalist and conservative in its image."[106] Nkrumah supported Foncha in the 1959 elections, however, because of his position toward Nigeria. Ghanaian diplomats spoke of Foncha as "our man." "Nkrumah did not want Nigeria to get too big."[107] Moreover, he sensed that Félix Moumié, the radical East Camerounian exile, supported a lost cause against the French in the East, and wanted a foothold next door, "to keep Ahidjo [the premier] in line."[108]

There was, finally, the growing awareness in Nigeria that various Nigerian dissidents were drawing support from Ghana. Chiki Obi, Aminu Kano, and Gogo Nzeribe all "received money from time to time, just enough to keep them in line," a Ghanaian diplomat posted to Lagos in early 1960 commented.[109] No doubt many Nigerians were disaffected by their government's pro-Western stance, and it was not unnatural for them to look to Ghana—whose support of them obviously went unappreciated in Nigerian official circles.

Relations were happier at the diplomatic level for a time. Nkrumah appointed a long-time resident of Nigeria as his commissioner, and the appointment was well received, as was that of Kola Bologun at the other

104 O. Awolowo, "Foreign Policy for Independent Nigeria," Ibadan, 1958. See also Interview: CF-5.

105 Interview: CF-28. For an interesting defense of Ghana's actions, see P.R. #335/62, 12 June 1962.

106 Edwin Ardener, "The Political History of Cameroon," *World Today*, 18, No. 8, pp. 346-47.

107 Interviews: CF-109, 20.

108 Interview: CF-109.   109 Interview: CF-112.

end.[110] Nkrumah's visit to Nigeria in February 1959 also dispelled doubts of his intentions, momentarily at least. He spoke openly of the causes of bad feeling, such as his deportation of Nigerians from Ghana, and his breaking of the organizational ties, by noting how small a proportion of the Nigerians in Ghana had been deported, and by suggesting that after Nigeria's independence, links could be reestablished. ". . . what stops us from having a common airline? A common shipping line? And even a common defence?"[111]

Throughout 1959 Nigerians reconsidered their attitudes toward Ghana. By September Awolowo reportedly felt that Nkrumah was "a much changed man,"[112] while by early 1960 an admirer of Nkrumah's such as Dr. Kalu Ezera, a radical NCNC member, could write that "even within the NCNC camp . . . there is a growing tendency to anti-Ghana-ianism."[113] The most salient explanation was the dynamics of the political process. After the Nigerian federal elections of 1959, Awolowo became federal leader of the opposition; the NCNC, as a result of its alliance with the conservative northerners, no doubt was forced to alter its attitude toward Ghana. But if the leaders of this diffuse party had dubious motives for their change, they no doubt had genuine qualms about Ghana as well. As McEwen said, "We did not know Nkrumah would become a dictator when we praised him so lavishly."[114]

Dr. Ezera's writings in this period are significant. "Nigerians bitterly resent being daubed traitors to the African cause for circumstances which are at present beyond their control." African unity could never become a reality until the states treated each other not with scorn and snobbery, "but with respect, sympathy, and understanding. . . . Yet . . . the two leading countries in West Africa whose combined weight . . . could easily shake the very foundation of imperialism in Africa, seem to be going in opposite directions. . . . And of course, all talk of African unity without Nigerian participation is moonshine."[115] A distinguished Nigerian civil servant later asked why Ghana and Nigeria had not learned some *Realpolitik*, taken into account the underlying geopolitical and economic realities of West Africa, and divided up areas of influence to unite the area.[116] His premise was that the two were fundamentally the same, that Nkrumah merely gave the impression of talking a different, more radical,

[110] See Kolawole Bologun, *Mission to Ghana: Memoire of a Diplomat*, New York, 1963, pp. 59-61.
[111] "Trip to Nigeria," Accra, 1959, pp. 8-10.
[112] See *Ashanti Pioneer*, 14 September 1959, Reuters Dispatch.
[113] Dr. Kalu Ezera, "Ghana and Nigeria: Toward Better Understanding," *Daily Times* (Lagos), 1 April 1960.
[114] Interview: F. S. McEwen.
[115] Dr. Kalu Ezera, *loc.cit.*   [116] Interview: CF-83C.

language. This was not the case. Nkrumah correctly realized that the nature of northern power in Nigeria made the type of union that he wanted impossible. There was no question of "respect, sympathy, or understanding."

Togo. On 27 April 1958, just after the IAS conference in Accra, Sylvanus Olympio's Union Togolaise, in alliance with a militant youth group, Juvento, won a victory in Togoland in elections supervised by the United Nations. Those who had supported integration within the French Union—Grunitzky, Ajavon, Meatchi—were out; those who seemed to be talking the language of African nationalism were in.

What were Olympio's intentions? *West Africa* cautioned that the "situation is a tricky one, and likely to present Ghana with a very real test of her foreign policy."[117] Ghana was to fail no test more thoroughly than this one. Within two years Togo was driven into a defense entente with the French, while Nkrumah contemplated military invasion; within three, there was to be enough subversion on both sides of the border to give both states justification for making substantial inroads on civil liberties; and within five, Olympio was assassinated—with a lingering suspicion lying on Ghana which weakened its prestige throughout Africa.

The underlying cause of the tragedy was a misapprehension of Olympio's intentions, shared by both the French and the Ghanaians. Thus the former opposed him before the election, and the latter after it had taken place. The French and their men in Togo argued that Ghana had an "imperialist design,"[118] and accused Olympio (before the election) of walking into a trap. Grunitzky's PTP regretted the inclusion of British Togoland into Ghana, and "maintained that [Olympio's party] was a small minority . . . seeking to bring about the integration of Togoland into Ghana."[119] Nkrumah simplified the situation into two alternatives (as he was similarly to do in January 1963 when Togo had gone full circle): there were those seeking union with France, and those who wanted Ewe union—ipso facto, union with Ghana. Had the wish been less the father of the thought, Nkrumah would have seen the logical flaw.

> Mr. Olympio (All-Ewe Conference) recalled that . . . his party had not favoured the solution which had made the Ewes in the former Trust Territory . . . under British administration citizens of the

[117] *West Africa*, 10 May 1958, p. 434.
[118] *UNGA*, IVth Comm., 18 November 1957, p. 707.
[119] *Ibid.*, "Report of the United Nations Commission on Togoland under French Administration," 1957, T/1343, p. 50, Para. 400.

new State of Ghana . . . [but] it had bowed to the decision of the majority and of the General Assembly. . . . His party considered that the only satisfactory solution would be to enable Togoland under French administration to become fully independent so that the two sovereign States . . . could then decide what relationship should exist between the two Ewe-speaking peoples. . . .[120]

Olympio only spoke of the need for a *modus vivendi* between the two, and at no point spoke of absorption of the one by the other. Indeed, the crux of Olympio's argument against the French had been that "Togoland . . . is a viable entity in itself."[121]

In April 1958 there was a more immediate failure of communication. Olympio had benefited from the impact of the IAS conference which took place soon before his election—a conference at which France had very much been the "scapegoat for colonialist sins."[122] But no evidence exists that Olympio's party received material support from Ghana in its campaign, as so many Ghanaian officials were afterwards to believe;[123] even if it had, this did not obligate Olympio to surrender Togo's sovereignty. On the very eve of the voting, the CPP had aided Juvento, but there was every reason for knowing that this group had an uneasy relationship, at best, with the Union Togolaise.[124]

There was a still greater failure. Nkrumah had decidedly not taken the measure of Olympio, despite numerous opportunities. Olympio, a self-confident and immensely successful businessman-nationalist, had been made a manager of the United Africa Company long before pressures for Africanization existed. He did not "permit the foibles of men to interfere with his principles or objectives,"[125] and it is easy to understand his lack of admiration for Nkrumah. Olympio dominated Togoland as the leader of an overwhelmingly successful nationalist party, but Nkrumah saw him mainly as a leader who could bring the territory into

[120] *Ibid.*, 8 November 1957, #697, p. 245, Para. 5.

[121] *Ibid.*, p. 248, Para. 44; "Report of the UN Commission, Trusteeship Council," Official Records of the 7th special session, 12-20 September 1957, C.U.T. memorandum, p. 87.

[122] *le Monde*, 30 April 1958.

[123] See Amb. S. W. Kumah, "Ghana-Togo Relations," *Ministry of Foreign Affairs*, Conference of Ghana Envoys, January 1962, p. 135, in which it is claimed that Olympio took advantage of the Ghanaian misconception that the two leaders shared similar views on Togoland so as to obtain financial support in his campaign. No evidence appears anywhere, however, that he received any whatsoever. Interviews: CF-10, 86.

[124] See *Ghana*, "Proceedings and Report of the Commission appointed to enquire into the Matters Disclosed at the Trial of Capt. Benj. Awhaitey," 1959, esp. pp. 198-200, Paras. 6933, 6952, 6965, and 6954. Juvento accepted 50 bicycles from the CPP on the eve of the election without informing Olympio of the gift.

[125] Interview: Sylvanus Amegashie.

Ghana. Olympio's objective had always been the "removal of the *présence française*,"[126] and his victory enabled him to negotiate with the French from a position of strength. Finally, he had a towering reputation in United Nations circles, and he was not without friends—from Sékou Touré to the Americans.[127]

A month after the election, Nkrumah announced at Ho that he intended to enter into "friendly discussions" with Togo's new government, and hoped to see the removal of "irksome customs barriers."[128] But he put the problem's solution in the context of Ewe reunification which, with its implication of the absorption of French Togo, had long since become unacceptable to Olympio. Olympio did indicate a willingness to discuss federation, carefully underlining the distinction between this and integration,[129] but he probably envisaged something different: an economic arrangement with Ghana and other West African states to save Togo from French economic control, and Ghanaian backing of Togo's currency.[130] The economic need was so desperate that he was prepared to gamble on the political consequences; indeed, there seems little doubt that, with astute leadership from Accra, Togo would be absorbed, having an economy about one-twentieth Ghana's in size. Nkrumah, obsessed as always by Ghana's independence, often noted that negotiations could not come until Togo's independence. In the intervening two years there was adequate time for potentially good relations to deteriorate. Given the best of will in Accra, Togolese nationalism would have increased in the absence of Ghanaian initiatives.

Thus Olympio began directing his efforts elsewhere. He discussed plans for a "French Union" with Sékou Touré in July 1958, which was to be a "union of equals" without representation in the French national assembly, and increasingly emphasized the need for a general West African federation, rather than one exclusively with Ghana.[131] Other things alarmed Accra. Olympio, in expressing his opposition to "integration" with Ghana, expressed his opposition even to the integration of ex-British Togoland with Ghana, a process that was proceeding apace.[132] What might appear to be irredentism on Togo's part was more a re-

126 James Coleman, "Togoland," *International Conciliation*, No. 509, September 1956, p. 33.

127 Olympio did not like Guinea's internal politics, but highly valued his friendship with Touré. The two held the distinction of having won West African elections in spite of French intrigue. See Eisenhower's comments on Olympio, *Waging Peace*, New York, 1965, p. 582, and Robert Cornevin's *Histoire du Togo*, Paris, 1959, p. 122.

128 *Daily Graphic*, 26 May 1958; *Times*, 27 May 1958.

129 Interview by Philippe Decraene in *le Monde*, 2 August 1958.

130 Interview: CF-86, a trusted adviser of Olympio's.

131 Interview by Philippe Decraene in *Combat*, 3-4, April 1958.

132 See Decraene interview in *le Monde*, 2 August 1958.

statement of an old hope than a plan of action, for Olympio was a realist, and knew little chance of reunification of the two trust territories existed; but he had the refugees from British Togoland to contend with. The irony was that Olympio and Nkrumah shared the same pan-African sentiments, and spoke the same language of African nationalism.[133]

Their differences led to practical consequences even by the end of 1958, owing to the intimate nature of the states' relationship, foreshadowed in the introductory preview. At that time two opposition MPs were detained in Accra for alleged plotting, part of which took place on Togolese territory, the government's report claimed.[134] Concurrently, there were reports of a plot against Olympio by Juvento, which had formally split from his party, and a section of which was in close touch with the CPP.[135] Lines were not clearly drawn at this point; some Juvento members were more strongly affected by family ties with Ghanaian opposition leaders, and Botsio gave the French a warning of Juvento's plans.[136] The point is that both governments were becoming apprehensive about activities across their border.

During 1959, Olympio began consolidating other friendships, having given up waiting for Ghana. Maga, the premier of Dahomey, was Togo's first official guest, and the Union Togolaise was represented at the Guinean party congress in September. Nkrumah realized that he was losing his chance of a union with Togo, and in October sent two officials to talk with Olympio. It was now Olympio's turn to wish to wait "until after independence," having come to suspect Nkrumah's intentions.[137] Later in October, Nkrumah gave a remarkable series of speeches in ex-British Togoland, stating that he would "see to it that [Togo] became the seventh region of Ghana. . . . Dr. Nkrumah told the large gathering that Togoland did not only belong to them by birth—but also it was their right."[138] From then until Togo's independence (on 27 April 1960), the two leaders exchanged insults regularly and diplomatic incidents multiplied.

Nkrumah was becoming obsessed with security in the Volta region, ex-British Togoland, and feared a repetition of the 1957 outbreak. The

---

[133] See *ibid.* Claude Welch points out that Olympio had long since warned that once British Togoland became part of the Gold Coast, chances of reunification would be lost. *Dream of Unity*, Cornell, 1966, p. 137.

[134] See *Ghana*, "Proceedings and Report . . . at the trial of Capt. Awhaitey," p. 199.

[135] *Ibid.*, p. 467, and *le Monde*, 7 January 1959.

[136] "Proceedings and Report . . . ," p. 285.

[137] Ministry of External Affairs, Report of Conversations between Olympio and Nkrumah, CFA-105.

[138] *Ghana Times*, 30 October 1959. Olympio's response is in *AFP Sp. outre-mer*, 1-2 November 1959.

government was also apprehensive of French intentions and, indeed, prepared security plans against the possibility of French intervention.[139] It was a bad assessment of French policy, and was ironic, for it was Ghana's actions that were driving Olympio for the first time to seek French protection. Shortly before Togo's independence, Nkrumah directed General Alexander, his British chief of staff, to conduct maneuvers at the border, the first since Ghana's independence, so as to frighten Olympio. Nkrumah also directed him to draw up an invasion plan.[140] Other stratagems were no more subtle. Having found "a document purporting to be a draft Constitution" for Togo that included ex-British Togoland, Ghana protested, claiming that Togo was plotting disturbances in Ghana, and was bridging the river Todzie "in order to facilitate the passage of insurgents into . . . Ghana."[141] The more compelling reason for this protest was probably Nkrumah's simultaneous detention of thirteen Ewe leaders.

Olympio resorted to ridicule, a weapon he was gradually developing to pierce Nkrumah's thin skin. "Whoever thinks that this bridge, more than the other bridges along the frontier, would facilitate an attack against Ghana has a boy-scout conception of military strategy. We would have thought that this tactic . . . was *depassée* since the burning of the Reichstag."[142] Elsewhere, he called Nkrumah's "bluffs" the "joke of the century" and most galling, referred to Ghana (along with Togo) as one of the "petit" states of West Africa.[143] There was in fact little likelihood of Ghanaian intervention, not only because of French and UN support for Togo, but because of the still strong restraining power of civil servants—and of a British general. Nkrumah had merely succeeded in losing good will in West Africa. By daring him to take his stratagems—and himself—seriously, Olympio had mocked him at a time when other governments were themselves reassessing "the Osagyefo." For that matter, the Ghana-Togo problem had ceased to be bilateral. At a conference in Accra in April 1960, the Nigerian Action Group spokesman, Chief Anthony Enahoro, suggested that West African frontiers should be guaranteed in concert by the West African states; failing that, Nigeria should guarantee Togo's borders.[144]

There was to be a last chance to start afresh. At some point prior to its independence, Hammarskjold intervened on behalf of Togo, still the UN's ward, urging Nkrumah to make a last attempt to improve rela-

[139] Interviews: CF-28, 55.
[140] By General Alexander's account.
[141] P.R. #233/60, 15 March 1960. See also *Ghana Times*, 16 March 1960.
[142] *Nouvelles Officielles du Togo*, 17 March 1960.
[143] *New York Times*, 24 March 1960.
[144] Reported in *Manchester Guardian*, 13 April 1960.

tions. Nkrumah agreed, to the surprise of many, and then invited Olympio to meet him at the border. Olympio replied that he was at home, and would be delighted to have Nkrumah for lunch.[145] Thus on Saturday, 11 June 1960, Nkrumah went with Ako Adjei, Dei-Anang, and others to Lomé. Olympio noted how grieved he was by the insulting speeches on the border. The Ghanaian ministry's report continued:

> . . . he asked the Prime Minister to clear the atmosphere and explain why Ghana was attacking Togo. Had Togo offended Ghana in any way. Dr. Nkrumah assured him that no offence had been committed by Togo.
>
> Mr. Olympio thought the first practical step should be by way of economic union. Dr. Nkrumah pointed out that economics implies politics. He thought Ghana and Togo should form a Political Union in which neither country would surrender sovereignty, but would co-operate closely in the matter of diplomatic relations, defence, and currency.
>
> . . . Mr. Olympio thought some of the difficulties in the way of political union were language and historical background, to mention only two. Political union was in his view a thing for the future, whereas an immediate practical step would be taken by way of economic union. [Moreover], British mandated Togoland . . . constituted a political difficulty. [Therefore, economic unity should come first, but the Prime Minister did not agree.] Here the Prime Minister said he had received the impression that Togo was trying to tie up with the French. [Olympio made it clear nothing was further from their intentions.]

Olympio persisted with his approach to unity, and, in the end, Nkrumah could only ask him to submit economic proposals.[146]

What stands out in the Ghanaians' minutes is Olympio's complete dominance of the occasion, and Nkrumah's failure to stand by any of his past accusations and criticisms other than that of links with the French; any sober reading of Olympio's politics throughout this period makes that particular statement seem bizarre. Nkrumah did not mention the reported constitution, the footbridge, the French security threat; these had been for tactical use, but they had been badly chosen tactics. Olympio would have scorned them as easily as he had done three months

---

[145] *Afrique Action*, 21 November 1960. A brief portion of the meeting is recounted in this interview with Olympio, which does not contradict the report by Ghana's own ministry, hereafter quoted from.

[146] MEA, Report of conversations between Olympio and Nkrumah, CFA-105.

earlier. The charismatic but unintelligent politician had encountered a statesman, and had been bested.

France and the Ivory Coast. France was most interested in Ghanaian developments, and soon after independence sent a skillful intelligence officer as its first ambassador. They supported a lost cause in fighting the idea of independence in West Africa, even if little contact existed between Ghanaian and French African leaders. The Ghana-Guinea union —which, whatever else it did, helped to sustain Guinea's independence for a year—gave the French reason to fear Ghana's influences; Eisenhower, for example, wrote that de Gaulle suspected "that considerable pro-Communist subversion was going on within the borders of many nations in the French community, with its local sources probably found in Guinea and to some extent in Ghana. . . ."[147]

The Ghanaians, for their part, had no use for the French. "They represented everything bad to us. But we did not know them, and we had no intelligence at that time to maintain contact with developments in their territories."[148] When the Quai d'Orsay suggested, in a letter from which quotation has already been made, that Ghana sought to "give effect to [its] designs" through the AAPC, Padmore responded that it was "a piece of cheek and impertinence on the part of the French government to address such a communication to the government of Ghana. . . . This remark certainly calls for the strongest protest."[149] But the only framework the Ghanaians had evolved for influencing the French African states was a monthly conference of African ambassadors and French African representatives that John Jantuah had formed in Paris. Padmore, it seems, was aware of divergent opinion that was spreading throughout the area, and the news circular issued from his office took note of hopeful developments.[150]

If Ghana's diplomats did not wish to give the impression of policies "inimical to any of our neighbouring states," and if Padmore wished to work with these leaders to encourage them to seek independence, Nkrumah had other ideas, particularly with regard to his most obvious adversary in black Africa, Houphouet-Boigny and, as already seen, with Olympio. To be sure, there was good reason to dislike Ivoirien policy. At a time when Ghana pledged £10,000,000 to a destitute state, and

[147] Eisenhower, *Waging Peace*, p. 429.

[148] Interview: CF-28.

[149] Padmore to Adu, 14 August 1958, CFA-12.

[150] See his reaction to the Malians' opposition to French nuclear testing, *Information Bulletin on African Affairs*, 2, No. 32. He was wrong, however, in stating that Keita was the first French African leader to oppose French atomic testing in the Sahara: Sylvanus Olympio had already done so.

87

had welcomed some five hundred nationalists to Accra (at the AAPC), the Ivory Coast was refusing to share its wealth with its poorer neighbors, and its people were rioting against, and expelling, foreign nationals from their country (4,000 of whom were Ghanaians who arrived home at the end of 1958).[151]

It did not necessarily follow, however, that Ghana had a claim on the southeastern corner of the Ivory Coast. Although Nkrumah felt an identification with the people of this area, brothers of his own Nzimas, this was only incidental to Ghana's claim; the success of the policy would challenge the cohesiveness of the Ivory Coast as a composite nation.[152] Given his policy toward dissident groups within Ghana, it is hard to believe Nkrumah was not hoping to shake Ivoirien confidence. Thus, from 1959, refuge and aid was extended to the "prime minister" of the Sanwi "provisional government," Armand Attié, who coordinated his activities with a non-Sanwi Ivoirien dissident, Camille Adam.

There was another area for pressure on Houphouet: his support of French atomic testing in the Sahara. Here Nkrumah had an issue that could appeal emotionally to all those opposed to Houphouet's policies. An editorial titled "Houphouet-Boigny—Stooge and Traitor" said the following: "The so-called Prime Minister of Ivory Coast—the puppet dancing savagely to the tunes of the French imperialist shampoolah—has done his worst . . .

"We sympathise with Houphouet-Boigny's mental defection in over-playing up his master De Gaulle's right to explode the Atom Bomb over poor defenceless Africans."[153] Houphouet's own attempts to belittle the concept of independence throughout this period[154] were doomed, but Nkrumah weakened his case by allowing such polemics to be used, and, more important, by putting forth the territorial claim. According to an Ivoirien diplomat, Houphouet had remained largely silent on this issue, so as to permit Nkrumah to discredit himself as much as possible, but after Nkrumah had made a new round of claims in early 1960 in the Western Region of Ghana, Houphouet said that he was obliged, "in the face of this new provocation, *purement verbale d'ailleurs*, to state clearly to Mr. Nkrumah that . . . he has neither the right, nor the means,

---

151 See *Daily Graphic*, 8 January 1959. It was an effective part of Ghana's strategy to dramatize the plight of the refugees.

152 For background to the dispute, see Zolberg, *One-Party Government in the Ivory Coast*, Princeton, 1964, p. 67, and for a thorough account of it, see Virginia Thompson, "The Ivory Coast," in G. Carter, ed., *African One-Party States*, Cornell, 1962, pp. 297-300. See also *Evening News*, 11 September 1959; Nkrumah, *Ghana*, pp. 261-62, 219; and *Debates*, 16 December 1959, pp. 632-34.

153 *Evening News*, 5 September 1959.

154 See *Ghana Times*, 5 September 1959.

to demand . . . the annexation of the least portion of the Ivory Coast."[155] Nkrumah's bluff was called, and little more was heard of these claims until later in the year. Houphouet would have had to seek independence whether or not Nkrumah had pressed for this, but by his methods he lost the basis for a genuine dialogue with, or a rational policy of pressure on, the Ivory Coast.

CONFERENCE DIPLOMACY, 1960

As late as August 1959, at a conference of the IAS foreign ministers in Monrovia, the nine independent states could agree to radical resolutions on every African issue of the day, except "African unity" which was barely mentioned.[156] Only Liberia and Ethiopia were conservative influences. By mid-1960, Africa had changed, and with it, the political balance of the group of African states. Cameroun and Togo were independent, the Entente states and the Mali Federation were arranging their independence, and Nigeria was waiting for its October celebrations. It was no longer to be so easy to find agreement.

Nkrumah's pan-African ideas were becoming increasingly precise, however. At the end of 1958, he had said that it was impossible to predict the form a union would take "until we have given careful consideration" to it[157] but, by early 1960, he made no such reservations and insisted on immediate union without, however, revealing how this was to be brought about. He also began speaking of the new danger Africa faced, balkanization, stating that the newly independent states were "designed to be so weak . . . that they will be compelled to continue to depend upon the colonial powers." It was a warning to be repeated throughout the ensuing six years, though it was not yet called "neo-colonialism." He had a remedy: Africa would be united by "an ideology —our common Africanism." To prevent balkanization, the Central Committee of the CPP decided "that arrangements should be undertaken to bring all freedom fighters in Africa together." Unlike past conferences, this one was to consist solely of African political parties "dedicated to and engaged in the struggle for African emancipation. Its main task will be to forge an ideology chain consistent with present-day African political thinking."[158] Put differently, he had decided to renounce the AAPC, the organization he had founded, to conduct alone the struggle he had begun in unison with the continent.

---

[155] Interview: CF-15, and *Abidjan Matin*, 9 February 1960.

[156] See resolutions in Legum, *Pan-Africanism*, pp. 183-87.

[157] Speech to the Indian Council of World Affairs, 29 December 1958, in *Bulletin on African Affairs*, 2, No. 72.

[158] Speech on the tenth anniversary of "positive action," *Ghana Times*, 9 January 1960.

Nkrumah had long since become disillusioned with the AAPC. It had produced meagre results. The Ghanaians did not like the secretary-general, Abdoulaye Diallo, and with Padmore's death, there was no one left who cared to utilize the organization. Nkrumah's new conference never materialized, for the second AAPC, planned for Tunis, was only weeks away, and attention throughout Africa was focused on it. Freedom fighters had agreed to work through the AAPC and, presumably, saw no reason to abandon its formal structure. Indeed, the Tunis conference was to show how much resistance Nkrumah had already encountered—or engendered.

There, the Pafmeca representatives formed a strong lobby to oppose the Ghanaians, particularly on behalf of Tom Mboya.[159] The Action Group delegates charged that a clique had prevented Nigerian representation on the steering committee, and had even removed Nigeria's identity card at one point, all to prevent Nigeria from playing "her proper role" on the continent.[160] But as Tony Enahoro's address shows, they fought back. "Our constitution is still not finally approved. Certain organs of the conference are in danger of lapsing into abeyance . . . we are . . . without a proper report on the work of the Conference . . . for the last fourteen months. Exactly what is the Conference doing to promote the liberation of Africa? . . . The Secretary-General reports that Africa has taken great strides forward since our first Conference. This is a stimulating thought. But to what extent is the Conference strictly responsible?"[161] The final resolutions further demonstrated the strength of the "anti-Ghana/Guinea" forces. The secretary-general was to become full-time, the steering committee was to be enlarged (and to include Mboya), and regionalism was praised. There was an emphasis on the need for better communications, transport facilities, regional cooperation. Catherine Hoskyns wrote that "African leaders seem sensibly to have come to the conclusion that political federation is the last and not the first step in unifying the continent."[162]

Thus Ghana had to discard that framework for action. But there were other frameworks left, and between Tunis and the birth of the Ghanaian republic they had all had their chance. The next meeting was a small one, of the foreign ministers of Ghana, Guinea, and Liberia. It was the sole attempt to make use of the Sanniquellie Declaration, and the results of it were nil. It began at State House, in Accra, on February 9th

159 On the Tunis conference, see Richard Cox, *Pan Africanism in Practice*, London, 1964, p. 34, and Catherine Hoskyns, "Tunis Diary," *Africa South in Exile*, 4, No. 4.
160 "They smelt Conspiracy in Tunis," *Daily Service*, 4 February 1960.
161 "IInd AAPC: Speech of Chief Anthony Enahoro," Tunis, 1960 (mimeo).
162 Hoskyns, *loc.cit.* Also see Legum, *Pan-Africanism*, pp. 243-46.

and lasted over two weeks, but the sole decision was the agreement "to recognize the independence and sovereignty of the state of the Cameroun and to extend to the new State a hearty welcome into the Comity of Nations."[163] Liberia had again stalled, arguing that no attempts at unification could be made prior to the independence of Nigeria, Togo, and others with independence dates; and that, in any case, there could be no discussion of "unity" until Cameroun had been recognized. Ghana and Guinea then made an empty concession, recognizing the existence of the state—not the government.[164] Like the AAPC, the Sanniquellie framework was emptied of significance. Nkrumah's insistence on political unity was growing rapidly in this period, and Liberia was the more determined to delay any action.

The next conference was entitled "Positive Action—for Peace and Security in Africa." For months Nkrumah had sought an effective response to France's nuclear testing in the Sahara, and thus made a call for African and other organizations to come to Accra for discussions. But after the original invitations had been sent, he broadened the agenda of the conference to include most of the questions of the day; it was thus to be a substitute for the gathering of freedom fighters he had proposed in January.

Opposition was quickly expressed. On March 12th the Emperor of Ethiopia wrote to Nkrumah questioning the propriety of raising "general questions affecting Africa" in addition to the question of atomic testing at a conference to be held so close to the second IAS Conference, scheduled for Addis Ababa the following June. Two days later Nkrumah responded: "It would seem a pity . . . at a gathering at which political parties throughout Africa will be represented not to at least touch upon other common problems, without however allowing them to overshadow the immediate issue of the tests. Some preliminary discussion, for instance, of the threat to Balkanize Africa and of ways of achieving closer union among African States, might pave the way to fruitful agreements later. Such preliminary discussions would not, we feel, in any way detract from the main discussions proposed to take place in your capital next June."[165]

The conference was held in early April, almost at the same time as the AAPSO Conference in Conakry. It made very little impact, coming as it did in the wake of so many fast-moving events. Campaigning for the presidential election and the plebiscite on the republic was draw-

[163] P.R. #183/60, 25 February 1960.
[164] Interviews: Adjei, Dzirasa, and Quaison-Sackey.
[165] His Imperial Majesty to Nkrumah, 12 March 1960, Nkrumah to H.I.M., 14 March 1960, CFA-9.

ing to a close in Ghana, and in the rest of Africa developments were of bewildering speed. Sharpeville, the demand for independence in the French territories, de Gaulle's proposals on Algeria, all tended to hide the conference from view in the African and world press.

The conference was designed to give Nkrumah a platform for comment on just these issues and, at the same time, to transform a successful domestic weapon, "positive action," into continental use. But for the first time since independence, it was difficult to be heard because of the importance and scope of the events elsewhere in Africa—the very events Nkrumah wished to affect. Thus did his speech convey an even greater sense of urgency: "it behoves each and everyone in the leadership of this struggle to endeavor to subdue his own little interests, his individual pride and ego and other petty considerations which merely serve to create needless obstacles in our path [sic]. The overriding importance of African unity demands the sacrifice of all personal, tribal and regional objectives and considerations."[166]

At the end of April another AAPC steering committee meeting was held in Accra, but it too was hidden from view, even in the Ghanaian press, this time by the reports on the Ghanaian election. Nor was much accomplished at the meeting; at the time Ghana was working to organize a united front of South African refugees, and was of course doing this outside the AAPC framework.

On the other hand, work was also going on to strengthen the purely Ghanaian organizations. At the end of May the Bureau of African Affairs was reconstituted—with Nathaniel Welbeck as chairman—to "intensify" its activities in the fight against imperialism.[167]

The real spotlight, in the meantime, was on the second IAS Conference in Addis Ababa. Ako Adjei led a large delegation to this meeting, and in his speech demanded that a union be formed. He dragged the Sanniquellie Declaration from its obscurity, and attempted to reframe it in political, supranational terms, although it was notable for the absence of an endorsement of such a pan-Africanism. This attempt to rewrite recent history fooled nobody. Indeed, this conference showed that resentment against Ghana had been mounting at the governmental level too. Maitama Sule, representing Nigeria's federal government, delivered a frontal assault on Ghana's "revolutionary" approach to unity, urging that Africa build from the ground up, not from the "top down." It was also important for its "unveiled attack"—as Colin Legum noted[168]— on Nkrumah himself: "if anybody makes the mistake of feeling that he

166 Nkrumah, *I Speak of Freedom*, p. 221.
167 *Ghana Times*, 27 May 1960.   168 Legum, *Pan-Africanism*, p. 192.

is a Messiah who has got a mission to lead Africa, the whole purpose of pan-Africanism will be defeated, I fear." The fruits of past miscalculations, insensitivity, indiscretion were all ripening at once. The new generation of leaders in the states just achieving their independence were not accepting Ghana's leadership and rejected both Nkrumah's ideas and style.

Worse, from this conference a secretariat might have emerged as a permanent organization with "a regular schedule of meetings," to "serve as a binding link between the independent African states . . . [that] will be the forerunner in the formation of [a] Union of African States," as Sule urged.[169] But there were two extremes that made the achievement of any such organization more difficult. Liberia, for one, proposed a delay until yet more states became independent. Having dangled the bait of a permanent organization as early as January 1959, Liberia now rejected it when a prestigious state proposed it; at Sanniquellie it had rejected the idea of forming a union, but had made clear that in a year the time would be ripe. Now it wanted to wait until even the East African States were independent. Quaison-Sackey concluded that "they would not even back their own proposals when these were taken up." But Ghana was equally short sighted: In his speech, Ako Adjei had admitted that "we must start from somewhere . . . whether with economic or cultural co-operation,"[170] but the delegation did not support the Nigerian proposal. In the end, there was no secretariat, and only a vague commitment to discuss African unity in the future.

Political pan-Africanism had receded considerably in two years, if it had not totally disappeared. Quaison-Sackey, writing in 1963, argued that "by the time of the Conference opening . . . something had gone wrong. The world press, it seemed, had begun to sow seeds of jealousy among [African] leaders, by claiming that Nkrumah of Ghana was attempting to achieve African unity simply because he wanted to dominate the whole continent."[171] Was it the world press's fault, or Nkrumah's? He had made quite clear, after all, that he was "prepared to serve under any African leader who is able to offer the proper guidance in this great issue" of political unity.[172] The disclaimer was meaningless, even damaging, since the problem of continental leadership was not in question. Only Nkrumah was thinking of it. Africa, in the meantime, had no supranational institutions, and since other states would not support these, he would not support an OAS-type inter-state organization. The groupings

[169] IInd IAS, speeches, Government of Ethiopia (mimeo).
[170] Government of Ethiopia, *loc.cit.*
[171] Alex Quaison-Sackey, *Africa Unbound*, New York, 1963, p. 192.
[172] Nkrumah, *I Speak of Freedom*, p. 221.

and counter-groupings of the three ensuing years were one inevitable consequence.

EXTERNAL RELATIONS

Nkrumah was gradually learning that he did not have to be a "perfect neocolonial leader" to preserve his loose links with the West; with the Ghana-Guinea union he found to his own surprise that he could do what he wished. Indeed, the international repercussions of the union were more amusing than serious. The French popular press thought the British were fishing in troubled waters, while Lord Beaverbrook chided Nkrumah for his action, as a breach of faith in the Commonwealth ranks.[173] Colin Legum feared that the "spark" lit in Accra would precipitate the "Commonwealth's greatest crisis,"[174] but the British government saw it as *West Africa* did, as "little more than the consolidation of an alliance,"[175] and the French were soon to see that their representatives received a warmer welcome in Conakry than did Ghana's.

Nkrumah was unfettered in his policy-making, because there was nothing he was doing at this stage that affected the great powers adversely. He was to feel even less restricted as 1960 approached, for as cold war tension rose in the world—and was introduced into Ghana—the West began giving greater attention to nonaligned leaders. He thus began taking steps to balance Ghana's nonalignment: Diplomatic relations were established with the Communist states, and it was decided to withdraw from the CCTA—the organization of the colonial powers, South Africa, and several independent African states.[176] It was anticipated, moreover, that finance for the Volta River Project would be obtained by mid-1960, after which the state could move in any direction it wished.[177]

Britain, the Commonwealth, and South Africa. After the All-African Peoples Conference, Ghana had an interest in cooling relations with Britain, at least publicly, for it was gaining in prestige from the effect the conference had had in British colonial territories. But Ghana's relations with Britain never went below a safe threshold. If Britain would not grant Ghana substantial foreign aid, it could do much to help Nkrumah consolidate the power of his regime. When the Queen's 1959 visit had to be postponed, the party press made enormous capital of the fact

[173] *Sunday Express*, 30 November 1958.
[174] *Observer*, 30 November 1958.
[175] *West Africa*, 29 November 1958, and *Debates*, United Kingdom, 596, pp. 556-57.
[176] This decision occasioned much dissent in the ministry.
[177] Interview: Sir Robert Jackson.

that a palace official had flown to Ghana to entrust Nkrumah with "the Queen's secret" (she was expecting her third child), that Nkrumah had flown to Balmoral where the royal family was vacationing and had been granted membership of the Privy Council as well.[178] The *Evening News* saw the new title as "a slap in the face for the Opposition in Ghana. They have always said that Nkrumah is a dictator. Now democratic Britain has spoken. . . . Kwame has recorded yet another triumph over his enemies and Ghana marches forward in her solemn pledge to help free Africa."[179] On his return, Nkrumah gave a conciliatory speech that was the first, according to Joe Appiah, that was "balanced and national in character."[180] Imperialism, Nkrumah had said at the Peoples Conference, "could come in different guises"; but the radical Ghanaians, and Nkrumah himself, had failed to recognize it (or had chosen not to resist it) when it came in its classic form.

British policy itself was changing rapidly in this period. MacLeod's new policy, Macmillan's winds of change (a phrase first used during his visit to Accra)[181] made it possible for Ghana's relations with Britain, at an official level, to remain warm much longer than they might otherwise have done. And, at a variety of levels Britons in influential posts in Accra made every effort to make their presence as inconspicuous as possible, further easing the postcolonial transition. Nkrumah, in the ghosted manuscript "My Task" said of the governor-general and the change to a republic, "Anyone less sympathetic to the true cause of Ghana might well have led us to proclaim ourselves a republic much sooner."[182]

There was no conflict with the large British firms; if these on occasion showed a certain venality in their activities,[183] Nkrumah was doing nothing to restrain them. On the contrary, he often went out of his way to help them.[184]

But had Ghana affected British policy? Except for the effect of the AAPC in the Rhodesias and Nyasaland at one point, it seems unlikely. The British press and public opinion had long since become disillusioned with Nkrumah's regime, as had the diplomats. Ghana's influence was,

[178] *Ghana Times*, 17 August 1959. It called a widely distributed photograph of Nkrumah with the Queen "Ghana's Most Treasured Picture."

[179] *Evening News*, 27 August 1959.

[180] *Ghana Times*, 7 September 1959.

[181] Macmillan briefly visited Accra en route to South Africa, the first visit of a British prime minister to an African member of the Commonwealth.

[182] "My Task," unpublished manuscript, p. 86, writer's files.

[183] See an antisemitic outburst in the Assembly, which was, by two accounts, inspired by British firms resentful of Israeli intrusions into their traditional sphere. *Debates*, 29 October 1959, pp. 68-69, 113-14, and Interviews: CF-27, 57.

[184] According to a United Africa Company official, Nkrumah helped secure an ideal location for the company's large new store in 1959. Interview: W. F. Pedler.

rather, that it existed, as an independent state, an ideal to which nationalists everywhere could aspire. British diplomats all said—half a
decade later—that Ghana had only nuisance value for Britain at that
time, and in terms of what Ghana was doing, this was surely true.

The implicit restraining influence the British exercised was probably
strongest in the Commonwealth framework; in some ways this was not
to change. But the Commonwealth itself had changed in the three years
since Nkrumah's first meeting. The tranquillity of former meetings was
impossible once the Tungku arrived for the 1960 conference, bound by
his parliament to challenge apartheid. Although Nkrumah, in his first
statements, remained reluctant to commit himself to any course of action, the Ghanaian press could not believe that their prime minister did
not have some strategy in mind.[185] Yet after three years, Nkrumah was
still committed to the belief that the "multi-racial example of Ghana"
could affect developments in South Africa, and in fact Adjei had invited
Foreign Minister Eric Louw to Ghana, when they met at the 1959 UN
General Assembly.

In contrast, on May 2nd, Sir Abubakar, in London for constitutional
discussions, asked publicly why South Africa should not be "kicked out"
of the Commonwealth.[186] Then, Louw gave an "astonishing" press conference (as the *Financial Times* termed it) before 130 correspondents in
which, *inter alia*, he used his invitation to visit Ghana as proof that
apartheid did not cause international tension, and noted he still intended
to visit there. Louw had attempted to "forestall the possible results of the
Prime Minister's 'informal talks' " on the South African question, and
thus it was that the Tungku stormed out of the conference room.[187] Nkrumah had still not acted. The *Ghana Times* editorialized: "BUT LET
THEM WAIT UNTIL KWAME NKRUMAH OF AFRICA HAS EXPLODED. . . .
HE IS LISTENING . . . AND WATCHING. WHEN HE SPEAKS IT WILL BE
FINAL. THE COURSE OF GHANA'S ASSOCIATION WITH THE COMMON-
WEALTH WILL BE FIRMLY MAPPED OUT."[188]

It was, however, through Louw that one learned that Ghana's invitation had been withdrawn. Nkrumah had first withdrawn it, said Louw;
then later and privately, he had said that the visit was still possible if a
Ghanaian cabinet minister could repay the visit. But "I have never heard
of an invitation with a condition attached to it . . ." Louw said.[189] Yet
the Ghanaian statement in 1959 had made absolutely explicit that the
need for reciprocity was inherent in the invitation.[190] Now the visit was

[185] *Ghana Times*, 2 May 1960. [186] *New York Times*, 3 May 1960.
[187] *Financial Times*, 5 May 1960. [188] *Ghana Times*, 9 May 1960.
[189] *Johannesburg Star*, 7 May 1960. [190] See P.R. #824/59, 17 October 1959.

canceled, which was what the *Ghana Times* called "Positive Action against apartheid."[191]

Nkrumah later justified his moderation by arguing that he had refrained from making any public declaration of policy while the conference remained in session;[192] it is true that when he spoke in Dublin the following week he put a caveat on continued Ghanaian membership in the Commonwealth. This was that if the mission of the UN secretary-general to South Africa should fail, "then the Government of Ghana . . . would find it embarrassing to remain in the Commonwealth with a Republic whose policy was not based upon the purpose and principles of the United Nations."[193]

Nkrumah, to be sure, made every attempt to appear to be in the forefront of opposition to the South African regime; he had South African refugees then in Accra flown to London for discussions with him, and sent for Quaison-Sackey to come for urgent consultations. But this was different from actually voicing his opposition in such a way as to precipitate a crisis over South Africa's application for continued membership, as a republic, in the Commonwealth. It was what the *Financial Times* called Louw's "sheer pigheadedness" that forced the issue and hardened attitudes.[194]

Nkrumah, clearly, had finally despaired of a moderate solution for South Africa, and on his return to Accra he said that Ghana could not "sit down and wait indefinitely" for a change of heart—and furthermore suggested the possibility of a policy of economic sanctions.[195] As the *Johannesburg Star* wrote, "In six months the winds of change have blown Dr. Kwame Nkrumah's views on boycotts from starboard to port." In January, under the "benign influence of Mr. Macmillan's presence," Nkrumah had said a boycott would do no good.[196]

He also began increasing the pressure on the South African exiles to form a united front. Accra had always been a logical place for them to gather, and Ghana had been helpful in a variety of ways. (Mrs. Geoffrey Bing had traveled to Rhodesia to assist them in obtaining transport; A. K. Barden actually got within South Africa—it was rumored—with £12,000 in his pocket to finance the flight of various African leaders.) Now Geoffrey Bing even attempted to fit together a government-in-exile, headed by Oliver Tambo, the ANC leader.[197]

[191] *Ghana Times*, 9 May 1960.
[192] Nkrumah, *I Speak of Freedom*, p. 223.
[193] *Ibid.*, p. 229.   [194] 11 May 1960.
[195] *Ghana Times*, 3 June 1960.   [196] *Star*, 3 June 1960.
[197] The effort failed, according to the PAC leader Nana Mahomo, because of the PAC's unwillingness to cooperate unless their president, Sobukwe, were named head of the provisional government. Interview: London, November 1965.

Even though Nkrumah was the chief supporter of the refugees from South Africa by mid-1960, they were already looking elsewhere for leadership. In the end, no groups were to be more disillusioned with him. For one thing, they doubted his commitment to their cause owing to his caution in the Commonwealth. For another, these well-educated men were not prepared to pay the price of deference to and praise of Nkrumah which was required to maintain his financial backing. "Once Padmore was dead, there was nobody in Ghana on our wavelength," Nana Mahomo said.[198] On the other hand, the *Financial Times* could write that Nkrumah "comes out well from the [Commonwealth] conference." He is acquiring "the mellowness and confidence of an elder statesman" of the organization.[199] Nkrumah at no point had directly criticized this club, membership in which he obviously enjoyed but which was very costly to his policy, bringing suspicion from Africans and few gains from the old Commonwealth states.

France and the Sahara Tests. If Nkrumah's dealings with the Commonwealth were demonstrating what gains moderation could bring, his dealings with France were showing what could be gained through direct opposition to a major power. France, because of its African colonial policy, was an appropriate adversary, but a frustrating one, as Ghana had no means of directly affecting developments in French African territories. Then France, in the year after America and Russia had ceased to test atomic weaponry, announced its decision to test atomic weapons in the Sahara, a decision which "outraged the whole of Africa."[200] Nkrumah was personally horrified, and in deciding to oppose the French, "was doing no more than expressing the indignation which all of us felt against using an area quite close to our land for testing these hideous weapons," as a governmental official wrote.[201] But such opposition could also rally opinion in French Africa, build Ghana's influence in the cross-currents of liberal world opinion, and dramatize Ghana's leadership in Africa.

On 3 July 1959 Ako Adjei handed a protest note to the French *chargé*: "Motivated as we are, by the spirit of humanity . . . we feel it our duty to speak not only for the people of Ghana, but also for all the African peoples."[202] The French rejected the appeal, and noted that "it was not understood why Ghana took upon itself the right to speak in the name

198 Interview: Nana Mahomo, London, December 1966.
199 *Financial Times*, 11 May 1960.
200 Letter to the author, CFL-A, 5 July 1967, p. 4.
201 *Ibid.*   202 P.R. #549/59, 3 July 1959.

of the other African states."[203] But they took it seriously enough to see that their African prime ministers defended their position.[204]

Ghana then took the issue to the UN and, with nineteen other powers, sponsored a resolution condemning France's plans.[205] The *Times* could observe, as a result of Ghana's persistence, that the "projected detonation . . . had brought to Africa the politics of Aldermaston."[206] But three months later, France tested. In its ostensible object, Ghana's policy had failed; the international team assembled in Ghana to march on the French testing ground were even turned back just beyond the Ghanaian border.

Nkrumah then announced that Ghana had frozen all French assets in Ghana, and within a week Gbedemah announced measures to implement the freeze.[207] When a second bomb was exploded two months later, the government placed further restrictions on transactions with the French monetary area, and recalled the Ghanaian ambassador from Paris. Exactly two weeks later French assets were "unfrozen."[208] But they had never truly been affected; French businessmen had found ways to circumvent the measures. Ghana had failed a very important test: It could not, or had not the will to, restrict business interests. The justification was that with the chance of a test ban treaty being signed in Geneva, the international situation had changed.[209] The real reason was something else, the "desire to avoid discouraging investment."[210] Indeed, when France again tested at the end of 1960, Ghana did nothing, while Nigeria, assuming Nkrumah would break relations with France, expelled the French ambassador.

In the meantime, Nkrumah had called the "Positive Action Conference" to focus attention on the testing. It had the effect of saving face for Ghana, but it probably narrowed France's room for maneuver only marginally. Nkrumah wrote that France had undoubtedly chosen the Sahara "to demonstrate to African states their political weakness,"[211] which it had demonstrated. The Ghanaians were learning that they had only a little to gain by "good behavior" at the tables of the larger powers, and that there was not much they could do to deter a great power from its set course of action.

[203] *Ghana Times*, 7 July 1959.
[204] See *Ghana Times*, 7 July, 8 August, and 10 September 1959.
[205] See Resolution 1379, UNGA, 840th Plenary meeting, 20 November 1959.
[206] 18 July 1959.
[207] P.R. #174/60, 13 February 1960.
[208] P.R. #295/60, 5 April 1960, #311/60, 7 April 1960.
[209] P.R. #344/60.
[210] According to *Economist Intelligence Unit*, No. 30, 21 June 1960, West Africa Series.
[211] *I Speak of Freedom*, p. 275.

The East. Within five months of its independence, Guinea had concluded a trade agreement with the Soviet Union; Ghana had none until late 1961. In October 1959, Sékou Touré visited Moscow, while the Duke of Edinburgh, in lieu of Ghana's head of state, visited Accra; Nkrumah could not have visited Russia in 1959 without seriously weakening his domestic position. Guinea became the anchor of the Communist states' relations in black Africa during 1959 and 1960, but no Ghanaian *agrément* was permitted for a Soviet ambassador until 10 April 1959. It was not until early in 1960 that Ghana sent an advance party to Moscow to open an embassy. There were no relations with China until July 1960.

Many factors produced this caution. Guinea, friendless at independence, anticipated no Western assistance, while Ghana had based its development plans around expectations of Western aid and investment. Many of the Guinean leaders had had experience in the East, and there were no interest groups in that country to militate against increased contacts with Communist states. But until late 1959, potential pressure groups in Ghana that wished to develop ties with the East were inchoate, with one exception. This was the group of foreign service officers, who wished to balance links with the West with new ones in the East, out of a genuine commitment to nonalignment, and, perhaps, out of fear that too lengthy a delay in establishing these ties would cause a reaction at some point—as indeed happened.

The senior civil servants knew the Communists were going to come, but fought to delay the opening of embassies in Accra, so as to gain time to prepare. "I did not think we had sufficient security apparatus to contend with the cold-war element that would be let in when we had both American and Russian embassies," one said.[212] Although the British were cautious in giving such advice, they convinced the Ghanaians that when the Russians came, they should be limited in number and movement—as they were.[213]

The old pan-Africanists' attitude has already been noted; Nkrumah's is more complex. Botsio thought that Nkrumah simply wished "to let sleeping dogs lie," so as to avoid opening himself to the charge in the West that he was "letting in the Communists."[214] He made many Westerners feel that he was even frightened of Russian designs, at one point going to the governor-general with a book on the KGB that he said disturbed him.[215] A foreign service officer sent to India for a course on intelligence said that Nkrumah instructed him to learn as much as pos-

---

[212] Interview: CF-28.
[213] Interviews: Botsio, Adjei. The restrictions, ironically, were never removed.
[214] Interview: **Botsio.**   [215] Interview: CF-70.

sible about Communism, which is what he would be dealing with, and of which he (Nkrumah) did not want anything.[216]

What is important to note is that prior to 1960 Ghana had nothing to gain by moving too far away from her Western friends. Guinea in the meantime could be the object of Western fears, while Ghana raised Western funds for Volta; whatever Nkrumah's long-range objectives, his actions suggest that this was his conscious or unconscious motivation.

To the extent that he concerned himself with the Afro-Asian Solidarity Organization, for example, it was to turn its concerns toward Africa. The Ghana delegation to the Tunis AAPC even sought to limit AAPSO's participation in the AAPC because of AAPSO's external concerns and its competition with it.[217] The AAPC was always outflanked on the left by the Cairo-based organization. Thus, even if he had the ultimate intention to make Ghana a Marxist-socialist state, there was no ambivalence about Nkrumah's immediate concerns: they were to put Africa on the map, to make it figure in Western and Eastern calculations; to focus maximum attention on African problems, which should be solved by Africans; that Africans, and African organizations should concern themselves with the liberation of Africa. (This was, of course, a negative concern. In practice he did not want other organizations concerning themselves with liberation.) The Solidarity Organization did not qualify, and as a result Ghana was outside the conflicts within it, in which Conakry, Peking, Moscow, and Cairo all had their parts.

The Egyptians had tried to draw Ghana into their organization. A Ghanaian political officer in Cairo reported late in 1959 that Nasser wished Ghana to fill its seat in AAPSO "to reduce the Russian preponderance,"[218] but Nkrumah refused to do even this. Meanwhile the radical African nationalist parties—like the UPC and MPLA—made their headquarters in Conakry, not Accra. It began to appear that on the African stage Accra was becoming to Cairo and Conakry what Delhi had become to Peking in Asia.

The Russians, for their part, could not have taken lightly the strong British influence in Ghana, and must not have known in which direction Ghana would go. But Ghana was important as a gathering place of British African nationalists, and was economically strong, so the Eastern states sought good relations with it. By late 1958 Eastern European

---

[216] Interview: CF-94A.

[217] *Ashanti Pioneer*, 28 January 1960.

[218] Debrah to MEA, 10 December 1959, CFA-60. At the subsequent AAPSO conference, Ghana's status was as a result downgraded. At the first conference, Ghana was given a seat on the permanent secretariat; in 1960, only on the less exclusive executive committee. "IIième Congres de Solidarité des peuples afro-asiatique," Cairo, 1960.

101

trade delegations began arriving,[219] and by late 1959 these countries were finding a greater receptivity than they had perhaps anticipated. Mikhail Sytenko, the Russian ambassador, arrived in August and began receiving much attention in the press.[220] He consolidated his position quickly, had easy and frequent access to Nkrumah, and from the start pressed him to move away from the West. Relations at legation level were agreed upon with Czechoslovakia in October, at ambassadorial level with Poland in December. Protocol officers, however, sought to enforce the limits placed on the Soviet embassy. A new group of Russians arrived in January 1960, which brought the number of personnel beyond their legal limit. Dei-Anang, who, when Adu was appointed cabinet secretary, became principal secretary at the ministry, recorded, "We must invite the attention of the USSR embassy to this discrepancy," which was done.[221] But the Soviets did not reduce the size of their staff, which suggests that Flagstaff House intervened on their behalf.

Ghana was reaching into the Communist world. Trade delegations were visiting all East Europe, and by July 1959 one had gone to Peking. In early 1960, F. E. Boaten, one of the first eight foreign service officers, opened an embassy in Moscow. In May, while Nkrumah was in London, Kojo Botsio led a parliamentary delegation to Moscow, a visit that was first mooted in 1957. It is clear that this marked a first turning point in Ghana's relations with the socialist countries. It was high-ranking and, according to Botsio, very well received by the Russians.[222] Botsio extended an invitation to Khrushchev to visit Ghana. It was accepted. More important, because more likely, on 20 June 1960 it was announced that Khrushchev had invited Nkrumah to visit Russia and that Nkrumah had accepted.[223]

It is evident that in this period the Russians shifted the emphasis of their interest in Africa from an "Afro-Asian bias toward pan-Africanism south of the Sahara."[224] Ghana was broadening its contacts, to make its nonalignment more assertive than it had been in the years immediately following independence, and its internal ideology was shifting in emphasis, making the shift the more important. Nkrumah, moreover, was be-

---

[219] But it seems—to judge by the communiqués—that Ghanaian civil servants were not rushing to sign agreements. See for example P.R. #1067/58, 26 November 1958, "Czechoslovak Trade Mission."

[220] His credentials were accepted by the governor-general on 13 August 1959, "on behalf of Her Majesty Queen Elizabeth II," CFA-10.

[221] Dei-Anang to E.W.A.B. Sam, director of protocol, 13 January 1960; E.W.A.B. Sam to I. S. Baikov, Counselor, U.S.S.R./Accra, 23 February 1960, CFA-14.

[222] Interview: Botsio.

[223] P.R. #489/60.

[224] See Mary Holdsworth, "Soviet African Studies 1918-1959," *Chatham House Memorandum*, p. 40.

coming worried that the Volta negotiations with America might fail, and wanted an alternative source of capital available. Russia, having decided that sub-Saharan Africa was important, was making more flexible the ideological criteria by which it chose its friends. Ghanaian and Russian interests were able to begin to converge, as the once revolutionary great power became more conservative and the little state of "bourgeois nationalists" became more radical.

But the irony in Ghana's position might be underlined by noting that its first diplomatic officer in Moscow went, as a matter of course and of necessity, to the British for advice and assistance in establishing the Ghanaian mission.[225] The speed at which Ghana was to change is indicated by the fact that the same officer, a few months later, was sent home, and almost lost his job, because of his alleged "neocolonialist mentality."

GHANAIAN STATECRAFT, 1957–1960

Ghana had made a name for itself internationally in these three years. To a large degree, its policies, in the words of one of their formulators, "were based on pragmatism and a desire to feel one's way in the maze of international jungle insofar as the interests of Africa were concerned."[226] Yet it is by no means clear that it had established the institutions with which to defend those interests or, indeed, to sustain a dynamic role internationally. Nor had it learned from the setbacks it had suffered. There were, too, disquieting developments on the domestic front which were bad portents for the foreign policy.

Diplomats, and Paradiplomatic Agencies. It had been a not unreasonable expectation of the career foreign service officers that, while the first ambassadors would of necessity be political appointees, the way would soon be opened for the senior officials to take up ambassadorships as more missions were opened. Yet the first real challenge to the professionalism of the service came in mid-1959 when Nkrumah made one of them an ambassador—Alex Quaison-Sackey, second most junior of the original eight. He had been a conspicuous member of the CPP, and justly called his appointment a political one. It was well known that Quaison-Sackey had been "very co-operative"[227] with the party in London, looking out for its interests while other civil servants were resisting such pressures. One officer offered his resignation from the service in protest

---

[225] Interview: Botsio, CF-33. [226] Letter, CFL-A, 5 July 1967, p. 4.

[227] Comment of Tawia Adamafio, who was comparing him to the "so-called civil servants" who refused to cooperate with the party at the high commission in London. *Ministry of Foreign Affairs*, "Conference of Ghana Envoys, January 1962," January 1962, p. 97. Also see Interview: CF-76.

(although Adu did not accept it), and the others felt equally strongly.[228] Fred Arkhurst was counselor at the UN (where he had done brilliant work), whereas Quaison-Sackey was only first secretary in London when the appointment was announced.

Quaison-Sackey's ensuing work at the UN was to justify his appointment—but the calibre of the purely political appointees was such as to justify concern. Few services are without their political appointees, but a young country does well to err on the side of caution in these affairs and trust its trained men; the senior officers, after all, averaged almost forty years of age in 1960. It was difficult to argue that a single political appointment—other than Quaison-Sackey's—had been prompted by a concern for external effectiveness, although several turned out to be suited to their jobs.[229] Some were made to get individuals out of the way, others were rewards for outstanding work for the party or large contributions thereto.[230] Of the 17 ambassadors, 5 had college degrees— while of the 67 career officers (as at 1 July 1960), 59 had B.A.'s, and of these, 17 had advanced degrees. It was not a situation in which confidence in one's superiors was likely.

There were other reasons to be skeptical of the ambassadors' quality. The Public Accounts Committee of the National Assembly wrote a scathing report on the operation of the overseas missions in mid-1960. Regulations were inadequate for the occasion, but such as they were they were commonly evaded; control from Accra was almost totally ineffectual. One ambassador, T. O. Asare in Bonn, had in five months drawn advances in salary and expenses at a rate four and one-half times his salary. He had at his disposal a Rolls-Royce and two Mercedes.[231]

Once the embassy's funds were in the hands of the head of a mission instead of the head of the chancery, little chance remained of running orderly missions. Nor was there any attempt to bring these practices to

228 Interviews: CF-33, 20.

229 E.g. Sir Edward Asafu-Adjaye, who projected successfully the image Nkrumah wished for Ghana in London at that time.

230 Bediako Poku, general-secretary of the CPP, was appointed to Tel-Aviv to make way for Tawia Adamafio in the party; Halm, in Washington, and Baidoe-Ansah were businessmen who had been active in the party and were large contributors.

231 *National Assembly*, "Report, Committee of Public Accounts, 1960," p. 10. See also *Ghana*, "Report of the Auditor-General . . . for the Financial Year Ended 30 June 1959," p. 15. Three years later the deputy foreign minister was still trying to collect outstanding sums from Asare. Even after demands from the cabinet secretary, and the head of the African Affairs Secretariat, Asare would write letters such as the following: "I have repeatedly informed you that in my capacity as Ambassador of Osagyefo the President I am not bound by any illegal, prejucicial and unproving [sic] ruling of the Deputy Minister of Foreign Affairs which basically undermines the dignity, respect and the security of the State."—Asare to Dei-Anang, 29 June 1963, in *Ghana*, Second Report from the Public Accounts Committee of the National Assembly, 1963, p. 16.

an end; Asare remained in Bonn another two years after the report was first publicized. It seems plausible to assume some appointments were made, indeed, to ensure tight control on "cuts" in contracts with firms of the country to which some men were accredited.

More serious, it was becoming obvious not only that political affiliation was a factor in promotion in the career service, but that ideology, such as it was, counted as well. Yet here was a dilemma. There were few enough Marxists in Ghana, and these could ill be spared for foreign missions; Nkrumah made his worst ambassadorial appointment in this period (J. B. Elliot to Moscow) less because Elliot was "ideologically sound"[232] than because he could be counted on not to oppose any of Nkrumah's plans.

Nkrumah knew—or so thought some of his confidants—that outstanding Ghanaian intellectuals and citizens would try to frustrate his particular plans of action, and therefore he had to send, on the whole, second-rate men. It is difficult to see how an educated and talented career officer like F. E. Boaten was to work under a barely educated party hack like Elliot; Elliot's recourse was to tell Nkrumah he was surrounded by "neocolonialist stooges" in Moscow.[233]

By late 1959, some officers already had difficulty in writing honest reports to Accra.[234] Ghana's diplomats were not geared to their foreign policy: either they were competent men enthusiastic about the opportunity to create the "African personality" in world affairs, but less eager to be Nkrumah's personal men, or they were incompetent political appointees not entirely aware of the way in which they were being used.

There was a further lack of calibration between foreign policy and the service: the network of embassies had grown too fast, before time had been allowed to develop sound precedents and good traditions. But other states were eager to establish relations with Ghana; Nkrumah was trying to unify Africa and extend his and Ghana's international influence, and embassies were necessary. As the *Estimates* suggested, "Since the 6th March 1957, the volume of external relations have increased beyond all expectations." In the original *Estimates*, provision had been made for London, Washington, Paris, Delhi, Monrovia; before the end of that financial year additional appropriations were needed for missions in Cairo, Tel-Aviv, Lagos, New York. Plans went ahead for more—Belgrade, Ottawa, Rome, until finally there were no more men. Indeed, by mid-1960 there were 35 vacancies in the service; in

[232] The phrase adopted in Flagstaff House to describe faithful "Nkrumaists."
[233] Interviews: CF-33, 109, 47A.　　　[234] Interview: CF-17.

105

the meantime, half the embassies had only one career diplomat posted to each, sometimes sufficient, but more often not.[235]

The Ministry in Accra also had its problems. At independence, the view prevailed that virtually all the career officers should be dispatched abroad to open embassies, rather than that a solid nucleus should be kept in Accra until the ministry was properly organized. It was understaffed, with the added disadvantage that it was organized like a home ministry, with only one channel of authority and no area desks.[236] Officers abroad felt they had inadequate guidance from Accra. Discussions of its reorganization began in early 1960, but within months of the reorganization, in late 1960, Nkrumah was virtually to dismember it.

Adu, the principal secretary until mid-1959, was one of the most distinguished and competent men anywhere in Africa; the threat to the ministry came after his time. His successor, Michael Dei-Anang, once a widely respected master at Mfansipim School, had risen to the top of the civil service in the governor-general's office. He knew little of foreign affairs, but he was fascinated by power and this eventually corrupted him. From the first he hesitated to disagree with Nkrumah, and he was appointed only a short time prior to the death of Padmore, the one radical with sufficient stature to stand up to Nkrumah. Furthermore, the ministry had never had a minister capable of making cohesive the implementation of foreign policy. Nkrumah held the portfolio until November 1958, and had too many other concerns to give close attention to the complex requirements of such a ministry. Botsio was there too short a time—five months—and, in any case, was more interested in economic affairs. Finally, on 7 April 1959, Ako Adjei got the job; he had led the UN delegations in 1957 and 1958, had attended many international conferences, and had handled some of the work of the ministry since independence. He was also appointed "because it was felt that he would be able to fall in line more easily with Nkrumah's handling of foreign relations."[237] But Adjei was a stubborn man, who eventually differed with Nkrumah on many aspects of foreign policy; Nkrumah, as a result, tended to work round him and, in consequence, the ministry.

No factor affected the formulation of policy more during this period than the death of George Padmore, and the subsequent rise in importance of his one-time assistant, A. K. Barden. To some, Padmore had been a man of few ideas, mostly bad, who had misadvised Nkrumah while pushing him to maximize his power. It is more pertinent to note

<hr />

[235] *Ghana*, Estimates, 1957, 1958, 1959, 1960. Also *Ghana*, Civil Service List, 1960.
[236] F. E. Boaten, "Brief Notes on Administrative Organization of the Ministry of Foreign Affairs," in "Conference of Ghana Envoys," pp. 175-76.
[237] Letter, CFL-A, 5 July 1967, p. 5.

that Padmore was the one person who commanded Nkrumah's respect (though some thought Nkrumah had become increasingly jealous of him by 1959)[238] and could generally prevent serious miscalculations. When he died, in September 1959, there was no one Nkrumah considered as eminent as himself on African affairs; a major restraint was removed. Nkrumah then announced that "in order to put the work begun by the late Mr. George Padmore on a permanent basis, the Office of Advisor to the Prime Minister on African Affairs will be converted into the Bureau of African Affairs." (BAA).[239] Nkrumah became acting director, and Barden, secretary. The latter was an ex-serviceman and ex-short-hand instructor, without ideological conviction, but with a love of money and power that was to find greater outlet as the years went by. His military experience led him to think he was an expert in "operations," and it was this aspect of the Bureau's work that he began to stress.[240] The Bureau, by late 1959, had virtually absorbed what was left of the AAPC.[241] In May 1960 the Bureau was established by statutory instrument, with Welbeck as chairman, and with John Tettegah, T. R. Makonnen, Mbiyu Koinange, Tawia Adamafio, and Andrew Djin as the members of the board.[242] This gave it complete independence from the ministry, further weakened coordination between the two, and increased the power of Barden who became director. Barden had only to report to the prime minister, and he was not slow to learn Nkrumah's weaknesses. Later events were to call into question his professed radicalism and devotion to Nkrumah.

Balance Sheet on the Eve of the Republic. After the outbreak of the Congo crisis, one scholar stated that a study of Nkrumah's role in African affairs since 1958 suggested that he had been consciously or unconsciously preparing Ghana for just such a crisis.[243] Certainly Nkrumah had given Ghana a special position in Africa and much note in the world; Paul-Marc Henry wrote that Nkrumah himself was "fast becoming the elder statesman of Black Africa."[244] He had increased the power of the state to the limit of its financial capacity in adding to the size of the army and the diplomatic corps. But for a small state, preparation for a crisis requires first of all some success in winning friends with whom

[238] Interviews: Botsio, Markham.   [239] P.R. #757/59.
[240] Interviews: Djin, Makonnen, Markham, D. B. Sam.
[241] The Bureau began publishing the AAPC *Bulletin*, and several individuals (e.g. Addison) had positions in both organizations.
[242] P.R. #386/60, 4 May 1960.
[243] L. W. Cone, "Ghana's African and World Relations," *India Quarterly*, 17, No. 3 (July-September 1961).
[244] "Pan-Africanism: A Dream Come True," *Foreign Affairs*, 37, No. 3 (April 1959).

107

one can coordinate policy. The state can, with skill, become the recognized leader in the councils developed with its friends.

In these regards Ghana had failed. Its key alliance at this point was at its low point. Touré had to be persuaded to attend the republican celebrations, and then "sulked" throughout.[245] Indeed, he was actively working against Ghana's interests. After Nkrumah's and Olympio's meeting two weeks prior to the celebrations, Touré sent an emissary to Olympio to warn him of the consequences of working with Nkrumah.[246]

Ironically, if a dominant factor from the African scene were to be singled out to account for the changing international role of Nkrumah and Ghana, it would have to be Guinea's indirect influence on Ghana. Sékou Touré had become the spokesman for a style of thought of which Nkrumah thought he himself should have the monopoly. Ako Adjei put it this way: "Touré was more nationalist, more left-wing, more pan-Africanist than Nkrumah ever was in those days. He wanted Nkrumah to break from the Commonwealth, to nationalize the firms, to make Ghana a socialist state. These were not possible courses of action, so Nkrumah instead started talking love to the socialist countries as a substitute, and this gained momentum, all out of proportion to the actual amount of socialism practised in Ghana."[247] Touré had a type of moral ascendancy over Nkrumah: his colonialist experience had been harsher and he was now the "most left" at a time when this carried status in the minds of many African leaders. In all, Ghana had got little from the £4,000,000 it had at this point given Guinea.

Furthermore, even if new hope existed for a *modus vivendi* with Togo, there was an absence of a working relationship that in itself was a source of weakness for Ghana. A political or economic union clearly in sight would have vastly increased Ghana's stature in Africa, creating momentum as well. So Ghana had generated no real movement towards unity anywhere—and "he who wins nothing, loses."

The sudden request for independence of the Entente countries attested, perhaps, to the indirect influence of the Ghana model, but in terms of actual influence thus accrued, it was a different story. Their request had caught Ghana almost by surprise, and suddenly there were to be more new states than Nkrumah had counted on, with few levers of influence for Ghana within.[248]

[245] Interviews: Gbedemah, Quarshie.   [246] Interview: CF-24.
[247] Interview: Ako Adjei.
[248] Nkrumah's independence message to each of the *Conseil* states was inappropriate, perhaps out of frustration: "It behoves us . . . to be watchful that the independence which each of us, whether singly or jointly as the countries of the Council of Understanding, seeks and accepts, is in truth a full and unfettered independence." *Ghana*

The All-African Peoples Conference in December 1958 was Nkrumah's finest hour, but the conviction grew on him that the euphoria there was itself sufficient as a basis for the continental union that he and many delegates had envisaged. He thenceforth utterly disregarded the regional pan-African prescription given by the conference, and he became less and less flexible on the question of continental union. Yet he could not work within that organization, and like all the other organizations he was instrumental in creating, he discarded it. There had been warning signals that Ghana could not play so cavalier a role. At the IAS foreign ministers' conference in Monrovia, in August 1959, the *Guardian* commented that Ghana's "grip" on the conference was "inconspicuous." Nigeria's absence, said another, made it seem like "Hamlet without the Prince."[249]

The absence of any continent-wide and effective secretariat that might have coordinated policy in the Congo crisis was also a grave weakness, for which Nkrumah could rightly be given part blame. That was not all; there had been numerous "wonderful resolutions" on cooperation of various sorts passed at the first IAS conference in Accra, then again at the second conference at Addis Ababa; in early 1962 Quaison-Sackey was to ask why these had "not been implemented."[250] Michael Dei-Anang gave one answer in the same discussion: "The reason . . . is that there is no effective machinery to do that."[251]

There was, finally, a fair measure of opportunism in Ghana's Africa policy, something which is seldom singled out when the end desired is attained. This is easily shown by Ghana's shift in its policy toward Algeria. At the 1958 IAS conference, the Ghanaians did not wish the Algerians even to be able to state their case, and as late as July 1959, radical foreign service officers had to work surreptitiously, apparently, to extend de facto recognition to the Algerian provisional government.[252] But by 1960, Algeria was a bigger issue, with African radicals often measuring a state's radicalism in terms of its support for Algeria. Aside from joint efforts within the United Nations and the granting of £5,000, Ghana had done nothing to aid Algeria. By mid-1960, however, it was trying to compensate for past caution. When the Tunisian foreign min-

---

Times, 23 June 1960. These states, as one of their diplomats once said, did not start with £200 million in their reserves.

[249] *Manchester Guardian,* 8 August 1959; *New York Herald Tribune,* European edition, 8-9 August 1959.

[250] In M. F. Dei-Anang, "Our Policy Towards African States," "Conference of Ghana Envoys, January 1962," p. 55.

[251] *Ibid.,* p. 56.

[252] Interview: CF-14. By this account, the young officers extended the recognition during an absence of Dei-Anang, the principal secretary.

istry called in the Ghanaian ambassador to suggest that Nkrumah, "in view of Ghana's influence in world affairs," do as Bourguiba had done and congratulate General de Gaulle on his olive branch extended to the FLN, so as to strengthen his hand, the Ghanaians refused. Dei-Anang recorded, "Until French Colonial policy in Africa has undergone a radical change it would constitute the sacrifice of an important issue of principle to congratulate General de Gaulle on anything."[253] Yet it was by such gestures that Ghana had always sought to help those in the metropolitan countries who wished a more enlightened policy toward Africa. The Algerians were not blind to the deficiencies of Ghana's support, or of Nkrumah's regime, as their first emissary to Accra, Franz Fanon, clearly showed.[254] Professor Mazrui's argument, that Nkrumah was "unequivocal in his support" of the FLN, and that this demonstrated his role in unifying Arab and Negro Africa, is historically inaccurate, and ironic.[255]

Ghana's external relations were beginning to diverge from what had originally been envisaged, and at the end of this period they were in flux. Nkrumah's close relations with Western leaders such as Macmillan were not sufficient to compensate for the extremely weak Western diplomatic presence in Accra. Nor was the Commonwealth—an organization which Nkrumah believed extremely useful—strong enough any longer to give him as big a platform as he desired. Friendships with Asian states such as India had been expected, and would have been natural, but these had not materialized, and there were no other states—other than the Communist—which at this point could fill the gap.

Ghana's nonaligned stance during this first period undoubtedly favored the West more than the East; Communist countries had been denied a base of operations in Ghana of the kind that they had found in Guinea. Ghana, a former colony, had rarely reacted to Western influence within the country. Finally, a self-styled Marxist prime minister was seen to be a model Commonwealth-statesman, whose views on international issues endangered no vital Western interest. If the party press was largely run and written by Marxists by mid-1960, it could also be argued that it was taken seriously by few. Writers like Idris Cox, a British Communist, were contributors, but at this point they fitted more into the "anticolonial" than the "pro-East" mold[256] for the most part—or so it seemed to many Western diplomats at the time.

[253] CFA-1.
[254] He was greatly distressed by what he found in Accra, during his residence there in 1960, and most of his criticisms about the new states in *Les Damnés de la Terre* derive from that period.
[255] See Mazrui, *Towards a Pax Africana*, p. 63.
[256] See *Evening News*, 17 April 1959.

If, at the end of this period, there were great ambiguity in Nkrumah's publicly expressed sentiments on international issues, the fact remained that Ghana's contact remained largely within the Western sphere. At the Positive Action Conference in April 1960, to which delegates came from various left-wing American and British organizations, there were no delegates at all from Eastern countries—other than Yugoslavia.

Nonalignment can be a dynamic concept. In 1957, it was acceptable as a stance, but hardly welcomed by either side; in 1960, after the break-up of the summit, nonaligned states could play a balancing act that gave them a voice in world affairs such as they were seldom to have again in the ensuing half-decade. Nkrumah sensed this as the period came to a close, and he began to call for the "uncommitted nonnuclear countries of the world, particularly of Asia and Africa, [to] summon themselves into a conference with a view to forming a nonnuclear third force."[257]

It had been simple to be just radical enough to be considered non-aligned (but not so much as to jeopardize the investment climate) when in sub-Saharan Africa only Tubman and the Emperor shared the lime-light. Now there were new voices.

The uncertain domestic scene had its effect on foreign policy, as well. On virtually every issue the government and the opposition were in dis-agreement; this point is well illustrated in a parliamentary debate on foreign policy: the government at one time saw Ghana as the inspiration of mass revolt in the Rhodesian Federation.[258] The opposition, on the other hand, saw Ghana's influence as acting on the white minority in Rhodesia, who adopted a preventive detention act similar to Ghana's.

There were changes of vast importance in Ghana; the founding of the republic is a turning point in this study, not alone because of its co-incidence with the outbreak of the Congo crisis. The domestic scene was sufficiently altered at this point to have wide effect on the foreign policy, with which, in this special case, it was inextricably linked. This is because of the change in the status and power of "The Osagyefo," as he was now known.[259] After the plebiscite for the presidency and the new constitution, a final part was—incredibly—added, giving the "First President" the power of legislative instrument, apparently the only con-stitution ever to do such.[260] What it meant was that Nkrumah now had the constitutional power to be what he had drifted toward during the

257 *Debates*, 4 July 1960, pp. 7-11.
258 *Debates*, 16 December 1959, p. 632.
259 Meaning "warrior," "victorious one," and came to mean "saviour, redeemer" in the world press—and often in Accra. From this time on his diplomats addressed him, in correspondence, in the imperial third person.
260 See W. B. Harvey, *Law and Social Change in Ghana*, Princeton, 1966.

past three years; it meant internal politics *could* "seem to fade into insignificance" as Nkrumah "concentrated more than ever on the freedom of all Africa and its Unity."[261] It had been the radicals in the constitutional commission who were responsible; they argued that the judiciary and the civil service could not be trusted to move with the revolution: Adu, Gbedemah, and Botsio had urged restraint.[262]

The other major change in the internal situation was the growth in strength of the CPP radicals themselves. There had always been loose, radical talk in the party, but only gradually were there issues arising where radical talk could conveniently be wedded to action. At first it came over questions like the establishment of an embassy in Moscow.[263] Gradually the true Marxists, such as Kojo Addison and Kofi Batsaa, were finding positions of influence, to reinforce the loose talk. But the growth of one person's power—Tawia Adamafio—was to link the Marxists and party opportunists together securely, until party stalwarts, like Botsio and Gbedemah, had been eliminated. Adamafio's rise to power was astonishing; a former opposition member, he had joined the CPP in London and had a reputation for blatant opportunism. On the other hand, he worked hard and liberally praised Nkrumah ("We all are at best a small star shining only through the grace of Kwame Nkrumah, our Political Central Sun and Author of the Ghanaian Revolution. . . . We must learn from Kwame Nkrumah's supreme modesty, humility, and simplicity of life."),[264] and power accrued to him rapidly, as it did to anyone in Ghana with those two characteristics. Moreover, he correctly sensed the direction in which Ghana—or Nkrumah—was tending, and made this movement, "to the East,"[265] his own.

With the growth in Nkrumah's power and the rise of the new CPP leaders came a new stage in the cult of personality[266] and in development of what was called an "ideology," around the leader. The *Evening*

[261] *West Africa*, 9 July 1960.

[262] Interviews: CF-28, 34, 57.

[263] In parliament a CPP member suggested Ghana should have embassies everywhere. Joe Appiah asked "Even on the Moon?" "We must go to Russia," was the emphatic reply. *Debates*, 28 July 1959, p. 1077. Those who wished to extend Ghana's diplomatic network as swiftly as possible were generally those beginning to press for a turn to the East.

[264] *Evening News*, 28 May 1960.

[265] The phrase itself was pregnant, symbolizing a fascinating unknown or dread danger, depending on the point of view.

[266] Consider the following editorial: "For in truth we affirm and proclaim, the taunts and jeers of imperialists and reactionary Pharisees notwithstanding, that if there is any man under the Sun whose every word and deed remind us of the Son of Man, it is Kwame Nkrumah." "Nkrumah Messenger of Destiny," *Evening News*, 14 April 1960. Throughout the Nkrumah period, Ghanaian journalists and ideologues showed greater familiarity with the King James Version than with the works of Karl Marx.

News, on Republic Day, devoted an entire issue to "Nkrumaism, which is launched today. . . . To the initiate Nkrumaism is a complex political and social philosophy which is still in gestation so long as the Leader continues to add to the principles by words and deeds."[267] The definition got little further; the deeds were revealing. "I had finished the preparations for the Republic celebrations [related a senior civil servant]. 'At this point, Prime Minister, having sworn the oath you will walk up to the dais, followed by your ministers, to receive the cheers of the crowds.' 'No,' he responded. 'I shall go up alone. This is my day now.' This was the turning point for Ghana."[268]

[267] *Evening News*, 1 July 1960.
[268] Interview: CF-28.

II

"Diplomatic Cockpit"

JULY 1960–JULY 1962

BOOK II

WITH THE OUTBREAK of the Congo crisis the Ghanaians had their first chance to exercise international influence. In the excitement they pledged their full resources for the Congo's rescue, yet their efforts failed to affect the outcome of the crisis. Nkrumah, for his part, did not estimate accurately where influence could be wielded. Events moved too fast in any case. As a consequence of the crisis, Ghana's relations with the East and West were put on an entirely new basis, for Nkrumah blamed the Western powers (not unjustly) for Lumumba's collapse, and the loss of what he considered to be his own foothold in the vital center of Africa. He ceased to disguise his sentiments on international issues, and a trip through the Communist countries compromised his nonalignment in Western eyes. Because of the polarization of world power at the time, the West considered it essential to block Soviet gains in Africa, and as a result Ghana roused more attention in Washington. With the great powers vying for the friendship of Ghana, it was easy for Nkrumah to misapprehend his own importance in world politics.

With the Congo crisis the radical wing of the CPP found new opportunities. The journalists and trade unionists whom Nkrumah was placing in control of the state's information and propaganda media pressed for tighter links with Communist states, and for the replacement of the corrupt old guard of the CPP. An economic crisis and domestic tension gave them their opportunity. Ghana's balance of payments position had deteriorated, higher taxes had been imposed, and the cost of living had risen: one consequence was a strike in September 1961 which paralyzed Ghana's economy and nearly led to Nkrumah's overthrow. At this point Nkrumah appears to have struck a bargain with the radicals which gave them what they had sought, while ensuring his own survival. Thus the party was represented at the twenty-second congress of the Communist Party of the Soviet Union, and the CPP's old guard was dismissed. The gains of the radicals almost cost Nkrumah the Volta scheme and the long-planned royal visit, but owing to his resourcefulness the Americans agreed, in the end, to finance the project, and the Queen's Ghanaian tour materialized and was a success.

In the aftermath of the Congo crisis Africa became divided into rival groupings, and between 1960 and 1962 the Ghanaians were striking out in all directions to form an organic union of African states that could succeed where the Ghana-Guinea Union had failed. Lessons that

117

might have been learned from that previous failure had not been drawn, however, and so the subsequent attempts fared no better.

For three years Nkrumah had had a clear field and *crédit illimité* for his African policies; but at the end of 1960 there were three times as many states as in 1958, and no framework through which Nkrumah could influence them. He already had offended most of the continent's leaders, in any case. Those states with which historical ties existed were now Ghana's staunchest adversaries. Pictures of Nkrumah in party offices throughout Africa were coming down, but not just because his own star was falling, rather because these parties now governed independent states with their own leaders. As intra-African rivalries mounted and as the threat of external manipulation appeared to grow, Nkrumah responded by demanding the increasingly less realistic goal of immediate union. Ghanaian diplomats found their advice on African affairs sought less and less in Flagstaff House, while the influence of those known as the "militants" mounted; but these ex-policemen and former typing instructors attuned to new opportunities merely gave Nkrumah advice that he wished to hear.

Nkrumah did not appreciate the new situation that prevailed in Africa after 1960, nor did he see the fluidity of relationships between the new states. He could yet have taken the lead had he seen the opening that Sékou Touré and the Emperor of Ethiopia saw for bringing the rival groupings together. The previous five years could have been written off as a period of trial and error, and reconciliation with his adversaries might have been achieved. The two-year period ends at a point where Nkrumah had awakened to these realities.

The balance in Ghana's international stance seemed at this same time to be redressed, as relations with the West improved. True, a congress of the CPP at about this same time approved of "scientific socialism" as the theoretical goal of the state, but it remained to be seen whether in fact "democratic socialism," or a "popular democracy" of the Eastern European type was to be the result. The period closes at a time when events could have gone either way. No bridges had been burned.

118

₀4₀

THE CONGO CRISIS AND

ITS REPERCUSSIONS

July 1960–February 1961

"La parole est créatrice"

SMALL STATES play small roles in settling international crises. The Ghanaians' involvement in Congolese affairs was, however, deep: they inspired the Congolese to play their part in their own nationalist drama, they assisted the Congolese in their preparation for independence, and their commander and troops played an important role in the UN command (ONUC) at several points. It was not unnatural for Kwame Nkrumah to feel that the old rules of power politics were to be discarded.

Ghana also assumed the position of Patrice Lumumba's defender in the last half of 1960, and because so much hinges on the nature of the relationship between Nkrumah and Lumumba, it is helpful to trace the evolution of their friendship. Until the eve of the Congo's independence, Ghana's support in fact went to Kasavubu, not Lumumba. Ehud Avriel, Israel's ambassador in Ghana at the time, met Lumumba in Léopoldville in January 1958. For their own reasons, the Israelis decided to back him, and financed his trip to the All-African Peoples Conference in Accra, where Avriel introduced Lumumba to Nkrumah.[1] Contact with Kasavubu, on the other hand, was made through a clerk in the American consulate, one of the many Ghanaians working in Léopoldville. Married to a member of Kasavubu's family, he served as a channel of communication between Kasavubu and George Padmore.[2] Kasavubu was the leading Congolese nationalist in 1959, and it appears that both Padmore and Nkrumah became convinced that he was the most easily influenced of the Congolese politicians as well.

At the 1958 Accra conference (which Kasavubu did not attend), Lumumba made no attempt to destroy Nkrumah's image of Kasavubu. On the contrary, he praised him as the *doyen* of Congolese nationalism

[1] Interviews: CF-27; 62, 9 February 1967.

[2] Interviews: Andrew Djin, 1 February 1966, T. R. Makonnen, 20 February 1966, and *ibid.*

119

in order to minimize the difficulties of a fragmented nationalist movement and to avoid jeopardizing his own position in Accra.[3] Ghana backed Kasavubu and ABAKO throughout 1959 (rather than Lumumba and his MNC) despite Lumumba's membership on the AAPC steering committee, and Holden Roberto's pleas to Nkrumah on behalf of his friend Lumumba.[4] Padmore's *Bulletin of African Affairs* devoted an issue to Congolese nationalist movements without mentioning Lumumba by name, while adding: "The Bakongo [led by Kasavubu], like the Kikuyu in Kenya, originally organised themselves to protect their tribal interests, but eventually became the spearhead of a national liberation movement."[5]

Support, however, was not well organized. When Kasavubu, Daniel Kanza, and others were rusticated to Brussels in April 1959, the Ghanaians decided to respond to their call for help by sending £10,000. Richard Quarshie, at the Paris embassy, dispatched it through contacts in Geneva with the help of Padmore's office.[6] It is more than likely, that others involved misappropriated part of it, that Israeli funds made up the difference, and that in any case, the Congolese quarreled over its apportionment.[7]

By early 1960, Ghana's policy began changing. Lumumba's strength was growing and this, in combination with Russian pressure on Nkrumah to support him, introduced an ambiguity into the policy.[8] There is no doubt, on the other hand, that Lumumba's experience in Accra in 1958 had added a pan-African dimension to his Congolese nationalism.[9] Nkrumah's regime gave him ideas for the Congo, and the two remained in contact through the AAPC. Ironically, it is unlikely that the Ghanaians ever influenced those ABAKO leaders whom they supported.

Ghana's price of admittance to the Congo prior to independence was an exchange of relations and information with the Belgians. Early in 1959, after the Belgians became aware of Ghana's contact among the nationalist leaders, they requested permission to open an embassy in

[3] The delegation was politically divided.

[4] Interviews: CF-62, 9 February 1967; 76.

[5] "Nationalist Movements in the Belgian Congo," *Bulletin on African Affairs*, 12, No. 11.

[6] Interviews: Richard Quarshie; CF-28; 62, 9 February 1967.

[7] Interviews: CF-27, 76.

[8] By one very authoritative account, Lumumba made contact with the East Germans while in Brussels for the January 1960 Round Table conference, after which the Russians decided to support his cause. It is possible that from this point, Nkrumah served as intermediary in transmitting funds from Moscow to Lumumba. Interview: CF-27. See also interview: CF-62, 9 February 1967.

[9] See, for example, C. C. de Backer, "Notes pour servir a l'étude des 'groupements politique à Léopoldville,'" Léopoldville, 1959, p. 6, and L. L. Alvarez, *Lumumba, ou l'Afrique Frustrée*, Paris, 1965, p. 31.

Accra. There was adequate basis for a *quid pro quo*. The Belgians sought better information on Ghana's intentions in the Congo, and hoped the Ghanaians would affect the nationalists in a particular way. The Ghanaians wanted as much involvement in the Congo as possible, having in their own experience seen the benefits of cooperation with colonial authorities, and wanting to be as well-apprised as possible on Belgian intentions.[10] In April 1959 the Belgians submitted the name of Gerard Walravens, former ambassador in Turkey, and Nkrumah gave the *agrément* without making the customary enquiries. The reputation of this man in high Ghanaian circles made less likely the type of cooperation both states sought.[11]

In the spring of 1960, Ghana learned that Lumumba intended to expel all Belgian nationals from the Congo if he came to power, of which the Ghanaians informed Brussels. "We thought that the Belgians might wish to have our good offices in persuading the Congo Nationalists to be reasonable. Ghana's motive . . . was to avoid instability and chaos which might invite the attention of the cold war."[12] A "Congo co-ordinating committee" was established—though not activated—at about this time, through which Nkrumah hoped to coordinate Ghana's various efforts in the Congo. Michael Dei-Anang traveled to Brussels trying to convince the Belgians of the seriousness of the situation, but made little headway.[13]

This involvement, although revealing a prophetic foresight on the part of the Ghanaians, could not have aided Ghana's cause in Lumumba's camp. It is not easy to find the evidence that "Lumumba's hero is Dr. Kwame Nkrumah," as Colin Legum claimed.[14] Lumumba's later actions were to belie this, making more cogent the observations of one of the most astute diplomats in Léopoldville during 1960: that Lumumba of course told people he admired Nkrumah, "particularly when he knew the praise would be repeated to Nkrumah. He understood precisely how to gain Nkrumah's aid and support, and abused him more and more as time went on."[15]

Nkrumah's paramount concern was to back the winner in a power struggle which was beginning to take shape in the Congo. Once the principle of independence was granted, Nkrumah began to focus much

[10] Letter to the author, CFL-A, 5 July 1967, and interview: Ako Adjei.

[11] Interviews: Ako Adjei, Richard Quarshie, CF-28. Walravens was alleged to have a highly developed taste for Ghanaian ladies.

[12] Letter to the author, CFL-A, 5 July 1967.

[13] *Ibid.*, and interview: CF-28. This was while Nkrumah was at the London Commonwealth Prime Ministers' Conference.

[14] Colin Legum, *Congo Disaster*, London, 1961, p. 95.

[15] Interview: CF-27.

of his African strategy around Léopoldville. After Lumumba emerged the strongest figure in the elections of May 1960, Nkrumah then, and only then, began to give him his strong—though hardly undivided—support, while publicly dismissing ABAKO as tribalistic.[16]

Nkrumah now sent Andrew Djin to Léopoldville as his representative; Djin gives an interesting account of his work in this period:

> The Belgians could not have been more co-operative, and would do anything I asked of them. My job was, of course, to insure a smooth independence, like ours—and to apply the reins on Lumumba. These Congolese were very unsophisticated, compared with the Ghanaians; they knew nothing of socialism, or politics in general; they were rowdy, and out of touch with the modern world. I had to convince them that they were on a stage, and that if their independence didn't go well, it would set back the fate of all Africa.[17]

This typically Ghanaian view of another African country gives insight into what was the great success of Nkrumah's Congo policy but what was to become its great weakness and failing. The Ghanaians, unlike the Congolese themselves, saw the crucial nature of that country's independence—but they failed to grasp the limits on their own ability to influence events there.

Djin, for his part, had been loyal to Nkrumah, and as the CPP had prospered, so had Djin. He had been managing director of a notorious CPP adjunct, the Cocoa Purchasing Company,[18] treasurer of the party and of the AAPC's finance committee, and a member of the board of the Bureau of African Affairs. Through all this he had grown richer. He had a less certain instinct with respect to foreign affairs; he was a clever Tammany Hall politician, now placed in the Congo, a borough that spoke a different language.

Thus, in the negotiations on the central question on the eve of independence (over the respective positions for Lumumba and Kasavubu), Djin thought he played the central role in convincing Lumumba "that he had to work with Kasavubu for strategic reasons, and that in time he could eliminate him."[19] Nkrumah, for his part, was always to give Ghana credit for the final agreement reached.[20] In fact, the Americans,

[16] Interviews: James Markham, and CF-62, 9 February 1967.

[17] Interview: Andrew Djin, 1 February 1966.

[18] See Dennis Austin, *Politics in Ghana*, 1946-1960, London, 1964, p. 341n, for a citation from an official government report on Mr. Djin's past activities.

[19] Interview: Andrew Djin, 1 February 1966.

[20] See, for example, Nkrumah to Kasavubu, 14 September 1960: ". . . as you yourself must know through my Ambassador . . . I was able to reconcile Lumumba and yourself," quoted in Nkrumah, *Challenge of the Congo*, London, 1967, p. 57.

the British, and the Belgians had a real interest in seeing the two Congolese leaders reconciled, and they were able to convince Djin that it was for him to arrange the reconciliation, knowing it would then appear more palatable. Unfortunately, the game was being played at a higher level than Nkrumah was prepared to acknowledge, and he took Djin's role as messenger very seriously indeed.[21] Even before the outbreak of the crisis, there were therefore two grave weaknesses in Nkrumah's Congo policy: he had entrusted the most delicate assignments to men unequal to their tasks, and he had come to believe that he had a position of influence in the Congo that was not his. For all this, Ghana had been intimately involved in the Congo's affairs. Nkrumah and Lumumba had discussed the possibility of a Ghana Congo union at their last meeting prior to independence, and Lumumba, despite his more pressing concerns, had not discouraged the idea.[22] He had too many needs that only Ghana, the most influential sub-Saharan state, could meet.

Finally, all that could have been done, had been accomplished. Ambassador Walravens, on behalf of the Belgian government, officially requested the government of Ghana to "recognize the new state with the least possible delay."[23] The Ghanaian fears were soon to be realized. Only one day after the first troubles in Léopoldville, Patrick Seddoh, a foreign service officer, cabled Accra (where Djin was at this time) that it was possible that the Congo news would give a "much exaggerated" view of the position there. Nonetheless, a "high-powered" mission should be appointed immediately, with a strong military presence included. "If the Congolese cannot maintain order, then perhaps a defence arrangement with the government of the Congo or with some other Independent African States" will be necessary.[24] It was a prophetic report, even if it did underestimate the depth of the trouble.

JULY–AUGUST: AN OPERATIVE FOREIGN POLICY

The next month was to be the most exciting period of Ghana's first nine years. Probably no new nation ever brought so much help to a brother state so quickly. At the beginning Ghana's aid came at almost every level of government. Doctors, engineers, and civil servants went. Ghana pro-

---

[21] Miss Hoskyns argues that Lumumba accepted Kasavubu as president because of Ghanaian pressure, irrespective of the great powers' wishes. The argument of several participants in the negotiations, that Lumumba's decision was based on his own assessment of where power lay, is far more persuasive. Interview: CF-27, and Catherine Hoskyns, *The Congo Since Independence*, London, 1965, p. 77.

[22] Interviews: Richard Quarshie; Andrew Djin, 1 February 1966.

[23] G. Walravens, Belgium/Accra, to Ako Adjei, 30 June 1960, CFA-113.

[24] Ghana/Léo. to M.E.A., 8 July 1960, CFA-115. Seddoh spoke fluent French and was a shrewd diplomat.

vided Lumumba with a flying secretariat on his July travels and, when he asked for his own plane, he got that too. True, Nkrumah's inadequate understanding of military matters helps to explain his willingness to send his entire fighting force to the Congo, and his mistaken view of Ghana's financial capacities led him to commit greater resources than Ghana could spare. But of such stuff is the heroic frequently compounded and, as an *Observer* correspondent wrote, "Whether their efforts are successful . . . the fact that they felt that they were capable [of so much aid] is an important advance along the road of Africa's self-respect."[25]

The mutiny began July 5th to 7th, and Katanga declared its secession on July 11th. The following day Nkrumah sent Lieutenant Colonel (later General) Otu, Djin, and two other diplomats to Léopoldville and, to their resentment, he sent Major General Alexander, his British chief of staff, twenty-four hours later. The foreign minister wrote Hammarskjold impressive details of Ghana's readiness. It could send two battalions and adequate stores immediately, and a radio-link which the secretary-general could also use. Quaison-Sackey was told that "We are standing by here on a 24-hour basis and would be glad to receive as soon as possible answers to the points raised."[26] By the next day, Ghana had chartered a ship to send matériel, and on Saturday, July 16th, 0400 GMT, the first Ghanaian troops left by R.A.F. Comet. Within two days, the secretary-general had requested a third Ghanaian battalion, and by July 19th all Ghana Airways flights had been canceled for the transportation of troops. Within a week of Lumumba's first request for Ghanaian troops, 1,193 were in Léopoldville; 192 more were waiting for transport in Accra with 156 trucks and 160 tons of stores.

The Congo coordinating committee, activated shortly after the outbreak of the crisis, was quickly becoming a high-powered group, with priority in all government operations, setting far-reaching precedents for the operation of Africa policy. A building was requisitioned for it; Richard Quarshie, a senior foreign service officer from the ministry, was made secretary; Kweku Boateng, minister of information and a radical, was its chairman at one point. Others, like Eric Otoo (later the director of intelligence) came into prominence through the committee, but it was Geoffrey Bing, the attorney general, who dominated it. By Quarshie's account, the rest of the committee was at a loss to know how to assess the developing crisis, whereas Bing, with experience from the Spanish Civil War, had no such trouble.[27] Significantly, the foreign minister was not a member; he declined when Nkrumah did not offer him the com-

25 Frank Pilgrim, *Observer Foreign News Service*, 10 August 1960.
26 Ako Adjei to Quaison-Sackey, 14 July 1960, CFA-115.
27 Interview: Richard Quarshie.

mittee's chair.[28] The members met each morning at 8:30 and again at 6:00. Staff men brought beds for twenty-four hour operations. Here the lengthy press statements and the closely argued speeches were written, and the technical aid was organized.

The bewildering speed of events in the first two weeks, and Ghana's role in them, made it easy for a passionate leader to believe that his state was playing a central part in a great international crisis. Indeed, Ghana had become "the diplomatic cockpit of Africa."[29] Foreign policy was no longer merely proclamatory. Ghana was a principal supplier of troops to the Congo and was on terms of special friendship with the government; Quaison-Sackey, next to Omer Loufti of the U.A.R., was in the most pivotal position among the Africans at the United Nations. General Alexander had become the "de facto commander of the UN forces in the Congo," according to the BBC, and had done "more to restore public calm than any other man in the Congo."[30] Throughout July, in whatever light Nkrumah viewed Western maneuvering, there appeared to be a basis for hope that the crisis would be settled quickly. It seemed clear (so the foreign minister cabled Quaison-Sackey) that as the difficulties were entirely occasioned by intervention "from outside," the secession "will automatically collapse . . . as soon as order is established in the other parts of the Congo"; which, it appeared, Ghanaian troops were in the process of doing.[31] It was, in all, a period of great hope.

By August, Nkrumah had reason to believe he could set in motion a grand strategy for Africa that would bring about the organic union he had long sought. He would construct bilateral unions with as many states as possible. All African roads would lead to Accra. When Lumumba, returning from New York, passed through Accra on August 8th, one of the most important events in the Nkrumah period occurred. In Nkrumah's private quarters, in the presence of only the most senior officials and in deepest secrecy, a Ghana-Congo agreement for union was signed: Ghana and the Congo were to be one. Lumumba's public allusions to the contrary on other occasions notwithstanding, it was a bilateral discussion.[32] The Guineans were not involved. The union was important not because it had a chance to be consummated, or because Lumumba could possibly have signed it in good faith, but because of the way Nkrumah

---

[28] Interview: Ako Adjei.

[29] A phrase apparently first used by Sammy Ikoku, *Evening News*, 23 July 1960.

[30] P.R. #577/60, 21 July 1960, transcript of BBC broadcast.

[31] Ako Adjei to Quaison-Sackey, 15 July 1960, CFA-115.

[32] Interviews: Richard Quarshie, Ako Adjei, Stephan Dzirasa, Enoch Okoh. See the text in *Challenge of the Congo*, pp. 30-31. See also Nkrumah's allusion to this in *Africa Must Unite*, London, 1963, p. 148. Also see *Evening News*, 29 July 1960.

envisaged it. He had gained mastery of Africa. It was later to be his conviction that this union (which existed only on paper) was snatched from him by "the imperialists."[33]

There were high stakes for Nkrumah in the crisis: it brought him his first opportunity to show international statesmanship as mediator, but such a role presupposed that the Congo not become a great-power pawn. On the outcome of the crisis depended his plans for the unity of Africa; to accomplish his ends, he had to maintain a position of influence with Lumumba. All of this made essential the restoration of order at the earliest moment. Owing to the background of Ghanaian-Congolese links prior to independence and Ghana's role in the first stage of the crisis, Nkrumah considered Ghana to be the arbiter of the situation by right, a right he became convinced he could exercise by planning his strategy at three different levels, and by working in the Congo through three different instruments. Firstly, there was his chief of staff, General Alexander, on whom he counted to restore order and to wield influence within ONUC. Secondly, there were his diplomats; he considered Lumumba's cause joined in his, and, to buttress the position of the Congolese prime minister and to maintain his own position with him, he depended on Ambassador Djin and his political officers. As a function of these two parts of his strategy, and as a third commitment, was his contingent in ONUC, and ONUC itself. He had been realistic enough from the first to realize that Ghana, or even all the African states together, could not compose the situation alone, and that the United Nations should therefore be involved. As a nonaligned leader of international stature who had shown faith, in practice, in the United Nations by committing his troops to it, he felt entitled to a position of influence in the councils of ONUC. His Congo policy was not to succeed, mainly because the crisis was deeper than he had envisaged. Worse, he was to lose stature and influence as a result of his Congo policy, and that was because of the nature of his strategy and its implementation, which must be examined in its three parts.

In the first week of the crisis, General Alexander did play an important part. Prior to the arrival of ONUC's commander, General van Horn, Alexander was the senior officer in Léopoldville, effectively taking charge, as his rank entitled him to do. His celebrated disarming of the Congolese troops in the capital city brought much attention to Ghana, and convinced Nkrumah that, through his own commanding officer, order could be restored. Yet the consequences of Alexander's act were to work against Nkrumah's objectives, as is seen by examining the dis-

---

[33] See Nkrumah, *Challenge of the Congo*, p. 31.

arming itself. Upon his arrival in Léopoldville, Alexander convinced Ralph Bunche, the Secretary-General's representative, and Vice-Premier Gizenga—acting in Lumumba's absence—to permit him to disarm the troops; otherwise the Belgians would do so themselves, causing further deterioration, he was convinced. Alexander had great success in accomplishing his mission but Lumumba, upon his return, refused to permit any further disarming, whereupon Bunche countermanded the previous arrangement with Alexander; in a few days the Congolese troops were again carrying arms, and tension in the city rose accordingly. A widely publicized dispute ensued between Bunche and Alexander over ONUC's priorities. Bunche felt that, however right Alexander may have been in believing that military necessities should take precedence over political objectives at that point, the United Nations had to subordinate itself to the legally constituted authority were ONUC to be a success. Alexander, on the other hand, considered that Bunche had not even "pressed my arguments over control of weapons with Lumumba, nor do I believe that Bunche at the time fully realized the implications of the weakening on this point."[34]

This dispute carried over to one between Alexander and van Horn, chronicled in the latter's memoirs.[35] The problem was that Alexander had no formal position in the Congo—beyond that of adviser to his president—making his continued presence in the Congo the more embarrassing. Alexander considered that van Horn, like Bunche, did not press hard enough for control of the weapons of the Force Publique and also "had very little respect for [van Horn's] professional ability."[36] Even if Bunche's view on the disarming of the troops was, in one scholar's view, "legally correct and authoritative,"[37] events were bearing out Alexander's predictions. Ironically van Horn came close to accepting Alexander's thesis, and found himself as much in disagreement with Bunche as had Alexander. Personal hostility between them, and Alexander's anomalous position in Léopoldville, made accord between them impossible.[38]

[34] Maj. Gen. Alexander to the author, June 1968. I am grateful to General Alexander for permission to quote from his extended comments written in response to many questions raised with him. See also his book, *African Tightrope*, London, 1966. For the Bunche-Alexander dispute, see Hoskyns, *The Congo Since Independence*, pp. 135-39.

[35] Maj. Gen. Carl van Horn, *Soldiering for Peace*, London, 1966, pp. 180, 146, 157.

[36] Maj. Gen. Alexander to author, June 1968.

[37] See E. W. Lefever, *Crisis in the Congo*, Washington, 1965, p. 35.

[38] The belief of van Horn, and of many Ghanaians, that Alexander sought a permanent high-ranking post in ONUC is unlikely to be correct. A professional soldier could not have considered a post under van Horn as equal to that of General Officer in Command of a country's army, particularly where the soldier was in a position of such influence. See also interview: CF-27. Alexander did, however, offer his services to van Horn as a field commander, but on the assumption that he would preserve his position in Ghana.

127

In a sense, both Alexander (and Nkrumah) on the one hand, and Bunche (and to a lesser extent van Horn) on the other were right. As Nkrumah was to repeat time and again, had order been restored, the position in the Congo would not have deteriorated. What Nkrumah failed to see was the implications of a British general appearing to take the lead in a tense situation where the confidence of the African government was a crucial factor, something which Bunche did see. Nkrumah refused to see why his general, who for a short time had played a most critical role, could not assume a position of leadership in ONUC; but the more Nkrumah propounded Alexander's thesis, the more he antagonized UN officials. In Nkrumah's later writings, it is suggested that many of the difficulties to which Ghana fell prey in the Congo were due to the miscalculations and split loyalties of General Alexander as Ghana's Chief of Staff.[39] But while Djin or Welbeck (Djin's successor) had bases of power in Ghana to a limited extent independent of Nkrumah, Alexander, as an Englishman, had only one fount of power, and that was the president's unfaltering belief in his abilities. No doubt some of Nkrumah's characteristics which were discussed in the first chapter are relevant in explaining his confidence in Alexander—his respect of the competent Westerner, and his fear that his own people could not be trusted with power. Even Nylander, Nkrumah's defense minister, was not privy to military strategy, while Alexander consulted almost daily with the president.[40] When Nkrumah had to choose between his loyalties to Lumumba and Alexander, he did not hesitate to stand by Alexander, thus confirming the argument that Nkrumah's interests in the Congo were not limited by his loyalty to Lumumba. Ironically, some observers have concluded that the only influence Nkrumah was ever able to bring to bear on the development of the Congo crisis came as a by-product of Alexander's presence and actions. Yet as Robert Gardiner has argued, Alexander had only brought Nkrumah "artificial influence"—that is publicity—which was hardly central to the African mission in the Congo. UN officials saw no reason why Nkrumah's writ should run in Léopoldville.

To maintain his position of influence with Lumumba, Nkrumah had given Ambassador Djin a brief to assist the prime minister in every possible way. It was not in Nkrumah's nature to make explicit to Djin where such diplomacy fell in his own priorities; he always left to his representatives the resolving of contradictions in policy. But the effect

---

[39] Nkrumah, *Challenge of the Congo*, p. 39n. He indicates that he dismissed Alexander for this reason. Alexander was dismissed for much different reasons, and not until September 1961. See infra, p. 185.

[40] Interview: Amb. C. T. Nylander.

was to make conflict between Ghana's soldiers and diplomats inevitable. On virtually every issue Djin and Alexander gave Nkrumah contrary advice—for obvious reasons. Each represented one of the increasingly contradictory arms of Nkrumah's Congo policy. Much of the conflict derived from Djin's failure to understand why Ghanaian troops could not take orders from the accredited representative of Ghana's president to intervene on Lumumba's behalf. But Alexander threatened Djin in a more basic way. As will be seen, all of the African diplomats were competing for influence with Lumumba, and it was vital to Djin that he preserve the preeminence he had possessed at independence. Increasingly, the major issue between Lumumba and Nkrumah was the white officers in the Ghanaian contingent—who were unsympathetic to Lumumba's designs—and the other African diplomats' primary means of weakening Ghana's influence was to stress Ghana's unreliability to Lumumba. Getting Alexander out of the Congo or, at the least, reducing his influence, thus became Djin's major goal.[41]

Botsio, Dei-Anang, Bing, and most of the others in Accra sympathized with Djin, as did Colonel Otu in Léopoldville, in whom General Alexander had little confidence. A report prepared for Nkrumah in Dei-Anang's office shows how civil servants began to question the Alexander legend, particularly with respect to his disarming of the Force Publique. "A few days before the arrival of the Ghanaian troops, Mr. Djin . . . had worked tirelessly to get the Congolese people . . . to see the importance of avoiding further clashes with the Belgian troops. . . . When General Alexander arrived . . . *the stage was set* for getting the Congolese people to bring a speedy end to the troubles." Moreover, it went on, a psychological situation had been created which threatened to leave a heritage of hatred. The Congolese people had expressed surprise at the color of the Tunisian soldiers' skin, as well as at the fact that Ghanaian troops were accompanied by so many European officers. Now that ONUC was entrenched, it concluded, "the presence of the General is superfluous since [Colonel Otu] is not only efficient but is politically acceptable."[42]

Such competition had serious implications for the implementation of policy. It was, for example, Nkrumah's intention from the beginning to restrain the Congo's volatile prime minister, particularly with respect

[41] Alexander writes that Djin was "anti-white" and "anti-Belgian." The first charge is not correct. Djin was simply jealous of Alexander, who was seemingly succeeding in his own objectives, which Djin demonstrably was not doing. See Alexander, *African Tightrope*, London, 1965, p. 34.

[42] "Brief Report on the Situation in the Congo," n.d., but presumably July 1960, by internal evidence, CFA-116. See also Dei-Anang to Djin, 25 August 1960, CFA-114.

to the question of Soviet aid—which, Nkrumah and Alexander knew, if accepted by Lumumba, would bring countervailing Western support to his opponents. Djin, on the defensive with Lumumba because of Alexander's presence, was undoubtedly reluctant to dissuade Lumumba, as Alexander claims. "He was too eager to keep Lumumba's ear, and echoed whatever Lumumba wished."[43] In Stanleyville, when Lumumba decided to issue an ultimatum to the United Nations (that, unless the Belgian troops were out of the Congo within twenty-four hours he would appeal for help from the Soviet Union), Alexander tried to convince him of the dangers in doing so, and, having failed, helped to circumvent the prime minister. This he did by alerting Bunche, who persuaded the Congolese cabinet to disown the statement, prior to Lumumba's return, which infuriated Djin. Alexander also claims that Geoffrey Bing played an equally critical, more conscious, role, in frustrating policy. "Not only did Bing stop messages emanating from Nkrumah, he also, I am told, failed to deliver messages which I sent from the Congo, although in most cases these were personal from myself to the President."[44] This is not possible to verify, but is in accord with Bing's style and his perceived interests. Quaison-Sackey, on the other hand, represented Nkrumah's commitment to the United Nations itself; he reinforced Nkrumah's and Alexander's sentiments, with respect to the Soviets, by "strongly recommending that our mission in Léopoldville be instructed to approach Lumumba with a plea for patience. This recommendation has the support of the Africa Group here."[45]

Nkrumah, however, failed to see where his influence could be wielded; and the Congo crisis was rapidly becoming too complex for Ghana to solve, even though Nkrumah had correctly diagnosed the dangers inherent in the situation. Thus he wrote to Hammarskjold that Lumumba had withdrawn the ultimatum "in accord with my personal request," although it was clearly Bunche's diplomacy that had counted.[46] By early August the Ghanaians were having no success whatever in restraining Lumumba. When he traveled to New York, Flagstaff House telegraphed Quaison-Sackey asking for "his utmost cooperation in ensuring that Mr. Lumumba confine his activities to his important mission to the United Nations" and not travel to Ottawa for a television interview where, by implication, he would be outside the reach of restraining influences.

[43] Interview: Major General Alexander.
[44] Alexander to the author, June 1968. See also *African Tightrope*, pp. 43-46, and Hoskyns, *The Congo Since Independence*, p. 137. Also interviews: Andrew Djin, and CF-51.
[45] Quaison-Sackey to Dei-Anang, 18 July 1960, CFA-121.
[46] Nkrumah to Hammarskjold, 20 July 1960, CFA-121, and interviews: Maj. Gen. Alexander, and CF-51.

Lumumba did not heed the advice, and in Ottawa contacted Soviet diplomats.[47]

There was cruel irony for Nkrumah in these developments. His objectives could be achieved only through Lumumba, whose weaknesses he understood. Yet Nkrumah's primary influence in the Congo was still the presence of the Ghanaian contingent, which was increasingly embarrassing, owing to its white officers. Nkrumah still accepted and propounded Alexander's thesis that order had to be achieved throughout the Congo before Lumumba, or indeed any Congolese, could govern.

The contradictions in Nkrumah's Congo policy also created problems for the UN secretariat. Nkrumah's faith in the United Nations had always been clear enough, and he had good reasons for wishing to see it play a key role in the crisis, at least in its early stages, in order to prevent the Congo from being drawn into the vortex of the cold war, in which circumstances Nkrumah knew his own influence would be minimal. Moreover, as a member of Nkrumah's Congo coordination committee said, "We felt that if we could attract the United Nations into the crisis, Ghana's stature would be augmented, because all the world would be focusing on us; more important, we could wield influence within the UN."[48] Not surprisingly, such a view of the United Nations led to conflict with its secretariat, for Nkrumah's interest in the outcome of the crisis was sufficiently strong to lead him to act unilaterally, or against ONUC interpretations, on various occasions.

The first conflict with New York, and the first test of Nkrumah's foreign policy in the Congo, came in the obtaining of transport from the great powers. He was determined to have the first troops in Léopoldville, but was totally dependent on the great powers to get them there. During those first hours, between July 12th and 15th, he was in such desperate need that he would have bought transport planes on the spot had he not succeeded in obtaining them by other means.[49] When he first approached the British for help, the first Security Council resolution authorizing the formation of a UN force had not been passed; they had every desire to help (so they claimed), but not until it was a United Nations operation.[50] Nkrumah, for his part, clearly intended to send troops with or without United Nations authorization.[51]

[47] Nkrumah to Quaison-Sackey, 19 July 1960, CFA-122. See also Hoskyns, *The Congo Since Independence*, p. 158.
[48] Interview: CF-95.
[49] Interviews: CF-8, 56.
[50] Interview: CF-101, January 1967. The British did, however, provide General Alexander with a plane in which to go to the Congo, before the UN resolutions were passed.
[51] See his press statement of July 13th, quoted in Nkrumah, *I Speak of Freedom*, London, 1961, p. 246.

Nkrumah also wanted a balanced participation by the great powers,[52] and while he waited for Hammarskjold to obtain the British and American planes that he had requested, Ambassador Sytenko of the Soviet Union offered Ghana the use of two Ilyushin 18's, which were accepted without reference to the UN secretariat. "It was this gesture, at a time when the ex-colonial power was delaying, that helped to determine the course of the next few years."[53] But from the secretary-general's point of view, Nkrumah had been too hasty in demonstrating Ghana's non-alignment. Hammarskjold was surprised, Quaison-Sackey cabled, that the "Ghana Government has seen fit to make a direct request to the Soviet Union for planes without reference to the Secretariat."[54] After the Western powers had agreed to supply transport, Nkrumah wrote to Quaison-Sackey that the provision of aircraft was inadequate, as only one of the three promised British Beverley's had arrived, and it was unsafe. "In any event for political reasons it is most undesirable that we should refuse Soviet Air assistance while accepting that of the United States and the United Kingdom. You should therefore press most strongly for clearance by Ghana of the use of Soviet Aircraft."[55] What started as a misunderstanding, arising from haste, foreshadowed grave differences between Nkrumah and the secretary-general at a later stage.

The records show growing concern in the secretariat during August over Ghanaian "unilateralism" in the Congo. Thus, ONUC had never been able to take command of Ghana's police contingent in Léopoldville, and in mid-August the contingent acted on Lumumba's request for protection, on orders from Accra. "The Secretary-General noted that the Ghana police contingent in the Congo forms a part of the UN force [wrote Quaison-Sackey]. . . . The Secretary-General requests the government . . . to give the necessary instructions so that henceforth the disposition of all members of the Ghanaian contingent in the UN force shall be regulated only through the United Nations command."[56] The dispute centered on the Security Council's resolution of July 14th which regulated the relationship of national contingents and ONUC. It also stated that members of the Congo government were to have "adequate

52 Interview: Quaison-Sackey.

53 Interview: CF-95; also interviews: Dzirasa, Ako Adjei, Sir Edward Asafu-Adjaye, January 1966.

54 Quaison-Sackey to Kweku Boateng, Congo Coordinating Committee, 18 July 1960, CFA-119.

55 Nkrumah to Quaison-Sackey, 19 July 1960, CFA-115A. There were sublevels of competition, too. Nkrumah requested four DC-4's from Egypt, and the next day Israel offered two Beverley's. Nkrumah to Quaison-Sackey, 18 July 1960, CFA-121, and Boateng to Quaison-Sackey, 23 July 1960, CFA-121.

56 Minister of Interior to Hammarskjold, 11 August 1960, in Quaison-Sackey to Ako Adjei, 12 August 1960, CFA-117.

protection" and, by reference to this, Ghana claimed that it had indeed acted in compliance with the resolution, even if at a higher, unilateral level of interpretation. "One of the inevitable facts of the UN administration is that it moves too slowly and often too late," said the Ghanaian reply.[57] A special formula was urged whereby protection might immediately be given when requested, after which the circumstances could be reported to the UN High Command. "The Government of Ghana considers that adequate protection of the members of the lawfully constituted central government, on whose invitation the UN forces are in the Congo, is a *paramount* duty imposed by the Security Council resolution."[58] The police contingent, which brought invaluable aid to Lumumba, was one of the few trumps Ghana had left in Léopoldville, and so it did not arrange to follow the secretariat's directive.

Ghana's problems went beyond those caused by the inherent contradictions in her policy. Other African states were not willing to permit Ghana to assume more influence in the Congo than they possessed, and their challenge to her influence began at the outbreak of the crisis. On July 12th Nkrumah had cabled every African head of state that reports from the Congo were so disturbing that "I have decided to send a special mission . . . to obtain first-hand information."[59] The replies showed, however, that there were limits to the amount of leadership which Nkrumah could assume. The Tunisians, in the process of mounting an equally ambitious (if less frenetic) effort cabled back that they looked forward to cooperating with Ghana "as well as with other African States *at the United Nations level.*"[60] Tubman publicly expressed his irritation at the dispatch of the Ghanaian mission, and Nkrumah telegraphed Asafu-Adjaye in London to the effect that if his views were sought concerning "President Tubman's statement that he regrets Liberia was not consulted, you should say that in view of the rapidly developing situation, Ghana felt it essential that the quickest possible action should be taken."[61] At the other extreme, Sékou Touré had already demanded that Nkrumah join him in breaking diplomatic relations with Belgium. Nkrumah replied that "such would be inopportune," and that he "would like to give further consideration to your proposal in the light of subsequent developments in [the] Congo."[62]

By August, competition among the African states, particularly be-

---

[57] Quarshie to Quaison-Sackey, 14 August 1960, CFA-120.
[58] Quoted in Quaison-Sackey to Ako Adjei, 12 August 1960, CFA-117.
[59] Nkrumah to heads of African states, 12 July 1960, CFA-115.
[60] *Presidence*/Tunis to M.E.A., 14 July 1960, CFA-121 (emphasis added).
[61] Nkrumah to Sir Edward Asafu-Adjaye, Ghana/London, 15 July 1960, CFA-115.
[62] Nkrumah to Touré, 15 July 1960, CFA-115.

tween Ghana and Guinea, had severely reduced Nkrumah's options. According to Anicet Kashamura, minister of information in Léopoldville, it was a situation where "everyone bargained for influence," and where the Guineans held several important cards.[63] They spoke French and were the most radical. According to Djin, they disagreed with every Ghanaian proposal at meetings, as if on principle.[64] There is little doubt that their most effective weapon was the presence of the white Ghanaian officers; their weakness was that they could not replace the concrete aid the Ghanaians were bringing Lumumba.

But the Ghanaians were also finding how difficult it was to aid the Congo. A loan of £2 million was suggested in July, for example, but was never acted on, so great was the chaos in the channels through which it would be distributed. True, an Africanization expert went to Léopoldville with technicians who organized electricity timetables, and they got several government departments working once again. But they found almost no Africanization. "The so-called ministers spent most of their time in bars."[65]

For the politicians and civil servants, "going to the Congo" was what one did to increase his influence in Accra. Dei-Anang, A. K. Barden, Kojo Addison, Ako Adjei, and many others found compelling reasons to board planes and spend time in Léopoldville. There was little doubt what they were doing. Empty adventuring by some of these set the precedent for later clashes with the Congolese government; it was the illusion of the other, more responsible, officials that such trips could lead to easy solutions, which were then pressed in Accra.

Throughout August Ghana began to get caught behind its triple-barrelled commitment in the Congo, and its initiatives began backfiring. One by-product of alleged Ghanaian interference in Léopoldville was a misplaced popular reaction against Ghana's military presence. As early as August 9th, the Ghanaian embassy reported that ABAKO supporters had demanded the withdrawal of Ghanaian and Guinean troops, in the course of a demonstration aimed primarily against Belgium.[66] But the crowds were wrong for (to the chagrin of Djin and to the growing embarrassment of Nkrumah), the Ghanaian contingent was firmly under UN command.

Lumumba's prime concern, meanwhile, was to "get the Belgian troops out of the Congo and then deal with Katanga."[67] If Nkrumah were to

---

[63] Interview: Anicet Kashamura, April 1965, Paris.
[64] Interview: Djin, 1 February 1966.   [65] Interview: CF-74.
[66] G. H. Arthur to Ako Adjei, 9 August 1960, CF-120. Alexander is convinced that Djin instigated the demonstration as a means of pressing Nkrumah to withdraw him.
[67] Hoskyns, *The Congo Since Independence*, p. 139.

retain Lumumba's confidence, he had to show results in solving the problem of Katanga's secession. But how? Ghana was far removed from the power struggle among the great powers at the United Nations over the interpretation of the Security Council's resolutions. It had cultivated a relationship with Belgium for just such eventualities, but with what persuasive argument could Ghana influence Belgium? Nkrumah could only summon its ambassador and "invite him to get in touch with his own government [so that he could] inform the Government of Ghana of the exact position of Belgium" on the Katanga question. Belgium replied, none too generously, that "the unity of the Congo is the work of Belgium. Any modification of the Congo's unitary statute can only be the result of Congolese efforts themselves."[68] It seems likely that Nkrumah at this point did not appreciate the extent of the hold that the Belgians and Tshombe had on Katanga, which is suggested by a memorandum of the same date to a Ghanaian embassy: "It appears to Osagyefo . . . that Mr. Tshombe's original attempts at secession have been overtaken by events and [Osagyefo] is of the opinion that a meeting of Independent African States in Léopoldville in the near future would be extremely helpful."[69] Nkrumah also telegraphed the heads of African states that if they stood together for the "complete and unconditional and immediate withdrawal of Belgian troops from Katanga . . . it will be possible to resolve the present crisis within the framework of the United Nations."[70]

More drastic proposals were necessary for Lumumba's benefit. On August 1st, Ghana had promised to give the Congo "all possible help," but it added no threatening alternative course were the United Nations not to fulfill its mission.[71] By August 8th the stakes were higher. The Security Council was going into debate, and Lumumba was making his way to Accra by way of Conakry and other African capitals. The Ghanaians, moreover, were forewarned of Guinea's promise to "put the Guinean armed forces in their entirety at the disposition of the Lumumba government."[72]

Understandably, Ghana had to offer more. On the day of Guinea's communiqué, Nkrumah announced to the press that he would ask the National Assembly to mobilize Ghana's forces remaining in Ghana to go

---

[68] P.R. #657/60, 6 August 1960, and Belgium/Accra to Hon. Ako Adjei, 8 August 1960, CFA-120. All Ghana could do was establish a special telephone circuit to facilitate the Belgian Embassy's communication with Brussels.

[69] M.E.A. to J. T. Speare, Ghana/Monrovia, 6 August 1960, CFA-116.

[70] P.R. #663/60, 8 August 1960.

[71] In contrast to Russian statements of the same day, it should be noted.

[72] Ghanaian Intelligence officers obtained a rough draft of the Guinean statement before it was even released. See CFA-116.

to Lumumba's aid if necessary. He did so on August 8th. His speech—an important one—stressed two themes. Firstly, the African states had been seen to be "technically competent to tackle any problem arising on the African continent." Secondly, if the United Nations failed in Katanga, Ghanaian and Congolese forces would "fight alone" against Belgium, in which case "Ghana and other African states would not be without aid and assistance from other countries, which value, as a principle, the concept of African independence."[73] Yet the African states had been forced to rely completely on the Western powers to move their troops to the Congo. As for the second theme, it was rendered irrelevant by the fact that only about three hundred fighting troops were left in Ghana. One journalist commented that "President Nkrumah has attempted and pulled off a feat of 'brinksmanship' with all the aplomb of a Foster Dulles and the clatter of a Khrushchev,"[74] but it fooled few others. If there were any doubt of Nkrumah's real strategy, the cabinet minutes of the same day dispel it: "The President explained that the policy of Ghana was not calculated to cause aggression . . . anywhere . . . on African soil. He was always guided by the fact that unless a policy of toughness was followed, the initiative in the Congo would be lost to the Belgian and other imperialist powers."[75] Indeed, Nkrumah sent a message to the secretary-general two days later reassuring him that in spite of press reports to the contrary, Ghana would stand by the United Nations, adding only the expected caveat, "so long as the United Nations [is] engaged in carrying out the mandate entrusted to it by the Resolutions of the Security Council."[76]

The Security Council's August 9th resolution, which stated "that the United Nations Force in the Congo will not be a party to . . . any internal conflict, constitutional or otherwise," was unnecessarily restraining from Lumumba's and Nkrumah's point of view. Hammarskjold had drawn an analogy with the intervention in Lebanon in 1958 to support the limited interpretation of the resolution but, as Nkrumah telegraphed Quaison-Sackey (using arguments of Geoffrey Bing), two states were in conflict in the Lebanese crisis, and the United Nations had sent in observers, not troops.[77] Obviously the Ghanaians wished ONUC to be used to crush Katanga's secession as quickly as possible.

Nkrumah saw the conference of Independent African States, scheduled for Léopoldville at the end of the month, as the last chance to improve

73 *Debates*, 8 August 1960, pp. 617-744.
74 *Observer Foreign News Service*, 14 August 1960.
75 Item 1, cabinet minutes, 8 August 1960, CFA-120.
76 Nkrumah to Quaison-Sackey, for Hammarskjold, 10 August 1960, CFA-120.
77 Nkrumah to Quaison-Sackey, 9 August 1960, CFA-114.

the situation with respect both to the position at the United Nations and the Congo itself. He instructed Quaison-Sackey that, if he were unable to obtain backing in the Africa Group and Security Council for a strengthening of ONUC's mandate, he should seek to postpone the issue until after the Léopoldville conference. "These [African] States should be given the opportunity of attempting to work out an agreed formula acceptable to all parties in the Congo."[78] Nkrumah still sought to confine the conflict as much as possible to Africa, with only the United Nations intervening from outside. Thus, while Lumumba and Hammarskjold drew further and further apart in the Congo itself Nkrumah still tried to restrain Lumumba and bid for time until the conference opened. He wrote to Djin that he must urgently "impress tactfully upon Lumumba and Kasavubu the importance and absolute necessity for them to cooperate with the United Nations in securing our objective in the Congo. . . . I am disturbed at Lumumba's present attitude toward Mr. Hammarskjold and I wish you to bring home . . . to him that the success of our whole operation can be totally undermined by any . . . hostility to the United Nations. . . . I would like to point out that African solidarity . . . is not sufficient unless it is backed by the United Nations."[79]

This was all to little avail for at the most crucial level—the prime minister's entourage—Ghana's influence had become marginal, largely because Lumumba, increasingly desperate, had begun to take Soviet and Guinean advice. On August 19th, Nkrumah informed Lumumba that he would "insist on white troops being withdrawn from the Congo as soon as possible,"[80] but he did not mean it, for a week later he sent Botsio to plead with Lumumba to accept Alexander and these officers.[81] Yet to maintain influence with Lumumba, some concession was necessary, and so he tried to develop an alternative strategy for solution of the crisis, one in which he himself could hold the reins of power. At General Alexander's suggestion, he proposed a "high command" of African armies, like the one that had been discussed in 1958.[82] Nasser sent military officers to Accra in mid-August to plan such a command and throughout that month the two leaders corresponded. As late as August 22nd, Nkrumah thought that both he and Nasser were going to Léo-

[78] *Ibid.*
[79] Nkrumah to Djin, 17 August 1960, CFA-123.
[80] Nkrumah to Lumumba, 19 August 1960, "Correspondence exchanged between Osagyefo Dr. Kwame Nkrumah and the Leaders of the Republic of the Congo on the Congo Situation," Accra, 1960.
[81] Interview: Botsio.
[82] See supra, p. 49. Alexander's claim to have first suggested the high command is widely acknowledged, even by General Otu, no admirer of his. Interview: General Otu.

poldville for the IAS conference, at which time "we can plan this all out together," as he wrote to Lumumba.

> The problem seems to me to be to convert the Congolese . . . army into an efficient fighting force within a very short space of time. . . .
>
> I think this can be done by the use of a military mission from the African states and by the recruitment from abroad of a number of key technicians. Great care and tact will require to be used in selecting these outside military technicians. . . .
>
> For the plan to be successful, we shall, however, still need the umbrella of the United Nations. I do not think anything is to be gained by calling upon them to leave. We should rely absolutely on Hammarskjold's specific statement: "We cannot, we will not, and we have no right to raise any resistance to any move by the Central Government to assert its authority in Katanga.[83]

It was then decided to hold the IAS meeting at ministerial level, so Nkrumah had to give up his plans for personal talks with African leaders. As the question of a high command was not even allowed on the agenda, the best the Ghanaians could hope to get was a counsel of moderation for Lumumba. Ghanaian hopes were very much out of date, as the Russians and Guineans had already evolved plans with him for the invasion of Katanga. The countermove that Nkrumah had feared, namely, the dismissal of Lumumba, came on September 5th, after the "invasion" had failed.

SEPTEMBER–NOVEMBER: NKRUMAH AND LUMUMBA

"The President names and revokes the Prime Minister," according to the *Loi Fondamentale* and thus, on September 5th, Kasavubu removed Lumumba from office as a consequence of his attempted invasion of Katanga. There can be little question that UN officials were " 'delighted' " by Kasavubu's actions—as Miss Hoskyns quotes one of them.[84] Whether they and the Americans had encouraged him is not verifiable, though it hardly seems unlikely. In Nkrumah's mind, it was beyond doubt. Even though it was possible to argue the rights and wrongs of Kasavubu's actions purely from a point of view that best accorded with one's own interests, there was a serious legal issue complicating the more basic struggle for power.

For the next six months, Nkrumah was to argue—in letters to peers, in speeches at the United Nations, and wherever else possible—that

---

[83] Nkrumah to Lumumba, 22 August 1960, CFA-121.

[84] Hoskyns, *The Congo Since Independence*, pp. 200-01. Nkrumah cites this passage in *Challenge of the Congo*, p. 36.

Kasavubu had no more legal right to dismiss Lumumba than the Belgian monarch to dismiss the country's prime minister over a difference in policy. Crawford Young emphasizes the weakness in that argument, however, by noting that a chief of state elected by parliament cannot be compared to a hereditary monarch. "Kasavubu, as the father of Congolese nationalism, was a political figure, not just a symbol."[85] Nkrumah's use of legal argument was so extensive because, with Geoffrey Bing playing a large role in strategic planning, it happened to be one of the more effective weapons in a rather limited armory.

But the consequence for Nkrumah of the new crisis in Léopoldville was that it now became almost impossible for him to maintain his dual commitment—to Lumumba and to ONUC. The problem came to a head on September 6th when the UN, using Ghanaian troops, refused Lumumba permission to broadcast on Léopoldville radio. Nkrumah argued bitterly that while Fulbert Youlou (and the French) gave Kasavubu access to Radio Brazzaville, Lumumba was denied access to what was, potentially, one of his most powerful weapons.[86] From the point of view of the United Nations and indeed from Kasavubu's, Lumumba having been dismissed no longer counted. In any case, "the strong do what they will, and the weak what they must." Lumumba made various attempts to gain control of the broadcasting facilities, but could not break the commitment of national contingents of the UN command, least of all the Ghanaians'. According to one of Ghana's ablest officers, it was a question of *Realpolitik*; General Alexander was convinced that had Lumumba made his broadcast, passions would be inflamed, European lives would be endangered, and Belgian paratroopers might move in, to cause yet further deterioration in the situation.[87]

The Ghanaian officers, by this time, had little use for Lumumba. Kashamura writes, for example, that Colonel Ankrah (as he then was) told Lumumba that "a government which has ceased to be in command of the situation is no longer a legal government."[88] Lumumba, in turn, accused Ghana of "treachery," said Djin, and Djin told Nkrumah that "although we were responsible for making possible the independence of the Congo, since the Country became free we have been a liability to Lumumba and the Congolese."[89]

Lumumba wrote to Nkrumah demanding that Ghana's troops grant him use of the radio, and Nkrumah's reply showed that he was still

85 Crawford Young, *Politics in the Congo*, Princeton, 1965, p. 327.
86 See Nkrumah, *Challenge of the Congo*, p. 36.
87 Interview: CF-51. See also *UN*, S/4506, and *Times*, 14 September 1960.
88 Anicet Kashamura, *De Mobutu aux Colonels*, Paris, 1966, p. 149.
89 Djin to Nkrumah, 12 September 1960, quoted in Nkrumah, *Challenge of the Congo*, p. 41.

eager to maintain a dual commitment. In letters that were subsequently seized from Lumumba's person and published, to the acute embarrassment of both parties, he had tried to restrain Lumumba. Lumumba was urged to adopt "tactical action," to work with his bitterest opponents, to keep the United Nations there and finally, with respect to external affairs, "especially where the Security Council and the United Nations are concerned, leave matters to me. . . . You may rest assured that on all questions I shall mobilize the Afro-Asian bloc. . . . Turn to me whenever you are doubtful about what you should do. My brother, we have been setting the pace for quite a while now and we know how to handle the imperialists and the colonialists. The only colonialist or imperialist I trust is a dead one. If you fail, you will have only yourself to blame, and it will be because you have not been willing to face the facts."[90] Colin Legum argued that the letter represented Nkrumah's attempt to "get in on Lumumba's 'wavelength.' "[91] Since Nkrumah knew how enraged Lumumba was with him and with Ghana, and since the letter reveals a degree of vanity unusual even for Nkrumah, it might also be argued that it was Nkrumah who was not "facing the facts." Nkrumah in this period refused to listen to objective reports from Léopoldville, and Ghanaian diplomats then in the Congo said that instructions coming from him usually took little cognizance of realities in Léopoldville.[92] Nkrumah's detailed instructions for "tactical action" showed how little he understood what was happening there. Power, at this stage, was exercised by "a group of nonpolitical technicians" and almost all the Lumumbaist ministers had been removed from office.[93] Nkrumah's advice was irrelevant. Had he appreciated Lumumba's delicate position, he would less likely have committed such explosive advice to paper. In any case, the letters were found and used by the Kasavubu supporters to their own ends.

In a separate letter, he did try to answer Lumumba's specific demand, and suggested that if Ghana's troops were to be placed at his disposal, "then you and your Government must find some way to declare that in this struggle, Ghana and the Congo are one."[94] The Ghana-Congo union agreement of August 8th would have to be invoked. Nkrumah might have taken his troops out of ONUC had Lumumba made the

[90] Nkrumah to Lumumba, 12 September 1960, quoted in "Situation in the Republic of the Congo, Report of the United Nations Conciliation Committee for the Congo," UN A/4711/Add.2, 20 March 1961, pp. 7-10.

[91] Colin Legum, *Congo Disaster*, p. 152.

[92] Interview: CF-104, and CF-76.

[93] Robert L. West, "The United Nations and the Congo Crisis: Lessons of the First Year," *International Organization* (Autumn 1961).

[94] Nkrumah to Lumumba, 12 September 1960, see note 80, p. 137.

gesture Nkrumah called for,[95] but he set a very high price on this and no doubt trusted that he could thus preserve faith—and face—with Lumumba, and a role in ONUC at the same time. Lumumba was not impressed and the next day, after a brief arrest, he gave Djin an ultimatum to secure the cessation of all the Ghanaian army's activities, failing which he would be "compelled to break off diplomatic relations with Ghana."[96] However, relations were no longer his to break off and Djin acted very much like a diplomat, by his own account refusing to be excited.[97]

The quarrel ended because of Lumumba's altered position. Convinced that his cause was hopeless so long as he remained in Léopoldville, he wrote to Nkrumah on September 17th, three days after a thirty-year-old Colonel, Joseph Mobutu, had seized power, that his government had decided to move the seat of parliament and government to Stanleyville. "The Congo-Ghana Union will be immediately achieved and I shall submit the plan for Parliament's approval. Kasavubu was the obstacle in the way of this Union. The Ghana Embassy should be transferred at once to Stanleyville. . . . You will have to send me military reinforcements at Stanleyville."[98] In fact, Lumumba was living under ANC guard, his arrest prevented only by the presence of UN troops. Within several days the balance of power had swung heavily against him. Nkrumah had missed his chance and, by all accounts, Lumumba would not forgive Nkrumah in the time remaining to him.

The next step was an attempt to reconcile Kasavubu with Lumumba. Djin's own reports to Nkrumah make clear how involved Ghana was in the process of negotiation at one level, but they understandably fail to show how peripheral Ghana's role was overall. In his address to the United Nations of September 23rd, Nkrumah commented on Djin's efforts: ". . . but for the intrigues of the colonialists, a document of reconciliation . . . drafted in the presence of my Ambassador in Léopoldville and approved by both Mr. Kasavubu and Mr. Lumumba would have been signed by them. Imperialist intrigue, stark and naked, was desperately at work to prevent this being signed."[99] To the extent that Kasavubu was prepared for a reconciliation with Lumumba, it was a result of the efforts of two UN officials, Jean David and Robert Gardiner, the first of whose efforts proved embarrassing. No doubt the Americans did press Kasavubu in a contrary direction, but the salient point

---

[95] According to Richard Quarshie, in interview.

[96] Quoted in Djin to Nkrumah, 15 September 1960, in Nkrumah, *Challenge of the Congo*, pp. 52-54.

[97] *Ibid.*

[98] Lumumba to Nkrumah, 17 September 1960, CFA-123.

[99] "Osagyefo at the United Nations," Accra, 1960, p. 7.

was, as Miss Hoskyns points out, he himself became convinced that reconciliation would be more fruitful with Mobutu, an alliance through which the Katanga question could be settled.[100] By the account of a distinguished Ghanaian then in the service of the United Nations, Djin's own conversations with Kasavubu got nowhere, thanks to the language barrier, but Djin deceived himself into thinking Kasavubu accepted the terms he had proposed.[101]

Because Ghana was compromised in Kasavubu's eyes, Nkrumah had somehow to sustain Lumumba's fortunes were he to retain any influence in Léopoldville. New factors reduced Lumumba's—and Nkrumah's—chances yet further. In late September, when Djin was preparing his return to Ghana to attend his long-neglected business interests, Nkrumah sent Nathaniel Welbeck to join him, despite Welbeck's diplomatic failure in Guinea the previous year. Djin had been powerless, but he described Welbeck as "reckless."[102] Welbeck loved addressing political rallies in Ghana, and loved doing so equally in Léopoldville. In both places he did this in the hyperbolic idiom of CPP politics. But with Ghana's position in the Congo at best a delicate one, the effect was for Welbeck—and his bumbling and, in general, drunken intervention —to become the object of Congo government attacks and the subject of ONUC jokes.

Kasavubu declared Welbeck *persona non grata* as early as October 4th. Nkrumah refused to accept Kasavubu's note, insisting that Welbeck remain at his post.[103] Nkrumah had already largely failed in his attempt to balance his dual commitment and this might have been an opportunity to cut his losses, either withdrawing his forces, or withdrawing Welbeck. It would have been rational for Nkrumah to have done the latter, since Welbeck's presence was openly provocative, while Ghana's real contribution to Lumumba was what the professional diplomats at the mission could do—and were doing—in providing a channel of communication between Lumumba and his supporters.

In choosing neither alternative, he lost what he himself considered his most powerful level of influence, the presence of Ghanaian troops in Léopoldville, and lost most of his remaining influence in the UN secretariat. By late September, Kasavubu had begun demanding the withdrawal of Ghanaian troops and by October 16th, on ONUC orders, they began to leave. There was, indeed, every military justification for

---

[100] Hoskyns, *The Congo Since Independence*, pp. 221-22.
[101] Interview: CF-56.
[102] Interview: Djin, 1 February 1966.
[103] See Nkrumah, *Challenge of the Congo*, pp. 80-81. Welbeck was *chargé d'affaires*, because Nkrumah could not obtain the *agrément* for a new ambassador.

rotation, since it was hardly fair that one contingent alone should have the benefits of service in Léopoldville. Nkrumah protested loudly, using Welbeck's contrived report that European and African traders had become nervous for their own safety as a result of the Ghanaian troops' departure; but to no avail. It was obvious that the government in power would not tolerate indefinitely the presence of troops in the capital whose national representatives were openly contriving against it. Gavin Young of the *Observer* wrote that it was hardly fair that the Ghanaian troops should be forced to "suffer such an indignity. Their conduct has been almost universally praised since their arrival in Léopoldville in July. They have been smart, courteous, and well-disciplined, but they have become unwitting pawns in a political game."[104] The soldiers had their revenge five and a half years later when they deposed Nkrumah.

Other consequences flowed from Nkrumah's decision, more disastrous to his immediate objectives. While the situation in Léopoldville became increasingly tense, the credentials debate began in the United Nations (between Kasavubu's and Lumumba's representatives) in which, as will be seen, lines became clearly drawn between Ghana and the Francophone states on the one hand, and between Ghana, the United States and its allies on the other. In the middle of it, there occurred the famous "Welbeck incident," the *coup de grâce* for Ghana's Congo diplomacy. Nkrumah had refused to permit Welbeck to withdraw. For that matter, Welbeck refused to leave, even though the *persona non grata* note had become, by this time, an expulsion order. The result was an all-night gun battle between the ANC and the UN contingent guarding the Ghanaian residence. One of the most popular ANC officers, Colonel Kokolo, was killed, which, according to a Ghanaian diplomat there, further enraged the Léopoldville crowds and the ANC against Ghana.[105] Welbeck was removed by General Alexander, lucky to be alive.[106]

According to Miss Hoskyns, it was Kasavubu's victory at the United Nations that was decisive in provoking Lumumba's escape. She also claims that the United Nations might have intervened to prevent his arrest (and, thus presumably his death) but for the fact that the Ghanaian troops, who were on duty in Kasai where the arrest took place, "were highly suspect and that relations between ONUC and the ANC were at their most tense as a result of the death of Kokolo."[107] It thus seems

104 Gavin Young, "Struggle for Influence," *Observer Foreign News Service*, 29 September 1960.
105 Interview: CF-104. See also "The Situation in the Republic of the Congo," *UN* A/4576, and A/4587/Add.1, 26 November 1960.
106 See Alexander's account of this in *African Tightrope*, p. 56.
107 Hoskyns, *The Congo Since Independence*, p. 273.

clear that Nkrumah's decision not to withdraw Welbeck had the gravest consequences. If it is accepted that an eventual comeback by Lumumba was still possible,[108] then it follows that Ghanaian diplomacy—or Nkrumah's failure to use diplomacy—was the difference between a situation in which Lumumba's fortunes could be improved, and the one in which it was possible for his opponents in Léopoldville to deliver him into the hands of Moise Tshombe and Godefroid Munongo. As it was, the Ghanaian mission closed two weeks later, and the professional diplomats left too, although diplomatic relations were never severed. In any case, with Lumumba under arrest, the situation in Léopoldville was hopeless for his supporters.

Yet Ghana had not been consigned to helplessness in this last phase. Following Lumumba's dismissal, it stood, along with the U.A.R., in an important symbolic role, maintaining a center of Lumumbaist strength—guarded by the United Nations—in the middle of the opponents' capital, and its diplomats might have continued to work quietly on Lumumba's behalf. Nkrumah failed throughout to realize that Ghana could not be involved in the real struggle for mastery in the Congo that occurred at the level of the great powers. In the end, Ghana's record amounted to "a sorry farce," in the words of a respected diplomat then in Léopoldville.[109] It was an unhappy finish to an episode that had begun in high hopes.

Most Ghanaians argue that the Congo operation evoked little interest among average Ghanaians, so distant a scene of action was it. But this was in spite of massive governmental propaganda. The posters on every corner, the constant campaigns for cigarettes and other comforts that soldiers away from home desire, were constant reminders of Ghana's involvement. The front page of the *Evening News* bore these headlines on one day:

OUR DETRACTORS ARE DOOMED IN THE BAR OF HISTORY

FORWARD TO A UNITED STATES OF AFRICA

DOWN WITH BELGIAN TREACHERY AND BETRAYAL

WOMEN ARISE[110]

The opposition wanted more attention paid to problems at home, instead of "foreign adventurism." Joe Appiah thought Ghana should *"festina lente,"* and another asked who would "bell the cat" of im-

---

[108] See *ibid.*, pp. 304-06. This is a contentious point, but several of the most senior UN officials dealing with the Congo did accept this, and favored it.
[109] Interview: CF-27.   [110] 19 July 1960.

perialism,[111] thus placing themselves in an unheroic posture. The CPP had its peace wing too,[112] but it did not counteract the war cries of the new radicals, best personified in Kweku Boateng, minister for information and broadcasting:

> When one recalls the heroic struggle of our President . . . and ponders upon the fact that this has led to the independence of the Congolese, and in turn, witnesses the dastardly assault upon it, it becomes clear that there is . . . only one solution to halt this imperialist counter-revolution, and that is the solution of war. . . . We must chase; we must harass, and we must fight these imperialists out of every street, hole and corner in the Congo! This is the surest way to consolidate . . . our hard-won independence.[113]

The North Koreans had repelled imperialist aggression, as the Egyptians had done at Suez. Now it was Ghana's turn to show similar courage and fortitude: "this implies the complete mobilization of all our forces." When the opposition accused Nkrumah of bluffing in asking for the mobilization of the armed forces, Krobo Edusei offered to lead the army into Katanga himself "and to fight until Tshombe and all his puppet ministers are . . . detained in the James Fort Prison."[114]

This debate was a charade, a substitute, perhaps, for an invasion Nkrumah wanted to lead. But it was in times of domestic crisis that the radicals made their gains, and thus was important. A convinced radical like Boateng, the minister of the interior, sincerely believed the sentiments he expressed, but the crisis served also as a convenient cover for imposing still stricter domestic laws. On August 24th, a new executive instrument came into effect which gave the government full powers of press censorship.

AFRICA DIVIDED

The African scene was changing very rapidly, not in the Congo alone. In a period of four months twelve territories had become independent, which left Ghana surrounded by potentially hostile sovereign states. Closely linked to Paris, they were to take positions on both the Congo and Algerian questions which would cause bitterness and division within the existing African camp at the United Nations. Ghana faced obstacles which it had not anticipated. It would have to break through its geographic isolation before it could organize any sort of union, and it had

[111] *Debates*, 9 August 1960, p. 685.
[112] See remarks of Prince Yao Boateng, *ibid.*, 19 July 1960, pp. 55-57.
[113] *Ibid.*, 9 August 1960, p. 697.
[114] *Ibid.*, 10 August 1960, p. 733.

to find a means of coping with the new challenge to African unity at the United Nations.

The Search for Allies. Nkrumah was developing the first true strategy in his Africa policy. By August 8th, he had two union agreements on paper, with the Congo and Guinea, and a third proferred to Togo. He had paid very little attention to the Mali Federation which became independent in June, for he seems to have considered it an "imperialist creation"; "if Modibo Keita were a true nationalist he would opt out of the federation in time," or so one official later described Nkrumah's contemporary thoughts.[115] The difficulties between the Senegalese and Soudanese sections of the federation were well known by late July, and so Nkrumah sent the deputy minister, Puplampu, with the resident minister in Conakry, Stephen Dzirasa, and Richard Quarshie, to Dakar for talks with Keita. By mid-August the federation was dead. The Soudanese were suffering a traumatic shock jolting them far to the left; their belief that the French were behind the breakup only confirmed Nkrumah's suspicions. Now, the courting began in earnest.

The Soudanese still clung to the broken federation, kept to its full name, and declared Bamako its provisional capital. Both its leaders and Senegal's wanted Ghanaian support. Keita visited Accra in early September and got precisely what he sought: "They reaffirmed their recognition of the Mali Federation and pledged their full support for its continued existence." The communiqué also recorded the two leaders' support of a political union of Africa; and Ghana promised financial aid.[116] Three days later Gabriel d'Arboussier headed a Senegalese mission to Accra, but the communiqué only noted Senegal's insistence on the "irrevocable nature of the decision" in the breakup, and the two parties together merely recognized "the absolute necessity for an African community."[117] Nkrumah had his man: Modibo Keita was a radical idealist with the highest regard for Nkrumah.

In late October, Nkrumah followed up his meeting with Keita, sending two ministers to Bamako. Following a week of discussions they agreed that a commercial agreement would be formulated, and that Nkrumah would visit Mali.[118] By early November, Mali's ambassador, Oumar Sow, had arrived, and it had already been arranged that each state

---

[115] Interview: Richard Quarshie.

[116] "Communiqué," P.R. #205/60, 9 September 1960. For background, see William Foltz's excellent study, *From French West Africa to the Mali Federation*, New Haven, 1965.

[117] P.R. #208/60, 12 September 1960.

[118] "Ghana Mission to Mali," P.R. #375, 21 October 1960.

would provide chancery and residence for the emissary accredited to it, saving foreign currency on both sides.[119]

Nkrumah then began planning his visit on a grand scale. The ministry, well aware of the limits imposed by the absence of guest facilities in Bamako, tried to limit the delegation to twenty (wrote Ako Adjei), but even that number was too small for Nkrumah.[120] Though shocked by the size of the retinue, the Malians were still prepared to give Nkrumah "a grandiose welcome."[121] *l'Essor,* the Malian party's newspaper, commented that it was Ghana who had gone to Guinea's rescue after the 1958 referendum, it was Ghana who had been one of the first to support the legal government in the Congo, and it was President Nkrumah who, on the morrow of the breakup of the Mali Federation, had spontaneously offered aid to their country. "Ces gestes sont de ceux que le Mali n'a pas l'habitude d'oublier."[122]

Nkrumah, drawing too many conclusions from the warmth of the reception, announced unilaterally on the first day that Ghana and Mali would have a common parliament, "while Bamako has preferred to keep its silence," wrote Samuel Doambo, a well-informed correspondent of *Afrique Action.*[123] Nkrumah had hoped for a *fait accompli* and once again he played his hand badly: "One does not force friendship in Africa."[124] *l'Essor* wrote nothing of the proposal, and the communiqué issued merely advocated political unity in its most general sense. Only three months earlier the Malians had seen another union of theirs broken: but the sympathy of most Francophone states with Senegal, Mali's ideological sympathies with Ghana on the great issues of the moment, and its economic need, were all to save Nkrumah.

There was competition for Mali, however. Houphouet had also gone to Keita's aid immediately following the federation's breakup, and hoped to bring Mali into his sphere, as well as to pay off old debts to his and Keita's common adversary, Léopold Senghor. Nkrumah's new strategy was to construct bilateral unions with every state possible, and the unlikely yet compelling solution he found was to try to bring the Ivory Coast into his own orbit by the new method, union. He took the first step to improve relations with Abidjan on August 7th, when he sent a large delegation to their independence celebrations. He invited Houphouet to Accra. At the end of August, Houphouet sent a delegation to Accra to see whether Nkrumah was genuinely prepared to discuss cooperation, and he agreed to meet with Nkrumah although not in Accra.

[119] Ako Adjei to Nkrumah, 14 November 1960, CFA-36.
[120] Ako Adjei to Nkrumah, 14 November 1960, CFA-36.
[121] *l'Essor,* 14 November 1960. [122] *Ibid.*
[123] *Afrique Action,* 26 December 1960. [124] *Ibid.*

On September 19th they met in Half-Assine, Nkrumah's birthplace, nearly equidistant from the two capitals. Ivoirien and Ghanaian accounts of the meeting do not conflict on important points. Nkrumah congratulated Houphouet on his independence, and then pointed out that the two states were the richest and most advanced of West Africa. "If they co-operated and joined forces they could divide up spheres of influence and together rule Africa. Houphouet replied that he was most eager to co-operate with Nkrumah, but to serve, not to rule, Africa."[125] Incredibly, Nkrumah had a written union agreement with him, to produce at the appropriate moment; but Houphouet so dominated this most bizarre meeting of the period, and stressed "co-operation" so consistently, that Nkrumah was never able even to mention the document.[126] The Ivory Coast became a member of the United Nations on the next day, and soon began opposing Ghana on numerous critical issues.

Some fluidity still remained in the West African scene through October. Sékou Touré made several overtures to Houphouet, and Modibo Keita attempted to keep all doors open, even with France. Almost unnoticed, Houphouet called together the other newly independent Francophone states, primarily to find a common position on the Algerian question. Up to the eve of the meeting it had been thought that Touré would send a representative; he did not, but Keita sent an observer.[127] The delegates found agreement not only on the question of Algeria, but—more ominous for African unity at the United Nations—on the Congo as well.

At a later date Quaison-Sackey wrote that these Francophone states "had been fully schooled by France about the activities of Ghana, Guinea, Morocco, and U.A.R., and they had come [to the United Nations] prepared to thwart us at every turn. Their opportunity came with the issue of the seating of the Kasavubu delegation. For the first time there was a great schism."[128] When two rival delegations arrived claiming the Congo's seat in New York, the radical states quite sensibly did not want the question of credentials voted on. But in November, apparently through the miscalculation of Sékou Touré ("he didn't understand how the UN operated," Quaison-Sackey commented)[129] the issue was forced. The Ghanaian delegation, after doing everything in its power to delay a vote, did what it could to effect a favorable outcome. In the process, all the mounting resentment against the Ghanaians burst forth in the speeches of the Abidjan bloc. When Quaison-Sackey said that "My true

125 Interviews: CF-15, 95, 113.   126 Interviews: CF-95, 115.
127 William Zartman, *International Relations in the New Africa*, p. 44.
128 Quaison-Sackey to Ako Adjei, March 1962, CFA-53.
129 Interview: Quaison-Sackey.

African blood boils in me at the prospect of the Congo's being dominated by Colonial Powers again, after all the efforts we have put in to
assure it of its complete independence," the Camerounian representative suggested that his comments were bordering on contempt . . . "we
are Africans just as much as Ghanaians and we shall not allow anyone
either to place the Congo under the trusteeship of any State whatever or
to try to carry on there the intrigues which certain people are busy
working in these corridors."[130] When the Welbeck incident erupted in
the middle of the debate, these same delegates were also quick to blame
Ghana for the loss of Tunisian and Congolese lives.

As a result of setbacks at the United Nations and in the Congo itself,
Nkrumah threw another ball up in the air. On November 21st, he wrote
Nasser and Touré that it was time to form a high command of African
forces and on November 26th he formally proposed it to all states which
had participated in the 1958 IAS conference, and to Guinea and Mali.[131]
Nigeria was not included, ostensibly because of its defense-training agreement with Britain (which differed from Ghana's only in that it granted
Britain certain over-flying and air-staging facilities). Guinea, for its part,
was less than enthusiastic. According to Ambassador Achkar Marof,
their distrust of Ghana's military establishment went too deep.[132] Nor
was Nasser quick to take up Nkrumah's proposals, probably for the
same reasons.

Nkrumah's first opportunity to give his proposal any momentum was
the visit of Emperor Haile Selassie, perhaps the one African head of
state he consistently admired during his nine years of power. The Emperor's visit was a great occasion for Ghana, but Nkrumah again misconstrued the possibilities of cooperation. What the Emperor wanted—
and what he was to succeed in getting after three more years of effort—
was an institutional framework for the IAS, as in the "Organisation of
American States, and the Arab League" (as he said in an address) which
was just what Nkrumah did not want. They only agreed to build a "Union
of African States," each conceiving the proposal in his own way, and
"to give urgent consideration" to the idea of a high command.[133] The
Emperor's next stop was Monrovia where, in the company of William
Shadrach Tubman, he clarified his thoughts. He denied that he had
agreed to do anything more than study Nkrumah's proposals and,

[130] *UNGA*, 18 November 1960, 918th meeting, pp. 26-29.
[131] See Nkrumah, *Challenge of the Congo*, London, 1967, p. 86.
[132] Interview: Amb. Achkar Marof, September 1965.
[133] "Toast Delivered by His Imperial Majesty," in "Visit to Ghana, by H.I.M. Haile
Selassie, December 1st-5th, 1960," Accra, 1960, p. 13; *Ghanaian Times*, 7 December
1960.

reportedly, added that "We believe that to sacrifice one's self for one's country is more important than to sacrifice one's country for one's self."[134]

By suggesting that a summit meeting be convened to study Nkrumah's plan, the Emperor was delaying action. Nkrumah wrote Touré that the Emperor had reacted favorably to the high command—as Nkrumah no doubt believed he had done—but "events are moving so fast in Africa and the situation in the Congo is deteriorating so rapidly that if we do not act now and spend time on sophisticated niceties of procedure, we may be overtaken by events."[135] Thus it became imperative to rebuild the Ghana-Guinea Union and, by adding Mali, to give momentum to his proposals of a high command and an organic union of African states. The choice, posed frequently, was between bringing a large group of states along slowly, or giving the appearance of speed with a few. Nkrumah always preferred the latter option—perhaps because he would otherwise be obligated to defer to colleagues like Tubman, who once again had seemingly thwarted his hopes.

The Ghana-Guinea-Mali Union. While the Emperor was visiting Ghana, Keita and Touré met for the first time since the *éclatement* of the Mali Federation and agreed to work toward unity, and to strengthen their ties with Accra. Such wounds as had existed between Bamako and Conakry were healed. But it was only as a result of the worsened Congo situation, Houphouet's second conference in Brazzaville on December 16th (which Mali did not attend), and Mohammed V's invitation for a conference in Rabat that Nkrumah was able to bring the three states together in a formal union.

On December 23rd, Nkrumah and Keita went to Conakry where, with Touré, they declared their states united. It looked to some as if Mali had been added to the Ghana-Guinea union. A whole new union had in reality been declared since, except at the United Nations, relations between Accra and Conakry could hardly be worse than they were throughout the autumn of 1960. Why did Modibo Keita and Sékou Touré now go along with Nkrumah? A Western diplomat in Bamako at the time described it as the high-point of Ghana-Guinea-Mali relations; it was the Malians' first international meeting, to which they went as "babes in the woods." Nkrumah was the outside force necessary to keep the other two together, and Touré was simply shamed into going along with Nkrumah because of the overriding importance of African unity. "The meeting brought together the strands of several movements;

---

[134] *West Africa*, 10 December 1960. See also *Daily Telegraph*, 9 December 1960.
[135] Nkrumah to Sékou Touré, 14 December 1960, CFA-126.

it was a psychological coming-together at a critical time. The president returned to Bamako to tell me he accepted the declaration for exactly what it said. In Africa, "la parole est créatrice."[136]

Nkrumah's past record with unions made success with this new one imperative. The beginning was not promising. According to Ako Adjei, Congo policy was first discussed on Christmas eve at the founding meeting. Their disagreements were profound. When Nkrumah came to Conakry a week later to take them on to the Casablanca conference, they could only agree, ominously, that if a majority at Casablanca favored withdrawal of troops from ONUC, Nkrumah would withdraw the Ghanaian contingent.[137] The states did favor withdrawal, but he did not withdraw his troops.

Shortly after the Casablanca meeting of heads of state, ministers of the three states came to Accra to study "political union, a common bank, and a common currency." Although it was scheduled for January 9th, the Guineans did not arrive until the 13th; the Malians, having greater needs, arrived on January 5th. Most decisions were postponed in hopes that agreement could be reached at a meeting of experts planned for April. The Guineans still wanted a common currency, but with Gbedemah as minister of finance, this was out of the question. The Malians, on the other hand, at least arranged help from Ghana on transport and financial problems and examined the possibilities of links with Upper Volta in order to give contiguity to their relationship with Ghana.[138]

By April, several events had further weakened residual trust between Ghana and Guinea. Touré, sensitive to questions of protocol, counted on Nkrumah's presence at his inauguration in late January, owed to him as a reciprocal gesture. When the Ghanaian plane arrived, Touré was on the tarmac but it was Botsio not Nkrumah who led the delegation. Touré never forgave Nkrumah.[139] In not going to Conakry, Nkrumah had probably acted on the advice of a new counselor, Habib Niang, a Senegalese Marxist who came to Ghana after the breakup of the Mali Federation. Niang, it was believed in Accra, had absconded with state funds in Guinea during a period of residence there. He thus had little interest in seeing Ghana's links with Guinea grow stronger, and he quickly gained a position of influence in Flagstaff House.[140] Tubman, eager to

<hr />

[136] Interview: CF-69, 18 November 1965. The citation in French is in Germaine Dieterlen, *Essai sur la Religion Bambara.*

[137] Interview: Ako Adjei.

[138] "Committee to Study Political Union of Ghana, Guinea, and Mali," P.R. #15/61, 7 January 1961.

[139] Interview: Dzirasa, resident minister in Conakry at the time.

[140] Interviews: CF-24, 85, 37.

take advantage of Touré's ill-will toward Nkrumah, immediately thereafter interested him in a new movement for African reconciliation, which
was to culminate in Monrovia in May 1961, with the formation of the
Monrovia Group.[141]

Nkrumah had more success in his relations with Mali during the first
half of 1961, in spite of the diplomatic appointment he had made. Salifu
Yakubu, an M.P. and ex-policeman, became Ghana's resident minister
in Bamako; he was uneducated and stupid, and in any event spent much
of his time in Tamale (in northern Ghana), a fact his government did
not know.

The new union had of course brought much attention to Ghana from
without, and it is noteworthy that at first it generated much excitement
within the foreign and civil services. One of the more radical diplomats
thought that it was "so dynamic in potential that it would create its own
conditions for take-off";[142] a more sober view was that of senior officials
in Flagstaff House, who wanted the union to succeed and be seen to succeed, as a federation of more manageable proportions than Nkrumah's
continental design.[143]

Casablanca. It is not clear whether Nkrumah was at first eager to attend
King Mohammed V's conference planned for Rabat in early January. By
one account, he saw it as a "regional" conference, in contrast to the
Ghana-Guinea-Mali union which he envisaged as a nucleus of an all-
Africa Union.[144] Others said he was eager to go in order to convince his
colleagues to maintain their troops in ONUC, the issue for which the
conference was ostensibly called. The King, in any event, had carefully
cultivated Nkrumah's friendship, and thought that Ghana's position on
Mauritania, to which Morocco had laid a claim, was less obdurate than
that of virtually all the other black African states.[145]

By the time of the conference, Nkrumah had to go—to prevent
ONUC's imminent disintegration. As Nkrumah's decision not to withdraw from the UN command was one of the most important he ever
made, and as this issue dominated the Casablanca conference, it is worth-
while summarizing at this point Ghanaian interests in the Congo. At the
end of 1960, Antoine Gizenga established a government in Lumumba's
name in Stanleyville; Nkrumah had too much respect for the efficacy of
Western power to believe that this regime could be sustained without
engendering increased Western assistance to Léopoldville and Katanga.
Hence the only institutional framework within which a return to legal-

---

141 Interview: Amb. George F. Sherman, Liberia/Accra.
142 Interview: CF-7.   143 Interview: CF-85.
144 Interview: CF-104.   145 Interview: Moroccan Embassy, CF-58A.

ity—and a position of influence for Nkrumah—could be realized was ONUC and the United Nations itself. Nkrumah well knew the map of Africa, and the Congo's strategic position. "He had made an enormous investment in a decent outcome, and the only way he could get a return was to keep the troops in, in hopes that their mission would succeed, preserving a position of influence for himself. He knew that if we withdrew, non-Africans with different interests would replace us," commented a Ghanaian diplomat.[146] Thus Nkrumah cabled the prime minister of Ceylon that the "UN efforts should not be paralysed. . . . As long as our troops continue to serve . . . I am sure that our combined efforts would help to retrieve the situation."[147] Were they withdrawn, he said in a broadcast, there would also be the "imminent risk of civil war, of the Spanish type."[148]

All his advisers pressed him to maintain the commitment. General Alexander stressed that only by keeping them in could he preserve any influence in the United Nations, and hinted that his importance would increase as others withdrew.[149] Moderates like Botsio and Gbedemah also felt strongly about Ghana's commitment and were supported by such leading civil servants as Enoch Okoh and Michael Dei-Anang. There was also the influence of Hammarskjold himself, who had gone out of his way to be courteous to Nkrumah despite their differences, and whom Nkrumah liked.[150] Perhaps the most important factor was that most of the Ghanaian troops were without experience in combat, and Nkrumah considered the Congo operation excellent training for them.[151]

In sum, Nkrumah felt a position of influence in the Congo essential to his pan-African plans. Hence his emissaries had intervened in the autumn to restore Lumumba to power. Their failure earned Ghana the opprobrium of the moderate states and of the Kasavubu/Mobutu regime. But the only means to restore "legality" was through ONUC, which for the moment supported Kasavubu and Mobutu. Once Lumumba's government had disintegrated and a new one had been established in Stanleyville, Nkrumah was not prepared to sacrifice his own plans on the altar of Lumumba's memory. On various occasions Nkrumah had refused to do Lumumba's bidding, and from the first Lumumba had been expendable in terms of his own strategy.

For reasons already discussed, Nkrumah's influence on the UN sec-

---

[146] Interview: CF-104.
[147] Nkrumah to Mrs. Bandaranaike, 10 December 1960, P.R. #480, 10 December 1960.
[148] "The Congo Situation," transcript of broadcast, 15 December 1960, Accra, 1960.
[149] Interview: Maj. Gen. H. T. Alexander, 7 June 1965, 17 February 1967.
[150] According to Mr. Quaison-Sackey, interview.
[151] This point was emphasized by all interviewed on the Congo question.

retariat had been minimal up to this point. No doubt its officials considered Nkrumah's intermittent threat to withdraw Ghana's forces as bluff. They may even have been encouraged to think that—by Ghanaians.[152] However much a foreign policy is dominated by a national leader, it cannot be understood solely in terms of his intentions, particularly when he holds views generally distinct from those of his diplomats and advisers.

By early 1961 ONUC faced a grave threat. According to Miss Hoskyns, "Hammarskjold was now convinced that if the United Nations were not given some additional powers, the force would have to be withdrawn."[153] According to British officers in the Ghanaian army, ONUC would have collapsed had Ghana withdrawn at this point.[154] The Egyptian and Guinean withdrawal was not serious, as these soldiers were largely ineffective. The Moroccan withdrawal was disastrous, and in combination with a Ghanaian withdrawal would have been fatal. Ghana's soldiers had been among the best, and it would have been impossible to maintain order in large parts of the Congo without them. Thus Ghana and Nkrumah were able to play an important role for the first time since early July 1960.

It follows that Nkrumah had to oppose Nasser's and Touré's efforts at Casablanca to elicit support for a general withdrawal from ONUC. Nasser and Nkrumah, in particular, argued long and hard and, from at least one point of view, Nkrumah was the victor. A lengthy prescription was given to the United Nations but, on Nkrumah's insistence, no time limit was inscribed within which the conditions were to be fulfilled.[155] As *quid pro quo*, Nkrumah agreed that Ghana would serve as a channel for Eastern arms going to Stanleyville, conditions permitting.[156] Nkrumah also had no choice but to subscribe to Nasser's view of Israel, and Moroccan views on Mauritania, and to grant *de jure* recognition to the Algerian provisional government.

Even more important to Nkrumah, he pressed "union" and met greater success at a conference of African states than ever before. True, the Casablanca charter called for what could only be seen as functional cooperation (despite Nkrumah's interpretation).[157] It was still a great step forward, and Nkrumah considered it "the most important result of the conference."[158] Indeed, the next six years must be seen as an ebbing of this strong pan-African tide, for never again did a group of states sub-

---

152 Interview: UN Secretariat, CF-109A, September 1965.
153 Catherine Hoskyns, *The Congo Since Independence*, p. 306.
154 Interview: CF-8.
155 See Nkrumah, *Challenge of the Congo*, pp. 104-08.
156 Interviews: CF-8, 104, 109.
157 See Nkrumah, *Challenge of the Congo*, p. 106. Also interview: Dzirasa.
158 *Ibid.*

scribe simultaneously to an assembly of representatives, a common market, and a high command. It is no wonder that during Africa's ensuing search for unity Nkrumah was reluctant to abandon the Casablanca charter.

Still, the rewards that Nkrumah and his large and competent delegation had won have to be measured against the limitations Casablanca membership imposed on Ghanaian policy. It was easy enough to accord higher status to the new Algerian envoy (who replaced Franz Fanon) so that he was now to be treated by Ghana "as an Ambassador for all purposes."[159] But there were several more serious consequences. It was appreciated in Accra that the two key members of the group were the U.A.R. and Ghana, as the only members of radical outlook who also possessed the means of implementing common designs. Thus occurred the sacrifice of the special relationship between Israel and Ghana—which Ambassador Avriel had foreseen.[160] Between independence and 1960, Ghana's imports from Israel had increased twelvefold to £810,000, while as late as 1959 Ghana had bought only £400 of Egyptian goods. Now, Ghana sought to replace Israeli products with Egyptian: after discussions of the high command began in mid-1960, Ghana switched a £120,000 order of cement from Israel to the U.A.R., and by 1962 Ghana was buying £315,000-worth of Egyptian goods. When Ako Adjei went to Cairo for discussions on the Casablanca charter, he noted that Ghana had now recognized Israel's imperialistic nature;[161] Madame Fathia Nkrumah inaugurated a new U.A.R.-Ghana air service. Officials in the Israeli foreign service office feared that they had lost much of what they had gained in sub-Saharan Africa,[162] when in fact all they had lost was a psychological position. They had long since gained their political objectives in Africa.

Ghana had, in fact, too many ties with Israel for the relationship to be altered at every level; nor were Israel's friends in Ghana prepared to stand by silently as political links weakened. Botsio, whose influence was now declining, gave an almost lyrical tribute to Israel at an Israeli trade fair in Accra in mid-January, which the Egyptians protested.[163] Nkrumah, nonetheless, made an informal visit to the fair eleven days later, but this was of much less importance than his formal reaffirmation, after Botsio's speech, that Ghana stood by the Casablanca resolution.[164]

[159] Ako Adjei to Michael Dei-Anang, 2 February 1961, CFA-128.
[160] See supra, p. 50.
[161] *La Bourse Egyptienne*, 25 January 1961.
[162] Interview: CF-104A.
[163] "Speech at the Opening of the Israeli Exhibition by Honourable Kojo Botsio, at Accra, 17 January 1961," P.R. #62/61, 17 January 1961.
[164] See "Press Reports Concerning Casablanca Resolutions," P.R. #78/61, 18 Janu-

Nkrumah wished cooperation in the "Joint African High Command" that Casablanca had approved at his urging, not merely for the crisis of that day, but for the future as well. Yet from the outset, the Egyptians were less ardent about establishing it. For one thing, they were disengaging from Orientale province, apparently permitting Gizenga's forces to fill the vacuum. They also wanted General Alexander removed before cooperation got underway on long-range planning: Egyptians and Ghanaians differed in their view of British generals. The U.A.R. minister for war did, however, come to Accra in early February while Ako Adjei was having talks simultaneously in Cairo. Then, after learning of Lumumba's death, Nkrumah called an emergency foreign ministers' meeting in the Casablanca cadre, which underlined Ghana's radical aspirations. Fawzi and five others came from Cairo, as much for consultation with Accra as for the meeting. The other states attended in a lower key, making the bipolar nature of Casablanca all the more apparent. The Guineans arrived on the eve of the last day and, being at the apogee of their radicalism, refused to sign the communiqué.[165]

The communiqué showed Ghana still refusing to sacrifice either line of its Congo policy; so Casablanca could have little effect. The United Nations was to be required to work through Gizenga's regime on the one hand, but ONUC was to be regrouped, not withdrawn.[166] It was not a serious proposition. Ghana's position on the UN command was as adamant as at Casablanca. In late March, Geoffrey Bing, for one, noted the continued individuality of Ghana's policy: "The Soviet Union's policy is in many ways unrealistic in that they are pressing at the same time for the removal of the Belgians, the punishment of the murderers of Lumumba and the withdrawal of the UN forces within one month . . . [do] we need to dissociate ourselves more positively from their policy on UN troops?"[167] Bing's question was not explicitly answered, but the policy stayed the same, even after the disheartening April massacre of forty Ghanaian soldiers at Port Franqui.[168]

Membership in the Casablanca Group, of course, necessarily involved recognizing the Gizenga regime in Stanleyville, which Ghana did on February 15th, following the announcement of Lumumba's death. But as Alexander continued to point out, it was impossible to combine mili-

---

ary 1961. See the Egyptian view on the Casablanca declarations vis-à-vis sub-Saharan African states, in "Casablanca Conference, January 1961," Cairo, 1961, p. 4. See also *Daily Graphic*, 30 January 1961, for reports of Nkrumah's visit to the Fair.

[165] See *Daily Graphic*, 20 February 1961.

[166] See the communiqué, in Colin Legum, *Pan-Africanism*, London, 1965, p. 210.

[167] Bing to Nkrumah, 24 March 1961, CFA-4.

[168] See Nkrumah, *Challenge of the Congo*, pp. 156-71 regarding the Port Franqui tragedy.

tary aid to Stanleyville with continued support of ONUC.[169] Yet Ghana had agreed at Casablanca to receive secret arms shipments from Russia and Czechoslovakia—which began arriving in late March. Nkrumah sent A. K. Barden and a trusted military officer on a mission to Stanleyville on February 23rd, and they returned in early March recommending large-scale assistance.[170] In late April, Nkrumah tried to have the arms flown in to Stanleyville and asked the Sudanese government for use of staging facilities on the grounds that the supplies were for support of the Ghanaian contingent in Kasai. The Sudanese knew Kasai could not be supplied from Stanleyville and that, in any case, the route to Kasai did not lie through Khartoum. Alexander, to be safe, alerted the British military attaché in Accra, who in turn asked the Sudanese government to turn down the request. In the end, Ghana sent nothing but money to Stanleyville.[171]

Nkrumah did appoint an envoy to Stanleyville, though not until April (and then only following Mali's lead), a Ghanaian who had resided in the Congo, whom Djin assisted in establishing an office. Gizenga, for his part, appointed Antoine Kiwewe, a former Lumumba minister, as ambassador to Ghana, Guinea, and Mali, but he only presented his credentials on the eve of the formation of the new, legitimate government in Léopoldville, and, in any case, he chose to reside in Bamako. Indeed, the Ghanaians—particularly Nkrumah—had never placed great faith in Gizenga and were in an unpleasant position. Step by step, Ghana had been pushed into a corner shared only by Communist and left-wing radical states. They had lost the confidence of the moderate states and of the West, but were unwilling to let their policy, except on symbolic issues, be determined by their Casablanca partners.

THE DEATH OF LUMUMBA

Lumumba's death, announced on February 13th was a watershed in Ghana's foreign policy and in Nkrumah's thinking. As such, it was the prelude to the shift of policy that reached its climax during Nkrumah's 1961 tour of the Soviet Union. Nkrumah had reason to feel bitter. Lumumba had invited Ghanaian troops before requesting UN assistance; Nkrumah had told the secretary-general that order could be restored within a week, had Ghana received maximum cooperation. In September, leading Western statesmen had praised him for his Congo policy, but by the end of the year the West and the Francophone African states held Ghana responsible for some of the most flagrant interference that

---

[169] Interviews: Maj. Gen. H. T. Alexander, 17 February 1967, CF-85.
[170] Interview: CF-104, and see Nkrumah, *Challenge of the Congo*, p. 153.
[171] Interview: CF-104, 8. See also Hoskyns, *The Congo Since Independence*, p. 292.

the Congo experienced, despite the fact that Nkrumah had designed his policy to prevent great power interference in the Congo. The charge rang true in all directions, particularly if the measure were normal international conduct. It is easy to understand Ghana's feelings about Western interference, and Nkrumah's own disappointment. Historians in the future might well see Nkrumah's policy primarily as a pioneering, if inept, attempt to bring Africa into the international system as a region capable of settling its own crises without external interference.

Nkrumah's rejoinder to his critics foreshadowed an intensified policy of interference for the whole continent. "How can Ghana pursue an isolationist policy [i.e., of nonintervention] in African affairs, when she is committed to a policy of African Unity?"[172] No more impressive was his continuing attempt to clothe his policy with a legal dress. When used as a basis for judgment in an anarchic situation, law is frequently a function of power, something Nkrumah knew well in Ghana's domestic affairs. And, in the Congo, it was something that could be argued both ways. He had lacked—and Lumumba knew it—sufficient power to affect the Congo situation more than marginally. He had failed to prevent radical states from withdrawing their troops following the Casablanca conference, and thus his continued importance varied directly with the importance his ONUC contingent was felt to have in New York.

He had been successful, in conjunction with the other Casablanca states, in maintaining sufficient pressure on the secretariat and on the Western powers so that when events favored a new course the Casablanca position was still a possible alternative course of action. In the wake of Lumumba's murder, new Security Council resolutions were passed that, in fact, accepted many of the Casablanca conference's demands. Yet it must be emphasized that if this pressure were a necessary precondition to successes in the Security Council, and if this had prevented some "easier compromise"[173] from being agreed upon, it had not been sufficient cause for the passage of a new mandate for ONUC. The Americans were prepared to support the resolutions because Lumumba was dead and because the Stanleyville regime was expanding at a rapid rate. From their point of view, it was necessary to counteract this movement—for cold-war reasons.

Miss Hoskyns has argued that the secretary-general's actions had tended to favor the West throughout; on the other hand, Hammarskjold obtained his own objective, as Professor Claude has argued, namely, the restriction of the cold-war arena. This had given his policies such

---

[172] "The Congo Situation," transcript of broadcast, 15 December 1960, Accra, 1960.
[173] Catherine Hoskyns to the author, n.d.

success as they had had.[174] Here, however, was the dividing line between Ghanaian and great power Congo policy. As Nkrumah said to the General Assembly in March, the UN objectives were beneficial and desirable, but they were "not essentially African objectives." Rather, they were "aimed at halting the cold war by achieving a compromise between the great powers and they reflect, in all their imperfections, the struggle of the great powers over issues which do not affect the Congo or Africa." What was at stake was "African unity, peace and security."[175] What Nkrumah wanted was a recognition of *African* paramountcy in ONUC, a precedent for which existed in the American position in the Korean War. But Nkrumah obviously could not get the privileged position in the command that he sought for Africa—and himself. Africa was not yet united: on the contrary, it was more divided than ever.

Though several of his goals were accomplished with the passage of the February and April Security Council resolutions, his vital interest was lost with the end of even the appearance of his influence in Léopoldville. It is not correct, therefore, to say that a new and more conciliatory American Congo policy designed by President Kennedy brought warmth into Ghanaian-American relations. As an American diplomat pointed out, Nkrumah was hardly so unintelligent as to fail to see that the new American policy, for all its support of a new command, and its warm reception in the Afro-Asian world, completely denied him the Congo.[176]

Because Africa was not yet strong enough to impose its own solutions on its own problems, Nkrumah accelerated his efforts to unite it. The institutions and resources would have to be developed, he concluded. Firstly, he put renewed emphasis on the need for an African ideology. In the presence of the Soviet Union's president (and only several days after Lumumba's death was announced), Nkrumah laid the cornerstone of the Kwame Nkrumah Institute of Ideology, at Winneba. He lamented the dearth of ideological education among the CPP stalwarts who, up to that point, had been in "death-grips with imperialism and colonialism, and it was a grim fight every inch of the way." Now there was time for such education, and it would not be confined to Ghanaians:

> . . . from my days in London up to the present, I have never once
> stopped shouting to all Africans about African unity. The sad episode
> in the Congo more than justifies my fears about the unwisdom to stand
> alone. . . . [But now,] I see before my mind's eye a great monolithic

[174] Inis Claude, *Swords into Plowshares*, New York, 1964, p. 291. See also Inis Claude, "The United Nations and the Use of Force," *International Conciliation*, No. 532 (March 1961).

[175] "Osagyefo at the United Nations," Accra, 1961, p. 16.

[176] Interview: CF-97, 26 October 1967.

party growing up [out of this Institute] . . . united and strong, spreading its protective wings over the whole of Africa—from Algiers in the north to Cape Town in the south; from Cape Guardafui in the east to Dakar in the west.[177]

Secondly, in seeking to exorcise the imperialists from Africa, following the Congo debacle, he developed, with the help of Geoffrey Bing, a new interpretation of what had gone wrong, and what was needed for the future. Bing wrote to Nkrumah from New York "the lesson of the Congo is that it is essential to have both a military and a technical ability to assist an emerging country so that the new government can become stable before it is exposed to cold war pressures. . . . On the technical side a great deal more needs to be done. The Congo situation has shown that perhaps the key issue was the control of banking facilities of the Congo; we must have our own economists and banking specialists trained,"[178] who would be useful in the unliberated parts of Africa. In point of fact, Ghana could not have supplied the technical ability needed in the Congo during the crisis. Robert West, at that time in a senior position in the finance ministry of the Congo, later noted that 150 Belgians had left that ministry early in the summer of 1960 and that, even with a consolidation of functions, there were 65 positions, a third of them at the highest levels, that could not be filled by Congolese.[179] Ghana did not then, or in subsequent years, have even a small percentage of this number to spare.

The Congo crisis was responsible for a division in Africa that Nkrumah had neither foreseen nor wanted; it would require two years of effort to heal. His attempt to regain the initiative with the formation of the Ghana-Guinea-Mali union got nowhere, for the union, like its predecessor, began moving backwards within a week of its proclamation. For varied reasons, Nkrumah had not seen fit to tailor his Congo policy to the Casablanca requirements, and thus failed to bring about working alliances with those powers; but as a member of the group, he lost the respect of the moderate states. He had designed his Congo policy to keep the cold war out of Africa; the crisis had introduced it despite his efforts. His interests in the Congo had significantly diverged from those of the Soviet Union, but the "thousands of cases of small arms and ammunition" that arrived in the spring from the East convinced the Americans that he was only biding his time before moving Ghana more closely in

[177] "Laying of the Foundation Stone of the Kwame Nkrumah Institute," 18 February 1961, Winneba, Ghana; Accra, 1961, pp. 5-8.
[178] Bing to Nkrumah, 23 March 1961, CFA-158.
[179] Robert L. West, "The United Nations and the Congo Financial Crisis: Lessons of the First Year," *International Organization*, 15, No. 4, p. 608, n.11.

line with Soviet policy.[180] The Russians sensibly realized that they had an important opening in Africa. All of Ghana's established interests had become subject to review by early 1961. The radicals—puritan and opportunist—thus had new opportunities to enlarge their power within Ghana.

From the outbreak of the Congo crisis to the consolidation of rival blocs in Africa early in 1961, it is difficult, in sum, to see where Nkrumah had moved events; rather they had controlled him. The effect of the crisis was for Nkrumah not unlike the effect of the 1948 war in Palestine for Arab leaders and for the remainder of his period in power these effects were to be important determinants in his foreign policy.

[180] Interview: CF-97, 26 October 1967. The quotation is from an inspired article in *Time*, 12 May 1961, pp. 21-22, and describes the arms shipments arranged at the Casablanca Conference.

161

◦ 5 ◦

EAST, WEST, AND NONALIGNMENT

July 1960–July 1962

"The word 'Socialism' has some evil connotations so that some people tend to shiver at the mere mention of [it]."—
AMBASSADOR BEDIAKO POKU[1]

IN 1960, Nkrumah and the Russians had failed to achieve their respective Congo objectives. In February 1961, the many different interests which their policies upheld were buried with Lumumba, in whose support they had been united. Ghana's relations with the East and with the West were transformed. Unless they are purely verbal and thus of marginal relevance, such changes do not occur overnight; indeed, step by step elements had been added to Ghana's foreign policy that were catalyzed by Lumumba's death and policy was then refashioned.

In Book I it was argued that, as late as mid-1960, Ghana's nonalignment still favored the West. True, in the ensuing two years Ghanaian politics oscillated from left to right, but Western positions of influence in Accra were on the whole being eroded, while new Eastern positions were consolidated. At the end of the period there was a new equilibrium in Ghana's nonalignment of sufficient delicacy to require but a small force to be tilted in either direction. The magnetic attraction of the East for Nkrumah was counteracted by his continued need of Western investment, of bringing the Volta negotiations to a successful conclusion, and of ensuring that he had the domestic benefits of a royal visit. But the West had already denied him his greatest victory, and in the process Africa had become involved in the cold war. Thenceforth Nkrumah began to take sides in matters which he had always considered irrelevant to African interests.

Related to this foreign policy shift was a power struggle between the radicals and the old guard of the CPP, the outcome of which severely limited Nkrumah's options. What were the issues in the struggle? Accord-

[1] *Ministry of Foreign Affairs*, "Conference of Ghana Envoys," January 1962, p. 48. Author's files.

162

ing to Botsio, it was a generational question. "Adamafio and the social-ist boys were out to get rid of Gbedemah and me. They took the posi-tions on issues they did because it was the opposite of our own. Ideology was a side issue: Adamafio was an ex-U.P. member."[2] Botsio's new man-sion embarrassed the regime, however, and provided ammunition for the radicals who, through the press, began a campaign to discredit the old guard early in 1961. Governmental proclamations of socialist inten-tions were victories for a faction, and Nkrumah's famous "dawn broad-cast" in April was their greatest victory up to that time.[3] On the whole, power and ideology were inextricably linked, for if ideology was not an issue with Adamafio, it was with the puritans, such as Batsaa, Baffoe, or Addison.

Elsewhere it is argued that there were few pressures on Nkrumah to advance the fortunes of either the opportunists or puritans of the left, that they now came into their own because Nkrumah had always in-tended it to be so, and for the first time, that he felt in a strong enough position to increase their power without threat to his own position.[4] If this does not exaggerate Nkrumah's power, it overlooks how subtly and shrewdly the radicals played their hand, and how easily influenced Nkru-mah was in general. The radicals represented a compartment of his radi-cal past and contemporary mind and were his radical conscience: but their maneuvering, demands, and exploitation of favorable circumstances accounted for their growth in power as much as did Nkrumah's volition.

The moves toward socialism had various implications for foreign policy. When Krobo Edusei complained that the "good name of Ghana . . . is being soiled . . . abroad" as a result of Ghanaian developments,[5] he meant in London or Washington, the cities the old guard frequented. Ghana's name was improving in the capitals from which the radicals were drawing strength. There were serious implications in this: here is the nexus of the most important effect of domestic policy on foreign policy and foreign policy on domestic trends. The more talk of socialism there was, the worse the investment climate became. When Western investment was not forthcoming, criticism of the West increased and justifications for seeking large Eastern credits and trade became more compelling. Ironically, the moves toward socialism had very few impli-

---

[2] Interview: Kojo Botsio.

[3] A summary of the speech is most readily found in Dennis Austin, *Politics in Ghana 1946-60*, London, 1964. Adamafio later claimed to have written it. *Evening News*, 1 June 1966. Sir Robert Jackson does not support this claim. Jackson to the author, 8 Febru-ary 1968.

[4] Richard D. Esseks, "Economic Independence in a New African State," unpublished Ph.D. dissertation, Harvard, Chapter vi.

[5] *Debates*, 25 April 1961, p. 90.

163

cations for the actual organization of the Ghanaian economy at this point.

The talk of socialism also adversely affected the popularity of the regime. There existed no grassroots support for socialist policies; the average person disliked even discussion of it and but for Nkrumah, it could never have come.[6] When a harsh budget was adopted in the summer of 1961 (on the quickly tendered advice of Professor Nicholas Kaldor), workers went on strike, disrupted the economy for a month, and almost brought about the regime's overthrow. The budget was associated with "socialism," but at this time Nkrumah accepted the minimum demands of the radicals in order to maintain their support in his struggle for survival, and he dismissed the old guard.

COUNTERVAILING FORCES, JULY 1960–AUGUST 1961

In April 1960, Kojo Botsio had led a large delegation to Russia. Now, early in August, John Tettegah went to Moscow with Tawia Adamafio. They were on the warpath and made it clear to Ghanaian diplomats there that, upon their return to Ghana, they would build socialism. In the Crimea, they visited Khrushchev who, according to Tettegah, promised them that if the West delayed over the Volta River Project, he would build it for them, just as he was building Nasser's dam.[7] When a report of their agreements with Khrushchev reached the press, they blamed the head of chancery in Moscow, F. E. Boaten, who was recalled to Accra and nearly dismissed from the service.[8] They also brought back exciting plans for economic and technical cooperation and for a substantial increase in trade. A fishing industry, various industrial enterprises, and the establishment of hydroelectric stations of medium capacity were envisaged. To pay for all this, "the Government of the USSR has extended to the Government of the Republic of Ghana a long-term credit in the amount of 160 million rubles."[9]

In its three years of independence, Ghana had sought aid for only one major project, the Volta scheme, and had spent two full years in negotiations with the Americans for it. Suddenly, £G14,700,000 was offered to develop Ghana, almost without asking and apparently with no strings attached. Almost simultaneously came the *agrément* for a Chinese ambassador from Peking, Huang Hua. If there were no relationship between the two events, their coincidence had symbolic domestic impor-

---

[6] This was a widely reflected view, at every level of society. See interview: CF-14.

[7] Interview: John Tettegah, in 1960 head of the Ghana Trade Union Council.

[8] Interview: CF-33.

[9] P.R. #773/60, 31 August 1960.

164

tance for the radicals, who were quickly injecting socialist content into party literature. This type of coincidence was to recur.

Relations with the Eastern countries developed apace throughout the remainder of 1960. Emmanuel Ayeh-Kumi, roving ambassador and perhaps the richest Ghanaian of the time, made a number of trips to the East, bringing back further promises of aid and trade.[10] Others went too. The minister of labour and cooperatives had gone in August 1960 with one delegation; others went to lay the groundwork for a protocol to the Ghanaian-Soviet agreement for economic and technical cooperation which was finally signed on 23 December 1960. This was on the eve of the formation of the Ghana-Guinea-Mali union and Nkrumah, at the same time, announced that Ghana would send 3,000 students to Russia and the East the following year to balance the 3,000 in the West.[11]

While Adamafio was in Moscow, a letter came from Eisenhower praising Ghana for its cooperation, efficiency, and promptness in the Congo.[12] It briefly appeared that Ghana's policy in the Congo had not affected its warm relations with Washington, which seemed all the more the case when President Eisenhower, in a major address, gave the concept of nonalignment much stronger endorsement than it had ever had from an American leader.[13] By late September, however, perception of the other's intentions had radically changed on both sides. Nkrumah was convinced, probably rightly, that Western powers had played a critical role in deposing Lumumba; yet from that date, Ghanaian diplomacy had all the appearance of a flagrant intervention in Western eyes.

The State Department, for its part, should have understood that Nkrumah's speech to the General Assembly of the United Nations on 23 September 1960 contained little that was new. It presented Nkrumah's solutions to most world problems—Vietnam, Korea, the Middle East, South Africa, and, most of all, the Congo. The speech, far from echoing the "Communist line" of the moment, was a vociferous enunciation of African, Ghanaian, and his own interests. He wanted the United Nations, for example, to "delegate its functions in the Congo to the independent African states . . . especially those . . . whose contributions in man and matériel make the United Nations effort in the Congo possi-

---

[10] See "Visit of Ghana Delegation to Czechoslovakia," P.R. #702/60, August 1960, and "Joint Communiqué of Hungary and Ghana," P.R. #1216/60.

[11] "Ghana Delegation to USSR on Co-operative Affairs," P.R. #686/60, 11 August 1960, and "Protocol to the Ghanaian-Soviet Agreement for Economic and Technical Co-operation," P.R. #1213/60, 12 December 1960.

[12] Quoted in *Ghanaian Times*, 3 August 1960.

[13] See *New York Times*, 21 September 1960.

ble."[14] It was following this speech, however, that Christian Herter, then secretary of state, commented that Nkrumah was "very definitely moving towards the Soviet Bloc."[15] (Eisenhower shared this view, saying in his memoirs that Nkrumah had left a meeting with him to go directly to the Assembly where he "cut loose with a speech following the Khrushchev line in strong criticism of Secretary-General Hammarskjold.")[16]

It is true that Nkrumah's first friendly meeting with Khrushchev (which took place in New York) could hardly have presented a greater contrast to his frosty session with Eisenhower.[17] For the moment, this had less importance than that Nkrumah publicly expressed his "personal appreciation of the way the Secretary-General has handled a most difficult task"[18]—while Khrushchev did seek Hammarskjold's dismissal. If Herter's remark was prophetic, it also had the effect of a self-fulfilling prophecy. The *Ghanaian Times* commented that "In the cold war, the West has not been clever, and has often walked as if blindfolded into the arms of the East. The Christian Herter blunder clarifies this point and confirms it."[19] Attacks on the United States in the Ghanaian press increased as interests diverged further and further. In America, the press began asking whether Ghana remained nonaligned.

Caution could still be detected in Accra. There was a significant period of delay before the government made public the communiqué of 4 August 1960. Elliot, the Ghanaian ambassador in Moscow, who did all he could to please the government to which he was accredited, pressed his own government to approve and publicize it, as "the situation is becoming embarrassing to me."[20] Nevertheless, over eight months elapsed between the time Adamafio and Tettegah brought home news of the £14,700,000 credit and the time that the cabinet approved it, so divided was the government.[21]

The visit of President Leonid Brezhnev in February 1961 was one of the important symbolic turning points in this year of change. He had

[14] "Osagyefo at the United Nations," Accra, 1960, p. 6.

[15] *New York Times*, 24 September 1960. Apparently Ambassador Wilson Flake in Accra had persisted in writing enthusiastic reports about Nkrumah. Herter, thus unprepared for Nkrumah's tirade, overreacted to the speech and, against the advice of several subordinates, made the quoted comment. Flake was soon replaced in Accra.

[16] David D. Eisenhower, *Waging Peace*, New York, 1965, p. 583.

[17] Interview: Sir Robert Jackson, 12 January 1967; CF-85, cabinet secretariat, 14 October 1966.

[18] Quoted in Nkrumah, *I Speak of Freedom*, London, 1961, p. 279.

[19] 29 September 1960. See also *Evening News*, 29 September 1960.

[20] Elliot to M.E.A., 12 August 1960, CFA-10.

[21] "Ratification of Protocol to the Ghanaian-Soviet Agreement for Economic and Technical Co-operation," P.R. #422/60, 29 April 1961.

not originally included Ghana in his itinerary, perhaps because it was still considered too "revisionist";[22] Nkrumah had, after all, vigorously opposed Russia's Congo policy and little more than talk about socialism existed in Ghana. But while Brezhnev was in Guinea, the Ghanaians hurriedly extended an invitation to him which he accepted the same day that Lumumba's death was announced.[23] He arrived on February 16th while President Senghor was still in Ghana on a state visit, a coincidence which proved embarrassing and a source of offense to the Senegalese.[24]

The joint communiqué issued by Nkrumah and Brezhnev recorded their "similarity of points of view . . . on the most important problems of international policy," although for the moment it was significant that Nkrumah spoke once again of the need to prevent the cold war from "penetrating into the African continent,"[25] a concern which Sékou Touré, for one, did not share at this time. The most important immediate effect of the visit was its encouragement for the radicals within the CPP, when they could utilize the martyrdom of Lumumba, their hero, to advance their own interests. It was from now on that they began to argue that Ghana could be developed by the Soviet Union alone; that there was no further need to pay attention to the West; that efforts should rather be concentrated on a major request to the Soviet Union for £100,000,000, to be made during the president's forthcoming tour there.[26]

The domestic fight came into the open. Gbedemah, strongest of the old guard, presented a memorandum to the cabinet in mid-March on Ghana's increasingly serious economic situation, in which he predicted what might befall the country if existing trends were not corrected. In a note of realism unique at this time, he asked how interested the Russians were likely to be in helping to repay Ghana's rapidly accumulating Western debts.[27] Such questions were brushed aside and he was demoted from the ministry of finance to the ministry of health.

The now more frequent and more radical pronouncements on global problems, issued from Flagstaff House, were significant pointers to the shift in thinking at the top. As little attention was paid to them anywhere else in the world, it is the actual change in the implementation of

[22] In the opinion of one adviser of Nkrumah's. Interview: CF-85.

[23] Dzirasa, the resident minister in Conakry, had not previously been alerted to the possibility of an invitation. Interview: Dzirasa.

[24] Interview: CF-43.

[25] "Stay of Leonid I. Brezhnev in the Republic of Ghana," P.R. #193/61, 18 February 1961; "Visit of H. E. L. I. Brezhnev," Accra, 1961, p. 3.

[26] Interview: CF-14.

[27] Cabinet Memorandum, March 1961, files of Komla Gbedemah.

167

policy that merits study. In October 1960, for example, the Afro-Asian Council in New Delhi, formed as a result of Chinese action in Tibet, asked Ghana to raise the question of Tibet at the United Nations.[28] It was an issue which Ghana, even as a nonaligned state, might consider as one of principle. But the ministry official concerned with the matter did not want Ghana raising the issue, as anyone who did "will be playing the role of a propagandist in the Western Camp,"[29] particularly if this occurred while China remained outside the United Nations. Adu's response to the council used only the latter argument, that "no useful purpose" would be served by Ghana's action so long as China was not a member of the United Nations, and this was clearly a defensible nonaligned approach.[30] But the former argument was increasingly typical of official policy in Ghana.

By early 1961, the ministry had begun to make its own contributions to the new radicalism. Almost simultaneous with the announcement of Lumumba's death, Harry Amonoo, a senior foreign service officer, was brought from Geneva to the ministry where he was to remain until transferred to Flagstaff House in 1963. An intelligent and hardworking diplomatist who preferred the office to the conference table or podium, he supplied the radical substance that had been largely lacking in the ministry. In February, for example, Ghana's embassy in Paris reported that South Korea wanted its UN representative, Channing Liem, to pay a goodwill visit to Accra while making an African tour, in order to raise support for South Korea's admission to the United Nations. Amonoo, at this time the protocol officer, recommended to Kofi, the acting principal secretary, that "as the Republic of Korea is pro-American and a divided state, the government should not entertain this goodwill Mission. All expenses should be borne by the Mission."[31] It now became a question of who could be the more unfriendly to the prospective visitors; Ako Adjei wrote to Dei-Anang that the delegation should be given no official recognition and that no press release should even mention them. "They should be treated as ordinary tourists."[32]

The "Sands of the Cold War"[33] were indeed shifting in Ghana. In

[28] J. Narayon, President, Afro-Asian Council, to M.E.A., October 1960, CFA-128.

[29] P.A.S. to P. S., M.E.A., 29 October 1960, CFA-129.

[30] A. L. Adu to J. Narayon, 10 November 1960, CFA-129.

[31] Ghana/Paris to Dei-Anang, 14 February 1961; H. R. Amonoo to A.B.B. Kofi, 24 February 1961, CFA-59.

[32] Adjei to Dei-Anang, 26 February 1961. Amonoo then reported for all ministries: "My ministry has directed that this delegation should not be given any official status . . . because Ghana is unwilling to fraternise with only one section of the people of Korea," a different reason from that he had given within the ministry. H. R. Amonoo to all principal secretaries, 25 February 1961, CFA-59.

[33] Arthur Schlesinger, *A Thousand Days*, London, 1965, p. 498.

May, J. B. Erzuah, Ghana's ambassador in Cairo, reported that the North Korean trade representative wished to bring a ten-man goodwill mission to Ghana in mid-June. He commented: "I am not convinced about the need, at present, for such a visit from the Democratic People's Republic of Korea. And, from my conversation with the Trade Representative, I am not impressed with the vague and undisciplined manner in which the visits are being planned."[34] Headquarters accepted these reasons for "discouraging the visit," and added that the timing was bad.[35] In fact, neither delegation came, but the difference in criteria regarding the two prospective delegations from a divided nation is interesting. In 1964 North Korea opened its embassy in Accra.

Ghana and the West. Numerous restraints on Ghana's movement toward the East remained during these first six months of 1961;[36] the most significant was probably Nkrumah's relations with John F. Kennedy. The new president had made America's Africa policy a major issue in his campaign, and had appointed advisers tending, as Nkrumah said to Kennedy, to give "hope and confidence for the promotion of better relations between Africa and the Western powers."[37]

The view from Washington, however, was now very different from what it had been in 1958. The Eisenhower administration had watched Ghana change its direction in foreign policy, and by the time Governor Williams entered the State Department, the shift was noted in Washington as a *fait accompli.* "There was as much to fear in their orientation at the beginning of our new administration as there was four years later," a senior official commented.[38] This did not mean that Williams, or Kennedy, lacked hope that Nkrumah could be influenced. But there was mounting pressure in Washington for a "less indulgent" attitude toward Ghana, particularly after three liberal Democratic senators returned from a short visit to Ghana openly criticizing the regime.[39]

Accra's view of Washington, on the other hand, was much improved; this despite Schlesinger's undoubtedly apocryphal assertion that relations had so deteriorated that the Ghanaian cabinet met to consider whether Francis Russell, the new American ambassador, should even

[34] Amb. Erzuah to P. S., M.E.A., 22 May 1961, CFA-59.

[35] Kumi to acting P. S., and to Honourable Minister, 30 May 1961; Kofi to Erzuah, 8 June 1961, CFA-59.

[36] A distinction may be made here between implicit restraints (economic structure, direction of trade) and active restraints (the efforts of diplomats, advisers). The latter is meant in this context.

[37] Nkrumah to Kennedy, 23 January 1961, CFA-130.

[38] Interview: CF-102, September 1965, Dept. of State.

[39] Senators Church, McGee, and Moss. See *New York Times,* 12 February 1961, for their report to the Senate.

"be allowed to present his credentials."[40] In a long letter to Kennedy at the time of Russell's presentation, Nkrumah made much of his own strong American ties and made it clear that he had no intention of troubling Kennedy "with complaints or with criticism of a past administration for whose actions you were nowhere responsible." Nkrumah used the occasion to argue the case for a new American policy toward the Congo, based on his own ambitions and desires, and urged Kennedy to effect the release of Lumumba. He ended by expressing the hope that "an exchange of correspondence such as this might lead to an agreed policy between the United States . . . and the independent States of Africa."[41]

Alas, Nkrumah was not yet Africa's spokesman, and, in any event, Kennedy's interest in improving relations derived from very different concerns. As Sir Robert Jackson put it, the Americans—and the British—were fearful that if Nkrumah moved too far from a nonaligned position, along with his Casablanca partners, Ghana would be lost to Africa, and the Western position would be seriously eroded, because of the near-total polarization in world politics.[42] Thus it was that Lady Jackson, a friend of Kennedy's for twenty years, urged him in the strongest terms to receive Nkrumah following his General Assembly address of March 7th. Although Lumumba was now dead, she felt Nkrumah could be influenced. "It is worth a risk and could possibly be a triumph," Schlesinger quotes her as saying.[43] The president agreed, and she was proved right. True, America's new Congo policy did not give Nkrumah what he personally sought, but Kennedy's assurances that America would work (for example) to eliminate Portuguese colonialism, and his virtual assurance that, pending feasibility rulings, America would build the Volta River Project, were sufficient to outweigh Nkrumah's Congo losses for the moment. Kennedy also accorded Nkrumah honors which were unnecessary by protocol (which were to be frequently recalled later), creating an even more favorable impression on a man who valued such gestures.[44] The emotional warmth with which Nkrumah viewed the new president and his family tended to balance the effect of the increasingly deep disagreements on policy which divided Washington and Accra.

40 Schlesinger, *A Thousand Days*, p. 497. No contemporary cabinet member interviewed remembered such to have happened, and all thought it the opposite of Nkrumah's reaction; Sir Robert Jackson concurs. See also CF-97, 26 October 1966. Nkrumah liked and respected Russell, and their personal relations were cordial.
41 Nkrumah to Kennedy, 23 January 1961, CFA-130.
42 Interview: Sir Robert Jackson, 12 January 1967.
43 Schlesinger, *A Thousand Days*, p. 498.
44 Kennedy welcomed Nkrumah at the airport personally, although it was not a state visit. See *Debates*, 18 April 1961, and 25 June 1961, p. 11.

Kennedy's gestures had counteracted Russian influence, buying time for American policy. By the time Ghana's nonaligned stance had lost credibility, Sékou Touré had moved Guinea away from its close identification with the Communist countries, and the Congo crisis was in important respects settled.

During 1960-1961, radical Africans began to call Ghana's membership in the Commonwealth into question. At their meeting of 8 August 1960, Lumumba had forced Nkrumah to agree that Ghana would withdraw from it when the two countries' union was consummated, and the Guineans continued to press Nkrumah toward the same end.[45] Ghanaian-British relations became increasingly strained in 1961 owing to the Congo crisis and on at least one occasion Nkrumah suggested that the Commonwealth might be adversely affected by developments there.[46] But the weight of evidence shows that Nkrumah still valued the access the organization gave him to British leaders, and the platform which membership gave him on world issues. Ghana's envoys in Africa evidently agreed, and at a conference they held in October 1961, concluded: "Those who criticized Ghana's continued membership of the Commonwealth should be told that it was not a question of links but one of practical results and that Ghana's membership of the Commonwealth rather enabled her to help other African states still under British domination."[47]

That Nkrumah had the Commonwealth in a "separate sealed compartment of his mind" (using, once again, Jackson's metaphor) is suggested by Ghana's voting pattern at the United Nations during a debate on South West Africa, at the time of the Commonwealth's conference in London. A resolution had been tabled that, in its revised form, called on "those members of the UN having close and continuous" relations with Great Britain to bring influence to bear toward a solution of the issue of South West Africa. The Ghanaian delegate "regretted that the approval of the draft resolution . . . was being artificially linked with the Commonwealth conference . . . because the two matters were entirely separate."[48] He was clearly acting on instructions in so speaking,[49] and in the end Ghana abstained on the resolution along with most of the

45 See Nkrumah, *Challenge of the Congo*, p. 31.
46 In a letter to Macmillan, 23 January 1961, quoted in *ibid.*, p. 103.
47 *President's office*, Notes of Conference of Ghana Envoys in Africa, 1961, p. 7. Author's files.
48 *UN Docs.*, A/4709, 15 March 1961. See also *UN*, A/C.4/L.671 Rev. 1 and Rev. 1 Corr. 1.
49 This is evident because in the debate of two days earlier Yameopke, the Ghanaian delegate, had refrained from taking any position for lack of instructions, and now proceeded to oppose the motion, unlike the Nigerians who had supported it from the beginning.

Commonwealth, while Nigeria, the Soviet Union, and sixty-six other states voted for it.

Nkrumah presumably concluded that the Prime Ministers' Commonwealth Conference was not the place for radicalism and, according to British ministers, his influence in that body continued to mount. This is well illustrated by Ghana's continued reluctance to risk disrupting it over the South Africa issue. When Nkrumah arrived in London from New York for the 1961 meeting, he was reported saying that he had "no wish for a showdown," and the *Daily Telegraph* observed that the chances were thus improved "that there will be no attempt to bar South Africa from the Commonwealth."[50]

Yet the same day Julius Nyerere gave Colin Legum a prepared statement, expressing his conviction that Tanganyika could have no place in an organization that included South Africa. Legum called Geoffrey Bing that evening informing him of the article and it was only at that point that Ghana too began preparing a statement for the following Sunday, March 12th.[51]

The fact that almost half the final communiqué was devoted to the question of disarmament, on the urging of Nkrumah and Nehru, indicates that Nkrumah's approach to the organization brought him the results he wanted in areas he happened to consider important.[52] The fact that South Africa was not expelled from the Commonwealth, but withdrew after the issue was drawn by Nyerere, was a sobering reminder to South African refugees of the difficulty in gaining support from such purportedly radical leaders as Nkrumah.[53]

Ghana's membership in the Commonwealth was clearly one other restraining influence in the months to come, but it worked in a more diffuse way than the new link with the White House. Criticism of Great Britain increased apace throughout 1961, particularly during Nkrumah's visit to the Eastern countries in the summer,[54] but up to that time channels of communication with Britain were always open. Duncan Sandys, then the Commonwealth secretary, remained closely in touch with Nkrumah, with whom his relations were cordial.

There were, moreover, close relations with a country such as Canada, whose aid and friendship Ghana always considered a consequence of Commonwealth links. A position paper of the ministry of foreign affairs

[50] *Daily Telegraph*, 10 March 1961, and interview: CF-103.

[51] Interview: Colin Legum. See *Observer*, 12 March 1961.

[52] See final communiqué, in *Times*, 18 March 1961.

[53] From this point on Ghana did attempt to take more direct action against the South African regime. See p. 224.

[54] In Budapest, the British Chargé walked out of a banquet after an attack on his country by Nkrumah.

showed how many ties and how many reasons for the close relationship existed. Canada had a "healthy understanding" of the type of economic problem developing countries faced, and was a safer provider of aid than its powerful neighbor; there was much trade, a common position with respect to Britain's entry to the Common Market, and the impressive attempts of Canada to preserve its own outlook on world affairs in the face of American dominance in North America.[55] Canada was ably represented, too, by an outstanding diplomatist, Bruce Williams, whose work enhanced the fabric and contacts that made the Commonwealth so important a part of Ghana's foreign policy at this point.

Pilgrimage to the East. Preparations for Nkrumah's visit to the East had been proceeding since spring, but the tour was only publicized a week prior to his departure, "because the programme was being changed frequently and nobody knew precisely where he would be and every care was taken to keep it secret," the foreign minister said.[56] By the time Nkrumah left, the political battles within the party seemed to have abated. Botsio and Gbedemah were both appointed to the Presidential Commission (which ruled in Nkrumah's absence) so clearly Nkrumah felt at the time that their wings had been sufficiently clipped. But he left on the very day that a harsh budget was introduced, which was designed to give the government new sources of revenue—through new taxes—without inflation; this to prevent further bleeding of the reserves. Jackson, Gbedemah, and Botsio thought different medicine was called for,[57] but Nkrumah overruled them and, obviously confident that the situation was in hand, set out with an enormous retinue (in which he prudently included most of the CPP's left wing).

What were the various expectations for the trip? Civil servants and foreign service officers felt that Ghana's nonalignment was not in balance until Nkrumah had been to the East.[58] It was after all a time when the prestige of the Communist states had never been higher, particularly in the third world; more to the point, there had been little contact between Ghanaians and Communists. The East held an allure and a mystique that strengthened radical hands. It was what the British had kept

[55] Richard Akwei, "Brief on Ghana's Foreign Policy Towards the Americas," in "Conference of Ghana Envoys," p. 201.

[56] "Conference of Ghana Envoys," p. 50.

[57] Interviews, Botsio, Gbedemah, Jackson. ". . . we were convinced that new taxes could not be collected (which proved to be the case) and that the new budget would cause strong political unrest. One of the most important factors in my own attitude here was the factor of security in relation to the Queen's visit." Sir Robert Jackson to the author, 8 February 1968.

[58] See interview: CF-85.

173

Gold Coasters away from;[59] now they would see for themselves. For the radical party men, the trip was the occasion for bold moves, in which they could augment their power and, possibly, Ghana's too. They felt Ghana possessed enormous leverage with Russia, and wished to ask not only for £ 100,000,000, but that Russia should make Ghana the distribution agent for all Russian aid to Africa.[60] This was ambition indeed. Nkrumah's objectives were entirely different; he seemed to have been more concerned with what he could do for the Socialist motherland. "In retrospect, it is clear that this trip was a pilgrimage for Nkrumah."[61] The itinerary alone gives an idea of its scope:

10—25 July:	Soviet Union
25—28 July:	Poland
28—31 July:	Hungary
31 July—3 August:	Czechoslovakia
3—8 August:	Yugoslavia
9—10 August:	Rumania
10—11 August:	Bulgaria
11—12 August:	Albania
14—19 August:	China
21 August—1 September:	Soviet Union (Crimea)
1—6 September:	Belgrade
7—15 September:	Soviet Union (Crimea)

He went with high expectations. They were more than sufficiently rewarded. Everything the Russians did reinforced Nkrumah's growing determination to accelerate the timetable of the "liberation movement."[62] The restraints on him that for so long had prevented him from showing his real sentiments on world issues virtually ceased to operate.[63] The Russians took him to see symbols of power, including an atomic reactor which they promised to reproduce in Ghana. More important, they took him on a 10,000 mile trip to Kiev, Leningrad, Irkutsk, and Tashkent. There the feasibility of a multinational state was given convincing proof of a kind that Nkrumah thenceforth never tired of describing. "The

[59] One distinguished Ghanaian commented as follows: "I blamed the British for the fascination that Ghanaians had of the East at this time, because the British had kept us so insulated from all Eastern influences." Interview: CF-28.

[60] Interview: CF-14.

[61] Interview: CF-85.

[62] See *Times, Daily Telegraph*, 11 July 1961. Interviews: Ako Adjei, CF-7, 85.

[63] Some disagree. Miss Catherine Hoskyns wrote the present writer, "Ghana started aligned to the West, and [these] gestures were a prerequisite for any genuine kind of nonalignment. This is a very basic point of interpretation." It is also essential to ask whether, even if these were "gestures," they were *intended* to have the effect Miss Hoskyns attributes to them and, more important, whether they did have such effect.

174

peoples of the Soviet Union, by so effectively welding many Republics and nationalities together into one great country, have demonstrated the effectiveness of political union (applause). This is [an] achievement which we can emulate in Africa where the conditions for unity are so favourable and the necessity so imperative."[64]

In a one hundred-page commemorative booklet published by Novosti Press Agency on Ghana government presses, an exchange is quoted that well characterizes the spirit of the trip:

> "Who settles labour conflicts in the plant?" the President asked [in a Kiev factory]. "Are there no strikes?" "We have no strikes and there is no reason for them," the director replied. . . . "And indeed, against whom should we go on strike? After all the power belongs to the workers and peasants themselves."
> "It's clear that you cannot strike against yourself," Dr. Kwame Nkrumah remarked with a smile.[65]

This was to have added significance in a few weeks' time, when a strike in Ghana—the delayed consequence of the July budget—almost overturned Nkrumah's regime.

As the trip progressed, Nkrumah's speeches went further and further along lines presumably calculated to please his hosts. He remarked at the end, for example, that "But for the Soviet Union, the colonial liberation movement in Africa would have suffered a most cruel and brutal suppression."[66] The left wing, led by Adamafio, cheered him on, calling for "more, more Osagyefo," at times even suggesting that Nkrumah make Ghana a formal Soviet ally in the manner of Cuba.[67]

Nor was the communiqué calculated to reassure Westerners that Ghana remained nonaligned. True, words may have been misinterpreted by overreacting Western diplomats. Thus, the Ghanaian text of a crucial clause said the following: "The Soviet Government informed the Ghanaian Government of the proposals of the USSR on the German problem. The Government of Ghana *appreciated* the proposals of the Soviet Government concerning a peace treaty with Germany and the settlement of the West Berlin issue on the basis of that treaty."[68] Ako Adjei, who had briefly joined the tour, related how he tried to explain to Dean Rusk at a later date that the key word, *appreciate*, was used in its strict sense, derived from Latin, to establish that Ghana had taken note of the Rus-

---

[64] *Visit of Friendship*, edited by Novosti (Moscow), printed by government of Ghana, Accra, 1961, p. 53.

[65] *Ibid.*, pp. 58-59.   [66] *Ibid.*, p. 92.   [67] Interview: CF-85.

[68] *Ghana*, "Joint Communiqués Issued during Osagyefo's Tours of Eastern European countries," Accra, 1961, p. 4 emphasis added.

sian position.[69] But there were two other elements, the first of which was possibly the result of mischief-making. The German question was one of paramount interest to the Russians, and it is significant that their translation from the Russian text into English said that the Ghanaians "viewed with *understanding* the Soviet Government's proposals concerning a peace treaty with Germany. . . ."[70] It is likely that the Russian texts confused an already loaded issue.

There is a second point. Whatever were the words used in the communiqué, Nkrumah made clear in all quarters that he sympathized with the Russian position on Berlin. He thought a situation that could not be changed should be accepted, but it did not occur to him that his position was weighted in one direction during a great world crisis.[71]

By this time the Russians undoubtedly understood what Nkrumah sought—a voice in the highest forums. Thus they encouraged him to speak out on precisely the issues where Russia did (and Ghana did not) have interests; out of vanity he did speak out. Nkrumah was not the only nonaligned leader taking this position, but it was the style and the vehemence with which he took this stand that separated him from his peers. The irony was heightened by the contrast with his earlier statements on Berlin. On the eve of his departure for Russia, he had appeared distracted by the importance the Berlin issue held in the world. At the National Assembly he noted that in contrast to Angola, "no one is dropping napalm bombs on the people of Berlin."[72]

He was also persuaded to spend a few unscheduled hours in East Germany. This, in combination with his statements on Berlin, enraged West German opinion. Although a minor effort was made to pacify Bonn, by the time of Belgrade in early September he was calling on the great powers to conclude a peace treaty with Germany, after which the nations of the world could all "recognize the existence of these two states, to enable them to co-exist peacefully."[73] In the context of this period, it is not surprising that thereafter Western governments considered Ghana's policy a bad example of nonalignment, and wondered how much longer Ghana would even claim to be nonaligned.

Seen from amidst the entourage, Nkrumah had gone from triumph to

[69] Interview: Ako Adjei.

[70] *Visit of Friendship*, p. 99 (emphasis added).

[71] Note that the German question appeared in every communiqué Nkrumah signed during the summer, including in Peking. This was at a time when the Chinese press virtually refused to acknowledge the existence of the Berlin question.

[72] *Debates*, 4 July 1961. He was at that point unconsciously taking a position similar to China's.

[73] *Ghana*, "Conference of Heads of State and Governments," Belgrade, Accra, 1961, p. 101.

triumph. If Russia promised nothing concrete but the purchase of 60,000 tons of cocoa[74] there were substantial economic gains made in the Eastern European states. It was sufficient that each should promise something, and not necessary that Ghana had any needs that could be filled by it; at its most ludicrous level, a report of a Ghanaian diplomat in Albania, regarding the agreements entered into in Tirana, noted: "It is odd . . . that the Albanian Government should enter into air services agreement with our country, indicating that the civil aircraft of the People's Republic of Albania would fly to Accra knowing full well that at present, it has not a single civil aircraft, and therefore no airways."[75]

In Vienna, before flying to China, Nkrumah instructed the ministry's legal adviser, Kweku Dadzie, to make arrangements for establishing missions in each country in Eastern Europe; the foreign minister noted (according to Dadzie) that there were not enough men, but to Nkrumah, in his state of mind at the time, this was an insignificant detail.[76]

He then went on to Peking. "In Russia it was multinationalism, and the industrial might that impressed him; in China it was the ideology— at least for a time."[77] It is no wonder he was impressed. According to *Hsinhua*, he was met by 500,000 people, 1,500 of whom were performing traditional Chinese dances at the center of Tienanman square. "The whole square rocked to the deafening clapping of hands, firing of firecrackers and beating of drums, gongs, and cymbals."[78] Thus he outdid his gestures of the previous six weeks, and signed a vague but symbolically significant "Treaty of Friendship" as well as numerous economic and cultural agreements. "It was Adamafio again. The Chinese had proposed the Treaty, and I stayed up all night arguing with Tawia over the necessity of a treaty, when we had already signed a communiqué. 'No, we must have more, more, more,' he concluded."[79]

NONALIGNMENT

1960 was Africa's year, but the period between the collapse of the Geneva summit in May 1960 and the Belgrade Summit in September 1961 was also the year of the nonaligned. At the September 1960 session of the General Assembly, when Khrushchev, Castro, Nehru, Macmillan, and numerous other statesmen descended on New York, the non-

[74] This turned out to be a questionable blessing. Russia bought cocoa when the price was low, and did not buy it in years when the price was high.

[75] Annual Report, Ghana/Tirana to M.F.A., 2 March 1964, CFA-23.

[76] Interview: Amb. Kweku Dadzie.

[77] Interview: CF-85.

[78] *NCNA*, 14 August 1961.

[79] Interview: CF-85. See also H. C. Hinton, *Communist China in World Politics*, London, 1966, p. 191.

aligned discovered their trump: the great powers were acutely sensitive to the direction of the wind in the third world.

At the New York session, Nkrumah was more eager to make an impact as a world statesman (according to one of his entourage)[80] than as an African president, and the proposal which had been developing in his mind during the previous six months could now be put before the Afro-Asian group itself. This was that the noncommitted world should make of itself a cohesive and organized bloc. He had failed to consider the implications of his proposal; which defeated the purpose for which most states had chosen nonalignment—as their leaders were quick to point out. The criticism was sufficient to lead him to clarify his views before the Afro-Asian group itself, where he gave assurances that he did not intend that such a bloc be "isolated from the two power blocs" within the United Nations.[81]

What is of even greater significance (for this study) was that Nkrumah found himself one of the "big five" of nonalignment at New York, along with Nehru, Sukarno, Nasser, and Tito; it is this group that proposed (and then withdrew) a motion urging Eisenhower and Khrushchev to hold talks.[82] Peers are acutely conscious of peers; these other nonaligned leaders were Nkrumah's most conspicuous peers at this point, and it became a matter of priority that Ghana should maintain a leading position in the nonaligned world.

But for the remainder of 1960 and in the first half of 1961, Nkrumah was to become so completely absorbed in African affairs that he was unable to sustain an active role in nonaligned affairs. It was at the point that Nkrumah no longer appeared to be a leader of the uncommitted that Ghana's position became more radical in the conferences of the nonaligned.

Tito's visit to Accra in late February brought questions of world peace momentarily to the fore again, and consolidated a friendship between him and Nkrumah that was to have considerable depth in the ensuing five years. Nkrumah wished to call a conference in Accra on disarmament. It is not clear what Tito advised in Accra but on his return from New York in March, Geoffrey Bing wrote in a report that Quaison-Sackey agreed with him that, in view of the "present and delicate" negotiations of America and Russia on disarmament, Ghana would be better advised to widen its concern; the advice was accepted.[83]

---

[80] Interview: CF-8.   [81] *Ghanaian Times*, 3 October 1960.
[82] See *UN Docs.*, A/4522, A/L.317. Also see Peter Lyon, *Neutralism*, Leicester, 1963, p. 178.
[83] Bing to Nkrumah, 24 March 1961, CFA-2.

The initiative had long since been Cairo's and Belgrade's. Sukarno had been calling for a second Bandung Conference since Chen Yi's March visit to Indonesia, and now Tito, ineligible for such a conference, returned from his tour to consult with Nasser. Together they called for a conference of the nonaligned, to be preceded by a preparatory meeting in Cairo in early June.[84]

It is by no means certain that Accra was receiving accurate information. Erzuah, Ghana's ambassador in Cairo, cabled the day after the Nasser-Tito communiqué that Sukarno and Tito were playing the leading roles, and that they wanted Ghana, Guinea, Mali, and the UAR to consult with them in Cairo immediately.[85] In fact it was Nasser and Tito who sent invitations, a few days later. There is no evidence that Ghana was a party to the negotiations taking place during May between Delhi, Belgrade, and Cairo, which helps to explain Ghana's anomalous position at the meeting that ensued.[86]

Michael Dei-Anang, by now at Flagstaff House, prepared the brief for Ghana's delegation to the Cairo conference. It called for inclusion of the problems of neocolonialism, disarmament, and "spheres of influence" on the agenda of the conference for which the Cairo meeting was the preparation. It put greater stress, however, on less ideologically motivated concerns: the question of sponsorship and setting, and whom to invite. Thus, Ghana was to make a "strong bid" for the conference to be held in Accra, or in one of the Casablanca states, "because of prestige reasons and the need to emphasize Africa's importance in the geopolitics of nonalignment."[87] But, as it turned out in subsequent instructions, if this could not be obtained, it was at least to be sponsored by the "big five" of 1960.[88] The first aim was not realized, and India made the second impossible. From the first, Delhi had held doubts about the advisability even of holding a conference of the nonaligned; yet Nehru was one of the five and, when India refused to be a sponsor, what was a slim and unprincipled claim to leadership by Ghana had no further basis. Ako Adjei cabled Nkrumah: "India is very unpopular. . . . By her insistence . . . it has become impossible to agree, even among ourselves, that the five

[84] See G. H. Jansen, *Afro-Asia and Non-Alignment*, London, 1966, p. 281, and pp. 278-91.

[85] Amb. Erzuah to Ako Adjei, 23 April 1961, CFA-3. Sukarno was not in Cairo at the time. Erzuah either misread the situation, wished to de-emphasize Nasser's role because of Nkrumah's sensitivities, or confused the issue with the Casablanca group's foreign ministers' meeting scheduled for Cairo the following week.

[86] G. H. Jansen's well-documented study shows no evidence of a Ghanaian role, nor do the files of the Ghanaian ministry.

[87] Brief for Ghana delegation to Cairo preparatory conference, as "submitted to Osagyefo, 1 June 1961," CFA-3.

[88] Dei-Anang to Ako Adjei, 8 June 1961, CFA-4.

179

states . . . should be cosponsors. . . . [Moreover, Indonesia, UAR, and Yugoslavia are unwilling to carry the idea forward, as it] would amount to discrimination even among the 22 states which have agreed to participate."[89] Yugoslavia thus proposed that all countries attending the Cairo preparatory conference be considered sponsors, a "very popular" suggestion, Adjei pointedly said.[90]

He was now instructed that if he could not obtain support for select sponsorship, "you should at all costs work for admission of Algeria and Gizenga's Government into Conference. . . . It is imperative for tactical reasons that Gizenga's Government should be admitted to Conference. You should work for this without fail."[91] Here again the question of whom to invite was brought up, and Ghana again collided with India. India sought broad participation—and wanted European neutrals, certain Latin American countries, and all African states invited. "This is quite fantastic but that gives you an idea of what India is thinking," Adjei cabled Accra.[92] Moreover, India was insisting that in particular invitations be issued to Senegal, Liberia, Nigeria, Tunisia, and Libya. But the Ghanaian leaders, during the spring of 1961, had revised their definition of nonalignment, particularly in the aftermath of the Monrovia conference, at which the moderate African states had demonstrated their strength. These five African countries "are committed and are aligned, and therefore Ghana as well as Indonesia, U.A.R. and Yugoslavia would not agree," wrote Adjei. Moreover, the Casablanca states had also agreed on a strict definition of nonalignment, he added.[93]

Yet its Casablanca colleagues were not prepared to back the rest of Adjei's demands once Ghana, having failed to dominate the conference, sought to win the radical sweepstakes by its insistence that Algeria and Stanleyville be immediately admitted. Adjei wrote that his delegation's line was that it would "walk out" were Gizenga not admitted.[94] The membership subcommittee decided—at the insistence of Burma, India, Cambodia, Ethiopia, Sudan, *and* Guinea and Mali—that only Algeria should be present.[95] Gizenga was not admitted. But Ghana did not walk out; it was not a credible threat, Ghana's presence not being wholly indispensable. Ghana in no sense held a paramount position in the nonaligned world of mid-1961.

During the summer of 1961, Nkrumah's views on cold war issues

[89] Ako Adjei to Nkrumah, 5 June 1961, CFA-4. India may have been unpopular, but Adjei was telling Nkrumah this because it is what Nkrumah wanted to hear, and because it conveniently covered Adjei's failure to accomplish his impossible task.

[90] *Ibid.*   [91] Dei-Anang to Ako Adjei, 8 June 1961, CFA-4.

[92] Adjei to Nkrumah, 5 June 1961.

[93] *Ibid.*   [94] *Ibid.*   [95] *Ibid.*

moved closer and closer to the Communist position, as already seen. On his return from China, he accepted Khrushchev's invitation for a vacation in the Crimea, and from there went to Belgrade determined to form a disciplined and cohesive bloc of the nonaligned world. On the eve of his departure for Russia the previous July, he had said that his year-old suggestion that the nonaligned world should form itself into such a bloc had "become a reality."[96] Whether this in fact had happened, or should be attempted, was the subject of intense disagreement at Belgrade, and the Ghanaians again clashed with the Indians. Ghana lost, because, as Jansen wrote, "The Indian elephant simply sat down and was discovered to be a singularly immovable object."[97]

As a result of Nehru's pressure, the overall consensus of the gathering and, most important, Nkrumah's desire to avoid press reports of a divided conference, Nkrumah added a partial disclaimer of his old beliefs: "Even though we are not here to constitute ourselves into a third bloc, yet, by this very Conference, we are constituting ourselves into a moral force, a distinct moral force which should be a balancing force and influence between the East and the West in the cause of Peace."[98] The issue was one of power. Quaison-Sackey, who was with Nkrumah at Belgrade, commented five years later: "In retrospect, it was as well that the conference did not constitute itself into a bloc; the world has become polycentric, and a bloc created then would have resulted in greater world tension now. But five years ago, it seemed more reasonable: it was based on an accurate analysis of the world at the time, in which it was power and organization that counted. It failed to take into account that foreign policy cannot be static, however."[99]

The remainder of Nkrumah's address showed why a bloc was impossible. He advanced seven proposals for world peace:

1. General and complete disarmament.
2. Two German states to be accepted and recognized.
3. Great powers to be urged to sign a peace treaty with Germany without further delay.
4. Complete liquidation of colonialism by 31 December 1962.
5. Three deputies to be appointed under-secretary-generals of the UN, representing East, West, and nonaligned countries.
6. Admission of China to the UN.
7. Africa to be declared nuclear-free zone.

[96] *Debates*, 4 July 1961. [97] Jansen, *Afro-Asia*, p. 303.
[98] *Ghana*, "Conference of Heads of State and Government, Belgrade," Accra, 1961, p. 99.
[99] Interview: Quaison-Sackey.

Every resolution—*qua* resolution—was at the time welcome to the Soviet Union, every one unwelcome to the United States. True, numbers 1, 4, 5, 6, and 7 could be seen as part of the general anticolonialist stance, yet, in combination with numbers 2 and 3, they constituted a hostile battery indeed; Nkrumah's commitment to nonalignment was once again in question. If a few other nonaligned leaders had taken the same position, it was with less vehemence. True, Nkrumah deplored the Soviet nuclear test during the conference. But the nature of his criticism showed that he was applying a double standard for testing by East and by West.[100]

There was a last act. Modibo Keita and Sukarno were designated to go to Washington with the conference's peace plea, and Nehru, who was going to Moscow on a long-planned visit, reluctantly agreed to carry the same message to Moscow. Nkrumah was returning to the Crimea and thus offered to accompany Nehru to Moscow to assist him in presenting the plea to the Soviet leaders, a gesture of which Nehru was unappreciative.[101]

From Moscow, Nkrumah went on to the Crimea. The savings-tax imposed in the new "Kaldor budget" had led to a strike of the railway and harbor workers in Ghana, and civil unrest was spreading throughout the country. Nkrumah was afraid to return to Ghana. D. S. Quarcoopome, head of the ministry's research (Intelligence) bureau, sent his colleague Ben Forjoe to Russia to plead with Nkrumah to return. He agreed to do so, ten days after the conclusion of the Belgrade conference.[102]

At this point it was much clearer than before in which direction Ghana's foreign policy would move. Ghana had not been greatly affected by Nkrumah's international radicalism, but the West had lost any illusions it might have held. Two years before, it could point to Nkrumah as an example of a self-styled Marxist developing his country with Western aid, and now it was hostile. In July 1961, Colin Legum wrote that none of the new African states "has succeeded yet in producing a leader to challenge his pre-eminence in Africa's emancipation struggle."[103] Yet

[100] "Warnings to mankind" were issued when Russia tested; direct criticism of the U.S. when it tested. Note too that Russia tested first, and America followed only eight months later with a series of atmospheric tests. See P.R. #998/61.

[101] See Jansen, *Afro-Asia*, p. 304; *Hindu*, 7 September 1961; Rawle Knox, "End of Bandung Era," *Observer Foreign News Service*, 7 September 1961, and interview: Dr. Peter Lyon.

[102] Interview: CF-94A. Both Nkrumah's admirers and critics were substantially agreed on one point about him, namely, what amount of courage he possessed.

[103] "A new Look at Dr. Nkrumah," *Observer*, 2 July 1961.

within two months, Legum, whose respect for African political and economic independence was nowhere in question, had written Nkrumah off.[104] This was representative of a growing disaffection among Western liberals who were becoming convinced that Nkrumah was betraying his own cause. The *Guardian* summed up one mood, when it commented on Nkrumah's suggestion that the great powers meet in Accra to discuss Berlin: "If credit is to rebound on the neutral host there are many with a prior claim. . . . The international inflation of Dr. Nkrumah derives from [Ghana's] strategic position in the cold war. Ghana was the first . . . to achieve independence. . . . Her leader thus came to be looked upon by the West, understandably but wrongly, as the architect of African independence and as the natural leader of an African 'bloc'. . . . Perhaps he is just a man to whom too much deference is paid."[105] From this point onwards, Western public comments were to be like this. But deference was the price Western governments, on the other hand, were prepared to pay, until that point at which the Russians and the Americans lost interest in Africa in general.

EXTERNAL RELATIONS, SEPTEMBER 1961–JULY 1962: THE PENDULUM

Nkrumah had hoped to found a pan-African state by leading the continent in a search for the political kingdom. The Congo crisis, the independence of the conservative-minded Francophone states, and the growing influence of radical advisers in Flagstaff House brought Nkrumah to the belief that the political kingdom alone could not resist outside forces. Neocolonialism had become too potent in Africa. At this point, Nkrumah might well have chosen one crusade and concentrated on it, but now he became convinced that without an economic revolution political independence would be impossible, and that economic independence could only come through socialism.

On his return from the Crimea, all his concerns for Africa had to be put aside. He had been abroad for more than two months and much had changed. The country was paralyzed by a strike which at the very least threatened his personal political position. The West, no longer considering Nkrumah's brand of nonalignment genuine, was making every effort—and using every card they had—to prevent him from "going over to the other side." Thus the Volta scheme, which Nkrumah thought the Americans had agreed in principle to finance, was placed in jeopardy. So was the royal visit, which Nkrumah needed more than ever to increase popular support for his regime and himself.

[104] Interview: Colin Legum.
[105] *Manchester Guardian*, 17 September 1961.

These subsequent three months were among the most turbulent and critical of the Nkrumah period, and the triple challenge Nkrumah faced was intimately involved with foreign policy questions; one relating to relations with the Soviet Union, another with Great Britain, and a third with the United States. Following these, the equilibrium in Ghana's external relations that appeared to be established during the first half of 1962 shall be examined.

Victory of the Radicals and Relations with the Soviet Union. In the spring, shortly after his return to Ghana from New York and London, Nkrumah delivered one of his most important speeches, the "dawn broadcast," in which questions of party unity, ideological training, and presidential power were discussed. The first two of these he had neglected to cultivate and develop during the past year of almost total absorption in foreign and African affairs. Equally important in the speech was his attack on corruption, that most discussed aspect of Ghanaian public life.[106] This gave the radicals, who had enjoyed fewer opportunities to indulge in the acquired practices of ministerial life in West Africa, a sharp propaganda advantage over the old guard.

Virtually nothing was done about it, however, and the discrepancy between Nkrumah's ideologies and Ghanaian realities appeared more glaring as a result of the trip East. He had taken the left-wing leaders along with him no doubt for reasons of security, but their presence gave them the opportunity to press for drastic changes in Ghana. In the Crimea, he received allegations that the old guard were plotting against him, with the help of the "imperialists."[107] At this time Khrushchev offered him advice and aid on his personal security, which, significantly, he turned down. But he had ample time to consider who were his friends before returning on September 16th.[108] The trip East had indeed "marked a distinct break with the past," as Krobo Edusei later said.[109]

On his return, Ghana appeared to be on the verge of upheaval. The opposition was reaping fast benefit, the old CPP guard was disaffected, and the radicals themselves were threatening his position. At first, he tried moderation with the strikers (despite the advice of the left wing),

106 It was later stated that Nkrumah himself, at the time of the broadcast, possessed £100,091 in cash assets. See *Ghana*, "Kwame Nkrumah Properties," Accra, 1966, p. 1.

107 Interview: CF-87, Jackson, and Botsio. Botsio (and Jackson) thought the take-off point for the allegations was simply the fact that he and Gbedemah were less than warm in their support of Nkrumah's budget during the parliamentary debates on it following Nkrumah's departure for Moscow.

108 Interview: CF-87. See the excellent study of this period by St. Clair Drake and Leslie Lacy, "Government Versus the Unions: The Sekondi-Takoradi Strike, 1961," in Carter, *Politics in Africa*, New York, 1966.

109 "Conference of Ghana Envoys," p. 154.

but they refused to return to work. Tawia Adamafio and his friends were said to have drawn up in Peking a list of those whom they considered dispensable to the regime and now came their chance to present it, along with a demand that rapid steps be taken to move Ghana toward socialism, as Colonel Nasser at that very time was doing in Cairo. Faced with their overwhelming pressures and the threat to his position which followed their mixture of intellectual conviction and opportunism, Nkrumah did what he believed was necessary for his survival—he adopted their program and accepted their demands.[110]

Nkrumah broadcast again, declaring that the strike was illegal and had revolutionary overtones. His birthday, Founder's Day, was to follow, on September 21st; it would be a national holiday, and after it, he said, the country must return to work. After all, "the entire nation recognizes that I am the Founder of the new State of Ghana," he said,[111] thus adding the element calculated to remove himself from Adamafio's grasp. He then dismissed those on the black-list. First to go was General Alexander. Gbedemah, Botsio, Welbeck, and their ministerial friends went next. Sir Robert Jackson was saved by the fear that with him might well go the Volta River Project as well as the Queen's visit, for which he was responsible.

Was Ghana "going Communist," as some journalists asked? Obviously not. To all but a handful of the puritan radicals, the Soviet Union was a peripheral ally in a fierce struggle for local power. On the other hand, what had happened was not a move "toward a more recognizable position of noncommitment in the cold war" (as Colin Legum described it).[112] In October, for example, Nkrumah sent a representative to the Twenty-Second Party Congress in Moscow, and although Mr. Ebenezer Kweah was a minor CPP official, it was a symbolically important step.[113] True, Guinea sent its party Secretary, Saifoulaye Diallo, but Ghana was a newcomer to such levels of intimacy in the international Communist hierarchy; as early as 1959, a Soviet representative had attended a congress of the Parti Democratique Guinéen.[114]

At the diplomatic level, the Russians were gaining substantial leverage

[110] Interviews: Sir Robert Jackson, Kojo Botsio, and CF-85. See also Austin, *Politics in Ghana*, London, 1964, p. 408; *Economist Intelligence Unit*, No. 36, 13 December 1961; and Roger Murray, "Second Thoughts on Ghana," *New Left Review* (March/April 1967), 42, 35.

[111] P.R. #893/61, 20 September 1961.

[112] "Is Ghana Going Communist (part 2)" *Observer Foreign News Service*, 3 October 1961.

[113] He was so unimportant that Ghana's ambassador in Moscow had not been alerted to his visit. See "Conference of Ghana Envoys," p. 51.

[114] See Alexander Dallin, "The Soviet Union: Political Activity," in Brzezinski, *Africa and the Communist World*, Stanford, 1963, pp. 24-25.

with Nkrumah; Ambassador Sytenko, an effective diplomatist, did much to advance his country's interests. By this time, Ghanaian policy was easily influenced; for example, the question of Ghanaian representation in Moscow. Nkrumah and the ministry had decided to move J. B. Elliot from Moscow to Rabat, and Dr. Bossman from Rabat to Moscow; Bossman had paid his farewell call on King Hassan when he received instructions to remain at his post. Sytenko had made clear that it was important to his government that Elliot remain where he was, "which was all the more reason he should have been transferred," F. E. Boaten commented (from a professional standpoint) at the time.[115] Sytenko's reason is very straightforward: Elliot advanced Russian interests with the Ghana Government.

Moreover, in June 1961, Nkrumah had established a "new organization set up to expedite economic arrangements with the Eastern countries,"[116] the Committee for Economic Co-operation with Eastern Countries (CECEC), with a dozen principal secretaries and ministers on it. Their job was to see to the transformation of the Ghanaian economy which, beginning in January 1962, they attempted for a time to do.[117]

The Russians, who for a long time had not known what Nkrumah sought, found him not only useful, but usable by the end of 1961. Their growing difficulties in Guinea (where Ambassador Solod was asked by Touré to leave the country) made it all the more important to have a secure foothold in Ghana. Thus Anastas Mikoyan visited Ghana at the beginning of 1962 to consolidate gains made during the summer of 1961. Mikoyan could possess no illusions regarding the amount of socialism in Ghana: Ako Adjei recalled an occasion where he met with the cabinet and jested that "none of you are socialists."[118] At the level where it counted, he appeared to accord Ghana a new status, and said that Ghana "had made great progress in building socialism in the country."[119] This is in line with neither contemporary Soviet prescriptions or formulae, and thus was gratuitous. But the Soviets must have had high hopes.[120]

The Domestic Political Crisis and Relations with Britain. British public interest in Ghanaian developments had existed since that country's independence, but throughout 1961 British journalists flocked to Accra

[115] Interviews: Amb. A.B.B. Kofi, and F. E. Boaten.
[116] M.F.A. to Ghana/Moscow, 2 June 1961, CFA-10.
[117] Minutes, CECEC, 1962-1966, see CFA-10-11, 13-25.
[118] Interview: Ako Adjei.
[119] *Tass,* 12 January 1962, quoted in Brzezinski, *op.cit.,* p. 35.
[120] I am grateful to Professor Robert Legvold for his helpful discussion of Soviet policy in this period. See his incisive study, *Soviet Policy Toward West Africa: 1957-1967,* Harvard, forthcoming.

reporting on what they generally considered to be the deterioration of a regime.[121] Concern over the erosion of civil liberties and the growing strength of the Ghanaian left came to a head over the question of the Queen's visit to Ghana, scheduled for November 1961; everyone involved appreciated how much her visit could strengthen Nkrumah's personal position. Evidence that this concern was motivated by fear for British investments in Ghana is hard to find: the wave of public sentiment, the force of which strongly affected the British government, was probably caused by the strangeness of the turn of events in a country to which Britain had felt proud to bring independence, and in which it had implanted its own traditions. "As Dr. Nkrumah is the heir to our powers, those he oppresses are in general the heirs to our traditions, among them men who have in the darkest time . . . spoken out in favour of free speech, the rights of minorities, and the rule of law."[122]

In Ghana, anger and resentment mounted, both within and without CPP ranks, at what was considered scurrilous and unjustified criticism. Patrick O'Donovan wrote that Ghanaians resented the "lack of sympathy" for them: "With all this goes an overwhelming longing for physical progress, for prestige and recognition, and an angry longing for the satisfaction of a special African hunger whose causes are only too obvious."[123] Ghanaian radicals, for their part, saw it as an opportune time to sever the British ties that had exercised so powerful a restraint on Nkrumah during the four previous years. While he was still in the Crimea, the *Evening News* attacked Britain in a way that brought the propriety of a royal visit clearly into question. "How can a so-called bankrupt nation [as British correspondents had described Ghana] play host to the imperial head of a bloated kingdom?" After Nkrumah's return, the *Ghanaian Times* named Britain as the "principal culprit" in Secretary-General Hammarskjold's death.[124]

Nkrumah and the British government faced difficult choices. Nkrumah knew how much a successful royal visit would bolster his popularity, but his more immediate problem was to ensure his own survival in Flagstaff House. He felt he had to risk offending the British government,

[121] The most significant of the articles was a two-part series by John White, in the *Times*, 13-14 June 1961. A government white paper written by Geoffrey Bing later in the year saw this as part of a "conspiracy" against Ghana, and compared that paper's campaign against Ghana with its campaign in the 1930's against Czechoslovakia. Nkrumah also frequently alluded to the articles.

[122] "Dr. Nkrumah at Home," *Daily Telegraph*, 16 October 1961.

[123] *Observer*, 29 October 1961. British criticism was one issue that appeared to draw the country together throughout the Nkrumah period.

[124] *Evening News*, 11 September 1961; *Ghanaian Times*, 20 September 1961. The government dissociated itself from the second charge.

thus jeopardizing the visit, by dismissing General Alexander and those moderate ministers whom the British trusted and whom the radicals insisted that he dismiss. The British government, on the other hand, feared that the cancellation of the visit could precipitate a seizure of power by the radicals, as well as a break with Britain and the Commonwealth. Yet if the Queen were advised to go, and if Nkrumah reaped the benefits of her prestige in Ghana, British public opinion might be offended.

Moreover, normal channels of consultation and communication between Nkrumah and Duncan Sandys, the Commonwealth secretary, had broken down. Only a few days after General Alexander's dismissal, Sandys flew to Accra for three days of talks with Nkrumah. There, Nkrumah used his normal tactics to disarm him: The press was free, and was not to be taken too seriously; he only sought to balance his ties with the West with new ones in the East so as to achieve a genuinely nonaligned position. His admiration of the British and respect for their record of de-colonization was nowhere in doubt.[125]

Sandys, however, had heard all this many times before, and made full use of his best card—the Queen. He told Nkrumah that although his comments were very generous, they were very different indeed from what he had been saying publicly. The British, after all, had kept close track of his speeches, and he had had nothing good to say about Britain, and nothing bad about the Russians, Sandys said to Nkrumah. But his words were so kind that they should be made public; he (Sandys) would therefore summarize them that night in the form of a communiqué that both could sign. When Sandys presented Nkrumah with his own summary of the generous tributes to Britain, in the form of a communiqué, Nkrumah was visibly shocked and said he would have to consult his cabinet. He returned with a version unacceptable to Sandys, who worked it back almost to its original form, after which Nkrumah twice returned to his cabinet, where it was finally accepted in essence as Sandys had first written it.[126]

Up to this point, there had been no question of the Queen's visit being canceled, but presumably this is not what Sandys had told Nkrumah. The communiqué was received soberly by the British press, happily for Britain, as it was an astonishing triumph for the Commonwealth secretary. Ghana obtained recognition of its policy of nonalignment, "neither leaning towards the East nor towards the West," but as its nonalignment had never been in question, this was, thus qualified, a concession to Britain. Furthermore, "President Nkrumah assured Mr. Sandys that

[125] Interview: CF-103. Also, interviews: CF-60, 85.
[126] *Ibid.*

he appreciated the fact that since the Second World War Britain had given independence to nearly 600 million people and had thereby set an example in the peaceful transfer of power which had been followed to some extent by other colonial powers."[127] President Nkrumah "welcomed" Mr. Sandys' statement that the British government did not attach "strings" to economic aid given; "accusations against Britain of neo-colonialism were therefore not justified." Nkrumah advised the peoples of the remaining British colonies "to rely on the declared intentions and good faith of the British Government and to press their case for early independence by constitutional means," a statement adding nothing to Nkrumah's stature in East Africa. They praised the Commonwealth, advocated disarmament, and even "papered over"[128] their total disagreement on the Congo question to take a united stand, even though, two weeks earlier, Nkrumah had used British policy in Katanga as a principal reason for dismissing Alexander.[129]

Nkrumah's actions in the ensuing weeks, however, provided new aggravations for the British press. When he detained fifty men in the aftermath of the strike—including Dr. Danquah and Sir Stafford Cripps' son-in-law, Joe Appiah—pressure against the visit mounted. Jeremy Thorpe, the Liberal M.P., visited Accra and returned to advise against the Queen's visit, on grounds of security. This was a pretense, if not a canard; he wanted more attention focused on what he considered the reprehensible features of a reprehensible regime.[130] Bomb explosions began in Accra, and whether they were done by the left, or by the opposition (who were united in having nothing to gain from a successful royal tour), it is clear that they were done to bring about cancellation. On the eve of the Queen's departure Sandys made another visit, this time to dramatize the precautions that had been taken. Unless the most serious of security threats existed, Her Majesty was virtually bound to go through with her visit, which was in accord with her wishes,[131] and with British interests. H.M.G. was well apprised of the grave consequences that would flow from cancellation at so late an hour. Through Sandys' tour de force, the British government had obtained the satisfaction it needed so that relations could be restored to a level where it could be seen that vital British interests were not threatened and that Britain continued to possess influence in Accra. "Honour had been served."[132]

---

[127] *Times*, 6 October 1961. [128] Interview: CF-103.
[129] See Nkrumah to Alexander, 22 September 1961, in H. T. Alexander, *African Tightrope*, London, 1965, p. 149.
[130] Interview: CF-108A.
[131] Interview: CF-60. [132] Interview: Sir Robert Jackson.

Ghana's International Stance and American Policy. On 29 June 1961, Kennedy wrote to Nkrumah that the United States could be expected to participate in the Volta River Project, subject to World Bank feasibility rulings; the letter arrived in time to be a "birthday present" on Ghana's Republic Day.[133] Throughout the ensuing summer, however, the new administration heatedly discussed its attitude toward nonalignment, and frequently took Nkrumah's shifting position as focus for the debate. Certainly, Washington circles were disillusioned over the West's prospects in the third world as a result of the Belgrade Conference and, on September 4th (during the Conference), Kennedy announced that "in the administration of [foreign aid] funds, we should give great attention and consideration to those nations who have our view of the world crisis."[134]

While the British public had been largely concerned about Ghana's domestic trends, in America it was Ghana's international stance that was under attack, and on September 21st Kennedy put American participation in the Volta River Project under review. What followed in the ensuing three months reflects many of the forces at work in a potentially classic neocolonialist situation. It was to be the biggest investment in Africa; Ghana was negotiating with the world's greatest power, with one of its many corporations whose earnings equaled Ghana's annual product itself, and with the World Bank, which, while skeptical from the first about the project, was prepared to follow the American lead.[135]

For two years, American initiative had been located in the State Department, which had pressed Kaiser to stand by the project while all but one of its corporate partners withdrew from participation in the aluminum scheme. By the time of Kennedy's inauguration, however, Kaiser was the more deeply involved, and although it had very little money tied up in Ghana at this point, it wanted the project to proceed. After all, as a Kaiser official said, "Where else could we get a 120,000 ton aluminum smelter, costing $150,000,000, of which 85% was supported by debts, 90% of that covered by the American government."[136] Thus, roles were to a large extent reversed; the first telephone call Governor Williams received at the State Department in January 1961 was from Chad Calhoun, Kaiser's chief negotiator for the project.[137] Kaiser

---

[133] *UPI* dispatch, 30 June 1961. George Weeks, UPI correspondent in Washington, generously made his Ghana files on this period available to the writer.

[134] Quoted in " 'Our View' and Ghana's," *New Republic*, 16 October 1961. Most liberal American journalists criticized Kennedy's statement.

[135] Interview: CF-64, September 1965.

[136] Interview: CF-35, July 1965.   [137] Interview: CF-102, September 1965.

190

sought the government's involvement for its own protection, but the State Department was now more cautious, particularly as Gbedemah's influence in Ghana began waning.[138]

Nkrumah had several important cards in his hand, knew it, and used them. In early October, he wrote to Kennedy saying that in view of the letter of June 29th, he had assumed America would participate in the scheme, especially as the World Bank had in the meantime reported favorably. Impresit, the Italian construction firm that had won the dam contract, had imposed a deadline of October 17th for a Ghanaian greenlight, and so "if your government wishes to send a further mission to Ghana [to review the project] I should be grateful if it could come in sufficient time to inform me of US Government's position . . . by 13 October."[139] Some sources, said the *Financial Times*, thought the letter was an ultimatum; if so, Kennedy returned the gesture in kind, in arranging for Impresit's deadline to be extended by sixty days.[140]

Kennedy then appointed a team to review the project, headed by a known conservative, Clarence Randall, who had visited Ghana the previous year, and whose reservations about the project and the Nkrumah regime were known. The other two were Abram Chayes, who, with Mennen Williams and his deputy Wayne Fredericks, was the only important supporter of the project in the administration, and Harry Shooshan, an official from the Development Loan Fund. Randall, however, instructed his colleagues to report separately. Their terms of reference from the White House were to find out "if Nkrumah is a Communist"; what the consequences would be were support for the project withdrawn; what the attitude of Ghanaians and other Africans was; and what were the inherent merits of the plan itself.[141]

A British diplomatist once observed that Nkrumah was "the most sophisticated African leader" in dealing with Western leaders;[142] if Sandys had called Nkrumah's bluff, Nkrumah showed himself fully capable of dealing with men who knew him less well. According to one of the team, he presented himself most persuasively as the "troubled head of state" deeply concerned about his people, and about the problem of achieving consensus in a fragmented society.[143] Thus the ideological ramifications of recent changes were minimized. At least two of the three reported that Nkrumah definitely was not a "Communist" (whatever this meant), a judgment amplified by a letter from Macmil-

138 See *Observer*, 1 October 1961.
139 UPI dispatch.
140 *Financial Times*, 3 October 1961.
141 Interview: CF-105A, September 1965.
142 Interview: CF-106.
143 Interview: CF-105A.

lan to Kennedy. Sir Robert and Lady Jackson also played a critical role in convincing Washington.[144]

The second question, the consequences of cancellation, was the most serious. Aswan and 1956 was in everyone's mind. For a decade Nkrumah had searched for funds for the scheme, and he had often justified delay in the implementation of party plans for "building socialism" on the grounds that the Volta scheme was not to be jeopardized. The party left had long advised him not to count on Western support for it, and were they now to be proved right, there was the possibility that they could convince him to take drastic steps to alter Ghana's relations with the United States. Those advising Kennedy were not permitted to forget this. In any case, what was the president to tell Nkrumah if it were cancelled? How was he to hide a political motive? This was Nkrumah's strongest card.

The attitude of others in Ghana and Africa also counted. The Nigeria lobby that was thought to exist in Congress vanished, in view of Prime Minister Sir Abubaker's recommendation that the project not be stopped. Even Olympio favored it. Their motive was the same as that which America was to adopt; Volta was for the people of Ghana, and it was to their longer-range welfare, not to the Osagyefo's, that one had to look. This was not sentimentality, but a careful calculation of Nkrumah's chances of surviving, measured against the popular loyalties that would be at stake in the post-Nkrumah era. Finally, there was the inherent merit of the plan. Randall concluded that the amount of money involved was too large, given the political risk and uncertain economic benefit. But the other two thought the scheme imaginative, with an excellent cost/benefit ratio, and recommended in favor of the project.[145]

Ambassador Francis Russell, however, was uncertain what Clarence Randall would recommend, and from his own soundings in Washington had concluded that Kennedy's final decision could go either way.[146] Thus, when Sir Robert Jackson and a young USIS officer informed him that Randall had divulged a negative conclusion, he prepared an eleventh-hour appeal to President Kennedy.[147] While Russell was not optimistic about Ghana's prospects under Nkrumah and believed that the project could make him invulnerable, he stressed to Kennedy that

144 See Arthur Schlesinger, *A Thousand Days*, p. 499.

145 Interviews: CF-105A, Sir Robert Jackson.

146 Interview: CF-97. This was not an unsound conclusion. World Bank officials had long thought the project was being oversold, and when the tide seemed to turn against the project, did not hesitate to criticize it. Interview: CF-64.

147 Interviews: CF-60, 97.

80 percent of the civil service and of the university faculty, and much of the population, were against the regime; their position had to be strengthened against the day when Nkrumah was no longer in power.

In the end, it was one of Kennedy's "very closest decisions," according to Sorensen.[148] On December 16th, Randall and Russell were able to give Nkrumah the good news, hours before Impresit's deadline was to expire. America had done what it had to do, and if within the year it was regretting the decision,[149] in less than five it was to be most grateful.

Randall and Russell tried to convince Nkrumah that it was in his interest to make Ghana's nonalignment stricter, but there was little they could do but hope. What effective argument did they possess? Even while Kennedy weighed the pro's and con's of the Volta River Project, Ghana's courtship with the Soviet Union had gone on, and the press had continued to attack "imperialism" and "neocolonialism." By the end of the year, America's status in Ghana was at a low ebb.[150]

This is well illustrated by noting the difficulty of keeping channels of communication open. Kennedy had made it clear that he wanted Ambassador Russell to have access to Nkrumah on issues of interest to himself (it is significant that such a promise had to be exacted). It took little to upset the delicate equilibrium. An American journalist, for example, unable to obtain a Ghanaian visa from the embassy in Washington, spoke of the difficulty to a friend at the White House in November, who in turn apprised Clarence Randall of the problem. Randall discussed the matter with Nkrumah during their meeting of December 16th: Nkrumah suggested that Randall "had been misinformed" on the question of the visa.[151] Ambassador Russell, for his part, did not permit the matter to be dropped, and in February wrote to Nkrumah reminding him of the journalist's difficulty. Nkrumah wrote that the journalist should have had no trouble in obtaining a visa and that Ghana's position had therefore been misrepresented. Russell replied thanking him, and added that "I hope you will let me know whenever you have any reason to believe that statements by any American officials are inaccurate."[152]

---

[148] Theodore Sorensen, *Kennedy*, London, p. 594. Schlesinger argues that Kennedy's mind had long been made up, an unpersuasive argument in view of the strong opposition to the project. Schlesinger, *A Thousand Days*, p. 499.

[149] See Schlesinger, *A Thousand Days*, p. 500.

[150] It is tempting to believe that this is because Nkrumah had attained his objective, and had no further need to still the radicals. Western diplomats in Accra at the time stressed that it was more likely because the tension had been so great in the autumn, and the rout of the moderates so complete; the new wave of anti-imperialist sentiment was in the circumstances a natural consequence. Interviews: CF-60, 97.

[151] Quoted in Russell to Nkrumah, 28 February 1962, CFA-52, 53.

[152] *Ibid.*

193

Nkrumah's irritation was apparent, however, in his reply to what was by then a dead issue: "I find it somewhat embarrassing that the White House should be approached with routine matters of this nature. It will be appreciated that if this practice is allowed to persist, it will not promote the happy relations that now exist between our two countries."[153] Nkrumah's reaction within Flagstaff House is apparent from Ako Adjei's letter to Ambassador Halm in Washington. "Osagyefo . . . is surprised and most unhappy that the American Ambassador . . . should have bothered him and wasted his precious time with such routine matters."[154]

Within the Kennedy administration, however, the question of whether the journalist amidst a free press should be able to visit a country being aided by the United States was more than trivial. The radicals thought Russell had been impertinent, though his request had been little different from similar and daily ones from Eastern diplomats.[155] The American ambassador had exercised what diplomats of beneficent great powers have usually considered their right, but this was no longer good enough in Accra. According to Ako Adjei, "A vicious diplomatic circle had developed in Accra. I became very upset when an ambassador broke form and went straight to Nkrumah without clearing the appointment at the ministry. It was the group of Eastern diplomats who began it; the French, British, and Americans were careful to avoid breaking a rule. Then they realised that the Communists were making the running and tried to go straight to Nkrumah too. But it was too late. In any case, the ministry had no power, and they knew it."[156] Volta or no Volta, the balance of nonalignment had begun to tip in one direction, a double-standard for judging East and for West having been accepted.

Domestic-Foreign Policy Relations, January—July, 1962. The "Eastward" line of development in Ghana's foreign policy which had begun with the Congo failures, and had progressed during the trip to the East, might have been seen to triumph completely by the summer of 1962. In July, the CPP called its first conference of significance, and the "Programme for Work and Happiness" adopted was rich in new departures: Ghana was to have a one-party state and Nkrumaism was, for the first time, defined as being based on "scientific socialism."[157] Economic thinking was changing *pari passu.* E. N. Omaboe, the government statistician,

---

[153] Nkrumah to Russell, 1 March 1962, CFA-53.
[154] Adjei to Amb. Halm, 1 March 1962, CFA-52.
[155] See Interview: CF-14.   [156] Interview: Ako Adjei.
[157] See *CPP,* "Programme of the CPP for Work and Happiness," Accra, n.d., pp. 5, 12, 7, 20.

wrote that the Ghanaian leaders had been profoundly impressed with planning in the East, and had come to the conclusion that the existing five year plan "was no plan at all. The decision was therefore taken to scrap it and to work on a new plan that would possess the basic characteristics of socialist developments plans."[158]

There was, too, Nkrumah's growing suspicion at this time that the CIA was his real enemy, a suspicion against which any small diplomatic gains by Ambassador Mahoney, Kennedy's personable new envoy, were irrelevant.[159] In May 1962, when Nkrumah won the Lenin Peace Prize, it might have been difficult to believe that Ghana's nonalignment could be prevented from proceeding further in the same Eastward direction. True, the pious sentiments expressed in joint communiqués of Ghana and its socialist friends, regarding disarmament, imperialism, or their desire to transform Africa into a "zone of peace," seemed meaningless in themselves, but the possibility always existed that one step would lead to another, and that pious sentiments would lead to coordinated policies.

Yet, equally salient developments opened a different set of possibilities in the first half of 1962. In fact Touré had won the peace prize and then asked a Russian ambassador to leave; in Ghana, the occasion of Nkrumah's winning was more notable for the praise directed to Nkrumah than for the praise directed to the benefactor. Krobo Edusei, in the Assembly debate, congratulating Nkrumah, compared him to Jesus Christ, and if this was in Edusei's character, it suggested how far Marxism had gone in Ghana.[160]

Most important, there was the domestic political atmosphere of early 1962, which had settled to such a degree that Nkrumah felt able to release 321 detainees, among whom were Dr. J. B. Danquah and Joe Appiah. This action breathed new warmth into Ghana's relations with the West, for several reasons. The Western press used the detention of distinguished Ghanaians to discredit the regime; when they were released, Duncan Sandys could, for example, go so far as to comment publicly that this constituted "an important step towards the restoration of confidence and normality."[161] For the fact was that the radicals made their gains in times of crisis, as in the heat of the Congo *débâcle*, or the Takoradi strike; in such circumstances, Nkrumah was susceptible

[158] E. N. Omaboe, "The Process of Planning," in Walter Birmingham, I. Neustadt, and E. N. Omaboe, eds., *A Study of Contemporary Ghana*, London, 1966, pp. 450-51.
[159] Russell left in early 1962 due to ill-health. William Mahoney, an Arizona lawyer, had campaigned for Kennedy in 1960.
[160] *Debates*, 17 May 1962, p. 326.
[161] *Times*, 7 May 1962. Sandys also noted that it was not his practice to comment on the internal affairs of other Commonwealth states, thus making his statement the more remarkable.

195

to their blandishments. In times of calm, civil servants wielded more influence. Western diplomats, particularly British, thus pinned their hopes for an improvement in their own position on a further settling of the political scene.[162] Indeed, on 1 May, the British and Ghanaian governments signed a new joint military services training team agreement, which provided for a continued close working relationship between the respective military establishments.

Moreover, those drawing up the new seven-year plan knew (as did their Hungarian adviser, Dr. Joseph Bognor) that Western investment was a prerequisite to its success; ministers never failed to claim that the new economic ties in the East were only diversifications from old colonial patterns, and that Western investment was welcomed. True, Adamafio, at the height of his power during these early months of 1962, was thought to be frustrating attempts to attract capital,[163] but other radical ministers explicitly defended the need for such investment even in private. Gbedemah, by now in exile, correctly predicted that it was illusory to "talk socialism" and expect to get Western capital,[164] but what is relevant is that Nkrumah and the government were at this point interested in improving their image in the West in hope of getting it. As a policy position paper of the ministry said,

> Accepting the important facts that the United States has the economic resources some of which we need, that the United States is the chief "financier" of the United Nations in which we have placed our trust and hopes, we should, therefore, accept the conclusion that it is in our interest to improve our relations with the United States. Admittedly there are difficulties, e.g., the basic American belief in a formal institutionalised opposition in politics . . . but with tact, patience and persistence a lot can be achieved in this direction.[165]

Ghana was also making new efforts in the cadre of nonalignment itself, which had stabilizing effects on the foreign policy. In June 1962, Nkrumah and Ghana were host to the "Accra Assembly," the "World Without the Bomb" conference. It was an off-shoot of the hopes and plans of early 1961 to hold a nonaligned conference, and was developed mainly by Bing and Nkrumah through the voluminous correspondence Nkrumah maintained with various leaders in the disarmament field. It was, in all, a carefully planned effort; preparatory meet-

---

162 Interviews: CF-51, 24 November 1965; 113.

163 Interview: Sir Robert Jackson.

164 Open letter of Gbedemah to Nkrumah, 5 June 1962, privately printed.

165 "Brief on Ghana's Foreign Policy Towards the Americas," in *Ministry of Foreign Affairs*, Conference of Envoys, January 1962, p. 205.

ings began in Accra in October 1961, and continued in Zagreb, in February 1962; an international preparatory committee assisted which included Ritchie Calder (as he then was). The National Assembly appropriated £ 50,000 to finance it, and Frank Boaten, a senior and outstanding Ghanaian diplomatist, was seconded to administer the office. Over a hundred delegates, among them some of the most distinguished members of the international left (Wayland Young, Dr. Homer Jack, Canon Collins, Sean McBride) attended, along with ten experts, including Dr. Oskar Lange and James Wadsworth.[166]

The conference clearly increased Nkrumah's prestige, as a nonaligned leader, in the West. The calibre of the conference membership and the care of the preparation meant that resolutions were produced that commanded attention. Thus, when Ghana took an initiative, it seemed as if the credibility of its nonalignment improved. This was probably because efforts planned in Accra involved Ghanaian civil servants and diplomats who could consider alternatives and options cautiously. When Nkrumah was attempting to gate-crash into areas where his credentials were less than compelling, outbursts usually resulted that jolted the foreign policy to the left.

Another framework of Ghana's foreign policy that had a positive feedback effect was Ghana's membership in the Security Council, which began in January 1962. Nkrumah, who had never given careful attention to United Nations affairs, now began watching developments there closely.[167] If Ghana had expected to wield real influence on the Council, it was to be disappointed, but there is no doubt that Quaison-Sackey brought considerable attention to Ghana through his well-written statements and agile diplomacy. Involvement on the Council tended in itself to be a moderating influence on Ghana and occasionally, at least, a cause for working with the West. In June, for example, Ghana pledged £ 100,000 for the purchase of UN bonds which, from a cold-war perspective, outweighed its agreement with the Soviet Union that the UN secretariat needed reorganization. Thus the pendulum had swung, East and West, reflecting external events, internal pressures, and chance. It was clear, by the middle of 1962, that Ghana intended to be radical and left-wing in its image, but it remained to be seen whether it would preserve its independence of both blocs in the future.

[166] See *Accra Assembly*, "Selections from the papers of 'The Accra Assembly,'" Accra, 1962. Also interview: F. E. Boaten.
[167] Interview: Quaison-Sackey.

ᵒ⑥ᵒ

POLICY IN AFRICA:

Diplomats Versus Militants

April 1961–July 1962

"MR. QUAISON-SACKEY: *Mr. Chairman, I think you will agree with me
. . . [that] it . . . embarrasses the President in using his name as a great
man . . . talking about Nkrumaism. . . .*

"MR. KOFI BAAKO: *We cannot help it. We shall have to talk about it
everyday and if the President himself asked us to stop talking about Nkrumaism we shall not stop—we the masses.*"[1]

ALTHOUGH the African continent was divided by the spring of 1961,
many leaders were seeking opportunities to bring the rival factions together. The motive of Senghor, Tubman, Abubakar, and Olympio in
calling the Monrovia conference was primarily to bring the Casablanca
and Brazzaville groups within one framework, and to this end they
brought in Houphouet, Touré, and Keita as sponsors. Several had the
additional incentive of countering the threat Ghana was thought to pose,
since it was believed that Nkrumah had recently made his first attempt to
overthrow a foreign government—Olympio's. There are several reasons
why Nkrumah was not to support the movement for reconciliation at
this stage. His relations with the individual sponsors (examined in detail
in this chapter) were bad. The decision of his own allies—Keita and
Touré—to join them in planning the conference presented Nkrumah
with a clear challenge.

There was, too, a rebellious current in Africa at one level of inter-
group relationships: the third All-African Peoples Conference was held
in Cairo in March 1961, and at it radicalism was triumphant. It was
also the last AAPC—and the one at which there was almost no Ghanaian influence.[2] The problem for statesmen was to discern which current

---

[1] "Nkrumaism," Conference paper two, *Ministry of Foreign Affairs*, Conference of
Ghana Envoys, January 1962, p. 44.

[2] See Colin Legum, *Pan-Africanism*, London, 1965, pp. 265-80; see also secretary-
general's speech, p. 4, in *Bulletin of the Secretariat*, AAPC, No. 2, 31 October 1961, for
the only evidence of Ghanaian activity within the AAPC.

—radicalism or reconciliation—flowed deeper. Touré gambled on reconciliation. Ambassador Achkar Marof said it was because Guinea had come to realize that the radical states were no more reliable as partners than the conservative states. In the Congo, he noted, a white general from Ghana had constantly frustrated Guinean objectives, and thus he and his colleagues concluded that they would have to work with all the states or be totally isolated.[3] Guinea was thus moving away from its earlier radical stance, a movement which was to culminate in the expulsion of the Russian ambassador at the year's end. Ghana was going in the opposite direction, as a result both of the Congo crisis and the struggle for power within Ghana. All the Monrovia sponsors, save Guinea and Mali, were "aligned" in the cold war, according to Accra's new terminology. Nkrumah, throughout 1961, was thus racing against time to apply the lessons of the Congo as he saw them, firstly by remodeling his foreign policy apparatus and secondly by pressing desperately for an organic union of African states.

The problem of maintaining any momentum in Ghana's Africa policy had become insurmountable mainly because of its aims, but also because of the continued disputes within the ministry and dissension within the foreign service. On April 8th, while Ako Adjei, the minister of external affairs, was in New York, Nkrumah made his "dawn broadcast" in which he announced that he would appoint a minister of state for African affairs, thereby removing African affairs from the jurisdiction of the external affairs ministry (which was renamed the ministry of foreign affairs). Unconsulted, Ako Adjei returned without permission to plead the cause of a coordinated foreign policy. He calculated that this goal would be still more elusive were African relations detached from the ministry.[4] But Nkrumah did not alter his plans; a few weeks later, in a fit of frustration at Flagstaff House, he ordered Michael Dei-Anang, secretary-general of the ministry, to remain in the vacated office of A. L. Adu from that moment, to form a presidential secretariat. "No discussion. Finish!" Enoch Okoh recalled Nkrumah saying.[5] Hence the origins of the African Affairs Secretariat. No action of Nkrumah's was to affect policy-formulation so decisively as this, for whatever chance had existed for developing a cohesive policy was now lost. On the other hand, revolutionary pan-Africanism had won the day. Nothing, organizationally, was to stand in the way of the intensification of the pan-African program. Militant advisers were henceforth able to press their goals in Flag-

---

[3] Interview: Amb. Achkar Marof.   [4] By his own account, in interview.

[5] Interview: Enoch Okoh, cabinet secretary, 1961-1966. Nkrumah appointed Imoru Egala as Minister of State for African Affairs, but Egala held office only briefly, and no successor was named. The creation of the AAS made his position redundant.

staff House directly, with the foreign ministry unable to add a voice of caution.

At the time of the reorganization, the moderate states held their conference in Monrovia. Called in order to bring the blocs together, it momentarily drove them further apart, thanks to a last-minute boycott by the Casablanca states whose attendance was expected. But the moderates made evident how much deeper were their ranks, which made a strong impression on Ghanaians. Dissent had all the while been growing in Ghana—chronicled in the preceding chapter—and both opposition and CPP used these two actions, Nkrumah's dismemberment of the ministry and Ghana's failure to attend Monrovia, as the starting point for an extraordinary parliamentary debate on foreign policy. It was to be virtually the last one before Nkrumah's overthrow. Joe Appiah, the opposition's foreign affairs spokesman, mounted a frontal assault on Dei-Anang's removal to Flagstaff House, on the political favoritism that was ruining the ministry, on the corruption rife among the political appointees in the foreign service, and most of all on Ghana's growing isolation. "We have tried to blaze that torch on the continent of Africa that others might follow. But when all that has been done [and] we find ourselves now the damned, the vilified, not by Europeans but by Africans, then it is time we sit up and take stock of ourselves. . . . Twenty nations, twenty states of Africa [at Monrovia] certainly cannot all be wrong. . . . The Osagyefo maintains that it must always be the majority . . . twenty states forming the majority as against five states [Casablanca] on the other side. . . . African Unity stands in danger."[6] The limits on the opposition were shown by the fact that Joe Appiah, their spokesman, had to aim his sweeping attacks on the foreign minister, whom he knew exercised no power; Appiah was in any case to be detained four months later.

The CPP made many of the same criticisms. Nathaniel Welbeck, whose party fortunes descended after Léopoldville, said that "We must not try to antagonise the countries around us. . . . We must walk and not run . . . to show that we are not going too fast. . . . (Appiah: *Festina Lente!*)—Yes, *Festina Lente.*"[7] The government's defense was revealing. Puplampu, the deputy minister, acknowledged the criticism, then added that it was not Ghana's fault "if other states do not have a long enough vision to see the dream which we cherish of the ultimate union of all African states. We do not seek to antagonise; we seek to make friends, but we seek to make friends in the cause of African Unity, on which there can be no compromise."[8]

[6] *Debates*, 25 May 1961, pp. 946-51.   [7] *Ibid.*, pp. 947-49.
[8] *Ibid.*, p. 1006.

GHANA AND ITS ALLIANCES

There remained enough ideological solidarity between Ghana and its radical allies for Nkrumah to prevent the movement for reconciliation from succeeding during 1961. Ghana, Guinea, and Mali, for example, never voted on opposite sides at the United Nations.[9] There were, as well, obligations emanating from the meeting of Ghana, Guinea, and Mali in late December 1960, and from the Casablanca conference of early January, namely, that the separate groups would continue to meet and consult periodically. Conferences, in this stage of the development of African diplomacy, were a dominant means of diplomatic communication, which was unfortunate. The well-prepared state could dominate a small conference, and unsophisticated politicians could easily be swayed by sentiments reinforced by the enthusiasm of their peers. As long as conferences remained so important, the relative impact of a meeting was crucial, and here, Nkrumah failed to realize that small conferences and groups which he dominated could only in the end lose to the large ones from which he absented himself.

The first real test of Casablanca, as a group with a separate and dynamic existence of its own, came in April 1961. It took the form of a conference of experts in Accra, called for at the January meeting, and was designed to prepare a draft protocol for the implementation of the Casablanca charter. During the five days of discussion, the delegations were able to draw up organizational charts for the political, economic, and cultural committees, but they quite clearly lacked authority to make substantive decisions. They could not even agree formally on a location for their headquarters, though Bamako emerged as a preference.[10]

The military committee evolved detailed plans for the operation of the Joint African High Command (JAHC) during this conference, however. It proposed a supreme council of the chiefs of staff, a permanent military staff commission, and a field command, but the JAHC's power was carefully circumscribed, even on paper. The supreme council, which was to meet twice a year, could only make recommendations to the political committee—the heads of state—which met only once a year. The Egyptians, moreover, saw to the inclusion of a phrase which highly embarrassed Ghana. "All members of delegations shall be nationals of their own respective Member states."[11]

The degree of commitment to the group differed between delegations. Ghana was supplying the dynamism. It wanted the deletion of clauses which limited the scope of the organization, or which implied that the

---

[9] See Thomas Hovet, *Africa in the United Nations*, London, 1962, p. 139.
[10] "Conference of Experts of the Casablanca Powers," Accra, 1961.
[11] *Ibid.*

members' commitment was parallel to that in other "regional" groups. Mali consistently took the most cautious view of Casablanca, and wanted the following clause deleted, in view of its relations with the EEC: "All Member States undertake to notify the Secretariat of all treaties and conventions to which they become parties after the entry into force of the present Protocol."[12] When the secretariat was finally established, it was Ghana that was prepared to grant subventions against its contribution of the following year in the absence of contributions from some members.[13] Ghana was also Casablanca's proselytizer; Nkrumah persuaded Bourguiba to send delegates to the April meeting, and a few months later Ghana was trying to bring Somalia into the group.[14]

A foreign ministers' conference, scheduled for late April, got under way in Cairo in early May. Its only achievement was the selection of Bamako as headquarters. The weakest link and worst possible city were chosen. By this time the Casablanca group was organized, at least on paper, but the conference at Monrovia, that began on May 8th, hid the Cairo meeting from view, thus encouraging the moderates still more.

Midway between the two Casablanca meetings—and prior to the Monrovia conference—came the first quarterly meeting of the Ghana-Guinea-Mali union. Whereas Ghanaian ministers, diplomatists, and soldiers had handled their state's work in the Casablanca group, Nkrumah kept the union very much in his own hands, for on its success hinged the momentum of his pan-African policy. How he persuaded Touré and Keita to withdraw from sponsorship of the forthcoming Monrovia conference is not clear. His intention matters less than the inescapable consequence of his success for all Africa.

One clue is in the financial relations between the three states. Ghana's worsening financial situation was reason in itself, first of all, to cease the large-scale subsidy of allies. In mid-March, Gbedemah had submitted a cabinet memorandum in which he urged that Ghana not disburse the remaining £6,000,000 due to Guinea (of the £10,000,000 loan promised in 1958) or the £5,000,000 promised to Mali. Ghana was no longer a relatively rich country: "We will not be able to give further financial assistance to other African countries."[15] The acceptance of his advice would have meant a *volte-face* in the policy of Nkrumah, who responded to Gbedemah in practical terms. He not only held out the prospect of the completion of the £10,000,000 loan, but also refunded

---

12 *Ibid.*

13 Interviews: CF-104, 115. The 1962-1963 Estimates show Ghana committed £9,800 for the political committee, £5,820 for the cultural committee, £8,300 for the economic committee, and £10,000 for the high command.

14 Budu-Acquah to Afriye, Ghana/Mogadisciu, 15 July 1961, CFA-119.

15 Cabinet memorandum, March 1961, files of Komla Gbedemah.

the £160,000 Guinea had paid on the £4,000,000 borrowed earlier. Now came the time for Keita and Touré to collect on Ghana's promises. Given Ghana's financial straits, Touré and Keita could not have expected success unless Nkrumah were to achieve something by his generosity. By one account, Nkrumah did not explicitly threaten to withdraw the promise if the two did not withdraw as sponsors of Monrovia, but by another account, the financial motive was certainly paramount in their minds.[16] On July 5th Guinea received £1,000,000 and Mali £5,000,000 from Ghana.

The final communiqué gave as reason for their nonattendance that "the majority of the countries participating [at Monrovia] . . . will be represented by delegates other than their Heads of State," and thus it should be "deferred to a later date."[17] The sense of solidarity was also sufficient for them to prepare a charter for the "Union of African States" (UAS), which was "to be regarded as the nucleus of the United States of Africa." It was a restatement of their declaration at Conarky the previous December, but it was a tribute to Nkrumah's persistence that he got it at all. It envisaged "concerted diplomacy," quarterly meetings of the heads of state, a common defense, and many joint popular organizations which in the long run became the most successful (though the least vital) aspect of the union.[18] With respect to political unification, it was the weakest of the long line of statements that had been issued by these parties.

The UAS posed a formal challenge to the rest of Africa, and in the short interval between the announcement of its formation and the beginning of the Monrovia conference, the sparring that was to characterize relations between Ghana and many of the Monrovia powers began. A Nigerian minister ridiculed the new union, composed as it was of only ten millions. They would have done better, he added, to attend Sierra Leone's independence celebrations, and then the Monrovia conference, at which they might have presented their new plan.[19] The Ghanaian press so viciously attacked the Monrovia conference—and Nkrumah's remarks were so unguarded—that the first Ghana-Nigeria press war was set off. It was then that the *West African Pilot* made its famous charge that "Dr. Nkrumah Must Be at the Head of Anything or Outside It," and Colin Legum aptly commented that "for the first time many of

[16] Interviews: CF-104, and Stephan Dzirasa.

[17] P.R. #426/61, 29 April 1961.

[18] See Legum, *Pan-Africanism*, p. 204. The charter was not, however, made public for three more months, and was never ratified by the National Assembly.

[19] Radio Lagos, 3 May 1961, in BBC transcription service, IV, No. 4454. Nkrumah did not go to Sierra Leone because he had long since offended Sir Milton Margai, the premier.

the things that had previously only been said in private were now a matter of public discussion."[20] They were to remain so for a long time to come. Nkrumah had obviously put greater stress on the UAS than on any other framework of action, partly because it embodied his dreams and also because his influence within other groupings was nothing like so great.[21] But by using it as he had, he made clear where responsibility for the continued division of Africa lay: in Accra.

Throughout the spring and summer of 1961 Nkrumah attempted to generate sufficient momentum to expand the Union, and he had several reasons for believing he could succeed. In February, Kanyama Chiume, of Nyasaland, had promised that his party, the Nyasaland ANC, would bring his country into the Ghana-Guinea-Mali union.[22] Throughout the spring there were moves leading to a rapprochement and virtual alliance with Chief Awolowo of the Nigerian Action Group, which culminated in the latter's June commitment to bring Nigeria into the union. Almost at the same time, Garba-Jahumpa of Gambia, a colleague of Nkrumah's from Manchester days, promised to bring Gambia into the union. True, Chiume's country was a long way from independence (and from Ghana), and he made the statement simultaneously with a private request for a large sum of money.[23] The Action Group constituted the opposition in Nigeria, but Nkrumah, far from precluding the possibility of a *boulversement* there, was attempting to bring one about. As for Jahumpa, Pierre N'Jie, chief minister of Gambia, had to point out that Jahumpa was not a minister in Gambia, and had recently been defeated in an election at which his party had won only a single seat.[24] Momentum could nevertheless be generated out of such commitments—or so Nkrumah thought, if only because he believed that he had supporters in various territories prepared to support the union.

A further possibility existed: giving the union geographic contiguity by bringing Upper Volta into it. It was not the interests of the UAS which motivated Ghana to work toward this end, however. By mid-1961, Ghana was isolated geographically and restrictions on contact with its three neighbors increased, failures of which domestic opinion was not unmindful. Ghana was also charged more and more frequently with "imperialist ambitions," particularly after the Monrovia conference. It was thus felt that Ghana had to take a "wild gamble" to prove

[20] Legum, *Pan-Africanism*, p. 55. See also *Ghanaian Times*, 1 May 1961.

[21] According to one Ghanaian diplomat, he once referred to Touré as "my foreign minister" at a UAS meeting. Interview, CF-7.

[22] *Daily Graphic*, 3 February 1961.

[23] Interview: Ako Adjei.   [24] 17 June 1961, BBC IV, No. 4491.

204

that the regime was willing to work toward unity with moderate states in a practical way.[25]

Upper Volta had equally compelling reasons to seek an *economic* arrangement with Ghana. There were over a half-million Voltaic laborers in Ghana, a promised land to these Mossi coming from the world's poorest country.[26] Political independence had also brought President Yameogo a flexibility which he could exploit in an attempt to maximize his country's influence in securing the economic help it needed. It had joined the Conseil de l'Entente because Ivoirien and French pressure made the alternative of joining the Mali Federation impossible. Yet in the ensuing year, Yameogo showed himself politically independent of both senior partners. He repeatedly broke Entente solidarity at the United Nations and refused to sign a defense accord with France.[27]

By January 1961, Yameogo had found himself at a crossroads: The Ivoirien finance minister (a Frenchman) refused to pay the customs rebates on a percentage basis to the Voltaic government as had been agreed in 1960. It looked as if Houphouet had decided to bring him to terms through economic measures. Yameogo had already made several gestures in the direction of Accra and by January, Ghana, for its part, had an immediate need of working with Upper Volta; it was the *"maillot manqué"*[28] between Ghana and Mali, and Mali desperately needed transport facilities between Bamako and the sea. During a recess of the January Ghana-Guinea-Mali conference of experts, a team of Ghanaian and Malian ministers visited Ouagadougou, and in February Yameogo sent a goodwill mission to Accra. That Nkrumah wished to move swiftly can be concluded from the speed with which he opened an embassy in Ouagadougou. He sent a hard-working northerner, George Wemah, who believed that links could be established, and who presented his credentials on February 12th with the comment that colonial barriers had to be torn down.[29]

The real impetus for an agreement was brought, however, by the Monrovia conference, the various competing national interests then taking a new turn. Yameogo, also isolated, developed his contacts with Nkrumah's partners: he visited Conakry in April and Bamako in May, and Touré came to Ouagadougou. Yameogo sought to be the peacemaker between competing West African groupings, something from which he had more to gain than any of his peers. He went to Accra in

25 Interviews: CF-24, 37, 45.
26 See P. C. Damiba, "Les Accords Haute-Volta-Ghana," *Afrique Action*, 30 August 1961; *ibid.*, 8 May 1961.
27 See S. Doambo, "La Nouvelle Orientation," *Afrique Action*, 27 February 1961.
28 *Ibid.*, 25 February 1961.
29 *Ghanaian Times*, 25 February 1961.

May and, while Nkrumah spoke of building African unity, Yameogo talked of economic cooperation.[30] Nkrumah flew to Upper Volta on June 13th for a five-day visit in the midst of a crowded schedule.

Having overplayed his hand in Mali in late 1960, Nkrumah now repeated his mistake in Upper Volta, calling for a single constitution for the two states which, as in Mali, went unreported in the local newspaper.[31] (Four years later, Yameogo commented that Nkrumah's 1961 proposal for a common constitution had made him and his colleagues laugh, as it would soon be violated: "Because, when we came to choose the head of the united state, I would be the first candidate, and you would see that he would no longer desire a common constitution.")[32] The lesson, if any, that Nkrumah had learned from his failure in Mali was that economic links had to be laid quickly after a union was declared in order to give it living reality. This time, Ghanaian and Voltaic experts were working out far-ranging proposals for the elimination of customs barriers between the two countries, a proposal that from Upper Volta's point of view offered an excellent solution to its problems. Goods and peoples would move freely across the border, customs rebates would be paid in full, and Ghana would make an initial loan of good faith. "Men always learn from their mistakes how to make new ones," A.J.P. Taylor wrote of the Austrians after the Crimean War, on the eve of the War of 1859. Nkrumah failed to appreciate that there had existed in Mali a radical idealism which gave Keita a strong ideological bond with him, that was to keep the union between their two states alive in some form for another two years; while in Ouagadougou there was simply a classical view of the national interest. Upper Volta was hardly likely to surrender its sovereignty, and would only work with Nkrumah so long as working with Houphouet seemed less advantageous.

In the absence of any counter effort by Houphouet, Nkrumah seemed to have won a substantial victory, but the lack of response itself raised the question whether *le sage d'Abidjan* was not operating at a higher strategic level. Houphouet had obviously concluded that Yameogo had to learn of Nkrumah's unreliability through experience, and in the meantime focused his own efforts toward reconciliation with Modibo Keita which, if successful, would isolate Ghana further in West Africa.[33]

Keita and Touré, for their part, sought a reconciliation with Houphouet, and neither was impressed by Nkrumah's failure even to inform

30 See "Maurice Yameogo in Ghana," *Ghana Foreign Affairs*, 3 (June 1961), 38-41; *AFP Sp. Outre-mer*, No. 4471, 25 June 1961.
31 *AFP Sp. Outre-mer*, No. 4491, 17 June 1961.
32 *Carrefour Africaine*, Ouagadougou, 28 February 1965.
33 See Interview, Amb. Aisse Mensah, Ghana/Accra.

them in advance of his arrangements with Yameogo—which in the Ghanaian press were heralded as bringing an imminent addition to the very Ghana-Guinea-Mali union of which the latter two states were equally a part. Their displeasure was expressed at the quarterly meeting of the UAS in Bamako just after Nkrumah's visit to Upper Volta.[34] Nkrumah expected them to join him at the ceremony at Paga on June 16th, where he and Yameogo were to tear down a symbolic wall between Ghana and its northern neighbor. They refused. Any chance of the union's expansion was therefore killed. This had been the only careful attempt made to expand it, and now it had been weakened—unless Nkrumah were to make a dramatic success of the new arrangements with Upper Volta.

Early in July the Ghana-Upper Volta joint commission concluded (successfully, it seemed) its study of the problems in this new agreement. Ghana immediately gave Upper Volta £2,000,000, a sum almost equal to the contribution customs rebates had made to the Voltaic budget.[35] From Yameogo's viewpoint, it looked too good to be true, and it appeared that Nkrumah had finally accepted the wisdom of an economic imperative in obtaining African unity. *Afrique Action*, appreciating that history backs winners, commented that Nkrumah had achieved a great success, and that "his 'unrealistic' views on African unity, as fragile as they seem in the immediate future, will surely have their day, at the same time that a policy of positive neutrality, for the poor African states, is seen to be profitable."[36]

Although the agreement appeared to bring impressive gains in trade, it lost its force—as did all of Nkrumah's unions—almost as soon as the ink was dry. This time it was a new villain, in the guise of the Ghanaian economy. The import surcharge, imposed that summer as a result of Nicholas Kaldor's advice, substantially increased the price of goods on the way to Upper Volta. The ministry of finance refused to refund the surcharge, and with Nkrumah in Eastern Europe, little could be done. By the time he had returned, the French bank, skeptical from the first about the union's prospects, and fearing (it was said) the Ghanaian pound's weakness, had already begun to refuse to carry out the functions assigned to it in the agreement.[37]

During the remainder of 1961, the interests of Ghana and its allies

---

[34] Interview: CF-14. It was said that Houphouet, to enrage Keita against Nkrumah, had only to instruct his envoy in Bamako to make regular enquiries at the Presidence, about the progress of Upper Volta-UAS negotiations—an old diplomatic trick.

[35] See *AFP Sp. Outre-mer*, No. 4480, 4-5 June 1961.

[36] 26 June 1961.

[37] Interviews: CF-14, 24. See *Banque Centrale des États de l'Afrique de l'ouest*, "Rapport d'Activité," 1961, p. 5. Also Interview: Amb. Aisse Mensah.

diverged further. The Monrovia conference provided evidence of the moderates' strength in Africa, as we have seen, and from this Touré and Keita drew the obvious conclusion. In addition, and as a corollary, they became convinced that they could achieve an African reconciliation through their former ally, Houphouet-Boigny. Nkrumah, however, had no basis for rapprochement with Houphouet unless he were to retrace far too many steps. Nkrumah had long since resumed his *revanchist* policies with respect to the Ivoirien-Sanwi people, and continued to aid their exiled leaders.[38]

The factors that had originally brought the Casablanca group together were also changing. During the summer, the Congo returned to a legitimate form of government. Egypt became reabsorbed in Middle-Eastern affairs, and the chances for an Algerian settlement were becoming brighter. True, several of the Casablanca committees met during the summer; in July the economic committee met in Conakry and decided to form an African common market. The military committee met at the Cairo Military Academy and named an Egyptian brigadier as commander-designate.[39] Approval, however, had to come from the political committee, scheduled to meet in Cairo at the end of August immediately prior to the Belgrade nonaligned summit.

The Cairo meeting was to be by far the most important meeting of the Casablanca powers. It had been called at the request of the UAS leaders who, at Bamako in June, had decided that consultation was needed prior to the Belgrade summit. They further wished to discuss the forthcoming Lagos conference called by the Monrovia powers for January 1962.[40] Yet on July 24th, at the end of his Russian tour, Nkrumah informed his ministry in Accra that he would not attend,[41] even though he knew he would be on holiday in the Crimea at the time of the conference, from which the journey to Cairo would not have presented formidable difficulties. Moreover, when the meeting was held, Sékou Touré, another of the three who had asked for the meeting, did not appear. It meant that the group was constitutionally disabled until another meeting could be held. The only possible explanation was that Nkrumah's interest in Casablanca had temporarily waned, at least partly as a result of his trip to Russia.

[38] Interview: CF-104. See P.R. 1200/60, 19 December 1960, in which Nkrumah promised to "pursue . . . vigorously" the reunification of Sanwi and Nzima territories. See *Ivory Coast*, Gov. press release, 13 March 1961, for Houphouet's response.

[39] See *le Monde*, 15 July, 31 August, 1961; *Observer Foreign News Service*, 15 July 1961.

[40] See Dei-Anang to Erzuah, Ghana/Cairo, 30 June 1961, and Dei-Anang to Bossman, Ghana/Tunis, 30 June 1961. CFA-57.

[41] Ghana/Moscow to MEA, 24 July 1961, CFA-14.

The Ghanaians were nonetheless trapped within Casablanca. Unable to see their way clear to lead the way to reconciliation, they publicly justified their commitments and in private appeared to believe in their public sentiments. At a seventeen-day conference of the heads of Ghanaian missions in Africa, convened by Michael Dei-Anang, growing self-deception (or a dangerous lack of candor) was apparent. Dei-Anang, for instance, described the Casablanca group as if it were an operative, successful organization. The JAHC, for example, comprised "the Chiefs of Staff of Member States and meets periodically with a view to ensuring the common defense of Africa."[42] Nor were the achievements of Casablanca limited to the "successful meetings from which recommendations are issued. . . . The vehement condemnation of colonialism at the recent Belgrade Conference is mainly due to the concerted action of the Casablanca Powers. No one doubts that the establishment [*sic*] of the African High Command by the Group helped to effect a change in the UN Policy in the Congo."[43]

In the rest of Africa, the realization grew that the competing groups neither reflected the underlying substructure of African inter-state relations nor served the continent's interest. Thus Sir Abubakar Tafawa Balewa went to Conakry in December 1961 for purposes of reconciliation, and Dr. Félix Houphouet-Boigny to Bamako for almost three weeks for the same reason. Their hope was to make a success of the Monrovia group's next meeting, a conference planned for Lagos in January 1962, at which the competing groups could merge. It is true that Nkrumah brought Presidents Daddah and Osman (of Mauritania and Somalia) to Accra during the autumn, but the purpose had been more to proselytize than to bridge the gap between existing groups. Ghana, in 1961, showed that no state could defy the continent's mood and remain the center of the movement for African unity.

THE SEARCH FOR UNITY IN AFRICA: DIPLOMATS AND DIPLOMACY

Michael Dei-Anang once told Ghanaian envoys that "since each of them abroad was both politician and diplomat, it was necessary that they keep the vital arm of a politician separate from the arm of diplomacy."[44] This well described Nkrumah's approach: at a higher level he kept his policy divided into two spheres, generally implemented by separate groups, diplomats and militants. The diplomats, for their part, made frequent attempts throughout 1962, after the January Lagos

---

[42] *President's Office*, "Notes of Conference of Ghana Envoys in Africa," October 1961, p. 41, CF-conf.

[43] *Ibid.*   [44] *Ibid.*, p. 22.

conference had failed to bring the blocs together, to convince Nkrumah to strengthen that arm of his policy which could heal Africa's schism.

Alex Quaison-Sackey, for one, did all he could to influence policy at this critical point. One lengthy report of his reveals both the tactics the diplomats used and their strategic thinking at its best. He emphasized, in the first place, that reconciliation was still possible, that the recently concluded Lagos conference had not resulted in a hardening of attitudes in Africa, as so many had assumed. The Emperor had said in his speech there that no "fundamental or irreparable rift" existed in Africa, but this had gone largely unnoticed. All African countries were committed to "detailed schemes of co-operation," but it was the French-linked Brazzaville group, "which almost always drag their feet."

> Nor has it been well publicized in the Western press that the particular countries were really not prepared to give a final seal to the Liberian draft charter on the establishment of an organisation of African states. What should be noted is that the other states, mainly the "Brazza-ville Group," were not prepared to disrupt their own union, by accepting a charter which they had not had sufficient time to study. It can be deduced . . . that the so-called Monrovia Group is really not a group at all. . . . [The split in Africa is more accurately termed] a bifurcation, which is still capable of rectification.[45]

Hope had come to exist, Quaison-Sackey went on, for Osagyefo had reformulated his own theories. In a major address to the National Assembly, Osagyefo had noted that, because of the many criticisms directed against his scheme for an organic African union, he had decided to add to it a new element, the devising of some constitutional structure which secured the objectives of organic union while preserving "the sovereignty of each country joining the Union."[46] Osagyefo had also noted in his address that new states were unwilling to give up their recently won sovereignty and, more important, he had stressed that Ghana did not seek to impose leadership. The little states nonetheless felt insecure, Quaison-Sackey added, for there was fear (and here was what he had been leading up to) of *subversion*. "This is offered as the justification for entering into military arrangements which often carry no real safeguard or commitment and are mere neo-colonial devices."[47] If they understood this—and were not afraid of subversion (from Ghana), they would be more susceptible to Osagyefo's call for a high command, and for harmonization of their respective foreign policies. "What seems

45 Quaison-Sackey to MEA, March 1961, CFA-54, 55.
46 See *Debates*, 20 January 1962, p. 8.   47 See note 45.

to require re-appraisal is not Ghana's objectives in relation to African unity, but a review of the methods and procedures hitherto employed, in order to dispel the misunderstandings I have earlier described."

By directing attacks on the Brazzaville group-states, Quaison-Sackey could proceed to advocate a policy of cooperation with certain members of the Monrovia group, in concert with Ghana's Casablanca partners. He well knew the limits on Nkrumah's conceptual powers, and had obscured the issue of sovereignty to turn full-circle Nkrumah's new formulation on that question. He was then able to use a traditional tactic, arguing that ends were similar and not in question, and that only the methods were wrong; knowing full well that nothing could have been more central to the debate current in Accra over the question of method. He concluded by advocating the following strategy.

What we have to do is forge firm links with comparatively richer territories like the UAR, Nigeria, Ivory Coast, and Ethiopia in an effort to reassure those countries which, because of their present lack of resources, are seeking European or American allies. The issue really involves Economics. Ghana can not carry the burden of financing her poor neighbours but we can, in concert with like-minded friends like the UAR divide the Brazzaville ranks and make them speak for Africa and not for France. The stakes are high and patient planning and prodding will be required.[48]

At this time, Nkrumah was considering appointing him foreign minister, so his views carried weight.[49]

Nor was Quaison-Sackey alone. Virtually the entire foreign service agreed with him. Even Michael Dei-Anang was sympathetic; he noted in January 1962 that there was "a great responsibility for Ghana to be sympathetic" towards the "African countries which appear to be appendages of France. This is bread and butter diplomacy . . . it is becoming very clear to us that the political entanglements of our African brothers are due mainly to economic necessity and the personal ambitions of certain leaders."[50]

---

[48] *Ibid.*

[49] Mr. Quaison-Sackey graciously permitted the writer to examine his own correspondence and diary on this question. Nkrumah first wrote him in February 1962 that he might be asked to return to Accra, enter politics, and replace Adjei, whom Nkrumah considered useless.

[50] *Ministry of Foreign Affairs*, "Conference of Ghana Envoys," January 1962, p. 70. Whether Dei-Anang was prepared to argue this position with Nkrumah is another matter, though it may be presumed that at this stage he still possessed some independent judgment.

Frameworks of Reconciliation. Domestic crises of the autumn of 1961 had made it difficult for Nkrumah to give attention to Africa policy. By the end of the year, America had committed the needed funds for the Volta scheme, the Queen had made a successful tour that bolstered the regime, and the country had a more settled air than during the preceding four months. From this new position of domestic strength, Nkrumah could begin uniting the continent. With the new year, it seemed that he had taken stock of Ghana's continental position and realized that all was not well. Hence his gestures of reconciliation in his speech to the National Assembly, one of which has already been noted. This was less than contrition, however. In a private address to his ambassadors, he attributed none of the blame to Ghana.[51] More significantly, his Assembly speech showed that he merely wished to improve the appearance of an argument that African leaders were rejecting with a new vehemence —namely, that organic political unity could be reconciled with a preservation of sovereignty. Nkrumah once again was learning how to make new mistakes.

Ghana's position on the Lagos conference demonstrated the dilemma of its diplomacy: its willingness to work toward reconciliation but only on its own terms; its desire to unite all Africa but its inability to shed useless friendships with states with whom it shared ideological bonds. For three months, the dominant concern throughout Africa had been to make a success of the Lagos conference. The Monrovia powers had called it—in conjunction, once again, with Touré and Keita—to provide a framework of reconciliation a second time. In October 1961, Dei-Anang had said that Ghana "might attend";[52] by early January it had been decided that Ghana would attend the foreign ministers' meeting but not the summit of heads of state which was to follow—unless the Casablanca foreign ministers, who were to consult in Accra, decided otherwise.[53] Ghana's position was thus generally hostile to the conference before the real difficulty, Algeria's lack of independent status, appeared. The decision even to attend the foreign ministers' meeting in Lagos was apparently a concession to pressure from the Casablanca group, two of whose members, Guinea and Mali, were its sponsors.

Thus the Casablanca ministers gathered in Accra (while their Monrovia colleagues gathered in Lagos) and a plane waited in Accra to take

51 *Ibid.*, p. 39.
52 *President's Office*, "Notes of Conference of Ghana Envoys in Africa," October 1961, p. 11.
53 See *Ministry of Foreign Affairs*, "Conference of Ghana Envoys," January 1962, statement of K. B. Asante, p. 57.

them on. The question of attendance was discussed all night: Dei-Anang's secretariat presented a paper in which it was argued that unless the Algerian provisional government were invited in advance, even the foreign ministers should not attend. Algeria's Arab allies' quite natural reservations were brought to the fore, and by 5:00 A.M. the group had decided not to attend.[54] A discussion of a few days later sheds some light on Ghanaian motives. It was pointed out that Nigeria had originally intended to invite Algeria, but pressure by the Brazzaville states caused Sir Abubakar to delay Nigeria's invitation to Algeria until after the members could consult.

> *Ako Adjei*: The result was that it would be left to the participating countries themselves when they met to decide whether or not Algeria should be invited. This was the crux of the trouble. France and other countries no doubt were working behind the scene, because it was quite clear that the French-speaking territories would have the majority if it came to the question of voting whether or not to admit Algeria to the conference.
> *Quaison-Sackey*: It is not a fact that the French-speaking countries are more than the other group. [They] are 12 out of a total of 28. . . .
> *Ako Adjei*: The idea was to break the backbone of the Casablanca Powers. If Algeria [be] isolated and the other member states attend then the Casablanca Powers [will have] stabbed Algeria at the back. If Algeria [be] voted out, the only course open to the Casablanca Powers would be to walk out of the Conference and this action would not be diplomatic. We therefore thought the wisest thing for us to do was to boycott the Conference.[55]

Abubakar had quite sensibly realized that the Brazzaville states, in view of their relations with France, could not permit Algeria to be invited in advance, but that they could not dare to oppose the will of the majority once the Casablanca states had arrived. Ako Adjei had no case.

The effect of the Casablanca announcement was sensational, and for the African unity movement at this time, disastrous. Tension had been high in Lagos, where the news was bitterly received. Quaison-Sackey wrote from New York that it had been reported, moreover, "that while most of the delegates in Lagos were willing to accept Algeria's non-participation as a valid excuse for the absence of the North African countries, they attributed other motives to Ghana, Guinea, and Mali; in particular they laid stress on the contra-distinction between the Mon-

[54] Interview: CF-24.
[55] "Conference of Ghana Envoys," January 1962, p. 104.

213

rovia emphasis on the 'inalienable right' of each African state to its own sovereign existence and the Ghanaian ideal of pan-African political union, involving the surrender of sovereignty by each state."[56] Thus, Ghana's Africa policy at the end of January 1962 stood exactly where it was eight months earlier, at the time of the Monrovia conference. There had been no movement.

There was, however, a diplomatic framework of action, that of the Independent African States, through which nonexclusivist tendencies in Ghana's Africa policy were reinforced, but whose objectives were in conflict throughout 1962 with Ghana's other commitment—to the Casablanca group. The "regular cycle of the Conference of Independent African States which has not been broken since 1958" (as Nkrumah wrote Bourguiba)[57] was an acceptable forum of reconciliation for Nkrumah, because Nkrumah had founded the IAS, and a conference in this framework would not dramatize the relative weakness of the Casablanca group.

If the IAS had no machinery—other than the African group in New York—it had developed a sufficient force of tradition for there to be a widely held assumption that its third conference would be held in 1962, in spite of Africa's existing split. At the second IAS meeting, in Addis Ababa in June 1960, it had not been possible to choose a site for the third meeting, so the conference president, Ethiopia's foreign minister, was delegated to select a site. In July 1960 he wrote to the Tunisians that, since Sudan and Morocco had withdrawn as contenders, and "as a result of views exchanged between the states which have offered to be host . . . I am now in a position to announce . . . that . . . Tunisia has been chosen as centre."[58] Ghana, for its part, replied to the Ethiopian government that it was delighted.

A year later, however, with Africa split, Tunisia had to move cautiously to lay the groundwork for the conference. While Nkrumah was in Russia, Ghana's ambassador in Tunis, Dr. Bossman, wrote to Accra that Tunisia still wished to play host and "would particularly like the prior support of Ghana before other states are notified of this desire." K. B. Asante (then acting principal secretary of the African Affairs Secretariat in Dei-Anang's absence) seized the initiative to stress that in 1960 Ghana had "already signified its consent to the Conference being held in Tunisia next year."[59] On 30 January 1962, as the Lagos

56 Quaison-Sackey to MEA, March 1963, CFA-54, 55.

57 Nkrumah to Bourguiba, 9 March 1962, CFA-51.

58 H.E. Mr. Yilma Deressa to MEA/Tunis, 28 July 1960, in Sadok Mokadden to MEA/Accra, 27 September 1960, CFA-47.

59 Principal Secretary, AAS, to Principal Secretary, MEA, 19 January 1962, CFA-47.

214

Conference of the Monrovia group ended, the formal invitation arrived in Ghana, with a proposed agenda, the result of talks between the Tunisian representative and interested delegations at the United Nations. The conference was planned for April 1962.[60]

That Ghana *officially* sought reconciliation became clear in its request that the agenda specifically include the question of merging the Casablanca and Monrovia groups. In the ensuing month plans were made and a delegation was named, after which an official requested Nkrumah's official consent. Asante, sensing that this risked jeopardizing a commitment, noted that "Ghana has already committed herself to attending the conference and it is not therefore necessary to seek Osagyefo's approval."[61]

A series of complications throughout Africa conspired against the conference. First, Morocco desired to postpone it, ostensibly because of the critical stage of the Franco-Algerian negotiations, and the allegedly hostile attitude of the Brazzaville states. Dr. Bossman, by now Ghana's ambassador in Rabat, was perhaps unaware that diplomats adopt the policy of the country to which they are accredited only at great risk to themselves. He wrote Nkrumah, "Sir, I humbly recommend postponement of All African People's Conference [*sic*] due in Tunis for Osagyefo's serious consideration."[62] Furthermore, the Monrovia states presented problems. On March 6th the African group met in New York, and all the divisive factors within came out. Quaison-Sackey cabled that the April date was inconvenient "in view of the fact that the Lagos Conference had drawn up a draft charter for the setting up of a Regional Organization in Africa and had recommended that a meeting of experts be held in three months. There followed a tempestuous discussion, Ghana and other Casablanca states while favoring a postponement till, say, June, were vehemently opposed to the imposition of any charter drawn up by a group of states [i.e. Monrovia]." Quaison-Sackey therefore recommended that Bourguiba be urged to make direct contacts with all states, lest the chance of reconciliation be lost.[63]

The Ghanaian ministry urged the Moroccan Embassy in Accra not to press for a postponement, as to do so was "likely to have unfortunate repercussions. It is necessary to keep alive the problem of the merging of the Casablanca and Monrovia Groups . . . otherwise the failure of the Lagos conference may result in a hardening of attitude of the Mon-

[60] MEA/Tunis to MEA/Accra, 19 January 1962, CFA-44.
[61] K. B. Asante to H. R. Amonoo, 26 February 1962, CFA-44.
[62] Bossman to Nkrumah, 28 February 1962, CFA-44. He meant, of course, to refer to the IAS conference.
[63] Quaison-Sackey to Ako Adjei, 7 March 1962, CFA-51.

215

rovia Group. The Tunis conference provides a good opportunity for a meeting of the Foreign Ministers of the two groups." Moreover, Algeria had attended every IAS conference (the note inaccurately pointed out), and no state could possibly object to its attendance "without standing condemned in the eyes of the world."[64]

Nkrumah pressed Bourguiba in similar terms to avoid postponement, and copies of this letter went to each Casablanca partner.[65] But the conference was postponed, and Bossman attributed this to the competition between Morocco and Tunisia for certain of Algeria's assets. (According to the Tunisian ministry, the postponement was due to an over-extension in Tunisia's own activities at the time.)[66] The conference was then rescheduled for September 1962, and the members of the Monrovia group, according to Quaison-Sackey's reports, wished to delay until the end of May before deciding whether to attend, precisely the eventuality Nkrumah had hoped to avoid.

The third IAS conference was never held, for the stream of events that was to lead to the founding of the OAU soon overtook it. Ghana's diplomats had done what they could to achieve a reconciliation. If Nkrumah had supported their efforts, he had also supported other efforts (examined below) without being aware of contradiction, which could only delay the merging of the groups. The reasons for this are threefold. As already seen, he would not sanction reconciliation if it were to be on Monrovia's terms, that is, if reconciliation were to take place at a conference called by the much more numerous Monrovia group. Secondly, his overriding commitment was to organic political unity, and the very smallness of Casablanca and its original threefold commitment to a high command, an assembly of the states, and an African common market, sustained his illusion that at some point it might provide the vehicle for organic union. Reconciliation, if it were only to achieve a loose diplomatic union of all the states, was always a peripheral consideration with him. Thirdly, he had spread his commitments so widely that he was unable to devote sufficient time to—or to think clearly about—activities in the Casablanca cadre. It is to the second factor that we now turn.

From its beginning, Casablanca had proposed and propounded ambitious plans, but they looked impressive only on paper. Appearances were important to Nkrumah, however. There was, for example, the meeting of the economic committee in Cairo from March 26th to April 3rd, 1962, where it was once again agreed to create a common market among the six states. Twenty-five percent annual reductions in customs duties were

64 MEA/Accra to Morocco/Accra, 7 March 1962, CFA-51.
65 Nkrumah to Bourguiba, 9 March 1962, CFA-51.
66 Bossman to Nkrumah, 17 March 1962, CFA-42. Interview: CF-30.

envisaged, until free trade existed between them.[67] At the time, Nkrumah was attacking the EEC and its relations with African countries and using what influence he possessed to prevent Britain's entry into it, and he thought an African common market was the logical alternative to association with the Europeans. Casablanca alone had proposed a common market, and Ghana was a member of Casablanca: It was characteristic of Nkrumah not to examine whether a common market within this group was feasible.

Mali, for one, could not afford to belong to an African common market at this stage. On its earnings from its European economic links it had based its economic planning.[68] This, in combination with Keita's reconciliation with Houphouet, convinced Nkrumah that Keita had lost his radicalism, so he sent Michael Dei-Anang with a senior diplomat to talk with him. In Bamako, by a Ghanaian account, Keita took the initiative in the discussion and lambasted Nkrumah, his tactics, and his strategy, and dismissed Nkrumah's plea for the Casablanca common market by caustically asking what products Nkrumah proposed to exchange in it. "I thought it a tremendous victory that we had Keita's support in trying to bring Nkrumah to a more sensible approach to African unity. When we returned to Accra, Dei-Anang insisted that he do the reporting to Nkrumah, the reason for which I appreciated when I saw his memorandum on the Bamako talks, which went something like this: 'Keita, as Osagyefo had wisely foretold, has sold out to the French. There is no further point in trying to work with him.' "[69]

Nor did other member-states evince interest. The U.A.R. was putting into effect its nationalization decrees of the previous autumn, and Ghana's economists were themselves preoccupied with the new seven-year plan. There is no evidence that any of the states took a Casablanca common market into consideration in their planning, and it was presumably convenient that Mali be considered the obstacle; as will presently be seen, it was difficult even to convoke a gathering to discuss Mali's objections. At a meeting in Tangiers in August 1962, the Casablanca secretary-general noted that the states had not ratified the agreement "by the date stipulated," and asked that they do so by January 1963, when it was to begin.[70] None did. Yet an influential minister—

---

[67] See *Economist Intelligence Unit*, West Africa Series, No. 35, 6 June 1961.

[68] Mali deemed "that the total disappearance of both fiscal and Customs duties within a period of five years would have serious repercussions on its finances and that the increase in the volume of its imports within the Common Market would have a counter-effect on other suppliers from whose exports it draws a considerable part of its budgetary resources," and on which its five-year plan was dependent. *Casablanca Charter Liaison Office*, "Report of the Liaison Office," Bamako, 1962, pp. 10-11.

[69] Interview: CF-14.   [70] "Report of the Liaison Office," *loc.cit.*

Kofi Baako—said in parliament in September 1962 that the Casablanca common market was "virtually created."[71] On such illusions did Ghana's Africa policy ride, and by such tactics as Keita described had Nkrumah lost what small prospects Casablanca did offer for cooperation.

Ghana also pressed for a payments union and a civil aviation agreement; so too an African development bank, with initial capitalization of $30,000,000[72]—this was to be taken up in time by the African states, but not until that minimum degree of inter-continental cooperation had been established with the merger of the two groups. Thus these plans never left the Casablanca drawing board. Nor was it only the lack of a political will; Casablanca never possessed a solid institutional framework. By the time its secretariat was fully established, in a dusty house several miles from Bamako's center, the group was fading away. From this office, the Moroccan secretary-general issued fruitless memoranda calling on the heads of state to implement their own resolutions, but he interested none of them. Nor was there liaison. Guinea had a representative neither at the secretariat nor in Bamako. The Ghanaian representative did not coordinate with his own counterpart at the Ghanaian mission in Bamako.[73] The secretariat had a grand plan for its own development, but was told by the heads of state that it "was too ambitious"; its revised plans, for information, legal, economic, cultural, and other departments were hardly less so—it requested $600,000 for the liaison office alone.[74] The secretary-general's report at the end of 1962 makes the general difficulty clear: states did not answer cables. The committee of experts on the common market, for example, were to meet on October 15th in Bamako, for which invitations were sent on August 31st. The first reply arrived October 12th. "In a last effort . . . the meeting was saved, though postponed by several days." Another difficulty was finances. "The Secretariat, with its various tasks, cannot afford to be left in the course of a financial year without the necessary funds to face its obligations, if only to settle the salaries. This is not a hypothetical case . . . we are evoking. It was a reality and a fact at the beginning of 1962."[75]

It is significant that Ouazzani's year-end report devoted six out of eighteen pages to various proposals for educational and cultural cooperation, in the absence of other news to report, and "in the absence of the Cultural Committee's report."[76] Institutes of African Studies at Tangiers do not, in any case, make a union.

Only the high command came close to an independent existence, and

[71] Debates, 14 September 1962, p. 294.
[72] See Bulletin de l'Afrique Noire, No. 230, 11 April 1962.
[73] Interview: CF-115.   [74] "Report of the Liaison Office," pp. 10-11.
[75] Ibid., p. 14.   [76] Ibid., p. 4.

this was a tribute to Nkrumah's persistence. In summer 1962, Accra was designated as headquarters, and Ghana moved quickly—under the administrative direction of General Ankrah—to establish it. The fourteen officers brought to the headquarters earmarked units from national forces for the command and drew up strategy. A Ghanaian officer toured the continent keeping members interested, and in April 1963 the officers traveled to Cairo for a military exercise.[77] The great summit of Addis Ababa, at which the Casablanca group was formally declared dead, was only a month away, so all their efforts were of little avail.

In any case, officers cannot plan strategy apart from their governments—and it was this factor that was sufficient to preclude further cooperation in any sphere. By spring 1963, relations between the states could not have been worse. Morocco's suspicion of Algeria followed hard on Algeria's independence in the summer of 1962. Guinea and Morocco had an extradition dispute. Nasser was allegedly supporting Ben Barka, the exiled Moroccan opposition leader, and Morocco had not recognized the government of Nasser's friends in the Yemen. Ghana's troubles with Guinea were mounting. Other factors paled into insignificance beside such basic obstacles.

Of the six states, Ghana had held the highest expectations for Casablanca. Ghana had supplied its dynamism. But there was a limit to the extent to which Nkrumah could ever cooperate with his peers, and here is the third reason Ghana's commitments were ambiguous and its efforts contradictory during 1962. It will be recalled that Nkrumah and Touré had not attended the first meeting of the political committee (in August 1961). The second meeting was scheduled for May, then June, 1962. Nkrumah wished it postponed until September, so that he could go from Cairo to the Tunis IAS meeting "without having to make a double journey."[78] He apparently still thought that the two frameworks were complementary to his own visions, however incompatible with each other. The U.A.R. wanted it as scheduled, probably for the attention it would thus focus on the world economic conference scheduled for July in Cairo. Nkrumah, however, had two unilateral Ghanaian initiatives coming to fruition in June, a conference of freedom fighters and one on disarmament. True, these were legitimate excuses for not traveling to Cairo, but were quite apart from the consequences his nonattendance could have for Casablanca. Nonetheless he deferred the decision whether to attend until the last moment and, in the end, sent the smallest Ghanaian delegation thus far: Ako Adjei, K. B. Asante, and one ministry official. Once again the political committee had failed to bring the heads

77 Interviews: CF-104, 51.
78 Dei-Anang to Quaison-Sackey, 16 May 1962, CFA-42.

of state together. Nkrumah's interest in Casablanca had for the moment waned, for Casablanca was manifestly not furthering the organic political unity for which he thought the group existed. His proposals for a continental government, circulated by the secretariat in Bamako, elicited not one response.[79] He was thus unable to use Casablanca as a framework through which a demand for reconciliation could be made, and he had found that he could not use it as a framework for his own ends; he had doubly lost.

Radical states could, however, use Casablanca for purposes of reconciliation. The policy of Sékou Touré, for one, was very purposeful throughout this period. He went to Cairo in June, made certain that the merging of Casablanca and Monrovia was demanded in the communiqué, and from there proceeded to Asmara, where he and the Emperor of Ethiopia had the most significant encounter in the history of modern Africa. From it emanated the Organisation of Africa Unity. Ghana had also advocated reconciliation, but Nkrumah had all the while pursued goals contradictory to it at the diplomatic level, namely, the strengthening of Casablanca's economic and military arms and the refusal to permit Casablanca to join with the Monrovia states on anything but Casablanca's terms, even though it was obvious to all that Monrovia was the continent's dominant force. Now it was too late. Moreover, the other arm of Ghana's Africa policy—that advocated and implemented by the militants—inevitably made Ghana's role a destructive one in Africa's search for unity. Nkrumah could not have pursued reconciliation purposefully, for too many in Ghana had an interest in bad relations with the Monrovia group's leaders, and because the deterioration of Ghana's relations with its increasingly confident neighbors had gone too far, as we shall now see.

THE SEARCH FOR UNITY IN AFRICA: MILITANTS AND INTERVENTION

The Liberation Movement and Ghana's Neighbors. The great increase in the power of the Ghanaian radicals, in the autumn of 1961, had vast implications for the formulation of Ghana's Africa policy. Their power derived from their commitment to scientific socialism, and they knew their positions could not be sustained were close links forged with such states as Nigeria and Togo, or with the other Monrovia group leaders, as diplomats like Quaison-Sackey advocated. Moreover, their own strength had been infused by such refugees from these very states as Bakary Djibo (Niger), Habib Niang (Senegal), and most importantly, Samuel Grace Ikoku (Nigeria), the most brilliant African at

[79] Interviews: CF-104, 115. See also *Africa 1962*, No. 13, 29 June 1962.

Nkrumah's court during the ensuing four years. A. K. Barden, director of the Bureau of African Affairs, had a vested interest in any policy of which his office would be the agent; hence his advocacy of intervention. It is through the B.A.A. that colleagues of his, like Ikoku, hoped to achieve power in Nigeria and elsewhere.

These men knew well that Nkrumah was both ambivalent and flexible in his approach to strategy and that, while he might not initiate an attack on an otherwise friendly—but moderate—country, he would not react negatively were someone else to do so. Following the Lagos conference, Barden attacked President Azikiwe for his widely publicized keynote speech there in which Ghana had been indirectly attacked. Barden, in his statement to the *Ghanaian Times*, spoke with greater virulence than had to date been used against other states.[80] There is reason to think that the Ghana government's claim that the article had not been officially authorized was in fact correct.[81] Yet once the damage had been done, Nkrumah could himself draw on Barden's arguments, causing relations with Nigeria to spiral further downward.

Although Nkrumah had always viewed intervention in independent Africa as one of the available tools for implementing his designs, he never decided specifically to adopt it as his policy. Rather, the broadening use of intervention came in large measure by accident and in response to specific challenges. Ghana's changing position in the southern African liberation movements is first discussed in this five-part section. The rhetoric of Ghanaian ideology alone demanded that Ghana play a large role in these movements. But Ghana was ill-placed geographically. Southern Africa was a new theater of interest to all the states because of the independence of Tanganyika from which, it appeared, events in the racist-dominated states could be affected. Of the independent African states, it was Ghana that held the initiative on the southern African question until 1961, but Ghana was too far away to hold the leading position in this new phase. It is likely that the feeling of estrangement from a movement it had helped to initiate fed the desire to use weapons of subversion—developed ostensibly for use against southern African regimes—against independent neighbors.

In the last four subsections, cases of alleged subversion are examined in the context of a study of Ghana's relations with these neighbors. In the first, Sierra Leone, "subversion" may be a misnomer, but the lack of consistency in policy-implementation, bad diplomacy, and the backwash from other Ghanaian ventures elsewhere stained Ghana's policy. In the second, with Togo, subversion was a consequence of Nkrumah's fear

[80] *Ghanaian Times*, 12 February 1962.   [81] See CF-24.

for his own security, and in the third, with Nigeria, subversion was central to strategy from the beginning. A final section, a study of Ghana's relations with the Entente countries, is a variation on each of these themes.

Freedom Fighting and the Bureau of African Affairs. Early in 1962, Kwesi Armah complained of the lack of any "working machinery" for the liberation movements.[82] A response to this came in the form of a conference of freedom fighters in June 1962, hastily organized by the Bureau of African Affairs. Despite Ghana's geographic disadvantage, Nkrumah hoped to achieve at this conference a breakthrough such as he had accomplished at the first AAPC; he sought to unify faction-ridden movements and to spearhead a united front for action against the racist regimes. He failed in both of these objectives, and the conference marks the end of Ghanaian influence in the liberation movement.

There are several reasons for Ghana's failure. For one thing, the organization established for Ghana's efforts in this very area, the Bureau, was coming into its own, and the stronger it grew, the weaker Ghana's position in the liberation movements became. Aloysius K. Barden, the director, was building a staff of ex-policemen, and ex-servicemen like himself, and his worst qualities were coming to the fore. No one, other than Adamafio, exceeded him in opportunism, but Adamafio at least was an artist in this game. Where Barden's talent lay, and why Nkrumah believed him an effective "militant" remains a mystery.

Consider, secondly, the relations between Ghana's leaders and the exiles first with respect to South Africa and, then, to Angola. The United Front of South Africa was domiciled in Accra, where it had been founded in 1960, and its leaders were in close touch with Ghana's leaders. Their assessment of Nkrumah's regime is important, and there is no doubt that they were unimpressed. During a visit to Ghana, Nelson Mandela wrote in his diary that the BAA had "turned out to be something quite contrary to what it was meant to be. Barden is systematically destroying Ghana."[83] Jokes at Nkrumah's expense began to spread across Africa regarding new techniques of obtaining Ghanaian largesse. Barden and Adamafio both sought to channel the funds granted through their respective offices (in Barden's case, more out of a seldom frustrated desire to share in them) and it became a favorite sport to outwit both men.[84] The South Africans were more cosmopolitan than Barden or Adamafio,

[82] "Conference of Ghana Envoys, January 1962," p. 55.

[83] The diary, captured by the South African authorities, is part of the Rivonia trial evidence. The citation was provided by Miss Catherine Hoskyns.

[84] Ako Adjei gave up even trying to play a part when he found it impossible to compel Nkrumah to separate genuine from personal requests, by his own account.

and hardly welcomed the relationship that existed between the amount of praise directed to Nkrumah and the amount of money received.[85]

The power struggle within Ghana also affected the health of the United Front. Adamafio and Barden favored Potloko Leballo and what became his wing of the PAC, while Ako Adjei favored the ANC. In December 1961, by which time the Ghanaian radicals had won the fight, United Front leaders as a whole reacted against what even Adjei termed "incessant spoon-feeding" by the Bureau.[86] The government responded by impounding the passport of Tennyson Makiwane, an ANC leader, and finally by expelling him from the country. After these events the ANC, according to Colin Legum, "wrote Nkrumah off."[87] Leballo, increasingly, became Nkrumah's most vocal supporter in refugee circles, while other PAC leaders, like Nana Mahomo, lost all confidence in the regime.

Ghana's treatment of the leading Angolan nationalists was even more exceptional. Holden Roberto, whose followers in northern Angola had begun the uprising of March 1961, had first gone to Ghana in 1958 (as "Joseph Gilmore"), prior to the AAPC, having been expelled from Léopoldville by the Belgians. He was there intermittently until 1960 when "I went to Léopoldville, because my comrade, the late Patrice Lumumba, had invited me. . . . We opened an office and edited a newspaper."[88] Ghana changed rapidly in the last half of 1960, however. The MPLA (Roberto's competitors), more radical in its theory if not on the battlefront, had gained Touré's support and, through a process that is not clear, convinced Nkrumah that Roberto was under Western influence. Roberto's testimony, at a private session of the 1964 OAU conference, continued:

> When Lumumba was arrested I had to spend nights hidden in Embassies, and notably in the embassy of Tunisia, because I did not want to be arrested, having been accused of communism. I have had to go to Ghana, to flee to Ghana to seek refuge. I had no money; I turned to the Conference [the AAPC]. At that time I was a Member of the Directive [steering] Committee . . . and asked the authorities if they could help me. This was the answer I got: The Government

[85] One tells the following story. He was met at the airport by Adamafio who said he could see Nkrumah only if liberal praise were promised. During the interview with Nkrumah, Adamafio interrupted the nationalist repeatedly, saying that the latter had something to tell Osagyefo—and when the praise was not forthcoming, he received taps and then kicks from Adamafio from under the table. Interview: CF-72.

[86] Interview: Ako Adjei.

[87] Interview: Colin Legum. See also *Ghana*, "Nkrumah's Subversion in Africa," 1966, p. 3.

[88] *OAU*: Cairo-1964 Verbatims, AHSG, 21 July 1964, p. 26.

223

of Ghana has given orders that we must not help you because you are
in the pay of America.

I said that in Léopoldville I was considered a communist, and
here I am considered to be in the pay of America.[89]

Ghana's loss of influence in the liberation movements is also ac-
counted for by a third factor, namely, what the refugees considered
Ghana's hypocrisy, and "racism in reverse" in its policy toward southern
Africa and its insistence on dominance of the refugee activities. The
United Front leaders had not forgotten Nkrumah's caution on the South
African question in the Commonwealth. Less justifiably, they did not
appreciate the efforts Ghana finally did initiate when its conciliatory
efforts in the Commonwealth reached a dead end. In March of 1961,
Geoffrey Bing noted that the financial position of South Africa was deteriorating and the social structure crumbling. He went further to claim
that Ghana was seen to be the most radical state in its South Africa policy
and the most generous in its help to South African refugees. For example, many of the United Front's members carried Ghanaian passports.
Bing asked what was "the most effective form . . . opposition can take
within South Africa,"[90] and reached a conclusion that did not impress
the African nationalists: Beginning in the spring of 1961, Bing organized a group within South Africa consisting mainly of white liberals, who
were to assist in finding asylum for threatened nationalists and to smug-
gle in explosives. What success Bing's group had was resented by both
ANC and PAC leaders, as it was felt that Bing had no faith in the competence of African leaders themselves.[91]

At the 1964 OAU conference, Nkrumah related his own efforts to
bring the Angolan groups together early in 1962. He had invited them to
Accra and pressed them to agree, formally, to a united front, which they
did. (According to Professor Marcum, he also offered to sponsor Roberto if he would move his headquarters to Accra.)[92] Nkrumah also
said that Roberto's group reneged on the agreement. Roberto, however,
argued that his party had already created a front—of his party and
several others—and that when the MPLA arrived in Léopoldville
(from Conakry) in late 1961, long after his own group had begun the
armed struggle, it had made no effort to cooperate.

[89] *Ibid.*, p. 27.
[90] Bing to Nkrumah, March 1961, CFA-2, 3.
[91] Interviews: CF-72, 14. This was probably too harsh a judgment; Bing was responsible for the escape of many of them.
[92] Interview: Professor John Marcum.

When we arrived in Ghana [in early 1962], the suggestion . . . Nkrumah had to make was to disband the Front which had already been formed and start from scratch.

We answered "We cannot do so, because we are already engaged in armed combat, and because we formed a front less than a year ago. . . . It is like somebody killing his child because he is expecting another." We refused. But President Nkrumah exerted his influence in order to have the document signed, which I, later on . . . deemed incompatible. . . .

. . . I had not wanted to speak up but President Nkrumah has forced me to do so, and if we are in difficulties [in 1964] Ghana is responsible for it. We are not in an election campaign, we are involved in armed combat. While I stand speaking to you here, we have brothers, friends, who are dying . . . and if the problem of Angola is being complicated, it will be thanks to Ghana. . . . Certain African countries are taking advantage of the weakness of our friends to create confusion. Ghana is the first, that is why President Nkrumah shows more interest than anyone else. . . .[93]

The point was that Roberto's front was in a position of strength throughout 1962. Prime Minister Adoula of the Congo was one of his closest friends, and his forces were on the offensive in Angola itself. But in the Africa (and Ghana) of the period, this was not necessarily what counted. At the June 1962 nationalists' conference in Ghana, the MPLA leader Mario de Andrade, Roberto's rival, stressed to Nkrumah that he aimed to build a Marxist state in Angola after victory, whereupon Nkrumah became deeply and emotionally committed to his cause.[94]

It seems plausible that a relation existed between Ghana's inability to affect events in Southern Africa when so much attention was focused there, and its growing desire to interfere in independent states in West Africa. The fact was that training camps were established for training freedom fighters from southern Africa; step by step other uses were found for them until they were as much for training refugees from independent states as for those from southern African territories. Barden had pressed Nkrumah all along to enlarge the facilities and the scope of training; the distinction between exiles from independent and nonindependent regimes does not appear to have existed in Barden's mind. He had his chance after Nkrumah's 1961 visit to Moscow produced aid in the form of a Russian commitment of two trainers and equipment. In late 1961, Barden established a camp in Mankrong, near his boyhood home; ac-

[93] *OAU*: Cairo-1964 Verbatims, AHSG, 21 July 1964, pp. 28-30.
[94] Interview: CF-29.

cording to a study of "Nkrumah's subversion in Africa," published by the NLC in 1966, "the first course offered at Mankrong began on 3 December 1961 but little was accomplished until the arrival of two Russian instructors."[95] In its first six months, the camp was something less than a success. The Angolan refugees feuded and the Russian instructors were unpopular. Only S. G. Ikoku's "Action Troopers" from Nigeria seem to have benefited from the training, although some of these, too, told amusing tales of bad planning and mismanagement.[96]

More important, the Russians apparently made a reappraisal of the project and, on the completion of the course running at the time, brought the trainers home and were never again directly involved. Relations with Abubakar's government had obviously become more important than training some dozens of ill-equipped Nigerians to try to overthrow it. The Russians also appear to have assessed the potential in Barden's empire and found it wanting. Sammy Ikoku, however, had by this time gained a position of sufficient influence in Flagstaff House to justify a new course at Mankrong for the training of more Nigerians; this began in September, and the trainers were those prepared by the Russians for this purpose.[97]

The desire to intervene in West Africa was spurred by another development, which had its turning point at the freedom fighter's conference of 1962. The CPP had always advocated nonviolence: at the 1958 AAPC this question had been a divisive one between Ghanaians and North Africans. By 1962, most of the states in a position to obtain independence without substantial violence were independent, while it was increasingly clear that the southern African regimes could be overthrown only by force. In this period, these regimes looked vulnerable to the type of force that could be mobilized by the independent states, and so it was hardly surprising that the old prescriptions against violence were discarded. The transition in Nkrumah's thinking—which was also a product of his general ideological hardening—was complete by the conference, and "blood and guts" rather than "positive action" was the keynote of his private advice to the delegates.[98]

But the delegates from the racialist redoubts were not looking to him

---

[95] *Ghana*, "Nkrumah's Subversion in Africa," 1966, p. 6. Interview: CF-37A.

[96] See the record of the Awolowo trial, *Nigeria*, "In re Omisade," Vol. 3, pp. 3, 7, 33-34; Vol. 4, p. 61; Vol. 9, pp. 23-27.

[97] *Ghana*, "Nkrumah's Subversion in Africa," Appendix J, pp. 82-83. The Ghanaian trainers were delighted to be on their own, having resented the Russians, who reportedly thought them something less than adequately prepared for the circumstances.

[98] See "Africa's Liberation and Unity," Address by Osagyefo the President to the Nationalist Conference of African Freedom Fighters, 4 June 1962, *Bulletin on African Affairs*, Vol. 2, No. 113, pp. 23-26, and interview: CF-29.

for the inspiration they had sought in Accra four years earlier. Nkrumah, for example, thought that much of the squabbling between rival nationalist groups would be avoided were each delegation to take the name of his party, the CPP.[99] It is not surprising that he was laughed at—nor is it surprising that his reaction was to redirect his attention to the neo-colonial redoubts on Ghana's borders.

Sierra Leone. There was every reason why Ghana could preserve correct, if not warm, relations with Sierra Leone, with whom it was linked by colonial traditions and the Commonwealth. Only a measure of sensitivity was required in dealing with this smaller, less rich, but proud people. Inadvertently, Ghana's policy created only hostility. While discussing balkanization in Africa in 1960, and with particular reference to those countries of less than three million people, Nkrumah had said "It is impossible to imagine that the colonial powers seriously believe that independence could be of much value to these African states in such a terrible state of fragmentation."[100] As Ghana's second high commissioner in Freetown said privately, the effect of this speech "died very hard."[101] Bad diplomacy compounded this effect. Nkrumah had appointed as the first commissioner a Nigerian born Sierra Leonian with a Ghanaian passport who, it was mistakenly thought in Flagstaff House, would be in a position to cultivate good relations. After Nkrumah's speech, the commissioner was called to Government House, where he insisted that the prime minister had not read Nkrumah's speech properly—not intending this as an insult. Sir Milton Margai reportedly had him removed, physically.[102] As one of his ministers wrote, "Sir Milton had a long and deep-seated mistrust of Kwame Nkrumah, especially after he began to suspect that [opposition leaders] all enjoyed sympathetic support from Ghana. The fact that the Chinese News Agency operated from Ghana only added to Sir Milton's suspicions."[103]

Relations improved after Sierra Leone's independence in April 1961. The new high commissioner, K. D. Gwira, said he was given the "warmest welcome" any Ghanaian had ever received at Sir Milton's hand.[104] Moreover, Ghana had potential friends in the government. Karefa-Smart, the foreign minister, "did not share [Sir Milton's] suspicions" about Ghana, "although as early as 1961 I began to complain that it

[99] Interview: Nana Mahomo, a PAC leader.
[100] *Debates*, 8 August 1960. See also *West Africa*, 15 October 1960, p. 1165.
[101] *President's Office*, "Notes of Conference of Ghana Envoys in Africa," October 1961, p. 42.
[102] Interview: CF-113.
[103] Dr. John Karefa-Smart to author, 23 March 1967. Also, interview: CF-13.
[104] "Notes of Conference of Ghana Envoys in Africa," p. 42.

227

was no longer possible to have the free access to Nkrumah—even when I visited Ghana—that I felt I should have as one who had known and worked with him since student days in the USA."[105]

In the summer, relations seriously deteriorated because of an incident for which the Ghana government bore only indirect responsibility. Two Ghanaian adventurers entered Sierra Leone illegally in August, and attempted to obtain money from the Ghanaian High Commission on the strength of a telegram they claimed was from the Bureau of African Affairs. Officials of the Sierra Leone government were convinced they were troublemakers of the Bureau.[106] In fact they were wanted in Ghana on criminal charges.[107] In Freetown, relations with Ghana had not improved sufficiently to prevent the incident from becoming a *cause célèbre*. The two were sentenced to six months imprisonment, and the press gave wide coverage to the affair, while Ghana made every effort to have the two extradited for trial in Accra.

Ghana's high commission then published a press release denying charges that the two were Ghanaian agents, ending by noting that the "Government of Ghana have never made it their policy to conduct espionage in any African country."[108] Sierra Leone's ministry protested that the release was of a political nature and should have been cleared with the ministry, and in a second note commented that the high commission "had sought to exonerate [itself] from an allegation [of espionage] that as far as this Ministry was aware had never been made."[109] The Ghanaians were damned whatever they tried to say or do. Karefa-Smart was away at the time; Sir Milton and the rest of his government remained convinced that the two adventurers were government agents although, as far as can be determined, they were not. They gave James Amissah, the Ghanaian political officer, twenty-four hours to leave the country even though his behavior had been proper throughout; he was the scapegoat for a desire to "contain" Ghana that was spreading throughout Africa.

Most interesting was the growing cooperation between those African states that wished to counter Ghana's activities. Gwira had been informed "that the Nigerian High Commissioner . . . played a leading part in seeing to it that the incident was given the widest publicity"; more impor-

---

105 Dr. John Karefa-Smart to author, 23 March 1967.

106 According to Dougall Reid, U.K./Ghana, and a senior official in Freetown at the material time. Interview.

107 Interviews: CF-13, 101. They had convinced Ghanaian officials that they were friends of Lumumba's, and had obtained large sums of Bureau money under such false pretenses.

108 Quoted in "Notes of Conference of Ghana Envoys in Africa," p. 44.

109 MEA/Sierra Leone to Ghana/Freetown, 15 September 1961, in *ibid.*, p. 46.

tant, a minor Ghanaian diplomat, of no high repute, was expelled from Monrovia almost simultaneously and, as Gwira told his colleagues the following month, "Correct to form, the expulsion of Mr. Boateng from Liberia was given prominence in the *Daily Mail* [Freetown] and on the very day that the news appeared in the papers we had information that the Permanent Secretary of the External Affairs Ministry had contacted the Liberian Embassy asking to be informed of how Mr. Boateng was expelled from Liberia so that his Ministry could do the same to expel my Secretary from Sierra Leone."[110] Without any doubt, Margai had been influenced by British advice in the Amissah case; Karefa-Smart noted that had he been there at the time, he would have "advised Sir Milton to deal with the matter differently."[111] Nonetheless, the incident could be seen as a natural reaction to Nkrumah's failure to take into account the sensibilities of his neighbors. The penalty had come after belated attempts had been made to improve relations. Diplomatic faux pas can be cumulative.

Togo. Ghana's policy towards Togo between 1957 and 1960 might be considered a form of ideological irredentism. Using arguments drawn from the history of the Ewe-unity movements, and his own interpretation of pan-Africanism, Nkrumah had tried to frighten Olympio into surrendering Togo's sovereignty. The main result of this policy was the strengthening of Togo's fragile sense of nationhood. The disputes, and the subversion conducted from both Togolese and Ghanaian sides of the border in the ensuing years, hardly derived from the mere failure to find a modus vivendi in the earlier period. Nkrumah's growing concern for his personal security—not entirely misplaced—made pan-African justification peripheral to his Togo policy after 1960,[112] and his attempts to turn Ghana toward socialism made an accommodation with the neighboring regime more remote.

The confrontation in Olympio's home, between him and Nkrumah in June 1960, had at least momentarily ended the hostility between them. The one had sought economic cooperation and the other political unity, and it was agreed that Olympio would submit economic proposals to Accra. Adu telephoned Olympio shortly after the meeting, to find that they were still talking a different language on economic and political priorities.[113] What ensued is recounted by Olympio in an interview published in *Afrique Action;* Sékou Touré, Olympio said, visited him

---

[110] *Ibid.*, p. 47.   [111] Karefa-Smart to author, 23 March 1967.
[112] A conclusion based on interviews with senior intelligence officials. Interviews: CF-87, 55.
[113] Interview: CF-28.

shortly after the republican celebrations in Accra, and told him that he wished Guinea included in the proposals for economic cooperation which Olympio had promised to send to Nkrumah. Sir Abubakar had visited Lomé as well, and invited him to the Nigerian independence festivities on 1 October. In the three months between Touré's visit and the Nigerian celebrations, Olympio had not completed his proposals, as a result of which Ako Adjei handed him a note in Lagos: "pressing me to expedite my project for economic cooperation. I responded by bringing the Ghanaian government up to date with respect to my discussions with President Sékou Touré and Sir Abubakar. The only response I received was a letter listing the restrictions that the Accra government was imposing at the frontier of Togo on the movement of merchandise and people."[114] For Nkrumah, Olympio's "breach of faith"[115]—in not confining himself to the terms of the understanding of June 1960—provided an excuse to take punitive measures against Togo in order to "bring home clearly and unmistakenly that the unity of Ghana and Togo is natural and inevitable" (as he said publicly).[116]

Olympio's friends—such as Sir Abubakar—urged him to seek redress through the United Nations. Olympio said that it was not necessary to "dramatize the matter" though he might bring it to a conference of African heads of state.[117] He had, evidently, succeeded in giving West African leaders grounds for suspecting Nkrumah, rather than himself, of bad faith. After finding that Ghana refused to be party to a multilateral guarantee of Togo's currency (without political unification), Olympio had nothing to gain by working out bilateral arrangements with Ghana and knew that within the West African context he would not be blamed for attempting to multilateralize the June agreements. Olympio was in any case convinced that Nkrumah's economic policies were leading Ghana to bankruptcy and that the steady flow of refugees into Lomé testified to Nkrumah's growing political difficulties. Olympio also took great pride in the progress of the Togo economy, and felt that his austere regime, despite unemployment, could eventually accumulate sufficient reserves to buy out French interests and make the country viable. He had thus concluded that he would have to work around Nkrumah, and began strengthening his contacts with other West African leaders.

114 *Afrique Action*, 21 November 1960. The reason for accepting this report is that the sections of it referring to Olympio's meeting with Nkrumah in June 1960 do not conflict with the record of Ghana's own ministry. See p. 86.

115 Nkrumah to Maga, 13 February 1962, CFA-150.

116 *Ghanaian Times*, 20 December 1960. This, perhaps Nkrumah's most remarkable foreign policy pronouncement, was stated often in the ensuing years. See also *Nouvelles Officielles du Togo*, 17 September 1960.

117 *AFP Sp. Outre-mer*, No. 4324, 17 November 1960, and *Abidjan Matin*, 17 November 1960.

Nkrumah responded by probing the weaknesses of his adversary. Olympio—never a convinced democrat—had become more stringent with his domestic opponents, some of whom went into exile in Ghana. S. W. Kumah, once a senior CPP leader and in 1962 Nkrumah's ambassador to Yugoslavia, considered those Togolese offering to help Ghana "either political failures or job-seekers,"[118] but their influence mounted. Dr. Simon Kpodar and Antoine Meatchi, both leaders of the pro-French party that governed Togo between 1951 and 1958, were exiled in Accra by early 1961, had access to Nkrumah, and continually assured him that the people of Togo were on his side.[119]

By early 1961, it was "a race against time to see whose policies would first lead to the collapse of the other regime. It takes two to make a conflict."[120] If it is not clear which party had done more damage to the other, it is obvious that tension on the border had weakened internal political stability on both sides. Now there was escalation, a new round of events, and no doubt who threatened first. In mid-May 1961, Theophile Mally, Olympio's tough new interior minister, announced the discovery of 44 Czech pistols, and 2,616 rounds of ammunition in Kpodar's home.[121] These had come from the shipments brought to Ghana from Czechoslovakia. Olympio had reluctantly entered into a defense understanding with France in 1960, as a result of tension with Ghana. Having done so, he wished not to be bothered by military concerns. "He trusted the French to keep the Ghanaians out, and himself with regard to the French within Togo," one of his closest advisers commented.[122] After the first arms plot he felt compelled to show Nkrumah that he was not defenseless, however, and knowing Nkrumah's concern for his own security, thought that by giving a few arms to some of the Ghanaian exiles in Togo he could serve warning on Nkrumah that two could indeed play the game.

In 1961, Nkrumah had formulated no general strategy of subversion for independent Africa: but there was now new experience from the Congo crisis, and a surplus of arms which had not reached Stanleyville. One Ghanaian diplomat commented that "we got out of this one fairly easily, because the plot was yet in its early stages. But hereafter Nkrumah made clear that Olympio was not to be allowed to stand in the way

[118] "Ghana-Togo Relations," in "Conference of Ghana Envoys," January 1962, p. 136. Kumah was a one-time Ewe leader.
[119] Kpodar was a former deputy of Grunitzky's regime, and Meatchi a former minister.
[120] Interview: CF-87.
[121] See *West Africa*, 20 May 1961, and *le Monde*, 12 May 1961.
[122] Interview: CF-86.

of African Unity."[123] This first arms plot was a response to circumstances, but it led to the evolution of policy.

Throughout the summer of 1961 tension mounted. Olympio used his old weapon, the argument that ex-British Togoland should join with the Togo Republic. Ghana issued a statement challenging his interpretation of the 1956 UN plebiscite, and then the Ghanaian press, while Nkrumah was in Russia, began an extended campaign of pressure. A "Ghana-Togo Union Movement" was to be launched on August 27th, at which time the frontier barriers would by an unnamed process "Breakdown."[124] Then, tactics were reversed, as was to happen again. The *Evening News* commented that: "In the highest reaches of our endeavour toward unity . . . we may have been guilty of some excess due, largely, to the ardour and sincerity with which we had embarked on our mission. If, therefore . . . we may have offended the feelings of anyone, we are sorry and trust that the new rapprochement may heal any wound unwittingly done. . . . Olympio, good evening comrade. . . . I understand that you are a good Christian, like myself. Well, forget the past and let's start afresh."[125]

As Ghana's internal problems mounted in the autumn of 1961—coinciding with the arrival in Lomé of the Ghanaian leader of the opposition-in-exile, Professor Busia—it was easy, and characteristic, for Nkrumah to detect a plot against himself. He thus began taking a still harder line. F. Y. Asare, the regional commissioner in the Volta region who, with A. L. Adu, had argued for a conciliatory policy towards Togo, was replaced by a "hawk," M. Boni. About the same time, the Ghanaian envoys in Africa met in conference and strongly urged that border conflicts with the Ivory Coast and Togo be settled. A committee was appointed to discuss the matter with the president. According to one ambassador present, Nkrumah expressed the conviction that there was little problem in this, as Houphouet and Olympio were soon to be out of the way. Nkrumah did, however, agree to examine the proposals the envoys had made for ending the difficulties, but a few days later Boni made a provocative speech at the frontier, which he must first have cleared with Nkrumah, demanding the union of Ghana and Togo.[126]

By November, Nkrumah apparently felt that public opinion would support a new attempt to overthrow Olympio, and he certainly felt that his own security was at stake, with opposition elements operating from

123 Interview: CF-24.
124 See *Evening News* throughout the summer of 1961, and particularly July 11th and August 12th.
125 *Ibid.*, 4 September 1961 (special issue on Ghana-Togo relations).
126 Interview: CF-98.

Lomé and bomb explosions occurring in Accra. Ghana's socialist measures were also threatened by the ease with which smugglers could take diamonds or cocoa out of Ghana to obtain higher prices in Togo, bringing back cheap whiskey and cigarettes. Ghana's pound was weakening, and currency speculation in Lomé weakened it further. On December 1st, Olympio foiled an imminent plot to overthrow him and his government. According to statements made in Lomé, the principal in the plot, Christian Abby, confessed that in April 1961, automatic pistols and ammunition had been transferred to the Ghanaian regional commissioner's residence at Ho, but that they were not distributed to him—and Kpodar—until late November. It was also reported that the Juvento radicals were involved and had been arrested.[127] Togo's left wing had apparently joined the reactionaries to overthrow a common enemy.

Olympio then left Togo for Tanganyika's independence celebrations and en route met with Houphouet-Boigny, with whom he never before had felt any need to consult. In Dar-es-Salaam he reportedly threatened to invoke Togo's defense pact with France if Ghana attacked. "In other words, what Mr. Olympio said implies that France is ready to attack Ghana on behalf of Togo as soon as the latter [Ghana] makes any attempt to defend herself against Togolese aggression," commented Ghana's *Evening News*.[128] It was a curious argument, but not so ironic as the fact that a Ghanaian white paper, alleging that a massive plot against *Ghana* had been launched from *Togo*, was published on the morrow of the day the coup in Lomé was supposed to have taken place. The Ghanaian press went still further:

> To forestall all the wicked intentions of this semi-foreigner [Olympio] who wants to precipitate a bloodbath on this part of peaceful Africa the *Evening News* today appeals to the government and people of Ghana to take immediate steps to mobilize vigilance squads . . . and TIGHTEN our links with those friendly powers whom we know are TEN TIMES stronger than the fifth rate power with which Olympio is deluding himself with a funny sense of false and impotent security. . . .
>
> Although we do not wish to whip up a war psychosis . . . we must remind this upstart that our boys—heroes of . . . two world wars and lately Congo—are among the world's finest soldiers.[129]

---

[127] *AFP Sp. Outre-mer*, No. 4660, 7-8 January 1962, *le Monde*, 6 December 1961.

[128] "Olympio Sells Togoland to France," editorial, *Evening News*, 13 December 1961.

[129] "Olympio: Africa's Number Two Tshombe!" *ibid.*, 15 December 1961. See Olympio's comments on the White Paper in *Bulletin Quotidien Information Togolaise*, 13 December 1961.

Olympio, on his return from Dar, said he wanted Nkrumah to live long, so that he would regret what he had done. He also commented that he looked forward to the forthcoming summit conference in Lagos.[130] Nkrumah had not only driven an anti-French statesman into a defense understanding with France, but had driven an "isolationist"—who had sought to avoid joining rival African groupings—into a leading position in the Monrovia group.

In every forum and at every level relations deteriorated. A good example, which also shows the delicate nature of the problem, is provided by the case of a Ghanaian union officer who was arrested in Lomé in mid-November. Two fellow officers went to secure his release, were briefly held, and were informed by the Togo police that their detainee-colleague was in fact a Ghanaian police detective who had "reported two women who were the wives of Ghanaian refugees" in Togo, so that the Ghanaian police could arrest the two women living back in Ghana. The incident led to a meeting in Flagstaff House, at which it was decided to close the border. Barden (director of the Bureau of African Affairs) and Tettegah (secretary-general of the TUC) used the occasion to press for a harsher policy. The "treatment being meted Ghanaian nationals . . . is becoming unbearable," Tettegah noted.[131]

Conflict fed on the presence of the exiled Ghanaians as well. Ghana publicly rejected the notion that there were any refugees in Lomé. When Paulin Freitas, Olympio's foreign minister, requested that the president of the UN General Assembly look into the problem caused by some 5,000 of them,[132] Quaison-Sackey claimed that their presence was part of "a daily and seasonal population movement."[133] Refugees they were, 5,700 of them according to the UN's investigation.[134] It was no small embarrassment that their plight attracted world attention. The Vatican, the Red Cross, America's "Food for Peace" program all sent donations, but Ghana's ambassadors were instructed to protest against the use of the word "refugees" in reference to any Ghanaians residing in Togo.[135] The problem obviously could not be solved without reconciliation between the two regimes. Yet, as there had been tension even when there

---

[130] *AFP Sp. Outre-mer*, 4643, 16 December 1961; see also *AFP Bulletin Sud-Sahara*, No. 825, 14 December 1961.

[131] W. B. Otoo to John Tettegah, 1 December 1961, and Tettegah to Ako Adjei, 7 December 1961. CFA-150.

[132] *UN Docs.*, A/c.3/593, 1026th Plen., 5 October 1961.

[133] *UNGA*: iiird comm., 1112th meeting, paras. 45-53.

[134] "Final Report on Assistance to Refugees in Togo," *UN Docs.*, A/AC.96/199, 9 April 1963. See also "Matchet's Diary," *West Africa*, 25 November 1961.

[135] Puplampu, Deputy Minister, MFA, to Amb. Halm, Ghana/Washington, 16 April 1962; Puplampu to Amb. Bonsu, Ghana/Rome, 12 May 1962, CFA-150, 151.

were few exiles, the existence of so many made it seem impossible that outstanding issues between the two countries could be settled. There was, for all that, to be a final opportunity.

We have seen that at the end of 1961 Nkrumah was rethinking his Africa policy, having discovered Ghana's tarnished image. At both conferences of his envoys (in October and January), his ambassadors made their opposition to his policy as explicit as was possible. Kumah, for example, said it was "utterly wrong . . . to work toward good relations with Togoland by using opposition elements in that country," and asked what Ghanaians would think were Olympio to do the same in Ghana.[136] Tevoedjre, the Dahomean diplomatist and politician, notes that, at Tanganyika's independence celebrations (December 1961), the vice-chancellor of the University of Ghana made clear that Nkrumah was interested in reconciliation on the Benin gulf.[137] This is hard to square with the allegation that Nkrumah had just attempted to overthrow Olympio, but the fact that the attempt had been foiled may have encouraged Nkrumah momentarily to try another tack; in any case, Nkrumah's policies were often contradictory at different levels. Tevoedjre relates that Nkrumah wished President Maga to mediate; Nkrumah had cultivated relations with Maga in order to isolate Olympio (witness the state visit of Maga to Accra in June 1961), and it was agreed that Nkrumah and Maga would meet. Maga would then bring about a meeting between Nkrumah and Olympio, and Ghana, in return, would interest itself in Dahomey's development.

The first step was successful: Maga and Nkrumah met in northern Ghana and although Nkrumah spoke harshly of Olympio, he did agree, according to Tevoedjre, to "accept the borders of the independent states for the moment, provided that we all undertake immediately a procedure for concerted diplomacy and co-ordinated defense."[138] In effect, Nkrumah was offering to recognize boundaries which were nowhere else in question in return for support for his pan-African policies. If this appeared to be a one-sided proposition, it must be remembered that this was the first time he had abandoned the explicitly *revanchist* character of his basic pan-African formulation about redrawing colonial boundaries. He appeared to keep his promise, by stating in his speech to parliament (in mid-January 1962) that "no one seeks a revision of present boundaries unnecessarily."[139]

The attempted reconciliation got little further. At the Lagos confer-

---

[136] "Ghana-Togo Relations," in "Conference of Ghana Envoys," p. 135.

[137] Albert Tevoedjre, *Pan-Africanism in Action: An Account of the UAM*, Cambridge, Center for the Study of International Affairs, 1965, pp. 42-43.

[138] *Ibid.*   [139] *Debates*, 20 January 1962, p. 8.

ence, Olympio suggested that a Benin union between Togo, Dahomey, and Nigeria might be possible[140] and, although he did not preclude Ghana's participation, he was suggesting military and economic cooperation that might bring Nigerian power up to Aflao. Ghanaian diplomats in Lagos cabled that "Olympio's call has been unanimously endorsed by all sections of the Nigerian public,"[141] but Nkrumah had no habit of appreciating the initiatives of others. The Dahomean, Togolese, and Ghanaian foreign ministers were able, nonetheless, to meet in Dahomey in February, and at this level there was no barrier to reconciliation.[142] When Maga then tried to bring the two presidents together on neutral territory, he encountered the basic problem. Nkrumah responded to Maga's invitation as follows:

> I told you that in an effort to harmonise our relations, I paid a visit to Togoland myself in June 1960, at a time when relations . . . had sunk to their lowest ebb. If Mr. Olympio had kept his word about the general understanding reached during that meeting, I am sure that all the unpleasantness, misunderstandings, and suspicions that have been allowed to grow up unnecessarily between us could have been avoided. [Thus, if Olympio is sincere] it will be for him to pay us a visit in Ghana. It is indeed for him to return my own gesture of goodwill.[143]

Olympio's case for refusing to go to Accra was strong. He had gone to Ghana's independence celebrations and Nkrumah had not gone to Togo's; indeed, at the time of Togo's independence Nkrumah had allowed his ministers to make provocative speeches at the Togo border, because Olympio had not seen fit to abandon Togo's sovereignty in Ghana's favor. In such circumstances, it was appropriate for Nkrumah to travel to Lomé to seek an accommodation. Later, when both men knew that Nkrumah had tried to bring about Olympio's murder, it was hardly diplomatically appropriate for Olympio to pay a state visit to Ghana. Both were instinctively sensitive to the diplomacy of prestige, and Nkrumah had no basis for insisting that Olympio come to Accra in preference to a meeting on neutral ground, unless he wanted the price to be too high for Olympio. Nkrumah remained adamant, and wrote Maga in late March that he was convinced ". . . that if Mr. Olympio is genuine and is not out to seize the opportunity to derive propaganda advantage to the prejudice of Ghana, he would agree to go anywhere in the effort to reach mutual understanding and reconciliation. You know how sin-

---

[140] See I. W. Zartman, *International Relations in the New Africa*, New Jersey, 1966, pp. 135-37.
[141] Wilmot, Ghana/Lagos, to K. B. Asante, A.A.S., 3 February 1962, CFA-150.
[142] Interview: Ako Adjei.   [143] Nkrumah to Maga, 13 February 1962, CFA-150.

cere we are . . . and appreciate that we have no claims whatever against Togo. If Mr. Olympio is not ready to go to Ghana, let us, Mr. President, leave the matter in abeyance for the time being."[144]

Olympio suspected that a visit in these circumstances would be nothing more than a diplomatic smokescreen for other activities, and was apparently convinced that nothing would deflect Nkrumah from his course. He felt that joining Ghana in a political union was less than ever a realistic alternative for Togo. As he said on "Meet the Press" in New York, ". . . with the present conditions in Ghana, nobody would willingly join [with such a] country unless by war."[145] By the time of Olympio's return from America in early 1962, there could no longer be any doubt that the two states were on a collision course.[146]

Nigeria. Africa's largest state became independent on 1 October 1960. By the time of the celebrations (which Nkrumah failed to attend), Ghana had taken a new radical turn, making the distance between the two even greater than in the period studied earlier. In November, Nkrumah proposed his African high command to all states independent since 1958, plus Guinea and Mali. Nigeria was declared ineligible, on the pretext of its defense agreement with Britain.[147] Six weeks later, Nigeria made the next move, by failing to attend the Casablanca conference. This was a consequence of the slight to their status that Nigerians thought Nkrumah had made, but as a consequence of their absence at Casablanca, the Nigerians increasingly looked to the conservative French-linked group for allies in the context of pan-African diplomacy.

It is ironic that the Ghanaian and Nigerian delegations worked closely together at the United Nations, and voted similarly. Ghana's diplomats wondered why this pattern of cooperation was not possible in Africa. Indeed, at the time of the Casablanca conference, Nigeria had been in a radical mood; on January 5th it broke relations with France over the issue of nuclear testing in the Sahara.[148]

---

[144] Nkrumah to Maga, 22 March 1962, CFA-150.

[145] Verbatim text of "Meet the Press," 25 February 1962, by Radio-TV Reports, in Ghana/UN to MEA, CFA-150.

[146] Consider this illustration. Sylvan Amegashie, a prominent Ghanaian and relative of Olympio's, visited Lomé and heard the Togo president's description of his visit with Kennedy. Shortly after his return to Accra, he was summoned to Flagstaff House, where Nkrumah, by Amegashie's account, raged at him in a manner reminiscent of those sessions conducted twenty years earlier in Berchtesgaden, solely because Amegashie had not informed him in advance of his visit to Lomé. After that, Amegashie thought it unsafe to go to Lomé at all, making an exception only for Olympio's funeral.

[147] See p. 149.

[148] Nigerian diplomats had thought Ghana would take a similar action. They learned with experience "that the Ghanaian bark was louder than its bite." Interview: CF-83.

During 1961 and 1962 Nigeria's relations with Ghana were so strained that there would have been a diplomatic break in traditional diplomacy. Difficulties were aggravated when Ghana and Nigeria found themselves in opposing African factions, but the basic trouble had deeper roots. Within Nigeria itself, the NCNC and Action Group were completing the process of reversing their traditional attitudes toward Ghana.

It is an oversimplification to ascribe the Action Group's change from hostility to near-alignment with Ghana solely to opportunism and its new position as the Nigerian opposition. A split in the party was in fact developing which reflected ideological divisions which had existed since the party's founding. Sammy Ikoku, for example, had always been a radical, having tried as early as 1951 to go to Eastern Europe to obtain funds for a socialist paper and party.[149] True, he wrote violently inflammatory articles against Ghana in 1958, but this was a brief concession—and in any event Ghana was no ideological beacon in those days. More important, radical Marxists had dissolved their own party—the United Working Peoples' Party—in 1954, and had left members free to choose between the Action Group and NCNC; most chose the Action Group, whose "efficient organization and methodological planning" had impressed them.[150] The Action Group was in many ways closer to the CPP than was the more diffuse and tolerant NCNC (the CPP's Nigerian ally in the late 1950's), and the NCNC's governing alliance with the Northern People's Congress made its reversal, vis-à-vis Ghana, almost inevitable.

In June 1961, Chief Awolowo traveled to Accra and held lengthy meetings with Nkrumah, after which he had only praise for Ghana. He called for Nigeria to join the Ghana-Guinea-Mali union, which would then have sixty million people. "What a mighty force that would be in world affairs!" he said.[151] In parliament, the Action Group adopted Nkrumah's pan-African approach. On a motion of confidence in the federation's foreign policy, Anthony Enahoro said that if it were passed, "it will be to the disgust of progressive elements throughout this country—a policy which advises functional co-operation among African states at a time when the climate of progressive opinion . . . is overwhelmingly in favour of organic union."[152] The Action Group was just beginning to send men to Ghanaian subversion-training camps, arrange-

[149] See Richard Sklar, *Nigerian Political Parties*, Princeton, 1963, pp. 82, 126.

[150] *Ibid.*, p. 270.

[151] *Evening News*, 13 June 1961. See also *Ghana Foreign Affairs*, Vol. 3, No. 3 (June 1961).

[152] *House of Representatives, Nigeria, Debates*, 4 September 1961, p. 2808. The Action Group was careful about what it praised in Ghana, nonetheless. See *ibid.*, 29 November 1961, p. 3548.

ments made during Awolowo's visit to Accra. Knowledge of these Action Group activities intensified the federal government's realization that it would have to assume greater leadership in pan-African movements to counter Nkrumah's appeal to "progressive" Nigerian groups.

In January 1962, after the Lagos conference, Nigeria's governing parties began taking the offensive. Of course Ghana had not attended the conference, Dr. Azikiwe's *West African Pilot* said: "Ghana has never made any concession on anything. First they would not discuss an African High Command with Nigeria because we signed a defence pact with Britain. We have now [on the eve of the Conference] abrogated the pact . . . what concession has Ghana made? . . . Every day we hear talk about African unity from Accra. Ghana has certainly taken some practical steps to demonstrate this unity by breaking up the West African Frontier Force, the West African Airways Corporation, and the . . . Currency Board."[153] A. K. Barden then attacked Governor-General Azikiwe, describing him as a puppet of the British crown. While Leslie Harriman, Nigeria's acting high commissioner in Accra, made enquiries to see if Barden's article indeed represented the official view, the press in Lagos made its most vigorous attacks on Ghana. Nkrumah was the "führer" of Accra, an "iron-fisted dictatorship" had been imposed on Ghana.[154] Doe, the new Ghanaian high commissioner, criticized the *Pilot* for "prejudging" the issue, but made an implicit retraction: Barden's article had listed him as director of the Bureau; Doe now stated that "The description of Mr. Barden as Chairman of the Bureau. . . was a statement of fact and was not an indication of the capacity under which he wrote the article."[155] In the relations of governments, such an assertion as Doe's must be accepted, and of importance, but to the *West African Pilot* (and to Nigerian officials) Barden was "no more than an echo of his master's voice. . . . We pity Mr. Doe. He is new to the country and has come at a tricky period. He has done his best, as his calling demands, to lie for his government."[156] At the same time, the prime minister of Nigeria's eastern region accused Ghana of interfering in a by-election there—where it was no secret that Ghana was helping to finance the small Dynamic Party's campaign.[157] This was only a prologue of the crisis on the horizon.

Despite sporadic attempts to de-fuse the press war, relations did not improve during the spring of 1962, and little was required to provoke a new round of insults. It occurred when John Tettegah, the secretary of

<hr />

[153] *West African Pilot*, 15 January 1962.   [154] *Ibid.*, 12 February 1962.
[155] *Ibid.*, 14 February 1962. See also *ibid.*, 16 February 1962.
[156] *Ibid.*, 13 February 1962.
[157] *Ibid.*, 17 February 1962, 21 May 1962, interview, CF-112.

the Ghana-financed All-African Trade Union Federation, made several trips to Nigeria in April and May, just prior to the Trade Union Congress in Ibadan (where competing Nigerian union leaders were attempting to merge their groups). These trips prompted repeated allegations of attempted subversion.[158] Tettegah asked why he had less right to "interfere" in Nigerian labor affairs than had the American-financed ICFTU, of which the TUC-Nigeria was an affiliate. Nigerian officials pointed out, however, that Ghanaian representatives were official agents of their government (Tettegah, for that matter, was an ambassador plenipotentiary); Nigerian labor leaders would hardly be permitted to lobby at Ghanaian trade union conferences. As Jaja Wachuku wrote to Ako Adjei, "the fact remains that this Cabinet Minister [Tettegah] arrived in Nigeria at a crucial time and engaged in activities designed to wreck all efforts by the Nigerian people to settle the dispute between the two rival factions of the Nigerian Trade Union Movement."[159]

Following the open split in the Action Group in May and June came Nigeria's greatest crisis up to that time. Those loyal to Awolowo in the western regional government were deposed by the federal government, and replaced by a faction from the Action Group which was willing to cooperate with the federal coalition. The *Ghanaian Times* saw this as "a carefully hatched conspiracy against this region."[160] Ghana was in the strongest position ever to take the offensive: domestic tension had eased, Nkrumah had released several hundred political prisoners, while independent Nigeria was making its first detentions. But the Lagos *Pilot* would not allow Ghana the upper hand: "The image of Ghana today is the mirror of the most terrible, pitiless, and primitive dictatorship in black Africa and in all Africa, she is in competition with only South Africa for first place as the premier graveyard of democratic institution. . . . If Balewa is a dark-skinned Englishman [as the *Evening News* had charged] Nigerians prefer him to a black Hitler."[161] If the NCNC's attitude was affected by shame for its role in the national crisis, this was not apparent in its press, in which anguish over Nigeria's detentions was expressed. The party had had enough of Ghana. It resented the constant slights that Ghanaians had, wittingly or unwittingly, imposed on Nigerian officials.[162] Moreover, it envied Ghana's position in African affairs. One

[158] See *Express* (Lagos), 3-5 May 1962.

[159] Wachuku to Ako Adjei, 14 June 1962, in *Ghana*, "Nkrumah's Deception of Africa," 1967, p. 51. Note that AATUF was not even an operative organization at this point.

[160] *Ghanaian Times*, 1 June 1962.

[161] *West African Pilot*, 6 June 1962.

[162] See Wachuku to Adjei (note 159), p. 48, in which various slights to the Nigerian prime minister and governor-general are recounted.

MP stated, "Wherever you go you always hear of Ghana; in New York, it is Ghana; in London, it is Ghana. We too want publicity."[163]

The crisis was fed, more basically, by the government's well-documented knowledge of Ghanaian subversion in the form of Awolowo's alleged plot to overthrow the Nigerian government (in late summer 1962). At his trial, the Action Group leader was charged with "an intention to levy war against our sovereign Lady the Queen, within Nigeria."[164] Two of the indictments against the Action Group leaders involved Ghana: firstly, that Awolowo procured the services of Dr. Oladipo Maja, son of a founder of the Action Group, relative of highly connected Ghanaians, and a deeply committed radical, to "arrange for the training of Nigerians outside Nigeria in the unlawful use of explosives, weapons, arms, and ammunitions in preparation for the said levying of war within Nigeria." Secondly, that various of the accused "attended, outside Nigeria, courses of training in the unlawful use of explosives, weapons, arms."[165]

The judge had two witnesses to overt acts of treason, as required. Maja, for his part, turned state's evidence, and claimed that he had acted as go-between in the arranging of training in Ghana, and that Nkrumah paid him £7,000 for purposes of organizing in Lagos (which he, like so many of Ghana's freedom fighters, spent on his personal and professional needs).[166] The other witness was Sanya Onabamiro, who claimed to have been a member of Awolowo's so-called tactical committee (with Tony Enahoro and Sammy Ikoku), which had allegedly been set up to obtain power "by means of violence." Onabamiro claimed that it was to him that Awolowo gave instructions that two hundred "boys" obtain military training in Ghana, and that other arrangements be made preparatory to a coup d'état.[167] There was further evidence by some of those who had received training in Ghana and, in addition, the corroborating evidence of frontier registers, airplane tickets, and air-travel cards. In the end, the judge found Chief Awolowo guilty of treason, and sentenced him to ten years in prison.

Is it plausible that Nkrumah and Awolowo envisaged the overthrow of the Nigerian government? A distinguished Nigerian civil servant later argued that this was preposterous; did Nkrumah seriously believe that

[163] *Nigeria, Debates*, 14 April 1962, p. 1690.
[164] *Nigeria*, "The Queen and Maja and thirty others in re Omisade," Vol. 1, p. 3. See also Richard Sklar's excellent article, "Nigerian Politics: The Ordeal of Chief Awolowo, 1960-65," in Gwendolen M. Carter, ed., *Politics in Africa*, New York, 1966. I am grateful for Professor Sklar's advice on the reading of the trial record.
[165] *Ibid.*, pp. 3-4.
[166] He used the funds to establish a medical clinic in Lagos. *Ibid.*, Vol. 9, p. 76.
[167] *Ibid.*, p. 67.

new leadership in Nigeria would not also turn on him? Did he not realize that he had everything to gain if Nigeria remained Africa's slumbering giant? Was not Nigeria the perfect strawman to be painted as a colonialist lackey? Could power be seized so simply?[168] By this time, it was characteristic of Nkrumah to assume that Africans everywhere were divided in their political loyalties only over his particular brand of pan-Africanism; he did not see that the option he offered had come to be considered—in most places—outdated. In Togo in 1963 and, indeed, in Nigeria in 1966, Nkrumah was to make the same assumption. Nor did he have the patience or subtlety for a classical Machiavellian policy. If it is not believed that Nkrumah thought "union government" both feasible and imminent, there is no satisfactory explanation for most of his policies.

As for Awolowo, the judge read mystical passages from his diary, which suggest that his mind had been "worked up to a state of absolute belief in the victory of his Party. The frustrations which he later experienced in the House of Representatives . . . could only have caused greater bitterness . . . and given him greater vigour to see that his ambition . . . were attained by any means whatsoever."[169] According to a Ghanaian diplomat, once posted in Nigeria, and a relative of Dr. Maja, Nkrumah and Awolowo both concluded a coup was necessary, once they saw that the NPC-NCNC alliance was permanent. Maja, he said, made numerous trips into Ghana, and the Ghanaians continued to think these efforts went undetected. Maja had thus arranged for large quantities of arms to be transported (by his father's fishing fleet) from Elmina Castle into Nigeria.[170]

The importance of the evidence is obvious. By early 1962 the Nigerians had detailed knowledge of Ghanaian subversion, and by summer of the same year, they had all the evidence that was later to be presented at the trial. They were able to discuss the evidence with their Monrovia colleagues from the time of the Lagos conference meeting in January 1962. The government had not protested at an earlier point for very good reasons. They knew what was occurring, considered (at first) that it was not too dangerous, and wished the Ghanaians to "exhaust themselves" before a Nigerian protest should make them more cautious.[171] Ghana's aim had been clear. Leslie Harriman, who remained in Accra as Acting High Commissioner because Abubakar refused to appoint a permanent envoy, said "They were probing, testing, hitting at every point

---

[168] Interview: Philip Asiodu. [169] ". . . in re Omisade," Vol. 9, p. 91.
[170] Ibid., and interview: CF-112.
[171] Interview: Ambassador Victor Adegoroye.

where we were weak. It was not just the camps; Ghana's external broadcasting services began in 1961, with messages of socialism and pan-Africanism aimed at our people. They were beginning to have effect."[172]

Ghana had been on the offensive, and by June 1962 the Nigerians were afraid that Nkrumah might succeed in placing a new constellation of forces in power in Nigeria. Thus, at the time of the western Nigeria crisis, Jaja Wachuku suddenly held a press conference to lay the gravest of charges. Before peace could come between the two countries, Ghana would have to cease its subversion, Nkrumah would have to curb his ambition to impose leadership on other states, and Nigerian nationals would have to be treated like Ghanaians in Nigeria. He concluded on the offensive: "If we used all the machinery available to us we could topple the Ghana government. It would not last twelve months. . . . We cannot agree with the policy of black imperialism which is raising its head."[173] Tawia Adamafio replied in kind—he was then acting foreign minister. "Not even a combination of Wachuku's colonial masters can topple the Ghana government, much less a neo-colonised regime like Nigeria's Federal Government."[174] The *Evening News* in Accra referred to Wachuku's "heat-oppressed brain" and, in Nigeria, a junior minister publicly demanded that relations between the two countries be broken. "They do not like us. They hate us."[175]

Three days after Wachuku's press conference, Doe, Ghana's envoy, was made to wait one hour before seeing the minister. The *West African Pilot* in Lagos headlined "Jaja gets tougher." It was clear that the crisis was having a cathartic effect on the demoralized Nigerian officials. The *Pilot* described "the sleepless nights" of Nkrumah and his regime, during which they saw "visions of their own corpses dripping with blood at the public square in Accra."[176] Harriman protested Adamafio's statement, but the note was refused.[177] Wachuku also sent a lengthy letter to Ako Adjei summarizing all the charges (while remaining suitably vague with respect to the training camps), threatening to take "appropriate measures to protect [the Nigerian government's] interests."[178] Then, while passing through Accra, he refused to leave his plane to meet briefly with Adamafio, whose own gesture—of champagne in the V.I.P. lounge— was gratuitous.[179]

The future of pan-Africanism, wrote David Williams, depended on

[172] Interview: Ambassador Leslie Harriman.
[173] *West African Pilot*, 11 June 1962. [174] P.R. #335/62, 12 June 1962.
[175] *West African Pilot*, 12 June 1962. [176] *Ibid.*, 13 June 1962.
[177] P.R. #359/62, 15 June 1962.
[178] Wachuku to Ako Adjei, 14 June 1962, in *Ghana*, "Nkrumah's Deception of Africa," 1967, p. 51.
[179] See interview: Puplampu.

243

good Ghana-Nigeria relations.[180] These relations were very bad. There had been a clear split in the advice given Nkrumah by diplomats and by militants. Over and over Quaison-Sackey had argued the importance— and possibility—of a close relationship with Nigeria, as already existed at the United Nations. Kwesi Armah, although a political appointee, was as ardent as Quaison-Sackey in arguing the same point of view. "What is actually worrying us is the positive boastfulness by the followers of Osagyefo. For instance Nigeria has got the impression that Ghana's main aim is to dominate . . . I think the followers are doing a great deal of harm to our African policy."[181] The "followers"—Barden, Tettegah, and other radicals—had won. They had continued to provoke Nigeria and, more important, had continued to press Nkrumah not to relent in his opposition to the Nigerian government. When Awolowo pressed his own case, they had encouraged Nkrumah to offer him such assistance as might install Awolowo in power as Ghana's ally in the Ghana-Guinea-Mali union. They had successfully counteracted the advice of Ghana's diplomats, who wished Ghana's relations with Nigeria to be the bedrock of its Africa policy. In the process of their victory they had their ranks infused with new blood, refugees from Nigeria whose presence was to provide Lagos with a new irritant. Nkrumah's options were all the more narrowed, as some of these exiles, and in particular Ikoku, found positions of importance in Ghana.

The Conseil de l'Entente. There were two ways for Ghana to end its growing geographic isolation. It could work with Houphouet—as Quaison-Sackey thought was possible—and through him, with other Entente states. Alternatively, it could split the Entente by developing strong links with Houphouet's partners. Nkrumah tried both policies, followed neither of them through, and ended with the worst of both worlds, namely, the continued hostility of the Ivory Coast and the eventual consolidation of ties among the Entente states.

The chief obstacle to reconciliation with Abidjan lay in the presence of Ivoirien refugees in Accra, but in early 1962 Nkrumah offered to return to the Ivory Coast several of the most important if Houphouet would free the imprisoned Sanwi "king" in return. According to Ivoirien sources, Houphouet did so, and sent one of the king's freed associates to Accra to bring the remaining refugees back to Abidjan—but he remained in Accra, and did not bring his tribesmen back to the Ivory

---

[180] David Williams: "How Deep the Split in West Africa?" *Foreign Affairs*, 40, No. 1 (October 1961). It should be noted that President Touré was trying to mediate the Nigerian-Ghanaian dispute.

[181] *Ministry of Foreign Affairs*, Conference of Ghana Envoys, January 1962, p. 55.

Coast. Indeed, *a feuille de chou* (as the PDCI called it), the *Voix du Sanwi*, was begun in Accra.[182] Nkrumah had once more shown bad faith. The Ivory Coast was beginning a period in which its growth rate was among the world's highest, while the Ghanaian economy was lurching from crisis to crisis. It is easy to see why Houphouet should have felt confident.

Opportunities remained open in the other Entente countries, nonetheless. From an economic point of view it was very much in Ghana's interest to develop ties with such close neighbors. In 1960 Ghana had an adverse trade balance of £3,649,000 with African countries; in 1961, of £5,513,000, much of which was with the Entente states. If Ghana could consolidate economic links with Niger and Dahomey, and make the Paga agreement with Upper Volta work, the Ivory Coast would clearly be on the defensive.

The only concrete issue dividing Ghana and Niger was Bakary Djibo's entrenched position in Ghana as a "freedom fighter." Djibo had once been secretary-general of the Niger section of the RDA and Hamani Diori had been president, but the two had broken when Djibo preferred to maintain links with French Communists after Houphouet's split with them in 1950; Djibo then established his own party, Sawaba, and became head of the government in 1957. But Diori took power after the 1958 referendum and Djibo was forced into exile by October 1959—first in Bamako, then in Accra.[183] By January 1960 Sawaba was publicly launched as a CPP affiliate.[184]

Ruth Schacter Morgenthau has argued that Diori's and Djibo's parties had "represented similar modernization forces, respectively in western and eastern Niger."[185] Djibo's regrouped Sawaba (freedom) Party became, increasingly, a fragment of the far left, advocating the familiar solutions often attractive to politicians in exile. At this stage in 1962, Nkrumah could have found sufficient *raison d'état* to sacrifice his relationship with Djibo, in order to cooperate with Diori. Djibo was not one of Nkrumah's close associates, and it was a period in which "Nkrumah could still talk with leaders like Diori."[186] Nkrumah invited him to Accra, hoping to convince him to support union government, and Diori accepted, hoping to convince Nkrumah to withdraw support from Sawaba.[187] Moreover, it was a time of rapprochement in Africa, and

---

[182] See "Si le ridicule tuait . . ." Une Mise au point du Bureau Politique du PDCI-RDA, *Fraternité*, Abidjan, 12 March 1965; also interview: CF-15.

[183] Ruth Schacter Morgenthau, *Political Parties in French-Speaking West Africa*, London, 1964, p. 318.

[184] See "New Party Joins CPP," *Ghana Times*, 5 January 1960.

[185] Morgenthau, *op.cit.*, p. 318.   [186] Interview: CF-14.

[187] Interviews: CF-14, 85.

Diori noted in Accra that it was Conseil policy "to extend its contacts with the anglophone states, for the sake of African reconciliation."[188] The visit went well in several respects. Diori praised Nkrumah, something which was always well received, and the *Evening News* thus considered him qualified to be "a linguist of Progressive Africa."[189] If neither obtained what he primarily sought, they agreed to begin discussions for a trade agreement, the first step of which was to be the visit of a Ghanaian trade delegation to Niamey.

According to Ghana's chargé in Niamey, Diori immediately after his return from Accra appointed economists to prepare the ground for a meeting with a trade delegation. But "their hopes seem to be marred by frustration and disappointment: the interest which the Government and the people had . . . seems to be waning completely. There is the general impression that Ghana made this promise as a camouflage to woo Niger."[190] Diori, he went on, had rebuked his ministers for not attending Ghana's national day celebrations, when he himself had been in Paris. But there was no reciprocal interest shown from Accra, and "this inattention being given to Niger Government's needs may be due to the keen interest Ghana takes in the Sawaba party"; recent reports on Sawaba's strength in Ghana disturbed Niger's government, and so Nigeria's influence was mounting in Niamey. Moreover, Niger had sent an ambassador to Accra, Ghana only a chargé to Niamey. Worse, as the ambassador in Accra was denied tax-free alcohol privileges, Niger had reciprocated in Niamey. Yet, "In fact Niger has a great respect for Ghana and they are all hoping for the day Osagyefo would set foot on Niger soil. I am . . . appealing to the Ghana Government to come out boldly with a declaration of not supporting the Sawaba Party and making a publicity out of it."[191] Niger had clearly taken careful stock of its interests, and persisted, unsuccessfully, in seeking an agreement with Ghana out of concern for its own economic independence and survival; moreover, in mid-1962, it still looked possible that the Paga agreement with Upper Volta could have a profound impact on relations in this part of West Africa. Yakubu, Ghana's chargé, thus noted, "Niger has realised that Upper Volta's progress . . . depends on Ghana's support and she now feels she must also enjoy such privileges. But to the peoples of Niger, it seems Ghana does not pay heed to them."[192] Up to the end of this period, Upper Volta was clearly the key to the struggle for influence in landlocked West Africa.

There was more for Ghana to gain in Dahomey than in Niger, and

188 *AFP Sp. Outre-mer*, No. 4015, 13 March 1962.   189 15 March 1962.
190 Yakubu, Ghana/Niamey, to AAS, 19 July 1962, CFA-33.
191 *Ibid.*   192 *Ibid.*

every reason why Ghana should succeed. Nkrumah had developed relations with President Maga, so as to isolate Olympio; Maga, for his part, sought to be the peacemaker on the Benin coast. Maga, moreover, had to be on good terms with Nkrumah, because his vice-president, Apithy, had long admired him, and the domestic position in Dahomey was delicate. Maga visited Accra in June 1961, where it was decided to establish a trade agreement between the two countries, the urgency of which was continually stressed from both sides. However, some Dahomean economists wanted more caution, fearing Ghana would re-export goods from third countries into Dahomey,[193] and insisted that the payment and trade agreement be separate (with Ghana providing £500,000 in convertible currency for the swing credit).[194] In March 1962, both sides were still pressing, unsuccessfully, for a meeting of experts, when Maga suggested one way Ghana could make matters simpler: "as far as our financial problems are concerned, *un geste du Ghana, dans le cadre de la solidarité africaine*, will be highly appreciated by my government and all the Dahomean people."[195] If Nkrumah wanted an agreement, he did not want it enough to override the strong opposition that could be expected from his ministries, had a *geste* large enough to be public been involved.[196] Since the last such grants (to Guinea and Mali) in July 1961, Ghana's overseas assets had declined from £118,050,000 to £70,720,000, or roughly 40 percent, and the ministries were desperately seeking to stop the economic bloodletting. At a cabinet meeting, the minister of finance and trade presented the conclusion of his experts— that "the Ghana pound [unconvertible] should be the operative currency in the Trade Agreement."[197] This made the price very high indeed, and thereafter postponement followed postponement.[198]

In mid-May 1962, the *Ghanaian Times* added the political insult necessary to wreck remaining chances. It criticized Dahomey for considering an alleged offer of American arms to its army. New nations, the paper said, needed tractors, not arms, unless, of course, the arms were to provide defense against "imperialist outrages." It concluded, irrelevantly, by noting: "When we purchased planes from the Soviet Union, [the imperialists] scowled and screamed. . . . YET WE DID ALL THIS

[193] Interview: Gustavo Doudjo, *Chargé d'Affaires a.i.*, Dahomey/Accra. It is interesting that many Ghanaian documents of this period refer to the existence of a trade agreement, which in fact was never signed.

[194] Cabinet Information paper, Cabinet Meeting, 16 March 1962, CFA-30.

[195] Maga to Nkrumah, 5 March 1962, CFA-30.

[196] This presumably did not preclude some private *gestes*.

[197] See note 194.

[198] Meetings were planned and canceled because of the difficulties of finding both parties available at the same time.

WITH OUR OWN MONEY."[199] Dahomey did not have such money, and denied there was truth in the allegation in any event.[200] Eventually Ghana tried to make amends by appointing an ambassador to Cotonou, but the trade agreement was not signed. Once more the militants had won, wittingly or unwittingly.

Despite such obstacles as the surcharge in Ghana's 1961 "Kaldor" budget—which made Upper Volta's imports through Ghana dearer than anticipated—there still existed the possibility of making the "Paga" agreement between the two states work. In Ouagadougou, as Philippe Decraene wrote, "the taste . . . for everything from the south rages. . . . In the streets the Ghanaian trucks have never been so numerous, and the women wear Ashanti jewelry."[201] Trade statistics also showed that the agreement had some force:[202]

	1957	1958	1959	1960	1961	1962	1963
U.V.→Gh.	£2,183	1,628	2,105	2,413	3,346	3,391	2,380
Gh. →U.V.	£ 66	274	207	536	373	996	443
Total	£2,249	1,902	2,312	2,949	3,719	4,387	2,823

New difficulties in the agreement arose throughout 1962, however, in addition to those caused by the Ghanaian tax surcharge, and obstructions allegedly caused by the French bank. The small Voltaic traders began complaining that they were unable to transfer funds from Ghanaian banks to those in Ouagadougou and, according to a Voltaic diplomat, pressed Yameogo for a change in policy.[203] Yameogo was also finding it was not easy to keep his distance from the UAM states—his French-linked allies. These states, meeting in Tananarive in September 1961 to sign a defense pact, chose Ouagadougou, the weakest link, as headquarters. Yameogo repeatedly made clear that Paga did not affect his country's membership in the Conseil de l'Entente, although it did. Yameogo and Houphouet were step by step moving closer to a rapprochement, and if this were to succeed, Paga would be finished.

For all that, Yameogo and Nkrumah still had sufficient reason—Yameogo, to nourish his country's political and economic independence, Nkrumah, to give evidence that he could work with moderate states—to wish to make the agreement work. They decided to meet in late July

[199] *Ghanaian Times*, 10 May 1962.
[200] See Virginia Thompson, "Dahomey," in Gwendolyn Carter, ed., *Five African States*, London, 1963. Also interview: CF-24.
[201] *Communauté-France-Eurafrique*, April 1962, p. 27.
[202] Taken from *Bank of Ghana, Quarterly Economic Bulletin* (September-December 1963).
[203] Interview: Amb. Aisse Mensah, Upper Volta/Accra.

to recast the agreement in view of the difficulties that had arisen. It was a desperate gamble for Yameogo because, in doing so, he once again had to risk breaking links with Houphouet, after their near reconciliation. On July 31st, Nkrumah and Yameogo met at Tenkodogo, in Upper Volta, where for a day and a half they discussed the problems in the Paga agreement. The talks were a success, resulting in the appointment of a joint commission to seek solutions for all the difficulties encountered.[204] The political will necessary for the agreement's success finally appeared to exist on both sides.

It was on his return from Tenkodogo to Accra that Nkrumah, while passing through the little Ghanaian town of Kulungugu, barely missed death from the grenade of an assassin. To protect his security, Nkrumah ordered all of Ghana's borders closed. The agreement with Upper Volta, for all intents and purposes, was thus rendered impotent. Yameogo, for his part, now had no choice but to look to Houphouet— the bonds with whom he had twice scorned—for survival. As penance, Yameogo became spokesman for Houphouet in that leader's struggle with Nkrumah for mastery in West Africa.

GHANAIAN STATECRAFT, 1960–1962

The Diplomatic Network. Concurrent with the shift of ideology in Ghana's governing party toward a militant socialism came a major transformation of the structure of government: increasing control from and by the president's office. After the "dawn broadcast" in April 1961, Nkrumah began assembling an array of new secretariats around him that superseded (or worked in parallel with) existing government agencies and ministries. Thus was a presidential "publicity secretariat" established to give Ghana's policies "quick and full publicity abroad" which then began competing with the ministry of information.[205] This did not bring the benefits of efficient executive control normally expected of parallel agencies in autocratic regimes: in a developing country efficient bureaucrats are scarce; now neither agency worked well.

The ministry of external affairs had had the responsibility for informing its diplomats of Ghanaian developments; much of this now came into the hands of the publicity secretariat, with the result that one ambassador could complain: "I get my information about Ghana through B.B.C. or diplomatic parties."[206] Altogether the president's office was

[204] Interview: CF-24.

[205] *Ghana*, "Annual Estimates," 1961-62, Vol. 1, "The President," p. 55. See also *Ghana*, "Report of the Commission of Enquiry on the Commercial Activities of the Erstwhile Publicity Secretariat," 1967.

[206] *Ministry of Foreign Affairs*, "Conference of Ghana Envoys," January 1962, p. 50. It was Amb. Poku (Ghana/Tel-Aviv) lodging the complaint. Others echoed it.

budgeted in the 1961-1962 estimates for £39,761,000 (including expenditure for development), or about a third of total government expenditure. Much of the increase was caused by foreign policy concerns. Actual expenditure for defense in 1959-1960, for example, had been £3,514,856; the estimates for 1960-1961 were £4,491,110 and for 1961-1962 £12,288,150. This was due (officially) to "operations in the Congo," the necessary expansion of the army volunteer force, required to support the regular forces at home, and the brigade still in the Congo.[207] Some of the increase, however, was caused by new equipment, required (at least in part) so that Ghana's armed forces remained at par with Nigeria's.

The most significant change, however, was in the contingency fund. Until mid-1961 this fund had been technically under the control of the ministry. It was now brought under Nkrumah's direct control, unaudited, and raised 500 percent from £100,000 (though according to Gbedemah, Nkrumah had wanted a 2000 percent raise).[208] It is this vote that most affected African policy. Freedom fighters now could be flown in and out of Ghana, with no concern for expense; African leaders could receive their private *"gestes du Ghana dans le cadre de la solidarité Africaine"*—as they indeed did—and pet schemes, to which civil servants voiced objections could be begun by presidential fiat. Unpopular agencies, such as the Bureau of African Affairs, could begin covert operations throughout Africa.

In 1959, Prime Minister Diefenbaker had lent Ghana the services of an official from his foreign ministry to make recommendations for the organization of Ghana's ministry of external affairs. Wardroper, the Canadian, and Peter Abban, a Ghanaian diplomat in administration at the ministry, had drawn up a carefully staged and ambitious plan for the expansion of Ghana's diplomatic representation. Within five years there were to be embassies in every important country. By 1961, even this plan was found lacking in scope and had to be discarded.[209] The original estimates to parliament for the year 1960-1961 had made provision for 22 embassies, the request for the following year, 44. Numerous supplementary requests were made and in the end funds were provided for 53 (a number exceeding Australia's).[210]

The expansion came in three areas. Firstly, there was an expansion

207 "Annual Estimates," Vol. 1, pp. 149-51.
208 *Ghana*, "Apaloo Report," 1967, pp. 27-28, and interview: Gbedemah.
209 Interview: Peter Abban.
210 By June 1962 only 44 embassies were in operation, owing to the difficulties in opening missions in African states.

into countries with which Ghana had come into contact as a result of its new international prominence and activity. For example, the Ceylonese had a representative at the first Casablanca conference, and by the end of that month, January 1961, Nkrumah had appointed a high commissioner to Colombo. Latin America was also becoming an area of interest. The ministry had long considered it "virgin diplomatic territory" in which the "African personality" could be projected, and from which "powerful diplomatic and political support . . . in the United Nations" could be elicited.[211] Bing was another proponent of this, and he urged that missions be opened in Brazil and other important states.[212] At the end of this period, a mission existed in Havana (where Quaison-Sackey was accredited), a new one was being opened in Rio de Janeiro, and interest in Bolivia was developing.[213]

Secondly and thirdly were the new missions in Africa and Eastern Europe. The speed and ease with which Ghana was able to exchange embassies with states of the second group, in contrast with those of the first, is worth noting. Nkrumah had decided that Ghana needed a "presence" in every African state. In French speaking Africa, however, Ghana had little success in establishing missions; not one was opened in equatorial French Africa, although budgetary provisions had been made. Relations with Togo were so bad that the question of diplomatic relations did not arise. True, there were missions in each of the Entente countries, but this followed from Nkrumah's agreement with Houphouet in 1960 to exchange ambassadors; these states needed to be well-apprised of each other's developments. With some African states, such as Senegal, Morocco, and Niger, the mission accredited to Accra had a higher—ambassadorial—status at first than did the reciprocal Ghanaian mission which was at the chargé level. The implication would seem to be that Ghana indeed wanted a presence everywhere in Africa while other states, appreciating Ghana's importance, wanted effective diplomats to report Nkrumah's moves.

On the other hand, ambassadors were appointed to Eastern European posts in January 1962, almost immediately after Nkrumah's 1961 visit to these countries. Each of the six new embassies received an appropriation of £29,730. It is true that these states already had missions

211 "Brief on Ghana's Foreign Policy Towards the Americas," by R. W. Akwei, head of American division, MFA, in "Conference of Ghana Envoys," p. 205.

212 Bing, *Memorandum* to Nkrumah, March 1961, CFA-119.

213 Nkrumah apparently was interested in attending the 10th anniversary of the Bolivian revolution; Adjei recommended against it on the grounds that other states were to be represented, and Bolivia would not therefore be able to "accord Osagyefo all the honours and specialised treatment to which he is entitled." Adjei went instead. Adjei to Nkrumah, 12 February 1962, CFA-52.

in Accra, but reciprocity had not been demanded when they were opened; they obviously had a different objective from that which a Ghanaian embassy could hold in their respective capitals. With one notable exception (Dadzie in Bucharest) the envoys Nkrumah appointed to the Eastern posts were not of a calibre to give Ghana's embassies more than symbolic functions, and in only a few cases was there a trained diplomat under the ambassador.

Ghana's ambassadors continued to be a mixed lot. There were, for example, a few very able political appointees, such as J. K. Quashie in Abidjan, who served his government well until political temptation proved too strong, after which Nkrumah was forced to withdraw him.[214] His reports combined useful insights with sufficient dogma to make them acceptable to Nkrumah. He had a sense of Ghana's national interest, beyond its pan-African ambition, and thus kept a careful watch on economic indicators in areas where Ghana and the Ivory Coast competed. It was difficult to obtain information on the timber trade, he said, as the Ivoiriens did not want to give "an idea of the vile exploitation of the labour force used on the industry," but noted that that country's real advantage lay in having an EEC preference (which was, he prophetically argued, the "real threat to Ghana").[215]

Those that had fully imbibed Nkrumaism, however, ended in trouble more quickly. Budu-Acquah, Adamafio's associate, was appointed to Somalia, where he attempted to strengthen the position of the pro-Africa faction led by President Osman, against the pro-Arab faction led by Shermarche, the prime minister. His line was that "African States should guard against the exploitation of religious and ethnic differences in their search for unity,"[216] which was at best a contentious argument in Mogadisciu. Ironically, he described himself not as a diplomat but as a "missionary."[217] He involved himself in a pamphlet war with another embassy, personally distributed copies of Nkrumah's speeches to the doorsteps of ministers, openly propagandized for AATUF, and in the end so alienated the government that while he was absent they suggested that his leave be extended indefinitely and that he be replaced by a Muslim (which was done). Happily, a political officer in the Ghanaian embassy in Addis Ababa, who spoke Italian, was able to undo much of the damage through quiet diplomacy, and Budu-Acquah was moved on to Conakry. Ghana had been the first black state represented in Mog-

[214] See p. 315.

[215] Quashie to Osagyefo, 26 April 1962, and Quashie to Managing-Director, Timber Marketing Board, 3 May 1962, CFA-28.

[216] *President's Office*, "Notes of Conference of Ghana Envoys in Africa," October 1961, talk by Budu-Acquah, 9 October 1961, p. 9.

[217] In an interview with the author.

adisciu, and Budu-Acquah spoiled his state's excellent opportunity to develop a close friendship there.

None was more personally successful, however, than Kwesi Armah, a delightful (and reputedly corrupt) Nzima who had originally been sent to London to guard party interests among Ghanaian students in Britain. As deputy high commissioner he had led a demonstration on Lumumba's behalf in Trafalgar Square, for which he was censored by the *Diplomatist*, a London periodical.[218] One British cabinet minister considered him "the most conceited man I ever met," but it was a reflection of his government's attitude toward Africa that Armah was not asked to leave.[219]

In July 1961, Sir Edward Asafu-Adjei, the high commissioner in London, protested Nkrumah's instructions that certain gilt-edged securities be sold to provide funds for Guinea and Mali, and sent Armah to Eastern Europe (where Nkrumah was visiting) to convince the president accordingly. Armah returned with a letter of dismissal for Sir Edward, and letters of credence to the Queen for himself. That high commission became the symbol of patronage, corruption, waste, and bad management,[220] but Armah became, before much longer, probably the most influential Ghanaian under Nkrumah.[221]

Yet by this stage the majority of Ghana's representatives had become apprehensive about the trends in Ghana's foreign policy, despite the fact that most of them were political appointees. At the first conference of envoys (in October 1961) much tension was held beneath the surface. After discussing the talk by A. K. Barden, the ambassadors concluded: "There is no need to help citizens from independent countries. Citizens of independent countries seeking assistance or political asylum should be told that the best way to carry on their struggle was to do it in their own countries."[222] They all knew this was not the policy. They had tried to influence Nkrumah's policy with respect to the Ivory Coast and Togo and had failed. At the next ambassadorial conference, in January 1962, regrets were expressed that Ghana had not been represented at Monrovia and most appeared to hope that Ghana would attend the Lagos conference.

218 See *Daily Telegraph*, 12 September 1961.

219 See *Daily Express*, 17 January 1961, which asks, "what would be the case if members of an Iron Curtain country had indulged in similar activities?" and interview: CF-103.

220 See *Ghana*, Auditor General's Report, for years endings 30 June 1961, 30 June 1962, and 30 September 1963, and interview: CF-14.

221 He was also a restraining influence on Nkrumah in many ways, being far-sighted enough to see what could result were the regime not stabilized, and powerful enough to be willing to make specific recommendations.

222 "Notes of Conference of Ghana Envoys in Africa," p. 22.

Reports from many of the ambassadors revealed a clear preference for functional cooperation, instead of Nkrumah's policy of organic unity. This was in part due to the ease with which their host governments could influence them, but it was also a reaction against the increasing incoherence of instructions from Accra and against the policies propounded there. By the end of 1962 the handwriting was on the wall, and they either "went along," or they did not report (something at which they were bad in any case). Some outside of Africa simply tried to go about their business, projecting a positive image of Africa. Nylander, in Ottawa, was the first black African diplomat there and he and his wife traveled throughout the country, while he spoke on general African problems.[223]

By the end of 1960 there were already very narrow limits of independence for the professional foreign service officers. Nkrumah instructed Richard Quarshie, a principal assistant secretary of the ministry, to prepare six men for imminent duty as heads of missions in newly independent African states. Quarshie replied that by ministry standards the men did not exist; so Nkrumah sent six trade union officials as the new chargés and commissioners.[224]

Promotions, even admission to the service, became increasingly dependent on party loyalty. In foreign missions, envoys complained that "certain junior officers took advantage of their party membership to be lax in their discipline,"[225] which was an understatement. In the ministry, Adjei periodically tried to frighten younger officers who did not have party cards, it was said. But no one was more frightened than Adjei.[226]

The ministry, as originally established, operated in the same way as the home ministries, with one principal secretary and one principal assistant secretary. This was considered overcentralized, and Ako Adjei spent considerable time in 1960 reorganizing it into four divisions (administrative, protocol, United Nations and economic, and African affairs), each under a principal assistant secretary, who worked through the principal secretary. As part of the reorganization process the senior diplomats were brought home to man the new desks.[227] Whereas too few of the senior men had been in Accra in the first period, they were now concentrated too much at home; the senior posts abroad, to which they

---

[223] Interview: Amb. C. T. Nylander, and interviews: Canadian High Commission, Accra, where Nylander's record was lauded.

[224] Interviews: Amb. A.B.B. Kofi, Richard Quarshie.

[225] "Conference of Ghana Envoys," p. 17.

[226] Adjei always had at least one officer present in his office to protect himself when he talked with Western diplomats.

[227] Interviews: Ako Adjei, F. E. Boaten. See also "Notes on Administration of Ministry of Foreign Affairs," by F. E. Boaten, in "Conference of Ghana Envoys," pp. 175-78.

aspired, were taken by political appointees. The result was excessive competition and feuding, of which Nkrumah was the beneficiary. Blocked at the top, with nowhere to go, they had to make peace or get out. Some benefited from the environment; most, like Frank Boaten and A.B.B. Kofi, reluctantly bided their time until respectable and isolated posts had been found for them.[228] Only a few of the senior officers were lucky enough to have been away throughout this period: Arkhurst was seconded to the ECA, and Major Seth Anthony had replaced Amonoo in Geneva. But the diplomats failed to present an alternative to Nkrumah's policy.

What finally wrecked the chance for a coordinated foreign policy was Nkrumah's division of the ministry. It meant that those left in the ministry's block near Black Star Square were seriously demoralized, knowing their colleagues at the African Affairs Secretariat over a mile away at Flagstaff House were at the center of activity. In fact Nkrumah's complaints against the ministry—which had led to its dismemberment—were not entirely unfounded. Ministry officials could not "think East," as Nkrumah wished them to do. He considered Kofi, the principal secretary, useless. Nkrumah's ideas were unrealistic, but on the smallest of issues officials could drag their heels and impede the implementation of plans; it took two months and several angry exchanges of letters before diplomatic plates were granted to the Algerian envoy in early 1961. The protocol officer had argued that the corps' *doyen* and the French ambassador would complain were the order implemented, owing to the provisional nature of Algeria's government.[229] But which came first, inefficiency and recalcitrance—or unwise policy? While the ministry had had a bad record on the auditor-general's queries on accounts,[230] it was argued that this inefficiency and sloppiness fed on resentment at the steady loss of status.

Moreover, no one was present to support their cause. The ministry had never been strong, but as Ako Adjei's influence slid, its position became pathetic. Even ambassadorial postings no longer came within its purview. Adjei, for example, only learned through the Ghanaian ambassador in Washington that Osagyefo had decided that that envoy "should return home in the near future to take up other duties in Ghana."[231] Kobina Kessie, ambassador in Peking (who had obtained the post

[228] Kofi was appointed High Commissioner in Rawalpindi in mid-1962; Boaten became head of the Accra Assembly.

[229] Ako Adjei to Secretary-General, MEA, 2 March 1961; M. Mamattah to S.P.S. Kumi, 21 April 1961; Kumi to Mamattah, 25 May 1961, CFA-1.

[230] See *Ghana*: "Report of the Auditor General . . . for Financial Year Ended 30 June 1961," p. 23, paras. 189-203.

[231] Adjei to Nkrumah, 7 May 1962, CFA-58.

through a shift in party loyalties) left China in the autumn of 1961 despite explicit instructions from Adjei to remain at his post; Adjei asked for power to dismiss him, for the sake of discipline in the service. Nkrumah instead appointed him to Cairo.[232] Month by month Adjei's obsequiousness increased: by March 1962 he would "crave the indulgence" to apprise Osagyefo of essential information.[233]

In sum, Ghana's diplomatic system was manifestly not working; its gears were not meshing. Ambassador Bonsu, Ghana's envoy in Italy, gave an interesting illustration of how great the difficulties had become:

> The Minister of Industries said in his address that the Ambassadors of Ghana should be investment agents for the Ghana Government. The purpose of opening missions abroad is for the Ambassadors to promote trade, to project the personality, culture and other related matters of their countries. But . . . I am afraid, these things have not been understood by some of us, because so many things happen that the Ambassador is out of the picture. I am supporting this case by the agreement signed between the Ghana Government and AGIP in Italy for [an] oil refinery. Even though I was travelling with the Director of that company on the same plane to Ghana, I was never told about this agreement until I saw in the papers the next morning that an agreement had been signed.[234]

Nkrumah by this time made any decision of importance, and only he and his immediate entourage were apprised of the position of vital matters; the price of this manner of government is always high.

Balance Sheet on the Eve of Kulungugu. For the past two years, Nkrumah had reacted to events, and Ghana looked as if it were on a pendulum. Nkrumah had expected to consolidate power and industrialize Ghana—with Western aid and investment. From his original view that he was severely limited by the Western concept of Africa, he had gradually discovered that he could take initiatives throughout the continent without engendering Western opposition. But the appetite had increased with eating, and when his plans included control of areas of strategic interest to the West (such as the Congo) his dreams were swept aside; the irony is that the West's opposition to him was only incidental to its opposition to, for example, Lumumba. The West did not think

---

[232] Ako Adjei to Nkrumah 11 November 1961, 18 November 1961. Adjei added, "I am taking every administrative step to ensure discipline in the Foreign Service and I believe that firm measures of this kind will help to strengthen the morale." CFA-52.

[233] Adjei to Nkrumah, 5 March 1962, CFA-53.

[234] "Conference of Ghana Envoys," pp. 83-84.

Nkrumah (or Nkrumaism) a danger in itself, but the very violence of his own reaction against the West during this period suggests that he had indeed considered the Congo (and similar areas) as his domain, snatched from him by the forces of imperialism. Likewise, the French had suddenly granted a form of independence to an empire, but it was not entirely as a result of forces he had set in motion, contrary to the beliefs of his followers. That the French maintained positions of influence in these countries only incidentally to prevent Nkrumah's dominion over them is shown by the case of Togo, where the French position was relatively weak, and Ghana's threat very clear. But he was forced to revise his timetable, his tactics, and his strategy, such as these had been.

Events within Ghana had also affected his policy, although Africa policy tended not to be affected by domestic events as much as external relations. He had hardly expected that by encouraging the radicals they would either become disillusioned with his brand of socialism, or that they would become prepared to take advantage of his weaknesses in order to entrench themselves at his expense. When they did both, he had to change courses dramatically.

The second conference of Ghana's envoys shows clearly the differences between groups affecting foreign policy. At one extreme were, for example, Kessie (in Cairo), Nylander (in Ottawa), Poku (in Tel-Aviv), and Baido-Ansah (in Tokyo); they wondered, in the words of Kessie, if Ghana could "rely" for its economic development upon countries "who always *say* they want to catch up with the West"[235]—instead of relying on the West itself. As to pan-Africanism, their views were also more traditional. Kessie commented that he did not think "common ideology is necessary to bring African States together. On the contrary I think it is common interest which will probably bring about African Unity."[236]

But an ideology of Nkrumaism had already been offered. Its chief proponent at this point was Nkrumah's sincerest follower, Kofi Baako, who had developed this theory over thirteen years. So far as Nkrumaism possessed definition, its terms included cultural and religious values; a general desire for world peace, goodwill, African unity; and a form of African socialism.[237] Those civil servants who had an interest in preserv-

---

[235] *Ibid.*, p. 82, emphasis added.   [236] *Ibid.*, p. 64.

[237] See Kofi Baako, "Nkrumaism," in *ibid.*, pp. 118-24. Ambassadors Quaison-Sackey and Jantuah destroyed Baako's concept in a discussion. Quaison-Sackey, as the one envoy praised by Nkrumah at the conference, was in a strong enough position to comment that he found very little in the philosophy that could make it a "real one." More caustically, he asked how much socialism there was in Ghana. Jantuah, knowing the extent of Baako's adulation of Nkrumah, mischieviously demanded to know the premise of Baako's philosophy. See *ibid.*, pp. 45-46.

ing illusions (such as Dei-Anang) said it was clear that Nkrumaism was "an advanced form of that philosophy propounded by Gandhi."[238]

Then there was the left. The radical opportunists, like Adamafio, did not want Nkrumaism defined; "while therefore we are very anxious to get a Bible of Nkrumaism we do not want to tie the hands of our Leader in a way that when he acts he will be accused of going against his own principles."[239] But the radical puritans had a definition and a program, and contempt for those who wanted corrupt versions of them. What mattered was—in their words—"scientific socialism."[240] Classes on Nkrumaism, at the Kwame Nkrumah Institute of Ideology, followed lectures on scientific socialism. Cecil Forde, one of the puritans, assured their excellencies that villagers would not be against socialism (as several "comrade-Ambassadors" had implied) if public statements were "vetted" beforehand;[241] the implications of this are obvious. To the puritans, African socialism was a barbarism. One act of fate would ensure that their definition of socialism—the Russian definition—merged with "Nkrumaism" as a concept. They were to get it.

There was a vicious circle in Nkrumah's domestic policy which also affected foreign policy options. He imprisoned opponents—such as Danquah—making more room for the radicals. This created an atmosphere of distrust which led to more violence, necessitating in turn yet harsher laws. This cycle made friendship with the West more difficult, as public opinion abroad hardened against the regime and created openings into which the Eastern states could move, strengthening their positions. This is not, necessarily, to praise Western values. The West was silent about Tubman's domestic excesses.[242] But Western diplomats rightly based their own hopes for improved relations with Ghana on an easing of the domestic situation.

There was also the economic side. The investment Nkrumah had hoped for from the West had not materialized, primarily because the confidence of business had never been gained by the regime.[243] Once Nkrumah had been East the problem was exacerbated. Ghana's image

---

[238] Ibid., p. 47. Compare Gandhi's statement, "There is no such thing as Gandhism and I do not want to leave any sect after me," Ghandhi Marg, 3, No. 2 (April 1959). Ambassador Dadzie noted at the meeting that "by the very nature of Nkrumaism the development of the philosophy cannot crystalise until after the death of the leader." "Conference of Ghana Envoys," p. 49. In interview Dadzie claimed that Baako later demanded to know if he therefore wished Osagyefo to die.

[239] Ibid., p. 95.　　　　　[240] Ibid., p. 78.　　　　　[241] Ibid., p. 73.

[242] On the other hand, Tubman did not claim to be the redeemer of Africa, and little had been expected from Liberia.

[243] Suppliers credits, that arrived in vast quantity after 1961, were not investments. See West Africa, 23 March 1966, p. 341.

in the West was bad and at this stage leading Ghanaians still wished to improve it. Usually, they blamed the Western press. Every potential Italian investor, said Ambassador Bonsu, received his impressions of Ghana indirectly from the British press, "which projects for Ghana the image of a repressive and totalitarian regime aligned with the East." Thus, the possibility of much-increased Italian investment in Ghana was "inhibited by fears of expropriation."[244]

Ghana's proclaimed attitudes on international questions nearly always coincided with those of the Soviet Union.[245] Of more importance, Western observers thought Nkrumah had been gullible at best in his relations with Russia. They wondered whether he understood the not too fine distinction between the bonds of sentiment on grand world problems (where his opinions were of a large irrelevance) and those bonds which gave to the Soviet Union strategic advantages throughout Africa. On the other hand, the basis for relations with the West was, among Ghanaian policy-makers, openly defined in terms of Ghana's economic interests. It is obvious that a contradiction existed, for Ghana's economic interests were demonstrably not being served by its foreign policy.

A ministry brief averred that Ghana had so far maintained the courage of its convictions, and "judged every political problem on its merits."[246] Western diplomats did not believe that this was the case. Had they been convinced, Ghana could then have accomplished what was its primary challenge, namely, reconciling friendship in the East with economic ties in the West. This obviously did not preclude the encouragement of trade with the East, although it necessitated a realistic assessment of how swiftly so much change could be accomplished in Ghana's traditional trade pattern. Moreover, despite so much talk of scientific socialism in the press, Ghana's new seven-year plan was no more socialist than India's. This needed saying. The party ideologists wanted to make such contradictions in the ideology and its practice apparent, in hopes that the ideology would then be accepted in practice and the plan be discarded. Certainly there was little point in having a development plan based on premises rejected by the radicals, who controlled the state's propaganda media. But if precept was to match practice, then these ideologists needed to be curbed.

[244] Amb. Osei Bonsu, "Policy Towards Europe with Particular Reference to Italy," in "Conference of Ghana Envoys," pp. 214-15.

[245] Exceptions given in a ministry policy paper were Ghana's opposition to the Russian "Troika" proposal—although Ghana sought a general reorganization of the Secretariat which, it was admitted, prejudiced its relations with the U.S.—and to Russia's resumption of nuclear testing. See "Ghana's Foreign Policy Towards the Eastern European Countries," in *ibid.*, p. 210.

[246] *Ibid.*

In Ghana's nonalignment, it should be remembered that East and West by mid-1962 were just canceling each other out: but this was the result of a dynamic process, of new Eastern strengths eroding entrenched Western positions. Any further changes would detract from what remained credible in Ghana's nonalignment. It was not too late for Nkrumah to make the policy credible; there was something in it for both East and West if he played it right. The balance in many respects was tipping to the East, but it was vital that this was not conceded, even implicitly, in Accra. "Nonalignment" remained an article of faith that, in discussing options, still imposed a certain discipline on decision-making. Hella Pick, writing in March 1962, suggested that Ghana was "more genuinely independent of outside pressure and influence than any of the other West African countries."[247] Ghana could have maintained the precarious balance that characterized its nonalignment in mid-1962, had it made Miss Pick's views credible to others.

There was a similar, if less hopeful, ambiguity in Ghana's Africa policy. For two years, Nkrumah had conducted an abortive search for allies who could be counted upon to advance the cause of African unity, and in the process had begun a policy of subversion about which most African governments were well-informed. The Union of African States, formed by Nkrumah in the spring of 1961, had as early as autumn 1961 lost everything but the force of sentiment. Dei-Anang had tried to rationalize this failure at that time by comparing it, implicitly, to Nasser's ill-fated union with Syria: "Guided, however, by the fate that has overtaken the States which rather precipitately rushed into political union, our approach had been one of caution and circumspection, involving the careful assessment of every consequence of our move towards the implementation of our aims."[248] The only tangible progress to which he could then point, however, was the existence of telephone links between Conakry and Bamako, and it is doubtful whether his audience was fooled. It still cost less to send a letter from Accra to London than to Conakry.

Moreover, Ghana's contacts with the nationalist leaders of Southern Africa were now on a new basis. They still praised Nkrumah, because they had learned that they got their money through praise. Now that Tanganyika was independent, however, Ghana was no longer a primary center of African "liberation." After the Conference of nationalists at Winneba, in June 1962, Dr. Banda was quoted saying that, whatever side Ghana was on, whether in "heaven or hell," he would align his

247 *Manchester Guardian*, 10 March 1962.
248 "Importance of Making Ghana's Foreign Policy Clearly Understood and Accepted," Appendix A, "Notes of Conference of Ghana Envoys in Africa," pp. 35-37.

country with it.[249] Banda, during his years in Ghana, had learned much from Nkrumah in the wielding of power. Moreover, he was to continue to receive money from Ghana for a long time. But would Banda align an independent Nyasaland with pan-African socialism and "Nkruma-ism"? What did Nkrumah expect of Banda, once in power in Zomba?

The real import of Nkrumah's truncation of the ministry—a symptom of the shift in Ghana's policy as a result of the Congo crisis—was only becoming clear at this time. Michael Dei-Anang, head of the newly created African Affairs Secretariat, had defended the division on the grounds that "the foreign policy of Ghana was African unity and independence." With the successful conclusion of the Volta negotiations and the Queen's visit, there was some truth in Dei-Anang's statement. To be sure, African Unity had always been Nkrumah's obsession—but the political struggle within Ghana and the long negotiations with the United States over Volta had in fact absorbed at least an equal amount of his energy. The Congo crisis had changed that, leaving an indelible mark on the operation (and the instruments) of his foreign policy. Apart from Nkrumah's efforts toward world peace, virtually all Ghana's external relations after 1961 were part of a backwash from the Congo crisis. Institutionally, the African Affairs Secretariat derived its precedent from the Congo coordinating committee, and by the end of this period, no ministry or secretariat absorbed so much of Nkrumah's time as this one.

Dei-Anang came close to admitting the realities of Ghana's position in Africa. But for Ghana's policy, he argued privately, "the greater part of this continent would still today be labouring under the yoke of colonialism." On the other hand, "It might be argued that this policy has so far brought no material advantage to Ghana, that it has rather brought her into bad odour with the imperialists without the compensation of gratitude on the part of those African states whose independence had thus been hastened. Ghana must not, however, look for gratitude in the discharge of what she conceives to be a moral obligation; she must find contentment in the reward of a satisfied conscience."[250] Such idealism in the articulation of foreign policies is not rare (more candor might be expected in a private briefing with one's own diplomats, however); this acute observation mixed with a meaningless rationale was, perhaps, typical of the period. Nkrumah's shortcoming was that he failed to perceive that his methods militated against his goal; that the "material advantage" so obviously sought would continue to elude him as long as he could not control his desire for it. Responsibility was also shared by those, like Dei-Anang who, beginning as restraining forces, increasingly supplied only arguments to justify policies they knew to be unrealistic.

[249] *Daily Telegraph*, 3 July 1962.   [250] See note 248.

The lessons to be learned from the failures of this period did affect Nkrumah to some extent. By mid-1962, a subtle shift seems to have occurred in his thinking that gave hope for Ghana's Africa policy. He had come to realize that African unity would have to come by way of the elected leaders themselves, through a diplomatic initiative. What caused this momentary change? For one thing, the AAPC had long since ceased to be an arm of Ghana's foreign policy, and it was easy to see that nothing could be gained through further use of its mechanism. The Russians also apparently helped to convince him that if African unity were to emerge, it would have to be by a different method from that which he had used.[251] The Russians themselves were hardly neglecting the use of diplomacy in their Africa policy. It was this strand, growing in importance, that motivated the last few Ghanaian efforts prior to the attempt on Nkrumah's life in the little town of Kulungugu. Early in 1962, Ghana had recognized the Cameroun government and now, in July, Nana Nketsia IV, cultural adviser to the president and vice-chancellor of the University of Ghana, led a goodwill mission to Yaounde. On July 23rd, Nkrumah sent a message to President Tubman, offering cooperation in a diplomatic initiative to heal the rift in Africa. On July 31st, as we have seen, Nkrumah traveled to Upper Volta determined to make the Paga agreement with that state workable, as a demonstration of Ghana's good intentions toward less radical states.

The first initiative failed because President Ahidjo's *sine qua non* of reconciliation was a withdrawal of active UPC refugees from Ghana. The Bureau of African Affairs had grown powerful enough to prevent a reconciliation that stood to jeopardize its own membership. As for the second initiative, Sékou Touré had too much to gain by maintaining his command of the movements leading toward reconciliation, and knew only too well how to outmaneuver his brother Nkrumah. Nor was a partnership of Nkrumah and Tubman as appropriate as one between Touré and the Emperor of Ethiopia. The third initiative was deadened by the Kulungugu assassination attempt, an event that could not be foreseen, but which was a product of the regime Nkrumah had himself created, and the results of which are central to the ensuing chapters.

[251] Interview: CF-14, 85.

III

Union Government and Scientific Socialism

AUGUST 1962–FEBRUARY 1966

BOOK III

A "RANDOM ELEMENT" exists in Ghanaian politics, Dennis Austin wrote, with which an analogy may be found in the physicist's "principle of uncertainty" in "the well-ordered molecular structure of the universe. . . . The state is indeed a well-ordered one in which things work well; yet the element of surprise is always present to astonish and, invariably, dismay, even the most sympathetic observer."[1] Any new state is so delicately balanced a system with, usually, so undeveloped a political culture, that the whim of an individual can shift the direction; a single event may send him askew. Such an incident was the assassination attempt on Nkrumah at Kulungugu. Before this happened (on 1 August 1962), the possibility had always existed that Nkrumah could stabilize both his regime and the Ghanaian economy, and make credible his country's nonalignment. He had, moreover, belatedly awakened to the fact that other states were carrying the standard of pan-Africanism.

The Ghanaian radicals had made slow but steady gains since independence; their gains were rapid, however, during domestic crises, the most significant of which was that provoked by Kulungugu. In international affairs, Nkrumah's emotional bias had always been toward the East but this had not been allowed to dominate his policy completely: now the old arguments for preserving ties with the West lost their restraining force, as the West was suspected of complicity in the attempt. In Africa, Nkrumah had always wanted an organic union but was beginning to appreciate the value of moderation to keep Ghana in the forefront of the pan-African movement; now his demands for a union government became more insistent, more precisely defined, yet even less acceptable. In both these areas the radicals benefited.

The immediate consequences of the assassination attempt, in Ghana's domestic, international, and African policies indicate the degree of difference between the new Ghana and that of only days before. Over 500 people were detained, and all the results of the May liberalization were lost. When bombings by opposition elements began in Accra (in September), security precautions were taken that far exceeded those following the 1966 coup,[2] no doubt of necessity. At the end of August Tawia Adamafio and Ako Adjei were detained. By October, Krobo

---

[1] Dennis Austin, "The Political Scene in Ghana," *Political Quarterly*, 33 (January-March 1962), 21.
[2] In 1966, no state of emergency was proclaimed, unlike 1962.

Edusei and Nathaniel Welbeck had been brought back to power, and Kojo Botsio had been "rehabilitated." It was not, however, a question of deposing radicals and bringing the CPP's old guard back to grace. Nkrumah had long since begun to suspect Adamafio's loyalties and would probably have detained him even had one security report implicating him in Kulungugu not come in.[3] A similar (if perhaps less severe) fate would probably have been in store for Adjei. Step by step Nkrumah had removed all power from his former roommate, but in June 1962 Adjei had been awarded an honorary doctorate at their common Alma Mater, Lincoln University, which put Adjei dangerously close to par with Nkrumah in an area where there was need of delicacy.[4] Whether or not Adjei and Adamafio were implicated in the attempt, it was a convenient excuse to detain them.[5] Botsio and Edusei's loyalties, on the other hand, were not in question, and they were solid administrators whose talents Nkrumah had sorely missed during the previous year; the appointments were not intended to have ideological ramifications. Botsio had devoted himself to his own return to power, for he continued to believe that the party, which was the fabric of his life, and for whose strength he was so much responsible, belonged as much to him as to Nkrumah. He began jockeying for the post of foreign minister (which he had briefly held in 1959), with the result that by November Nkrumah had put aside the idea of bringing Quaison-Sackey back to Ghana to enter politics and the foreign ministry.[6]

Those who made clear gains in both power and ideology were the party ideologues, the "Socialist boys" who edited the papers and directed the Kwame Nkrumah Ideological Institute. The *Evening News* called Adamafio a "Dr. Jekyll and Mr. Hyde," its kindest tribute to him, and said he had been the "imperialist agent" who, "like Oliver Goldsmith's famous character, had one stock phrase for every occasion to cover his hollow mentality."[7] True, the net could have been cast wider,

[3] According to a former official of Nkrumah's security apparatus. Interview: CF-87.

[4] A point also made by Ambassador A.B.B. Kofi, who noted that Nkrumah scratched the "Dr." off Adjei's name on a delegation list in the summer of 1962 (even though Nkrumah's own Doctorate had the same origins). See *Evening News*, 29 August 1962, where by implication, Kofi's point is echoed.

[5] After the 1966 coup, members of the then defunct United Party, by then in positions of power in the new regime, stated that in fact the assassination attempt was organized by UP elements, and not by Adjei, Adamafio, and Crabbe.

[6] See note 49, p. 211.

[7] *Evening News*, 6 September 1962. The Ghanaian press was not the only one to have a field day. Richard Beeston, a correspondent of the *Sunday Telegraph*, expelled from Ghana in September, called the atmosphere in Accra "hysterical" and noted that the Ghanaian press had called Adamafio "everything from a vampire to a sex maniac." *Sunday Telegraph*, 2 September 1962.

to include some of those who replaced Adamafio.[8] But the Marxist convictions (and credentials) of the editors, Heymann, Batsaa, and others, were less in doubt, and a few months after Kulungugu, Nkrumah implicitly accepted their cause as his own. On December 1st the publication of *Spark* began: its purpose and inspiration were made clear enough by the name, but it also gave Nkrumah a medium through which he could say the things he dared not put in diplomatic notes and speeches.[9]

The backwash of Kulungugu into Ghana's domestic affairs lapped dramatically on the state's role as liberator of Africa. There had been, for example, rival factions of the Union des Populations du Cameroun living at the African Affairs Centre in Accra for some time. One group, led by Massaga, wished to assume the UPC's leadership after the death of Félix Moumié in 1960 and called themselves the "true revolutionaries." They came to Ghana after expulsion from France, and they included serious ideologues.[10] The other group was an offshoot of the "One Kamerun" movement of Southern Cameroons, formed in 1957 during Moumié's exile there. Ntumazah, its leader, was more moderate. Massaga's group, not surprisingly, had the support of Habib Niang, the increasingly powerful Senegalese adviser of Nkrumah, and of A. K. Barden, director of the Bureau of African Affairs; when Massaga's men threw bombs into the cabins of Ntumazah's men, Ntumazah was blamed. In the heat of the moment the authorities imprisoned the Ntumazah group at Nsawam, fearing they were also involved in bombings in Accra.[11]

The Bureau of African Affairs continued to try to organize all the groups into more cohesive frameworks, with no success. In early September a liberation front of the parties still in Accra was formed, but it included only Sawaba, UPC, Sanwi, BCP (Basutoland), UNIP (Northern Rhodesia), and a "United Front" from Togo.[12] The Ghanaian government gave facilities, equipment, and money to the front, but there

[8] See particularly the series of articles by Kweku Akwei, in the *Evening News*, beginning 3 September 1962; Akwei, in interviews with the writer, spoke of his efforts to "dialecticize."

[9] According to members of the African Affairs Committee and of the cabinet secretariat. This is a fundamental point. In their view (and the author's) *Spark* is one of the most important primary sources for indications of Nkrumah's thinking at a particular time. Interviews: CF-14, 85.

[10] Massaga was widely thought to have helped write Nkrumah's philosophical testament, *Consciencism*; another member, Tchaptchet, wrote articles for *l'Etincelle*, a journal in French based on, but not identical to, *Spark*.

[11] Interviews: CF-29, 87. See also Legum's important article in *Observer*, 19 August 1962, on this subject.

[12] See *AFP Special Outre-mer*, No. 4865, 11 September 1962, and *Ghanaian Times*, 10 September 1962.

was little to unite them. For UNIP, the front was peripheral. The Sanwi group was probably the most ineffective in Africa, unless one of its functions was considered to be the aggravation of Ghanaian-Ivoirien relations. The Togo group was just an arm of Nkrumah's Togo policy. Ironically, this first attempt to organize the nationalists came after Ghana had ceased to be a primary center of African liberation. After Kulungugu, the atmosphere in Ghana was hardly conducive to the purposes of the freedom fighters, and the state was conspicuously far from the real scene of the struggle farther south. Thus even this small front was a failure from the start, making all the more dramatic the comparison between Ghana's position at this time in the liberation movement and that at the time of the 1958 AAPC.

Ghana's relations with its neighbors were affected in an equally adverse manner. On the very eve of Kulungugu, Presidents Yameogo and Nkrumah had finally found the political will to make the 1961 Paga agreement succeed; its import was immediately shorn by Nkrumah's order that the border be closed (for reasons of security), in violation of all agreements with that state. President Yameogo thus had nowhere to turn but the Ivory Coast, and this drastically upset the balance of power in West Africa. President Houphouet-Boigny now had a *cordon sanitaire* around Ghana in which he, and the French, through their alliances with Dahomey and Upper Volta, held the dominant influence. Within a month of the assassination of Olympio in January 1963, the *cordon* coincided with Ghana's land boundaries.

The Union of African States—the Ghana-Guinea-Mali union—by now a body dependent solely on ideological sentiment, died a similar death. Upon hearing the news from Kulungugu, Presidents Modibo Keita and Sékou Touré immediately arranged to visit Accra in a gesture of solidarity with Nkrumah at his worst hour. Habib Niang was able to convince Nkrumah that it was not in his interest, however, to receive his two brothers (it was certainly not in Niang's own interest). Keita and Touré had to be asked to return from their airports to their capitals.[13] Later that month Touré began a frontal assault on Nkrumah's pan-African ideas and methods; if not the cause, Kulungugu was clearly the catalyst. Working in coordination with the Emperor of Ethiopia, Prime Minister Abubakar of Nigeria, and President Houphouet-Boigny, Touré maintained his momentum up to the time of the founding of the OAU.

Moreover, from the time of Ako Adjei's detention in August 1962 to Botsio's appointment in March 1963, there was no foreign minister, and

13 Interviews: CF-24, Budu-acquah. See also p. 151.

268

a far less orderly procedure in the conduct of foreign policy than there had been in the past. This was due also (and most of all) to the effect the assassination attempt had had on Nkrumah himself: The Kulungugu affair was the primary cause of the dislocation of Ghana's foreign policy in the last years of his rule. A certain frenetic quality developed in his running of the affairs of government. Officials of the cabinet secretariat no longer could restrain him from making policy statements that compromised his own desire to play a role in world affairs. Moreover, temptations which he had long held at bay could no longer be resisted. For a decade money had flowed about him, but it was always for the cause. His own bank balance had always been in the red up to the time of Kulungugu, his confidants said; they had always had to restrain him from too much generosity to those whose causes were joined in his. But now, "the Ayeh-Kumi's of the world got to him, and to his deficiencies in character was added a new one, avarice."[14]

The next chapters chart Ghana's course on two different maps: the dominant political forces in the world, and Africa and its pan-African movement. Ghana engaged in a search for a role as a member of a broad antiimperialist camp, a "Socialist Commonwealth." New ties with the Soviet Union helped to determine this course, as did Ghana's adoption (at the official level) of that state's ideology, scientific Socialism. Another assassination attempt led to a tightening of security links, the demand for more economic ties with the Soviet Union, and more Socialist measures within Ghana itself.

In Africa, while Sékou Touré and the Emperor organized the OAU, Nkrumah dispersed his representatives across the continent with instructions to press for "union government," to avoid all use of the word "charter"—which implied diplomatic links rather than organic unity—and to convince his peers that his concept was plausible and, in any event, inevitable. Nkrumah finally realized the extent to which Ghana was outside the mainstream of pan-African diplomacy at the summit conference in Addis Ababa when Ghana was not appointed to the liberation committee created there. Thenceforth, he fought the new Organisation of African Unity, and Chapters 8 and 9 recount his struggle to bring about "continental union government" in the face of the OAU's more modest attempts at diplomatic unity.

The fortuitous conjunction of events after Kulungugu created the rationale for new policies: but before these could become effective their justification had substantially altered. Thus Nkrumah consolidated his Communist links, only to find that by 1965 the world, from East to West,

---

[14] Interviews: CF-28; also 85. Ayeh-Kumi was the very rich Nzima adviser of Nkrumah's who was widely considered notoriously corrupt.

was bored with Africa. The new radicalism neither defeated imperialism nor compensated for the loss of Western support. Nkrumah increasingly perceived himself as Africa's Castro, and Ghana as Africa's Cuba, genuinely threatened by a great power and with a mission to liberate the rest of a continent. Had this been so, he might have held the support of his people.

EXTERNAL RELATIONS:

The Limiting of Ghana's Options
August 1962–September 1964

THE CONDUCT of Ghana's relations with non-African powers in the year following the assassination attempt at Kulungugu possessed a strange duality in character. On the one hand, Nkrumah had established ties with the Soviet Union which were vital in character. The link with British intelligence, which had survived the harshest tests during Ghana's first six years of independence, was cut. Nkrumah asked the Soviet Union to fill the vacuum. Shortly after Kulungugu he sent a cable to Khrushchev expressing his eagerness also to receive aid in presidential security if the offer made in the Crimea a year earlier was still valid. The premier swiftly sent one of his own senior security officers to advise Nkrumah on steps that needed to be taken.[1] *Spark* began publication, and all the Ghanaian papers increased their Marxist content on a dramatic scale; they began to use Eastern press agency reports as their own. Khrushchev now sent a senior and very capable ambassador to Ghana, Georgi Rodionov, who presented his credentials on November 26th.[2] He quickly established a preeminence in Accra that no diplomat had enjoyed since the departure of Ehud Avriel in 1960.

On the other hand, Nkrumah had established these links and had vastly increased the power of the CPP's Marxist elite, with the intention of reinforcing his own control of the state. A Marxist ideology was to be propagated, but this was to be done only by the information media under his direction. The cultural centers of the Soviet Union, the UAR, and Israel were thus closed in November because they were distributing propaganda adverse to the interests of the Ghanaian party.[3] The American and British information centers escaped closure because (it

[1] Interview: CF-87.

[2] Ironically, this was exactly the same time that Andrew Tully's book, *The CIA: The Inside Story*, gained wide circulation in official circles in Accra. Hundreds of copies were bought by the government for distribution in Ghana and other African states to provide proof of Ghana's thesis on the nature of America's intentions. See its review in *Evening News*, 27 November 1962.

[3] Interview: the Rev. Stephen Dzirasa (Deputy Foreign Minister).

271

was said) these were different in kind from the others. Also relevant was the American readiness to withdraw its entire aid mission were the American (USIS) library closed. AID was the one American program never attacked in Ghana by the press, and for good reason. Its projects, largely in the agricultural sector, were unobtrusive and successful.

The regime had realized that its need of the West had increased.[4] The seven-year development plan which was to begin in January 1963 depended heavily on Western investment, and even Joseph Bognor, the Hungarian economist who advised the government during 1962, stressed that Ghana could not expect to industrialize with its own resources and was forced to rely on the West. Building of the Volta dam was proceeding on schedule, but Kaiser Aluminum of California had made no binding commitment to construct the smelter which was to use the dam's electricity (and on which the viability of the Volta scheme depended). Kaiser had no intention of building it without investment guarantees from the United States government, so the American diplomats did not lack the means to exert pressure. The need for foreign investment was stressed in many of Nkrumah's speeches at this time. A new investment law was passed in early 1963 that offered greater inducements to Western businessmen to come to Ghana;[5] Nkrumah, for his part, made every effort to accommodate the American and British envoys where investment was concerned.[6] He was also capable of appointing an old "imperialist" like Sir Patrick Fitz-Gerald, a Unilever official in the process of retiring from business in Ghana, to run the foremost state corporation.

Up to the time of Kulungugu it was possible to maintain such an apparently contradictory policy; now it was not, even if this were not perceived by the Ghanaian government. It only remained to be seen what form Ghana's closer relations with the non-Western world would take. The old dichotomy of words and deeds that had existed in varying forms since independence had taken a new turn.

NEW TIES WITH THE SOCIALIST WORLD

Nkrumah had now made the symbolic commitment to the Soviet Union for which it presumably had been waiting. Few elements in a state system are so vital to its sovereignty as security at the center, and Nkrumah was

[4] See R. Esseks, "Economic Independence in a New African State," unpublished Ph.D. dissertation, Harvard, 1967, for an excellent analysis of the economic-political nexus in this period.

[5] See "Legal Backing for Investment Policy," *Ghana Foreign Affairs*, Vol. 2, No. 2.

[6] Western diplomats could also, on occasion, affect noneconomic actions; when the Ghanaian press accused Britain, America, France, and Germany of complicity in Kulungugu, the four ambassadors protested strongly, and Nkrumah expressed official regrets to the embassies in question. This was, however, exceptional. See *Times*, 24 September 1962.

hereafter to entrust this, in part, to a state unconnected with Ghana through either tradition or sentiment. Obviously the Russians were pleased about developments in Ghana, as a year earlier they had lost their strongest foothold in sub-Saharan Africa (in Guinea) when President Touré asked Ambassador Solod to leave.

By the time Nkrumah had made this commitment, however, another line of development in Ghana's relations with the Socialist states had become significant, one which worked against Nkrumah's desire to secure relations with them. In 1960 and 1961, civil servants and politicians had possessed every reason to be enthusiastic over the massive offers of aid and trade from the East but, by late 1962, disillusionment was widespread. If ties with the Eastern states were to grow still stronger, the popularity of Nkrumah's regime could suffer accordingly—which is what happened,[7] limiting Nkrumah's options in large measure.

Viewed in retrospect, short-lived ties between states may be expected to show weakness from the moment they are established; Ghanaian criticism of the links with the Soviet Union came almost as soon as Nkrumah had returned from the Crimea in September 1961. Krobo Edusei traveled to Moscow shortly thereafter to negotiate the terms of the various agreements for trade and credit made during the past year and found to his surprise that the Russians were the hardest bargainers he had ever encountered.[8] Civil servants after this began to examine the agreements carefully and found elements in them that were something less than favorable. A first, though minor, point of disagreement was salary scale for experts coming from Moscow. The ministry wrote to the Soviet Embassy in Accra that "Ghana's experience with the UN and the Governments of Western Europe and North American countries has been that the actual salary of the expert is normally paid by the country or agency providing him, and it is hoped that a similar arrangement could be made [with] the U.S.S.R."[9] At this stage, Nkrumah was prepared to back the ministry, and he wrote to Khrushchev asking for modifications; this brought results. Khrushchev replied that:

> The Soviet Government, being guided by the interests of furthering the friendship and co-operation . . . has given favourable consideration to the ideas set out in your letter and has found it possible to meet halfway your wishes . . .

[7] The implication, that personnel from the East were not popular in Ghana, is a surprising one to many, but one about which there was no disagreement. See a further discussion of this point in the author's study, "Parameters on Soviet Policy in Africa: Personal Diplomacy and Economic Interests in Ghana," in Raymond Duncan, ed., *The Soviet Union and the Third World*, Boston, forthcoming.

[8] Interview: Krobo Edusei.

[9] Ministry of Foreign Affairs to USSR/Accra, 30 November 1961, CFA-11.

The Soviet Side expressed its consent to a 50% average decrease in the salaries . . . and it also agrees to the Ghana side bearing no expenses in respect of granting "installation" allowances to the experts, of paying for their insurance and for the transportation of their luggage.[10]

Throughout 1962 difficulties increased. The Ghanaians were accustomed to dealing with Western businessmen and governments with whom speed was an important commodity. Russian plans moved slowly, and bargaining was time-consuming, because negotiators were allowed no flexibility in arranging terms with their Ghanaian counterparts. In the contract negotiations for the construction of state-owned collective farms are found typical difficulties prejudicing good relations. Ghanaians were not unaware of the difficulties the Russians themselves had had in establishing such farms, and were not happy to find that the Soviet contract "with the exception of one or two clauses . . . dealt almost exclusively with the sale and delivery of Soviet machinery and equipment, and very little with the organisation, establishment, and management of the State Farms."[11] Indeed, the realization that the Eastern countries were so deeply interested in the export of plainly uncompetitive machinery was a major cause for suspicion. What civil servants sought was Soviet responsibility for the success of the state farms, and shrewd Ghanaian negotiators included one clause requiring that the manager of each be a Russian specialist, with full responsibility for three years, after which time a trained Ghanaian would replace him. They also demanded that the Soviet Union "guarantee the quality and smooth operation of the equipment and machines delivered," which were very much in question.[12]

As was so often to be the case, it was Nkrumah himself who nullified the efforts of the Ghanaian negotiators. Sytenko, the Russian ambassador at the time, argued that were the Soviet Union given responsibility not only for the "productive aspect" of the farms (which was not in question), but also for the "efficient management of the farms as designed, planned, and executed by them," it would in fact mean their "interference in Ghana's internal affairs." To the dismay of CECEC, "Osagyefo agreed."[13]

Others were working at cross-purposes. John Elliot, Ghana's ambas-

---

[10] Khrushchev to Nkrumah, 2 December 1961, CFA-10, 11.

[11] Minutes, Committee for Economic Co-operation with Eastern Countries (CECEC), 23 May 1962, CFA-17.

[12] Draft by ministry of agriculture for state farms contract, 23 May 1962, in CECEC minutes, 23 May 1962, CFA-18.

[13] Minutes, CECEC, 23 May 1962, CFA-18.

sador in Moscow, consistently advanced the Russian case in negotiations without reference to Ghana's interests or actual needs. Those working under him in the embassy were dismayed by his approach, while the Russians continued to insist that he remain in Moscow.[14] The most important problems deriving from the agreements with the Socialist countries were far more basic to the nature of the Ghanaian economy, however. Credit had been offered which led to proposals for numerous projects, ranging from a gold-refining factory (U.S.S.R.) to a motel near Accra (Bulgaria), but the Ghanaians soon discovered that the agreements by no means committed the Eastern countries to total financing of the projects. The planning commission found that the contract with Russia for a proposed prefabricated-panel factory did "not even show the total cost to Ghana Government of signing it." This was followed by the startling realization that local labor and civil engineering costs would account for as much as two-thirds of the total cost in some projects. However great the Eastern contribution, it was clear that Ghana's resources were too limited to undertake so much.[15]

By June 1962 the problems created by the agreements were felt to be sufficiently numerous to warrant a broad review. At CECEC it was proposed that a subcommittee be appointed, "in view of the many anomalies now coming to light."[16] This was done, and the Ghanaians came to an irresistible conclusion, namely, that the contracts were "devised largely to meet export drives in Machinery and Equipment."[17] As for the machinery itself, another report indicated that "the matter of the frequent breakdown of Soviet vehicles and equipment . . . involving the Government in unwarranted repair costs should be brought to the notice of Osagyefo."[18]

The hope was that the agreements could be converted into the "turnkey" type, whereby accepted projects would be designed, engineered, and built by the Eastern countries, and handed to Ghana completed. The plan was to seek additional credit to cover these additional costs which, it was thought, could best be accomplished through the importation of building materials and consumer goods "to such an extent that Ghana will have an unfavourable balance [of trade] with each of them." The balance would then be converted into local currency to pay for local materials and labor. *"The problem is that so long as Ghana sells more*

[14] Interviews: CF-85, 14. He remained there until the 1966 coup.
[15] Minutes, CECEC, 6 June 1962, CFA-17.
[16] *Ibid.*
[17] "Report on Subcommittee" (appointed to review contracts with Eastern countries), Minutes, CECEC, 15 August 1962, CFA-18.
[18] "Recommendations of Committee as a Whole," Minutes, CECEC, 27 February 1962, CFA-14.

to these countries than she buys, the additional credit sought in this manner cannot be obtained."[19]

The problem was how to "buy more than sell," given the comparatively sophisticated Ghanaian market. Ghana had always maintained a favorable trade balance with the Eastern bloc; Russia wanted cocoa, for instance, but had little to offer of appeal to Ghanaians in return. Therefore, when the contract with Russia was renegotiated in early 1963 to provide 15-20,000,000 rubles for the Russian consumer goods—with which CECEC wished to defray the costs of various projects—little progress ensued. Sir Patrick Fitz-Gerald, managing-director of the state-owned Ghana National Trading Company, made clear some of the difficulties in this matter. The Russians, he said, wanted GNTC to buy Russian cars. But what about spare parts? Russian cameras were unsalable; they had no English instructions. Russia was not alone in causing problems:

> The Chinese representative was of the opinion that the newly appointed Managing-Director of GNTC was likely to discourage trade between Ghana and the bi-lateral countries. . . .
>
> This seems . . . very . . . peculiar . . . as . . . the . . . Director has had no dealings at all personally with the Chinese representative. . . .
>
> The Managing-Director, as an experienced trader, is desirous of helping the Company to obtain goods at the cheapest price—*from any country in the world*—so long as the quality and type . . . are acceptable to the Ghanaian market and so long as delivery dates are adhered to. . . .[20]

No doubt Fitz-Gerald was sincere, for Nkrumah had made this otherwise inexplicable appointment knowing he could not afford to waste Sir Patrick's real knowledge of the Ghanaian market. The Ghanaian market, however, was still free, and the regime was trying to move Ghana toward Socialism through ill-conceived state projects, financed by the sale of unwanted goods, on an uncontrolled market. Cement came in from Russia that was not liked, and since contractors were able to obtain supplies from traditional sources, the Russian product hardened on the docks. It was suggested that imports of American and Canadian flour be blocked in favor of supplies from Russia, but this met obstacles of a different kind. One principal secretary thought that "in order not to disturb the favourable trade balance with the two coun-

[19] "CECEC Memorandum by the Minister of Industries and Chairman of C.E.C.E.C. Subject: Review of Contracts-Progress Report," in Minutes, CECEC, 15 August 1962, CFA-16.

[20] Sir Patrick Fitz-Gerald, to Secretary, Bank of Ghana, 14 January 1963, CFA-21, 22.

tries the suggestion should be ignored."[21] It was that favorable balance which made possible the purchase of VC-10 jets, Italian marble for presidential lodges, and Ghana's far-flung network of embassies. The entire process was doomed from the start.

By the end of 1962, little progress had been made in solving these questions. True, the Hungarians had accepted the Ghanaian proposals half-way, but only the Poles and the Chinese showed real interest in accommodating the Ghanaians: the Poles, no doubt, because of their interest in developing long-range ties with Ghana; the Chinese, perhaps, because of their short-range and urgent interests.[22] In the ensuing two years, little further progress was made in integrating the projects into the Ghanaian economy.

It was not merely the style of Russian negotiations that affected the Ghanaians' view of their benefactors, nor was it only suspicion of their motives. Ghanaian elites objected to the projects themselves. One example is that of the state farms. These were never anything but financial disaster, and were always unpopular. Just after the state farms contract with Russia was signed, a diplomat posted in Sofia wrote his view of collectivized agriculture to the ministry: "On some of the State Farms [in Bulgaria] . . . labourers are 'Time Watchers'. . . . The contrary can be found on the private farm [where] the family . . . [does] not look for the closing time. In fact the attitude of the labourers on the [state] farms is like our former P.W.D. labourers in colonial days . . . there is no incentive, no push, no interest, and no love to do the job . . . . food is scarce because the State has killed the ZEAL, the vim and love of farming from the REAL farmers."[23]

An example of growing resentment among leading Ghanaians toward the policy of Communist states toward Ghana and, in this case, Africa, is the Bulgarian incident of February 1963, involving the community of African students in Sofia. Tired of what they considered inadequate support, discrimination, and poor educational facilities, these students were involved in conflicts with the Bulgarian authorities, and it would appear

[21] Minutes, CECEC, 27 February 1963, CFA-14.

[22] Polish technical experts were always quick to assure their Ghanaian counterparts that they came to Ghana as professionals, not as ideologues, which was appreciated. After the 1966 coup, they were excepted from the anti-Communist fervor generated by the new regime. As for the Chinese, their difficulties in the rest of Africa, their soft loans, and attempts to do anything the Ghanaians wished suggests they urgently needed a base of operations in Africa, this in addition to the normal ties they had a right to, and did, seek.

[23] "Report of Trip around Bulgaria," Amb. Appah-Sampong, to MFA, 11 July 1962. This was actually written by Peter Abban, then first secretary of the embassy in Sofia. CFA-16.

that Ghanaian students were in the forefront of the movement.[24] Nkrumah sent Kwesi Armah and Victor Woode (of the high commission in London) to investigate. Armah, for one, was sufficiently distressed with what he found to recommend that all Ghanaian students be brought home immediately. Nkrumah, for his part, resented the manner in which the issue had been exploited in the West, and compared Bulgaria's treatment of Ghanaians with the sustained discrimination against Africans in America.[25] Armah had always been something less than a convinced Socialist, but now had personal experience against which to measure Ghanaian ideology and his own instincts; his real sentiments were thereafter scarcely doubted by the officials with whom he worked.

An example of growing Ghanaian suspicions of Communist hypocrisy centers on trade between the East and South Africa. After the founding of the Organisation of African Unity in May 1963—where all the African states agreed to cease trading with South Africa—the question of Eastern trade ties with the racist regime was brought to the fore by articles in the *Observer*, which suggested substantial duplicity on the part of several Socialist states.[26] Harry Amonoo, then principal secretary for relations with Eastern Europe and China, cabled all diplomats responsible to him that "We intend to question our Socialist friends in Accra concerning these articles. Meanwhile you should make discreet enquiries."[27]

In Sofia the charges were "emphatically" denied, particularly as the Bulgarians had seen the *Observer*'s articles.[28] In Peking, where the questions posed were more delicate, the Chinese ministry was asked to "refute the allegation made in the BBC broadcast of 16 June 1963 . . . to the effect that . . . China has placed orders for grain with the South African government."[29] The Ghanaian secretary in Peking thought there was some truth in the charges made, "since the Chinese have not been able to refute the broadcast news as requested by this mission."[30] What had happened was that Chen Yi had attended Republic Day celebrations at the Ghanaian embassy on July 1st, where he indicated that the democracy loving Chinese people would do everything possible to aid the freedom loving African peoples in their just struggle against the

[24] See, for example, "Africans Still in Bulgaria Won't Attend Classes," *Washington Post*, 22 February 1963, in which an interview with the Ghanaian ambassador is quoted.

[25] Nkrumah's attitude shocked many officials. See interviews: CF-7, 14.

[26] The articles are by Colin Legum and Stanley Uys, in *Observer*, 9 June 1963.

[27] H. R. Amonoo to Ghana missions in Eastern Europe, Russia, and China, 13 June 1963, CFA-12.

[28] Appah-Sampong to MFA, 9 July 1963, *ibid.*

[29] Ghana/Peking to Ministry of Foreign Affairs, Chinese Peoples Republic, 19 June 1963, *ibid.*

[30] Ghana/Peking to MFA, 4 July 1963, *ibid.*

South African fascists. But these official pronouncements, the Ghanaian said, "should be taken with a grain of salt. The People's Republic of China, like all Socialist countries, is not unaware of the effective role which hypocrisy plays in international affairs."[31] He predicted that the Chinese embassy in Accra, if it did reply, would follow the same line as Chen Yi, and in this he was right.[32]

Then new charges were made in the press, this time by the South Africa Foundation, the semi-official nature of which was known by the Ghanaians. It claimed that trade between China and South Africa, which came to less than £500,000 in 1962, in January-February 1963 alone stood at £2,500,000. Ghana sent a note to the Chinese embassy saying it "would be grateful for the Embassy's comments on these trade figures." The embassy's reply was not calculated to be convincing: "The Government of the People's Republic and the Chinese people have all along cherished profound sympathy and extended resolute support to the South African people in their just struggle. . . . Based on this stand, the Chinese Government severed all economic and trade relations with the South African colonial authorities as from July 1960."[33] In mid-September 1963 Amonoo wrote Flagstaff House that the ministry did not believe the Chinese reply.[34]

In both his domestic and foreign policy, Nkrumah had increased his commitment to the Socialist cause, despite the growing unpopularity of Ghana's new relationships. Thus was he forced to rely more heavily on the Marxist radicals, and to reject—and to discourage—dispassionate criticism of the bilateral agreements, and of Eastern policy, from civil servants and technical advisers. In the language of David Apter, Ghana had become a mobilization system requiring higher levels of coercion to attain the new goals, with a consequent "loss of information" passed up through governmental channels.

NONALIGNMENT AFTER KULUNGUGU

Nkrumah did not cease to stress Ghana's commitment to a nonaligned foreign policy after the assassination attempt but, over the following year it became a tactical, rather than a strategic, commitment. True, a domestic basis still existed for nonalignment, given the goals of the seven-year plan, but the government's inability to match its on-going policy to the precepts of the plan meant that this became, step by step, an ideal on

[31] Official Secretary, Ghana/Peking, to H. R. Amonoo, 4 July 1963, CFA-41.
[32] *Ibid.*, 7 July 1963.
[33] MFA/Accra to China/Accra, 13 August 1963; China/Accra to MFA/Accra, 28 August 1963, *ibid.*
[34] H. R. Amonoo to P.S., A.A.S., 12 September 1963, CFA-12.

paper possessing no relationship to Ghanaian development. The nature of decision-making even further eroded the coherence of Ghana's non-alignment, as judged by other states. Ghana became, as a result, less and less objectively nonaligned, even if it remained subjectively committed to the policy. Nkrumah and the press could not resist passing judgment on every conflict arising in the world, which on the one hand made unlikely the type of mediation Nkrumah wished for himself, and on the other destroyed friendships with a number of states.

For the most part, it is not easy to see what was happening in 1962 and 1963. Ghana's disjointed responses to international crises, however, provide more cross references in this attempt to locate Ghana's position on the map of the Afro-Asian political movements. It is only in view of later developments that a pattern can be discerned in the starts and stops making up Ghana's diplomatic and ideological responses to problems in this part of the world where, G. H. Jansen argues, two opposing principles were becoming dominant: Belgrade nonalignment (and the search for peace) and Bandung solidarity (and the anti-colonial struggle).[35]

The most obvious change in Ghana's position within the nonaligned world was due to Nkrumah's position on the Sino-Indian war. Although Ghana's relations with India had never been warm, there were many links between the two states. In early 1962, however, Pakistan saw an opening in Accra. Nkrumah's reply to a letter from President Ayub indicates the lines of Pakistan's proposal. "I am indeed gratified that you should sound me and even enlist my support to settle the Kashmir question. . . . I have already taken steps for my representative on the Security Council to sound members on the two proposals which you put before me. . . . I trust that these constructive suggestions by you will be acceptable to Pandit Nehru."[36] Arrangements were quickly made to exchange embassies, in view of "the close personal relations of Osagyefo and Ayub Khan,"[37] and Ghana sent a career diplomat to Rawalpindi. India sent an emissary to press its own case, but Nkrumah had already taken the field-marshal's bait: The salient point of Ghana's policy on Kashmir was a request that the contenders use a "third-party as mediator—that is, the good offices of an outstanding world statesman [sic] who is acceptable to both India and Pakistan."[38] India's position was that there was nothing to mediate, a position toward which Nkrumah would

[35] G. H. Jansen, *Afro-Asia and Non-Alignment*, London, 1966, Chapter 17.

[36] Ayub Khan to Nkrumah, 20 April 1962; Nkrumah to Ayub Khan, May 1962. This may be a classic case of Nkrumah's naiveté (and vanity) in the exercise of diplomacy. CFA-53.

[37] Memorandum, MFA to Nkrumah, n. d., presumably May 1962. CFA-53.

[38] Adjei to Nkrumah, 11 June 1962, CFA-58.

in any event have been ill-disposed. It is also clear that Nkrumah, under the influence of the Ghanaian editors and the Chinese ambassador, had long since come to believe that India was a decadent state, particularly after his disputes with Nehru at the Belgrade conference.[39]

The vital issue in Ghana-Indian relations was to be China, not Kashmir, but the new ties with Pakistan were important in weakening Ghana's relations with India prior to the Himalayan border conflict. During the summer of 1962 Ghanaian officials began to receive unsolicited information on India's dispute with China, and China was thought to make the more convincing case. Western propaganda for the Indian side inclined Nkrumah toward the Chinese case in any event, diplomats said.[40]

In early July, Nehru himself "expressed his desire to pay a visit to Osagyefo the President . . . in the last week of September," after the Commonwealth Conference;[41] this was in return for Nkrumah's visit of December 1958, and no doubt was intended to win Ghana's support on the border question. The proposal was accepted, but Nehru was told in Lagos, on the eve of his visit to Ghana, that it would be better for him to postpone it, in view of the serious security threat in Ghana at the time.[42] A few weeks later, on October 20th, China attacked Indian territory.

Prime Minister Macmillan immediately offered arms to India. Nkrumah wrote to him criticizing this action. In disregard of Commonwealth convention, the letter was published. "Are you sure that by giving support . . . to one side against the other you will be able to increase the chances of bringing an end to hostilities?"[43] He then contrasted Macmillan's action with his own. He had been in contact with both sides, trying to find a basis for ending the conflict. In his reply, Macmillan expressed surprise that Nkrumah should object to aid given to a fellow-member of the Commonwealth, to which Nkrumah replied, also publicly, that the Commonwealth was not a military alliance. There was, he wrote, a need for mediation, by countries with ambassadors in both combatant states (for example, Ghana), which would be prejudiced if third parties took sides.[44] The *Evening News,* meanwhile, made its sympathies explicit: Britain was a "shameless sales agent for instruments of mass destruction";[45] on November 21st it headlined—in the largest type it possessed—"CHINA ENDS WAR." As an Indian paper argued,

[39] Interviews: CF-7, 87. See pp. 179-82.   [40] Interview: CF-7.
[41] Ako Adjei to Nkrumah, 12 July 1962, CFA-58.
[42] Interview: CF-7.
[43] Quoted in *Evening News,* 1 November 1962.
[44] *Ibid.,* 3 November 1962.   [45] *Ibid.*

Ghana had in fact taken sides. Nkrumah, by making his letter to Macmillan public, and by rebuking both Britain and India, had compromised Ghana's relations with India beyond repair.[46] Nkrumah, who had long wanted a nonaligned bloc in world affairs, was the first to bring comfort to an enemy of the founder of the nonaligned movement.[47]

Ali Mazrui has argued that Macmillan's position was the residuum of the "Pax Britannica" that existed during the days of the white Commonwealth, and that Nkrumah had merely underlined that Commonwealth membership did not presuppose defense accords with fellow members.[48] This misses Macmillan's point. Britain's aid to India was a result of its close bilateral ties with that state, and of the new Western desire to "contain" China. Macmillan had not made multilateral Commonwealth links a justification for British assistance, and the issue only arose *after* Nkrumah had publicly criticized Macmillan for offering assistance. It was at this point that Macmillan suggested Commonwealth ties as a relevant basis for Britain's aid to India, vainly hoping to appeal to Nkrumah's own Commonwealth sentiment.

Did Nkrumah wittingly discard the mediator's role he thought he had with respect to Pakistan and India, and China and India? By one account, the original statement on the Sino-Indian war had been a mild one, written in the cabinet secretariat, to which Geoffrey Bing (by now a special assistant at Flagstaff House) made drastic revisions.[49] He is said to have had no difficulty in convincing Nkrumah of the new statement's merit.

At one level of his thinking, Nkrumah was genuinely distressed at the outbreak of violence in Asia, which weakened the Afro-Asian solidarity that did exist at this point. Therefore, it was not wholly a search for prestige that led him to offer Accra as venue for a conference on the dispute. Mrs. Bandaranaike, however, successfully arranged one in Colombo in early December. Nkrumah sent Puplampu, the deputy

[46] Editorial, *Independent Indian Express*, quoted in *West Africa*, 10 November 1962.

[47] Major Seth Anthony, Ghana's high commissioner in Delhi, attempted to ameliorate the effects of Nkrumah's statement, about which he had not been consulted but was nonetheless "cut from the lists" of his Indian associates, so irritated was India by Nkrumah's action. Interview: CF-17.

[48] Ali Mazrui, *Towards a Pax Africana*, London, 1967, pp. 150-51. See also C. W. Newbury's comment on Nkrumah's action, in Newbury, *The West African Commonwealth*, London, 1964, p. 96.

[49] Interview: CF-52, London, 24 November 1965. This source, being British, may make the claim suspect, particularly as members of the former cabinet secretariat in Flagstaff House were unable to confirm it (they did, however, confirm that Bing was responsible for the final draft). On the other hand, that British diplomats in Accra had access to such types of information is hardly in doubt; moreover, sparring between Bing and more restrained Ghanaian officials was frequent on such matters. Interviews: CF-85, 87.

foreign minister, Ofori-Attah, the minister of justice, and Richard Akwei from the foreign ministry.

According to one of these, Ghana's was the least partial delegation; the U.A.R., wanting "no reward for aggression," was the most openly pro-Indian, and Cambodia, perhaps, the most pro-Chinese.[50] The Ghanaians alone came with a program for discussion: for a ceasefire, for withdrawal of forces, for direct negotiations. "The representative of Ghana's Redeemer was not overawed by the immensity of the task," G. H. Jansen wrote, representing the Indian view.[51] A more detached study is W. F. van Eekelen's in which it is noted that the Ghanaians, "although objecting to the use of force to settle disputes between Afro-Asian countries, seemed favorably disposed toward Chinese ideas about disarmed zones and quick negotiations on the fundamental issue."[52] But this is the way Nkrumah looked at all conflicts, rather than a sign of bias on his part toward China's case. The Ghanaians reportedly threatened to refuse to sign any communiqué from the meeting with Chinese officials in Peking if they did not concede certain points, and an eleventh-hour message from Nkrumah to the Chinese leaders made the same point.[53]

Nkrumah's opposition to the holding of a third Afro-Asian Solidarity conference (planned for January 1963 in Moshi, Tanganyika) also demonstrates Nkrumah's distress at dissension within the ranks of the developing nations. Although there was a long background of hostility between Ghana and the solidarity organization (AAPSO), it remains significant that during the Colombo negotiations he cabled the organization's headquarters in Cairo that "a meeting of the . . . Solidarity Conference at this time would be unfortunate and may weaken Afro-Asian solidarity. [Sino-Indian negotiations are at a delicate stage.] Statements might be made which could seriously prejudice the chances of success. . . . I most earnestly call upon your executive to give consideration to a postponement of the proposed meeting for the time being."[54] The ensuing meeting was most notable for the divisions shown in the Communist camp, hostility between China and India, and Indonesia's attempt to bar Malaya's representative from the meeting.[55]

Indonesia's confrontation of Malaya, a third issue, makes clear that Ghana at this stage did not extend automatic sympathy to the proponents

[50] Interview: CF-7. See also Jansen, *Afro-Asia and Non-Alignment*, pp. 330-51.

[51] *Ibid.*, p. 338.

[52] W. F. van Eekelen, *Indian Foreign Policy and the Border Dispute with China*, The Hague, 1964, p. 121.

[53] Interview: Puplampu, CF-7.

[54] Nkrumah to AAPSO Secretariat, Cairo, 11 December 1962, CFA-62.

[55] See Jansen, *Afro-Asia*, pp. 373-74.

of a second Bandung (China and Indonesia). Prime Minister Lee Kuan Yu of Singapore wrote to Nkrumah shortly before the Moshi conference, urging Ghana to oppose Indonesia's attempt to bar Malaya from the meeting. In the brief eventually written by the director of Middle-Eastern and Asian affairs, it was argued that the problem should be considered an international, not an internal one. Otherwise, the possibility of a UN solution which had been proposed by U Thant, "to the relief of many," would be precluded. "I would therefore not recommend that Ghana associate itself with such a thesis except in the limited sense of not supporting direct military or other intervention between any one of the territories involved and another." His diagnosis of the political situation in Malaya was realistic if radical, and devoid of dogma. He wrote that Britain was trying to preserve its strategic position at Singapore and that Lee was trying to balance Communist elements, while Indonesia was overreaching itself. His proffered solution was one based on the principle of self-determination, with referendums held in territories like Borneo, with UN observers present.[56]

Ghana did support Malaya (and Malaysia) in the future, the more so as tension increased between that country and Indonesia. For the moment, however, Ghana's sympathy did Malaya no good. Nkrumah had received Lee Kuan Yu's letter on 31 January 1963 but since the ministry did not act on it for ten days, it was too late for Ghana to make any efforts at the Moshi conference at the beginning of February.[57] The delay itself was probably due to the ennui at the ministry in the post-Kulungugu period. There was, as yet, no minister. The capacities of the ministry were in any case overstretched; in writing his brief, the desk officer noted that all his information was from newspaper reports.

The guiding interest in policy toward the Middle East was Nkrumah's desire to develop as many links as possible with Nasser (short of prejudicing Ghana's beneficial economic ties with Israel); and his less important and less relevant desire to settle the "Middle-Eastern problem." (Nkrumah "wanted a separate state for Arab refugees from Palestine as a compromise between their being absorbed in an existing Arab state . . . and their being re-absorbed in Israel. . . . This proposal became [increasingly] explicit.")[58] Trade with Egypt almost doubled between 1961 and 1962 (almost entirely in Egypt's favor), while political links multi-

[56] "Memorandum on Malaya," by H.V.H. Sekyi, Director, Middle Eastern and Asian Affairs, MFA, 11 February 1963, CFA-35.
[57] Lee Kuan Yu to Nkrumah, 29 January 1963. Michael Dei-Anang severely reprimanded the principal secretary at the MFA for the delay. Dei-Anang to P. S., MFA, 10 February 1963. CFA-35.
[58] Botsio to the author, 7 July 1966.

plied through the Casablanca group framework and, more significantly, through direct personal ties.

Israel's position in Ghana was increasingly defensive in this same period. Its trade there was nearly halved and, although it was able to negotiate a continuation of the long-standing trade agreement, its offer of scholarships for Ghanaian students (to study in Israel) was turned down in April 1962.[59] There remained ample room for diplomacy in Accra, however. The Israeli ambassador who followed Ehud Avriel was almost necessarily an epigone, but just prior to Kulungugu an outstanding diplomatist, Michael Arnon, was appointed. Master of the use of overt and unsubtle persuasion, he dared his country's opponents to come into the open. With Botsio's return to power he had an important ally, and he found old Israeli contacts like Welbeck malleable as well. He understood Nkrumah's weaknesses perfectly, never failing to take advantage of them. In a letter to Nkrumah—in which he was refuting charges made against Israel—Arnon enclosed a book of "Poems from an Emerging Africa," just published in Tel-Aviv: "It takes its motto, as you will see in the marked passage in the Hebrew introduction, from a passage from your memorable address in 1958 discussing the emergence of the African personality."[60] At a later date he sent a BBC transcript of a major speech of Nasser to Botsio: "As you will see even any mention of the word Africa is missing from the fifteen pages of the transcript. . . . The passages in which President Nasser stressed his major preoccupation with Arab affairs are underlined in red."[61] A minor threat, the proposed visit of the ex-Mufti of Jerusalem, produced from Arnon ten pages of documents, including a copy of a letter from the ex-Mufti to Hitler in 1944. Bediako Poku, a friend of Israel's posted there as Ghana's ambassador, was also mobilized for the cause; he cabled Accra that the ex-Mufti planned "to visit African countries to preach hatred against Israel."[62]

A greater threat Arnon had to counter was the possibility that Nkrumah (or the press) would venture into the world of UN resolutions and make comments that would further compromise Israel's ties with Ghana. After the Iraqi crisis in early 1963 (in which Kassim's radical government was overthrown), Nkrumah could not resist speaking out, and in an interview with a Reuters correspondent expressed his alarm at the

[59] Minutes, CECEC, 2 April 1962, CFA-19. These also show that an agreement on agricultural aid was negotiated at the same time as the trade agreement. Sending Ghanaian students to Israel was one thing; developing Ghana's resources was clearly another.

[60] Arnon to Nkrumah, 21 February 1962, CFA-37.

[61] Arnon to Kojo Botsio, 12 August 1963, CFA-38. Nasser's speech was delivered on 23 July 1963.

[62] Poku to Ministry of Foreign Affairs, 29 November 1962, CFA-37.

"grim possibility of the re-establishment and strengthening of neo-colonialism in the Middle East." Even Russia came in for criticism (for its early recognition of the new regime). He went on to reiterate his proposal that a new state should be created in the Middle East and, moreover, that Israel should be kept "within the limits laid down by the United Nations."[63]

There was reason for the Israelis to be concerned. The *Evening News* stated that the interview had "obligingly identified the President with the 1947 boundaries, and the capitalist-imperialist vested interests have so far succeeded in preventing the carrying out of the UN decision of 1947,"[64] which Arnon considered "superseded not merely morally and practically but also juridically."[65] The head of chancery in Tel-Aviv wrote to the ministry that Osagyefo's proposals had hit Israel as "no less than a 'Bomb-shell,' " and to the instructions that he should explain the statement as best he could he replied that the Israeli public demanded "that the one who did the declaring should be the one to do the explaining."[66]

Nkrumah had a variety of advice to choose from. Ben Frojoe, in intelligence, suggested the following:

> The Israeli Opposition Party started to taunt the Government that Osagyefo meant the 1947 resolutions and that their experts were being wasted in Ghana. . . . But any elucidation will bring Egyptian hornets' nests around Ghana's ears.
>
> It is therefore suggested, that the Publicity Secretariat should instruct the Broadcasting to say simply that the statement did not make any specific reference to the 1947 UN resolutions.
>
> This will preserve the diplomatic vagueness of the statement which has baffled both Israel and Egypt.[67]

Arnon, in the meantime, had been busy. He spent four days lining up support, and then sent a note to the ministry of foreign affairs asking if "the Ministry could be kind enough to confirm its understanding that the 'limits' mentioned in the interview refer to the borders agreed upon in the United Nations sponsored Armistice Agreement of 1949; the only border that Israel has ever had and with which it was admitted . . . to . . . the United Nations."[68] Nkrumah notified Golda Meir, then

[63] *Ghanaian Times*, 22 February 1963.

[64] *Evening News*, 23 February 1963.

[65] Quoted in a letter from Richard Akwei, MFA, to Nkrumah, 26 February 1963, CFA-37.

[66] Mochia, Ghana/Tel-Aviv, to MFA, 27 February 1963, CFA-38.

[67] Forjoe to Nkrumah, 25 February 1963, CFA-38.

[68] Arnon to MFA, 25 February 1963, CFA-37.

Israel's foreign minister, that 1949 was meant. In diplomatic circles, Arnon attributed his success to the efforts of Ambassador Bediako Poku, who happened to be in Accra at the time, and to the background of close Ghanaian-Israeli ties, but he was too modest.[69] Once again the Egyptians had been outmaneuvered in Accra, in the issue that was paramount to them even there; the Cairo government politely ignored Nkrumah's proposals for settlement in the Middle East, and continued to wonder what caused his "naiveté" with respect to the "realities" of his friendship with President Nasser.[70] As to the specific proposal itself —for the creation of a new state—even the Ghanaian ministry of foreign affairs had to comment, "About how the Arab state is to be established we are still in the dark."[71]

Whether or not Nkrumah appreciated the distinctions between the 1947 and 1949 boundaries of Israel, in his *Reuters* interview he had clearly intended to give support to the Eygptian position. The Israelis, however, were "simply too entrenched"—in the words of one Israeli diplomat—and had so many residual ties in Ghana that they could still undo the harm done to their position there when Nkrumah tried to weaken it.[72] He had sought to strengthen his relations with the U.A.R. in the African context through the Casablanca framework but, as already seen, he had met little success. His efforts to improve his relations with the U.A.R. in the Middle-Eastern context had no greater success. This reinforced the distinctive character of Ghanaian nonalignment. Neocolonialism existed, it was rampant, but in the developing Ghanaian thesis, it was reserved to Ghana to decide which states were neocolonial, and which were threatened by neocolonialism; this was true at least through 1963.

Ghana was being drawn into relations with Communist states, however, that in the end were deeply to affect its foreign policy as well as the nature of its nonalignment. This is suggested by carrying forward the examination of its relations with the two Koreas begun in an earlier chapter.[73] After Kulungugu, the North Koreans began propounding their cause at Ghanaian embassies. Twice in August the Ghanaian ambassador in Prague received calls from his North Korean counterpart, but he noted that he had "as far as possible refrained from any discussion that would commit the Ghana Government."[74] The South

---

[69] See letter to the author, 22 March 1967, CFL-A.

[70] Interview: CF-96.

[71] Ministry Minute, on letter of Nkrumah to Akwei, 26 February 1963, CFA-37.

[72] Interview: CF-21, September 1965.

[73] See pp. 168-69.

[74] H.B.K. Marrah, Ghana/Prague, to Ako Adjei, 13 August 1962. The same process occurred in Conakry. Ghana/Conakry to MFA, 5 August 1962, CFA-57.

Koreans were once again trying to advance their cause; they as well as the North Koreans were planning a trade delegation to Ghana. Thus the ministry prepared a position paper on the Korean question, the original draft of which went as follows:

> If Ghana were to state a preference it should be based principally on its national interests and then on UN resolutions. It appears that apart from our great interest in world peace, our direct interests are not at stake in this problem. The Korean problem is no longer a threat to world peace. Our preference, if any, should therefore be in support of the country which enjoys UN recognition [i.e. South Korea]. In our strict neutral position, however, we should have quiet relations with both Koreas. Our efforts should be directed to finding a just and acceptable solution to the problem of a divided Korea. It is obvious that the two visiting missions are a cover-up for efforts to lobby the Government of Ghana to take sides. . . . We should avoid the trap.[75]

The ministry official was doubly out of touch with the Ghana of October 1962. While taking note of official policy already defined (with respect to Germany and world peace) his brief suggested a preference for noninvolvement and, worse, for the "pro-American" half of Korea. Changes made in the draft at Flagstaff House reveal some of the tendencies that were developing. Enoch Okoh, the cabinet secretary, was "inclined to suggest that both delegations should be allowed to come," knowing Nkrumah's appreciation of a lively diplomatic arena. The changes he made (placed in parentheses) to the ministry's final recommendation are revealing: "Our relations will be one of *coolness to* (friendship with) both Koreas and will therefore *be not to encourage exchange of visits* (engage in relations) with either country although limiting political relations with South Korea on the analogy of our relations with West . . . and East Germany."[76]

Nkrumah approved, whereupon others began adding their comments. Amonoo took exception to the statement that Ghana should in normal circumstances recognize that country having UN recognition. ". . . Ghana's position on the Korean problem at the UN has been that the UN resolutions are not valid because the North Koreans are unable to attend the UN sessions whilst the South Koreans can owing to American pressure."[77] Michael Dei-Anang, quick to catch the trend of thought, added

[75] "Position Paper on Korea," Ebenezer M. Debrah to Principal Secretary, MFA, 26 October 1962, CFA-57.

[76] Comment of Enoch Okoh, on E. M. Debrah to P.S., MFA, 26 October 1962, 31 October 1962, CFA-57.

[77] H. R. Amonoo to Director, Middle East and Asian Affairs, and to Director, United Nations Affairs, MFA, 9 January 1963, CFA-56.

that "the only thing that colours . . . a visit [by the South Koreans] is the strong US control of affairs in South Korea. There is however, no harm in allowing the delegation to come to Ghana."[78] But the South Koreans once again cancelled their visit, without explanation. The North Koreans came and, although the final policy laid down at the time of the visit was that "we should cultivate relations with both sides short of diplomatic relations,"[79] this delegation was able to lay the groundwork for the establishment of diplomatic relations and the opening of an embassy in Accra by the end of 1964.

Only at the United Nations, where Ambassador Quaison-Sackey continued to protect the autonomy of his mission, did Ghana's policy have a semblance of coherence and consistency during 1962 and 1963. In 1962, Ghana voted against Israel in the Security Council when that state was accused of an infraction on Syrian territory, as the merits appeared to the Ghanaians to favor the Syrian case. The following year, Ghana voted for Israel when Syria appeared to have made a similar infraction on Israeli territory. Quaison-Sackey justly termed his own speeches before the Security Council on the Cuban Missile Crisis of October 1962 as "perfect non-alignment."[80]

That the basis of Ghana's voting was African interests is demonstrated by a factor analysis of voting in the 18th session (1963) of the General Assembly.[81] Within the cluster of 24 states with which Ghana's voting shows the greatest similarity (all but one of which are in Africa and Asia) Ghana had the highest coefficient of solidarity (.88) with respect to the voting pattern of this group in general. Ethiopia's cohesion

---

[78] Comment of Dei-Anang, 25 February 1963, on Brief of 26 October 1962, CFA-56.

[79] Akwei to Nkrumah, 25 February 1963, in which "the policy laid down by Osagyefo" is cited. CFA-56.

[80] Interview, Alex Quaison-Sackey. Ghana, the U.A.R., and Cyprus were delegated to express the concerns of "some fifty member states" about the situation. (*UNSC*, 1024th meeting, 24 October 1962, p. 10, P. 60, speech of Riad, the U.A.R. representative.) Quaison-Sackey's statement was tightly argued and balanced, much more so than Riad's. Sackey said, for example "There is thus a genuine fear that the Western Hemisphere is threatened by Cuba's military build-up, while Cuba is afraid of attack from its neighbours . . . which is the reason for its defence measures." He proposed that the U.S. give a written guarantee that it had "no intention of interfering in the internal affairs of Cuba and taking offensive military action," and that Cuba "should also give a written guarantee . . . that it has no intention whatsoever of interfering in the internal affairs of any country in the Western Hemisphere and taking offensive military action against any country." *Ibid.*, p. 17, PP 97-98.

[81] Bruce Russett, "Discovering Voting Groups in the UN," *American Political Science Review*, 60, No. 2 (June 1966). In a factor analysis such as this, groupings are not pre-selected; that is, votes of the Afro-Asian Group at the UN (for example) are not analyzed by computer. Votes are analyzed globally to see what natural groups (rather than formal caucusing groups) emerge. Naturally there is substantial coincidence between formal caucusing groups and groups emerging from the factor analysis.

289

within this same group is .82, India's .75, Algeria's .74, Morocco's .58. Equally revealing results appear when the voting of the states within this cluster of 24 are compared with the voting of the only monolithic cluster in the United Nations at the time, the Soviet Union and the states of Eastern Europe. Of the Afro-Asian states with which Ghana is naturally grouped 19 of the 24 in the analysis had higher coefficients of solidarity with Communist bloc voting, and thus exhibited closer affinity to the Communist positions on cold war issues. Ghana's coefficient is .17; Mali's, the highest in the group of 24, is .42. Ghana's is closest to Tunisia and Ethiopia in this regard.

The backwash of Kulungugu had affected every aspect of Ghana's external relations except its work at the United Nations. A new basis for relations with the Communist world had developed despite the growing conviction in many circles that Ghana's interests were ill-served thereby. The vagaries of Nkrumah's position on international issues had eroded the foundations of her nonaligned stance; as there was no relationship between these policy ventures and Ghana's interests as perceived by her diplomats, these individuals became still less relevant instruments of Ghana's foreign policy.

PERMANENT REVOLUTION

Ghanaian Politics after the Second Assassination Attempt. There was no chance for the crisis atmosphere in Ghana to settle during the last three and a half years of Nkrumah's rule. As will be seen in the following chapter, the founding of the Organisation of African Unity in May 1963 posed new challenges to Nkrumah, which led him to press even harder for both a Ghanaian and African revolution. Domestic events in the latter part of 1963 drew Ghana's foreign policy further along the path followed after Kulungugu. The sequence of events is in itself instructive, and suggests that the "random factor" rather than plan remained the fundamental determinant of the pace by which changes could occur.

The autumn of 1963 was an active time for party ideologues, who met with Nkrumah in a "Philosophy Club." *Spark* noted that a "Theory of the Revolution" was needed before the revolution itself could begin, so the ideologues began supplying one. Their program called for a "revolutionary political organ," a program of activities that would meet the "absolute necessity and immediate needs" of the masses, and finally— and of most importance to judge from the efforts expended—revolutionary propaganda to "raise the level of the people's anti-imperialist

290

consciousness."[82] By mid-October, Nkrumah had publicly accepted the ideologists' program. In an interview in *Paese Sera*, he stressed that "There is no such thing as [African] 'Socialism' . . . there is only one Socialism."[83] Moreover, he noted that he had written a theory of the African revolution, which only awaited publication. The first two requirements of the masses could be attended to. How?

Nkrumah was soon to answer this question in practical terms. The preventive detention act was extended and expanded so that it far surpassed South Africa's as an instrument of control; a new security services bill, which delegated vast powers to Nkrumah for the creation of new mechanisms of security, was passed. In December, he could thus create the presidential detail department and reconstitute the division of military intelligence so that it came under his authority. He also refashioned the research division of the ministry so that it, too, was directly under his authority, and had sufficient manpower and equipment to keep a close watch on Ghanaian exiles (and, at times, Ghanaian diplomats). The opposition had no illusions about the aims of the new legislation.[84]

The judiciary remained autonomous. As the *Economist* noted, "its supreme test" was to be its judgment in the Adamafio-Ako Adjei-Crabbe case.[85] On December 9th, they exercised their independence, and declared there was insufficient evidence to convict the three of conspiring to assassinate Dr. Nkrumah at Kulungugu. Nkrumah revoked the appointment of the Chief Justice and by Christmas had declared their decision null and void. A week later, a policeman in Flagstaff House attempted to kill Nkrumah. The Western press was incredulous. Suspicion (unwarranted) that this was staged for political purposes seemed to gain credence when the aftermath included the detention, once again, of Dr. J. B. Danquah, a shake-up in the police (in which Commissioner John Harlley lost some of his powers), and the announcement that the final stage of the revolution would be consummated in a plebiscite through which Ghana would become a one-party state. The single party was to "serve as the leading core of all organizations of the people," and the judiciary was to be brought under political control. To no one's

[82] "A Theory of the Revolution," *Spark*, No. 40, 13 September 1963.

[83] Interview by Giorgio Dignorinia, 5 October 1963, reprinted in *Spark*, No. 45, 18 October 1963. The party had, of course, long since adopted "scientific Socialism" (*vide*, "Work and Happiness," *Accra*, July 1962), but Nkrumah had been careful not to use the term himself in public until this point.

[84] See *Debates*, 25 November 1963, Vol. 34, pp. 962-1012, in which the Security Services Bill is passed. One member asked "How can we condemn South Africa . . . when we repress and oppress our own people?" (p. 969).

[85] *Economist*, 23 November 1963, 758. See also Austin, *Politics in Ghana*, London, 1964, pp. 412-13.

surprise, 92.8 percent of the voters said "yes" in the last week of January.[86]

There followed a series of accusations and demonstrations against the Western powers, with each of which the ideologues added to their string of victories. On the eve of a visit by Averell Harriman—who was coming to serve what was planned as a final warning on Nkrumah—the *Ghanaian Times* could offer the *quid pro quo* of the radicals' victory:

NKRUMAISM

Ever since Karl Marx gifted the world with his thoughts and worked on the scientific laws of social development, and ever since ... Lenin employed the principles and teachings of Marxism to unfurl the flag of Socialism in the revolutionary struggle ... the national liberation movement ... has produced men of international outlook who have enriched the Socialist commonwealth with their positive contributions. . . .

One such genius is Kwame Nkrumah of Africa.

That is why we in these parts speak of Marxism-Nkrumaism. . . . Nkrumaism, therefore, springs from the one great fountain of scientific Socialism.[87]

Shortly thereafter the text itself, *Consciencism*, was unveiled. It included explanations of categorical conversion, and set theoretic terms, such as:

$$U \underset{pa\ 1\ \dots\ k}{G} \longleftrightarrow [(\overset{\nearrow}{pa}+na) \underset{0\ G1}{\searrow} + (\overset{\nearrow}{pa}+na) \underset{0\ G2}{\searrow} + (\overset{\nearrow}{pa}+na) \underset{0\ G_{k-1}}{\searrow} + (\overset{\nearrow}{pa}+na)Gk] \underset{0}{\searrow}$$

or, put another way, the progress of liberated territories to a union of African states.[88]

Although the cause of this development is not the subject of this book, a tentative explanation placing events concerned with Ghana's external relations in perspective can be suggested. In the first place, the progression in Nkrumah's stated philosophy to "scientific Socialism" can clearly be seen as a result of the reverses he had experienced in his plans to unify Africa. For the ideologue, the failure of a policy presupposes a villain, and, since the cardinal supposition in Nkrumah's thinking was that union government was feasible and inevitable, the villain, by elimination, was imperialism and neocolonialism. This led to closer ties with the Russians, chief advocates of scientific Socialism, the CPP's new

[86] See "The Issues at Stake," *Spark*, No. 59, 24 January 1964.
[87] *Ghanaian Times*, 18 March 1964.
[88] Kwame Nkrumah, *Consciencism*, London, 1964, pp. 112-13.

ideology, and a gradual acceptance (in theory) of the corollaries of this ideology. In the second place, new security measures and more repression were a natural concomitant to the failure of his domestic policies. Prices and taxes were rising, and the common man could see little more from his sacrifices than new monuments to Nkrumah's growing power.[89] Thirdly, the "Socialist boys"—the party ideologues, the editors—were prepared to praise Nkrumah in a manner that enhanced the cause, Marxist Socialism, on which their own positions depended. Less determined and more principled men (such as A. L. Adu) had been unwilling to go to such lengths to propound their own ideas.

Finally, there is the quixotic, emotional, and unstable character of Nkrumah himself. If one accepts the explanation of a senior and highly competent intelligence officer, of the events of December 1963, much of the rest follows. By this account, Nkrumah had reluctantly accepted the verdict of the judges on 9 December. Kweku Boateng, minister of the interior (and himself a radical), had told the editors that they could not hold a press conference condemning the verdict. But Khaw Swanzey (the attorney-general) and the editors pressed Nkrumah, alleged there was evidence that the judges had taken a huge bribe (presumably from foreign interests), and within two days were able to call their press conference.[90]

By revoking the judge's appointment, Nkrumah broke Ghana's last real link with the liberal world. Having taken one drastic and far-reaching step to make the state what he no doubt had long wished it to be (but had lacked the will, and the cadres, to make it) his appetite increased. The second assassination attempt, coming when it did, heightened his distress and his determination to reconstruct Ghana along Socialist lines. *Consciencism* had long been written (probably by Habib Niang and Massaga, the UPC dialectician) but, by the timing of its publication, it reinforced an already long series of coincidences, happily for the radicals. Africa, an "optimum zone of development," in the Marxist sense, would have its "optimum centre of resistance" to imperialism, and the job of uniting the continent would no longer be an effort devoid of ideological content.[91] Ideologically, Ghana had moved almost

[89] It was not difficult, however, for Nkrumah to find support for his action. The *Economist Intelligence Unit*, for example, described the events of January as follows: "By imposing a party dictatorship Dr. Nkrumah may have created the necessary and in many ways distasteful strait-jacket for forcing Ghana's transformation, political and economic, into the first truly modern society in Black Africa." No. 45, West Africa Series, 18 March 1964.

[90] Interview: CF-87. This account was widely substantiated.

[91] See *Spark*, No. 40, 13 September 1963. The authorship of *Consciencism* was a subject of much controversy after the 1966 coup. It was widely believed that Willie Abrahams had written it, but it seems more likely that he only revised it.

imperceptibly along a road to Marxist Socialism, but this particular sequence of events gave justification and a sense of urgency for making far greater changes than those which had taken years to accomplish in the past.

The repercussions of these changes in the Ghanaian political scene should be considered. "Years of Imperialist domination," wrote the *Ghanaian Times* in April, had imposed on Ghana "values and attitudes antagonistic to Socialism," and thus the party had to "invade the ramparts of counter-ideological formulation."[92] This it did. The Marxist Forum, founded at Legon by serious intellectuals in early 1964, suddenly became the Nkrumaist Forum, whereupon interest nearly disappeared.[93] The Kwame Nkrumah Institute of Ideology at Winneba took on a much fuller program. "We use the Institute to sharpen comrades' minds the way a pencil sharpener takes care of pencils," Kweku Akwei said.[94] In May, civil servants, MP's, and diplomats took turns having their "ideological baptism" at Winneba.[95] Enoch Okoh, cabinet secretary and head of the civil service, stated that Ghana's civil service was now geared to the revolution, a statement which helped to ensure that it was not. Men with a sense of humor still existed in Flagstaff House. Whereas at a similar meeting two years earlier, Ghana's diplomats could make at least muted criticisms of their country's foreign policy, this time they could only listen. Professor Abraham told them that their personal philosophy "should be within the framework of a national philosophy or ideology" (Nkrumaism). The president told them that Ghana needed servants of humility, service, and dedication. They were said to have left after two weeks with "fresh zeal."[96]

THE DIPLOMATIC EQUIVALENT: RUSSIA, CHINA, AND NONALIGNMENT

The Soviet Union made substantial gains in this period. In late October 1963, Kweku Akwei, the increasingly influential secretary for ideology of the CPP, led a delegation to Moscow for a month's study of the ideological and propaganda work of the CPSU, partly at the Soviet Higher Party School (making them, apparently, "the first, non-Communists accorded this privilege").[97] He and his colleagues returned in time to

---

[92] "On Party Ideological Education (3)," editorial in *Ghanaian Times*, 29 April 1964.

[93] According to Professor Conor Cruise O'Brien, in his review of *Neo-Colonialism*, in the *New Statesman*, 26 November 1965, pp. 831-32.

[94] Interview by the author and William A. Butler, July 1964.

[95] *Ghanaian Times*, 30 May 1964.   [96] *Ibid.*, 28 May 1964.

[97] According to Wolfgang Leonhard, quoted in Legvold, "A Comparative Study of Soviet Policy Toward Six West African Countries in the Post-Colonial Period," unpublished Ph.D. dissertation, Fletcher School of Law and Diplomacy, 1967, p. 177.

give the party a fresh injection of ideology during the critical months from December 1963 to May 1964. More important, Russia's role in Ghana's security was increased. After the January assassination attempt, Russian officials had easy access to whatever intelligence data they wished in Flagstaff House. A large group of Ghanaians was sent to Moscow for a two-year course in counterintelligence.[98] Gestures of solidarity and friendship multiplied; Nkrumah sent Kofi Baako to Moscow as his personal envoy, to celebrate Khrushchev's birthday in April 1964.

Nor was any doubt left that Rodionov had become one of the most influential men in Accra, with the ability—and willingness—to affect policy decisions. Botsio gave, as one example, his own proposal to zone Ghana's Eastern embassies in 1964.

> I argued with Nkrumah that a united Africa could afford embassies in every capital of Eastern Europe, but that Ghana in the meantime could hardly afford surrogate expenses for the continent. I wanted to close all the embassies but Prague, realised that this was asking for trouble, so suggested we leave a skeleton staff in every capital but Prague, with the Ambassador there overseeing the work in the other cities. Rodionov, however, was able to convince Nkrumah that Ghana should keep its embassies there.[99]

Rodionov, by many accounts, had no hesitation in criticizing recalcitrant civil servants and diplomats in his discussions with Nkrumah. One study of alignments of states with the two great powers, based on 1963 data, concluded that Ghana was the "fifteenth friendliest state" to the Soviet Union, an enumeration leaving few states between Ghana and the states of Eastern Europe.[100]

Is this possible? Where in fact did Ghana stand with respect to Russia —and to China, Communism in general, and nonalignment? In the first place, Nkrumah's desire to maintain full control in Ghana could still, in practice, not be in doubt. Ghana was not Russia's "satellite." On the contrary, Ghana was "not yet Socialist," as the editors of *Spark* wisely wrote a week before the January referendum.[101] What, then, did Russia want, in addition to the considerable economic benefits it obtained through its ties with Ghana? It obviously had no interest in continental union government,[102] less indeed than had the CPP radicals.

[98] These were completing their course in February 1966, and went thence to Conakry with the deposed Nkrumah.

[99] Interview: Kojo Botsio.

[100] "Measuring International Alignments," by H. Teune and S. Synnestvedt, *Orbis*, 9, No. 1 (Spring 1965), 180.

[101] "Ghana is not yet Socialist," *Spark*, No. 58, 17 January 1964.

[102] V. Kudryavtsev, of *Izvestia*, wrote "It may well be that some of the ideologists of

There is no evidence that the Russians ever gave Nkrumah assistance in his attempts to unify the continent.

On the other hand, a personal relationship had developed between Nkrumah and Khrushchev who, for his part, probably overestimated Nkrumah's actual influence in Africa. More important were changes in Russian policy. Such warm relations between Ghana and the Soviet Union would not have been possible five years earlier, even had it been the Ghana of 1964 espousing scientific Socialism to the Soviet Union of 1959. The splintering of the Communist bloc (in the first half of the 1960's), the seemingly concomitant growth of America's willingness to use its enormous power, and increasing Russian consumer demands made flexibility in matters of ideology a necessity for Russia. Ghana could, therefore, be permitted to use Russian trademarks without accepting traditionally incumbent discipline.

Moreover, the Russians wished to encourage "progressive" forces in the "national liberation movement" and, as Nkrumah increased Ghana's involvement in radical causes outside Africa, Khrushchev must have seen further justification for strengthening Russia's ties with Ghana. The more important (and increasingly fruitful) interests Russia had been developing in Algeria and the U.A.R. reinforced this tendency. Finally, the Russians appear to have decided to make a virtue of what Khrushchev considered necessity. As a consequence of these various strands, a new Russian approach to the developing world was adopted which lasted until shortly after Khrushchev's fall. According to Robert Legvold, "Khrushchev sometime late in 1963 [apparently] encouraged a group of liberal intellectuals to devise new theoretical formulations describing internal developments within the radical African states, and later, over opposition from within the Party leadership, he himself took up their 'revisionist' conclusions as part of a policy adventure intended to dredge the continent for other Cuban-style conversions to socialism."[103] This was not enough, however, for the building of a long-term relationship between Russia and Ghana.

Ghana's relations with China also appeared to grow in warmth, though not as a consequence or effect of the Russian-Chinese split. Huang Hua

---

African unity who propose the establishment of governmental organs on an all-African scale right away are running away with themselves. But that is an expression of their dreams. . . . But I think that these projects are premature because of the highly diverse pattern of social and political conditions and foreign policy orientations." "Africa: Answer in Unity," *International Affairs*, Moscow, No. 8 (August 1964), 75. It was for these very reasons of differing orientations that Nkrumah, of course, would not consider economic links with neighboring regimes.

103 Legvold, "Comparative Study of Soviet Policy," p. 218.

became the second most influential diplomatist in Accra.[104] In January 1964 Chou En-lai paid a five-day visit to Accra, during which new credits were pledged to Ghana exceeding those made in August 1961. In the communiqué the favorite concerns of each party were included: China praised Nkrumah's efforts to unite Africa. Ghana praised China's sympathy for the African struggle. China was able to enhance its position on issues where important differences existed with Russia. Both parties sought an "Afro-Asian-Latin American-People's Anti-Imperialist Conference." Both sides advocated disarmament, if "the complete destruction of existing nuclear weapons and their stockpiles" was effected.[105]

Yet it was not a convincing communiqué. It was most significant for the routine pledge of "full support for the anti-imperialist and anti-colonialist struggle in Africa, Asia, and Latin America." No basis was found, however, for cooperation in effecting the liquidation of imperialism. China, for instance, offered Ghana assistance in the training of freedom fighters, but Nkrumah (according to participants in the talks) discreetly turned down the offer.[106] What is the significance of this? A general hypothesis is suggested by the Ghanaian diplomatist charged with responsibility for the surveillance of Chinese activities:

> Ghana-China friendship was a front. It was all "show."
> Nkrumah believed that China had to have a conspicuous position in the world of Ghanaian ideology, because he suspected that in the final analysis they were right in their view of the liberation movement.
> But basically he feared them. He instinctively trusted Russians, he instinctively distrusted Chinese. He was, simply, scared that the Chinese did not have his own best interests at heart, and I had clear instructions to watch their movements closely.[107]

Given Chinese—as compared with Russian—ideological rigidity in this period, it is not difficult to understand why they did not praise Ghana's efforts to "build Socialism" (there was no mention of Socialism in the communiqué). The Russians translated Nkrumah's books for wide distribution in their country, and could hail Nkrumah's contribution to Marxist thought, but the Chinese in the age of Mao could hardly be expected to follow suit.

Nkrumah did not like the Chinese—if this analysis is correct—but, solely because of their position as the largest Communist state, he gave

---

[104] Interview: Kojo Botsio. By all accounts Huang Hua was exceedingly shrewd. A senior party official, he had headed the Western Europe and Africa divisions of the Ministry of Foreign Affairs in Peking before being accredited to Accra in 1960.

[105] Communiqué, in "Chou En-Lai in Ghana," Accra, 1966, pp. 6-10.

[106] Interviews: CF-87, 85.   [107] Interview: CF-87.

them an important place in Accra. There were, in actual practice, few partisans of the Chinese position in the CPP. Akwei disliked the Chinese as much as did Nkrumah, and the ties of the editors of the Ghanaian papers were almost entirely with Russia and Eastern European states. Only a few, like Tettegah, seemed to have indicated a preference for the Chinese.

Here is one more cross reference on the map of movements in the third world. In 1961, Ghana was a state being blown from a "pro-West nonaligned stance" to a "pro-East nonaligned stance." The next point came when friendship with both Russia and China was so warm, and the threat of imperialism so obsessive, that Nkrumah no longer wished Ghana's foreign policy defined in terms of nonalignment.

The shift in Ghana's position is made more explicit by examining Ghana's ideological and diplomatic position on two issues, the first being the growing hostility between Russia and China. The Ghanaian press at first tried to prove that this was a product of the imperialists' imagination, which was no longer feasible by late 1963. *Spark*, therefore, began trying to refute ancillary Western arguments, namely, that China did not have peaceful intentions, and that the Soviet Union would collude with the United States.[108] Nkrumah was very grieved at the disunity in the Socialist camp. As he cabled a meeting of AAPSO in Nicosia (in September 1963), "Our goal should be to seek the unity of the Socialist countries, for it is only through this unity that they can support us in our struggle against imperialism and colonialism. It should be our concern at this conference to appeal to China and the Soviet Union most strongly to eliminate their differences."[109] The point of importance is not that Nkrumah could obviously not affect the rift; rather, it is the peculiar way he saw it. If there were to be a world in which Marxism, Leninism, and Nkrumaism were to be forces joined in the struggle against imperialism, national or ideological differences in the Socialist commonwealth had to be resolved.

The other thread in the fabric of this change was the position on non-alignment itself. Ghana had consistently taken less than an active interest in the AAPSO from its founding in Cairo in 1957 but by the end of 1963 Nkrumah had little choice but to shift his attitude. For one thing, new links with the Communist countries made a commitment to the "national liberation movement" necessary, a movement the Russians hardly saw as confined to Africa.[110] Afro-Asian movements had lacked appeal

108 "World Socialist Unity," *Spark*, No. 39, 6 September 1963.

109 "Osagyefo Sends Message to Afro-Asian Solidarity Conference," P.R. #422/63, 30 September 1963.

110 See, for example, *Mizan*, September 1963.

for Nkrumah not just because they were directed by other leaders and states; there were racial overtones that he did not like. The compelling solution was to link Latin America with the same broad anti-imperialist front, in whose affairs he had begun taking great interest. In the same message to the Nicosia conference he thus urged that "Afro-Asian solidarity . . . be reinforced with firm links embracing the Latin American states," which would "destroy any manifestations of racialism that can upset our anti-colonial and anti-imperialist struggle."[111] Ghana steadily increased its interests and activities in this new world. At the AAPSO meeting in Algiers in the spring of 1964, Ghana invited the organization to hold its fourth conference on its own territory, which in itself was of immense importance.

Ghana's position on both the planned second nonaligned conference and the second Bandung conference is also interesting. The former conference had received its most recent impetus in a communiqué of President Nasser and Prime Minister Bandaranaike in October 1963, and in extensive joint efforts of Tito and Nasser; the second Bandung conference in the several declarations of Indonesia, China, and Pakistan during the last half of 1963. The two conferences became competitive in several ways, as is argued by G. H. Jansen: "Behind Second Belgrade lay a new dogma of world peace and behind Second Bandung lay an old dogma of anti-colonialism. But what really gave force and pungency to the competition between the two conferences was that they became identified with one side and the other in a struggle between Russia and China."[112] Even had it not been bound by special ties with each movement, Ghana could not choose between the two movements, because of its desire to maintain close links with both Socialist camps. At Belgrade in 1961, Nkrumah had told Sukarno that Ghana would support a second Bandung,[113] and this was reiterated during the visit of Chou En-lai. In April 1964, a significant caveat was placed on Ghana's participation, however, when Botsio cabled Subandrio that "A Second Asian-African Conference will be useful if it is confined to concrete problems capable of being resolved without bringing dissension within our ranks."[114] As Kashmir, Malaysia, the Sino-Indian dispute, and the Sino-Soviet dispute

[111] "Osagyefo Sends Message to Afro-Asian Solidarity Conference," P.R. #422/63, 30 September 1963. This tendency was reinforced, among Ghana's diplomats, by the simultaneous preparations for the first United Nations Conference on Trade and Development. Nkrumah, for his part, even on the world level, saw the "political kingdom" as more important than the "economic kingdom," and never appeared to attach great importance to UNCTAD, at least in comparison with his other concerns.

[112] Jansen, *Afro-Asia*, p. 371. See also *le Monde*, 12 February 1964, for the similar argument of Paul Tankovitch at the material time.

[113] Noted in Ephson (Ghana/Cairo) to the P.S., MFA, 30 June 1962, CFA-60.

[114] Botsio to Subandrio, 6 April 1964, CFA-61.

could thus not be on the agenda, it remained to be seen where the Ghanaian solidarity makers could find a basis for any discussion at all.

Far more important is Ghana's attitude toward the nonaligned conference. A week after *Pravda* had made Russia's support of this conference public, Fred Arkhurst, principal secretary at the ministry, telegraphed all missions that Ghana had agreed to participate, "with the proviso that 'nonaligned countries' should be expanded to a 'conference of Developing Countries' or a 'conference of new emerging states'. . . . The reason is that the word 'nonalignment' is considered to be too narrow and inadequate."[115]

It is difficult to consider Ghana's foreign policy as a nonaligned one in the period after the second assassination attempt. To the extent that international issues dividing East and West were of relevance, the policy was designed to bring aid and comfort to one party. From an objective viewpoint, this can be nonalignment only in its most technical sense, indicating an absence of formal alliance with great powers.[116] Even from his subjective viewpoint, Nkrumah was using nonalignment in a tactical manner, and at critical points preferred not to use the term at all. The wheel had turned almost full circle.

GHANA AND THE UNITED STATES

Nkrumah's attitude toward the United States changed from suspicion to hostility in the early months of 1964. In one sense this was the other side of the Russia-Ghana coin, but the catalyst for the shift was the unexpected events in both countries, the most important of which was the assassination of Kennedy. It was not that the "Kennedy-Khrushchev-Nkrumah pyramid," which had established a dialogue between East and West (as the *Evening News* argued)[117] had been torn down—Nkrumah was not this devoid of a sense of proportion. By 1963 Kennedy may have regretted that "he had not been tougher"[118] with Nkrumah in 1961, but Nkrumah for his part never lost his admiration for Kennedy, and a thin layer of cordiality was preserved in official relations as a result.

Buried with Kennedy was America's Africa policy. If the change were not immediately felt in Washington, it certainly was in Accra.

115 Arkhurst to All Missions, 29 February 1964, CFA-61. According to Botsio, in interview, there was some question in the minds of other participating states at the time whether Ghana intended to participate in a second nonaligned conference, and that Tito pressed Nkrumah personally to make known Ghana's intentions.

116 See also "Non-alignment in the Third World: The Record of Ghana," by the author, in *Orbis*, February 1968.

117 *Evening News*, 1 December 1963.

118 Schlesinger, *A Thousand Days*, p. 500.

Against the judgment of numerous diplomats and advisers, Kennedy had charted a dynamic and admired course for America in Africa, and with Kennedy gone there was no one to advocate what was in any event an unpopular cause. His successor was a man who particularly disliked courting or even appreciating the sensibilities of leaders of small states with whom America had policy disagreements.

Underlying the deterioration of relations was Nkrumah's growing fear of the CIA. At some point in 1963 Kennedy had written a letter to Nkrumah in which he promised explicitly and personally that the CIA did not threaten his regime. He also stated that he would make personal efforts to ensure that the CIA did not work at cross-purposes with his own foreign policy.[119] Yet it is difficult to believe that America's case to Nkrumah was entirely convincing, notwithstanding the fact that Nkrumah, by all accounts, would believe the thinnest evidence of CIA activity. The most important nonofficial American in Accra, for one, did not believe that White House and CIA policy were the same.[120]

The CIA was not blamed for the assassination attempt of January 2nd, an indication to the Americans that Nkrumah's problem was very serious indeed. Rather, the Ghanaian press emphasized that housecleaning was needed at home during this period of the state of the "irreconcilability of class antagonisms"[121] (as Lenin was quoted). But events in Ghana had been too much for Western liberals, and throughout January the American press reflected this hardening. The *New York Times* itself seemingly endorsed Senator Dodd's earlier accusation that Ghana had "gone Communist," when Lloyd Garrison, its West Africa correspondent, wrote that diplomats in Accra were "almost unanimously" of the opinion that Ghana was "rapidly becoming an undisguised Marxist state"; Senator Dodd added a new blast of his own.[122]

As the campaign for the January referendum got under way, with anti-imperialism propaganda at a new high, the editors convinced Nkrumah

[119] Although the author did not see the letter, there was no substantial difference in the description of its contents by American and Ghanaian diplomats, or by Ghanaian intelligence officers. See interviews: CF-41, 87, 112.

[120] Interview: 39A.

[121] *Spark*, 17 January 1964, No. 58. See also *BBC*, Accra in English for Africa, No. 1147, 8 January 1964; and *New York Times*, 6 February 1964.

[122] "Ghana viewed as Going Marxist," *New York Times*, 18 January 1964. Diplomats interviewed by the writer in the summer of 1964 and during 1966, who had been present during this month, were less than unanimous about the wisdom of Garrison's article. They felt that the important point was that the distance between CPP goals and Ghanaian realities had only been widened. There were no economic measures taken parallel to the political changes. Also see "Introduction of Senator Dodd," in "Ghana Students in US Oppose US Aid to Nkrumah," *Committee of the Judiciary, United States Senate*, 29 August 1963, 11 January 1964.

that the CIA had been involved in the assassination attempt. Shortly after the votes were in, several hundred CPP militants (and those otherwise unoccupied) demonstrated at the U.S. embassy—they chanted slogans and pulled down the flag. T. D. Baffoe, editor of the *Ghanaian Times*, was reported as saying "We will massacre you as you massacred the people in Korea and Germany, in Cuba and Panama."[123] That it was a carefully staged demonstration is not in doubt, although the government officially rejected the allegation that it had had anything to do with it.[124] Ambassador Mahoney could not gain access to Nkrumah, but protested verbally to Botsio during the demonstration. On February 5th, the *Ghanaian Times* said that the "dopes and drunks who run the Murder Incorporated called the CIA are after the blood of Osagyefo." Although the government expressed regret over the demonstration and dissociated itself from this comment, Mahoney was recalled for consultations.[125] In fact the Americans were bewildered by the turn of events in Ghana.[126]

On Ambassador Mahoney's return to Accra, Nkrumah persisted in his refusal to discuss events of the previous month with him. A bottleneck of the worst sort existed, in which the Americans obviously had to make the next move. Thus was the oldest card of all brought out for its last play—the Volta River Project. The Kaiser Corporation was at this point committed to buy thirty years of electricity, but under no commitment to build a smelter to use the electricity. In the Oakland headquarters, Ghanaian developments seemed sufficiently distressing for it to be actively considered whether Kaiser should withdraw, rather than pour good money after bad. This was a credible threat: all its purchases and plans had been withheld pending the final review with the Department of State, the guarantee of which was vital. The Department, for its part, wished to send Edgar Kaiser to Accra to clear the impasse between Mahoney and Nkrumah, as Kaiser's relations with Nkrumah had remained warm. Kaiser wished to be assured of American intentions before undertaking this mission, if only to be certain about the factors affecting his decision on the smelter. In mid-February, a discussion was held at the White House that included the President, the Secretary of State, Harriman, Governor Williams, Kaiser, and Kaiser's close friend John McCone,

---

123 *New York Times*, 4 February 1964.

124 *Ibid.*, 8 February 1964.

125 *Ibid.*, 7 February 1964, 14 February 1964; *Ghanaian Times*, 5 February 1964. It is a characteristic irony of the period that, while the Peace Corps was being attacked in the press for alleged subversive activities, 80 more volunteers were requested by the Ghana government.

126 This is a theme running through American press reports in February. The Americans had not yet realized that they had left the Kennedy era; it seemed to them that they had merely aided Ghana (very generously at that), and were being thanked with hostile demonstrations. See *Washington Post*, 11 February 1964.

Director of the Central Intelligence Agency. By one account, Kaiser was assured that the CIA "was not active in any way" in Ghana, whereupon he left for Accra.[127]

His mission was a success. Arrangements were thus made for a visit by America's most venerable diplomat, Averell Harriman, who was to reinforce the gains achieved by Kaiser. Sir Robert Jackson arrived in the meantime, wearing United Nations and Volta hats. He helped to set the stage for Harriman's visit by making it clear to Nkrumah that unless Ghanaian-American relations improved, there would be no smelter and no industrialization.[128] Harriman came in late March, and used strong language indeed. According to Rusk's later testimony to the Senate Foreign Relations Committee, it was made very clear that the United States was not about to proceed with further cooperation on the Volta scheme if Nkrumah were "to steer Ghana down a road that is hostile to the U.S. or American interests there."[129]

In the short-run, Harriman's mission was also a success. Anti-American articles disappeared from the press during April and May, and Mahoney once again became a frequent guest at Flagstaff House. Kaiser made his own calculations. He sent a group of Ghanaian Socialists and engineers on a tour of America and, as he is said to have seen "progress" in their attitude at the end, he made his decision to proceed with the smelter by July.[130]

What had Johnsonian diplomacy accomplished? While Harriman was in Accra, the press and cabinet ministers stressed the African character of Ghanaian Socialism, and denied that it had any cold war relevance.[131] This was, however, incongruous, in a period in which *Consciencism* was launched. One of the best American diplomats thought that it was Nkrumah who had used the Volta card, by playing on American fears of the repercussions were the smelter not built.[132] Nkrumah's affectionate greeting to Khrushchev in May, when the premier was in Egypt dedicating the Aswan Dam, was pointed, in this regard. Other experienced diplo-

[127] Interviews: CF-39A, 60.

[128] Interview: CF-60.

[129] Quoted in *Guardian*, 10 July 1964. See also House of Representatives, Foreign Assistance Act of 1964, *Hearings before the Committee on Foreign Affairs*, 6 April 1964, pp. 124-45, and pp. 159-61.

[130] Some, like Kofi Batsaa, editor of *Spark*, refused to join the tour. T. D. Baffoe, editor of the *Ghanaian Times*, had entertained doubts about Nkrumah's policies in the presence of Kaiser officials, however; he went, and apparently his doubts increased. See his articles in *Ghanaian Times*, beginning 22 May 1964. See also *ibid.*, 14 April 1964.

[131] See, for example, "Speech of Krobo Edusei" at a dinner attended by Harriman: "The Socialist programme to which we are dedicated is not borrowed from anybody but springs from our own traditions." P.R. #153/64, 24 March 1964. See also *Ghanaian Times*, 21 March 1964.

[132] Interview: CF-41.

mats thought the Americans had been foolish to send Kaiser and Harriman: An ambassador in Mahoney's position should be able to re-open communication on his own terms. Indeed, the average Ghanaian newspaper reader could only have believed that yet another world leader had come to pay his respects to the Ghanaian president.

For the moment, tactical nonalignment seemed to be working. Were Ghana's options being increased? On the contrary, they were becoming fewer. Kaiser was to proceed with the Volta smelter, but the atmosphere during these months ensured that the investment needed to complement the Volta project would not be forthcoming: In 1964, foreign investment was one-tenth of what the seven-year plan envisaged and projected. Ghana's problems were not being solved; as a result of its foreign policy, it was losing its old friends, and gaining new ones whose sincere interest in Ghana's economic welfare was either minimal or badly misplaced.

THE OAU AND THE "AFRICAN REVOLUTION"

August 1962–July 1964

"If we go fast we shall surely achieve success. If we go slow we shall go to pieces and perish."—KWAME NKRUMAH

IN THE MONTHS following Kulungugu, Ghana's Africa policy lacked all strategy. Of this its diplomats were acutely aware: a political officer in Cairo, Anthony Ephson, wrote to the ministry that Ghana should reconsider its priorities. Asian problems, he said, were subsiding, but "There are major outstanding issues in Africa which are still to be resolved. The frequency of international conferences has been on the increase . . . have we, indeed, adequate personnel to enable us to attend?"[1] Michael Dei-Anang, who directed the African Affairs Secretariat at Flagstaff House, carefully sifted Nkrumah's information, but the failure of all Ghana's African initiatives up to this point had been so pronounced that even Nkrumah was aware that the pan-African lead was no longer in Ghanaian hands. In June 1962, Sékou Touré and the Emperor of Ethiopia had decided to work together to merge the Monrovia and Casablanca Groups. Nkrumah, desperate to regain momentum in his policy, concluded that if this unlikely alliance were possible, then he could himself work with the president of Liberia toward the same end. On July 18th his most influential diplomat, Kwesi Armah, delivered the following letter to Tubman:

> I . . . have the honour to call upon Your Excellency to consider the advisability of summoning a conference of the Foreign Ministers of all the Independent African states at the earliest opportunity . . . so that they can consider the best means of bringing about a meeting of the Heads of State . . . as soon as possible.
>
> I am sure that such a conference initiated by you which I am ready to sponsor along with any other Heads of State who feel as we do now will be a happy augury for the unity and solidarity of the African continent.

[1] Ephson (Cairo/Ghana) to MFA, 25 August 1962, CFA-60.

In view of our joint efforts in the past to achieve these ends, I am confident that I can rely upon Your Excellency for maximum co-operation in securing that all the Independent African states will forget the past and meet in an atmosphere of harmony and brotherliness.[2]

Tubman, who had learned from the past, now had Nkrumah exactly where he wanted him and did not discourage his effort. Kulungugu followed, and it was five weeks before Nkrumah could send a high-ranking delegation (Dei-Anang, Okoh, and Asante) to Monrovia to discuss methods of achieving reconciliation in Africa. Following the delegation's return, Nkrumah wrote Tubman that he was "encouraged not only by the sincerity, earnestness, and forthrightness with which you examined the proposals [for reconciliation] I humbly submitted to you, but also by your declared willingness to support all efforts to ensure the unity of our continent."[3] However inappropriate an alliance between Tubman and Nkrumah seemed, there is no question of Nkrumah's sincerity in making the effort. He continued to support a foreign ministers' meeting in the IAS framework at Tunis, on the grounds that the summit conference at Addis Ababa would otherwise fail, retarding the achievement of African unity.[4] He also opposed another Casablanca group meeting. The King of Morocco requested his support for a meeting of the Casablanca political committee in early October, and Dei-Anang telegraphed Ambassador Bossman in Rabat:

It is most imperative that nothing should be done which would give the impression that in spite of [our efforts for reconciliation] it is desired to crystallize the difficulties represented by the existing political grouping. . . .

Apart from this, Osagyefo is very preoccupied at present with urgent affairs. . . . It is not therefore possible to give a categorical answer . . . to King Hassan's enquiry. You should accordingly use your discretion in returning a non-committal reply in as tactful a manner as possible.[5]

There was the rub. Osagyefo was preoccupied with the situation created by the Kulungugu crisis of the autumn of 1962. If the assassina-

[2] Nkrumah to Tubman, 18 July 1962, CFA-58.
[3] Nkrumah to Tubman, 30 August 1962, CFA-42.
[4] H. R. Amonoo, A.A.S., to Ghana/Tunis, 8 November 1962. At this late stage Nkrumah continued to press for an IAS meeting, as this was the only framework in which he might wield substantial continental influence; it was clear by this time that if the Addis Ababa conference did succeed, its success would be attributed to the Emperor and Touré.
[5] Dei-Anang to Bossman, 5 October 1962, CFA-43.

tion attempt had not altered his belated decision to press for reconciliation in Africa, it prevented him from realizing that the initiative lay too firmly in other hands to be seized. Diallo Telli, Touré's emissary, had visited eighteen capitals by August 1962, gaining support for a summit conference in Addis Ababa. Dzirasa, Ghana's resident minister in Conakry, was not given even minimal information about Guinea's efforts, which included the formation of a seven-state group to work silently toward the dissolution of Africa's blocs. Ghana was not included, something it confirmed only on November 12th.[6] This was a bit late.

On October 9th President Touré had attacked Nkrumah from the most prestigious platform of the world. He said to General Assembly delegates that Africa had no need of "philosophical formulae or doctrinal theories; it needs honest co-operation . . . unity cannot mean uniform institutions . . . still less can it mean the creation of a single African party or a single African super-state. One of the major obstacles to [unity] has, in the past, been the widespread conception that it had to be formed around a single state or a single man." The delegate of Upper Volta said Touré was "speaking as the true spokesman of Africa today," as indeed he was.[7] The first anti-Nkrumah offensive had begun.

By year's end, Nkrumah still vainly hoped that an IAS conference could be held in Tunis, and so he appointed a delegation. Ghanaian diplomacy had again been overtaken by events. The Monrovia group met in Lagos in December to adopt its charter. Stephen Dzirasa, by now deputy foreign minister, met with Liberian Secretary of State Grimes, and Ketima Yifru, the Emperor's foreign minister, at the Accra airport as they proceeded to the Lagos meeting. Yifru then returned to Accra after the conference to "deliver the Emperor's invitation [to the Addis Ababa Conference] in person." Dzirasa told Nkrumah that "I further asked . . . what sort of material will constitute the basis of discussion . . . at the Foreign Ministers' Conference [of the Addis Ababa summit]. He said that the Casablanca Charter and the Charter of the Lagos conference will be used. . . ."[8] To this Dei-Anang added: "This indicates that we have to work fast on Osagyefo's proposals otherwise undue weight will be given to consideration of the Charters of the Casablanca and Monrovia Groups."[9]

[6] The African Affairs Secretariat asked Ghana's UN mission on 20 October 1962 about the group's existence, which was confirmed in a cable from Quaison-Sackey on 12 November 1962. Ghana's delegation in New York was at this time playing an important role in negotiations to achieve reconciliation within the Africa group, this in contrast to Ghana's role in Africa. CFA-43.

[7] *UNGA*, 1148th meeting, 9 October 1962, p. 56, PP 22-30; 1153rd meeting, 15 October 1962, p. 81, PP 95-96.

[8] Dzirasa to Nkrumah, 19 December 1962, CFA-43.

[9] Dei-Anang to Nkrumah, *ibid.*

Over Christmas, while Nkrumah attempted to intimidate the government of Sylvanus Olympio in Togo, his advisers thus reworked his pan-African ideas into a fresh proposal for continental African unity. Ghana was now to have an Africa policy. As far as Ghana's moves were concerned, it was the events in Togo that interested other African states, however.

THE TOGO AFFAIR

The plots against Olympio of 1961 had been financed by Ghana, and after Kulungugu—which had caused Nkrumah to fix almost all his attention on personal security—there was increased pressure by Ghanaian militants in Flagstaff House to try once again to depose the Togolese government; Nkrumah was receptive to the idea, mainly because he felt he would not be personally safe until a friendly regime existed in Lomé, owing to the presence of Ghanaian refugees there. It was, of course, *both* sides of the frontier that were "astir with irredentist activity,"[10] but between the two groups of refugees there were important differences in motivation. The Ghanaian refugees in Togo opposed Nkrumah largely for ideological reasons—opposition for which there was diminishing outlet in Ghana—while Togolese refugees in Ghana opposed Olympio for any reason presented but not for ideology. It is important and ironic that Nkrumah did not perceive this.

Meatchi and Kpodar, two Togolese ex-deputies of Nicholas Grunitzky's French-puppet regime of the 1950's, goaded Nkrumah to action, but later events were to prove that they had at heart their own interests, rather than pan-Africanism or Nkrumah's security. They could not easily have proved that they commanded any popular support whatsoever in Togo, but they had unqualified success in convincing Nkrumah that the masses of Togo supported *him.*

The Ghanaian refugees, for their part, had a meeting ground in Togo and a few, such as Gbedemah and Busia, obtained passports and presidential hospitality. Evidence which Ghana published late in 1962 did prove that some of those involved in Kulungugu had taken sanctuary in northern Togo, near the Ghanaian border (where they were, in fact, detained by the Togolese police). But proof that the prominent Ghanaian exiles were directly involved in the assassination attempt is tenuous, and proof that the Togo government was involved is nonexistent. Nevertheless it was shown that Togolese officials had helped to send inflammatory propaganda into Ghana, and had aided in the importation of

10 Colin Legum, *Observer Foreign News Service*, 8 January 1963.

arms *into Togo*.[11] That Olympio ever spearheaded an attempt on Nkrumah's life is not easy to believe, in view of his caution and understanding of Nkrumah's character. Olympio's main concern was Togo's survival as an independent state. He tolerated and, at times, encouraged the Ghanaian refugees because, according to one of his advisers, "they were his *atout*; expelling them would have deprived him of bargaining power and fed Nkrumah's ambition."[12]

Olympio had tried to reinforce his own position by following up his proposals of February 1962 for cooperation among the Benin states. In late August he brought about wide-ranging discussions between Dahomey, Nigeria, and Togo,[13] but no substantial cooperation ensued. The government in Lagos was well disposed to Olympio and, as evidence of Ghanaian involvement in Nigerian affairs mounted, had increasing justification for working with him against Nkrumah. A senior Nigerian official later expressed regret that Nigeria had not been sufficiently farsighted in this period. "A few million pounds would have propped Olympio up sufficiently for survival."[14] But, he noted, as a result of Nigeria's break in relations with France, the transportation of arms across Dahomey into Togo (as was contemplated) would have caused grave difficulties. More important, the Sardauna of Sokoto, prime minister of Northern Nigeria, had little interest in seeing links develop between the southern Nigerian regions and tribally similar neighboring states. Nor was Dahomey prepared to give Togo support, possibly for reasons that do it no credit.[15] Olympio thus began discussing the possibility of signing a formal defense accord with the French and, in the meantime, according to *le Monde*, the French government declared its intention to stand by the defense understanding already linking Lomé with Paris.[16]

Throughout the autumn of 1962, the explosions which began in Accra after Kulungugu continued, taking over a dozen lives; the Ghanaian regime laid the responsibility at Olympio's door. On December 7th Ghana began threatening its neighbor. In a note written by Geoffrey Bing, an attempt was made to find a legal basis for Ghana's own activities against Togo. Ghana, it said, would never contest the right of

[11] "Exchange of Notes between the Governments of Ghana and Togo," Accra, 1962, pp. 11-13.
[12] Interview: CF-86.
[13] See *Ashanti Pioneer*, 22 September 1962.
[14] Interview: CF-83D.
[15] Many Ghanaian officials said that Dahomey's position was linked to substantial gifts its leaders had allegedly received from Nkrumah. No proof of this was obtained by the author, however.
[16] 21 January 1963.

309

refugees to use constitutional or even revolutionary methods to secure a change of regime in their own country.

Indeed, the Government of Ghana completely accepts the view that where a Government has ceased to enjoy the support of the majority of the people and endeavours to maintain itself in power by force every effort should be made to achieve a change by peaceful means and that a resort to force is justified when all other means to end oppression have been tried and have failed. The basic condition . . . is that *such a desire to end an unpopular regime is backed by the will of the people.*

A curious distinction was then drawn between such acts and those of "a dissident minority in . . . Togoland designed to coerce . . . Ghana by means of assassination, terrorism, and indiscriminate murder." Togo was to repatriate these individuals immediately; if they did not do this "the Government of Ghana will have no alternative but to institute such measures as may be found necessary to protect the safety and security of the State of Ghana and its citizens."

Olympio replied twelve days later, asked for proof of the allegations, declared that refugees in Togo could only remain so long as they did *not* engage in any political activity, and ended by noting that Togo, for its part, could not protest against measures designed to protect Ghanaian citizens, "as long as such measures do not in anyway undermine the territorial integrity . . . of the Togolese Republic." On December 19th Ghana sent another, more detailed, note to the French Ambassador for transmittal to Lomé. This included evidence of Togolese "complicity" at Kulungugu, and again warned of "the dangerous international consequences" were Togo not to comply with Ghana's demands.[17] Quaison-Sackey was instructed to take copies of the notes to U Thant "on the basis that the situation might result in complications which could be a threat to peace."[18]

The Ghanaian notes included an astonishing revision of the law of asylum and, in traditional diplomacy, implied the gravest of threats. Ghana could not have it both ways: it had recognized the right of refugees to live in Togo but, in order to justify its own attempts to overthrow Olympio, assigned to any refugees the right to engage in revolutionary activities. It had to hang that right on difficult legal grounds, as Dr. J. B. Danquah, president of the Ghanaian bar, pointed out in a letter to the ministry of foreign affairs. "By what indications" he asked, "or at what point are we to tell whether a Government established by law had

[17] "Exchange of Notes between the Governments of Ghana and Togo," Accra, 1962, pp. 1-5.
[18] Dei-Anang to Quaison-Sackey, 27 December 1962, CFA-151.

310

become 'an unpopular regime'? How is 'the will of the people' . . . to be known or ascertained?" Danquah, only six months out of detention, presumably had another interpretation as to which regime was in fact described in the note, and as to which group of refugees, on the legal grounds outlined in the note, had a right to overthrow the government of its own country. Ghana was now grouped "with the evil-minded nations of the world—those who advocate force."[19]

Embassies in Accra assumed Nkrumah was planning something more serious than those ventures of the past. Quaison-Sackey was told on December 27th, however, that "for the time being no direct action is contemplated, as the reaction of the Government of Ghana would depend on the reply of the Government of Togo."[20] Togo did not reply to the notes. British officials gave Olympio the direst warnings for his security —he still had no personal guard.[21] In his last interview, he noted that since Ghana's last attempted coup in Togo he had been "very much on the lookout" for what Ghana might do.[22] Early Sunday morning, January 13th, Sylvanus Olympio was murdered.

That the assassination was carried out by Togolese soldiers who had left the French army cannot be disputed. Ghana's role in setting the stage is another matter, and it is for this that a revulsion against Nkrumah spread across Africa, at a critical time for Ghanaian diplomacy.

After the 1966 coup d'état in Ghana, an illiterate Fulani named Jacob was released from detention who, in his testimony to the Ghanaian C.I.D., claimed a part in the events of January 13th. He alleged that Nkrumah sent him to the regional commissioner's house at Ho near the frontier with orders to "organise people . . . to go to Togoland to assassinate" Olympio.

> I was kept in the dark in respect of certain aspects of the operation.
> [I recruited 36 men, and] some Ex-Servicemen from Lomé helped me
> do the training. . . . The training lasted for three days and on the night
> of the fourth day we invaded the Residency of the late Olympio,
> with an assignment to assassinate him. At dawn [the] men I took from
> Accra returned to the Camp. . . . In Accra I reported myself to

[19] Dr. J. B. Danquah to MFA, date unclear, presumably mid-December 1962, CFA-151.

[20] See note 18. Another bombing occurred in Accra on 8 January 1963, Ghana's "Positive Action Day," and Nkrumah may have acted in the ensuing days on the assumption that the explosion was planned in Lomé. It is difficult to believe, however, that Olympio at this stage would have permitted any such action, as he knew through his intelligence how tense Accra was.

[21] Geoffrey Dawson (U.K./Lomé) was in frequent contact with Olympio, through his friend Bonito Olympio, and with Sir Geoffrey de Freitas, the British High Commissioner in Ghana. Interviews: CF-86, 52.

[22] BBC transcript, sent by Ghana/London to MFA, Accra, 16 January 1963. CFA-151.

311

OSAGYEFO, but before reporting, the OSAGYEFO invited TETTEGAH to his office. . . . After the narration . . . Kwame NKRUMAH told Mr. Owusu-Sekyere to take me into custody until further notice.[23]

Although the authenticity of the document is not itself in question, the allegations are difficult to verify, as officials in the post-Nkrumah era were not eager to discuss this episode. It is widely claimed, however, that Nkrumah had worked himself into a frenzy of unusual proportions during this period, and that Bureau officials (and Meatchi) made frequent and secretive night trips to the border.[24] Nkrumah's December notes made some Ghanaian initiative imperative in order to prevent Olympio from winning a dramatic psychological victory. Jacob's failure to describe the crucial part of the operation lends support to the hypothesis that a Ghanaian plot was simply overtaken by events in Lomé. Nkrumah and Bureau militants in any event took credit for the assassination in selected quarters, much as they were to do after the first Nigerian coup of January 1966.[25]

The limits of a small new state in attempting to intervene beyond its borders are underlined by the events of subsequent days. The first announcement of the coup on Togo radio stated that the Togolese presidency was "entrusted to Mr. Antoine Meatchi, now in refuge in Ghana."[26] As Meatchi was a conservative northerner from the same tribe as 70 percent of the army, the choice was not surprising. The soldiers wanted pay, however, and only the French ambassador—who did not want Meatchi[27]—was in a position to guarantee their pay. The next day, Cotonou Radio, well-informed even on an hourly basis, noted that there was as yet no agreement on Meatchi, "on the grounds that he spent all his political exile in Ghana"; Kpodar, for his part, gave this as a

[23] "Statement by Jacob Fulani, Unemployed Male of No Fixed Abode, at Accra Station, CID Headquarters, 26 February 1966," CFA-200.

[24] Interviews: CF-29, 87, 86.

[25] By this hypothesis, Jacob crossed into Lomé, was dazed by subsequent events, and returned to Accra unaware that his own men had not played the crucial role. It was not in his interest to stress this failure when discussions of the appropriate reward took place in Flagstaff House. Nkrumah detained him, in order to insure that if credit were to rebound to Ghana for the assassination, it would occur at the place and time of Nkrumah's choosing. There is good reason to wonder what the role of the French Ambassador in Lomé was, given the Olympio family's conviction that he precipitated the murder by the manner in which he dealt with the Togolese soldiers' demand for pay. The Ambassador may have felt that Nkrumah could be trusted to muddle the Togolese waters enough to obscure whatever happened in Lomé.

[26] *Lomé Domestic Service*, 10:25 GMT, 13 January 1963.

[27] Interviews: CF-46, 49. The French considered that he was insufficiently *compréhensif* and stupid.

312

reason for the rejection of Meatchi,[28] but French pressure was probably more compelling. While Nkrumah publicly denounced those accusing Ghana of complicity in the murder, the French candidate, the former Togolese prime minister, Grunitzky, was brought into office.

Nkrumah in any event would have had grave difficulties intervening militarily after the coup, which he is said to have wished to do. A week earlier he had committed a second battalion to the Congo. Few Ghanaians believed that his generals were prepared to obey orders to intervene. The British explicitly forbade seconded British officers in Ghana's navy and air force to take part in such a venture and thus the army could have had support from neither sea nor air.[29] In fact only the Recce squadron was dispatched to the border. Within Togo, the French were familiar with the situation. Whatever the extent of French complicity, it is clear that Nkrumah had fallen into a trap.

Once in power, Grunitzky needed Nkrumah's goodwill and recognition. Nkrumah wanted his own security guaranteed (and, therefore, the expulsion of Ghanaian refugees), and the Ghanaian economy made safe. There was much to bargain about. Nkrumah privately appointed Barden as his "minister plenipotentiary" for negotiations with Togo who, with the Rev. Stephan Dzirasa, began arranging talks. At first Ghana was negotiating from a position of weakness: Touré was demanding an international investigation in order to embarrass Nkrumah. Dei-Anang cabled Quaison-Sackey that, as it was important "to do nothing to arouse the resentment of the Provisional Togolese Government," the investigation should be opposed at all costs.[30] At the first Ghana-Togo meeting, on January 24th, Ghana promised to open the border, and to remove certain import restrictions on agricultural produce. On February 7th Grunitzky came to Accra, where he and Nkrumah agreed to respect "the principle of noninterference," the "territorial integrity of each state," and the "international sovereignty of each Republic"—concessions to Togo. Nkrumah wished to discuss a common monetary zone and offered to guarantee the Togolese currency. Most important, Nkrumah wanted Grunitzky to take strong measures to rid Togo of Ghanaian refugees.[31]

Two weeks after the border was opened, it was again closed, without explanation. Special branch and the presidential detail department

---

[28] *Cotonou Domestic Service*, 0615 GMT, 14 January 1963. Interview: Dr. Simon Kpodar. Ambassador of Togo in Ghana, 1963-66.

[29] Interview: CF-52. Both the Navy and Air Force were dependent on British officers.

[30] Dei-Anang to Quaison-Sackey, 29 January 1963, CFA-105.

[31] P.R. #69/63, 12 February 1963, and interviews: CF-87, 55.

had made it clear that they could not guarantee presidential security while Ghanaian refugees still resided in Lomé, where President Grunitzky was under increasing pressure from Nigeria and other states not to appease Nkrumah on this issue.[32]

Worse, on March 18th Ghanaian security officials in Lomé kidnapped a Lebanese businessman named Hadad who, allegedly, had been speculating with Ghanaian currency, thus weakening the Ghanaian pound still further. At a meeting between officials from both governments on April 4th, "The Togolese delegation stated that they would like to be convinced that Mr. Hadad was not abducted from Togolese territory because it was Togo's duty to protect foreign nationals on her soil. The delegation asked to see Hadad and they were informed it was impossible." By this time the Grunitzky regime was in a position of weakness vis-à-vis Ghana, having found how difficult it was to obtain international recognition. It thus momentarily accepted Ghana's assurance on Hadad's case, though under pressure, presumably from the French, to intervene.[33] It was decided to settle the issue at a meeting on the frontier. On April 10th, however, the ministry received instructions from Flagstaff House that the proposed meeting should not be held. "Ghana Government should be allowed to deal with the case as she thinks fit."[34]

In the months after Olympio's murder, questions of security and economics had spoiled the opportunity that had existed for reconciliation. The discussions between experts and the agreements that had been concluded therefore came to naught. These failures proved that the issues between Ghana and Togo transcended personal rivalries: The Togolese now knew that they were unlikely to find agreement possible with Ghana so long as Nkrumah remained in power, and Nkrumah now saw that he could not gain control over Togo through a change in leadership there. Togo's new leaders were ideologically less well-disposed to Nkrumah than Olympio had been. It is not surprising that Ghanaian officials noted that Meatchi, Togo's new vice-president, refused to favor Ghana on any issue and became more anti-Ghana even than Gru-

[32] Interview: CF-87. The question of the refugees was obviously paramount in Nkrumah's mind. On January 15th Nkrumah called in British High Commissioner Sir Geoffrey de Freitas, to tell him he had heard "that some Ghanaian citizens had sought refuge in the British embassy in Lomé," according to Sir Geoffrey's account. Two days later de Freitas wrote Enoch Okoh, Nkrumah's cabinet secretary, that he "now" knew that this was incorrect. CFA-158. Many of the Ghanaian refugees in fact fled to Lagos shortly after Olympio's murder.
[33] "Summary, Meeting of Ghana-Togo Experts," MFA, 4 April 1963, CFA-105. According to *Togo-Presse* (19 March 1963), Hadad had smuggled £15,000. The French, of course, had no interest in seeing a reconciliation between Ghana and Togo.
[34] Minute to P.S., MFA, 10 April 1963, CFA-105.

nitzky.[35] By now it was an old story. Ghana had backed opportunists or, simply, conservatives who used Ghana's support to their own ends and who when in power foreswore all obligations to Nkrumah and his government.

One other West African incident, in combination with the Togo affair, was enough to consolidate the new alliance that was to make the May summit conference possible. At almost the same time as the Togo coup, it was discovered that J. K. Quashie, Nkrumah's favorite ambassador, had assisted in a plot against the president of the Ivory Coast. Houphouet wrote to Nkrumah asking that Quashie be recalled, and Nkrumah twice refused. Houphouet then threatened to publicize the incident as widely as possible, whereupon Nkrumah withdrew him, re-assigning him to Léopoldville.[36] Although Houphouet's diplomacy was characteristically quiet, it seems unlikely that he would have persisted with such low-keyed pressure had Quashie's involvement been deep. But the evidence was sufficient for Nkrumah not to wish it exposed, and it was sufficient to give added momentum to the anti-Nkrumah offensive, in which the next move was Touré's.

The Guinean president used the Togo affair as an excuse to bring relations with Ghana to a new low point. Although he later made clear that he knew Ghana was not responsible for the murder of his close friend Olympio, he felt subversion had gone far enough in West Africa.[37] "The people, party, and government of Guinea have learned with surprise of your country's recognition of Grunitzky's government," he telegraphed Nkrumah. Mourning was declared, and Olympio was pointedly declared a hero to the Guinean army.[38] Ghana gave no ground. The *Evening News* addressed Touré as follows: "FALLEN STAR: How are you and your NATO associates going to conduct an enquiry into the death of the late . . . Olympio? Presumably you may prefer to invade Togo FIRST! Ye Gods, save the world from this crop of Balewa's fawning sycophants."[39]

It was indeed Balewa and his government in Lagos that had reacted

[35] Interviews: Botsio, Dzirasa, CF-115.

[36] Interview: CF-15. See also the account in "Si le Ridicule Tuait . . . ," policy statement of the PDCI, *Fraternité*, Abidjan, 12 March 1965.

[37] Interviews: CF-37, 87. On January 14th Resident Minister Budu-Acquah cabled Nkrumah from Conakry that Guinea radio had stated that the assassination was an "internal matter" (CFA-151). Incomplete transcriptions of Guinea radio broadcasts do not show this; in any case it seems clear from the other evidence that Touré did not consider it an "internal matter."

[38] *BBC*, IV, 1158, Conakry radio, 21 January 1963. See also *Africa 1963*, No. 8, 12 March 1963.

[39] *Evening News*, 15 January 1963.

most seriously to the assassination. Jaja Wachuku, Nigeria's foreign minister, had delivered a note personally in Cotonou on the very eve of the coup proposing that Nigeria and Dahomey urge Ghana and Togo "to settle [the] rift amicably."[40] Wachuku was not certain that Ghana was responsible for the ensuing coup, but blamed Nkrumah for setting the stage, and wished to serve notice on Ghana to keep out of Togo's affairs.[41] At a press conference he, therefore, stated that "for purposes of security, Nigeria considers her boundary extends to the Ghana-Togo border," and called a Monrovia group meeting to investigate Olympio's murder. The *Evening New* responded that "Nervous Jaja Wachuku has once again brayed like a neocolonialist ass."[42]

The conference was held in Lagos. Two ex-ministers of Olympio's government accused both Ghana and France of complicity, but produced no convincing proof.[43] The conference, however, had a broader purpose: to publicize the matter further; to discredit Ghana still more; to prevent Grunitzky from handing Ghanaian refugees over to Nkrumah; and to raise the price of recognition of his regime. It succeeded in these objectives, and also brought together in common cause those West African leaders wishing to reconcile the existing African factions. Thus, in mid-February, Keita (who was as disturbed as Touré by the Togo affair), Touré, and Houphouet met in the western section of the Ivory Coast, discussed Togo, and, according to *Jeune Afrique*, concluded a *"sainte alliance"* to combat subversion jointly in their three countries.[44]

THE SEARCH FOR UNITY IN AFRICA, ROUND TWO

On New Year's Day, 1963, Nkrumah submitted the results of Dei-Anang's Christmas efforts with each African head of state and government. The proposal was the most precise formulation for union government ever produced in Accra, calling for a common foreign policy, joint economic planning, a common currency, and a common defense system. It was a statement of what was to be achieved—once the political will existed.

To implement the above proposals, a Central Political Organisation with its own constitution would have to be drawn up as a matter

---

[40] Interview: CF-83B.

[41] Doe, High Commissioner, Ghana/Lagos, to Dei-Anang, 12 January 1963, CFA-151.

[42] "Nigeria Is Not Yet Free," editorial, *Evening News*, 23 January 1963.

[43] See Albert Tevoedjre, *Pan-Africanism in Action: An Account of the UAM*, Cambridge, 1965, p. 45. See also *l'Essor*, Bamako, 26 January 1963.

[44] Alipui, Ghana/Abidjan, to MFA, 13 February 1963, CFA-105, and *Jeune Afrique*, 25 February-3 March 1963.

of urgency. It is suggested that this Union of African States should consist of an Upper House and a Lower House. *This* [it emphasized] . . . *does not in any way interfere with the internal constitutional arrangements of any state.* The overriding concern . . . would be to give political direction in regard to the implementation of the proposals.[45]

Allies were needed to generate the political will, but a basis for ascertaining which states could be trusted had to be found. For the radical elite, the answer was derived from a re-interpretation of the past five years of intra-state relations in Africa. This done, states were classified into groups—according to their "neocolonial" affiliations. The prelude to the historical reconstruction was a booklet published by A. K. Barden in September 1962. His critical point was that the first resolution of the 1958 IAS Conference (that African States would "pursue a common foreign policy") was virtually a mandate for union government. Barden illustrated the unanimity of the conference on this point by quoting similar praise of the conference's host, Prime Minister Nkrumah, by both President Tubman and the Tunisian delegate.[46] Yet the resolution had clearly indicated that the states were merely to *coordinate* their efforts so as to project the "African personality" effectively. Here, in Barden's study, was the myth of Eden all over again, in which was obscured all the lessons of 1958: that unity had come through caution, that Nkrumah had gained in prestige through lack of self-indulgence, that unanimity had come through carefully worded and inclusive proposals that brought the participants forward together.

Early in 1963, *Spark* carried a series of articles, "The Concept of African Unity," that in fact was Barden's analysis carried still further.[47] The role of imperialism was more thoroughly infused into the analysis, and the lines along which imperialism worked were carefully delineated. The remedy, to the counterattack which imperialism had mounted after the "days of unanimity" in 1958, was the same prescribed thenceforth for every African difficulty, weakness, or failing, namely, union government. Step by step articles in *Spark* led to the dénouement, the categorization of African states by their neocolonial attachments. This was unveiled on the streets of Addis Ababa two days after the summit itself had begun, in a special issue flown to Ethiopia for the occasion.

The first group, of Ethiopia, Nigeria, Liberia, and Congo-Léopoldville, was controlled by "Anglo-American Imperialism." Investment in

[45] Nkrumah to Heads of Independent African States, 1 January 1963, CFA-201.
[46] *Awakening Africa,* "Conferences of Independent African States," with preface by A. K. Barden, Accra, 1962, no page numbers. According to Dr. Z. Cervenka, Sammy Ikoku wrote the booklet. Cervenka to author, 20 May 1968.
[47] The series began with *Spark,* No. 7, 25 January 1963.

these states came from Britain and America; security and defense was "planned, run, officered, and largely financed" by the same powers. Congo was the surprise in this group but, as it had applied to Canada, Italy, Israel, Belgium, and the United States for help in modernizing its forces and equipment, it was, according to the Ghanaians, obviously controlled by Anglo-American imperialism.[48] French imperialism, controlling the second group, was the most perfidious in maintaining colonial links even between the African states in question. The states of "radical African nationalism" (Ghana, U.A.R., Mali, Tanganyika) were those that "plumb for thorough-going decolonisation and for organic union of African states. They want a single African charter which will create one Africa."

As for the "overlap" states, Guinea, for instance, was a state where "French and Anglo-American imperialism are striving for supremacy under that country's recent move to rehabilitate herself with the West," though it was conceded it had strong connections with states of radical African nationalism. Somalia and Tunisia, the "floating states," moved between different groups according to what, it was disparagingly implied, were their national interests.[49]

At the same time as this reconstruction, the diplomatic mechanism of Nkrumah's policy was shifted into high gear. By the end of January, thirty-one states had accepted Ethiopia's invitation to Addis Ababa, and there could be no further doubt that a meeting of significance was soon to occur. Nkrumah sent emissaries to most states of the continent in an attempt to prevent the emergence of an African charter based on Ethiopia's and Liberia's long-standing designs. Such a charter would not only *not* bring African unity, it was argued, but would also open Africa to the control of "Group 1" and, thus, to the control of Anglo-American imperialism. Envoys were instructed to avoid use of the word "charter," and to plead that Addis Ababa be used to create the atmosphere, to serve as the take-off point, for the preparation of union government itself.[50]

A few of the Monrovia leaders, like Maga, promised more support than they later gave, but most were cautious. Houphouet, for one, traveled from Yammasoukro to Abidjan to meet K. B. Asante, and commented that African unity was the end for which each state was working.[51] He was planning a surprise for Nkrumah at Addis Ababa.

---

[48] Presumably Ghana was in this group until 1961, having obtained its aid exclusively from the Western powers, Israel, and India.

[49] "Power Interests Behind the Trends at Addis Ababa," *Spark*, 24 May 1963.

[50] Interviews: Puplampu; Botsio; Makonnen, 20 February 1966.

[51] Interview: CF-24; and Botsio, 16 February 1966.

The Casablanca states, for their part, wanted a meeting to plan strategy prior to the summit—but not for planning union government. In no case did Botsio (who visited the radical capitals) obtain promises of support for union government in the member states of this defunct group,[52] and it is hard to believe that he explicitly asked for it in the terms Nkrumah had directed.

The real problem lay in the discrepancy between the position in a particular capital and what was reported to Nkrumah. The militants had created an atmosphere of high expectancy in Flagstaff House; Africa was going to have union government—or Nkrumah would not attend the summit conference (it was surely in the militants' interest that he not attend). Diplomats and politicians alike were reluctant to disabuse the president of his illusions, as much from fear that pessimistic reports would encourage him to boycott the summit, as from fear of the displeasure courted by reports of unsuccessful missions.

Thus on the eve of the summit conference Nkrumah had a most imprecise view of the African situation. Guinea, Ethiopia, Nigeria, and the Ivory Coast had long since taken the lead, and throughout these months their pace was maintained. Sékou Touré in one day visited both Houphouet and Keita. Abidjan Radio called it a period of "militant diplomacy . . . The phrase is very well chosen and is particularly adapted to the new and invigorating atmosphere existing in Africa ever since several demagogues tried . . . as the frog in the fable, to inflate itself as large as the ox."[53]

On April 28th Ambassador Ebenezer Debrah submitted Ghana's agenda proposals for the "Creation of a Political Union of African States," to His Imperial Majesty's foreign ministry. The proposals of Liberia and Nigeria were as expected; more ominous were the Algerian proposals, which called for a "union of African states," but one structured around a charter and permanent secretariat (perhaps thus explaining Algeria's absence from *Spark's* group of "radical African nationalists"). Ethiopia's proposals were of the greatest interest, for the preparatory machinery was in their hands, and they had firm ideas indeed. Their agenda proposals, distributed on May 12th, called for the establishment of an "Organisation of African States," a charter, and a permanent secretariat.[54]

[52] Interview: Botsio. See also *La Bourse Egyptienne*, 24 February 1963, *Times*, 5 May 1963.
[53] *BBC*, IV, No. 2126, 16 March 1963.
[54] *Addis Ababa*, Records of the Summit Conference of Heads of African States, No. C4/4/154.

Ghana then began what one of its diplomats called psychological warfare, using every weapon in its armory to press its goals. On May 11th Nkrumah's long-planned new book, *Africa Must Unite*, was published.[55] On May 13th Botsio set out with the first plane-load of Ghanaians, including Welbeck, Quaison-Sackey, Dei-Anang, Barden, Budu-Acquah, and fifty others. The CPP flag was unfurled at the airport, Ghanaian papers were distributed in the streets.

It shortly became known that the Emperor was not merely seeking an OAS-type charter, but had secured the services of a Chilean expert on the OAS to assist in drafting an African charter. To the Ghanaians, this proved that imperialism was behind the call for a charter. The reasons for Ambassador Manuel Trucco's presence were straightforward. Many pan-African charters had been devised in Africa in the preceding several years, and the countries with which these documents were identified each hoped that their charter would serve as the basis for the new all-African charter; Jaja Wachuku, for one, was particularly insistent that the Lagos charter be used. The Emperor, taking into account such pride, went outside the African context for constitutional advice, so that every country could agree on the results. As no other delegations were advocating union government, there was no apprehension about Trucco's presence outside the Ghanaian camp. Ironically Ghana received an unintended benefit from the Emperor's arrangements. Wachuku, incensed that his charter was to be discarded, was prepared to cooperate with Ghana for the first time since Nkrumah had broken up the British-West African links in the late 1950's.

The foreign ministers' meeting was nearly a disaster, not just for Ghana. Botsio's proposals were quickly voted down but, as the ministers could not agree on other proposals, a subcommittee was appointed (which included Ghana) to draft an agenda and a charter for the heads of state. Little optimism was left in Addis Ababa.

According to Clyde Sanger, the major uncertainty by Sunday, May 19th, was whether Nkrumah would attend; he reported that some delegates wondered if his presence would be "useful" in view of what was thus far agreed upon for the agenda.[56] It was at least in part a calculated uncertainty on Nkrumah's part. At one point Dei-Anang came to the Ghanaian delegation with new instructions, namely, that Nkrumah would not come unless the foreign ministers supported union government. This

---

[55] This consisted, in part, of an updated version of the manuscript the Israeli ghost-writer, Moshe Pearleman, had prepared for Nkrumah in 1959, which presumably was revised by Flagstaff House aides. Dennis Austin called the book "an inelegant mixture of rambling argument and unrelated comment on Ghanaian politics." *Politics in Ghana*, p. 39.

[56] *Guardian*, 20 May 1963.

was bluff. But clearly a debate had been raging between such radical advisers as Tettegah, Batsaa, Budu-Acquah—who argued that Nkrumah should not attend—and the diplomats, who had every interest in his presence at the conference. Colin Legum wrote that "By using the summit as a sounding board and by refusing to compromise, Dr. Nkrumah believes he can get a groundswell of political opinion which in time will overcome the less radical ideas of his contemporaries."[57] This was one strand of his thinking, but the primary reason he attended was no doubt less subtle. He thought he would be listened to. One Ghanaian diplomat suggested that "he was so accustomed to his orders being taken in Ghana that he could not believe the process would not repeat itself in Addis Ababa."[58] He had, after all, never attended a large gathering of African statesmen. It also seems at least plausible that he did not wish to be left out—along with only King Hassan and President Grunitzky.

He arrived Sunday, May 19th, the same day that the subcommittee handed a draft charter and amendment to the secretariat for the consideration of the heads of state. Since January, talk of a charter had been forbidden in Accra; now one had been presented. Nonetheless, Ghana's influence in the subcommittee was considerable. There had been no end of difficulties in preparing it; the report observed that the subcommittee "was confronted with the same problems as those which had previously found expression during the work of the charter; refusal to discuss immediately a preliminary draft charter on the basis of the Ethiopian text, and the wish to refer this document for study, in view of its decisive importance for the achievement of African unity, to a committee of experts approved by the Heads of State."[59] Put differently, the conservative states had combined forces with Ghana to prevent results. But if Ghana had not infused the submitted text with the substance of African unity as defined in Accra, it had successfully filled it with the spirit and language of African unity. The Ghanaians had transformed a technical, legal charter into a call to arms, said Quaison-Sackey.[60] On this was based the Ghanaian argument that Nkrumah should in the end sign it. For all that, Nkrumah insisted on pressing forward for true union government.

The atmosphere had in the meantime been transformed with the arrival of the remaining heads of state and government, every one of whom was greeted at the airport by the Emperor. His elaborate preparations were bearing fruit. Virtually all the support Nkrumah had antici-

---

[57] "African States Chart Campaign for Continental Freedom," *Observer Foreign News Service*, 25 May 1963.
[58] Interview: CF-13. [59] *Addis Ababa*, No. C4/6/156.
[60] Interview: Quaison-Sackey.

pated quickly disappeared. It was not the "loud confident talk" of some Ghanaian delegates that hurt Ghana's position, nor the braggadocio about Olympio's assassination (as Sanger described it).[61] Nor was it the forces of neocolonialism, for all the states of "radical African nationalism" but Ghana added to the groundswell of support for the charter. Ghana was asking for something no state was prepared to offer.

One by one the leaders outlined their hopes and thoughts. Nasser called for an "African League," with periodical meetings of the heads of state. Ben Bella's dramatic speech did not mention political unity, not as a slight to Nkrumah, but because Nkrumah was not all that mattered at Addis Ababa. Only Milton Obote called for the surrender of sovereignty.[62] Still, few delegates failed to take Nkrumah seriously. He remained the most conspicuous leader in black Africa even if, as the *Times* said, "other leaders, with other ideas, have come to maturity."[63] One diplomat, Ambassador Ahmad Jamal of Sudan, felt Nkrumah spoke in the role of hero; the ministers had enjoyed voting down each of Botsio's proposals one after the other the week before, he said, but now they listened.[64] What was important about Nkrumah's speech was not his proposal that the conference lay the groundwork forthwith for union government, but his insistence that Africa must have its due. It was the testament of a confident visionary, rather than of a self-seeking and short-sighted dictator. Thus it was important that Nkrumah sign the charter, and what his intentions were became a major item of suspense.

Why, in the end, did he sign it? Some officials were convinced throughout that he would: but Habib Niang, Barden, and all the Ghanaian editors were urging him not to sign, on the assumption that the OAU would collapse as a result. Some of the diplomats, however, darkly hinted that the OAU might just possibly carry on without him. Others pressed him with the argument that the charter was imperfect, but a beginning. He had accepted the 1951 Constitution of the Gold Coast in order to destroy it: could he not do the same again, so Africa could have the union government that the masses yearned for? Shortly before signing was to take place Nkrumah requested a brief adjournment, on the basis that the charter had only been completed the day before, and needed further examination. The Emperor used the time to good advantage, and in the presence of only Botsio urged Nkrumah to sign.[65]

61 *Guardian*, 20 May 1963.
62 *Proceedings of the Summit Conference*, Vol. 1, Sec. 2, Addis Ababa, 1963, CIAS/General/INF/8, pp. 7, 2, 3.
63 *Times*, 27 May 1963.
64 Interview: H. E. Ahmad Jamal, Amb. of Sudan/London, 19 November 1965.
65 Interviews: Botsio; Dzirasa; Quaison-Sackey; Ribeiro.

His signature, on May 26th, seemed to herald a new moderation on Ghana's part. "The extraordinary sight of Dr. Nkrumah embracing the absolute monarch . . . must not turn out to be a piece of pure hypocrisy," wrote the *Financial Times*.[66] Nkrumah had increased his stature. It appeared that the tide of Kulungugu had receded. There was now an African organization that translated institutionally what African brotherhood amounted to. It was pan-Africanism's finest moment, and the form the old movement had now taken had the endorsement of every leader on the continent. Nkrumah was leader of the movement's left wing, his first time in this position since the independence of Guinea five years earlier. "It appeared he had learned a lesson at Addis Ababa, so isolated was he," a Nigerian diplomat commented. "I remained sceptical."[67]

GHANA AGAINST THE OAU

On his arrival in Ghana from the Addis Ababa Conference, President Nkrumah expressed to reporters his happiness "that the political unification of the African continent, my life-long dream, is here."[68] In praising the OAU, it seemed as if he had decided to make a virtue of necessity. The first year in the life of the OAU coincided, however, with a period of intense domestic change within Ghana, as seen in the preceding chapter. New links with the Communist states, a second assassination attempt in January 1964, and the increasing power of the Marxist elite made all the more difficult the compromise with more moderate states that was necessary were Ghana to confine its African politics within the OAU framework. More specifically, the success of the summit conference presented Ghana with challenges on four major questions. Its policy differed from that of the new continental organization with respect to the construction of a pan-African secretariat, to liberation in nonindependent Africa, to the construction of regional associations, and finally to the harboring of refugees and the conducting of subversion.

Four Conflicts. Ghana's first dispute with the OAU appeared to some to be over semantics, but beneath it lay the central concept in Nkrumah's plan for a continental union government. The officially accepted version of a "Special Resolution" of the summit conference had called for the establishment in Addis Ababa, forthwith, of a "Provisional General Secretariat that will operate until the Charter of the Organisation of African Unity is applied." It was to be assisted by an "expert commit-

66 "The African Summit," 27 May 1963.
67 Interview: Alhaji (the late) Isa Wali, High Commissioner of Nigeria in Ghana, 1964-66.
68 *Times*, 29 May 1963.

tee" composed of delegates from the Congo (Brazzaville), Ghana, Nigeria, Niger, Uganda, and the U.A.R.

Obote and Nkrumah had made a proposal that closely resembled this one, but its purpose was vastly different. According to a Ghanaian cabinet information paper, it was for a "provisional *commission* of officials and experts [to] be appointed to examine the various proposals contained in the charter . . . including the establishment of the permanent Headquarters and other organs envisaged under the Charter."[69] Nkrumah's design was to use the "commission" to bury the plan for a secretariat once and for all, and then to begin preparations within the commission for a union government, as if his earlier strategy for the summit conference had in fact succeeded. For this purpose he intended to send a large delegation to Addis Ababa. The issue came to a head in June when, according to both the draft officially accepted at the summit conference and the Ghanaian draft, the commission, or provisional secretariat, was to meet.

The Ethiopians, for their part, had lost no time in establishing a provisional secretariat. Through E. M. Debrah, Ghana's talented ambassador in Addis Ababa, they cabled Accra that the Ghanaian delegate to the secretariat should proceed to Ethiopia. Botsio gave his approval. Nkrumah did not.[70] A cabinet paper noted that the Ghanaian interpretation was that the provisional committee, or secretariat, consisted of a number of countries taking an equal part in its work, whereas the Ethiopians maintained that their government was responsible for the secretariat's work, merely *assisted* by six individual delegates from the six named states.[71] It was vital to Nkrumah's strategy that there be more than one Ghanaian in the secretariat if his strategy of overwhelming it was to succeed. Ethiopia remained adamant. Debrah telegraphed that the provisional secretary-general (already appointed by the Emperor) had said that the wording "provisional commission" was not accepted at the summit conference, nor was the part of the Uganda amendment which associated six countries with the provisional secretariat. Debrah argued—on behalf of Ethiopia's case—that if

[69] Cabinet Information Paper, by the minister of foreign affairs, 21 June 1963, CFA-50 (emphasis added).

[70] E. M. Debrah to H. R. Amonoo, 18 June 1963. Memo of Botsio to P. S., MFA, 21 June 1963, CFA-45.

[71] Quoted in MFA to Ghana/Addis Ababa, 22 June 1963, CFA-50. K. B. Asante, Ghana's best diplomat in this period, wrote to H. R. Amonoo when the latter arrived in Addis Ababa: "I personally recollect calling the attention of Osagyefo's advisors to the fact that a subsequent resolution has modified the original [one] establishing the Secretariat. . . . The view of the Secretariat [the A.A.S.] is that the matter should be dropped. The Ghana delegation may, however, act as if the original resolution was operative." So much for the weight of diplomatic advice. Asante to Amonoo, 9 July 1963, CFA-49.

Uganda's amendment had been adopted, the provisional commission, with two senior officials and experts from each state, "would be excessively large. . . . It would be preferable to make Ethiopia responsible for the provisional secretariat although six senior government officials from other states must be added." He noted that Ghana was free to bring as many experts as it wished, but that only one could be present in the conference room.[72]

From the first Nkrumah had been unenthusiastic about Ghanaian participation in a secretariat, however provisional. Now, he was more strongly opposed than ever. Kwesi Armah, whom he had named his representative for any negotiations that might ensue, argued persuasively, however, that he and his team would, through its hard work, stagger the secretariat and force it to recognize the necessity of producing plans for union government. Nkrumah was convinced—Armah could, better than any other Ghanaian, manipulate him—and the delegation left July 11th after Armah's paean at the airport to "a Continental Government—the end of our toils and tears and the vista of a new hope on the horizon."[73]

Armah and his team of secretaries, four diplomats, and lawyers drafted memoranda and proposals until the early hours of every morning throughout the weeks at Addis Ababa, flooding Nkrumah with reports of their progress. Botsio cabled Armah that "Osagyefo [is] greatly impressed with your initial successes and your businesslike approach. He feels hopeful about your efforts."[74] What they were trying to do was buy time, time in which Ghana would become involved in the OAU, time in which Nkrumah could adjust to a horizon without union government. The main task at Addis Ababa was to prepare for the first regular foreign ministers' meeting, scheduled for Dakar in early August, and Armah's version of the agenda, in a telegram to Nkrumah, is revealing: "Under item 'Political and Diplomatic Co-operation' on agenda a progress report will be presented to Dakar Conference touching on a central political direction leading to the establishment of a Continental Government for Africa."[75] What Armah then labeled "other business" was the list of real issues for discussions at Dakar. It was remarkable enough that a progress report under the rubric of "Political and Diplomatic Co-operation" could be construed to mean that union government was gaining ground. But by this time, arguments were not admitted that

[72] E. M. Debrah, Ghana/Addis Ababa to H. R. Amonoo, A.A.S., 26 June 1963, CFA-50. Debrah was obviously attempting to convince Accra of the correctness of the Ethiopian position.
[73] P.R. #301/63, 11 July 1963.
[74] Botsio to Armah, 20 July 1963, CFA-48.
[75] Armah to Nkrumah, 20 July 1963, CFA-48.

did not pay obeisance to union government—which Nkrumah, more than ever, believed to be immediately realizable.

By August, Ghana's diplomatic sails had not yet been trimmed. Nkrumah was still to realize how formidable were the enemies of union government. When the Senegalese Foreign Ministry asked that delegations to the Dakar conference be limited to four, Nkrumah sent sixteen.[76] Botsio led the delegation, and was assisted by Armah, Amonoo, Barden, and the editors of the Accra papers. The first blow was the undoing of Kwesi Armah's work in Addis Ababa. As he said himself in one of the early sessions, "We felt that, if the subject of political and diplomatic co-operation were put on the agenda, it would enable the Foreign Ministers to consider it first and foremost, and it would give them an opportunity to draft a clear constitution for the United States of Africa. But *the Foreign Ministers would like it taken off the agenda.*"[77] As a result, the Ghanaians worked even harder to prevent a secretariat from being established, and an administrative secretary-general from being appointed, "lest these functional units of co-operation become generally accepted prior to the advent of the Continental Union Government."[78] Indeed, this was the strategy for an entire year.

Ironically, Ghana's rapprochement with Nigeria was furthered through these two questions. Nigeria wanted Lagos as the site for the secretariat, and Jaja Wachuku, Nigeria's colorful foreign minister, was prepared to be difficult if frustrated. On August 9th a secret vote was taken in which Addis Ababa was selected by simple majority. But Togo and Morocco, not yet accredited members of the OAU, had voted, and Wachuku demanded that the question be passed on to the heads of state—a year later. Ambassador E. K. Dadzie, of Ghana, found justification for supporting Wachuku's stand in "principles, realities, and rules of procedure," and asked that a subcommittee be appointed "to make a proper recommendation" to the heads of state—a year later. When another vote was taken on a subcommittee report on this question, Ghana and Nigeria alone did not participate in the vote and, in combination with several other states, were able to stall the choice of Addis Ababa.[79]

The same pattern was repeated with the nominations for the post of secretary-general. Guinea's Diallo Telli was the only nominee at this stage, and Nigeria and Ghana again raised objections. During an in-

76 Botsio to P. S., MFA, 28 July 1963, CFA-48.

77 *OAU* "First Regular Conference of OAU Foreign Ministers," Dakar, August 1963, verbatim transcripts (mimeographed), 6 August 1963, pp. 30-31, CF-conf. (emphasis added).

78 Interview: CF-24, 3 July 1964.

79 "First Regular Conference of OAU Foreign Ministers," 10 August 1963, pp. 31-37, 50.

terminable debate, Botsio urged that "those things must be done properly, according to principle," which meant, never.[80] The Guineans wished that "the organisation might as soon as possible cease to be provisional and throw hesitation aside," but Ghana and Nigeria's opposition on this score was also successful.[81] Ghana then made various attempts to get at the back door what had been refused at the front, through proposals for "unity" that could be accomplished within the Addis Ababa charter as it stood. The Ghanaians presumably had in mind an evolution of the charter into a union government, Burkeian fashion—the difference being that the evolution was to take place overnight.

Nkrumah's growing desire to fight the OAU was fed by bitterness arising from defeat in the second area of conflict—liberation. While a leader in his position might have rationalized the failure to achieve union government in one conference, there was no way to rationalize the fact that Ghana had not been appointed to the liberation committee (the committee of nine).[82] Ironically, five members had received aid from Ghana for their own independence movements.

Modibo Keita was primarily responsible for choosing the nine and, although some Ghanaians, like Botsio, professed not to understand the basis of his choices, it should be obvious. Keita was aware of the tactics Ghana used in African movements and probably felt Ghana would find it difficult to share the initiative within the committee structures. He was also pressed by the freedom fighters themselves to keep Ghana out. These had either encountered personal difficulties with Nkrumah, had come to suspect that Ghanaian funds earmarked for them had been diverted by Barden, or simply wished to avoid the difficulties that, by this time, were associated with Ghana.

There were other reasons for Ghana's exclusion. If the sovereignty of individual African nations were accepted, it was obvious that liberation wars launched from an independent state would have to be guided according to the precepts of that state; and wars would only be launched from states neighboring on the unliberated territories. This did not in itself preclude Ghana from membership but, as it did mean that all the "neighboring states" (Tanganyika, Congo, Senegal and Guinea) had a

[80] *Ibid.*, p. 80.

[81] *Ibid.*, p. 60. See also editorial, *Daily Graphic*, 16 August 1963, and *Spark*, 27 September 1963, in which Telli is viciously attacked.

[82] This affected not only Nkrumah. At the 1964 Lagos OAU foreign ministers' meeting, one Ghanaian said, "we leave it to the conscience of the leaders . . . some of whom are here in this hall to acknowledge the humble assistance of Ghana of which we are justifiably proud." *OAU*, "Council of Ministers, Lagos Conference, 24-29 February 1964," Lagos, 1964.

prior claim to seats on the committee, the remaining five seats were the more highly prized.[83] In membership also lay the status symbol of the day, and so such states as Ethiopia and Nigeria could claim membership, as the reward for their role in organizing the summit conference. Thus was no room found for Ghana. The strength of its desire to belong is reflected in the effort made by Ghana's high commissioner in Kampala to reserve one of the three positions as under-secretary on the committee for Ghana. This too was unsuccessful.[84] Shunned, Ghana decided to fight.

On June 29th Oscar Kambona, Tanganyika's foreign minister, cabled that the voluntary contribution to the liberation committee was due by July 15th. On July 9th Nathan Quao cabled from the New York mission that Ethiopia was requesting Ghana's contribution; by the time of the deadline, Algeria had contributed £70,000, Guinea £20,000, Tanganyika £30,000.[85] Ghana, first in liberation, made no contribution.

The next chance to fight came at the Dakar foreign ministers' conference. Copies of the committee's report had found their way into the wrong hands at Dakar, and the Ghanaians used this as their first basis of attack. The big guns were saved for the most galling point—the preeminence of the "neighboring territories" in the liberation struggle. Harry Amonoo said to the delegates that the committee rather should have consulted "certain countries which, on the question of liberation, have had great experience." No one listened, so the Ghanaians began making petty suggestions—that the secretariat of the liberation committee should include only two people, for example.[86]

Ghana's frustration over its exclusion from the committee mounted after the Dakar conference. On October 25th *Spark* carried a many-faceted attack on it, in which the OAU's position on Ghana's list of priorities was clearly revealed. In the days of Casablanca and Monrovia, it said, at least the conservative states could not prevent the radical states from helping the liberation movement. Now imperialism had emasculated the liberation movement: it had found the soft spot within the OAU, the liberation committee, by working through its client states. Imperialism could either "cripple the liberation movement or . . . push [the unliberated territories] along lines that will permit the setting up of neo-colonial regimes." *Spark* then proceeded to reveal much of the substance

[83] The freedom fighters, in a joint memorandum to the heads of state at Addis Ababa, also urged that "The site of the African Liberation Bureau should be geographically close to the still non-independent territories." *OAU*, 1963, CIAS/Gen/INF/40 p. 2.

[84] D. B. Sam, Ghana/Kampala, to A. K. Barden, B.A.A., 9 July 1963, CFA-49.

[85] Ghana/Dar-es-Salaam to MFA, 29 June 1963, Nathan Quao to Richard Akwei, MFA, 9 July 1963, CFA-49.

[86] "First Regular Conference of OAU Foreign Ministers," 8 August 1963, pp. 19, 23.

of the committee's secret June report; this had leaked—but it hardly helped to make the committee's strategy still more widely known.[87]

The committee had exceeded its authority and, worse, it had "transferred the primary role in helping liberation movements to the neighbouring countries," which gave control to imperialism. Proof—for *Spark* —lay in the committee's recommendation that Holden Roberto's Angolan provisional government be recognized: Prime Minister Adoula, an imperialist agent, had blackmailed the committee into this. The article did not, however, seek to explain Algeria's heavy support of Roberto's group.[88] It concluded that African states of radical nationalism must bypass the committee to work for "the fuller realisation of Addis Ababa." This Ghana proceeded to do.

The third challenge to Ghana as a result of the founding of the OAU was a by-product of the new position on regional unity in Africa. In the summer of 1963, after the Addis Ababa conference, the role and position of the French-speaking states' organization, the *Union Afrique et Malgache* was, on the one hand, widely brought into question, while on the other, efforts to bring about federation in East Africa were greatly stimulated.

By the time of the Addis Ababa conference, both the Casablanca and Monrovia groups had been abandoned, having failed in their primary objectives. The Union of African States (the Ghana-Guinea-Mali union) was likewise discarded: at Addis Ababa, Touré had unilaterally announced its dissolution. There was no zest for sacrifice displayed, as the group was long since dead. By comparison, the UAM had gone from strength to strength, which from Ghana's point of view was an error to be set right.

Ironically, it was Touré who began the attack on the UAM. For over a year he had directed his efforts toward bringing the OAU into being. Having succeeded, there was no comparable challenge to absorb his energy. When the French-linked states that he had so recently worked with did not dissolve their regional/political organization, despite the formation of the OAU, he appeared in his former radical guise. Thus

[87] A point also made by the *Observer*, 24 November 1963. See *Spark*'s response, "Whose Secret Have We Leaked," No. 51, 29 November 1963.

[88] Ben Bella's recognition of Roberto was embarrassing. As a result of the liberation committee's difficulties during the summer, Ben Bella became impatient and expressed his frustrations about the committee during a visit to Ghana. His reasons were different from Nkrumah's, which did not stop the latter from claiming him as an ally. See "Ben Bella in Ghana," *Ghana Foreign Affairs*, Vol. 2, No. 3 (November 1963), and "Behind Ben Bella's Visit," *Spark*, No. 35, 9 August 1963. Interestingly, *Spark* saw on the horizon "conditional independence" for Angola, "under which both Portuguese and U.S. Imperialism will be accommodated."

was laid a basis for reconciliation with Ghana, were Ghana to place Guinea on its list of those states displaying a commitment to "radical African nationalism"—a process of elegant simplicity which was to bear much repetition in the ensuing two years. By July 3rd Touré was sufficiently incensed at the UAM states to share his frustration with Nkrumah. Nkrumah replied that he, too, had been "greatly concerned about the possible use of delaying tactics to interfere with the objectives which we [sic] laid down at Addis Ababa."[89]

The regionalist's conspiracy—as Ghana considered it—looked still wider. Ambassador Debrah in Addis Ababa reported that the *Voice of Ethiopia* radio had commented that the OAU "should rely upon groups like the [UAM] which have already proved their effectiveness." Debrah, knowing the precise line Nkrumah was taking at the moment, added: "My understanding is that the Addis Ababa Conference has ended all Group Organisations in Africa. I believe you should ask our Ambassador in Ivory Coast or wherever the headquarters of the so-called UAM is to make enquiries."[90]

According to Albert Tevoedjre, the former Dahomean diplomat and UAM official, UAM members were in fact bending under the pressures of the radicals, and there existed a significant division of opinion within the group about its future—which could be exploited.[91] Ghana's position was too rigid to take advantage of this. Upper Volta was perhaps the most flexible state within the group but, as its relations with Accra were rapidly deteriorating with the development of a boundary dispute, Ghana's diplomats could do nothing to influence it. The Ghanaians attempted to infiltrate the UAM's meetings, but singularly misconstrued what was occurring at them.[92]

Ghana was only skirmishing with the UAM states at this point; despite the far greater importance to her of these West African French speaking states, Ghana's real battle in 1963-1964 was against the East African Federation. Nkrumah's own dislike of regional links was of long stand-

[89] Quoted in K. B. Asante, A.A.S. to Budu-Acquah, Ghana/Conakry, 17 July 1963, CFA-48.

[90] E. M. Debrah to H. R. Amonoo, 18 June 1963, CFA-45.

[91] Albert Tevoedjre, *Pan-Africanism in Action: An Account of the UAM*, Cambridge, 1965, p. 52.

[92] Obianim, Ghana/Cotonou to K. B. Asante, A.A.S., 23 July 1963. CFA-48. *Spark*, No. 42, 27 September 1963, tried to argue that France was seeking a bargain "in which the skin of the UAM would be exchanged for the living body of the OAU," that is, that the political functions of the UAM would be abandoned in order that French influence could be extended throughout Africa, at the expense of a strong OAU. In 1964 the UAM did briefly shed its political functions (changing its name to the UAMCE), but it is doubtful that France supported the temporary conversion. See Tevoedjre, *Pan-Africanism*, p. 52.

ing, but his ideas had only crystallized as a result of his 1961 trip to the Soviet Union. In an important address shortly thereafter he had stressed that local associations, regional commonwealths, and territorial group-ings, as opposed to union government, would be "just another form of balkanisation."[93] His policy was soon implemented, at the 1962 PAFMESCA conference in Addis Ababa, where a delegation of Ghanaian militants attempted to weaken that organization by claiming supremacy for the virtually defunct, Accra-based All-African Peoples conference.[94]

By the time of the founding of the OAU, the proposed East African Federation offered the most exciting prospects of unity anywhere on the continent. On June 5, 1963, President Nyerere and Prime Minis-ters Kenyatta and Obote signed a declaration of intent which seemed to point directly to early federation. Throughout the summer, the attitude of Prime Minister Obote and Ugandan officials progressively cooled, from fear that Uganda would gain least in such a union. Moreover, "three was an awkward number," as a Tanganyikan minister de-scribed the situation. Nkrumah had worked hard at Addis Ababa in May to convince Obote that such a federation would be an obstacle to African unity. David Bosumptwi-Sam, Ghana's high commissioner in Kampala, was a personal friend of Obote, and labored throughout the summer to reinforce Ghanaian-Ugandan links. The high commission in Kampala was reinforced with an additional (and agile) diplomat, George Nipah, transferred from Dar, and by several executive officers from Flagstaff House and the Bureau of African Affairs.

Nkrumah began writing lengthy letters to the leaders involved, stating his fear that federation would be a tool of British imperialism, like the French-linked associations in West Africa, and a monumental impedi-ment to continental unity. Nyerere's reaction can be gauged by a cable from Quaison-Sackey to Nkrumah:

> I have had long discussions with President Nyerere today at his request [while Nyerere was on a visit to the U.S., U.K., Canada, Algeria, and Guinea] regarding Osagyefo's letter which President Nyerere showed me. Nyerere was openly distressed by the tone of the letter and feels that he has been misunderstood. He believes that the

[93] *Debates*, 22 January 1962, p. 8.

[94] This was in February 1962. The Ghanaians had allies there. Several delegates, in Ghana's pay, echoed the Ghanaian line. Oginga Odinga even publicly thanked Ghana for providing funds for him to attend the conference. See *Pan-African Freedom Move-ment for East, Central, and Southern Africa*, "Report of the Conference at Addis Ababa, 2-10 February 1962," Addis Ababa, Africa Dept. of the Foreign Office, for and on behalf of the PAFMECSA Secretariat, 1962, espec. pp. 52-53, 71, 57.

formation of one federal state in East Africa within the context of African Unity will further the cause of Union of African States which, as Osagyefo knows, is dear to his heart.[95]

More serious efforts than letter writing were undertaken, however. Barden was introducing agents who operated, however ineptly, throughout East Africa in attempts to penetrate Government House in Dar-es-Salaam, and to bribe organizations in Uganda that could be calculated to oppose federation. Some Ghanaian agents were recruited under a false flag.[96]

Ghanaian diplomacy in East Africa showed a "new cult of bad manners" (as Gordon Craig described Italian diplomacy under Mussolini). When Joseph Murumbi, of Kenya, suggested publicly that Tanganyika and Kenya alone might form a federation, attacking Nkrumah (by implication) for good measure, Bosumptwi-Sam replied through an advertisement in the *Uganda Argus*:

> Judging from Mr. Murumbi's career which is marked by opportunism, it is not surprising that he should have distorted and entirely perverted evaluation of African leaders of international stature and repute like Osagyefo.
> By playing to the gallery of the imperialists . . . Mr. Murumbi has proved himself an adroit puppet. His vituperations have revealed in time his neo-colonialist stand . . .[97]

Murumbi had merely noted that Nkrumah had once advocated West African Federation, and Sam quite incorrectly denied that this was ever the case. This statement was not out of line with the general character of Sam's diplomacy.

Nkrumah's attitude was a result of several factors. Until 1960 he had been a popular symbol of African liberation in East Africa; he had aided political movements there, and cultivated the leaders. It was difficult for him to accept the new situation, in which his advice and help were neither needed nor wanted. Bediako Poku, who succeeded Sam in Kampala, thought "jealousy" explained the better part of Nkrumah's attitude, and so did much of the rest of the world. True, the fear that from East Africa would emerge a more powerful leader than himself was a factor in his policy, but there were sincere ideological convictions as well. Botsio, for instance, stressed that Nkrumah genuinely believed the proposed federa-

[95] Quaison-Sackey to Nkrumah, 18 July 1963, CFA-48.
[96] Interviews: CF-29, 91.
[97] *Uganda Argus*, 28 October 1963. Professor Donald Rothchild first directed my attention to this statement.

tion to be an imperialist trap. Nkrumah had never visited East Africa, and could only compare it with the British West Africa of the late 1950's, as he remembered it.

It is obviously not Ghana's opposition to federation that caused the breakdown in the East African negotiations. As Joseph Nye notes, the Ugandans began using Ghana's interpretation of pan-Africanism to prevent the ideology of pan-Africanism "from serving as the simple directive to federation that it had been in June. No longer was the burden of proof of ideological legitimacy entirely on those who opposed federation."[98] Ghana had simply given the Ugandans an ideological basis for strengthening their own case against the Tanganyikans and Kenyans.

Ghana's real "achievement" was the lowering of its own prestige throughout Africa. Up to the time of the formation of the OAU, no East African leader had failed to take Nkrumah seriously; after this, few could. Nor did they continue to listen in silence. In December, Nyerere said, "We have heard the curious argument that the continued balkanisation of East Africa will somehow help African Unity. [Such an argument] attempts to rationalize absurdity."[99] This was only the first round.

In the long run, Ghana's fourth challenge from the founding of the OAU was the gravest. This is the question of subversion and, by implication, refugees; while in the last half of 1963 it was just becoming the principal issue between Ghana and its neighbors, it was to assume enough importance almost to wreck the OAU, and more than any other issue to contribute to Ghana's isolation in Africa.

At Addis Ababa, President Houphouet-Boigny succeeded in including in the charter a clause of "unreserved condemnation, in all its forms, of political assassination as well as of subversive activities on the part of neighbouring states or any other states." The only issue between the Ivory Coast and Ghana was that of Nkrumah's support of the ragged band of Sanwi dissidents. Houphouet's patience was nearly exhausted. Confronting Nkrumah and Botsio at the summit conference, he told them in the course of a four-hour discussion that Nkrumah would have to stop this support "if he was to have his support in the African struggle."[100] Houphouet was granting Nkrumah his last chance.

Michael Dei-Anang drafted a position paper in June on the question of the refugees, which elucidates the ambiguity (and growing hypocrisy) of Ghana's position. He noted that a new policy was needed with respect

---

[98] Joseph Nye, Jr., *Pan-Africanism and East African Integration*, Cambridge, 1965, p. 197.

[99] Republic Day Broadcast, 12 December 1963, quoted in *East African Standard*, 13 December 1963.

[100] Botsio to author, 9 August 1966.

to the freedom fighters as a result of the conference, less for those from nonindependent territories, than for those "who consider that it is their duty to ensure that popular governments . . . replace reactionary and puppet regimes in independent territories still under the control of external forces." The problem was that

> as long as conditions . . . assist the maintenance of a power-drunk minority whose welfare takes precedence over the needs of the masses . . . discontent cannot be stifled.
>
> In order, nevertheless, to preserve the spirit of unity engendered at Addis Ababa, it will be necessary to formulate a definite set of principles to govern the presence of these elements in our state. Since we spear-headed the struggle for continental union, we must be careful not to do anything to jeopardise . . . the attainment of this union.
>
> Our own example in the creation of a Socialist pattern of society . . . is the best lever for changing the reactionary conditions . . . in other parts of Africa.

Dei-Anang went on to describe the agreement between Osagyefo and Houphouet. Ghana could grant hospitality to Sanwi people, but only on condition that the government and institutions of the Ivory Coast, "which have been established by the will of the people," were respected; Ghana would give the Sanwi no material assistance and would allow no speeches or articles to be given or written against the government of the Ivory Coast. When Osagyefo had implemented these agreements, arrangements would be made for a further meeting between the two presidents at which "wider discussions for a closer understanding and integration of policies . . . can be undertaken."[101]

What does Dei-Anang's draft mean? Were the "definite set of principles" only to be formulated, or to be implemented as well? Was the Ivory Coast governed by a "power-drunk minority," or was it "established by the will of the people"? To make it acceptable to Osagyefo, all the shibboleths of his ideology had to be honored. To bring him to accept the restrictions (for such was obviously Dei-Anang's intent and interest) involved a veritable orgy of verbal gymnastics.

Nkrumah's intentions became clear soon enough. In early July, he stated to the national assembly that freedom fighters from independent states and resident in Ghana would be forbidden from doing "anything whatsoever" against the government of their country: He quickly nullified the injunction by adding, *sotto voce*, "tactical."[102] The assembly

[101] "The Problem of Freedom Fighters from Independent African States," memorandum by Michael Dei-Anang, 9 June 1963, CFA-45-46.
[102] *Debates*, 3 July 1963, and interview: Botsio and CF-84.

rang to peals of laughter, without echo in the diplomatic gallery. So began the last stage of the collision course between the two ranking leaders of West Africa.

The irony was that at this stage the refugees were doing little to "eliminate neo-colonialist influences" in Africa (as Nkrumah had said was their duty); rather they were cleverly protecting their comfortable positions in Accra. By their presence, Nkrumah both lost the opportunity to repair Ghana's links with some states and found a deterioration in relations with others. The influence he gained over the course of events in those states, through the subversion undertaken or propaganda issued by the refugees in Ghana, was marginal in almost every case.

The tactics of the refugees is best illustrated by the example of Samuel G. Ikoku, the brilliant Nigerian Marxist wanted in Nigeria for treason. Through Kojo Botsio's careful efforts, a near-working relationship was established between Ghana and Nigeria at the diplomatic level, as has been seen. In September 1963 Botsio took the unprecedented step of traveling to Lagos to heal existing wounds, and his trip was an unqualified success. Ikoku, *de facto* editor of *Spark*, had every reason to fear a rapprochement between the two states, and so when the Awolowo trial ended (shortly after Botsio's return) with a verdict against himself and other Action Group leaders, *l'Étincelle* asked "Who has bound the hands of the judge in Lagos?" *Spark* gave one answer, an insult to Lagos that was bound to ruin Botsio's efforts: "There might be disagreement as to terminology in labelling the present regime in Nigeria. One thing however seems clear. It is something agreeable to the imperialist circles in Britain."[103]

The process of reconciliation was supposed to be completed by the naming of a new Nigerian high commissioner to Ghana, Alhaji Isa Sulaiman Wali, but shortly after the Alhaji's arrival Ikoku successfully obliterated any possibility of cooperation. The dispute now revolved around Ikoku's wife, who wished to join her husband in Accra. Nigerian immigration authorities had prevented her departure, but when Prime Minister Sir Abubakar's attention was called to the incident, she was permitted to leave. Khow Richardson, the most prominent Ghanaian refugee in Nigeria, wrote an open letter to Ikoku at Flagstaff House praising the Nigerian government and damning the Ghanaian government which, in refusing to permit the departures of the families of Ghanaian refugees, had shown no similar spirit of charity. In retaliation, Ikoku wrote to Richardson, also publicly, and addressed his letter to Sir Abubakar's office. Alhaji Isa Wali gave a statement to the press

[103] *l'Etincelle*, 15 September 1963, Vol. 2, No. 2, and *Spark*, editorial no. 2, No. 40, 13 September 1963.

(not carried in the Ghanaian papers) protesting Ikoku's letter, which he called a "deplorable attempt to poison the present cordial relations" between the two governments. Ikoku *was* employed by Flagstaff House, Isa Wali pointed out, whereas Richardson had no contact with Government House in Lagos, thus making Ikoku's letter all the more insulting.[104]

Dei-Anang then summoned Isa Wali to Flagstaff House, where he accused him of prejudicing good relations by issuing such a public statement. Isa Wali retorted that the difference between the Nigerian refugees in Ghana, and the Ghanaian refugees in Nigeria, had to be pointed out. Dei-Anang disingenuously tried to convince the Nigerian high commissioner that Ikoku was not a government official, that he was an employee merely of an independent statutory organ, the Bureau of African Affairs. This was a lie, and Isa Wali knew it. From then on, "I simply tried to mark time in Ghana until the inevitable happened," he commented.[105]

By entrenching themselves in Flagstaff House, and by continuing the polemics in the press, the refugees ensured that Ghana's relations with other African governments would continue their downward spiral. The ingredients of a sophisticated policy of subversion were finally being added to the Ghanaian scene, however, as the number of refugees increased, and as relations became so bad with other states that overthrow of their regimes became a compelling means for Ghana to end its growing isolation. These other states, the intended victims, were finding in the OAU an instrument with which they could blunt the force of the Ghanaian offensive, enraging Nkrumah all the more against the organization. As a result of the challenges the OAU presented to it in four areas, Ghana had arrived at a policy by the beginning of 1964, and a strategy. The policy was continental union government. The strategy was the use of every means of propaganda, subversion, and, on occasion, diplomacy, to achieve it, and to oppose head-on any constructive effort to build anything short of it.

OAU Diplomacy, 1964:
Towards a Continental Union Government

The period of hope following the Addis Ababa conference nearly gave way to a period of despair at the beginning of 1964. The Algerians were

---

[104] See *Daily Express* (Lagos, 21 February 1964). See also statement of the Ghanaian High Commissioner, Lagos, *ibid.*, 20 February 1964, in which it was claimed that Ikoku was a "free-lance journalist." See also *Ghanaian Times*, 17 February 1964.

[105] Interview: Alhaji Isa Wali, and "Record of His Excellency's Conversation with Michael Dei-Anang, 25 February 1964," First Secretary, Nigerian High Commission/Accra to Ministry of External Affairs, Lagos. The late High Commissioner graciously permitted me to examine his correspondence with his ministry.

at war with the Moroccans, the Somalis with the Ethiopians, East African armies were in mutiny, and the French were demonstrating their willingness to intervene in Africa to protect their interests (in Gabon). Most worrisome to Nkrumah, the termination of the United Nations Command in the Congo was impending, raising the spectre of a seizure of power by General Mobutu or Moise Tshombe.[106] Behind the frenzy of Ghana's diplomacy in Africa during the next eight months was Nkrumah's fear that the imperialists were reversing the direction of the African liberation movement through their interventions on the continent, and that if union government were not immediately realized, it would never be. As a result of the first threat, Ghana began pressing once again for the formation of an African high command, and, as a result of the second, accelerated still more the drive toward union government. The growing realization that Ghana was not in the continent's mainstream led to further attacks on the liberation committee. Ghana's reaction to these three perceived threats drove her prestige down still lower.

The Defense of Africa. At the end of October 1963, the OAU Defence Commission met in Accra, and Kofi Baako, Ghana's defense minister, outlined Ghana's four proposals. These were for a supreme command headquarters "responsible for the Defence of the Union"; for regional headquarters; for a "Joint Services Strategic Reserve Command"; and for a joint intelligence organization. Nkrumah was not actually envisaging the command any differently in 1963 than he had in 1960, with respect to the privileged position that he felt Ghana must play within: in October he was actually thinking about having Algerian and Ghanaian troops alone replace the UN Command in Léopoldville.[107] Few of the OAU delegates in Accra were interested in Baako's proposals in any case, the more so when he tried to enhance the proposals with talk of a "strike force," and other impracticable designs. As was pointed out, there could not be a union army before there was a union. Ghana was told once again that it could not get at the back door what had been refused at the front.[108]

Yet the need for defense cooperation in Africa was real. Nkrumah, characteristically thinking of optimal solutions for Africa's problems, was right to press for a high command. His military officers were convinced that his plans were feasible, a conviction reinforced by the similar

[106] Nkrumah's predictions on this score were correct. See Nkrumah to U Thant, 17 December 1963, in "All-African Force for the Congo," Accra, 1963, p. 4.

[107] The proposals are summarized in *OAU*, "Council of Ministers, Lagos Conference, 24-29 February 1964," Lagos 1964, CFA-conf. See also Nkrumah to Botsio, 2 October 1963, in Nkrumah, *Challenge of the Congo*, p. 231.

[108] Interview: CF-31.

views of their fellow Nigerian officers.[109] The proposals were, however, merely referred to the heads of state who were not to meet until July 1964, nine months later. This was not wholly due to the forces of imperialism within the OAU; the manner in which Ghana pursued policy lost her even the advantage of idealism, and her diagnosis was right for the symptoms but not for their cause.

Thus, after the East African mutinies of January 1964—which accentuated Nkrumah's sense of urgency—Ghana's envoy in Dar-es-Salaam, a former trade unionist, translated Nkrumah's frustrations into more bad-mannered diplomacy. Nyerere later described it this way: "We experienced army mutinies in East Africa and had to go through the humiliation of asking for assistance from a former colonial power. But in my country . . . the Ambassador of a brotherly African State celebrated and rejoiced, and I am forced to request that he be removed. . . . And what was the reason for this rejoicing at the humiliation of a fellow African country? Union government."[110]

Nkrumah saw Nyerere's difficulties as an opportunity to underline the fragility of separately constituted African states or federations. The *Ghanaian Times* editorialized that "the concept of regional federation as a substitute for continental African unity has been largely destroyed by the sequence of events in East Africa."[111] Nyerere, on the other hand, saw the occasion as an opportunity to strengthen African solidarity, by asking that "the problems arising from the mutiny . . . be dealt with in a way which will foster, and not harm, the common objectives of African Unity." He requested an extraordinary foreign minister's session in Dar-es-Salaam. Premiers Obote and Kenyatta did not join him in making the request, though their armies had also experienced mutinies.

Botsio's instructions were to press for a high command, and he and his deputy, the Rev. Stephan Dzirasa, both claim that in a private meeting with Nyerere they were assured that this would not be resented. Botsio and Nyerere were friends, and Nyerere would have known that Botsio was bound by instructions. Nyerere's opening words to the conference make clear, however, that he drew a distinction between Botsio's personal position and the Ghanaian delegation's brief from Nkrumah: "The presence of British troops in Tanganyika is a fact which is too easily exploited by those who wish to divide Africa or to dominate Africa (applause). Already it is clear that there are some people who will

[109] Interview: CF-51, office of the G.O.C., by permission of Maj.-Gen., the late Emmanuel Kotoka.
[110] Speech at Cairo OAU conference, July 1964. Quoted in *BBC*, IV, No. 1611, 22 July 1964.
[111] 4 February 1964.

seize upon this opportunity to play upon natural fears of neo-colonialism, in the hope of sowing seeds of suspicion between the different African States."[112]

In the conference discussions, Oscar Kambona, Tanganyika's minister of external affairs, made clear that the high command was not on the agenda, and repeatedly underlined that the conference had one single responsibility, namely, to decide whether African troops would be offered to replace the British forces that were keeping order in Dar-es-Salaam at that moment. Botsio interjected, however, that he did not "think it consistent with our dignity or integrity to bring back the troops belonging to powers which were formerly occupying the territory as colonial powers," something which was not in question, and he reopened the question of a high command, which had been closed in Accra the previous October: "Since this organisation was established in Addis Ababa last year we have already had one such meeting to deal with this sort of question, and now we have this resolution before us. Therefore we must provide for any such contingency, because if we are to be summoned together frequently for such purposes, I think we should be a laughing stock."[113] He then proposed that the conference add the question of a high command to the agenda for the forthcoming regular foreign ministers' meeting, scheduled for the end of that same month in Lagos. Uganda, seeking to embarrass Tanganyika for having summoned the special conference, alone supported Ghana. Most delegates felt that the rules of procedure prohibited any discussion of Botsio's proposal at an extraordinary conference; even Algeria opposed Ghana: "We cannot anticipate situations which might occur in any part of Africa without knowing the details."[114] Nyerere got his African troops—from Nigeria—and by submitting so painful a national problem to the OAU he added to his own prestige in Africa.

The Ghanaian press remained as concerned as ever about imperial ambitions in East Africa. In early March, Duncan Sandys, the British Commonwealth secretary, traveled through these countries, and the *Ghanaian Times* commented that he was "hopping around East Africa with many wares in his neo-colonialist basket. . . . There is the grand design of an East African Federation with Britain holding the purse strings. We can't mince words about this whole exercise. It is sinister. It is outrageous. It is neo-colonialism in its most venomous form. And the more we view it, the more we wonder whether the mutinees which have

---

[112] *OAU*, "Second Extraordinary Session of Council of Ministers, ECM/1, Confidential Verbatim Record," February 1964, p. 4, CFA-conf. I am grateful to Catherine Hoskyns for permitting me to examine her copy of this conference report.
[113] *Ibid.*, pp. 51, 12-20.   [114] *Ibid.*, p. 41.

339

supplied the pretext for these moves, were not really inspired from Whitehall."[115] Ironically it was Tanganyika that refused all offers of British military support; Uganda, Ghana's ally, accepted a British military training mission.

By the time of the regular OAU foreign ministers' conference, Ghana had dissipated much of the potential support for a high command. Ghana pressed for it every chance it had at Lagos, but the proposal became a political football passed from committee to committee. As a Kenyan delegate said at one point, "the Hon. Delegate of Ghana can wait until we come to this part of the item before giving us his views," and when this point came, the chairman pointed out that "there is no question of the establishment of [an] African High Command" but that recommendations for the study of it were merely on the floor.[116]

It was a delicate question; members wondered what function a high command would have with respect to internal disorders. The Ghanaians stated that the command would have no role to play in such circumstances—although its principal justification was "that in some of the countries the young armies mutinied." It was a very confused presentation and, in the end, the Ghanaian motion (that its proposal be examined by a special subcommittee set up to examine political questions) was rejected; it had three votes supporting, six against, and fifteen abstentions.[117] The one journalist informed on the proceedings of the conference (writing in *Africa 1964*) said that "the O.A.U. showed masterly diplomacy in shelving a point of discord," and he was right.[118]

Ghana's other causes of the moment fared no better. By this time, other states had joined Ghana in criticizing the OAU liberation committee. But while it is not clear that Ghana's criticism had caused them to speak out, there is no doubt that Ghana's criticism was affecting its own reputation in Africa, and bringing others to the committee's defense. "Delegates were astonished by the unjustified attack made by Ghana on the activities of the Committee," said the summary of discussions (at Lagos) on the committee's work.[119]

The Ghanaian delegation at first tried to claim that *Spark*—in which the main attacks on the committee had appeared—was not the voice of Ghana's government, and that, in any case, "juridically the disclaimer of the Ghana delegation is sufficient." Having disclaimed the attack of *Spark*, the delegation repeated the paper's charges, and added new ones.

[115] Editorial, 3 March 1964.
[116] *OAU*, "Council of Ministers, Lagos Conference, 24-29 February 1964," Lagos, 1964, CFA-conf., pp. 294-95.
[117] *Ibid.*, pp. 289, 292.   [118] *Africa 1964*, No. 6, 20 March 1964.
[119] *OAU*, Lagos, 1964, p. 121.

The Verbatim Report of the Liberation Committee had shown that "some Distinguished Delegates were scared of the word military assistance," one Ghanaian said, and in the colorful idiom of OAU politics he added a more serious complaint: "This co-ordinating Committee became, as we feared, a kindly old lady who hired out during the night her rooms to various men and their girl friends for an hour each couple and yet powerfully insisted that nothing immoral took place in her rooms."[120]

Ghana had not contributed to the committee but contributions, the Ghanaian delegates maintained, were voluntary. Oscar Kambona noted that every country but four had contributed, and three of those had promised their help. He hoped that "before the end of the conference" the Ghanaians would announce that they, too, would contribute. At Addis Ababa, a Ghanaian had said he knew the committee would fail—from the moment it was appointed, he added—so Ghana was attempting to make its prophecy self-fulfilling.[121] Other delegations mounted an attack. Liberia said that if countries felt they had no obligation to make voluntary contributions, "then we are about to have a precedence in this Organisation which might have the ultimate effect of running it on a rock."[122] Not even Uganda supported Ghana on these questions, as it had a vested interest in the committee—it was a member.

The attack was sufficient for the Ghana delegation to say, on whose authority it is not clear, that "the Ghana Government has already decided to make a contribution. But for one reason or another the money has not been paid in yet."[123] No such decision had been made. Ghana's position on this issue clearly conditioned the response Ghana elicited with its most important proposals at Lagos, for union government. These, presented in various guises, met the same fate as did its proposal for a high command.

At first Ghana was direct, but the mood on the first day was such that little time was wasted disposing of Ghana's scheme. "Continental Government was rejected at the Addis Ababa Conference," said the Liberian delegate. The Sierra Leoneans had a face-saving solution, in proposing "that a Committee be set up to examine possible political action which will further promote the unity and solidarity of the African states." Guinea explained that the proposition as it now stood "was not one for continental government but for the setting up of a Study Committee to study ways and means of promoting African Unity."[124]

Two days later the political committee met to consider this proposal of the plenary session. Botsio said that action was needed "in line with

120 *Ibid.*, pp. 122-24.   121 *Ibid.*, pp. 126-29.   122 *Ibid.*, p. 141.
123 *Ibid.*, p. 128.   124 *Ibid.*, pp. 349-50.

the uncompromising mood of the African masses for more effective political and diplomatic actions." What this would be was not in doubt, namely, "some sort of machinery by which political direction can be given." Tanganyika favored Sierra Leone's proposition, but on the limited interpretation of the committee's brief—that ways of reinforcing the article of the charter which called for political and diplomatic *cooperation* could be investigated. Algeria supported the creation of the committee, too, "with the very precise task of studying the items which we have entrusted to them." The Committee was to endure only for the length of the conference, otherwise only Brazzaville would have been willing to support it. It was established.[125]

In the new committee's discussions, the Ghanaians furthered Botsio's suggestion that "some sort of machinery" was needed by an analogy with the Security Council of the United Nations. This was a major—and risky —concession by the Ghanaians, as Nkrumah did not accept so "minimal" a demand for another sixteen months. Africa was not ready for this, either. Senegal said it "sounds very good . . . but surely the Organisation of African Unity has already suffered too much from the spectacular tactics employed by some, particularly those who were not anxious in the first place that the O.A.U. should be formed. . . . Already it is rumoured that there is to be a future Security Council within the O.A.U. within which two or three countries represented here dream of having the power of veto." Africa should stop being afraid, the Senegalese said. It should admit that it is not ready for a continental union government, toward which Ghana's *Comité de Vigilance Politique* was an intermediary step.[126]

Still the Ghanaians continued. Botsio said that "We have taken upon our shoulder the heavy burden of uniting the various African states. . . . There is no reason to amend the Charter, but it must be made dynamic."[127] It was this contradiction in terms that came under attack. Tunisia pointed out that the charter made "no mention of executive powers, for the organization as such." Even the Ugandans were opposed, as their legal expert had found that the suggestion involved supranational considerations which the charter did not allow. Ghana, in the end, only obtained a resolution noting that the committee had had inadequate time to consider its brief, and thus member states were requested "to submit to the Provisional Secretary-General any suggestions which they feel may promote the unity and solidarity of the African continent."[128]

In his general report to the Lagos conference, the provisional secretary-general observed that the OAU had "become overnight the

125 *Ibid.*, pp. 89-91.   126 *Ibid.*, pp. 235-36.   127 *Ibid.*, pp. 237-39.
128 *Ibid.*, pp. 239-40.

authentic voice of Africa."[129] While it was the heyday of the OAU, it was "now the fashion to disparage anything Ghanaian," as one Ghanaian delegate said at Lagos.[130] One reason this was so is obvious: Ghana was fighting the OAU.

The *Ghanaian Times*, nonetheless, headlined that "Delegates [at Lagos] favour Union Government."[131] There was thus no way to pass the unmistakable lessons on to Nkrumah. Ghana could have had more success than it did on such issues as nonalignment and Rhodesia had it not fought the OAU on the issues of union government and the high command, which were what mattered in Flagstaff House.

The Eve of the Summit: Ideology and Diplomacy. Between the Lagos conference and the July summit of the heads of state in Cairo, the campaign for union government and revolution in Africa gathered momentum in Accra. Any shortcoming of the OAU was attributed to the fact that the organization had a diplomatic basis, rather than one of organic political unity of the states. The failure of the organization to solve all of Africa's problems was similarly accounted for. The lack of progress in liberation in Africa was, by equally loose logic, tied to the failure to effect a union government. Before May 1963, the *Ghanaian Times* wrote, the anti-colonial struggle "commanded a sense of urgency because it enjoyed clear direction and unqualified inspiration from individual African capitals, mainly Accra, Cairo, and Algiers. . . . Now . . . the anti-colonial struggle has been . . . linked to a world-wide diplomatic jamboree." The last stage of the liberation struggle, it said, "is hardly negotiable. The price is blood and bullets."[132]

H. M. Basner, the South African Marxist who had recently joined the inner circle of Flagstaff House, attacked Kenneth Kaunda for promising to establish "a centre in Lusaka to give administrative training to people from surrounding countries still engaged in a struggle for independence," as opposed, presumably, to "blood and bullets"; this was 3 April 1964, before Zambia's independence. But the diplomatic bias of Kaunda's position was explained in terms of the claim that he and his party had not had to fight for independence; the British government had dissolved the Federation of Rhodesia and Nyasaland, as a result of pressure of "the African Revolution," meaning, of course, Ghana.[133]

What in concrete terms was Ghana doing, on the other hand, to further the "African Revolution"? By early 1964, the Bureau of African

---

[129] *Ibid.*, p. 28.   [130] *Ibid.*, p. 122.   [131] 25 February 1964.
[132] "Decolonization: Government of African Union Can Make It Effective," *Ghanaian Times*, 4 July 1964.
[133] H. M. Basner, "What Does Dr. Kaunda Mean," *Spark*, 3 April 1964.

Affairs had reached a new prominence in Accra. Its own subversion training camps, however, had no impressive accomplishments; since the Russian trainers had left in mid-1962, the Ghanaians were forced to rely on their own men who, by all accounts, were of limited competence. Not long after the Addis Ababa conference Nkrumah had, all the same, given Barden sufficient power to put men in Ghanaian missions anywhere on the continent to circumvent the work of the professional diplomats. By early 1964, Barden had a large number of operatives in the field on whom Nkrumah increasingly relied for the implementation of his Africa policy. What were the Bureau men doing that was so important? Was their role functional, or was it simply to titillate Nkrumah's fancy?

One example that shows both the tension between diplomats and militants, and the actual work of the militants themselves, is a report from some of Barden's men in Northern Rhodesia (as the territory then was). Here, there were old and solid contacts, and every reason to hope to see an ally emerge. The government in Northern Rhodesia was going to have many vacancies in its civil service following independence, Barden's agents wrote, owing to the departure of many expatriates. Ghana could help to train Zambians to fill these places. But the acting prime minister, Kamanga "has visited Ghana before; this man is not 'so sure' about Ghana, for he said so. . . . He asserted, 'the source of our information about Ghana is through the press and radio. We sometimes neglect or waive some of these things . . . but at times we get so confused that we don't know what to believe. . . .' I explained to him the present role of the imperialist press against Ghana." The responsible official at the African Affairs Secretariat observed the following, largely on internal evidence:

> The activists do not use any unusual channel of communication. They get their information and make their contacts through ministers, etc. To approach these persons they style themselves ambassadors (that is why they are addressed your "Excellency"). . . . Therefore their work does not supplement that of normal diplomacy. They try to practice modern diplomacy and are ill-equipped hence the troubles with the execution of our policy. It is also significant that the discussion here is about civil service matters about which the activists know very little. The Acting Prime Minister is bound to see through this and lose confidence in our ability to help.[134]

[134] Report of BAA on Northern Rhodesia, 16 February 1964; minute, A.A.S., 16 May 1964, CFA-39.

The reaction in Northern Rhodesia can be guessed from the action of the regular, not the acting prime minister. Nkrumah, on the advice of Barden, tried to appoint one of Barden's activists as Ghana's first high commissioner in Lusaka. Kenneth Kaunda would not permit the British to give the *agrément*.

Barden had become an increasingly powerful influence on African policy. When reports appeared that Kaunda wished to establish diplomatic links with Pretoria (as Ghana had wished to do between 1957 and 1960), Barden wrote to Nkrumah that such a move would play "directly into the hands of a vicious circle comprising U.S.A., Britain, West Germany, and Verwoerd's apartheid Government," and urged him to take the matter up with Kaunda. Nkrumah wrote Kaunda that "I would like to believe that there is no foundation in it, and that it is only symptomatic of the methods of our enemies who seek to create confusion within our ranks . . . I would like to believe that my reaction can be confirmed."[135] Kaunda had come to Accra often for inspiration in the early days of his country's struggle for independence, and Nkrumah was unable to accept that he was now dealing with the head of the government of a soon-to-be-independent state. Admittedly it was different to press for relations with South Africa at this time, compared with the earlier period when Ghana sought to do so. Kaunda had a difficult problem to resolve, in relation to the racist regimes, however, and, particularly in view of Nkrumah's early efforts vis-à-vis South Africa, it was tactless to offer Kaunda such gratuitous advice. Thus were potential allies lost.

Kojo Botsio and such temperate and informed diplomats as K. B. Asante were not ignorant of the trend, but were often ignorant of the specifics of Barden's policy. This is exactly what Nkrumah intended. They were the men who had to plead with foreign diplomats in Accra to ignore the attacks in the press, and who had to point to the existence of reservoirs of goodwill for Nigeria, Senegal, America, and other countries in Ghana. Nkrumah well understood that the less they knew about Barden's work, the more convincingly would their denials of Ghanaian subversion be made. The fact that Botsio (rather than a radical) remained foreign minister meant that he had to be listened to on occasions, but his attempts to affect Africa policy in any fundamental way got nowhere. He tried to fire Barden without success, and he could not even keep informed of the regular work of the African Affairs Secretariat and the African Affairs Committee.

[135] A. K. Barden to Nkrumah, 27 April 1964; Nkrumah to Kaunda, 30 April 1964, CFA-39.

The overall effect of the African Affairs Secretariat was no more healthy than that of the Bureau. In attempting to counteract the Bureau's influence, its head, Michael Dei-Anang, contributed significantly to the strain in relations between Ghana and other African states. A pattern had emerged in Dei-Anang's discussions with African ambassadors. For instance, after the Bureau's journals had attacked one country during the autumn of 1963, that country's ambassador was instructed by his own foreign ministry to protest vigorously. Dei-Anang asked him why he bothered with such "bourgeois imperialist diplomatic formalities," denied he or the president had authorized or even seen the articles, and he ended by claiming that the Bureau was an independent agency and refused to accept the protest.[136]

Certainly, none of the diplomats in Accra had any illusions about the relationship between *Spark* and Nkrumah, but the lack of an explicit relationship permitted Dei-Anang to skate on the thin ice officially maintained between the two. When one government begins to act paranoiacally, it is sometimes better to preserve diplomatic illusions. Had Dei-Anang not continued to deny the existence of a relationship between the two, other governments would have been forced to accept the articles as formal statements of Ghanaian government policy, and react accordingly. Hypocrisy can hardly be added to insult indefinitely, however.

It was in these circumstances that Ghana's drive for continental union government went forward. The decision not to relent was reinforced from several directions, one of which was the position of the continental labor movements. Since 1961, John Tettegah and the Malian labor leaders had sought to make the All-African Trade Union Federation something more than a paper organization and, in June 1964, at its second conference (in Bamako) they succeeded. One hundred delegates, from 36 countries, representing 37 national unions, gathered to plan strategy against colonialists, neocolonialists, and imperialists; radicalism was triumphant. After the conference more than 60 of the delegates came to Accra where they were entertained in "the historic Ideological Hut at Flagstaff House."[137]

Hope also derived from new successes in presidential diplomacy. Messemba-Debat, who had overthrown the Abbey Fulbert Youlou in Brazzaville, visited Ghana for five days in May and found wide agreement on radical issues with Nkrumah. He did not commit the Congo

---

[136] Interview: CF-43.

[137] *Ghanaian Times*, 17 June 1964. See also *AATUF*, "Reports and Resolutions," Second Conference of the AATUF, Bamako, 10-14 June 1964, Accra, 1964. See I. Wallerstein, *Africa, The Politics of Unity*, New York, 1967, pp. 193ff, for a thorough discussion of the role of AATUF.

to the immediate creation of a union government but Nkrumah, for his part, was convinced he had a new ally.[138]

Sir Albert Margai, Sierra Leone's new prime minister, also became an ally. He was interested in maximizing his own power in Freetown, and thought he could learn much from Ghana's leader. In mid-June, Botsio and Amonoo traveled to Freetown to give him a message, and its importance was underlined by the status of its carriers. Margai agreed to assist in the struggle to create union government, though it is not possible to believe that sincere ideological convictions were involved. Even the new state of Malawi, which became independent on the eve of the Cairo conference, was seen as a potential ally. A plane-load of Ghanaians, including Krobo Edusei and 32 members of the police band, traveled to Blantyre for Dr. Banda's celebration.[139]

The most remarkable development in Ghana's drive toward union government was within Flagstaff House itself. What if the government were not formed at Cairo? Ghana could not wait forever, it was argued, and so it should form a nucleus of the continental government with Mali, Algeria, and Upper Volta, which would give concrete demonstration of the advantages union brought, presumably as the Ghana-Guinea-Mali union was thought to have done three years earlier. It was not considered relevant that at this time Ghana had an increasingly bitter border dispute with Upper Volta, which made impossible the geographic contiguity sought: so Nkrumah would have to eat up Upper Volta on his way to Bamako and Algiers.[140]

Finally, union government was the subject of dedicated planning in various circles in Accra. Economists and editorialists wrote lengthy articles showing why union had to be accompanied by Socialism: "for on a laissez-faire basis . . . a big state like Nigeria or the Congo would become the centre of capitalist investments from abroad [from which] the tariff-free zones of the rest of Africa [could be penetrated]."[141] The final result of union government, a united and strong Africa, was vividly described in the press by scholars at the University.

In July Tshombe became premier of the Congo. An imperialist dagger had indeed been thrust into the heart of Africa. But now there was

[138] Interview: Botsio.
[139] See *Ghanaian Times*, 4 July 1964.
[140] Interview: CF-24, 3 July 1964, A.A.S. Upper Volta accused Ghana of demarking the border in its favor, and its foreign minister made a bitter speech at the Cairo OAU conference denouncing Ghana. See *OAU*, "First Regular OAU Conference," Council of Ministers, verbatims, pp. 71-89. It would appear that Upper Volta was in the right. The border was officially demarcated in 1968, and Ghana made the concessions then that Upper Volta had demanded in 1964. See also Tettegah to Nkrumah, 23 September 1964, in *Trade Union Congress, Ghana*, "Trade Unions in Chains," 1966.
[141] *Ghanaian Times*, 8 June 1964.

347

a remedy, the African revolution: *Consciencism* was its scripture; Kwame Nkrumah, Osagyefo of Africa, its high priest; "union government," its litany. Michael Dei-Anang, head of the African Affairs Secretariat, published a new poem, "Kwame Nkrumah—A Shaft of Light."[142]

While the ideological fires blazed in Accra, at least some Ghanaian diplomats, engaged in the "diplomatic jamboree," continued to concern themselves with such mundane things as the national interest. One interesting case illustrating the handicaps under which Ghana's diplomats labored in this period is the negotiations with Senegal for a trade agreement, which came to their unhappy termination at the same time as the Cairo conference.

The Ghanaian representatives in Dakar sought to use every channel to develop ties between the two countries which was, if nothing else, reciprocation of Senegal's expressed interest. Dr. Foli, the ambassador, wrote Nkrumah shortly after presenting his credentials in June 1962: "During the presentation, President Senghor expressed a strong desire to sign a commercial agreement with Ghana and has asked me to tell Osagyefo of his preparedness to send a delegation to Accra for this purpose. Please, allow me to convey to you my best wishes for Osagyefo's well being. I am, Your comrade in the interest of Africa."[143] By October Foli had received no indication of interest from Ghana, though "the matter was raised again by President Senghor who informed me that members of his Cabinet have unanimously agreed to sign a trade agreement with Ghana."[144]

There were compelling reasons for such an agreement, more from Ghana's side than Senegal's. In the first quarter of 1962, over half of Ghana's fish imports came from Senegal, while Ghana exported almost nothing to Senegal.[145] Foli was sufficiently embarrassed by the delay to tell reporters in Dakar that negotiations were soon to be forthcoming, "to make them feel Ghana is not discriminating against Senegal." Accra did not get the point, for proposals and counterproposals that were soon advanced by Senegal got nowhere. Nothing further was done until mid-1963, when Senegal again pressed for an agreement.[146]

Nor was progress made at this time. For one thing, Senegalese fishermen who held import licenses in Ghana were not allowed to remit foreign

---

[142] *Ibid.*, 1 July 1964.   [143] Foli to Nkrumah, 27 June 1962, CFA-31.
[144] Foli to P. S., A.A.S., 6 October 1962, CFA-31.
[145] P. S., Finance and Trade, to P. S., A.A.S., 24 July 1962, CFA-31.
[146] Reported in *Daily Graphic*, Accra, 5 October 1962. See Foli to P. S., A.A.S., 8 November 1962, for Foli's justification for his action. CFA-31.

currency from Ghana, although they were entitled to it. The ministry of trade in Ghana, in its now normal muddle with ex-Ambassador Djin as minister, thought the Senegalese government was engaged merely in "debt collection on behalf of overseas suppliers" (as if this were not its responsibility in such circumstances). K. B. Asante, as usual, tried to clear up the difficulties and suggested that "deeper issues" were involved, including "hoarding"[147]—which had become a fact of Ghanaian life.

Ghana then began quibbling, as was inevitable where no political will existed. Senegal proposed 5 November 1963 for negotiations, but Ghana made no move, because Senegal had not formally accepted Ghana's proposals in principle. A Ghanaian diplomat in Dakar wrote the African Affairs Secretariat that "One would have thought that by proposing the fifth of November . . . and Dakar for the opening of negotiations, the Government of Senegal had by implications already accepted our proposals as basis for negotiations."[148] A memo in reply did not help. Ghana was "as keen as Senegal to have a trade agreement," but everything had to be explicit. On the other hand, it was gratuitously added that, "As to pressing for a formal invitation, I would not myself insist too much. The idea first came from the Senegalese . . . but that is no reason why we should make it appear that Dakar is begging us to conclude a trade agreement."[149] It could not appear otherwise. The Ghanaians did not go to Dakar, and it was finally left to the Senegalese to ask if they could come to Accra.

The delay this time was for important reasons. Ghana now demanded that a payments agreement also be concluded, using Ghanaian currency, although it was known from experience that this presented special difficulties for a country with convertible currency guaranteed abroad. Foli was, by this time, angry.

> I would like to observe that in the interests of African Unity, this negotiation should not be delayed more than is necessary. The opinion which prevails in Senegal, even among the ordinary people is that Ghana advocates African Unity but is not willing to sign a trade agreement with Senegal. They admire our efforts but these little setbacks make them feel that they are factitious. . . . The time has now come for us, in the interest of our Union Government, to get around the African states not only by words but by deeds.[150]

[147] P. S., ministry of trade, to K. B. Asante, P. S., A.A.S., 30 October 1963, and Asante to P. S., ministry of trade, 7 November 1963, CFA-31-32.
[148] Head of Chancery, Ghana/Dakar, to P. S., A.A.S., 20 February 1964, CF-32.
[149] Memo of B. G. Godwyll, MFA, 4 March 1964, CFA-32.
[150] Foli to P. S., A.A.S., 23 July 1964, CFA-32.

Exactly three days earlier, in Cairo, when Nkrumah had persisted in raising the issue of union government through back door and side door, despite continual defeat, Senghor had commented: "I think we have already pronounced ourselves on the fact that we cannot, at present, form a Pan-African Government. So if, each time, we go back to each item, and indirectly raise the question of a pan-African government, we will never finish. . . . Let us, if we so wish, once again discuss the pan-African government. . . . [But] We will not build Africa if, every time we are beaten, we try to bring the problem up again."[151]

The other side of this coin was simply that, by the end of 1964, Senghor knew that he himself was beaten in his attempt to get a trade agreement. Negotiations were put aside, and the Senegalese concluded that there were other ways to build African unity than by trying to convince Ghana to sign a trade agreement. In 1965, Ghana imported £58,000 of commodities from Senegal; its exports there were worth £120.

The Cairo Conference. Botsio arrived in Cairo in mid-July for the foreign ministers' meeting, with inflexible instructions to press for union government and a high command. In the debate on union government, Botsio argued that Africa had underestimated the neocolonialist structure of the former colonial powers, and Africa had, in countering the threat, achieved nothing more than the Latin American states with the OAS—"with only paper co-ordination." "The President of Ghana," he warned, "cannot forever keep silent about this dangerous position."

> Some people also maintain that a union government of Africa is not practicable. It is difficult to see what is meant by such a statement. . . . The Ghanaian proposals . . . are easier, cheaper, and more effective to implement than the numerous commissions, meeting often and only issuing reports. . . . Our draft constitution emphasises that under a Union Government, the sovereignty of individual states will be preserved and in fact strengthened. There is therefore no purpose in any Member State hesitating, regarding the establishment of a Union Government.[152]

Did Botsio take his *simpliste* formulae seriously? None of his colleagues did, but they replied with tact, in various ways trying to bury the issue. Mongi Slim noted the "hesitation" in beginning discussion, and cautioned that "silence on such an important matter might well give the

---

[151] *OAU,* "First Regular OAU Conference of Heads of State," AHSG/PUS (I), verbatims, 20 July 1964, p. 27.

[152] *Ibid.,* CM (III) (L)/SR.2; First Committee (Political), 14 July 1964, pp. 2-3.

impression that it is agreement on the immediate creation of an African government." But when they did begin Botsio was quick to suggest that the ministers only take note of the proposal, for no one was more embarrassed than he.[153] Alas for Botsio, the discussion had only begun.

Malagasy wondered how the government could be reconciled with an "increase in sovereignty"; Senegal and Dahomey wanted regional planning first. Guinea tried to salvage the concept of ultimate union, but went no further. Cameroun's foreign minister, however, would not allow Guinea's minister to save Botsio's face: The question had been discussed at Lagos, and had not had adequate study, let alone agreement, he said. Africa needed cooperation, not "fictitious solidarity." He urged the ministers not to wash their hands of the matter by passing the proposal on to the heads of state. For "What have you washed your hands of? After all, it is our interests that are at stake. Is Africa to play this dangerous game and dabble in hypocrisy?" The proposal, he suggested, could be registered at the OAU's secretariat and studied when "African solidarity" had begun. Algeria, like Guinea, tried to help Ghana, and went furthest in advocating union as an ultimate goal. The U.A.R. executed the *coup de grâce*. From this point in the conference the Egyptians used the proposal of a special "communication committee" (in fact already provided for in the charter) as a diversionary technique, probably by design and, certainly, in effect.[154]

Botsio finally chose to ignore the near-universal rejection of his proposal, and proceeded "to express our sincere thanks to all those who have spoken very warmly of Ghana and of our leader," a speech apparently designed for Nkrumah's *post facto* approval. Finally the Chairman, Kenyama Chiume of Malawi, appointed a committee of Ghana, Togo, Liberia, and Tunisia to draft a report for the heads of state.[155]

Nkrumah had ample warning of the conference's mood. For reasons already suggested he was in no mood to compromise, and his left wing encouraged him at each opportunity. On July 26th he thus delivered what was, in the circumstances, the most trite, gratuitous, and insulting speech he had ever given. Every argument that delegates had repeatedly heard from Ghana was dragged out, and given forth in a steady ring of clichés. All of his direst predictions had been fulfilled. Union government had to come immediately, and then every African problem would be solved. The conference should not appoint a permanent secretary-general, nor should it choose a permanent headquarters. No, "the status quo should remain," because union government, he implied, was coming whether they liked it or not. He concluded his speech by sug-

[153] *Ibid.*, p. 9.   [154] *Ibid.*, pp. 17-36.   [155] *Ibid.*, p. 42.

gesting that if the OAU were not ready to establish the union government immediately, "those of us who are ready to do so" could go away from Cairo "having agreed to the establishment of a Union Government of Africa."

"Public speeches are a dangerous diplomatic weapon: they hit someone, but usually the wrong party," A.J.P. Taylor wrote. President Julius Nyerere listened to the speech and, after Nkrumah's attacks on the proposed East Africa federation and what Nyerere thought was an accusation that Tanganyika was an imperialist agent, decided that enough damage had been done. In the sessions remaining before his own speech he was seen writing, obviously recasting his speech.[156]

According to Botsio, Nkrumah's own speech had been reconstructed in part at the last minute; thus several references in it were ambiguous. As one result, Nyerere misread Nkrumah's attack on the liberation committee. Nyerere was right in saying that the only reason Ghana had criticized the committee was that the Addis Ababa conference "had committed the unforgivable crime of not including Ghana on the Committee." Nkrumah—and Nyerere quoted—had said:

> The choice of the Congo as a training base for freedom fighters was a logical one and there was every reason to accept the offer of the Congolese Government to provide offices and accommodation for the representatives of the Liberation *Committee* [i.e. movements]. Africa's freedom fighters should not, however, have been exposed to the espionage, intrigues, frustrations and disappointments which they have experienced in the last 8 months. What would be the result of entrusting the training of freedom fighters against imperialism into the hands of an imperialist agent?[157]

Nyerere incorrectly concluded that Nkrumah believed that the headquarters of the liberation *committee* should have been in Léopoldville, and had instead been located in Dar-es-Salaam, a place of "espionage and intrigue" (with freedom fighters trained, at that, by an "imperialist agent").[158] Nkrumah had referred only to the Congo in this section of the speech, and had meant to say "Liberation *Movements*," as indicated in the quoted passage. His mistake made Nyerere's misunderstanding

[156] Interview: Botsio.

[157] Quoted in *BBC*, IV, No. 1611, 22 July 1964.

[158] Nkrumah's speech, as quoted by Nyerere, by OAU transcripts, and by *Spark*, says "COMMITTEE" at the bracketed point in the quotation. The official version of the speech, "The Quest for a United Africa," Accra, 1964 (printed after the conference), uses the word "MOVEMENTS" at the crucial passage. There is no question that Nkrumah meant "movements," by all accounts. Nkrumah obviously knew the "committee" was headquartered in Dar.

natural, although Nyerere's reading of it is contradicted on internal evidence.[159] Yet there was enough in Nkrumah's speech that Nyerere did get right to make this confusion almost negligible; certainly most African governments at the time were not interested in the clarification.

What Nyerere stopped by his speech was the politeness about union government. Tanganyika had, as he pointed out, practiced unity by uniting with Zanzibar; less "preaching" about unity was needed. He mocked union government as the panacea for every difficulty that Africa encountered, and also added his own invective: "to cap this whole series of absurdities, after all the wonderful arguments against unity in East Africa, we are now told again, at this very rostrum, that those who are ready should go ahead and unite. Those who are ready should now go ahead and unite. Now we have the permission to go ahead. . . . If I were a cynic, I would say we of the United Republic of Tanganyika and Zanzibar are ready. I would ask Ghana to join our United Republic. But I am not a cynic."

Nyerere's suggestion was no less logically compelling than any of the long line of Nkrumah's proposals, and now they were publicly declared to be nonsense. Nyerere had merely said that the Emperor wore no clothes. The most significant fact is that it was said by a member of *Spark*'s "Group 1," by a "Radical African Nationalist." The speech was also significant as an opening of the sluice-gate for anti-Ghana feelings on many issues throughout Africa, and it signaled the beginning of the last stage of an "anti-Nkrumah offensive" that was gaining support across the continent.

Nkrumah had been severely humiliated among his peers. Nonetheless, he remained an African head of state, and the group was learning how to channel conflict; it decided to hold its second conference of heads of state in Accra, as the Ghanaians had suggested. Nkrumah could be expected to see two alternatives for the final discussion of union government at this conference. He could retreat from the principle and give the conference a happier conclusion and himself room for maneuver in the critical year to come. He would thus show that Ghana was not unwilling to work along functional lines, and hopefully his peers at Accra might see the wisdom of organic ties. On the other hand, he could try once again to force a grudging acceptance of the principle of union government in the hope that with this he could turn the principle into reality.

He chose the latter course. He had staked his reputation on the success

[159] According to Botsio, Nyerere later apologized for the misunderstanding, but according to Tanzanian sources, the apology was only directed to the specific point, not to the substance of the speech.

of his plan for African unity, and he lacked the flexibility to know how to retreat. The result was still greater humiliation, for the principle itself had been unequivocally rejected by all but four states. Only in the case of Uganda was there public (if dubious) acceptance of immediate union.

The final day of the conference, July 21st, began with a discussion of OAU finances, and nearly every issue offered a new opportunity for a head of state to deal Ghana a blow. When Kenyatta suggested that the liberation committee be increased in size, Bourguiba rejected the request on principle, for the committee, he said, should be small, and the request was made only because "certain African [presidents] oppose the Committee because they are not members of it." Cameroun wanted the liberation committee's budget integrated with the secretariat's budget, so the contribution to the committee would be compulsory; Mali, for one, agreed.[160]

It was also attempted to arrange financial contributions so as to relieve Ethiopia of its sole responsibility for the OAU budget, and Nkrumah (who, according to Ghanaian diplomats, was not following the discussion) made what he thought would appear to be a conciliatory gesture. Ghana would, he said, grant the £100,000 that the organization needed.[161] But Nkrumah's colleagues were more interested in principles, and felt that Nkrumah was trying to regain the initiative by a display of Ghana's wealth. His contempt of the OAU had been made far too clear to permit a less cynical interpretation of his offer. Abubakar made the least kind cut during the conference (for which Nkrumah was to have his revenge eighteen months later) in retorting to Nkrumah's gesture— only one country had not contributed to the committee, "and that was Ghana and so I cannot understand now why Ghana should say that it would pay towards the cost of the Secretariat. We would take what they pay now, as a cost toward this Liberation Committee which they did not pay before. And now, if they pay for this Liberation Committee and they are generous enough they could give an advance to the Secretariat."[162]

When Nkrumah again brought up the high command, Ahidjo made the most amusing attack through a paraphrase of Ghanaian doctrine: the greatest threat was "subsidised subversion tele-guided from other African States"; if these states were not trying to overthrow other governments by violent means, the function of the high command would cease to exist.[163]

160 *OAU*, Cairo, AHSG/PV7 (I) 21 July 1964, pp. 10-11.
161 Interview: CF-14, and *OAU, ibid.*, p. 22.
162 *Ibid.*, p. 26.   163 *Ibid.*, p. 41.

Despite these attacks, Nkrumah insisted on bringing up union government. Sékou Touré, the chairman, noted that the committee named at the foreign ministers' session had only asked the heads of state "to declare itself on the principle."[164] But Nkrumah insisted on pleading his case, and it is interesting to see what he said amidst his peers:

> What I am suggesting . . . I didn't say we should set out on this table and within five minutes establish a Union Government. . . . My point was this, that it is a central factor in the political life of the African continent, since it is going to be a vital issue let us at least accept in principle the possibility of the establishment of a Union Government of Africa. . . . But I say let's say that we should start here and then, and get all the functions and I put forward the suggestion also that we have been able to agree in principle to the possibility of the establishment of Union Government in Africa. I say let's submit it to the . . . Jurist's Committee . . . so . . . what I am saying is . . . if it is a good idea then what I put forward is this: Let us give a chance to our Jurist's Committee. . . . But I want to make it clear. I didn't come here to say—I know Rome wasn't built in a day but Rome started somewhere before it became Rome.[165]

Touré, as chairman—and Nkrumah's ally—tried to summarize the argument as logically as possible and Keita even added that the gap that had "separated our friend . . . from the majority . . . was narrowing." Apithy of Dahomey evoked memories of Nkrumah's 1947 London pan-African gathering which he had attended, and supported Nkrumah, by this time a picture of pathos. Sir Abubakar let them go no further. An African government was a dream, he said, "Or a nightmare." Nigeria, for its part, would never surrender its sovereignty. "This request, Mr. Chairman, is indirectly a vote of no confidence in the Organisation of African Unity. When we started this Organisation only a year ago we were working, progressing and now we are trying to impose something." Union government might come, so might world government, he said.[166]

The Emperor of Ethiopia, who knew that at this point it was conceding nothing to grant Nkrumah some concession, and who possessed a sense of dignity, sought to blur the distinctions Sir Abubakar and others were making. "The proposal of His Majesty [said the interpreter] is to examine the draft, not to reject it."[167] But Cameroun did not want to examine something that could not be implemented "before five, ten, fifteen, or even twenty years," and Bourguiba suggested that the appointment of such a committee would reduce the credibility of the OAU.

[164] Ibid., p. 45. [165] Ibid., pp. 46-47. [166] Ibid., p. 52.
[167] Ibid., p. 55.

Messemba-Debat tried to salvage the Emperor's suggestion, when President Nasser, the host, spoke from some experience: "The question of unity has always been thorny. . . . We should speed up the process leading to the realization of the *making of unity*. The last step . . . should then be the constitutional unity. We should discuss first the ways of unifying the systems adopted in our Armed Forces. Next how to use our own currencies in internal transactions." Thus, he said, the proposal should be entrusted to a committee that would consider the "makings of African Unity," which meant, of course, Article 11 of the OAU Charter.[168]

Nkrumah tried one last time.

> Mr. Chairman, I intended to speak last, but since—(interruption) my point is this: I think that the point of view which has been put forward by my colleague and friend President Nasser is no different from the matter I have been trying to put before the House. My point is this: this idea, whether it is dream or not—because most ideas that are bred throughout the whole world first come out of the brain of man—so it must be a dream before it comes down to earth. What I am putting forward is this: refer this matter to a Committee as President Nasser has said and let them study—I am quite sure that with the studying of the fundamentals, the economics it will lead eventually to what you people call political economy; you cannot divorce and tell the fundamentals from economy. There are cultural problems, social problems, and all these problems which must be studied. If you begin from the economic and cultural side, before you get to the end, you are in the political implications of the whole problem. And so the idea which I put forward is this: let us refer this to a Committee—let them study. And the report that will come out of it will be the only thing. They might even say "We have found out, after we have studied the reports that you must study the economic situation first." Some of you have been talking . . . (interruption) so I think let them study it and report to us.

Nkrumah did not see the distinctions his colleagues had belabored, and in the end it would seem from the text that they had ceased to listen to his incantations. Tubman finally agreed to Nasser's proposal, but asked, "Does that mean that we are accepting the proposal in principle or that we are simply referring it to this Committee—are we accepting the principle? No, Mr. Chairman, they say no." Sékou Touré added "no," indeed, "the principle here is not admitted."[169] With that union government expired.

[168] *Ibid.*, pp. 63-68.   [169] *Ibid.*, pp. 72-73.

DIPLOMATIC CONSEQUENCES
August 1964–February 1966

". . . It is [often] not the sensitive, flexible and versatile mind of the diplomat, but the rigid, relentless, and one-track mind of the crusader that guides the destiny of nations. The crusading mind knows nothing of persuasion and compromise. It knows only of victory and defeat."
—HANS MORGENTHAU

A REBELLIOUS CURRENT was once again flowing through Africa: there was another crisis in the Congo. Ghana was, despite its defeats at Cairo, not without allies.[1] Kojo Botsio and a dozen of his ministerial colleagues from the old Casablanca group, East Africa, Somalia, and Brazzaville had met during the Cairo conference to discuss the return of Tshombe to power in Léopoldville and the outbreak of fighting in the eastern Congo. Agreeing that these developments were intolerable, they resolved to remain in close contact. They met again at an extraordinary OAU foreign ministers' conference in Addis Ababa (in September 1964), and had plans, never to be fulfilled, for meetings in Khartoum and Accra. Their concern was the Congo, but they discussed the possibility of formalizing the group for broader purposes; this plan never matured because of the strong sentiment on behalf of the OAU.[2]

With almost any issue of concern to the radical African nationalists, Nkrumah might have taken the lead and increased Ghana's influence; he did do this with the Rhodesia question. The question of continental union government, however, interested no one. His urgent messages to his peers asking for coordination and cooperation on such questions as the 1964 Congolese rebellion lost their force, because he insisted on

---

[1] The Ghanaian press, however, insisted on describing the Cairo conference as a Ghanaian triumph, giving the last period of Nkrumah's rule a very inauspicious beginning. For the benefit of those who heard reports of Nyerere's speech denouncing Nkrumah—on the BBC—Nkrumah said upon his return that if the British press and imperialist agents "only . . . knew the depth of solidarity and understanding created at the Cairo conference . . . they would be more discreet." *Ghanaian Times*, 31 July 1964.

[2] Interview: Botsio.

placing his proposals in the framework of the need for union government.[3]

Since its inception Nkrumah had treated the OAU with contempt, partly because of Nkrumah's policy of union government, more importantly because Ghana could not dominate the OAU. At Cairo, Ghana offered Accra as a sight for the 1965 OAU meeting, for understandable reasons of prestige: this would be its first chance to be a part of the organization's "in-group." Yet the choice of Accra posed a dilemma: Could Ghana sponsor a conference of an organization the objectives of which it rejected? This was resolved with the demand, posed almost daily in the Ghanaian press from September 1964 onwards, that the OAU effect a union government in Accra. Hardly had Accra been selected than Nkrumah began sketching elaborate plans for a conference headquarters, the scope of which led many to conclude that Nkrumah envisaged the new buildings as an African capital. "Job 600," the remarkable £10,000,000 complex which was to be used for two weeks at the most, made Nkrumah the subject of jokes throughout the world.[4] But these missed the point. Obviously Ghana could ill-afford the project with the economy in such disrepair (although Nkrumah did assume that the project—and the conference—would be a useful public diversion at a time of stress); the complex more significantly underlined the extent to which Nkrumah counted on the emergence of union government at the conference. Important objectives in the domestic sector were pushed aside, and Nkrumah told one visitor that this was done because they would be irrelevant or redundant when union government was achieved.[5]

Elsewhere in Africa there were new and imaginative—if premature—efforts to break away from the stagnant patterns plaguing Africa. President Senghor was pressing for an association of the riverine states of Mali, Mauritania, Guinea, and Senegal. There were proposals for a free trade area comprising the Ivory Coast, Liberia, Sierra Leone, and Guinea. Nigeria initiated a cooperative effort for the development of the Chad basin and was negotiating border and customs agreements with its neighbors.[6] The Equatorial African Common Market was under

[3] See his telegram to the Emperor of Ethiopia regarding the Congo rebellion, quoted in Nkrumah, *Challenge of the Congo*, p. 264.

[4] According to Botsio, in interview, Nkrumah began at the Cairo conference itself sketching plans for the complex (Botsio himself favored the building of badly needed estate houses to house the delegates, the cost of which would have been one-tenth that of Job 600).

[5] Interview: CF-113, January 1965, London.

[6] See particularly E. O. Obayan's interesting paper, "Economic Integration and African Unity," Ministry of Economic Development, Lagos, unpublished manuscript.

way. As the prospects for regional groupings brightened, the OAU began to encounter difficulties. Many commission meetings had to be canceled for want of a quorum.[7] The OAU needed less ambition and a greater pragmatism to give it the solid foundation it lacked. For one thing, the French-linked states of West Africa were not sufficiently integrated into —or committed to—the OAU to wish to risk sacrificing their short-run interests for the organization's sake. Old colonial ties were not dying easily, and subversion plotted in Accra which was aimed in part against them forced some states to assess their commitment to the OAU; the old debate about the nature of the OAU was transformed by mid-1965 into the question of whether the organization could hold a meeting or, indeed, survive at all.

Since 1961, Ghana had plotted subversive acts against independent African states. It is only after the founding of the OAU that subversion became a central part of a strategy for uniting the continent, rather than merely a response to temptation and circumstance; as much as any reason, this was because of Ghana's exclusion from the OAU's liberation committee and the attendant humiliations. As late as January 1964, Ghana was still cautious about subversion, and turned down Chinese assistance that was offered. Then the times changed. In mid-April, A. K. Barden proposed to send activists to Cameroun, the Ivory Coast, Senegal, Dahomey, Niger, Upper Volta, Algeria, Togo, and Brazzaville for the following reasons:

a. Ghana has made it clear that the stage is reached where imperialism, apartheid, and neocolonialism must be fought by armed revolution.

b. As the leading African nation fighting against these evils Ghana must make available to the Freedom fighters greater facilities for training.

c. Osagyefo has indicated that training must be intensified forthwith.[8]

The summer of 1964 brought more changes. Nkrumah's failure at the Cairo OAU conference drove him to move up the timetable of revenge. There was also the new imperialist threat in the Congo, where Moise Tshombe had taken power. On the night of 27 November 1964, General Barwa and the Russian military attaché supervised the loading of a transport plane with arms destined for Juba and, ultimately, the Congo-

[7] Thus the Defence Commission could not meet in December 1964. See *West Africa*, 26 December 1964, p. 1461.

[8] Barden to Nkrumah, 28 April 1964, in *NLC*, "Nkrumah's Subversion in Africa," Accra, 1966, p. 8.

lese rebels based in Stanleyville.[9] From the point of view of the Americans, this was Ghana's most significant interference.[10] Though it takes few arms to cause trouble in that part of the world, this was part of a multilateral effort in which the initiative was not Ghana's. True, few things obsessed Nkrumah at this time more than the Congo situation. But we have it on authority of Thomas Kanza, then spokesman for the Stanleyville regime, that Nkrumah was not a key leader in sustaining or supporting the rebellion. The rebels did not even keep him informed about their negotiations or their struggles among themselves because, as Kanza said, "Nkrumah bargained with information to advance his own position with other African leaders, and we could not afford to jeopardize our security."[11]

Ghana's inability to make effective use of subversion as an instrument of policy was primarily because aspirations did not match capacities. There is, for example, the case of Leballo's South African-PAC militants who wished training in Ghana. A. K. Barden, director of the Bureau of African Affairs, went to Dar-es-Salaam in 1964 to arrange to bring about twenty-five of these men to Accra for advanced training. Most of the men had already received some training in Peking, and all were educated. Barden was incapable of acknowledging that limits to Ghanaian capabilities existed. In consequence, when the PAC militants realized they could learn nothing in Ghana and became restless, the administration detained them to forestall a mutiny. Barden had to endure the humiliation of asking the Algerians to give them the training they sought.[12]

Aid from the Chinese thus became crucial, and in August 1964 Barden was able to negotiate a contract with them for assistance in subversion-training, though apparently without Nkrumah's permission.[13] In October, five guerilla experts arrived and began planning courses at the Half-Assine camp, where "the students had become demoralized over the elementary training . . . they were receiving."[14] As Barden had proposed on August 21st that the camp be expanded to absorb 500 students, the Chinese came just in time for his purposes.

Only when Nkrumah had discovered how misplaced had been his confidence in Barden could Ghana pose a genuine threat to the West African equilibrium. Nkrumah had not made Barden an MP in mid-

[9] Interview: CF-31. This is the report of one of the best observers of Ghana during the period, a neutral official trusted by most parties in Accra.

[10] Interview: CF-41, U.S. Embassy/Accra.

[11] Interview: T. R. Kanza.   [12] Interviews: CF-29, 87.

[13] How he managed this is obscure. Interviews: CF-29, 87. See "Nkrumah's Subversion in Africa," p. 7.

[14] "Nkrumah's Subversion in Africa," p. 7.

1965, presumably because he had grown too powerful. So intense was the effect of his exclusion that he had to be placed in a mental hospital. From there, the man who had praised Nkrumah more than any other wrote him threatening letters.[15] With Barden's demission, however, the bureau became a far better organized agency. It was in effect split into several parts, with General Barwah assuming responsibility for the training camps. The last stage of Ghanaian subversion had begun. From this time on Chinese (and East German) assistance might have led to a level of competence which would have made Nkrumah's regime very dangerous indeed had the 1966 coup not intervened.

How did Ghana's remarkable president preserve his illusions in these last years? For one thing, it is not entirely coincidental that Nkrumah's dreams about a union government had developed parallel to the increasingly authoritarian character of the state. Ghana, more and more, was a place where one shattered illusions at his own peril. At the very time that the conservative states gathered in Nouakshott in reaction to Ghana's subversive maneuvers, the squalid domestic scene in Accra spotlighted Nkrumah's lost ground as an African leader. The death of Dr. Danquah, on 4 February 1965, while in solitary confinement at Nsawam prison, brought out the petty viciousness of the regime. Mass executions did not occur in Nkrumah's Ghana; instead there was the death in detention of the man from whom the Osagyefo had gained his start in Ghanaian politics, the man whom Padmore called "the doyen of Gold Coast politicians."[16] President Azikiwe commented that it was an irony of history that he should die "in a detention camp barely eight years after his country had become free from foreign domination."[17] *Spark* snarled like a chained dog, and called Zik's comments "empty phrases culled from bourgeois capitalist philosophy." The only regret expressed in official statements was that the government had been "disadvantaged" by the death before the prisoner could be brought to trial.[18] Because of its attempt to tarnish Danquah's fame, the government met with a wave of revulsion in many countries, particularly Nigeria. The verdict in the Kulungugu treason trial was decided four days after Danquah's death.

[15] Interviews: CF-29, 14, 87. Curiously, Nkrumah proposed to remove the problem caused by Barden's presence in Ghana by appointing him ambassador to Rumania, an appointment made after Barden's illness, and which he was unable to take up. Interview: CF-29.

[16] Padmore, *Pan-Africanism or Communism*, p. 175.

[17] *West Africa*, 13 February 1965, p. 182.

[18] "Your attitude does you no credit," statement of J.A. Owusu-Ansah, High Commission of Ghana, Lagos, *Ghanaian Times*, 17 February 1965. By one undoubtedly truthful account, Nkrumah planned to release Danquah on 6 March 1965. Whether he would in fact have done so is less clear and, in any event, is irrelevant: Effect, not intent, matters in politics. Interview: CF-87.

Nkrumah's former colleagues and roommate, acquitted in December 1963 by an independent court, were sentenced to death by a politically reliable jury.

Communication diminishes in such a system. Even those hostile to Nkrumah praised union government on public occasions, and sometimes even the Western press seemed to join in. Keith Kyle, an able journalist, argued that for Ghana, "continental union is not only a political ideal, but an economic necessity," for without the expanded trade in Africa that union would bring, its economy could never advance to a mature level. "It is fair to say that a lesser man than Nkrumah would have been sorely tempted to chuck revolutionary ideals for a generation on the grounds that for the time being the human material is not there. But this option would be unreal: in this game one gains or loses ground and can never stand still."[19] Was this satire, or ingenuous nonsense on Kyle's part? In 1965, Ghana's trade with African states decreased by about 50 percent because of strained relations with neighbors and mismanagement and corruption in import licensing.

Nkrumah's power became nearly absolute in this period. Botsio described the results of the 1965 constitutional revisions as follows: "The MP's . . . were nominated not by their constituencies, but by the so-called Central Committee and according to the . . . Constitution, if Parliament refused to elect as president a candidate proposed by the Central Committee, it was the Parliament which was dissolved, and not the presidential candidate thrown away for a new one. Note: the members of the Central Committee and Parliament were nominated by him!"[20] Thus was Nkrumah reelected president by a parliament named entirely by him, after an election where no popular or legislative votes were cast. It meant that the last election of a "bourgeois capitalist type" had been held nine years earlier, prior to independence. It was Ghana's "first Socialist parliament," as the press said.[21]

As seen in retrospect, the central question in Ghana's external relations during this period was who would bail Ghana out of the nearly desperate situation into which it had descended. So far had the economy fallen that even Nkrumah began to allow his decisions to be affected by economic considerations, if only marginally. In the twelve months fol-

[19] Keith Kyle, "Dr. Nkrumah's New Man," *Spectator*, 4 September 1964.

[20] Kojo Botsio to the author, 28 July 1966. Kofi Baako publicly commented, "We don't want to have situations like those in Italy where Parliament tried 17 times unsuccessfully to elect a new President." Aaron Ofori-Attah said the country did not want spurious nominations by "any self-seeking clique." *Ghanaian Times*, 22 May 1965; see also editorial, *ibid.*, 2 June 1965.

[21] See *Spark*, No. 124, 3 September 1965.

lowing the Cairo summit, prices rose by 33 percent. In 1965 Ghana achieved its lowest recorded peace-time growth, .02 percent, compared with the planned 5.7 percent, a rate easily achieved in the Ivory Coast.[22] Ghana's foreign policy, by this point, could have helped the economy only marginally, so complete were the failures of Nkrumah's past policies. There were still adequate opportunities to make the situation worse, and these seem to have been exploited.

Some of the most experienced observers thought a genuine struggle for Ghana's political loyalties was still being waged, and that it had reached its most crucial point. The failure of Eastern credits and aid to solve any of Ghana's problems, the concomitant creation of unexpected new ones, together with the low quality of products bought from the East all might combine to make Ghana turn back to its traditional friends, so the argument went.[23] Indeed, to the astonishment of many, Nkrumah gave an Easter speech on the economic situation in which he blamed internal factors for the difficulties, without once attributing Ghana's problems to imperialism, colonialism, or neocolonialism. At a later stage he even attributed the low 1965 price of cocoa to the law of supply and demand, rather than to imperialist machinations.[24] He also began making discreet soundings in Brussels as to the possibility of a Ghanaian application for associate status in the EEC—this after years of fighting even the idea of such a relationship between African and European countries.[25] He invited an IMF and World Bank mission to Ghana, publicly accepting their conditions for support. In May, Kojo Botsio was sent to Eastern and Western capitals to seek new support, of over a billion pounds from the West. Nkrumah conspicuously increased the power of avowedly pro-Western economists, like Albert Adomako at the Bank of Ghana.

This was all done too late. The Western governments thought that these moments of rationality were at best only short hesitations on a steep downward slide. For years Nkrumah had hidden his real intentions, they thought, and while professing friendship with the West had led his state on a reckless and ultimately calamitous course. Now, guarding

---

[22] The 1964 *Economic Survey* was characteristically blunt in criticizing the government for its economic policy in this period. It was often said it could do this because nobody in Flagstaff House bothered to read the annual survey.

[23] Interview: CF-113, May 1965, London.

[24] See "Our Economic Situation," Easter Message by Osagyefo, 17 April 1965, Accra. Also "Osagyefo Addresses Farmers on the Cocoa Situation," P.R. #278/65, 22 September 1965.

[25] Interviews: CF-113, May 1965, London, and CF-58, 8 November 1965, London.

their hands, they played his old game. If there is no evidence of their collusion in the 1966 coup, there is reason to think that Western economic pressures would by the spring of 1966 have made the regime's survival very unlikely.[26]

The Soviet Union did extend a two-year grace period prior to repayment of credit but, as Komla Gbedemah had predicted four years earlier, they offered Ghana no foreign currency for it to repay its far more pressing Western debts. Increasingly, it looked as if the East was not prepared to look out for a country unwilling to look out for itself. The Russians had apparently revised their estimate of Ghana's importance as well, and "began to fear that by supporting Nkrumah they were stunting the growth of socialism in Ghana," one official said.[27] They wished to preserve privileges already accumulated, but hoped this could be done inexpensively. It was a costly, though understandable, miscalculation.

The state of Ghana's foreign service and its foreign ministry sank to new lows in this last period. In June 1965, Alex Quaison-Sackey was named foreign minister, replacing Botsio, who took over state planning. In case Quaison-Sackey entertained any illusions about his ability to affect Ghana's foreign policy, Botsio was given continuing responsibilities at the ministry, and was appointed chairman of the Ghanaian delegation at the Accra OAU conference, to the embarrassment of many. Quaison-Sackey had hoped to bring African affairs back under the ministry, and to boost morale in the foreign service. But after the coup d'état, Michael Dei-Anang, in Ussher Fort Prison, "told me that at the time of my appointment, Nkrumah had told him that 'Quaison-Sackey is not going to preside over the dissolution of the African Affairs Secretariat.' "[28] Not even the appearance of influence on foreign policy remained with the ministry. It is Dei-Anang, whose jurisdiction was African affairs, who prepared the lengthy brief on Vietnam for Nkrumah and the delegation that accompanied him to Peking in February 1966.[29]

---

[26] For example, credit for consumer goods—on which the stability of the regime depended—probably would not have been extended after 1 April 1966 by the large expatriate firms. Such action was within their power and their rights. Western diplomats were in close touch with the businessmen in question. It is difficult to believe that Nkrumah could have survived the riots and demonstrations that would ensue from the food shortages.

[27] Interview: CF-87.

[28] Interview: Quaison-Sackey. Kwesi Armah was offered the ministry, but turned it down so that he could take the ministry of trade, where he could better serve his personal interests.

[29] Mr. Quaison-Sackey kindly showed me the brief, as prepared by Dei-Anang.

THE ANTI-NKRUMAH OFFENSIVE:
LOMÉ, NOUAKSHOTT, ABIDJAN, LAGOS, AND ACCRA

The less reasonable a creed is, the more it is sought to establish it by force.—JEAN-JACQUES ROUSSEAU, as quoted by Dr. Félix Houphouet-Boigny[30]

It was of cardinal importance to Nkrumah's prestige and to the stability of his regime that the OAU conference scheduled for Accra in 1965 be successful. Militant-refugees from neighboring states, however, were well-entrenched in Accra and, as already seen, had new opportunities to prepare for intervention in their home territories with the arrival of the Chinese trainers in the autumn of 1964. A third strand in the West African diplomatic skein at that time was Houphouet-Boigny's. Never given satisfaction by Nkrumah over the Sanwi leaders following their discussion at Addis Ababa in 1963, he was loathe to attend the 1965 OAU summit from the time that Accra was chosen as its site. The presence of politically active Ivoirien refugees in Ghana, in combination with his long-standing aversion to Nkrumah, was sufficient cause for him to wish to avoid bolstering Nkrumah's standing by attending the meeting.

Houphouet's sentiments were intensified when in September 1964 Sawaba leaders in Accra began making obvious preparations for intervention in Niger. On the night of September 26th, commandos armed with submachine guns and automatic pistols left Ghana; the first party, according to Nigerien evidence, arrived at 5:00 A.M. on the morning of October 4th, and assassinated several villagers before being seized.[31] Thus warned, the Niger authorities, with French help, could await further parties "with open arms,"[32] finding in the process ample documentation of the commandos' strategy and aims. Ghana might be expected to avoid publicizing its feelings about Hamani Diori's government at so delicate a moment, but it was characteristic of the regime in such situations to brag, and it was in the interests of the refugees in Ghana to lead them to do so. *l'Etincelle* printed a Sawaba declaration of 20 September

---

[30] Embassy of the Democratic Republic of the Congo, London, "Extraordinary Conference of the African and Malagasy Common Organisation [OCAM] Held at Abidjan, May 16th 1965," p. 4.

[31] As presented at the Lagos Foreign Ministers' meeting in June 1965. See speech of Adamou Mayaki, in *Government of Nigeria*, Verbatim Report of the Fifth Extraordinary Session of the Council of Ministers of the Organisation of African Unity, 10-13 June 1965, pp. 17-18.

[32] Interview: Ambassador Tiecoura Alzouma, Niger/Accra.

1964, in which Sawaba warned that it would impose "its will on the traitors" who governed Niger.[33]

Armed with precise documentation of the commandos' activities, Presidents Houphouet, Yameogo, and Diori informed OAU secretary-general Diallo Telli that they would not attend the summit unless these activities were ended, and the offending refugees were expelled from Ghana. Telli attempted to mediate and, briefly, he appeared to meet success.[34] On November 19th Nkrumah wrote Houphouet—after sending a delegation to hear his demands—that the presence of refugees was a residue of artificial colonial barriers and, moreover, that it appeared that "this unhappy phenomenon is being used as a kind of pin-prick against us personally, and as a means of diverting attention from the urgent need for unity of thought and action in Africa." But with normal relations restored following the adoption of steps now being outlined, he went on, they could work together toward "the achievement of some sort of a federal Union Government for Africa." All that mattered was his promise that Djibo, the Sawaba leader, Ehounoud Biley and Fattoh Elleigand, Sanwi leaders, and others were to leave Ghana.[35] Houphouet was appeased, but remained skeptical.

Nkrumah may have intended to keep his word, but the refugees acted quickly to protect their privileges. On 14 January 1965, he again wrote Houphouet, this time of his desire to find countries willing to receive the refugees in question. Having been unsuccessful he had, "with the greatest reluctance, decided to allow the refugees to remain in Ghana on the clear understanding that they do not undertake any subversive activities whatsoever against their Government."[36] On past performance, the promise was worthless, and the explanation less than credible.

Nkrumah's bad faith and the mounting evidence of Ghanaian subversion in West Africa precipitated an offensive of surprising momentum against both Ghana and the Accra summit itself. The result was that by the summer of 1965 Ghanaian diplomacy in Africa became a defensive diplomatic holding operation with only one objective, namely, to force African heads of state to follow through individually on their collective commitment to attend the 1965 summit in Accra. Nkrumah was prepared to make tactical retreats at every stage to appease Houphouet, without making concessions of substance in his policy or aims.

[33] l'Étincelle, No. 21, 15 October 1964. See also No. 22, 1 November 1964.
[34] The autumn diplomatic moves are recounted, in detail, in Government of Nigeria, Verbatim Report (of the Lagos 1965 OAU Foreign Ministers' Meeting), pp. 12-15.
[35] Nkrumah to Houphouet-Boigny, 19 November 1965, quoted in ibid., speech of Kojo Botsio, p. 35.
[36] Nkrumah to Houphouet-Boigny, 14 January 1965, quoted in ibid., p. 35.

But a conservative current began flowing through West Africa, which enabled Houphouet to gain the offensive to the end.

The ensuing drama of West African diplomacy in 1965 was in five acts. Aside from Nkrumah, Houphouet-Boigny was always the principal actor, but attention was focused at different stages on five cities, the first being Lomé, the reef upon which were wrecked so many of Nkrumah's past hopes.

As seen earlier, the murder of Olympio did not lead to harmony between Ghana and Togo. True, reciprocal support at the level of OAU diplomacy had ensued: Ghana (unsuccessfully) supported OAU recognition of Grunitzky's regime at Addis Ababa, and in return the Togolese, always careful not to antagonize Nkrumah, had refrained from overtly opposing various Ghanaian proposals for continental government.[37] Such a relationship could not survive in the face of continued friction along the frontier. Ghana had been unwilling to reopen the border and, on 23 January 1964, Togo finally closed the border from its own side.

Nkrumah demanded a far-reaching agreement between the two states designed to prevent any financial difficulties for Ghana that might come from an open frontier. He proposed that the Bank of Ghana and the Ghana National Trading Company open branches in Lomé, while the two states worked out common financial and monetary policies. (Vice President Meatchi of Togo later said "they decided that goods could circulate between the two states—but not people.")[38] Though President Grunitzky wished to take only one step at a time, there was no question of his desire for cooperation. In August 1963, apparently at Nkrumah's request, he sent Simon Kpodar, formerly a refugee in Ghana from Olympio's government, to serve as his ambassador. He kept him there, even though Ghana did not reciprocate for a full year. He even consented to Nkrumah's appointment, in 1964, of the old pan-Africanist Edwin duPlan as Ghanaian ambassador, disreputable as he was, even though it was obvious why Nkrumah wanted an official of the Bureau of African Affairs in Lomé. Four years after Togo's independence, Ghana thus possessed an ambassador in the capital of its closest neighbor.[39]

---

[37] This is apparent in all the verbatim transcripts of OAU meetings drawn on for this study.

[38] Interviews: CF-104, 115, and *Jeune Afrique*, 7 March 1965.

[39] Kpodar was appointed 14 August 1963. *Gouvernement du Togo*, Decret 63/101. Kpodar was at first an embarrassment to the diplomatic corps in Accra, due to his former presence in Accra as a refugee, but as the distance between his and Nkrumah's government grew, his standing improved dramatically. As for duPlan's appointment, see

Grunitzky continued to press for reopening the border, and in October 1964 it seemed that his efforts were to be rewarded. Nkrumah promised to come to Aflao for the occasion. But at the last moment he canceled, and he also canceled two separate dates in January 1965.[40] Fear for his own security still determined Nkrumah's relations with Togo, and increasingly it looked as if the border would stay closed so long as Nkrumah remained in power. Grunitzky, in the meantime, had no alternative and did what was expected of him, in view of his past record. He began a rapprochement with Houphouet (who had opposed recognition of his regime in 1963) and he moved Togo into the French African organizations from which Olympio had so long kept it. Defense and monetary agreements were signed with France, and the French ambassador became, by statute, doyen of the corps in Lomé.[41]

Relations with Ghana deteriorated in other respects. Smuggling increased and recorded trade decreased. DuPlan, by several accounts, tried to bribe important officials in Lomé, sometimes with success.[42] He was seldom sober. J. K. Yankson, Ghana's political officer—and an intelligence officer as well—had to guard his own moves because of hostility felt by Togolese toward Ghana. More ominously, incursions by border guards occurred regularly.[43] It looked as if Nkrumah hoped for an incident that could be used to justify keeping the border closed.

On January 16th, only two days after Nkrumah had written his fateful letter to Houphouet, Ghanaian guards pursued two Togolese villagers on their own soil. The villagers got help at the *poste de douane* of Segbe from the *adjutant chef*, Francois Pinheiro. The Ghanaians killed him, and then sought to find reinforcements to bring the body across the border "so as to allege . . . that the incident took place on Ghanaian territory." This time, the Togolese were prepared. Within an hour, Togolese police were able to verify that Pinheiro had died in Togo, and that the shots had been fired from the Togolese side of the border. Worse for Ghana, Apedo-Amah, the foreign minister, brought duPlan to the scene to examine the corpse and its location the same afternoon, so that it would be juridically impossible for Ghana to disclaim responsibility.

Grunitzky's comments at the time credentials were presented, *Togo-Presse*, 19 September 1964.

[40] See *Togo-Presse*, 30 October 1964, 21 January 1965, and *AFP Sp. Outre-mer*, 29 October 1964, No. 5515.

[41] See *le Monde*, 5 February 1965, *AFP Sp. Outre-mer*, No. 5337, 28 March 1964, No. 5219, 8 November 1963, and *Journal Officiel de la Republique Française*, 10 June 1964.

[42] Interviews: CF-29, 49. See also *Togo-Presse*, 20 January 1965.

[43] Interview: CF-115. See also the Togolese *compte-rendu* in *Togo-Presse*, 18 and 20 January 1965.

DuPlan was persuaded to return to Accra and make Ghana's responsibility clear, thus ruining, if unwittingly, Nkrumah's scheme. The latter, enraged by the turn of events, added insult to the murder, in what *Togo-Presse* called "un curieux geste": on January 19th he sent Botsio to Aflao to open the Ghanaian side of the border.[44]

Feeling ran high in Togo, not so much over the incident, as over eight years of provocations by Nkrumah. On January 20th the Togolese parliament resolved that the incident should be reported to the OAU. There were demands that Togo join Houphouet's Entente, and the government surprised Ghana by announcing that Togo's side of the border would not be opened until satisfaction for the murder had been obtained.[45]

Ghana did not apologize. The press repeated the old canard of an "anti-Ghana Conspiracy," developed to "stir our brother African countries against us" because Ghana was against neocolonialism, for African unity, and for scientific Socialism.[46] Nkrumah dismissed duPlan;[47] repercussions multiplied and history repeated itself. There was new Togolese-Nigerian cooperation, but because of Lomé's restored links with Paris, not of the type that might have developed between Olympio's government and Nigeria. The *Pilot*, in Lagos, even called for a defense pact, since "some states" did not respect the spirit of the OAU. "Only last week we heard noises about 'our brothers in Togo separated from us by colonial divisions.' To Togolese, such veiled words mean no more than expansionist dreams. . . . Nigeria's 'political' frontiers should extend to Lomé." Apedo-Amah, however, made clear that Togo had stronger friends than Nigeria on whom to rely.[48]

The second act in the anti-Nkrumah offensive took place in Nouakshott, the capital of Mauritania, at which was formed the *Organisation Commune d'Afrique et Malgache* (OCAM). The diplomatic antecedent to the organization was the old UAM which, in 1964, as a result of pan-African pressures, the French-linked states had converted into the

---

[44] *Ibid.* Ghana did not present its own version of the events until a week later, and even then it did not contradict the details of the Togolese version. A high-ranking neutral official made a detailed investigation of the events of this week, and permitted the author to examine his reports to his own chief. CF-31.

[45] One member commented, "Qu'avec le Ghana, il faut agir avec vigueur." *Togo-Presse*, 21 January 1965. See also *ibid.*, 20 January 1965.

[46] "The Anti-Ghana Conspiracy," *Ghanaian Times*, 26 January 1965.

[47] In taking Togolese instructions, duPlan had shown himself ignorant of the most basic rules of representation. Togolese officials learned of his demission from him, which compounded the damage. This was reputedly during one of his revels after his brief return to Lomé. See "Des Apaisements qui Tardent," *Togo-Presse*, 4 February 1965.

[48] *West African Pilot*, 26 January 1965, *AFP Sp. Outre-mer*, No. 5587, 24-25 January 1965, and *Fraternité*, 4 February 1965.

UAMCE, the *Union Afrique et Malgache pour Co-operation Economique*. Houphouet, never happy about the conversion of the organization into a politically sterile grouping, had long sought an opportunity to give it back its political functions. The now increasingly tense relations between the Ivory Coast and Ghana gave Houphouet additional incentive, and the Segbe incident gave him the certainty that the time was right for a major campaign against Ghana.

The Ivory Coast was in a strong position to take the lead in this offensive. During 1964 the domestic political scene had quieted, as the economy showed unparalleled growth. Upper Volta was firmly back in the fold of the Entente, as was Dahomey, long-absent from the alliance as a result of its dispute with Niger which was now settled. Thus Houphouet had a regional power base for a continental policy. Just after the Entente's February meeting—its first in over a year—and shortly before the planned UAMCE meeting in Mauritania, Presidents Diori, Grunitzky, Mba, and Yameogo gathered in Abidjan to plan strategy for Nouakshott.[49]

There, fourteen states agreed to join Houphouet's proposed organization, OCAM, and to scrap UAMCE. Also at his urging they buttressed Tshombe's position in the Congo. A badly chosen focus for the group's first efforts, it was in part a reaction to the threat to the doctrine of sovereignty of the radical states, who had claimed the right to intervene in the Congo because of Tshombe's past record. More particularly, they resolved to "condemn energetically" the action of certain states, "notably that of Ghana," which had welcomed agents of subversion on their soil; and to boycott the Accra summit.[50]

The conference had another result, namely, to give the participating states the self-confidence that they had lacked since independence. African nationalism had always been defined in Accra or Conakry; ideology was an important component of prestige in West Africa and the radical states had always reaped the benefits.[51] The Ghanaian press had called these leaders traitors and stooges, and their reaction had been to go to the Élysée for reassurance. Now that they were on the offensive, it almost seemed that they had chosen to advance Tshombe's fortunes in order to annoy Nkrumah.

The West African equilibrium appeared to shift, as the challenge to

[49] See *West Africa*, 13 February 1965, and "Les Etats Africains se regroupent à nouveau selon leurs affinities et leurs options politique," Philippe Herreman, *le Monde Diplomatique*, No. 132 (April 1965).

[50] *West Africa*, 20 February 1965, p. 203.

[51] See I. W. Zartman, *International Relations in the New Africa*, New York, 1966, pp. 56-57.

Nkrumah became multilateral. When Nkrumah called OCAM's charges against his subversion "ridiculous," the PDCI in Abidjan published their version of Nkrumah's policy toward the Ivory Coast since 1957. It ended, "Kwame Nkrumah, with his *dada* of intercontinental government, only envisages . . . a single union, the impossible union, the union around his person, around the 'Osagyefo,' the saviour! *Eh oui!* Kwame Nkrumah clothed in the skin of a saviour, of a new messiah! *Vraiment, si le ridicule tuait.*"[52] Yameogo became the spokesman for the Entente. This was in part his penance for Paga, but it is also because Houphouet preferred to remain above the battle.[53] In a *compte-rendu* of Nouakshott, Yameogo hit hard: Ghana's early independence had made Nkrumah think he had a mandate from God "to command the African universe." Yameogo was himself for continental government, he said, but Ouagadougou would be the seat, Maurice Yameogo would be the president. "It is then that you will see the sham sincerity of Mr. Kwame Nkrumah manifested."[54] The OCAM states would not go to Accra for the OAU conference, he added, unless all the refugees were sent away.

There were less direct consequences of Nouakshott. On March 12th several hundred Ghanaian students demonstrated at the USIS library because of American support of Tshombe, whom OCAM also supported, and then moved one block to the Nigerian High Commission, to protest the alleged involvement of Nigerian mercenaries in the Congo. The main result of this bitterly resented accusation was the tightening of links between the Entente states and Abubakar's government. Nigerian diplomats suggested that this event as much as any served to bring Nigerian student, labor, and other radical groups around their own government and against Nkrumah's.[55]

The public response in Ghana to Nouakshott was an intensification of the campaign of denigration against the Entente states and against Nigeria. The press developed the theme that the conference had served non-African ends; it had done a "great job for global imperialism."[56] But which imperialism? Now came a subtle contribution to a theory of modern imperialism. At Nouakshott, the Ghanaian theorists noted, de

[52] "Si le Ridicule Tuait . . ." Mise au Point du PDCI-RDA, *Fraternité*, 12 March 1965.

[53] Yameogo was in a strong position to carry the Entente's standard. No important Voltaic refugees lived in Ghana (aside from the Malam of the Ghanaian army), and Upper Volta had no defense agreement with France to which Nkrumah could point.

[54] "Compte-rendu du recent sommet du Nouakshott," by President Yameogo, *Carrefour Africain*, Ouagadougou, 28 February 1965.

[55] *West Africa*, 20 March 1965, p. 322, and interviews: CF-83B, 83C, 100, and Alhaji Isa Wali.

[56] *Ghanaian Times*, 20 February 1965. See also H. M. Basner, "To Nouakshott and Back," in *ibid.*, 22 February 1965.

Gaulle had been honored only out of sentiment; when it was appreciated that the conference had supported Tshombe and damned the Chinese (friends of de Gaulle's), then it became obvious that Washington controlled these states. Proof was subsequently seen in the reception Yameogo received on a state visit to America at the end of March. At a time when American interest in Africa was at a low point, the administration did much to flatter Yameogo in a way that further boosted Entente morale, if not its prestige in Africa. At a press conference in Washington, Yameogo ridiculed Nkrumah and made clear that there could be no compromise on the question of subversion.[57] *Spark* said Johnson had written the lines spoken by Yameogo;[58] but if American and Entente interests coincided, it was largely a result of Nkrumah's policies. Ghana had done the wrong sums; the subversion Yameogo spoke of was real.

For all this, the Ghanaian regime began to realize that it was in trouble, and it began making serious efforts to recoup its losses. It sought to drive a wedge between those OCAM states where Houphouet's influence was strong and others, like Cameroun, Mauritania, and Congo-Brazzaville, whose orientation was more radical or who were unaccustomed to pressure from Abidjan. Nkrumah thus began courting President Ahidjo, with the intention of proposing a deal on Camerounian refugees whom Ahidjo considered threatening. Messemba-Debat dissociated his government in Brazzaville from the accusations made at Nouakshott against Ghana and, step by step, he, Ahidjo, and Ould Daddah of Mauritania moved away from OCAM itself.[59] Their shift was not solely a result of Ghana's efforts, but it showed that Ghana could use diplomacy to its advantage when Nkrumah was so prepared.

There was also an attempt to strengthen old ties with Touré and Keita. Botsio made an unpublicized visit to Conakry and Bamako and arranged a meeting between the three presidents for March 14th. By his account, Touré and Keita expressed their own irritation at the OCAM states, but urged Ghana to settle the refugee problem within the OAU guidelines—that refugees not be permitted to engage in political activities. At the ensuing meeting of the three presidents, they also urged that Nkrumah scuttle continental government, and that he work wholly within the OAU charter.[60] This strengthened the position of Botsio and

---

57 *le Monde*, 1 April 1965, which reported Yameogo saying "Je montrerai qu'il n'est ni l'homme miracle ni l'homme vedette qu'il cherche à incarner."

58 *Spark*, 8 April 1965.

59 See "Debat Rejects anti-Ghana campaign," *Ghanaian Times*, 24 February 1965, and "Ahidjo advocates strong relations with Ghana," *ibid.*, 3 March 1965. Also interview: Botsio.

60 Interviews: Botsio, CF-14. Ben Bella's simultaneous arrival in Bamako, and the

Ghana's diplomats, who had long urged the same thing; they now felt Nkrumah might be persuaded to take such advice.

Nkrumah did briefly appear to be trying a new tack. At the end of March he gave a major address to parliament in which conciliatory moves on several foreign policy issues were announced.[61] First came his notice that the border with Togo was to be opened. Ghana had in fact already expressed regret over the January incident, and had offered compensation. The leaders in Lomé either did not consider that Ghana had offered sufficient redress, or they had raised their price for reconciliation, for they still refused to open their side of the border until such further issues as the 1963 kidnapping had been settled. Nkrumah in any case was only doing what he had to do, for the joint Ghanaian-Togolese commission appointed to investigate the incident had attributed the blame unequivocally to Ghana, thus rendering Nkrumah's parliamentary gesture somewhat irrelevant.[62]

Nkrumah also announced that negotiations would be undertaken with Upper Volta and the Ivory Coast for the reopening of Ghana's borders with these states. On the eve of Yameogo's departure for Washington, Botsio had flown to Ouagadougou, where he offered to settle all outstanding issues between Ghana and the Entente states, hoping to prevent Yameogo from attacking Ghana too openly in America. But the Voltaics were irritated by his visit, as Flagstaff House had not given their ambassador in Accra enough time to advise his head of state of Botsio's impending arrival. Nor was Botsio able to offer a good price. By his account, Yameogo made clear that until the refugees were expelled from Ghana, the Entente would not be interested in any discussions. Yameogo added that the Ivory Coast and Upper Volta had never closed their borders with Ghana; as Ghana had unilaterally closed its side, it had only to reopen its own side if it truly wished open borders with its neighbors.[63]

---

subsequent trip of Ben Bella, Keita, and Touré to Conakry gave rise to speculation that Nkrumah was purposely excluded from a gathering of radicals. Botsio denied this. See also *Africa 1965*, No. 8, 23 April 1965, which tends to corroborate Botsio's opinion.

[61] "A Year of Decision for Africa," Address by Osagyefo the President, 22 March 1965, Accra, 1965. See the comment on the address, *West Africa*, 3 April 1965, p. 363.

[62] *Ghanaian Times*, 22 February 1965; *Togo-Presse*, 5, 8, 10, 29 April 1965; *West Africa*, 27 February 1965, 222, 231, 17 April 1965, 217; and Radio Lomé, 8 April 1965, cited in *Africa Research Bulletin*, April 1965.

[63] Interviews: Botsio, Ambassador Aisse Mensah, Upper Volta/Accra. See also Radio Ouagadougou, 24 March 1965, cited in *Africa Research Bulletin*, March 1965. It is difficult to believe Nkrumah ever intended to open the borders. After the coup, he made as one of his primary criticisms of the new regime its opening of the frontiers. "All economic control will collapse . . . all the thieves [will have] a free hand." BBC, ME/2140/B/7, Conakry Radio, 17 April 1966.

Finally, in this same week at the end of March, Nkrumah commuted the death sentences of those allegedly involved in the Kulungugu assassination and announced that detainees who did not threaten the state's security would be released in due course.[64] These were in fact foreign policy issues, so much did they color the view of Ghana from the outside. Giving Adjei and Adamafio twenty-year sentences, instead of death, was not considered a great concession by those who did not believe them guilty, however. The promise to release detainees was the result of Lord Russell's intervention, and it was claimed that 100 were released three months later. Nkrumah's intention of releasing still more was reversed on the advice of his illiterate bodyguard, Ambrose Yankey, though possibly Nkrumah simply sought political benefit from a promise he never intended to keep.[65]

One correspondent thought Nkrumah's new line had been decided upon during a period of meditation in Half-Assine during February.[66] The evidence is stronger that a hardening of his attitude occurred at that time. Prior to his departure for his week of meditation, he met all his economic experts and was astonished to find them telling him the exact state of the economy. He reportedly raged at them for having "deluded" him for so long, and he insisted that they take whatever steps were necessary to correct the trend. Yet when he returned from Half-Assine, he ordered vast new expenditures, particularly for Job 600: It was pleasurable to think Ghana had no economic crisis, so this was declared to be the case.[67] Thus Nkrumah was responding to Houphouet's challenge, as well as to Touré's and Keita's pleas, by intensifying his drive for union government on all fronts.

The competition between Houphouet and Nkrumah escalated in April, and the African focus was soon to be on Abidjan. Ammunition for Houphouet's next round came by way of Niamey. On March 19th a once-imprisoned dissident from Niger named Ahmadu Diop, allegedly

---

64 See *West Africa*, 20 February 1965, 217; Nkrumah's "Address to Parliament," 26 March 1965, Accra, 1965; "Task Ahead," Address by Osagyefo, 12 June 1965, Accra, 1965.

65 Interview: CF-87. Russell maintained a voluminous correspondence with Nkrumah. Russell, aware of Ghana's bad press, wished the Ivory Coast to be exposed for committing the offenses Ghana was accused of, and he hoped the release of detainees would improve Ghana's image, as it surely would have.

66 See *West Africa*, 3 April 1965, 363.

67 Interview: CF-85, Cabinet Secretariat. The *Ghanaian Times* editorialized: "Osagyefo . . . the Nation's Fount of Honour enters the sixth day of fasting and meditation today. In quietude and self-denial, he meditates with himself on the milestones so far covered in the great pilgrimage." Also see *Evening News* during his period of meditation to examine the dispensations issued.

trained in Nanking and in Ghana, set out from Accra, arriving in Niger on April 10th. On April 13th, during the Muslim Tebaski festival, Diop threw a grenade at President Diori who was praying—amidst a crowd of 20,000. One boy was killed, three Malians and three Nigeriens were seriously injured, but Diori emerged unscathed.[68]

The repercussions of this second attempt were, compared to the January Lomé incident, in proportion to the political importance of the murdered Togolese adjutant and the president of Niger. Houphouet's party issued a statement saying that the attempt, "far from creating a psychosis of fear as the inspirers hoped, will give a new *élan* to the courageous struggle of the militant masses of the PDCI-RDA against the agents of Chinese imperialism."[69] Just prior to the attempt, the Entente states had met in Abidjan to plan a campaign for the admission of Léopoldville to OCAM. Now Nkrumah supplanted Tshombe as their chief concern. Foreign ministers and leading politicians of the Ivory Coast and its partners went to Dakar, Brazzaville, Fort Lamy, Addis Ababa, Nairobi, and elsewhere requesting support for a boycott of the Accra summit. Diori and Yameogo themselves went to Yaounde, where they had little success, and to Lagos, where they appeared to have more.[70]

But was Ghana implicated in the attempt against Diori, which prompted Houphouet's crusade? It is difficult to know whether the assassin was an actual agent of Ghana, or whether he had merely been trained in Ghana, and then let loose to do as he wished. Nkrumah called the allegation a "monstrous fabrication," and asked why Ghana would attempt to assassinate a leader at the very time it was hurriedly preparing to welcome him to the OAU summit conference.[71] If this were so, there was also the question of Nkrumah's purpose in authorizing the training (by Chinese colonels) of Nigeriens in guerilla warfare, both before and after the attempt on Diori's life. The reaction of the Ghanaian press was predictable. "Is it too far-fetched to suggest that the attack on Hamani Diori was the work of agents of imperialism and neocolonialism aimed purposely at creating a pretext for increased hostility against Ghana, and through Ghana, against the OAU?"[72] It surely seems to be

---

[68] See *Togo-Presse*, 14 April 1965, *le Monde*, 15 April 1965, and *Fraternité*, 23 April 1965.

[69] *Togo-Presse*, 17 April 1965.

[70] See *West Africa*, 1 May 1965, 479. At this time it appeared certain that Abubakar would not be willing to attend an OAU conference in Accra. His comparison of Ghana and Nigeria as the "ant and the elephant" enraged the Ghanaians. See *Ghanaian Times*, 24 April 1965.

[71] "Statement on Allegations Concerning the Attempted Assassination of President Hamani Diori," Accra, 1965.

[72] "Crush This Big Lie," *Ghanaian Times*, 23 April 1965.

too far-fetched if one considers how much more compelling was the simpler explanation. Ghana alleged that the CIA had attempted to kill one of its own agents, and that the Diori attempt could not possibly "fit into Ghana's aims and objectives."[73] This last was patently false.

More important, could Diori's government *know* that Diop was trained in Ghana, assuming that he was? If not, Houphouet's offensive was only a struggle for prestige, with the Entente exploiting the animosity of other states toward Ghana to convince them of subversion emanating from that state. In fact the Entente diplomats knew precisely where the training camps were and had publicized their location long before these were revealed to the world after Ghana's 1966 coup d'état. They had their own agents within the camps and capitalized on the inability of Ghanaian militants to keep secrets. It would not be difficult for Niger's agents to keep track of a man like Diop, who had a record of subversion.[74]

It is true that only conservative states were attacking Ghana. More radical states, such as Tanzania and, in the end, Nigeria did not wish to jeopardize the summit conference over Nkrumah's caprices. But these two states were part of a pan-African tradition that the Entente leaders did not share. Tanzania, moreover, was comfortably distant from Mankrong and Half-Assine, though Nyerere's reaction to Nkrumah—at Cairo—had been as hostile as Houphouet-Boigny's when Ghanaian policy threatened Tanzanian objectives. Nigeria's leaders, for their part, lived under the illusion that their state was strong enough not to be threatened.

African unity, such as it had become, was again fractured and, although the underlying cause continued to be the Congo, attempts to resolve the difficulties were blocked once again by Accra. It is not easy to perceive Nkrumah's strategy in this period. His popular base in Ghana was too thin at the end of his five year term even to hold a plebiscite, and so he held an election without votes. Although it looked doubtful that there would be a summit conference in Accra, the Ghanaian press made the meeting the main prop of the regime. "Showboy" would be in trouble without a conference and should have been aware of the danger. The success attending Houphouet's diplomatic maneuvering increased the precariousness of the Accra summit. Although Entente missions had

73 "Who's Subverting Who," *ibid.*, 19 April 1965.

74 Diop, according to the Niger statement, had been previously imprisoned for over a year. See *Africa Research Bulletin*, April 1965. In numerous interviews with Entente diplomats prior to the 1966 coup, the writer found them well-informed as to the location, size, and scope of the Ghanaian camps. Their data could be compared with that publicized by the new regime following the coup. What frustrated the Entente and Nigerian diplomats was that the rest of the world, for the most part, refused to accept what was occurring.

met no success outside of West Africa, Houphouet could count on eleven of the fourteen OCAM members' support. Nkrumah's response was to increase his attacks on these very states. "OCAM has exposed itself as the American group of states in Africa," he said in interview. Denying that Ghana carried on subversive activities, he argued that the numerous coups d'état and other African problems could be prevented by union government: "man can help on the unfolding of history. He cannot stop it unfolding."[75]

Houphouet, concluding that there was no point in attempting to mollify radical opinion (particularly in Accra) called an extraordinary meeting of OCAM in Abidjan shortly thereafter to rally his followers and to arrange the admittance of Tshombe's Congo to their number. The aims of the OAU and OCAM were not contradictory, but complementary, he said. The states of OCAM sincerely believed in the OAU. "WE WILL GO ANYWHERE TO TAKE PART IN THE WORK OF THE OAU EXCEPT TO ACCRA."[76]

Nigeria's government was not in a position to join Houphouet's crusade, or to boycott the Accra summit, thanks to domestic political pressures, as Sir Abubakar explained to Presidents Yameogo and Diori when they visited him. He took the situation seriously enough, however, to begin diplomatic overtures soon after their visit for the holding of a special foreign ministers' conference, to resolve the conflict and save the OAU. On April 24th he formally proposed an extraordinary session of the Council of Ministers to the OAU secretary-general who, in turn, communicated the request to each state on May 4th.[77] Nkrumah replied two days later that "such a meeting is unnecessary and is not in the interest of the OAU and African Unity." To the Nigerian government, the African Affairs Secretariat wrote that it believed "a dangerous precedent would be set if the unanimous decision of the OAU [to meet in Accra] is allowed to be set aside by the grumblings of those who imagine and nurture grievances."[78] But by June 2nd the required two-thirds of the states had agreed to the meeting, with only the U.A.R., of those re-

[75] *Sunday Express*, 23 May 1965, interview by Dapo Fatogun. Reprinted in untitled pamphlet by Ghana Government, 1965. Nkrumah almost never gave interviews at this stage.

[76] See note 30.

[77] See Abubakar to Diallo Telli, 24 April 1965, ECM/2/Appx.1(v), and Secretary-General to all Member States, 4 May 1965, *ibid.*, in *Government of Nigeria*, Verbatim Report of the Fifth Extraordinary Session of the Council of Ministers of the Organisation of African Unity, Lagos, 10-13 June 1965, p. 97.

[78] Nkrumah to Secretary-General, OAU, 6 May 1965, in *ibid.*, p. 97, and A.A.S. to High Commissioner of Nigeria/Accra, 28 April 1965, in *ibid.*, pp. 103-04.

377

plying, supporting Nkrumah in objecting to the conference.[79] Ghana, called to account, had no choice but to attend; Houphouet's group, seeing the conference as a continental platform for its charge against Nkrumah, was enthusiastic.

Nkrumah instructed Botsio, who led Ghana's delegation to the Lagos meeting, to avoid the question of refugees and subversion if possible, and to refuse to discuss it were it raised. He was to take a strictly legal position on the question of venue for the summit conference, and to argue that the OAU was irrevocably committed to meet in Accra.[80] The instructions were irrelevant to the conference that ensued. Refugees and subversion were its subjects, and the choice of Accra as the site for the meeting was never in question; as every delegate quickly perceived, the issue was whether Ghana could make enough concessions to appease Houphouet so that he and his followers would attend the summit. As Prime Minister Abubakar said in his welcoming address on June 10th, "Since Cairo . . . a lot of water has gone under the bridge. . . . It is not a question of your being asked to revoke or modify the Cairo decision. . . . You are to prepare the ground before it can hold. . . . You cannot ignore the serious threat of a boycott."[81]

No one present at this tense conference—and confrontation—underestimated the danger, and few were optimistic about a solution. Secretary-General Diallo Telli, in his report, said that "this constant pressure and diversity of interest have never been so intense and diverse" in Africa as in this period. "The important point is that world public opinion is seriously disquieted as to what will become of the great, generous and realistic ideas that gave birth to the Organisation of African Unity. World opinion is not unaware that the Organisation . . . is at a stage at which, unless special sacrifices are made, it may founder in chaos."[82]

On June 11th the Ivoirien, Nigerien, and Voltaic foreign ministers laid their charges. Camille Aliali recounted the tangled history of the Ivoirien-Ghanaian relations of past years, noting that the dilemma was that only a few months prior to the summit Ghana had "not even started to give effect to the resolutions" agreed to between the two heads of state the previous year. True, Nkrumah had bowed to public pressure and sent several Sanwi leaders to Cairo, but as he had promised them they could return and was in fact supporting them in Cairo, and as others remained in Accra, the situation remained threatening.

79 ". . . the United Arab Republic Government fears that such an Extraordinary Meeting will lead to a series of frictions and diversity in opinion." Mahmoud Riad, Minister of Foreign Affairs, U.A.R., to Secretary-General, OAU, 14 May 1965, in *ibid.*, p. 100.
80 Interviews: Botsio, CF-14, 24.   81 Verbatim Report (see note 77), p. 3.
82 *Ibid.*, p. 8.

As Africa has only one IMMORTAL REDEEMER at the moment, the other Heads of State, poor mortals, must see to their security. . . . But more important than reasons of security is the question of dignity. How can we agree to go to Accra when it has been proved that so-called political refugees attend official occasions in Ghana? Regrettably there have been cases, all too frequent, of refugee leaders being given the places of honour to which the official representatives of our countries were entitled. It would certainly be undignified to accept such humiliating situations.[83]

Much the most stirring moment of the conference was the address of Adamou Mayaki, foreign minister of Niger. In meticulous detail, he described Ghanaian-based incursions into his country. "Here are some examples of some of the weapons we have taken from some of the commandos who attacked the Port of Poso which is near Lake Chad: they had two automatic machine guns, two sub-machine guns, two automatic pistols and a dozen rounds of ammunition. . . . Those who attacked the post of Tera had ten automatic pistols, with 2,500 bullets, three sub-machine guns with five hundred bullets. . . . All this is being done with a view to impressing the masses and to creating anarchy." Some commandos were still operating in Niger, he said. Fifteen had been captured, and all stated that "they were trained, organized, and armed in Ghana with a view to coming to kill in my country. At the present time, training camps and death camps exist . . . in the following places: Mampong, Hasi, Osini, Aksim, Konongo, and Siniani. . . . I know that Ghana, faced by my detailed argument, will speak of imperialism. . . . They will accuse Washington, Belgium, London, Brussels, and Bonn in order to defend themselves. . . . (But) the commandos did not come from Belgium, London, Washington . . . and Bonn."

In this affair . . . the only imperialist we can refer to is Ghana. . . . If this subversion does not cease immediately it will lead to intervention in our countries by foreigners such as China, Russia, or America. The example of President Nkrumah is a direct invitation to all foreign forces who wish to intervene in Africa. The example of Dr. Kwame Nkrumah towards our country is a tragic confrontation between ideologies which are foreign to the African conceptions. If Africans will not be very careful with the examples of . . . Nkrumah, Africa will be rapidly dragged into the cold war, and this will bring to us chaos and anarchy. President Ben Bella was perfectly right when he uttered the prophetic words at the last conference in Cairo, "We must all accept one another as we are if we wish to remain united."[84]

83 *Ibid.*, pp. 12-16.   84 *Ibid.*, pp. 16-26.

Botsio was in trouble. If he adhered to Nkrumah's instructions, the planned summit could not avoid collapse. The best he could do was to "play it by ear,"[85] to take advantage of logical gaps in his colleagues' speeches, counter their charges, and claim good faith on Ghana's part. It was probably the best speech he could make, in the circumstances, but his one miscalculation was to make a statement known to be false. He denied that the Bureau of African Affairs involved any refugees other than those "from dependent countries." Worse, "We categorically deny that there are camps in Ghana against any independent African country."[86] Few, by this point, had any remaining doubts that the camps existed, for purposes much transcending their original brief.

A reconciliation committee, chaired by Joseph Murumbi, the Council's chairman, and composed of the Ethiopian, Gambian, Malian, Nigerian, and Tunisian representatives, now began attempting to mediate. On June 12th Aliali put forward his demands to them:

1. All political refugees in Ghana to be repatriated;
2. All political parties (of refugees) in Ghana to be dissolved;
3. Repatriation of refugees to be definitive, and not temporary;
4. A commission to be appointed to observe implementation of all OAU decisions;
5. The question of refugees and subversion to be on the agenda of the Summit conference.

If these conditions were accepted, OCAM heads of state "might modify their position," he said, and attend the summit.[87] Botsio expressed Ghana's readiness to send refugees away during the conference period and, if no country would receive them, to send them outside Accra for the duration of the summit. He demanded that any solution proposed not be directed solely at Ghana, since the question of refugees "was not peculiar to Ghana. It was a basic problem" throughout Africa. He flatly rejected any suggestion of a commission, as proposed by Aliali, as an infringement on Ghana's sovereignty. Moreover, time and again he refused to accept item two, on the grounds that the CPP was the only legal party in Ghana—using a legal pretext to cover the existence of political-refugee groupings within the country.[88]

Finally, it came time to compromise. Upper Volta noted that since Botsio had denied the existence of such political parties, "the committee should seek a wording which would save the face of the parties to the dispute." Mali suggested that, instead of a commission, Telli and

[85] Interview: Botsio.   [86] Verbatim Report, pp. 31-40.
[87] Summary of Proceedings of the Reconciliation Sub-Committee, in *ibid.*, p. 81.
[88] *Ibid.*, pp. 81-87.

Murumbi be asked by Ghana to examine steps taken in fulfillment of the Council's resolutions, to which Botsio agreed. This was not enough. The draft resolution presented back to the Council, which incorporated Mali's proposal and did not require Ghana to expel refugees definitively, was unacceptable to the complainants.[89]

There could be no question of voting on the draft, as this would only split the organization further. The minister from Léopoldville stated that "a situation has arisen, in which we will democratically submit to the vote [that which] we will not be able to convince our heads of state about."[90] On the contrary, consensus had to be achieved. Botsio, for his part, was only worried about what Nkrumah would accept. He bargained hard, but there was no way to end the impasse on the question of the finality of the refugees' expulsion. As recriminations increased, hope receded. Then, proposals by Mongi Slim and Murumbi saved the day—and the organization. Sensing that Botsio could not make further concessions before his colleagues—but that he could in the corridors, they brought about a suspension of the meeting. Exactly 43 minutes later the contending parties returned in agreement, to the prolonged applause of the house. At the conference's opening, Telli had stated what was "uppermost on everyone's mind, namely, that today more than ever the miracle of African Unity and solidarity must again take physical shape."[91] As at Addis Ababa two years earlier, it had. The crucial paragraph had been reworded to satisfy all parties:

> Notes with satisfaction the guarantees and assurances given by the host government and all practical steps already taken and those it has decided to take in order to ensure the full success of the next meeting of the Assembly of Heads of State and Government, and particularly the measures reaffirmed by that Government to send away from its territory before the conference all those persons whose presence is considered undesirable to countries of their choice and to forbid the formation of any political groups whose aims are to oppose any member state of the OAU.[92]

Botsio and the diplomats with him hoped that with this commitment Nkrumah would feel compelled to do what they had never been able to convince him to do, namely, rid Ghana of the refugees. Nkrumah was en route to the Commonwealth conference during the meeting, so Botsio had not been able to request new instructions during the negotiations at Lagos. Nkrumah, who tended not to appreciate the undertakings of others, declined to be bound by Botsio's pledges—since he had not him-

[89] *Ibid.*, pp. 85-90.   [90] Verbatim Report, pp. 61-62.   [91] *Ibid.*, p. 9.
[92] *Ibid.*, p. 65.

self authorized them.[93] This posed a serious dilemma, to which Nkrumah responded, characteristically, by denying its existence. In an August speech to the national assembly he referred to his address of July 1963 in which he had stated that refugees were not permitted to engage in political activities; this was delivered in answer to the OAU's demands. Yet in that earlier speech the policy as stated was intended to be understood as a joke.[94]

In this same speech Nkrumah cited trade and various forms of bilateral cooperation that could be begun with other African states. Economic and trade missions should be attached to Ghana's African embassies, he said. Was he serious? Seven days earlier it had been decided at Flagstaff House that the exchange of instruments with Niger—all that was now needed to bring to conclusion three years of negotiations for a trade agreement—should not take place because of the "hostile attitude of Niger authorities," and this despite the pleas of Ghana's ambassador in Niamey that the Niger government was eager to proceed with the agreement.[95] Economic and trade missions were obviously still to have lower priority than those of the Bureau of African Affairs.

Thus tension mounted in the summer of 1965. Few of the refugees were sent away, and diplomats found no indications that the main part of them would be. To no avail, Joe Murumbi came and pleaded tearfully that Nkrumah not jeopardize the summit.[96] Nigeria complicated Nkrumah's dilemma. At the Lagos meeting Abubakar, as host and conciliator, had not asked that Sammy Ikoku be expelled from Ghana, but he thought it hardly appropriate to attend the summit in Accra if Ikoku were present.[97] He was soon to have a basis for a deal with Accra.

By the end of the summer, delays in constructing the incredible conference complex, Job 600, forced Ghana to request a postponement of the summit until October, a date which competed with that of Colonel Boumedienne's Second Bandung conference due to take place in November in Algiers. Two-thirds of the OAU members were required to give their assent to the change of date, for which purpose Alex Quaison-Sackey, now foreign minister, proposed visiting Lagos to enlist Nigerian support. According to Alhaji Isa Wali, he lost much of the potential goodwill from the gesture by insisting that he travel that same day, and that he be permitted to see Prime Minister Sir Abubakar on arrival. "Diplomacy is based on reciprocity, and we could never see Nkrumah so

93 Interviews: Botsio, CF-14.

94 "Sessional Address, 24 August 1965," Accra, 1965, p. 8. See pp. 334-35.

95 Hagan, M.F.A., to P.S., A.A.S., 16 August 1965, and Amb. Placca, Ghana/Niamey, to P.S., A.A.S., 15 July 1965, CFA-27.

96 Interview: Quaison-Sackey.

97 See *West Africa*, 1 May 1965, 479. Also interviews: Isa Wali and CF-100.

promptly. We needed time in any event to plan a strategy for getting Ikoku out of Ghana," Isa Wali commented.

The plan they evolved was that Nigeria would accept the new date to make its commitment to African unity unambiguous. They would then request that Sackey's visit be returned by a visit of Senator Dan Ibekwe, minister of state for Commonwealth relations. Ibekwe would surprise Nkrumah with a request that Ikoku be sent away from Ghana prior to the conference; Ghana's good faith would be tested. The plan worked, but not without a request by Nkrumah that if Ikoku were expelled so would be Nkrumah's enemy Khow Richardson, from Nigeria. The Nigerians told him there was no connection between the two requests. The conference was to be held in Accra, not Lagos. Nkrumah asked if brother states dealt with each other in this fashion. "We told him that a brother was in his rights to refuse to visit his brother unless mad dogs were removed from the front yard."[98]

In October all eyes turned on Accra. Despite the postponement that was obtained, the atmosphere there remained hectic. Work on Job 600 continued around the clock, as bullet-proof glass was fitted into the viewless windows, and as the imported furniture and fittings were put in place. The foreign reserves were all but depleted, as wines, eggs, and consumers goods were flown in from Europe to convince delegates that all was well in Ghana.[99] Tension with Algeria, over the competing conferences dates, was still high, and Houphouet remained adamant that all refugees leave. In early October, Secretary-General Diallo Telli, President Keita, and others made moves to bring Nkrumah and Houphouet together. At Nkrumah's request, they arranged a meeting in Bamako for October 13th, a week prior to the opening of the summit.

Houphouet went to Bamako with his Entente partners and now raised his price of attendance. The communiqué showed his and Nkrumah's agreement that the "families of the political refugees who were once resident in Ghana and have been deported in accordance with the resolution of the Lagos [conference] shall join the persons deported. The deportation of such persons and their families shall be final." Most importantly, Ghana agreed to request the assistance of the Entente's Accra embassies to "detect and deport" persons opposed to their governments, a concession Entente diplomats had not succeeded in obtaining

98 Interview: Isa Wali.

99 See *Ghana*, Economic Survey, 1965, p. 20, para. 88. Windows in Job 600 were above eye-sight so as to protect heads of state from assassination; Nkrumah, as usual, failed to separate his own obsessions from the concerns of his peers.

at the Lagos confrontation.[100] Such demands suggested that Houphouet would not attend under any circumstances. Nkrumah's willingness to compromise appeared to be shown through his acceptance of the additional conditions.

The issues were more complex. Nkrumah had returned some UPC refugees to Cameroun, following a September visit by Botsio to Yaounde, where an agreement had been concluded. According to Entente diplomats, Houphouet now tried to ensure that President Ahidjo made visible efforts to reintegrate the refugees into society, so that Nkrumah could see that the other refugees would share the same fate (as Houphouet had promised).[101] Since Ghana's neighboring states constituted a special category in Nkrumah's mind—as Entente diplomats knew—Houphouet had to be certain that the agreements of Lagos and Bamako be honored. Additional conditions for attendance had to be imposed at Bamako, because Nkrumah had lied, insisting that the refugees *had* left, when everyone knew that most of them were still in Ghana.[102] Houphouet's strategy was to demonstrate to Nkrumah that no harm would come to the refugees if deported, while at the same time imposing upon him such humiliation that any peace made would be real and not just another smokescreen. He was unwilling for the Ghanaian people to see Nkrumah breaking his commitments with impunity. On the other hand, if peace were not made, he was prepared to do anything in the realm of public diplomacy to bring down a regime that he felt was in its last, and most dangerous, stage. In the end, the leading refugees left—though not before Nkrumah had given them round-trip tickets—but their families and principal followers remained.[103] Ghana refused to permit the Entente diplomats to locate and name those they wished deported.

Eight states did not, therefore, attend the summit—those of the Conseil de l'Entente, Togo, Gabon, Chad, and Malagasy. These lost prestige in the short run for not having honored the spirit of African unity. Botsio, too, thought the demands of the Entente ambassadors were excessive; "diplomats cannot go around pointing out people they want deported." But such were the terms of the Bamako summit. Nkru-

[100] "Communiqué," P.R. #303/65, 14 October 1965.

[101] Interviews: Ambassadors Léon Amon, Ivory Coast/Accra; Aisse Mensah, Upper Volta/Accra; Tiecoura Alzouma, Niger/Accra.

[102] There was much deceit on this issue. Dei-Anang, according to the Entente and Nigerian diplomats, would say that the refugees had left, when they had just been sighted in Winneba or elsewhere.

[103] The refugees played their hand skillfully. Diplomats at Flagstaff House thought that with the Bamako agreement they were finally rid of the refugees. "But they were cleverer than we were, and continually pressed Nkrumah not to surrender to Houphouet's demands. He genuinely felt sorry for them. 'These men are human beings and cannot just be kicked out and left to their fate,' he said to me at one point." Interview: CF-14.

mah had only grudgingly sent away the most conspicuous refugees—like Bakary Djibo and Sammy Ikoku—and as such had violated both the letter and spirit of the Bamako agreement.

Following the conference, he used the absence of the eight to justify bringing back the refugees. He did not, of course, bring back the Camerounians because, as Botsio said, Ahidjo had attended the summit.[104] But would Nkrumah have refused to permit Bakary Djibo to return from Nairobi had President Diori attended? Abubakar came to Accra, yet he had hardly left when Sammy Ikoku returned from Moscow.[105] Houphouet failed to attend not out of fear for his security with refugees still present, but because he had correctly gauged Nkrumah's intentions; Nkrumah had refused to go to Canossa, so Houphouet refused to go to Accra. After the years of Nkrumah's insults, abuse, and subversion, Houphouet was perhaps justified in refusing him satisfaction now.

The main significance of the conference thus lay in its being held at all. The pity was that so much more might have been accomplished. Ironically, Nkrumah was finally coming to understand the necessity of working within the OAU (at least at one level). He even accepted the pleas of Botsio, Harry Amonoo, Quaison-Sackey, and others to "meet African wishes half-way" by not demanding the continental union government which the press had been promising for a year as the outcome of the conference.[106] Instead he called for the establishment of an "executive committee" similar to those quietly proposed by Ghanaian delegations (acting without authority) at Dakar in 1963 and Lagos in 1964. For Nkrumah this was the bare minimum, but even so he could not get it. Nor was there even the two-thirds vote necessary to establish a committee to study the possibility of revising the charter in order to make an executive committee legally possible. Had he argued for an executive committee two years earlier, and geared his diplomacy to such an objective, there might have been a happier outcome now.

[104] Not all the Camerounian refugees were deported, but those whom Ahidjo specified were. Those whose pictures were widely publicized following the coup, in subversion camps, were those who had been threatened with expulsion if they remained reluctant to undergo training, and whom Ahidjo did not consider a threat. Interview: Botsio, and CF-29.

[105] Ikoku traveled on a Zimbabwian passport, as E. Madley. Interview: Alhaji Isa Wali.

[106] The issue of Ghana's attitude toward the OAU had been hotly debated in Flagstaff House throughout 1965 and, to a degree, even in the press. See Budu-Acquah, "Crisis in the OAU?" *Ghanaian Times*, 10 May 1965, and "Telli's Report," *Spark*, No. 149, 16 October 1965. Nkrumah only accepted the "revisionist" view when extraordinary pressure was put on him, just before the conference's opening, to the effect that he would otherwise appear foolish. The diplomats did not wish to be humiliated among their peers on home ground, and were thus willing to court Nkrumah's disfavor. Interviews: Botsio, Budu-Acquah, Quaison-Sackey, H. R. Amonoo.

Nkrumah's reaction to this defeat was at first to threaten withdrawal from the OAU.[107] Although the Emperor and Sir Albert Margai easily dissuaded him, there is no doubt that he was prepared to admit failure for the first time.

NKRUMAH'S LAST AFRICAN DÉMARCHE

How is union government feasible when "the U.A.R. and Tunisia are not on friendly terms, Morocco and Mauritania are not on friendly terms, Ghana and Ivory Coast are not on friendly terms, Ghana and Upper Volta are not on friendly terms, Ghana and Niger . . . (Interjection: inaudible) (Laughter) (Applause)"—HASTINGS BANDA in the Malawi Parliament.[108]

In the four-month interval between the Accra conference and the coup, African developments took second place to international concerns at Flagstaff House. Some officials thought that Nkrumah, by the end of the year, had bowed to the necessity of working through the OAU. This may be so, but another side of his policy had become more significant. He had developed far more sophisticated means of subversion than ever before with which to pursue the goal of union government. The conference itself was marked by such technological advancements as the wire-tapping of hotel rooms and even bar tables. Through the aid of East Germany, Ghana had available far more elaborate methods of undermining other African governments, including a new "Special African Service" set up by two East German agents, which was to report to Nkrumah directly—without even going through Bureau channels. Its budget for 1966 "included C207,290.00 for general expenses and C289,920.00 for operating expenses."[109]

From the beginning subversion had been, in part, one of Nkrumah's responses to his growing difficulties in influencing the march of African history; his use of it usually followed a frustrating defeat. He was becoming desperate following the summit conference, for he was losing all his friends, even his most faithful admirers of an earlier period. In the Malawi parliament, Kumuzu Banda referred to his erstwhile hero as an idiot.[110] It was not clear until the eve of the summit whether President Obote would even send a delegation, so much had relations with Uganda

---

[107] Interview: CF-14.

[108] *Malawi*, Debates, 9 November 1965, p. 219.

[109] See *Ghana*, "Nkrumah's Subversion in Africa," 1966, p. 34. Also see pp. 28-33, 37-40. The new service was barely operational by the time of the 1966 coup.

[110] Or so Nkrumah interpreted Banda's remarks. See *Malawi*, Debates, 10 November 1965, p. 275. Ghana protested the remark, and so Banda had the Hansard volume revised. Interview: CF-14.

deteriorated since 1964.[111] There were several indications that he was preparing for more serious assaults on his enemies. In the first week of 1966 came a new round in the struggle with the Ivory Coast president, and a new attempt to obscure Ghanaian objectives.[112]

The major event of the four months was the Nigerian coup of January 15th. Ghana's response to it indicates a type of development that might have ensued had Nkrumah himself not been overthrown. Even during the brief period of reconciliation between Lagos and Accra in the months following the formation of the OAU, Ghanaian interference in Nigerian affairs had continued. This took the form of subsidies for trade unions affiliated with Accra's All-African Trade Union Federation, particularly during the Nigerian dockers' strike in 1963 and the general strike in the summer of 1964;[113] arranging for the transportation of Nigerian radicals to Moscow, without knowledge of their national authorities;[114] and much the most crucial, the importation into Nigeria of ammunition, 120 consignments of which were apparently dispatched during the grave election crisis at the end of 1964.[115]

In none of these cases was the Ghanaian role central—in leading the workers to strike or in fomenting the near-breakdown of the Nigerian system in the election; the substructure of Nigeria was sufficiently fragile for these to develop of their own accord. But settlement of the strikes was more difficult, and the number of lives lost in the election was much greater as a result of Ghanaian intervention. Diplomatic harassment brought a focus to the Nigerians' resentment at Ghana's unhelpful role.[116]

Nor was Nkrumah's involvement in the disastrous coup of 15 January

---

[111] Interview: CF-14.

[112] Ivoirien authorities caught some B.A.A. agents engaged in espionage and imprisoned them. In retaliation, Nkrumah detained some innocent Ivoirien laborers under contract to work on a French-financed hotel at the Accra airport. In January 1966, Quaison-Sackey and Amonoo traveled to Abidjan to try to negotiate an exchange of prisoners, but Houphouet, who received the envoys from a sickbed, observed that there was no basis for reciprocity as the Ivoiriens were not guilty, and concluded that Nkrumah had merely sent them to put a smokescreen around his own plans. Interviews: CF-15, 49, 14.

[113] See *Trades Union Congress*, "Trade Unions in Chains," Accra, 1966.

[114] See Tettegah to Amb. G. Rodionov, U.S.S.R./Accra, 16 July 1965, in *ibid.*, no page number. Also interview: CF-100. The issue was not that Nigerians could not travel to Russia, but that they could not travel anywhere without proving they had the resources to support themselves abroad. This they could not do with respect to Russia without revealing illegal activities within Nigeria.

[115] After the 1966 Ghanaian coup, the NLC permitted the director of Nigeria's Special Branch to examine the records of Nkrumah's subversion, the report on which Alhaji Isa Wali permitted the author to examine.

[116] Three senior Ghanaian diplomats were declared *P.N.G.* after their unannounced arrival in Lagos during the election crisis. As one was the head of the intelligence division, the Nigerians suspected the worst; whatever their purposes, they had broken form at a delicate time for Nigeria.

1966 as great as he attempted to convince his entourage and the public; nonetheless, it seems clear that Ghana had a role in it; his desire to claim credit for it is beyond doubt and very revealing. According to High Commissioner Isa Sulaiman Wali, the Ibo conspirators in Lagos had, as one might expect, been in contact with Sammy Ikoku. According to his mission's reports, Isa Wali was alerted hours after the coup that Colonel Zanlerigu—of the President's Own Guard—left Accra with Ikoku; they returned several days later with Major Ifeajuna, one of the principal conspirators who, after the rebellion's backfire, was much wanted in Lagos. In the meantime, Nkrumah sent sheep for sacrifice and celebration to Ikoku's house.[117]

As soon as the coup was announced—and possibly some hours before—Nkrumah began working around the clock to strengthen the radical Majors' position in Lagos, even though it should have been clear almost from the first that they had failed in their objective of installing a radical government. On January 17th, flanked by Ikoku and another Nigerian exile, Nkrumah announced his recognition of the new regime; which was diplomatically impertinent as Ghana had received no official request for recognition. Nigerian diplomats in Accra and Flagstaff House officials now engaged in a duel of wits to discredit the other party in the eyes of General Aguiyi-Ironi's new government, the result of which was the general's public acclaim of his high commissioner.[118] Once again Nkrumah was wrong in thinking Africans would divide only for or against *him*, and wrong in thinking that Ghana could determine in a positive sense the course of events elsewhere in Africa. It only possessed an infinite capacity for mischief.

On the occasion of the announcement of Sir Abubakar Tafewa Balewa's death a week later, Nkrumah delivered what *West Africa*, in its most strained euphemism of the Nkrumah period, called the "most striking comment" of those tributes paid. Nkrumah said that Sir Abubakar "died a victim of forces he did not understand and a martyr to a neo-colonialist system of which he was merely the figurehead. . . . The

---

117 Interview: Alhaji Isa Wali. Ifeajuna's presence was common knowledge in Accra by the end of January. According to intelligence officers in the Ghanaian army, Nkrumah offered the major whatever he wished were he to succeed in assassinating General Ironsi. Isa Wali was able to repatriate Ifeajuna, who was later executed by the Ojukwu regime in Enugu.

118 Isa Wali had refused to attend the press conference at which Nkrumah announced his recognition of Ironsi's government, as "the relations of government are based on official communications, and I had not informed Nkrumah of any change of government." Quaison-Sackey then wrote Ironsi trying to discredit Isa Wali. Ironsi responded in February by appointing Isa Wali chairman of a delegation to an OAU special conference which, nonetheless, he could not attend, as he was busily obtaining his revenge in Accra—by celebrating the downfall of Nkrumah.

tragedy of Sir Abubakar was that he never realised that for Nigeria the choice was either immediate political unification of Africa or Nigeria's disintegration. He scoffed at the idea of African Unity. Thus he was destroyed by those very pressures and forces which only a continental union government could have eased."[119] Flags flew at half-mast in Dar-es-Salaam and elsewhere throughout Africa. The Ghanaian public received Geoffrey Bing's prose, which Nkrumah found perfect for the occasion, with incredulity. Most observers realized that a coup in Ghana had to come soon since Nkrumah was no longer inhibited by any standard of decency and was no longer guided by any sense of what could aid his cause.

THE WESTERN FULL HOUSE

For all the homage paid to nonalignment, Ghana's policy in this last period was one of almost implacable hostility to the West in word and deed. In part this was the consequence of—and natural development from—the policies Nkrumah had long since set forth, but it was also a reaction to the increasing international aggressiveness of the leading Western power. The crucial change in American-Ghanaian relations occurred over foreign policy-ideological differences, as in an earlier period of change; while, once again, the change in relations with Britain resulted from domestic-economic developments—when £50,000,000 of investments looked neither safe nor profitable. Britain, with its own economic problems, and its need to protect its investments in Ghana, had diminishing direct influence in Accra. Britain was also withdrawing from empire, and Nkrumah, by 1966 the senior Commonwealth leader, was thus able to play a relatively more equal role in his dealings with London. Yet residual British influence, of an indirect kind, remained strong; a fact which was ultimately to lead to Nkrumah's undoing. America, moving in a direction opposite to Britain's, came to discover how much leverage it possessed in Accra; the roots for the dominant role it assumed in Ghana following the coup d'état exist in the last period of Nkrumah's rule.

The turning point in Ghanaian-British relations probably coincided with the departure (in late 1963) of Sir Geoffrey de Freitas, who had been high commissioner for two years. He had arrived in January 1962 with much hope of influencing Nkrumah—although, by that time, most British diplomats in Ghana wondered if it were worth the effort. For a

[119] *West Africa*, 19 January 1966, *Ghanaian Times*, 24 January 1966. The writer was in Bing's office while the statement was drafted. Enoch Okoh, the cabinet secretary, tried to alter it drastically, but Bing had already short-circuited him by sending a carbon to Nkrumah, who was, reportedly, delighted by Bing's draft.

short time he succeeded, but when he left, discouraged and disheartened, there was general agreement that Britain thenceforth could only mark time until a new regime appeared.[120] The first manifestation of the United Kingdom's loss of interest was perhaps in the appointment of Sir Geoffrey's successor. As the Commonwealth Office's nominee could not accept the appointment, a relatively junior officer was substituted to forestall the appointment of a Foreign Office diplomat.[121] So much for Ghana's priority in Whitehall.

The change in commercial relations is more important. After Ghana's new investment act was passed in 1963, prospective British investors visited frequently. It looked as if a genuine and profitable partnership between British capital and Ghanaian Socialism could exist within the framework of the seven-year plan. But Nkrumah assigned every attractive slot in the plan to the state sector and bought out private investors whose success was politically threatening. Once Andrew Djin, the former ambassador to the Congo, was appointed minister of trade, all hope of a workable import licensing system disappeared. Graft, hoarding, corruption, and maladministration became endemic to the system so that it became impossible to plan investment rationally. By the end of the year British commercial officers considered the investment act a dead letter. The fear that remained was not that British concerns might be nationalized, but that Ghana's economy would deteriorate enough to render British investments worthless.[122]

British influence in Ghana, however, was still impressive. Lord Mountbatten's visit in October 1964 was worth the visit of several Russian astronauts and strengthened the position of the British military training missions still serving Nkrumah's regime. Harold Smedley, the new high commissioner, turned out to be one of the best diplomats in Accra during this period.

The important link between the two countries was, however, increasingly the Commonwealth. Nkrumah's moderation at the 1964 and 1965 prime ministers' conferences astonished Smedley, Duncan Sandys, and Sandys' successors. Nkrumah's proposal for a Commonwealth secretariat proved to be one of the most important to be made at those meetings. Such an office had been proposed by Sandys himself in 1961, but without results; by 1964 the Commonwealth office had come to feel that they had everything to lose if the planning mechanism of the prime

120 Interviews: CF-52, 89, 106.
121 Interview: CF-113, December 1966, London.
122 Interviews: CF-89; and CF-90, 11 November 1965, United Africa Company, London.

ministers' meetings were placed in other hands, and hoped the proposal would be forgotten. When Nkrumah resurrected it, they obviously could not oppose it.[123]

Through adroit use of the Rhodesian issue in this period Ghana accumulated political capital with which it could counteract its growing isolation in Africa and gain substantial leverage with Britain as well. The Ghanaians first seized the initiative on this issue in 1963 after the Addis Ababa conference,[124] at which point the immediate objective was to prevent London from turning over the assets of the Federation of Rhodesia and Nyasaland, soon to be dissolved, to the Salisbury settlers. By mid-July, the carefully documented memoranda of Geoffrey Bing— who made this his personal cause—had been distributed by Ghanaian missions to every possible medium of publicity. One of Ghana's advantages was its membership in the UN Security Council. African states wanted the Rhodesia question raised in the General Assembly, where they could contribute, but Bing convinced Quaison-Sackey that new information on the military build-up in Rhodesia required immediate action by the Security Council.[125]

At the Security Council session an effective presentation by Quaison-Sackey—contrasting with a vain attempt by the British representative, Sir Patrick Dean, to drive a wedge between Ghana and other African states—enhanced the smaller state's prestige. The United Kingdom was moved to one of its rare Security Council vetoes, but even British diplomats conceded that Ghana had gained much for itself in directing attention to this issue.[126]

While thus currying African support, Nkrumah sought to keep his lines with Whitehall as clear as possible. At both the 1964 and 1965 Commonwealth Conferences Nkrumah played the "moderate African, telling Albert Margai to shut up" and trying to find a basis for compromise between the British government and radicals like Nyerere.[127] But after the 1965 conference he concluded that Commonwealth prestige was to be bought only at the cost of jeopardizing his primary

[123] Interviews: CF-103, 10 November 1965, London; CF-106. This was one of Nkrumah's most imaginative diplomatic exercises, and one which much impressed the British, however reluctant they were to develop the secretariat.

[124] Here again Ghana's exclusion from the OAU's liberation committee was an incentive to action, in this case with a constructive result.

[125] Interviews: Quaison-Sackey, Bing, CF-14.

[126] The Uganda representative commented, "The issue before this council is not a Ghanaian issue, as the representative of the United Kingdom has endeavoured to make you believe, but an African issue." *UN Docs.*, Security Council debates, 13 September 1963, No. 1066, p. 13, para. 82. Also interview: CF-106.

[127] Interview: CF-103, 10 November 1965, London.

ambitions. For that reason he determined to assume a position so radical as to be just slightly left of Nyerere's.[128]

As the possibility of a declaration of independence in Salisbury increased, Nkrumah put more pressure on Whitehall. At the Accra OAU summit the Ghanaians wielded great influence on the Rhodesian question; with their superb information-propaganda mechanism and their well-prepared and well-informed delegates, they ensured that radicalism carried the day. British diplomats thought that the Ghanaians had in fact raised the stakes whenever a consensus had emerged, narrowing Wilson's options.[129]

A week before Rhodesia's declaration, Harold Wilson returned to Britain from Salisbury by way of Accra, in order to meet with Nkrumah for discussions which took place at the airport. Before Wilson's departure, but after Nkrumah had taken leave of him, the British High Commissioner handed his prime minister a Ghanaian *aide mémoire* outlining the Ghanaian position on Wilson's proposed royal commission. Purportedly it set forth the considered Ghanaian views following upon the Nkrumah-Wilson talks. Diplomatic courtesy and Commonwealth convention required that the substance of the talks be kept private. In fact the memorandum had been written (by Bing) prior to Wilson's arrival and subsequently was given to the press. In the British view, Nkrumah was guilty of inexcusable indiscretion, repaying Wilson's courtesy and inconvenience in briefing him on the Rhodesian negotiations by acts of rudeness.[130] From Nkrumah's point of view, since the Commonwealth amenities conflicted with a higher African interest, they had outlived their usefulness. He may also have suspected Wilson of trying to score points among radicals by consulting with him. In any case the meeting was significant: after years of equivocating on British colonial interests, Nkrumah was prepared to cast off Ghana's ties to the Commonwealth in order to enhance its position in Africa.

By the end of November, after Salisbury's "U.D.I.," Nkrumah was pressing for military sanctions against Rhodesia. He urged mobilizing an African force for the purpose, to be guaranteed by the permanent members of the Security Council or, ominously, by "one of them," which "would be sufficient."[131] He asked parliament for authorization to form

---

128 Interview: Quaison-Sackey.

129 Interview: CF-106, British High Commission, Accra. See also *Observer*, 24 October 1965.

130 See "Aide Memoire Given to the British Prime Minister by the President of Ghana on the Occasion of His Visit to Accra, 31 October 1965," in *Ghana*, "Statements on Southern Rhodesia by the President and Government of Ghana, October 1965 to January 1966," Accra, 1966. Also interviews: CF-106, Quaison-Sackey.

131 "An Address by the President of Ghana to the National Assembly in Accra, 25 November 1965," in "Statements on Southern Rhodesia . . ." p. 17.

392

a militia, and announced that recruitment would start immediately. It would mean a mobilization on a scale which "must entail considerable disorganisation of civilian life," for "in a crisis of this nature we must put military necessity first." The speech had a familiar ring—it sounded much like one given over five years earlier in the heat of the Congo crisis. It was psychological warfare again, but the limits to the influence of a small state even with respect to its own supposed sphere of influence were underlined anew. This was 1965, not 1960. In the five years that had passed since the heady days midway through "Africa's year," the continent's importance in world affairs had dramatically declined. There was not to be any international intervention in Rhodesia to which Nkrumah could hitch his own star. The United Nations had not fully recovered from a year of paralysis deriving from the Congo crisis itself.

It seems likely that Nkrumah realized the empty nature of his own moves. Five years earlier he believed that Lumumba's regime could be stabilized by international action, but in this new crisis he sensed that the white Rhodesian rebels might succeed in their objectives.[132] As his instincts were, in the short run, right, he might have saved Africa from a painful humiliation by opting to continue trying to influence Britain from within on the question of Rhodesia.

At first the possibility of a break with Britain had no support. British officials thought Nkrumah may have considered a withdrawal from the Commonwealth and that, in any case, he was trying to find the minimal gesture to preserve his leadership of the left and leave relations with Britain intact. The decision was made for him. In the course of the special OAU meeting on Rhodesia in Addis Ababa, a gust of emotion swept the hall leading to a resolution that all member states break relations with Britain unless certain stringent conditions were met within the next several days. The Ghanaian diplomats were apprehensive, but felt compelled to join the chorus.[133]

To the embarrassment of most African heads of state, OAU members thus found themselves called upon to break relations with Britain, which offered little hope of universal acceptance, let alone effectiveness. In the ensuing debate in Accra over whether to make the break, Quaison-Sackey argued on principle, that it had to be made. Kwesi Armah was more pragmatic.[134] Nkrumah hesitated, reconsidered, then on December 16th announced his decision to follow the OAU resolution.

---

[132] Interview: CF-14.

[133] Interviews: CF-106, CF-14, Quaison-Sackey.

[134] Armah was flatly against a break in relations. The British thought Quaison-Sackey hypocritical, but it is probably a reflection of the relative security Armah felt in his own position that he was able to give such conservative advice. Quaison-Sackey from the beginning of his tenure as foreign minister felt insecure in his position.

It was a strange and sad development. The diplomatic corps, ministry officials, and Nkrumah himself did everything possible to ease the difficulties for the British staff. Most of the British officials believed that regardless of what happened in Rhodesia they would not be back in Accra while Nkrumah was still in power. The British military training missions—including a brigadier—stayed. The commercial section of the high commission very efficiently continued to exercise the political functions of the mission. It was a curiously British way of solving the problems caused for both sides.

One step was leading to another, however. Nkrumah proclaimed that the Commonwealth had failed in its mission and that Ghana, at the next OAU meeting, "would therefore propose that all African states sever such links as stand in the way of African Unity or impede its progress."[135] It sounded like an admission that Commonwealth membership had affected his policy, as it indeed had done. One step was also leading to another for those Ghanaians who saw the last restraints on Nkrumah's behavior being removed. Chief among these was the officer corps of the army, so many of whom had been trained at Sandhurst, Mons, or Camberly.

Numerous issues divided Washington and Accra. American support of the Congo's premier, Moise Tshombe, was a major one.[136] Lyndon B. Johnson even declined to receive an OAU mission—which included Foreign Minister Botsio—that was in Washington in an attempt to mediate the 1964 Congo crisis. Nkrumah felt threatened more personally by the United States on other fronts. By spring 1965, he was convinced that the Americans were trying to wreck his OAU summit, a fear reinforced by the prominence Washington gave to Upper Volta's president on a state visit there. The visit had been long planned, but there is little doubt that the Americans were using it, in part, to reinforce those opposing Nkrumah, of whom Yameogo was the current spokesman. Nkrumah became further convinced that Washington was driving the cocoa price down as a means of toppling his government, but with no suggestions as to how the price could be manipulated. His greatest fear was of the CIA. There can be no question that the CIA had a presence in Ghana and that it maintained contact with Nkrumah's opponents in exile. For all this, Nkrumah exaggerated the threat beyond all reason,

[135] "An address by the President of Ghana to the National Assembly in Accra," 16 December 1965, in "Statements on Southern Rhodesia . . ." pp. 21-22.

[136] Note that Nkrumah never broke relations with Tshombe; he valued too highly the information with which Quashie, his ambassador, supplied him.

accrediting to that organization an interest in Ghana out of proportion to Ghana's significance.[137]

On the other hand, Nkrumah's policy on occasion could be pragmatic. Ground for the VALCO aluminum smelter was to be broken in December 1964, and Edgar Kaiser and George Woods, president of the World Bank, had come for the occasion. This was just after the American-Belgian intervention in Stanleyville, and the Ghanaians had not yet made the anti-American demonstration that characterized the response in capitals of other radical states, though one was planned by students at the University of Ghana. The vice-chancellor, Conor Cruise O'Brien, was pressed by the American ambassador, a personal friend of his, not to permit it. O'Brien's response was that he would neither forbid nor encourage a demonstration. Then the minister of information—a radical—called him and also requested that he prevent any demonstrations, to which O'Brien's response was the same. Upon being asked the origin of this unusual request, the minister reportedly replied, "Edgar [Kaiser] is here."[138] A very feeble demonstration was in fact held in Legon, at the University, serving only to show that passions in Accra could be controlled when vital interests were at stake.

For their part, the Americans began to take a serious view of the threat that Nkrumah now offered. In the past they had dismissed his machinations as of only nuisance value, or even as a help to the American cause because of the counterproductive means he used to advance his ends. By mid-1965 all this was changing as concrete American interests began to be affected.[139] Nkrumah could threaten the status quo in Africa; he could undermine regimes friendly to America; and he could transmit substantial aid to the Congolese rebels. As late as 8 June 1965, in the presence of Major-General Barwa and Major-General Gorshenin, the Russian military attaché, 142 cases of machine guns were loaded into the Russian freighter *Gulbeni* at Tema to be sent to Pointe Noire for distribution in the Congo. He was building a £6,500,000 air-base in northern Ghana, with a three-mile long strip, thought by the Americans to offer excellent staging facilities for Russian planes en route to Havana. Intelligence facilities which the Russians and East Germans were developing with the Bureau of African Affairs were bound to complicate American efforts throughout Africa. It is not a surprise to learn that during 1965 (according to one report) Communist intentions

---

[137] See CF-41, record of interviews at U.S. Embassy, Accra.
[138] Interviews: CF-40A, 84 (14 September 1965, New York).
[139] Interview: CF-41, U.S. Embassy, Accra.

in Ghana were the subject of discussion at the highest NATO level.[140] The Volta Project was no longer a high enough trump for the American hand.

Ghana's economic crisis was intensifying so rapidly that long-range objectives of attracting American investment to complement Volta had to be put aside in any case; Ghana's needs were more urgent, for which purpose Nkrumah began trying to conciliate Washington. The real issue was whether the economy could be salvaged in time to avert long-term disruption, a question that Nkrumah naively expected Washington to resolve in Ghana's favor. What was needed was a massive loan, and here was America's new card. But the People's Solidarity conference (AAPSO) held in Ghana in May 1965 confirmed in the Americans a long-growing disinclination to provide help. A thousand-million pound request made to the Western powers in the spring of 1965 was simply referred in each capital to the IMF;[141] Nkrumah had no illusions about the extent to which America's word counted in that institution. For his efforts to mediate in Vietnam he also needed American approval. In a further effort to placate Washington, the press became more temperate, and for the first time it added disclaimers that polemical articles reflected official policy.

The Americans were merely amused. They no longer hoped for any substantial changes in Nkrumah's foreign policy. Convinced also that he was incapable of moderating his capricious economic program, they ceased to fear that his downfall would be long delayed. Evidently satisfied that his gestures deluded the Americans, Nkrumah sent instructions to Ambassador Ribeiro in Washington to press for surplus (PL-480) food needed to meet Ghana's deficit. Ribeiro made no headway. He thought, however, that relations had improved since the anti-American demonstrations of February 1964, and when President Johnson made polite enquiries about his work, he complained about Ghana's lack of success— and Guinea and the U.A.R.'s success—in having its request for food met. Ribeiro was convinced that through White House intervention Ghana was to get its food—at which point Nkrumah's newest book, *Neo-Colonialism*, was published. Ribeiro learned through the press a few days later that Ghana's request had been turned down.[142]

140 Interviews: CF-31, 14.

141 Interviews: CF-46, Quai d'Orsay, 1 April 1965; CF-58, Commonwealth Office, 8 November 1965.

142 CF-98. Amb. Ribeiro was one of the many of Nkrumah's political appointees who was more comfortable in the West than the East, and who wished to think that relations with the West were better than they in fact were. It is otherwise impossible to understand how he could have been so misled about the nature of relations between the two countries at this time.

Neo-Colonialism reached the public during the visit to Ghana of a World Bank evaluation mission. If the question of timing was bad, the question of authorship was worse: Nkrumah could not resist taking credit for manuscripts handed to him by others.[143] For months the Americans had lodged protests about press stories seeming to reflect Nkrumah's own attitude toward America. The response from Flagstaff House was that the authors were free to write as they pleased. Now some of the articles appeared under Nkrumah's name, but the American objections elicited from him only hurt surprise that anyone took such "theoretical" efforts as this book seriously. He left the impression almost of suspecting that the Americans knew the authorship to be a fraud; and for that reason appeared to be aggrieved that he was held to account for views which were written by others.

In December, a month later, Nkrumah complained publicly with reference to the expected American aid that "food so heavily laden with strings would prove indigestible," and professed to see in the American refusal an "isolated incident" marring otherwise friendly relations.[144] The firmness of the United States clearly had made an impression. There was new evidence of the same sort in late January 1966 when former Ambassador Mahoney and other Americans were brought back to Ghana for the dedication of the Volta dam. Nkrumah used the occasion to hail what the U.S. had accomplished in the Volta project, as exemplifying the "dual mandate" to develop the third world which America had assumed. At the state opening of parliament shortly thereafter, not one word was spoken in criticism of American policy in Vietnam.[145] It was a curiously pro-American period, as Ghanaians said.

But the United States was now playing a wholly new hand. Mahoney had left in the summer of 1965 and because of strained relations no successor was sent until the end of the year. The new ambassador, Franklin Williams, an Afro-American of national distinction whose undergraduate career at Lincoln University had overlapped Nkrumah's, was possessed of a curious confidence, like Mahoney's three years before, that Nkrumah could yet be redeemed. For that reason alone many of the diplomatic corps in Accra thought that Williams was being used as a smokescreen to cover American hostility. As could be guessed, the Americans were calculating carefully what might be the odds for a coup. The deputy chief of the U.S. mission, Oliver Troxel, played his hand very skillfully, as did his equally able successor, John Foley. Influential

---

[143] The book was written by five non-Ghanaians, it was said after the coup.

[144] "The Great Tasks Ahead, Osagyefo's New Year Message, 31 December 1965," Accra, 1966, p. 5.

[145] See "Sessional Address, 1 February 1966," Accra, 1966.

Ghanaians were all the while pleading with them that no new assistance be extended to Nkrumah, lest (depending upon the speaker's viewpoint) it delay the inevitable confrontation with economic reality or extend the life of the regime itself. When the coup took place, the Americans had not been involved but were nonetheless well prepared to take advantage of the new hand they had now been dealt.

THE SOCIALIST COMMONWEALTH

As Nkrumah and the radical elite looked at Ghana's relations with the Socialist countries, the main problem was the international schism in the "anti-imperialist" world. They wished, in theory, that they could resist choosing between Moscow and Peking. One writer even suggested that a united stand "against involvement in the ideological dispute will in itself prove to be a deciding factor in resolving it."[146] But in practice Ghana had to choose. In early 1965, Michael Dei-Anang, analyzing Ghana's position on those issues dividing Russia and China, found on most of them that Nkrumah sided with Peking. "In the final analysis the Chinese are right," Nkrumah was quoted as saying.[147] On grand ideological issues he did side with Peking, but on issues of practical relevance he sided with Moscow. Ghana, unlike Guinea, signed the test-ban treaty, because Nkrumah thought testing and everything associated with atomic war abhorrent. Disgusted by Chinese tactics at the fourth AAPSO conference held in Ghana, he was still more disappointed by them when they proved indifferent to his attempts to mediate the Vietnamese war. He remained frightened of them internally, and after the Ben Bella coup placed their activities at the training camps under the supervision of his most loyal officer, General Barwah.[148] As for Russia, he expected it to industrialize Ghana in the post-Volta stage.

The real issues for Ghana in its relations with the Socialist countries were economic, as even Nkrumah was beginning to appreciate toward the end of his period in power. These revolved around the questions of the implementation of the 1961 credit agreements, the practices employed by the East in the payments agreements, and the Socialist countries' insistence on buying commodities from Ghana at world market prices.

By 1965, less than half of the credit promised in 1961 had been ex-

[146] H. M. Basner, "The Indivisibility of Non-Alignment," *Ghanaian Times*, 21 May 1965.

[147] The document itself was apparently destroyed in the fighting of 24 February 1966. Its contents are based on descriptions in interview. CF-14, 85, and Botsio.

[148] Interview: CF-87. Barwah at the same time was made Commander of the Ghanaian army, replacing Maj.-Gen. Arthur Ankrah.

pended. A report from the Ghanaian embassy in Tirana, in response to a request that it seek out areas for cooperation, makes clear how basic some of the problems were.

> "unfortunately the quality of this country's products and the level of its university education are so low that the ambassador found it impossible to advise our Government . . . to send Ghanaian students . . . or Ghanaian specialists . . . to Tirana.
>
> In short, our country, Ghana, is far ahead in all spheres of Development, and the Albanians rather have much to learn in our country. There is no doubt that even our average secondary school is better equipped . . . than the so-called Albanian State University.

As for the specific products that could be exchanged under the 1961 trade agreement, the writer was led to comment that "the beer could not last a month without moss forming at the bottom of the bottle. The cigarettes were just like raw tobacco wrapped up in pieces of paper."[149] Difficulties with Albania were at best a caricature of the problems with the major Communist states; nonetheless, the problems in implementing the agreements with the Soviet Union, for example, detailed in an earlier chapter, had not abated by 1965. Contracts worth £5,607,234 had been signed with Moscow by the beginning of this last period, only a third of the total commitments. This was due to the slowness of Soviet negotiators, Ghana's lack of funds to undertake its part of the joint projects, and the concomitant unwillingness of the Soviets fully to convert their projects to the turn-key type.[150] Few of the projects contracted for were completed by the time of the 1966 coup.

Difficulties with the bilateral payments agreements were equally irritating to the Ghanaians. Her missions in Eastern countries were usually forced to deposit sterling with the host government when ordering goods from convertible-currency countries. The Committee for Economic Cooperation with Eastern Countries

> discussed the issue at length and unanimously agreed that the practice is not in consonance with the provisions made in the Bilateral Payments agreements . . . [which] provide for Clearing Accounts, and in these accounts payments in currencies other than the contracting parties' currencies should not arise. . . . Against the above practice it should be noted that the position is not the same with withdrawal in Ghana banks by members of the Rumanian embassy since they can obtain practically all their requirements in Ghanaian currency.[151]

[149] Annual Report, Ghana/Tirana to M.F.A., 2 March 1964, CFA-22-23.
[150] See CFA-15.   [151] Minutes, CECEC, 14 August 1963, CFA-24.

Thus a Ghanaian attaché in Bucharest could not use *leu* to buy a Mercedes, while his Rumanian counterpart in Accra could—and did—do so. The same was true for buying airplane tickets in most of the bilateral countries, leading the Ghanaians to conclude that they were being used as a "cheap source of foreign exchange."[152]

One of the very few issues for which the Ghanaian press ever criticized the Socialist countries was their practice in buying Ghanaian raw materials at world—i.e. Western—market prices. The price of cocoa in 1965 was its lowest in over a decade, and the Russians (who, in the 1961 agreements with Ghana, had reserved to themselves the right to buy whenever they chose) bought enough to last more than one year. The *Ghanaian Times* editorialized that on the one hand the downward fall in the terms of trade of the developing countries "has resulted from the desire of the imperialist nations to exploit the primary producers." On the other hand, "there is a fundamental contradiction between the acceptance of this thesis and the present attitude whereby the Socialist country also pays the same price which the Western countries, because of their desire to exploit, have contrived to pay."[153] There also existed a growing, though unproved, suspicion that Ghanaian cocoa sold to Russia in exchange for out-of-date Soviet machinery was then sold on Western markets, providing the Russians with hard currency. To remove grounds for the suspicion, the Ghanaian-Soviet trade protocol of January 1965 included the stipulation that "goods . . . shall not be re-exported to a third country except with the prior approval in writing" of the second party.[154]

There is, of course, another side to the question of Ghanaian-Eastern relations, namely, the Communist states' view of Nkrumah's regime. At the beginning of the last period the Ghanaian press could headline "Osagyefo's Books are Very Popular in Soviet Union,"[155] but shortly thereafter the fall of Khrushchev brought in new leaders for Russia. These men were more cautious. With them, as *Mizan* wrote, "the almost visionary optimism of earlier years" in the Soviet view of Africa gave way to "a more hard-headed attitude."[156] As ideology now had less, and trade had more, importance, the Russians began exploring the possibility of opening an embassy next door in Abidjan in 1964; their relations with Nigeria grew steadily warmer. In the early days of

[152] Interview: CF-99A.

[153] "Ghana and the Socialist Countries," *Ghanaian Times*, 26 July 1965.

[154] Soviet Union-Ghana Trade Protocol, 6 January 1965, in CECEC minutes, n.d., CFA-22. Nkrumah decided in 1965 that Ghana would thenceforth sell cocoa only for cash, although he did not hold his Socialist friends to this.

[155] *Ghanaian Times*, 25 September 1964.

[156] "The USSR and Africa 1966," *Mizan*, 8, No. 1, p. 38.

Ghana-Soviet friendship, Nkrumah appeared to be Africa's most important leader. It is hard to believe that in 1965 Kosygin was unaware of the decline in Nkrumah's prestige.

Ambassador Rodionov himself was substantially free of dogma in evaluating the regime. Though the Russians continued to say that Ghana, along with Algeria, Guinea, and the U.A.R. was "within sight of Socialism,"[157] Rodionov knew differently. Nor do articles published in Marxist journals after the coup permit another view.[158] The personality cult in Ghana bothered the Russians, according to Botsio, and though they never talked about it or ever spoke to Nkrumah about it, "it was obvious they did not like it." About the economic problems, however, they were very vocal. Botsio wrote: "In 1965 a team of Soviet experts wrote up an appraisal of the economy and recommended putting more energy and resources into productive enterprises and less on social and other projects. This was practically ignored." Equally firm were their views on the party; the Soviet team, Botsio wrote, "recommended a democratisation of the top branches of the Party machinery. . . . This was also ignored."[159] Botsio and Rodionov discussed these problems at length, each no doubt hoping the other could persuade Nkrumah to correct the dangerous trends.

Ghanaian intelligence officers emphasized the Soviet concern in the areas of security where they had responsibility. Instead of the strong, intelligent men they wanted to assist them, Ambrose Yankey, Nkrumah's crony, supplied them with his illiterate and feeble friends. And what, it was asked, could Marxists be expected to make of the Ayeh-Kumi's of this world?[160]

As for the Chinese, it may be doubted that the informed among them held a high opinion of Nkrumah. But as the importance of Africa grew in their ideology, the Chinese sought to preserve what few beachheads of influence remained to them in Africa. Indeed, at the end their influence appeared finally to be growing, for it was they who advised Nkrumah on the formation of the "people's militia" at the end of 1965.[161]

Meanwhile, more than merely Moscow and Peking competed in the Ghana arena for political influence and advantages for trade. The Cen-

[157] *Ibid.*, p. 38.

[158] See the important discussions at the Cairo conference of radical African parties in October 1966, reported in *World Marxist Review*, No. 12 (1966), and No. 1 (1967).

[159] Botsio to the author, 29 July 1966.

[160] Interview: CF-87. It was widely suggested among key Flagstaff House officials that Ayeh-Kumi's growing power was one of the most disturbing factors to the Russians in Ghana. At best, Ayeh-Kumi was an avaricious capitalist.

[161] Interviews: CF-42, 14. The militia was created, but organization of it could not proceed because of lack of funds in the treasury.

401

tral and East Europeans, unlike the other Communist states, sought mainly to develop long-term economic relations with Ghana who, as a result, treated them after the coup differently than it did the Russians and Chinese. A final group included those smaller states with special interests who came to Accra to increase their own international prestige. Albania, North Korea, and North Vietnam were in this category, as would have been Mongolia, with whom Ghana agreed to establish relations at the end of 1965. Of all the foregoing the most important state obviously was East Germany, whose competition with Bonn must be considered in any analysis of Communist diplomacy in Accra.

The East Germans had only trade mission status in Ghana, but the twenty men on their staff suggest a broader role. Karl-Heinz Kern, one of the ablest diplomats in Accra, developed a network of contacts in the CPP so that its own propaganda machinery provided the main channel of support for his cause. Kern wanted consulate-general status for the trade mission, and CPP radicals were willing to support his request. From 1963, news articles about West German Fascism and East German progress became frequent in the press. Their campaign was climaxed in September 1964 by a visit to Ghana of Herr Paul Scholtz, a G.D.R. deputy prime minister.[162]

The West Germans lacked neither cards to play nor friends to play them. As Ghana's third trading partner, she could make her influence felt throughout the economy. Little aid had been given to Ghana—only the DM20,000,000 Volta bridge—but Bonn was careful to leave open the possibility of more, according to West German diplomats.[163] In the private sector a great number of West German firms had made available suppliers' credits. Few businessmen had Nkrumah's confidence as much as did Noe Drivici, a Rumanian working from a West German base, who induced him to conclude agreements covering some £50,000,000-worth of somewhat dubious projects.[164]

Nkrumah's position on the German question at the second Non-Aligned Conference at Cairo in 1964 contrasted sharply with his insistent calls for recognition of East Germany in 1961. This time he did no more than urge the conference to "call upon the two Germanies to . . . find a solution to the problem of German unity."[165] Moreover, he suggested that since the conference members had no interests in the German dispute—being nonaligned—they could put their good offices at

---

[162] See *Ghanaian Times*, 30 September 1964, 7 October 1964.
[163] Interview: CF-103A.
[164] See *West Africa*, 26 March 1966, 341.
[165] "Peace and Progress, Speech Delivered by Osagyefo at the Second Conference of Non-Aligned States," Accra, 1964.

the disposal of the Germans. The change in Nkrumah's attitude was probably due to his discovery that Ghana did have an interest in the matter. The cabinet discussed East Germany's status that same autumn, and decided not to raise it. Botsio commented that recognition would have "unduly upset our trading relationships," and would have burned the country's fingers in European politics[166]—but he had to work hard to counteract the efforts of the CPP radicals. The foreign ministry followed his approach; whenever Flagstaff House requested professional advice on raising the status of the East German trade mission, the ministry would take its time while urging the West Germans to be patient.[167]

The West Germans, for their part, countered the East Germans by introducing their own publication, a weekly newsletter that soon equaled *Spark*'s home circulation, and may well have surpassed it in influence among Ghanaians. Thus East Germany could make only gradual increases in its influence: in spring 1965, when Ghana was negotiating for massive assistance from West Germany, the press attacks ceased in every paper save *Spark*. But by January 1966 the attacks in all the press had reached such a peak that the West Germans became very worried indeed. Among the Western powers their relief was greatest when the coup occurred.[168]

The Communist presence in Accra, then, was far from a single, unified political force. The relations of the Eastern states with Ghana, complex and evolving, were developing independently, with ups and downs that left it unclear what they would have become in another year. Long the most influential of these states in Accra, the Soviet Union was believed by many observers to be losing interest in Ghana very rapidly by 1966. Given the size to which Ghana's economic debt had climbed, the Russians at that point might have made Ghana very dependent on it, in the manner of Cuba, if on a much smaller scale. As they did not choose to take this option, the next move would have been up to Nkrumah. He had already come a long way in a period when Russian interest was clearly waning. He planned to sign a "Treaty of Friendship" with the Russians during a visit to Moscow after his visit to Peking[169] in February 1966. Communist front institutions, like the Youth Festival, were finding Ghana prepared to welcome them. Nkrumah is said to have intended to "close the gap" (in the words of a Russian diplomatist)[170]

[166] Botsio to the author, 29 July 1966.
[167] Interviews: Botsio, CF-71, 103, 112.
[168] They were thus the first to recognize the new regime.
[169] According to Quaison-Sackey, who said Rodionov wanted the treaty so that Ghana's relations with China would not appear to be warmer than its relation with Russia.
[170] Interview: CF-31A, Russian Embassy/Accra.

between Ghanaian ideology and practice, upon his return from Peking, in the manner of Nasser in 1961. Had he done so, the Communist states could not have contracted their commitment to Ghana as rapidly as they might wish.

NONALIGNMENT, SOLIDARITY, AND WORLD PEACE

In the foreign affairs of Ghana the final period of Nkrumah's rule co-incides with the interval between the second nonaligned summit conference at Cairo (October 1964), and the first "Tricontinental" conference, at Havana (January 1966). During 1964 the competition between the "Belgrade" and "Bandung" movements ended in the merging of the two. As G. H. Jansen explains, Belgrade merged itself with Bandung, "not because of a congruence of political ideas or attitudes . . . but because of the timidity of the non-aligned in the face of the steadily-growing cohorts of the Afro-Asians."[171] Ghana expressed no formal preference between the two movements in 1964, but the aggressiveness of Ghana's diplomacy helped to make the merger inevitable, with the consequence that nonalignment as a formal movement was down-graded. At Cairo, in a speech that reflected as much as any the attitude of the more radical states, Nkrumah said: "There is such a thing as peaceful co-existence between states with different social systems; but as long as oppressive classes exist, there can be no such thing as peaceful co-existence between opposing ideologies. . . . We cannot co-exist with imperialism, we cannot co-exist with colonialism, we cannot co-exist with neo-colonialism."[172]

During this period Ghana was represented also at the abortive meeting of the Second Bandung in Algeria, played host to the fourth Afro-Asian Solidarity Conference (in Winneba), and took a leading role in the Tricontinental conference in Havana. By the time of the coup, as the various diplomatic strands came together, it was at last becoming clear where Ghana was tending in the third world.[173]

The Bandung strand began at Belgrade in 1961, when Sukarno and Nkrumah discussed the former's plans for a second Afro-Asian conference. As early as August 1962 the Ghana cabinet was on record recommending participation in such a conference, and this position was reaffirmed during Chou En-lai's visit of January 1964.[174] From the first

---

[171] Jansen, *Afro-Asia*, p. 384.

[172] "Peace and Progress," Accra, 1964.

[173] It should be stressed that activities in this sphere never approached "union government" in importance in Flagstaff House, with the result that Ghana's position within these Afro-Asian movements could be more easily affected by Communist diplomats, or even by Ghanaian diplomats.

[174] See memorandum of M.F.A. to cabinet, for the cabinet meeting of 21 August

it was made clear that Ghana was "NOT interested in playing host," as Ben Bella had obtained Ghana's support for Algiers as a conference site, this at a time when Ghanaian-Algerian relations were at a peak of cordiality.[175]

But the Ghanaians, particularly Botsio, made their participation contingent on the absence of divisive issues. The ministry wished only "purely economic, cultural, and social problems facing our countries at the present time" to be discussed.[176] Sukarno's foreign minister, Subandrio, tried to impress Botsio with the "urgency" of this conference, and proposed holding a preparatory meeting of foreign ministers at Djakarta. Botsio, who had just returned from UNCTAD in Geneva, knew that many foreign ministers were not going, and Dei-Anang wrote to him, on Nkrumah's behalf, to decide for himself whether to go.[177] In the end Botsio sent the Rev. Mr. Nimako, High Commissioner in Colombo, to save currency.

The preparatory meeting was held in mid-April 1964. The records make several important points about Ghana's position in the third world. Only ten African states appear to have been invited; eight attended. Arkhurst, at the ministry, made explicit that Ghana wished all African states to be included.[178] The Ghanaian delegate stated that "he would like to see all of them invited to the second Afro-Asian Conference, including all members of the OAU." More remarkably, he urged that the liberation movements recognized by the OAU be invited as well, despite Nkrumah's hostility toward Holden Roberto, and toward the liberation committee in general. Botsio's explanation of this departure from policy is that he and the ministry were responsible for Nimako's brief.[179]

The preparatory conference was plagued by the question of membership; China wanted Russia, Indonesia wanted Malaysia to be excluded from the Algiers conference. Here Ghana carefully walked a well-trod path, in trying to avoid the former question. While Guinea objected that "the Soviet Union was . . . a European country . . . politically . . . a

---

1962; and cabinet's acceptance of this proposal, noted in H. R. Amonoo to Ghana/Cairo, 30 August 1962, CFA-60.

[175] Arkhurst, P.S./M.F.A. to Nimako, High Commissioner/Colombo, 23 April 1964, CFA-61.

[176] S.P.O. Kumi, Director, Middle Eastern and Asian Affairs, to P.S. and Minister, M.F.A., 4 April 1964, CFA-61.

[177] Subandrio to Botsio, 8 March 1964, and note by Dei-Anang, added to this letter. CFA-61.

[178] Arkhurst to Nimako, 6 April 1964, CFA-61.

[179] Organising Committee, Second Afro-Asian Conference, "Proceedings—Meeting of Ministers in preparation of the Second African-Asian Conference, Jakarta, 10-15 April 1964," pp. 12, 70, CFA-conf., and interview: Botsio.

. . . single entity [with its] capital . . . in Europe," the Ghanaians merely considered the Soviet Union, Israel, and Malaysia as "doubtful cases." It suggested that in each case the decisions could "best be decided through informal discussions or alternatively a small group of not more than five . . . set up to work out a draft on the matter." Beyond this, Ghana only emphasized the need for "urgency" with respect to economic development.[180]

Despite Indonesia's efforts, however, the Second Bandung was postponed until June 1965. By mid-1965 it could no longer serve as a barometer of Ghana's position on third world questions, for by now the Accra summit was much in jeopardy. In itself a conference in Algiers was seen to divert attention from Ghana's OAU conference. Nkrumah's feelings about the Second Bandung were intensified when, on its eve, he received news of the ousting of Ben Bella by Boumedienne, together with an intelligence report that the Chinese were implicated in the coup.[181] China's unseemly haste in recognizing Boumedienne, and its opposition to further postponement of the conference, gave Nkrumah ample reason for refusing to join Guinea in supporting the Chinese cause. Moreover, by August, Nkrumah's conference and Boumedienne's were in direct competition over prime dates.

The postponement of the Algiers conference to November brought a reversal in Chinese and Indian/Russian roles. China now opposed a conference, while India and Russia urged one. Ghana was represented at the ill-fated gathering that did take place, while Guinea, Mali, and Tanzania, wittingly or unwittingly supporting the Chinese, absented themselves.[182]

For other reasons Ghana did not become deeply involved in this strand of the Afro-Asian movement. Though Nkrumah and Sukarno, China's ally, seemed to talk the same anticolonial language, and much as Nkrumah liked Sukarno's idea of the "new emerging forces," there was disagreement on so many specific issues that no real cooperation was possible. The press publicly deplored Indonesia's withdrawal from the United Nations, and Nkrumah expressed opposition to Indonesia's designs on Malaysia. When Subandrio, with a large delegation, came to Accra in June 1965, these points were reiterated. The only promise he

---

180 *Ibid.*, pp. 41, 58, 13. Ghana's support of Malaysia was, however, explicit. A telegram from the M.F.A. to Ghana/Washington on 25 June 1964 said, "We are . . . in favour of Malaysia's participation." S.P.O. Kumi to Amb. Ribeiro, CFA-61.

181 Interview: CF-87. The Russians were presumably the source of the intelligence report.

182 See *Economist*, 3 July 1965; *New York Times*, 28 October 1965; *le Monde*, 29 October 1965, and Jansen, *Afro-Asia*, pp. 394-99.

received from Nkrumah was that Ghana would attend Sukarno's conference of the new emerging forces.[183]

Thus with respect to the Second Bandung and the radical states in Africa and Asia, Nkrumah's attitude was not unlike his attitude toward Russia and China. The grand pronouncements of the Sukarnos and the Chinese appealed to him, but he found it difficult to accept their individual policies.

A more interesting line of development in Ghana's third world diplomacy ended with the Havana conference. At a 1964 council meeting of the Afro-Asian Peoples Solidarity Organisation in Algiers, Ghana invited that organization to hold its fourth conference in Accra. Ghana's interest in Latin America was in the meantime increasing. Ambassadors were already in Argentina and Brazil and, in 1964, Richard Akwei was sent to Mexico City. Ties, too, were developing with Castro, whom Nkrumah had met in 1960, in New York. At first Ghana had not pressed for close relations, mainly to avoid antagonizing the Americans.[184] By 1965 such considerations were less compelling. In January 1965 Che Guevara, to the delight of Ghanaian radicals, visited Accra, to urge revolution in the developing world.

By April 1965, a month before the solidarity conference was to begin at Winneba, the Ghanaians once again became apprehensive of that organization, this time for new reasons. Nkrumah did not want the "Socialist commonwealth" further disturbed by new Sino-Soviet polemics, particularly on Ghanaian soil, and the ministry for its part had never been enthusiastic about the conference. The announcement that Ghana would be unable to hold the conference until after the OAU summit was, in effect, a cancellation. Although the Russians were not thought to attach great importance to the solidarity organization at this point, they presumably intended to derive some benefits from the Winneba meeting, for they persuaded Nkrumah to reconvene it, obviously a humiliating move for Ghana.[185]

From the beginning of the conference, in early May, Nkrumah sought to dampen potential hostilities. There never was a chance. Hardly had they arrived than the Chinese protested what *Hsinhua* called a "so-called photo and books exhibition" set up by the Russians, because of the

---

[183] Botsio noted that Ghana and Indonesia were sufficiently far apart in distance to preclude trouble between Nkrumah and Sukarno. Ghanaian diplomats were irritated even by Nkrumah's willingness to attend the NEFO conference. See also "Think Again Brothers," *Ghanaian Times*, 7 January 1965, and interviews: Botsio, and CF-31.

[184] Interviews: Botsio, Quaison-Sackey.

[185] Interviews: Botsio, CF-14, 87. See also *Egyptian Gazette*, 4 April 1965, 11 April 1965.

inclusion of "anti-Chinese pamphlets."[186] But the Chinese had allies among the Ghanaians. At the conference opening, Nathaniel Welbeck, as chairman, read fraternal greetings from the Chinese, but not from the Russians. More pointedly, the *Ghanaian Times* printed alongside its daily news of the conference a map of Afro-Asia which did not show even the Asian portions of the U.S.S.R. Rodionov's complaint about the newspaper's map was to no avail.[187]

The Russians benefited more, however. They wanted a conference planned in a new framework that would include the Latin American movements, particularly since the next solidarity meeting was planned for Peking. They got it.[188] But though Nkrumah had the same objective, the Soviet success was frustrating to him. In his speech, "True Freedom for All," Nkrumah asked "who has the right to jeopardise the unity of the anti-imperialist world?" He urged that the conference's main pre-occupation be to "strengthen our solidarity"—meaning, of course, to improve relations between China and Russia.[189] Yet relations between those two countries were further exacerbated at this conference.

The Winneba conference, however, marked the final turning point in the regime's relations with the United States. Though Ghanaians said nothing new in Winneba, their acting as host to such a conference had very serious implications in the view of American diplomats who, at this point "gave up on Nkrumah."[190] Ill-feelings were mutual. Anti-imperialist fervor was inflamed by the daily American bombardment of North Vietnam begun three months earlier, and the American invasion of the Dominican Republic of only one week before. Nkrumah had a long record of compromise with "imperialism," despite oft-repeated assertions to the contrary; his holding the conference in Ghana tended to affirm that there would be less compromise in the future.

Ghana now had recognition as one of the third world's most radical states, a position of some diplomatic importance. The Moroccan delegation gave up its place on the Havana preparatory committee to make way for Ghana, a sign of Ghana's transition from opponent to pillar of these movements. At the Havana conference the following January,

186 *Hsinhua*, No. 050958, 10 May 1965.

187 Interviews: CF-31; Welbeck, 23 February 1966. How Welbeck could so conduct himself is not clear; either Nkrumah was uninformed on what transpired or wished to show his lack of appreciation to the Russians for forcing him to hold the conference.

188 See "Moscow and 'Afro-Asia,'" *Mizan*, Vol. 8, No. 2, pp. 57-60.

189 " 'True Freedom for All,' Speech Delivered by Osagyefo Dr. Kwame Nkrumah at the Fourth Afro-Asian Solidarity Conference, 10 May 1965," Accra, 1965, p. 10.

190 Interviews: CF-41, 77, U.S. Embassy/Accra.

John Tettegah became one of the highest officers in the new tricontinental organization created there.[191]

Ghana had come full circle in nine years. In 1957 it evinced little
interest in the solidarity organization, and had very warm ties with
Israel, which was the principal adversary of AAPSO's host country and
chief supporter. By 1966 Ghana was a chief sponsor of AAPSO, while
relations with Israel, after a diplomatic incident during the OAU Summit conference, had reached a low ebb.[192]

Nkrumah's last initiative in foreign policy sought peace in Vietnam.
Like so many of his efforts, here there was a solid beginning; then as
the situation changed the genuine opportunity to exert influence was lost
in pursuit of illusions; professional judgment was subordinated to personal ambition.

If Western states could "write off" a head of state, they could also
give him a "real opportunity to be taken seriously again."[193] Prime Minister Harold Wilson proposed to do so with Nkrumah. At the June 1965
Commonwealth conference, Wilson eagerly included Nkrumah, as the
only leader with credentials acceptable in Hanoi and Peking, in the
mission he wished to send to Vietnam; it was no wonder that the BBC
called him the "Key man."[194]

President Nyerere, a man of greater principle, had refused membership, but the Ghanaians from the beginning were elated by the opportunity. Nkrumah's own enthusiasm can be judged by the fact that he did
not resign from the mission when his conditions for accepting membership were not met.[195] There were grave dilemmas, of which the most
dangerous lay in appearing to be "used as a 'tool of U.S. imperialism.' "[196]
Fully aware of the hazards, Nkrumah walked a careful path that summer. While at Helsinki, Nathaniel Welbeck damned the Americans, and

[191] See *Ghanaian Times*, 13 May 1965, 17 May 1965 and 5 January 1966; Ernst
Halperin, "Peking and Latin America," *China Quarterly*, No. 29, pp. 149-150.

[192] Nasser refused to dine at the conference banquet were the Israeli ambassador,
previously invited, permitted to be present. This marked the end of the Ghana-Israel
saga, even if Israel still had many influential friends in Accra. At the time that Tettegah
—an old friend of Israel—was in Havana, one Israeli diplomat commented that Ghana's
attitude toward his state was one of " 'permitting' Israel to continue to aid Ghana's
development." Interview: CF-104B.

[193] "Nkrumah's Return," *Economist*, 24 July 1965.

[194] Quoted in *Ghanaian Times*, 21 June 1965.

[195] These were that Australia withdraw its troops from, and that New Zealand drop
its plans to send reinforcements to, Vietnam; and that a united Commonwealth appeal
be made to Washington to halt its attacks on North Vietnam.

[196] Editorial, *Ghanaian Times*, 14 July 1965.

at home the Ghanaian press blamed the United States for the Vietnam war; Nkrumah himself made clear that negotiation, of a sort not wholly unfavorable to the Americans, was essential, and he pressed Peking to receive the Commonwealth mission, which from the beginning they had refused to do.[197]

The North Vietnamese had a difficult problem to handle. They knew that Nkrumah believed in their cause, but understood only too clearly why he wanted the Commonwealth mission to succeed. They made the situation much easier both for themselves and him, by extending him an invitation to visit Hanoi not as a member of the Commonwealth mission, but as president of Ghana. The *Ghanaian Times* called this "a glorious victory for humanity"; the British apparently realized that the only hope for the Commonwealth mission lay in Nkrumah's hands. The *Economist* asked Wilson to ask himself, "What can I do for the Osagyefo?"[198]

But in Accra Britain and the Commonwealth had a lower priority than in earlier days; for one thing, Ghana's economic (and political) position was precarious on all counts, and for this Nkrumah needed to find a remedy. Resolved that he himself, without help from the Commonwealth mission, would bring peace to Vietnam, as a preliminary to solving Ghana's problems, he immediately sent a mission to Hanoi to try to lay the groundwork for negotiations. The Ghana delegation, headed by Kwesi Armah, included Dr. Bossman, Capt. Hassan and, most important, F. S. Arkhurst.

At the time opinion in Accra was divided between the politicians who thought Nkrumah, in order to increase his prestige, should travel to Hanoi whatever the mission reported; some diplomats, who also thought he should go, but in order to convince the North Vietnamese that negotiations were needed; and the more cautious and realistic diplomats and civil servants, who thought it better to delay until there was assurance that a trip could be fruitful.[199]

Armah's mission, ill-starred from the beginning, was empty of results but full of consequences. Moscow refused to make it possible for the group to go to Hanoi by way of Irkutsk, which cost them several days'

[197] See Nkrumah's own statement, *Ghanaian Times*, 25 June 1965. See also, for the points of view of H. M. Basner and N. Welbeck, *ibid.*, 12 July 1965, and 20 July 1965.

[198] "Nkrumah's Return," *Economist*, 24 July 1965. This article, generally favorable to Nkrumah, did not reflect any deeply felt desire in the Commonwealth Office, or in the State Department, to "rehabilitate" Nkrumah, as some thought. In those two departments, the article was rather thought to reflect the influence of Barbara Ward, Lady Jackson. Interview: CF-58, London, 8 November 1965.

[199] The discussion, and much of that which ensues, is based, in the first instance, on the extensive and authoritative reports of a neutral official in Accra to his chief, kindly made available to the author. Also interviews: Quaison-Sackey, Alhaji Isa Wali, CF-14, 20.

time and much inconvenience, and apparently convinced Arkhurst that the Russians did not favor negotiations.[200] In Hanoi President Ho Chi Minh told the mission that victory might come before the end of the monsoon, so that negotiations were irrelevant and undesirable, but that he would welcome a visit by President Nkrumah. According to the same report, he expressed his fear for the safety of the Ghanaian president, as American planes were attacking closer and closer to Hanoi. The mission took this as a sign that if America were willing to stop bombing during Nkrumah's visit there would be a better chance of negotiations. But they returned in early August to report that, on balance, a visit by Nkrumah was not justified, as Hanoi did not wish to negotiate at the time. This fitted neither the Ghanaian line on Vietnam, nor, more importantly, Nkrumah's own desire to end the war. The immediate plan was to ignore the report, although Arkhurst thought this would make the ultimate accounting more difficult.

The very night of the mission's arrival home, Quaison-Sackey was sent to Washington with a letter for Johnson. The letter did not refer to possible negotiations with Hanoi, for Hanoi had not welcomed any. It was rather "a general appeal for peace, with no clear indication of any willingness on the part of Hanoi to take any new steps. . . ."[201] President Johnson gave Quaison-Sackey fifteen minutes, long enough to assure him that Nkrumah would be in no danger from American bombing, as the American Embassy in Accra was also assuring Flagstaff House.[202] It was a clever way of ignoring what Nkrumah really wanted.

Nkrumah was increasingly frustrated. His friends in Vietnam and China had more important priorities than to please him, and the Americans were unwilling to strengthen his hand by making even the smallest concession. It looked to all that Nkrumah's prospective trip would only be a bid for prestige.[203] Nkrumah hurt his own cause by reporting inaccurately on Armah's mission in well-informed quarters. As Nigeria had been a member of the original Commonwealth mission, Alhaji Isa Wali was irritated that he had not been officially informed on the results of Kwesi Armah's mission. Nkrumah called him in only to give him a very

[200] The Russians claimed the plane was full; but they were usually prepared to make room nonetheless. See also *Times*, 22 July 1965, and *Daily Telegraph*, 2 July 1965.

[201] *New York Times*, 7 August 1965. The article cited paraphrases Nkrumah's letter, which the White House presumably made available to the *New York Times*'s correspondent.

[202] See *Times*, 7 August 1965, and *Guardian*, 9 August 1965. The Americans obviously had no interest in making a martyr of Nkrumah. At this time, planes still could land regularly in Hanoi. Whether the Americans in fact wanted negotiations at all is not relevant to this discussion. There is no evidence to suggest that even if the Americans did wish talks with Hanoi that Nkrumah's efforts could have brought these about.

[203] Interview: CF-49.

411

scant report.[204] Nkrumah then insisted—so Isa Wali reported to Lagos—that the Americans were entirely at fault, that the failure of Armah's mission was due to American intransigence (which perhaps it was, though at a different plane of events), but that the Americans had in fact agreed at his own request not to bomb Hanoi during his prospective visit. Isa Wali knew this last was untrue, and asked elsewhere how diplomacy could be "based on a lie." Thus did he conclude that it was to be a "stage-managed affair, something at which Nkrumah is a past master"—to boost his sagging prestige.[205]

At first Nkrumah was persuaded not to make the trip. But after the OAU summit conference he had less to occupy him, and as the Americans had turned down his request for PL-480 foods, while the Russians refused new credits, his domestic troubles were deepening. Eventually, at the end of January, he decided he would go to Hanoi and to Peking as well. He wanted to include Washington, but the Americans, loathe to give him cause for new domestic advantage, would not entertain this possibility.[206] At Flagstaff House, Enoch Okoh had, with Dei-Anang, discreetly placed minutes and plans for the trip at the bottom of his "in" basket, hoping that he would defer his visit indefinitely. Now having made up his mind to go, although usually leaving all details of his trips to them, Nkrumah began making his own plans.

Flagstaff House officials and favorites became frightened. The advice in every quarter was against the trip. No one in or outside Ghana, save Nkrumah, wanted it. Over the weekend of February 18th, Okoh removed personal items from his desk; reports came in that officers were plotting a coup d'état in Kumasi.[207] On Sunday, T. R. Makonnen, last of the old pan-Africanists in Ghana, wrote to Nkrumah a cynical letter of praise, comparing the trip of his long-time friend to that of Jesus to Galilee.[208] The next day, February 21st, Nkrumah left, the huge jet filled with guards, friends, aides, and ministers. Diplomats at the airport wondered if he would return.[209] En route to Cairo, he is said to have asked if the plane could turn back without landing. Apparently told that it could not, he must have decided that he, too, had reached the point of no re-

[204] This included a brief, uninformative letter for transmittal to Prime Minister Sir Abubakar, dated 11 August 1965. Files of Alhaji Isa Wali, who permitted the author to examine his correspondence with his ministry on this issue.

[205] Isa Wali to P. S., M.E.A./Nigeria, 12 August 1965, in *ibid*. Also interview: CF-31.

[206] Such was consistent with American policy toward Ghana, if it is accepted that Nkrumah could not have brought about negotiations with Hanoi.

[207] Interviews: CF-85, 87.

[208] Interview: T. R. Makonnen, 20 February 1966.

[209] The author found several of these diplomats at the airport placing bets on the possibilities (and time) of a coup.

turn, although President Nasser encouraged none of his illusions.[210] He stopped in Pakistan, to present to President Ayub, who made a special trip to receive him, a plan for peace in Kashmir, which officials at the ministry had hurriedly prepared on the eve of his departure without the knowledge, however, of Ghana's diplomatic representatives in Pakistan and India.[211] He arrived in Peking on Thursday, February 24th, only to learn that the army and the police, with the support of the Ghanaian masses themselves, had deposed him in the manner of their forefathers.

[210] See interview of Eskine Childers with Nasser, "Nasser's Front Door," *Guardian*, 27 April 1966.
[211] Interviews: CF-17, 99.

413

•10•

"THE PENALTY OF FAILURE"

THE COUP D'ÉTAT, an occasion of greater celebration in Ghana than independence nine years earlier, flowed logically from Nkrumah's domestic and foreign policies. Yet the regime had substantial accomplishments to its credit as well, to which historians will give due attention. The summary of those in the field of foreign policy by A. L. Adu, one of Ghana's most distinguished sons, reflects the sentiments of many Ghanaian diplomats.

> Ghana succeeded in making the impact of African diplomacy felt in international forums and international organizations. Ghana succeeded in mobilizing Africa's efforts towards the emancipation of the dependent territories. Ghana succeeded against formidable obstacles of inertia and opposition, in making the idea and ideals of African unity accepted all over Africa as the ultimate objective for all African states, whatever disagreements there might be on the ways and means of achieving this objective. Ghana succeeded in making Africans everywhere feel proud of their Africanness and in a real sense in galvanizing the spirit of "African personality" in international organizations. Most of these successes are due to the sense of dedication, of purpose, of single-mindedness, and the inspired leadership of Dr. Nkrumah.

Still, "in politics it is not enough to begin well," Adu continued. "You must also finish well, otherwise you are likely to suffer the fate of all unsuccessful politicians and prophets. Because of the grave mistakes which Dr. Nkrumah committed, he has had to pay the penalty of failure."[1]

As understood in this study, foreign policy is something more than the statement of a government's international intentions—although we have noted that the aspirations to which Ghana gave voice were not without importance. Foreign policy is the combination of statecraft and statesmen, negotiation and diplomats, and of all the constituent elements used to project a nation's image and safeguard its interests abroad. Its success is a product of the competence with which the foreign policy

[1] A. L. Adu to the author, 5 July 1967.

instruments are wielded in their interaction within the international system. In this final chapter, we shall attempt to assess Ghana's foreign policy through the refraction of the several lenses employed throughout this study to examine the unfolding of the policy. We begin with an examination of Nkrumah's role, for Ghana's foreign policy was from the first his in character and stamp; it was most significantly a reflection of Nkrumah's characteristics and desires, of his perceptions of how the international system worked, and of his reactions to external events.

THE FAILURE OF GHANA'S FOREIGN POLICY:
NKRUMAH AS A STATESMAN

Max Weber, in his lecture "Politics as a Vocation," tells us that "three pre-eminent qualities are desirous for the politician; passion, a feeling of responsibility and a sense of proportion."[2] Nkrumah's passion and devotion to a cause were never in question. He stimulated bureaucracies to high efficiency, and inspired the most dispassionate civil servant through the strength of his convictions. But Weber understood passion to mean something other than what by 1960 appeared to be excess in Nkrumah's statecraft. A cabinet officer devoted to Nkrumah observed: "He loved extremists; the radical freedom fighters, having no responsibility, had free access to him because they advocated his causes so passionately— and praised him so liberally. Yes: he considered 'extremism in the cause of African unity as no vice, moderation in its cause no virtue.' "[3]

Nkrumah's passion inhered in words and in preference, but his diplomats always said that when the time came for action, "his bark was louder than his bite." Caution in his statecraft made the passion seem ironic if not contradictory. C.L.R. James has described how Nkrumah told him that he wondered if he had been correct, on leaving prison, in waiting for six years "and not driving straight ahead for independence, even if such a course had demanded armed insurrection" instead of co-operation with the British governor.[4] Nkrumah rationalized the choice by saying that a smooth transition of power in the Gold Coast would encourage the same process in other territories, and added, "I called for what I termed at the time 'tactical action.' An American friend jokingly suggested that 'tactful' action might have been a more appropriate name."[5] The choice he made did have the intended effect, but what he had done in practice was later to collide with his view of himself as a

[2] Gerth and Mills, *From Max Weber*, New York, 1968, p. 115.

[3] Interview: CF-85. The paraphrase of Barry Goldwater's famous phrase came in response to a mention of the American senator's name by the interviewer.

[4] C.L.R. James, "Notes on the Life of George Padmore," unpublished manuscript, p. 57.

[5] "My Task," unpublished manuscript written for publication under Nkrumah's name by Moshe Pearlman, p. 27.

Marxist revolutionary who had gained power through armed struggle with the imperialists. As his objectives moved beyond his reach he talked more and more of an African revolution and trapped himself in his talk. Africa in the period under review was not ready for the revolution he said it wanted; his passion was discredited by its disparity with his own past behavior. For that matter, Ghana itself, where the problem of corruption was becoming increasingly embarrassing to its friends, was very far from being the revolutionary state he claimed he led.

Caution was clear in all his policies. With respect to South Africa, he hesitated until 1960, when Eric Louw, foreign minister of South Africa, forced the issue of his country's membership in the Commonwealth. It was a man of principle—Julius Nyerere—who in 1961 altered the Commonwealth fundamentally by his statement that Tanganyikan and South African membership of the Commonwealth were incompatible. As Dennis Austin has argued, caution equally characterized his policy in the Congo and on the Casablanca group.[6]

Nkrumah was often considered an opportunistic statesman; in foreign policy this is a judgment of the degree of accomplishments in terms of goals, not of motivation. Ghana's principles were loud and radical, but Nkrumah's actions were outflanked for years on the left by such peers as Sékou Touré. After the Kulungugu assassination attempt, Nkrumah tried to compensate for the caution in his earlier policies. This was not passion, rather what Simmil called "sterile excitation."[7]

[6] See Dennis Austin, *Politics in Ghana 1946-1960*, London, 1964, p. 397. Ghana, in the last years of Nkrumah's power, was frequently accused of hypocrisy on the South African question, sometimes fairly, sometimes not. In 1965, for example, Ghana was asked to contribute to the UN special fund for the victims of apartheid; it refused, on the grounds that it supported South African freedom fighters in Ghana. A Ghanaian diplomat protested that such was "a unilateral action; even if it is in the framework of the OAU [which it was not] I venture to say that it does not release the . . . Government of its obligations under the UN charter." Still Ghana did not contribute. See J. B. Phillips, Ghana/Geneva to MFA, 8 January 1965, and Kuntoh to P. S., A.A.S., 20 January 1965, CFA-23. When a conference on sanctions was held in London, Ghana contributed £500, one-fourth of what was requested and of what Algeria gave—although the first-class air tickets of the Ghanaian delegates cost £632. See Ronald Segal to Nkrumah, 29 January 1964, Kwesi Armah to E. Okoh, 12 February 1964, F. S. Arkhurst to Armah, 7 April 1964, *ibid*. These are examples of pettiness in policy owing to Ghana's inability, at that point, to maintain the lead in the anti-apartheid movement. Some hypocrisy did exist with respect to Ghana's trade links with South Africa. Most trade was cut off, but some links continued to exist, particularly through the Black Star Line, owned by Ghana. The A.A.S. wrote the Line's president that, "Pending a continental application of the two resolutions [of sanctions against South Africa passed by the OAU and the conference of nonaligned states at Cairo] a statement should be issued by the Government denying that there is any trade whatsoever with South Africa," in spite of the admitted existence of these. 29 October 1964, *ibid*. East African leaders in particular were convinced that Ghana had made far fewer sacrifices than their states on this issue.

[7] Quoted in Gerth and Mills, *From Max Weber*, p. 115. See Professor Conor Cruise

In any case, passion, Weber warned, is dangerous unless "responsibility to the cause" is "the guiding star of action." Nkrumah's failure in this regard stems most evidently from his inability to accept Ghana fully (and solely) as his constituency, and this profoundly affected his sense of priorities. He was embarrassed by Ghana's size, and saw Africa as his stage, but he was judged—the more so as colonial frontiers became increasingly rigid—by his performance as president of Ghana. Between 1957 and 1960, Nkrumah balanced his responsibilities and his passion to a large degree and, whatever his longer-range motives for doing so, he allowed his concern for Ghana's development to temper his passion for foreign affairs. His prestige was greatest during those years: If there is no causal connection between this fact and his attention to Ghana's needs, there certainly was a causal relationship between his fall in prestige after 1960 and his failure to look after his own people.

His fatal flaw was undoubtedly his lack of any sense of proportion. There were several ways of explaining (and sometimes justifying) the local development of the "cult of the personality" (a phrase which the Russian diplomats in Accra, among many, came to use very frequently). Professor K.A.B. Jones-Quartey had this to say of its origins:

> At Lincoln he always brooded about Africa's lack of a "national" symbol or myth. Britain had its monarchy, America had its flag, and the Constitution, etc. But what had Africa? No crown, no constitution, no flag, no rallying cry, no focal point—nothing! It was imperative, Nkrumah insisted, to develop a myth—some national symbol somewhere. . . . Eventually this symbol turned out to be—Kwame Nkrumah himself, and the whole African case then assumed the form of a pyramid in his own mind. Africa was its base, Ghana was somewhere in the middle, and at the top—Kwame Nkrumah. But I want you to understand that at this point it was to him a question of filling a vacuum which plainly existed. I believe he genuinely could not find this needed symbol and therefore decided to fill the gap with himself. Thus did he himself come to justify (or rationalise) the praise.[8]

Apologists often said that the cult was a device used to preserve party solidarity; others said it was an antidote for the lack of any solidarity. Considering how far it developed, it might be seen more simply as the symptom of something deeply wrong in Nkrumah's character and, at the

---

O'Brien's brief description of Nkrumah's "passion" in the last years, *Observer*, 27 February 1966, p. 1.

[8] Prof. K.A.B. Jones-Quartey to the author, 23 March 1968. Jones-Quartey attended Lincoln with Nkrumah. The citation is Jones-Quartey's own elaboration and clarification of the notes taken in interview with him, 3 February 1966.

417

least, a symptom of great insecurity. To accept a thesis sometimes propounded, that the cult comes naturally to the African, that he praised Nkrumah only as he praised his chief, is to confuse ritual with required sycophancy.[9]

The cult was hardly a passive affair, or one which developed only at a late stage. Kofi Baako announced the publication of a treatise on "Schaekism and Nkrumaism" as early as 1949,[10] and that was only the beginning. Would Julius Nyerere have named himself chancellor of both universities of a country within a month, giving his name to one of them? Could Nehru have entitled his autobiography *India*? The cult was not just symbolic of domestic supremacy; it affected decision-making in foreign policy. Advisers who praised him liberally rose rapidly in influence, as happened with Tawia Adamafio. General Alexander has written that the "last person" to see Nkrumah was the one whose advice was taken; it might also be the one who praised him the most.

This lack of proportion led to a gravely distorted view of his own importance in the world. True, in its widest setting the initial thrust of Nkrumah's foreign policy made some impact on international relations, and Ghana's early independence combined with his own high standing in Africa brought him international acclaim. By 1960 there was sufficient experience among diplomats and party elite to recognize the limits of a small state in translating momentary impact into permanent influence. But the circumstances of the time played on a natural tendency of Nkrumah's; with the attention given to neutralist spokesmen like him in the 1960-1962 period, he became one of the first such leaders to confuse the concern of the great powers for Africa's needs with Africa's ability to maneuver among and to influence the great powers. Ironically all this occurred at a time when the very basis of his standing was being eroded, as his Africa policy suffered reverse after reverse. Nkrumah thought he was becoming more and more important when in fact, because of the shift of the spotlight from the nonaligned leaders after 1962 and because of his own diminishing hold on his African power base, the reverse is the case.

He never ceased trying to earn the mantle of world statesmanship through offers to mediate in a great international crisis: to the Middle Eastern states from 1958, to the Indian subcontinent from 1962; indirectly to the Chinese and Russians from 1964, directly to the Cypriots, and Sudanese, and to the Vietnamese, Chinese, and Americans from

[9] Moreover, to accept that such obsequiousness as Nkrumah demanded is natural to the African (as he himself is said to have claimed) involves us in a rejection of Nkrumah's noblest belief—namely, the equality of the races.

[10] Noted in Kofi Baako, "My Hatred for Imperialism," Accra, n.d., probably 1949.

1965. Mediators are sought. Nehru was asked to mediate in the fifties because he was a man of stature who *had* led a revolution—who had spent eleven years in jail—and who ruled a country fifty times Ghana's size.

No doubt Nkrumah's lack of proportion would have appeared different on the wider stage that he wanted; in the same context Thomas Kanza noted that de Gaulle's Fifth Republic political style would appear ludicrous were he prime minister of Holland.[11] But de Gaulle was President of France—and Nkrumah was neither president of Nigeria nor of a hypothetical African super-state; he was president of Ghana. He could not accept that his stage was limited to Ghana, but the more he insisted that he should not be so confined, the more enemies he made. He might have remained on the broader stage he briefly held, had he been less insistent that it was his by right. When he finally—and dimly —perceived that he did not in fact possess the stature he had hoped to attain, he permitted the cult to go to new lengths, no doubt as compensation. Komla Gbedemah, who had nurtured and solidified the strength of the CPP during Nkrumah's year in prison, justly wrote from exile, in 1962, "Osagyefo, Fount of Honour, Father of the Nation, Messiah, Teacher, Redeemer, Leader, Ideological Mentor, the Infallible. . . . Truly President Kwame Nkrumah, you have succeeded uniquely in making Ghana a land without glory for all but your high high Dedication."[12]

Nkrumah's political failure cannot be attributed solely to his loss of a balanced passion, a sense of responsibility and of proportion, in successive periods of Ghana's development. Weber assumed the statesman to be a man of some intelligence but, in the case of Nkrumah, this quality bears examination. Consider his call for an African union government, and how he explained it. There were great emotional reserves of support throughout the continent, for the concept of a united Africa that could take its rightful place in the councils of the world. In a later section, the strategy he employed to obtain the union will be examined; consider at this point only how he understood it.

He had opposed federalism in Ghana ostensibly for the good reason that Ghana was too small to afford any division of power. He then used Ghana as a paradigm for Nigeria and the Congo, attacking federalism in those far larger states. He went still further: he used unitary government as a paradigm for the entire continent, called for the elimination of colonial boundaries, and sought to develop a continent-wide single

[11] Interview: T. R. Kanza, 9 February 1967, London.
[12] "Open Letter of K. A. Gbedemah to Dr. K. Nkrumah," 5 June 1962, privately printed and distributed.

419

party that in itself would make any division of power within such a united state impossible—with all political power effectively wielded from some central capital. It was defensible in theory but not in practice to argue that an East African federation would be a backward step from African unity since it would divert attention from the grander scheme. In seeking everything he got nothing, but he was apparently unable to see any contradictions in this position. Togo, for example, could be the "seventh region of Ghana," but not a federal partner with it. Economically weak Guinea was to be organically joined with Ghana. Indeed, three dozen heads of state were to throw off their state's sovereignty, by which, through a mysterious process, their sovereignty was to be increased—but Togo, for one, was always to throw off its sovereignty in favor of a single, specific state. Ambition alone cannot explain such concepts.

In the last years of his rule, according to Botsio, he finally accepted that a degree of federalism might be conceded in the union government, that the colonial divisions (i.e., boundaries of independent states) could be preserved to a degree. He developed an image of an African Union of Socialist Republics after his trip to the Soviet Union in 1961. But where is the basis of the comparison—and the African mother Russia? His increased "flexibility," his willingness at the end to press only for an "Executive Committee" of the OAU, for example, was simply a concession that he would "permit" something that was nowhere in question. Long debates took place in Flagstaff House over these concepts—but "in a false quarrel there is no true valour."

Jones-Quartey explained his intellectual difficulties in these terms:

> Of all the elements in his complex personality, one stood out clearly to those who knew Nkrumah better than others—his essential inarticulateness. He had charm, a sort of delightful gaucherie, explosive mirth, and so on. But he was plain inarticulate in serious, unrehearsed discussion. For one thing, he never had a firm foundation in English, but I suspect in his own language he might still have the same problems. It was not just a question of verbalisation, but of thought processes itself. Hence the jumpiness and often the incoherence of his speech in serious conversation, resulting in the puzzlement and disappointment many people have had after single meetings with him. ... In a debate—let's say like one of those famous Kennedy-Nixon TV clashes—there would have been a catastrophic disintegration in Nkrumah.[13]

[13] Jones-Quartey to Thompson, 23 March 1968.

420

When he confronted Olympio in June 1960, and when he tried to explain his approach to union government to his peers at Cairo in 1964, this disintegration seems to have occurred. His bargaining ability with his peers was also affected; thus Sékou Touré got £4,000,000 in 1959 from him in a situation where a cleverer head of state than Nkrumah would have demanded more in return.

The inarticulateness may be linked to his compartmentalized mind and to what Thomas Hodgkin called the "essential eclecticism" of his learning.[14] One of the well-springs of the foreign policy was his own commitment to Marxism-Leninism but, because he had not considered the relationship of such an ideology to the African context, and, because he was able to work all the same with Westerners and, at least at first, proclaim to them his commitment to their cause without foreseeing the consequences of such unrelated and inconsistent policies, he was, in the end, trusted by no side. He was unable to study an ideology whole but very willing to extract lines and phrases that appeared useful whatever their original context; Botsio thus argued that Nkrumah used Marxism largely as a directive—and a pretext—for increasing his power. A thoughtful Briton argued that Nkrumah could "get carried away with his own dreams" for lack of a philosophy of life, because he had no coherent framework of thought and nothing to guide him but political ambition.[15] Nkrumah, in all, was a "marginal man,"[16] intellectually insecure, insistent, for instance, on the use of an honorary doctorate, which most statesmen possess but few have the immodesty to use. Thus he was willing to put his name on badly written books of dubious value not realizing that, ultimately, these could only detract from his reputation, particularly as the identity of the true authors became known.

His "singlemindedness," Adu said, launched the "African personality," but in the end it was his undoing. He lacked flexibility. Sir Robert Jackson suggested that he shared with Farouk an inability to judge what was possible, in contrast to a supple autocrat like the Shah. Ghana's foreign policy was Nkrumah's, and a reflection of his moods and ambitions but, at a different level, this study is an account of his inability to foresee the consequences of his actions or perceive the changes occurring in the environment. He was so easy to influence that his foreign policy might have gone in other directions had the pressures on him been dif-

[14] Quoted in Austin, *Politics in Ghana*, p. 40.

[15] Interview: CF-70, 13 October 1965, London.

[16] Sigmund Neumann's phrase. Note also the importance of Nkrumah's origins—from an insignificant, marginal Ghanaian tribe, like so many of the individuals Neumann applied his phrase to. See a related point by Father O'Connell in "Senghor, Nkrumah, and Azikiwe: Unity and Diversity in West African States," *Nigerian Journal of Economic and Social Studies*, 5, No. 1 (March 1963).

ferent.[17] A good foreign policy, however, should never be so fortuitously determined nor should it founder on the weaknesses of one man, for it should never be based on one man alone.

The Failure of Ghana's Foreign Policy: The Components of Statecraft

For all this, Ghana, as we have said, had its successes. Were those which A. L. Adu credited to her foreign policy a result of the statecraft practiced during these nine years? Let us first consider Ghana's foremost instrument for leadership, namely, her symbolic position as the center of black African aspirations. Nkrumah had become an important symbol to millions of Africans even before independence and, between 1957 and 1960, his articulation of African ambitions stirred the continent, accumulating for Ghana immense political capital from which to draw in later years. The first conference of Independent African States, organized by Adu in 1958, launched the "African personality" in international diplomatic circles, and the first All-African Peoples Conference, organized by George Padmore in the same year, stimulated the forces of nationalism in every African territory.

Thomas Hodgkin—as quoted earlier—argued that Ghana's foreign policy would be largely judged "on the extent to which its leaders . . . succeed in identifying themselves with the principle of Negro-African liberty. This is less a matter of speeches than of policies."[18] True in any continent, the concluding observation was particularly cogent in Africa at its low stage of social and economic development. Organization was needed, otherwise widespread sentiments could not be channeled as supports for a policy. But as the constructive diplomatic initiatives of 1958 were very largely not followed up, it is reasonable to ask whether those accomplishments cited by Adu were not a result of the speeches and in spite of the policies, insofar as they occurred after 1958.

Nkrumah could, owing to his prestige, force conservative leaders to take cognizance of the new Africa. His speeches—what he symbolized for the continent—affected, for example, Tubman's options. Bold moves like the Ghana-Guinea union put the conservatives on the defensive. But the strategy of such men as Houphouet-Boigny and Tubman denied Nkrumah the fruits of his personal standing among political leaders;

17 Gbedemah and others have argued, for example, that had Ehud Avriel represented the United States instead of Israel between 1957 and 1960, the subsequent years would have been very different. Thus is underlined an essential point, namely, that if the roots of Ghana's foreign policy may be seen in Nkrumah's past, this is a necessary but far from sufficient explanation of why the foreign policy went the way it did.

18 See Preface.

when the Ghana-Guinea union first showed fissures, both leaders were able to exploit these.

The problem was that carefully thought out objectives, to which the various components of statecraft could relate, did not exist, at least after 1962. After that point, the whole decision-making process was never capable of withstanding the various strains put on it. Hitherto, there had been one very conspicuous diplomatic success, the Volta River Project: in enquiring why Nkrumah found funds for it, and why it did not thenceforth serve as the base for the industrialization of Ghana, one sees the distinction between an objective related to the components of statecraft, and one not so related.

The project was one of the most imaginative and most ambitious schemes in the third world, and succeeded owing to exhaustive preparation and great persistence. The entire diplomatic mechanism was involved in this: ministers, diplomats, advisers, friends of the state's leaders in Britain and America, all had their part. Throughout the extended negotiations, the Ghanaian leaders maintained a realistic view of their own bargaining position, and were thus taken seriously.

Once the Volta dam had been built, Ghana received very little investment from the West and little benefit from the enormous credits extended by the East, for there was no coherent policy tied to the instruments available for the development of the Volta industrial scheme; the dam had been, after all, only a means to an end—Ghana's industrialization. By the time the project neared completion, the CPP was committed to "scientific Socialism," but Nkrumah had not paused to consider whether the West would be willing to invest in a country whose long-term aim was nationalization. The plans for making Ghana Socialist deeply involved foreign policy, as this was to be achieved through making agreements for credit and trade with Socialist states. There was little preparation or forethought as to the negotiations or to possible consequences of such agreements. Nor was there any attempt to relate these to overall economic strategy—a seven-year plan was launched that very much depended on Western investment for its success. In the end, there was one group of influential policy-makers advocating the proliferation of agreements with the Socialist states, on ideological grounds, and another, seeking to rationalize the entire developmental process and seeking to salvage what was left of the seven-year plan.

Nkrumah's statecraft within Africa is that by which he will finally be judged—and here it was more deficient than outside the continent. Was the fault wholly Nkrumah's? One diplomat blamed the entire foreign service apparatus: "In the case of African affairs . . . I tried to woo

423

Barden [of the Bureau of African Affairs] so that I could influence him. It was not easy. Sometimes I succeeded; sometimes I failed. But when one tried one found [that it was not] too difficult . . . to get sense to prevail."[19] This is the argument of one of Ghana's outstanding diplomats, who did much to ameliorate the diplomatic problems caused by Nkrumah's policy, but he avoids the central point, namely, that from an operational point of view, the premise of the policy was mad. Diplomats could argue Barden out of a particular course of action. Eric Otoo, the accomplished head of the intelligence network, could assure Nkrumah that Barden did not, for example, have Kikuyu's in the Kenyan highlands ready "to strike down Kenyatta in the name of Osagyefo," as Barden is said to have claimed.[20] Enoch Okoh, the cabinet secretary, and K. B. Asante and Michael Dei-Anang of the African Affairs Secretariat, could judge Nkrumah's moods, discreetly place certain papers at the bottom of his desk work, and hope for the best.[21] But in the end, the Bureau was more influential in shaping policy than the other foreign policy agencies because its officers told Nkrumah what he wished to hear. The diplomats could not have persuaded Barden to foreswear pressing for union government, for it was on this advocacy that Barden held his high and lucrative position.

We argued at the end of Book II that Ghana's diplomatic network had ceased to function effectively by the time of Kulungugu; to the extent that it even existed in the last period it was mainly a mechanism for personal policies. It might appear that there were parallel agencies duplicating the work of each other; organizationally this is correct, but it is not what in fact developed. There was only one network with power—with the Bureau of African Affairs as its apex—which misled and deluded Nkrumah in a way that he himself wished, and another, with the ministry of foreign affairs at the center, which was reduced to helplessness for a large part of the time, its officers defining their tasks as, for the most part, the averting of the more costly errors.[22]

Flagstaff House was the center of what Thomas Hodgkin suggested had become something of a "palace regime."[23] A contingency fund of £2,000,000 made the good life there possible, but it was not a good

---

19 Letter to the author, 2 June 1967.   20 Interview: CF-87.

21 One senior and effective diplomat wrote, "I avoided asking questions at the wrong time. Dei-Anang taught . . . this. He would choose the correct moment for raising awkward issues. Nkrumah's mood was most important. Dei-Anang had a very alert and ingenious mind and he would not if he could help it give Nkrumah the chance to jeopardize what he thought was in the country's interest." Letter to the author, 2 June 1967.

22 Interview: CF-20.

23 Thomas Hodgkin, "African Angels," *New Statesman*, 23 June 1967.

diplomatic nerve center. Competent men like Eric Otoo were competing with illiterate men like Ambrose Yankey to give advice on intelligence, and the Russians were present to affect the process according to their interests. Geoffrey Bing was present to counteract the restraining influence of men like Okoh. Dei-Anang, by 1963, had too many interests in the regime to play a constructive role, and in trying to preserve his own and Nkrumah's illusions he committed the basic diplomatic sin, namely, using the obtrusive, inelegant lie.[24] Thus he earned the enmity of nearly every envoy in Accra, and was the chief administrator, by the end, of Nkrumah's foreign policy in all its facets.[25] By the eve of the coup, K. B. Asante had found a place at the OAU Secretariat, and the refugees had found their way back to Accra after the OAU conference to press Nkrumah with new determination for a policy of subversion. These were not good omens.

The foreign service, for its part, was demoralized. There were 57 embassies at the end and, although 10 of them now had professional diplomats as their heads, the political appointees were of an even lower standard than before.[26] The professional diplomats knew they were closely watched in Accra and abroad, and were unwilling to jeopardize their careers or their families by taking forceful action. Those who saw the futility of Nkrumah's policy tried to preserve their own professional integrity by stressing—in conversation and negotiation—aspects of the policy, such as Rhodesia, that a radical leader might have made central to his foreign policy. But they were not otherwise exercising their professional abilities, and felt that they were largely wasted abroad. They realized that no one in the ministry read their reports, so they stopped reporting with regularity; Botsio noted that one embassy went a full year without reporting home. To the extent that they were embassies without functions, they brought Africa no credit. When they did report, it was often in such a way as to make Ghana fair game for its opponents.

Consider, for example, a routine question of policy during the period of friction between Algeria and Ghana over the rivalry of OAU and Afro-Asian conferences, a few months before the coup. Ambassador Heymann, a CPP militant, had urged that Ghana participate in a trade

[24] Consider an example given by Nigerien Ambassador Tiecoura Alzouma, in an interview: "I visited Dei-Anang to protest an article in *Spark* that viciously criticized my government. He insisted that Nkrumah and the government had nothing to do with *Spark*, whereupon I pointed to another issue on his desk, No. 100, with the lead article entitled, "Why I Founded the *Spark*,"—by Kwame Nkrumah.

[25] The briefs prepared for Nkrumah's trip to Hanoi were even prepared in Dei-Anang's office, to the intense annoyance of Quaison-Sackey, the Foreign Minister.

[26] Botsio, in an interview, commented on his difficulties in persuading leading party men to accept ambassadorial posts: too many advantages inhered in staying at home.

fair in Algiers despite the tension. This was done, if on a small scale, after which he cabled Flagstaff House (to justify the decision): "Politically, the participation of Ghana has taken the wind out of the sail of the ruling Junta. . . . Locally, public opinion is not very happy about Ghana's appearance on the Fair scene for obvious reasons, although this, in no way, affects the high prestige Ghana enjoys among the Algerian masses."[27] The meaning of this was obscure enough: but from it Dei-Anang wrote to Nkrumah three weeks later that the decision to participate in the fair was "sound and expedient," and that in spite of the "present tension" between the two countries, "Ghana generally enjoys a high prestige among the masses."[28] In the meantime the French ambassador in Ghana was obtaining from France's not inconsiderable diplomatic sources in Algeria very accurate assessments of Ghana's standing in Algeria. These were passed on as a matter of course to Paris and thence Accra. The French ambassador kept his Entente friends well briefed, at a time when they wished to prevent the success of the Accra OAU summit conference, and could find French assessments of the Algerian position with respect to its conference very useful. Thus did Ghana's adversaries effectively probe at its weak spots.

Ghana could have done much through diplomacy at the international level. Nkrumah rightly appreciated that there were many enemies of African success, but he need not have played into their hands. If the international deck was stacked in 1957 against the small developing state trying to make some impact on international relations, it was during the subsequent decade that the "north-south" division in international trade came to the forefront of world attention; "regionalism," of the type Ghana could have backed in West Africa, became a byword of progressive statecraft in international thinking. But Ghanaian diplomacy at the top was not geared to these developments, in which it might have played a prominent role through its own example.[29]

For an example of what was possible in the foreign policy as a whole, consider what the Ghanaian team at the United Nations was able to do as an autonomous subunit of Ghanaian statecraft. It was the best, or one of the two best, African delegations in New York, and it realized that only one crusade could be fought at a time, and this crusade was to advance African interests. During most of the Nkrumah period,

27 Amb. C. Heymann, Ghana/Algiers to P.S., A.A.S., 6 September 1965, CFA-54.
28 Dei-Anang to Nkrumah, 27 September 1965, *ibid.*
29 Ghanaian diplomats abroad often attempted to apply their efforts to strengthen movements toward regionalism and stressed the importance of the work of UNCTAD. This was, however, unrelated to the main thrusts of foreign policy and, therefore, of little relevance.

426

Quaison-Sackey was a dominant force in the African Group, proof of which was his own election as president of the General Assembly at a time when Ghana's popularity was low. He had kept Nkrumah's predilections from affecting his diplomacy, and had worked to ensure that states like Nigeria acted with Ghana on international issues, even when relations between the two states at home were close to breaking point. Russia, it was said, sought to use its position in Accra to influence Ghanaian voting, but was visibly unsuccessful. Ghana pledged $20,000 to the United Nations in its financial crisis, on Quaison-Sackey's pleadings; this when Western diplomats expected that Ghana, as a result of Russian pressure, would take a neutral position—or would even directly side with Russia—were a vote taken on member-contributions at the General Assembly. A strong United Nations was in Ghana's interest; Nkrumah knew this, and Quaison-Sackey was able to deter him from betraying his convictions.[30]

It was not easy, even under the auspicious circumstances in which Ghana was launched as a state, to establish a diplomatic network which could compete with the older powers. A British minister commented that Ghana (and African states in general) had no diplomacy, that he never worked through their representatives in London, but through the British High Commission in Accra or directly with Nkrumah.[31] This was his preference, but it was also a necessity when Ghana's high commission in Belgrave Square was in such disorder. A true statesman would have considered the bypassing of his accredited representatives as an affront. Yet Nkrumah trusted very few of his envoys and virtually never consulted them; apparently he saw the African personality best projected through ostentatious cars and noisy diplomacy, and little understood—as his Russian friends did—what "great triumphs" could be gained "at small risks" through diplomacy.[32]

Before diplomacy can achieve anything for a state, the diplomats themselves must be able to preserve what respect their state does enjoy in the ministries to which they are accredited: to do which they must possess adequate information and a sense of timing. Nkrumah's style, and view of diplomacy, made this impossible. Consider one example of what this cost. Kwesi Armah in 1962 echoed a complaint of all his fellow envoys of not being told of government decisions. He noted that he was not informed in advance of the dismissal of General Alexander, and was

[30] Interviews: CF-22, 41, 93, 94, 85.
[31] Interview: CF-103, 10 November 1965, London.
[32] "Totalitarian Approaches to Diplomatic Negotiation," in G. A. Craig, *War, Politics, and Diplomacy*, London, 1967, p. 231.

"called to the foreign office and advised to clear the air."[33] He had obviously been called to the foreign office to be made to feel uncomfortable; every relevant office in Whitehall knew what had happened. That was not all. Ambassador Elliot, Ghana's envoy in Moscow, commented directly to Armah: "I think the British Government must have been informed direct of the reasons for dismissing Alexander because when I arrived in Moscow the British Ambassador there seemed to know the reasons given to the British Government and appeared to be satisfied and in sympathy with the reasons."[34] This was *diplomacy*—on the part of the British—of a level that Ghana's professional diplomats were capable of, had they been given a chance. Ghana had a tough, intelligent corps ready to take advantage of the favorable speeches being made about African aspirations in this period, and could have done much to encourage their host countries to translate these sentiments into policies, given intelligent guidance. By 1962 they knew Ghana's stock was low. In 1964 Africa's stock was low, too, and part of the blame was Nkrumah's. Meanwhile his diplomats were obliged to go from chancery to chancery seeking support for his request of several billion dollars of aid in the spring of 1965 to pay for his excesses. Ghana's foreign policy was not a revolutionary one, just a bad one.

Whatever problems existed in Ghana's first five years because of the divergence of goals between Nkrumah and his diplomats were partially compensated by the energy that Nkrumah brought to the implementation of Ghanaian policy. Distinctions between what Nkrumah and the diplomats wanted were blurred by the very rapidity of the turn of events. But in the last four years, Nkrumah's desires were so divorced from what rationally could be construed as the interests of any group in Ghana that the state as such no longer possessed a foreign policy: there was only the course of a dictator expending a nation's resources to achieve unrealistic ambitions and objectives. "The diplomat . . . has it in his power to bungle a good, and avoid the worst consequences of a bad, foreign policy," Hans Morgenthau writes.[35] Because Nkrumah did not understand the stuff of which foreign policy is made, the Ghanaian diplomats failed. They failed to avert the consequences of Nkrumah's misunderstanding of the way the international system worked, but they are the unsung heroes of Ghana's foreign policy for their attempts.

BALANCE SHEET ON THE EVE OF THE COUP D'ETAT

During the period of this study the dominant force in the Middle East was "Nasserism" and the drive toward "Arab unity" tied to it. "Nas-

---

[33] *Ministry of Foreign Affairs*, "Conference of Ghana Envoys, January 1962," p. 52.
[34] *Ibid.*
[35] Hans Morgenthau, *Politics Among Nations*, New York, 1963, p. 545.

serism" was not an ideology, but it was a force that no power could afford to belittle, however many its setbacks and failures. Nkrumah's foreign policy was designed, in the first instance, to bring him the fruits that Nasser's foreign policy brought the U.A.R. and, in a more controversial sense, the Arab peoples. It was the job of Flagstaff House to assure Nkrumah that he benefited similarly from the "African revolution," interpreted in terms of "Nkrumaism." "African unity" became the most important diplomatic term in sub-Saharan Africa but, after 1962, the mainstream of the drive to "African unity" came not from Accra, but from Addis Ababa, Dar-es-Salaam, and other capitals.

The reasons for the differences between Nasser's and Nkrumah's degrees of success are obvious. We said at the outset that no international movement succeeds without the backing of a strong power; if "Arab unity" was proportionately less successful than international Communism, it is partly because, within the system of states that it wished to affect, it was proportionately less powerful than Russia in its system. Compared to Ghana, however, Egypt was obviously blessed by its strategic setting and relative size within its region. This location gave it an international importance, as well, that no part of West Africa possessed.[36] Moreover, Nasser had a secure domestic base, and an unquestioned popular following. Nkrumah was shown not to have a secure domestic base, and his popularity was in doubt after 1961. "Nasserism" had an enemy, Israel, that preserved some unity in most of the Arab world, and, in the period studied, Nasser was considered central to the defeat of Israel. "African Unity"—the diplomatic abstraction of the OAU in black Africa—had an enemy, racism in Southern Africa; yet "Nkrumaism" benefited not at all from this, an Accra base for operations against apartheid being too far from the scene of struggle. Partly as a result, Nkrumaism increasingly stressed neocolonialism, imperialism, and so forth, as the prime enemy.

In 1960, the Congo crisis precipitated a split in Africa. If the effect of the crisis on Nkrumah was similar to that of the first Palestine war on Arab leaders, the effect on African leaders as a whole was different; Israel remained as an element uniting Arab states, but the Congo crisis drove African leaders apart. Throughout the crisis Ghana attempted to show how much an African state could do for a sister state, and it etched in the memory of many African leaders the fact that Africa had to cooperate if they were ever to solve their problems without outside

---

[36] "In relationship to Africa as a whole, Ghana has limited strategic importance. . . . It is doubtful that West Africa, in whole or in part, would become the scene of major operations in the event of a Third World War. There is little of strategic value in the area that would make it a target for conquest." *U.S. Government*, "Special Warfare Area Handbook for Ghana," January 1962, pp. 524-25.

interference. But what sort of cooperation? The Emperor of Ethiopia and Sékou Touré saw that Africa needed a "useful minimum" of co-operation, since "maximum cooperation" was not possible.[37] Nkrumah's greatest failure in this period was to delude himself into thinking that a paper union with Lumumba could be used to build his African union. By early 1961, after Lumumba's death, he was calling for maximum unity throughout Africa and gearing his foreign policy to this demand.

If Nkrumah brought the politics of unity to the African continent, he divorced himself from its mainstream at pan-Africanism's greatest moment, the founding of the OAU. Ghana fought the organization during most of its first two years, which brought union government no closer, and forced the OAU secretariat and member governments at their meetings to spend a disproportionate amount of time dealing with the problems Ghana created. There were many areas where Ghana could have taken the initiative and leadership on the radical issues of the day, but Ghana's influence was dissipated by Nkrumah's unique vision of what was essentially a mirage. Nkrumah lacked neither ideas nor dynamism, and in fact diagnosed many African problems accurately. His prescriptions for all of them were the same, however; they were also counter-productive.

At the other level of his Africa policy, his relations with neighboring countries, there was a still less understandable failure. This policy had long since become one of personal *Realpolitik*, a policy based not on considerations of general national advantage but on personal security, largely as the result of the form of internal government which had developed in Ghana when there was no outlet for opposition. Martin Wight notes that: "Neighbouring states are usually enemies . . . common frontiers are usually disputed, and your natural ally is the Power in the rear of your neighbour."[38] And he calls this part of the "pattern of power." Nkrumah tried this game too, but with the wrong players, or with those in too small a league. He was using, for example, Dahomey as a wedge against Togo, who shared many of the same radical pan-African aspirations, when he could have used a relationship with Nigeria, to bring tiny Dahomey and Togo into a West African economic union, organized and possibly dominated by the superior economic power of Ghana. As it was, Nkrumah ironically "helped to forge a bond of shared

[37] A distinction made by Muhammad Heikal in reference to the Arab states in the aftermath of the 1967 Middle East war. Quoted in Gavin Young, "Arabs Move Towards 'Unity' Summit Talks," *Observer*, 9 July 1967.

[38] Martin Wight, "The Balance of Power," in R. Butterfield and M. Wight, eds., *Diplomatic Investigations*, London, 1966, p. 149.

430

hostility to Ghana" between Nigeria and the French speaking states of the former Brazzaville Group.[39]

Nkrumah's attempts to launch an African revolution in his last years of power found no more success, and did not even draw on the lessons to be inferred from the failure of the AAPC in earlier years. A movement launched from one state involves interference in others—but there must be a mechanism through which such interference may be made to succeed. In this context Professor Binder writes that "nowhere is the definition of an internal affair so anomalous as among the Arab countries."[40] Nasser intervened throughout the Middle East, but, if Hussain and Faisal were unappreciative, Nasser's own past successes and Arab tradition meant that there was little moral fervor in condemning such intervention in other Arab capitals. More important, the mechanism existed through which a movement of some dimension could be mounted: "Racial sovereignty," Mazrui's term, was relevant for a discussion of the Arab world, where Saudi dockers at one point awaited word from Cairo before loading oil to the West. Even a leader without Nkrumah's faults could not have developed such a network of influence in black Africa. Indeed, there was so little history on which the new leaders of black Africa could fasten in nation-building that the colonial frontiers became inviolable.

In short, Nkrumah had failed to grasp the most important result of the emergence of independent states in Africa, namely, that however close the links that nationalists from different territories may have had as students, or as pan-African militants in London, once these nationalists were leaders of independent states they would be unprepared to surrender their sovereignty, the most valued asset in their small treasuries, and would react to subversion accordingly.

Moreover, Ghanaian intervention was symmetrical to nothing;[41] no other African state was intervening in Ghana's affairs, unlike, for example, American and Russian espionage and subversion which have developed in reaction to each other. Houphouet's own counter-thrust to it in 1965 was only as successful as Ghanaian intervention had been at that point, but had there been one conspicuous Ghanaian success, Houphouet would have found broader continental backing and no doubt been able to induce East African leaders to stand up for the principle of noninterference that had been violated.

[39] Mazrui, *Towards a Pax Africana*, p. 66.

[40] Leonard Binder, "Nasserism: The Protest Movement in the Middle East," in Morton Kaplan, ed., *The Revolution in World Politics*, New York, 1962, p. 159.

[41] For the concept of symmetry in world politics, see David Finlay and Jan Triska, "Soviet-American Relations. A Multiple Symmetry Model," *Journal of Conflict Resolution*, 9, No. 1 (March 1965).

431

The "African revolution" launched from Accra was *Opéra Bouffe;* it failed because the leader was incapable of estimating the limits of his resources, the size of his following, and the capabilities of his followers. In chasing the whirlwind Nkrumah brought Ghana's economy closer and closer to bankruptcy and had the coup not occurred, he might have lost his few non-Ghanaian adherents in the same way that his plans for a "militia" misfired—the money became unavailable.[42] The last director of the Bureau of African Affairs had this to say of freedom fighters who came to Accra: "None of them took him seriously. They came here, shouted slogans about Nkrumaism and union government, picked up their checks, gave their duty speech in praise of Nkrumah elsewhere—so that he could see that he was getting his money's worth—and then they just did the Highlife. In the last years even the most apparently devoted followers, like Mokhehle, had seen through him."[43]

If it be granted that Nkrumah kept the idea of a united continent alive in the minds of the African peoples, it must be accepted that by his methods he antagonized most African statesmen and alienated them from a cause of which many were potential supporters. His commitment to the old ideal was costly in another way. "A man's reach should exceed his grasp, or what's a heaven for?" Robert Browning, Max Weber, Karl Mannheim, and others have honored the role of the chiliastic, utopian vision as a recurring historical force. But are such sentiments prescriptions for policy? Foreign policy runs on realism, only loosely related to the aspirations that guide it. Soviet foreign policy has never been judged a failure for its lack of success in Communizing the world precisely because national interests have been kept closer to the fore than those of international Communism. But union government was held to be desperately necessary, inevitable, and easy to effect—this was the premise of Ghana's Africa policy. "Demonstrating the need for an institution does not bring it into existence,"[44] however, and there was ample evidence available that it would not be simple to achieve. According to Nkrumah, African leaders had only to shed their "petty sovereignties" and let history "unfold"; allies were chosen according to whether they were expected to aid in effecting the union government, but the list had to be shuffled constantly, since Nkrumah failed to realize that no other government kept union government as an option at any level. Thus did Nkrumah expose Ghana's Africa policy to ridicule.

With the other major thrust of the foreign policy in its last years, "scientific socialism," Nkrumah was not isolated within Ghana. A small,

---

[42] See *supra*, p. 401.   [43] Interview: Ofori Baah.
[44] Kenneth Waltz, *Man, the State, and War*, New York, 1965, p. 228.

dedicated band of men praised and supported Nkrumah, and proclaimed Nkrumaism, because it was defined as being a part of the mainstream of Marxism-Leninism, and because the state was now committed, in theory, to the implementation of their program. In this case
there were also other states, thirteen of them in Europe and Asia, which
shared these goals and which encouraged the practice of "scientific
socialism," although they were all dismayed by the disparity between
Ghanaian theory and practice.

Ghana's commitment to this theory was doubly costly to the success
of its foreign policy—firstly, internationally, and secondly, in Africa.
Realism in policy dictates that statesmen set their sights at attainable
goals (at least in private) and allow sufficient flexibility in public
pronouncements to avoid trapping themselves. Despite Nkrumah's
proclamations and beliefs, socialism was not feasible in the Ghana of
his day. There was never any sign that his regime had the capacity for
discipline to implement socialism of the Bulgarian, North Vietnamese,
or Cuban varieties. The cadres for such a policy did not even exist;
"there were only five good Ghanaian Marxists," a Russian diplomatist
said. Nkrumah's Marxism appeared as a mere caricature of what is accepted as the real thing, eroding the prestige of the foreign policy, and
making the credibility of its nonalignment, in Botsio's words, "a joke."

Nkrumah could have proclaimed socialist goals while preserving a
nonalignment acceptable in both Washington and Moscow. He could
have continued to develop ties of a more enduring variety with the
Russians and built on the ties already existing with America (that had
been cultivated so carefully between 1957 and 1960), in order to obtain
the industrial investment to complement the Volta project. But accepting "scientific socialism"—an ideological import—meant that Washington would no longer be interested in preserving a working relationship with Ghana. Having become too involved with Russian diplomacy,
he lost his own ability to discriminate between varying Western intentions. Nasser in the same period made no such mistakes; he kept his
options open by keeping his relationship with the Russians defined in
terms of national interest, and by keeping his domestic equivalents of
Ghana's "socialist boys" locked up or away from his office.[45]

Commitment to this ideology also cost Ghana influence in the one
area where Ghana's weight, cohesiveness, and human resources entitled

---

[45] Compare also the relationship between a talented journalist like Muhammed Heikal
and Nasser, whose desires Heikal reflected; and that between Samuel Ikoku, a brilliant
theoretician who allowed Nkrumah to use *Spark* as "a channel for saying all the things
he did not wish to put in diplomatic papers" but who himself used *Spark* to draw
Nkrumah along a path chosen by himself.

433

it to real influence, namely, West Africa. No state of influence in that region—or elsewhere in sub-Saharan Africa—was likely to accept "scientific socialism," and Ghana's acceptance of it discredited its other objectives in their minds. At the level of Ghana's relations with its immediate neighbors, the result was even more ironic. Nkrumah and his Marxist advisers considered it unthinkable to threaten Ghana's "socialist progress" by developing economic links with these states, since this would have entailed a close harmonization of economic policy.

What gains, then, did acceptance of the theory bring? Most of the Eastern credits were granted when Nkrumah's intentions were still a question mark in Moscow's or Peking's eyes and Ghana's economy in "imperialist's" hands. It was not incumbent on Nkrumah to proclaim their ideology in order to obtain their aid. As it was, by the time of the coup, only C55,100,000 out of C115,000,000 had been utilized from the Eastern credits, because of the difficulty in implementing—and finding domestic finance for—Eastern projects.

It can be argued that because of the oppressiveness of world imperialism Ghana was justified in working toward the strengthening—or creation—of a world "socialist commonwealth," in preference to, for example, economic unity in West Africa. Even had such a commonwealth existed, how much could Ghana do within it to further these ends? Might it not have accomplished more by accepting the realities of geography, size, and power and by working toward the creation of an economically united West Africa untied to either franc, pound, or dollar? As it was, Ghana only acted as a magnet for opposition elements from other states in the region who came to Accra and by their presence severely limited Nkrumah's options.

Commitment to scientific socialism also disturbed soldiers and policemen who, in 1966, piled the concept, along with that of "continental union government" on top of the wreckage of the regime. They turned to the Americans to get the economy moving, and made peace with their neighbors, opening long-closed frontiers, while Nkrumah, from Conakry, berated them on both counts. Both these policies, because of the soil in which they were implanted, and the way they were cultivated, entangled him and his regime.

In the final analysis, Nkrumah's foreign policy might be compared with Juan Peron's in Argentina. In the terminology of Gustavo Lagos, it was a prestige-seeking policy to which the effective—economic and geopolitical—status of the nation did not entitle it.[46] Peron followed a policy of trying to tilt with the giants—which in the end meant with

[46] Gustavo Lagos, *International Stratification and Underdeveloped Countries*, Chapel Hill, 1963, p. 149.

windmills. He survived after 1953 by mortgaging his regime in Washington, and joining in a defense alliance with the United States. Nkrumah, like Peron, sought his country's economic independence and, had the Ghanaian coup not occurred, some equally humiliating solution would have to have been found for Ghana's economic crisis to avert intolerable hardship among the people. This was the more so as the great powers lost interest in black Africa. When the Americans found that they could intervene in Stanleyville and provoke only a verbal response from Moscow, they for the most part came to believe Africa was unimportant. The Soviets had also lost interest; by the end of 1965 they were not willing to underwrite Nkrumah's regime despite the opportunities that might be thought to have been open to them. The U.A.R., on the other hand, with its strategic location, was in a better position and, when its economy faltered, the great powers had an interest in preventing its collapse.

Any developing state will seek to raise its effective status in world politics. How can this best be done? Every elite group in Ghana saw the necessity of unity of some sort in West Africa in order that Ghana could increase its power and prestige and the economic strength of the region. Nkrumah thought he was the only true Ghanaian pan-Africanist, but his method for unity in West Africa failed. Consider the Ivory Coast. Robert Cornevin once said it had no foreign policy: "Its diplomats only seek to bring in investment and to increase its economic status. It waits for Nkrumah's downfall, by which time it will be in a position to begin constructing the wider economic links in West Africa that would give it the benefits of a larger market."[47] That is a foreign policy. When Houphouet visited the United States, he minimized the formalities and spent most of his time attracting investors in New York. As Professor Lagos said of the developing states (and as E. H. Carr has observed is ultimately true of any state) "the economic status of the nation is the basic component of real status."[48] By 1965 Houphouet's critics were beginning to grant him grudging acknowledgment of his apparent success, which was due less to the principles of economic development used than to his own astute statecraft.

Until 1960 Nkrumah spent more of his time trying to improve Ghana's economic status than in seeking to fulfill the mission of a historic movement. His prestige and the movement's success were greatest in this period. After 1960, his foreign policy was oriented toward the search for power; the chance to increase Ghana's status through domination of

[47] Interview: Robert Cornevin, 18 March 1965, Paris.
[48] Lagos, *International Stratification*, p. 198, and see E. H. Carr, *The Twenty Years' Crisis*, London, 1962, pp. 117-32.

its region, to be achieved through economic union, was lost. It is not suggested that pan-Africanism was a poor choice as the first principle in foreign policy. "Emotions and not intellect provide the dynamic force in history,"[49] and the emotional power of pan-Africanism could have been harnessed to the rational aims of Ghana as a state, particularly in West Africa. Houphouet had no fear of "continental union government," for he knew it was not an option: but he had much to fear from a coordinated Ghanaian drive to unite West Africa through economic links. These would have compensated for Ghana's small size, and could have driven a wedge through the most effective counter-force to a radical pan-Africanism in West Africa—the "French" system. Between 1957 and 1960, Nkrumah might have laid the basis for such West African economic and political cooperation. Instead, he broke the few elements of cooperation among the British colonies, partly because he could not believe that these could be used to further other than British ends, partly because he could accept no restraining forces.[50] The ties linking the French colonies together and with France were not wholly broken, however. This limited the degree of economic independence which these new states possessed, but it was, ironically, the presence of these links that was to be a major element in the isolation of Nkrumah's regime. Moreover, within a year of Nkrumah's downfall, Mali, once Ghana's partner in a union and beneficiary of Ghanaian largesse, had decided to return to the franc zone, the most important strengthening of the "French" system in several years.[51] At that same time, the bet Nkrumah had struck with Houphouet ten years before came due. It was won while Nkrumah was in refuge in Guinea, the country that had forced the Ivory Coast to seek political independence. But Guinea was destitute. The economic

49 J. Frankel, *The Making of Foreign Policy*, London, 1963, p. 170.

50 In the first half of 1968, two years after the coup, this action of Nkrumah's was one of the few that still reminded the world press of him. In April 1968, West African states met in Monrovia to attempt to form some sort of economic union in the region but their failure was almost total. The *Economist* reported that "The greatest barrier [to cooperation] is the absence of cohesion among the English speaking states of west Africa. . . . President Nkrumah's profoundest mark on the region was his wanton destruction of all significant links between Nigeria, Ghana, Sierra Leone, and Gambia." 11 May 1968, p. 37.

51 And two and a half years after Nkrumah's downfall, soldiers overthrew Modibo Keita and his regime. Like their fellow-officers in Accra, the new Malian leaders formed a "National Liberation Committee" and, so it appeared early in 1969, set out, in an imitative fashion, to perform the same tasks in their smaller arena as did the National Liberation Council in Accra. It seemed possible that Ghana's chances for influence as a "model" in Africa would be almost as great in its post-Nkrumah period as in the earlier period, given the frequency of military coups in the Africa of the late 1960's, and the obvious need for some state to demilitarize successfully, as Ghana was trying to do in 1969.

kingdom had proved to be more elusive and more important than the political.

The fact that Nkrumah did give many Africans "pride in their Africanness" might outweigh the almost complete failure in his statecraft and make less severe the judgment of him by future generations. President Nyerere, in his denunciation of Nkrumah at Cairo in 1964, thought perhaps Nkrumah anticipated this: "Some people are willing to use their very great talent to wreck any chance of unity on our continent as long as some stupid historian could record that they wanted African unity when nobody else actually did."[52] Historians are not always stupid, and those in the future will surely note that Nkrumah was not alone in wishing to see Africa united and free of external manipulation; those who do consider Nkrumah the greatest African of his period are hardly likely to have reached this conclusion from an analysis of his foreign policy. Perhaps it was in the nature of the Africa of this period, when events moved at so bewildering a speed and during which the continent itself was so much in the grip of other forces, that the history of these years could not be the biography of its leaders. Certainly this point eluded Nkrumah, whose greatest failing was his inability to see the limits of the influence of one man bound to one small state.

[52] Address of President Julius Nyerere to First Regular Conference of Heads of State, OAU, Cairo, 22 July 1964, quoted in BBC, IV, No. 1611.

APPENDICES AND INDEX

A Note on Sources

"All sources are suspect," A.J.P. Taylor wrote in the bibliography of *The Struggle for Mastery in Europe, 1848-1918*; how much more true in the study of a contemporary period. Ghana's foreign policy is partly of interest because it was controversial in the period studied, making it more important for the writer to confine himself, so far as possible, to the cautious use of what primary sources of material are available and to avoid using, so far as possible, the large amount of sometimes excellent but nonetheless secondary commentary that abounds in the literature. It would be misleading to include in this study a lengthy bibliography of those publicly available documents and books of which use was made (and which are footnoted) or which bear tangentially or directly on the subject; this book is not essentially based on this literature. For those wishing to pursue the subject matter further, adequate bibliographical essays exist.

Much of the material utilized in this study was compiled prior to the coup d'état that overthrew the regime of President Nkrumah in early 1966. It would be idle to deny, however, that the writer was a special beneficiary of the coup, as significant documentation was made available after and as a result of it, following some six months' of requests for such assistance. Restricted material to which access was gained before or after the coup falls into three categories.

1. Verbatim transcripts of meetings of the heads of state and foreign ministers of the Organisation of African Unity. These well illustrate Ghana's position in the cross fire of continental diplomacy which so much dominated the African scene in the 1963-1966 period. The several thousand pages of documentation involved have been placed on microfilm in the Rhodes House-Bodleian Library at Oxford, and also in the Hoover Institute at Stanford, where they will be made available to interested scholars in due course. The same holds for the 800-page records of the first Independent African States Conference, and certain material issued by the Secretariat of the Casablanca Conference.

2. Official Ghanaian documentation. In the fight for Flagstaff House on February 24, 1966 and in the ensuing days, much of the diplomatic correspondence of the Nkrumah regime was destroyed. Some material of interest remained in the Ministry of External Affairs, however, and the writer was granted access to some of this. No restriction or qualification was placed at any time as to what conclusions could be drawn from this material. Throughout this study, citations to this refer to the writer's files, labeled "CFA-" with page numbers, for the benefit of scholars who might be interested in pursuing issues in question.

441

3. Interviews. These constitute a principal and perhaps the most suspect source. In most cases it was possible to check assertions of fact made by those interviewed against official records, or against other interview sources. Diplomats at the Ghanaian ministry, in addition, were requested to make use of the official records in replying to questions. Otherwise unconfirmed assertions of fact are accepted without qualifications only from those whose other statements and assertions had been checked and found consistently accurate; it is a pleasure to record that a large number of diplomats and public servants may easily be placed in this category, and that few attempts appear to have been made to mislead the scholar. Wherever feasible sources have been identified, but in the majority of cases this was not possible without breaking commitments. As a result, all interview records have been numbered "CF-" with reference to private files, and will be available in due course to scholars that are interested, if there be any. All interviews that took place in Accra between February 24, 1966 and the close of that year are not dated; the date is given in all other cases.

No doubt many will find the method by which restricted sources have been cited in this study unsatisfactory. The alternative would, however, have been to follow a dangerous precedent which is being followed with increasing frequency: making no reference to source whatsoever when confidential materials are used. In a day when more and more social scientists work with or advise governments and can gain access to data which is unavailable to others, including interviews, it would seem incumbent on the scholar to be explicit in indicating that a source does exist for a point of quotation. The reader may otherwise be led to believe that the point made comes under the heading of "general knowledge," that the citation does not merit identification, or, worse, that the writer is justifiably elliptical or inexplicit because of his "inside" knowledge.

Beyond these restricted materials, several well-informed diplomats and institutional representatives made available to the writer their own official records and files, with the definite understanding that no reference would be made to these; therefore they have been used only as a check on material that could be quoted or otherwise identified. A collection of miscellaneous and scarce publications by various agencies, bureaus, and offices in Ghana used in the study have been placed in the Edward Ginn Library of The Fletcher School of Law and Diplomacy, Medford, Massachusetts. These include circulars and pamphlets issued by George Padmore's office, the AAPC, the Bureau of African Affairs, the Ministry of Information, and the President's office.

Available primary material used in this study include the very sophisticated publications of the Ghanaian government; the annual economic surveys, auditor general's reports, and estimates. In addition, parliamentary debates and white papers of the government have been used, as noted in the text.

Recourse to the press as a source of factual information has been made only when unavoidable. The reading of (and drawing upon) a newspaper over a given period of time as a social document is most valuable, and much time was expended reading the *Evening News, Ashanti Pioneer, Ghanaian Times, Spark,* and other Ghanaian periodicals. Often it was possible to trace official statements to the government's Press Releases (labeled "P.R." in the footnotes), kindly made available by the Ministry of Information. In addition, the following papers have been used, for the entire period under study, as general sources: *The Times, Le Monde, The New York Times, The West African Pilot* (Lagos), *Togo-Presse* (Lomé), *Hsinhua* (Peking), *L'Essor* (Bamako), *La Bourse Egyptienne* (Cairo), *Carrefour Africaine* (Ouagadougou), *Daily Service* (Lagos), *Fraternité* (Abidjan-weekly), and the *Observer* and *Sunday Times* of London. Special note should be made of *West Africa,* published weekly in London, and invaluable to students of any discipline studying countries of ex-British West Africa.

Finally, several important books and articles on which I drew for background material or data must be mentioned. The definitive study of Ghanaian politics is Dennis Austin's *Politics in Ghana, 1946-1960* (London, 1964). Also enormously helpful were the following: David Apter, *Ghana in Transition* (New York, 1963); J. D. Esseks, "Economic Independence in a New African State," Ph.D. dissertation (Harvard University, 1967); Catherine Hoskyns, *The Congo Since Independence* (London, 1965); Thomas Hovet, Jr., *Africa in the United Nations* (London, 1963); G. H. Jansen, *Afro Asia and Non-Alignment* (London, 1967); Colin Legum, *Pan-Africanism* (London, 1965); Colin Legum, "Socialism in Ghana: A Political Interpretation," in Robert Friedland and Carl Rosberg, *African Socialism* (London, 1964); Ali Mazrui, *Towards a Pax Africana* (London, 1967); Ruth Schacter Morgenthau, *Political Parties in French-Speaking West Africa* (London, 1964); Kwame Nkrumah, *Challenge of the Congo* (London, 1967); George Padmore, *Pan-Africanism or Communism? The Coming Struggle for Africa* (London, 1956); Claude Welch, *Dream of Unity* (Cornell, 1966); I. William Zartman, *International Relations in the New Africa* (New York 1966).

APPENDIX B

Organization of the Ministry of Foreign Affairs, 1961–1966

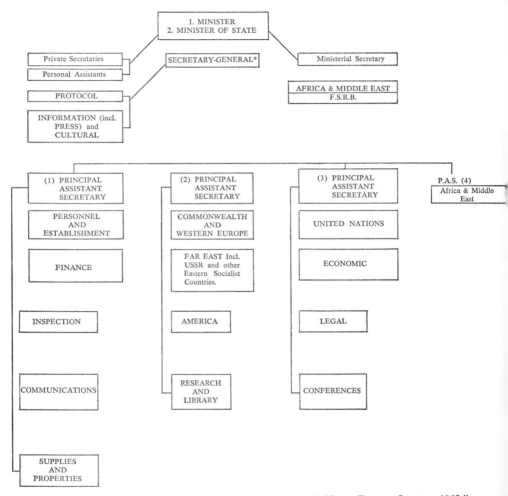

Source: *Ministry of Foreign Affairs*, "Conference of Ghana Envoys, January 1962."

* The office of Secretary-General existed only briefly; by late 1961 it was renamed "Principal Secretary," after Michael Dei-Anang moved to Flagstaff House.

APPENDIX C

PART I: GHANA'S DIPLOMATIC RELATIONS AND NETWORK

States with diplomatic relations with Ghana	Status of Ghana's mission: E=embassy; H.C.=high commission; L=legation; CH.=charge d'affaires; Date of estab. of dip. rel. (DR); or, date apptd. 1st Gh'n envoy (E.A.); or, date of agrément for 1st Gh'n envoy (ag), or, approx. date of opening of Gh'n mission (O); or, date of presentation of credentials of 1st Gh'n envoy (PC)	Status of 2nd party's mission in Gh'n; or, Date apptd. 1st envoy to Gh'n (E.A.); or, Date of agrément of 1st envoy to Gh'n (ag); Date of presentation of credentials of 1st envoy to Gh'n	Feb. 1966 dip. personnel (+ envoy) in 2nd party's mission	Jan. 1964 A grade Gh'n officers in mission, professional diplomats (— envoy)	B—exec. grade personnel in Gh'n mission, + ed. press attachés	C—clerical grade personnel in Gh'n mission	Feb. 1966 Gh'n envoy: political appointment (P); career officer (C)	Diplomatic dislocations
Albania	E; DR Jan. 62	E; 62	3	—	1	1	P	Gh'n emb. closed 1966
Algeria	de facto recog., 7/11/59; de jure recog., 1/61; 1962-O	E; 4/5/60-PC	5	—(2)[5]	2	1	P	Gh'n emb. closed 1966
Belgium	E; 1965-O (amb. resident in The Hague)	E; 11/9/59-ag; 1/13/60-PC	2	—(3)[5]	—	—	P	
Brazil	E; 1962-O	Legation; 1961-O; E; 1960-O	3	1	1	1	P	Gh'n breaks DR 12/6/60; re-est., 1962
Bulgaria	E; 1/62-O	E; 6/18/61	3	—	1	1	P	Gh'n emb. closed 1966
Cameroun	E; 12/28/65-PC	E; 1960-O		—	—	—	P	Gh'n emb. closed 1966
Canada	HC; 1957-DR; 1/61-PC	HC; 1957-EA	5	1	1	1	C	
Ceylon	HC; 1/24/61-ag	HC; 1961-O	2	—	—	—	P	
Congo-Braz.	E; 1965-O	—	—	NA	NA	NA	P	Gh'n emb. closed 1966
Congo-Kinshasa (Léopoldville)	E; 7/1/60; 7/15/60-PC	—(Stanleyville régime: apptd. nonresident amb., 4/61)	—	1(2)[5]	—	1	P	Gh'n emb. closed 1966; Gh'n recog. of Stanleyville régime, 15/2/61; reversion to Léo, 9/61
China	E; 7/6/60-DR; 10/22/60-ag	E; 8/8/60-ag	9	1	2	2	P	Gh'n emb. closed 1966
Cuba	E; 60-O; nonresident amb.	E; 1/5/60-O	5	1	1	—	P	Gh'n emb. closed 1966
Czechoslovakia	E; 1/62-O	E; 3/18/60-EA;	9	—	1	1	P	
Dahomey	E; 6/20/62-EA (amb.)	E; 1961-O		NA(1)[5]	2	1	P[1]	
Denmark	E; 66-O	E; 1961		—(1)[5]	NA	NA	(C)[1]	
Ethiopia	E; 6/3/59-ag	E; 4/10/59-PC		—(1)[5]	2	1	C(p)[1]	
France	E; 57-O (amb. resident in U.K.; 1959-res. in Paris)	E; 3/57-O	12	4(3)[5]	3	1	P(c)[1]	

States with diplomatic relations with Ghana	Status of Ghana's mission: E=embassy; H.C.=high commission; L=legation; CH.=charge d'affaires; Date of estab. of dip. rel. (DR); or, date apptd. 1st Gh'n envoy (E.A.); or, date of agrément for 1st Gh'n envoy (ag), or, approx. date of opening of Gh'n mission (O); or, date of presentation of credentials of 1st Gh'n envoy (PC)	Status of 2nd party's mission in Gh'n; or, Date apptd. 1st envoy to Gh'n (E.A.); or, Date of agrément of 1st envoy to Gh'n (ag); or, Date of presentation of credentials of 1st envoy to Gh'n	Feb. 1966 dip. personnel (+ envoy) in 2nd party's mission	Jan. 1964 A grade Gh'n officers in mission, professional diplomats (— envoy)	B—exec. grade personnel in Gh'n mission, + ed. press attachés	C—clerical grade personnel in Gh'n mission	Feb. 1966 Gh'n envoy: political appointment (P); career officer (C)	Diplomatic dislocations
Germany, Demo. Rep.	E; 59-O	Trade Commission	8	1(3)[5]	3	1	P	Trade Commission closed 1966
Germany, Fed. Rep.	Resident ministry, 1/59—5/63	E; 58-O	—		2	1	C[2]	DR broken, 2/66
Guinea	Emb—5/63-66	Res. ministry, 59-63					P	Gh'n emb. closed 1966
Hungary	E; 1/8/62-EA	E; 11/24/61-EA	4	1	1	1	C(p)	
India	HC; 1957-O	HC; 1957-O	5		1	1		
Indonesia		DR—3/18/61	4				P	
Iraq		E; 4/21/60-EA	2	1	2	1	P	
Israel	E; 1958-O	E; 1957-O[3]	4	1(3)[5]	1	1	—(P)	
Italy	E; 1961-O	E; 1959-60-O	3	2				
Ivory Coast	E; 9/60-DR; 3/16/61-PC	E; 1961-O	3					
Japan	E; 1/21/60-PC	E; 7/10/59-PC (chargé)	5	1(2)[5]	2	1	P	
Kenya	HC; 12/12/63-O	L; 5/26/59-O	2	NA(2)[5]	NA	NA	P	
Lebanon	E; 1966-O	E; 7/21/60-PC	2	—(1)[5]				
Liberia	E; 1957-O	E; 3/14/57-O	4	1(2)[5]	1	1	P	
Libya	E-CH; 2/1/60-ag		3	—(1)[5]	3	1	P	
Mali	Resident ministry—12/60	Resident ministry—12/60	3	—(1)[5]	2	1	C	
Mexico	E; 1964-O	E; 1964-O	4					
Morocco	E; 8/3/61-EA	E; 2/3/61-ag.	5	1	NA	NA	P	Gh'n emb. closed 1966
Netherlands	E; 1965-O	E; 1/20/59-PC	2	NA(1)[5]	2	1	P	
Niger	E-CH; 62-O	E; 61-O	10		3	1		Gh'n emb. closed 1966
Nigeria	Commission; 59-O; HC; 10/1/60-O	Commission; 4/20/59-ag.; HC; 10/1/60	2	2			(c)P	
Pakistan	HC; 3/23/62	HC; 3/23/62	2	1	2	1	C	
Poland	E; 5/18/62-EA	E; 12/31/59-EA	7		1	1	P	
Philippines		E; 63-O. No chancery, nonres. amb.	1					Gh'n emb. closed 1966

Table of Ghanaian and foreign diplomatic representation (continued)

Country	Ghana's representation	Partner's representation					Term	Remarks
Rumania	E; 62-O	E; 62-O	4	—	2	1	C	Gh'n emb. closed 1966
Rwanda	E; 65-O	—	—	NA	NA	NA	P	
Saudi Arabia	—	E-CH; 3/30/60-DR; E; 1/9/61-ag.	3	1(2)⁵	2	1		
Senegal	E-CH; 4/21/61; E-62-O⁵	E; 6/24/59-ag.	3	—(2)⁵	2	1	P	
Sierra Leone	Commission: 60-O; HC; 4/27/61-O	HC; 61-O	2	—(2)⁵	—	1	P	Gh'n HC status lowered 1966
Somalia	—	—		—	—	—	P	Closed 1966
Sudan	E; 60-O; E; 7/27/61-EA	E; 60-O	3	—	1	1	P	
Sweden	—	E; no chancery, amb. resident in Monrovia	3	—	—	—	P	Closed 1966
Switzerland	E; 65-O amb.: also in Geneva	E; 62-O	3	NA	NA	NA		
Tanzania	HC; 62-O	E; 62-O	—	—(2)⁵	1	1	C	Gh'n HC status lowered 1966
Togo	E; 1/21/63-DR 9/2/63-Emb. opened 9/64-PC	E; 63-O, PC	4	—(1)⁵	1	1	P	
Tunisia	E; 1/1/5/60-EA	E; 1960-O	—	1	2	1	P(c)	Tu. emb. closed 1964
Turkey	E; no chancery-66 (amb. res. in Rome)	E	3	—	—	—	P	
Uganda	HC; 63-O	HC; 64-O	3	1	2	1	P	Gh'n HC status lowered 1966
USSR	E; 1/14/59-DR; 1/7/60-EA	E; 4/10/59-ag.	10	2(3)⁵	3	1	P	
UAR	E; 5/9/58-PC	E; 58-O	7	1(2)⁵	—	1	P	
United Kingdom	HC; 3/6/57	HC; 3/6/57	16	4(7)⁵	26	5	P	DR broken by Gh'n, 12/16/65 re-est, 3/66
United Nations New York	Perm. mission, 9/57-O		26	5	3	1	C	
Geneva	Perm. 59-O		6	1(4)⁵	1	1	C	
USA	E; 3/6/57	E; 3/6/57³	2	4	5	2	P	
Upper Volta	E; 6/12/61-PC	E; 61-O	—	—	2	1	P	
Vietnam, Demo. Rep.	3/65-DR	E-CH; 11-6-65-PC	—	—	—	—		
Yugoslavia	E; 3/24/59-DR; 1/7/60-EA	E; 3/24/59-charge apptd.; 8/15/60-EA; 65-O	3	—	2	1	P	
Zambia	NA		NA	NA	NA	NA	NA	
African Affairs Secretariat, 1/64			NA	11(4)	23	16		
Ministry of Foreign Affairs, 1/64				35	133	19		

¹ Parenthesis indicates presence of such a representative at some time other than February 1966.

² "B" grade career officer, appointed during the period of strained relations 1963-66, when Nkrumah wished the mission kept at a low status.

³ Indicates presence of a consulate prior to Ghana's independence.

⁴ Although the Ghana-Guinea-Mali Union was dissolved in May 1963, Ghana and Mali continued to entitle their representatives to their former partner's capital as "Resident Minister," the term used during the period the union existed.

⁵ Numbers in parenthesis in this column indicate the number of "A" personnel as of October 1966, after the coup d'état, if there was any shift in the number.

APPENDIX C

Part II: The Components of Ghanaian Statecraft: A Functional Chart

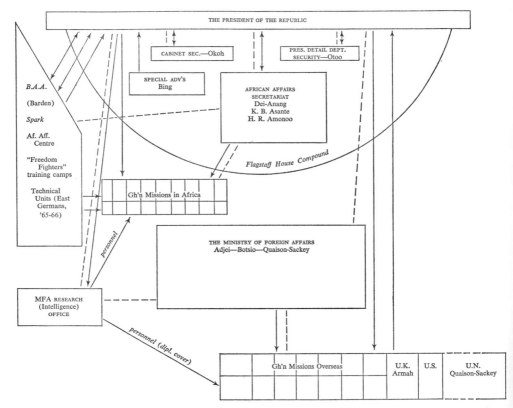

Distance of boxes from President denotes relative influence in policy formulation
Size of boxes denotes size and scope of office's activity vis-à-vis foreign policy
Broken lines indicate institutional channels of authority
Solid lines indicate effective power flows: arrows in direction of the President denote
  influence on Nkrumah; arrow in direction of component indicates President's ability
  to use it as effective instrument of his policies.

448

APPENDIX D

PART I: ANNUAL BUDGETARY ESTIMATES

	MEA-MFA	Af. Aff. Sec.	Min. of Defence	Contingency Fund	B.A.A.[6]	Intell./Research
57-58	$1,530,000+		[included in MEA 57-58]			
58-59	$3,420,000+		$ 9,350,000	[$280,000]+	[$33,000]+	[$140,000]+
59-60	$4,780,000+		$11,300,000	[$280,000]+	$42,500[1]	[$140,000]+
60-61	$5,300,000+		$12,600,000	[$518,000]+	$57,800[1]	
61-62[2]	$6,480,000+	$1,320,000*	$42,000,000	$1,400,000[1]	[$215,000]*	
62-63	$5,980,000	$3,060,000*	$40,600,000	$3,060,000[1]	[$448,000]*	
63-64	$6,780,000+	$2,880,000*	$39,700,000	$4,200,000[1]	[$307,000]*	[$568,000]+
65[3]	$5,040,000	$3,550,000*	$47,000,000	$2,800,000[1]	[$307,000]*[5]	$5,180,000[4]

SOURCE: Statistics are taken from *The Annual Estimates*, Government Printer, Accra. Bracketed figures are included in the budget of the heading denoted by a similar mark (* or +). Conversion to dollars is made at the then official rate of £G1=$2.80, and rounded to the nearest thousand. Figures include supplementary estimates but, after 1961, these were passed with such frequency that it is not clear if all appropriations are included, making the figures given conservative in all probability. Information published in *Ghana*, "Nkrumah's Subversion in Africa," 1966, suggest that figures given for the Bureau of African Affairs are very conservative, but it is likely that additional moneys indicated in that publication are in fact from the presidential contingency fund.

[1] Budgeted under the President's Office account. African Affairs Secretariat Funds also are in this account but under the larger heading of "The President," and, unlike those in the contingency fund, were audited.

[2] This includes supplements for three extra months, due to a change in the fiscal year.

[3] In 1965 the fiscal year was made to coincide with the calendar year.

[4] $568,000 of this sum is for the MEA Research Office and is included in the MEA budget given. The remainder is for presidential "special services."

[5] "Nkrumah's subversion in Africa," page 34, indicates that $580,000 (C497,210) was budgeted for the "Special African Service" for 1966, implying that this East German established intelligence-adjunct of the BAA spent considerable sums in 1965.

[6] Includes appropriations for the African Affairs Centre.

APPENDIX D

PART II: DIRECTION OF GENERAL TRADE, 1961–1965

	1961				1962				1963			
	Imports C'000	%	Exports C'000	%	Imports C'000	%	Exports C'000	%	Imports C'000	%	Exports C'000	%
Sterling Area	140,143	41.0	90,646	32.8	108,869	38.8	97,157	35.2	119,870	38.8	83,342	31.9
Of which United Kingdom	124,358	36.3	79,366	28.7	96,809	34.6	86,815	31.5	102,802	32.8	73,663	28.2
Of which African Countries	2,150	0.6	3,574	1.3	1,486	0.5	2,851	1.0	6,938	2.2	1,903	0.7
European Economic Community	74,362	21.7	88,075	31.9	62,611	22.3	77,213	28.0	79,272	25.3	74,659	28.6
Dollar Area	37,690	11.0	68,141	24.7	31,776	11.3	54,043	19.6	27,425	8.8	44,107	16.9
Centrally Planned Economies (U.S.S.R., China and other Countries of Eastern Europe)	18,737	5.4	13,128	4.7	20,890	7.5	24,502	8.9	34,318	11.0	35,798	13.7
African Countries excluding those in Sterling Area	23,038	6.7	4,217	1.5	17,285	6.2	6,881	2.5	14,234	4.5	2,887	1.1
Japan	26,494	7.7	3,900	1.4	18,578	6.6	5,916	2.1	19,327	6.2	8,880	3.4
Other	17,366	5.1	7,910	2.9	17,467	6.3	10,366	3.7	15,266	4.9	11,582	4.4
Parcel Post	4,963	1.4	259	0.1	2,712	1.0	10	0.0	3,283	1.0	5	0.0
Total	342,792	100.0	276,324	100.0	280,188	100.0	276,086	100.0	312,998	100.0	261,262	100.0

	1964				1965			
	Imports C'000	%	Exports C'000	%	Imports C'000	%	Exports C'000	%
Sterling Area	103,402	35.4	72,535	26.4	110,810	28.9	64,768	23.8
Of which United Kingdom	80,059	27.4	63,420	23.1	99,125	25.8	56,619	20.8
Of which African Countries	10,529	3.6	1,958	0.7	5,201	1.6	2,706	1.0
European Economic Community	67,109	23.0	80,897	29.4	82,171	21.4	75,709	27.8
Dollar Area	33,811	11.6	62,923	22.9	40,510	10.5	50,529	18.6
Centrally Planned Economies (U.S.S.R., China and other Countries of Eastern Europe)	46,318	15.8	32,530	11.8	100,990	26.3	57,917	21.3
African Countries excluding those in Sterling Area	16,783	5.8	3,593	1.3	10,669	2.8	2,526	0.9
Japan	15,641	5.4	9,806	3.5	16,626	4.3	6,270	2.3
Other	7,049	2.4	12,850	4.7	20,933	5.4	14,537	5.3
Parcel Post	1,752	0.6	2	0.0	1,352	0.4	3	0.0
Total	291,864	100.0	275,136	100.0	384,061	100.0	272,259	100.0

C1.00=$1.16 at contemporary valuation.

INDEX

service training, 18-20; attitude toward pan-Africanism, 20; reaction to Quaison-Sackey's appointment, 103-04; stabilizing effect of foreign service, 197; and CPP membership, 254

France: and AAPC, 62-63; relations with Guinea, 71; relations with Ghana, 87, 98-99; atomic testing in Sahara, 88, 91, 98-99, 237; and UAM, 330n

freedom fighters conference, 222, 226-27

Freitas, Paulin, 234

Freitas, de, Sir Geoffrey, 314n, 389

"Ga Shifimo Kpee" movement, 30

Garba-Jahumba, I. M., 31, 204

Gardiner, Robert, 56, 141; resentment of Padmore, 23; on Gen. Alexander, 128

Garrison, Lloyd, 301

Garvey, Marcus, 6, 12, 20

Gbedemah, Komla, 53, 55, 173, 419; organizes CPP victory, 3; personal background of, 17; defense of Ghana-Guinea Union, 69-70; negotiates with Guinea, 76-77; on economic situation 1961, 167; dismissed, 185; and VRP, 191; on foreign investment, 196; on loans to African states, 202; and Togo, 308

German question, 176

Germany, Democratic Republic: subversion aid, 386; relations with Ghana, 402-03

Germany, Federal Republic: relations with Ghana, 402-03

Ghana: popular attitudes, 16-17; foreign nationals in, 17; foreign investment, 20; expatriates, 20-23; independence celebrations, 28; Ga Standfast Association, 30; anniversary celebration, 31; relations with Arab states, 46-51; opposition party in, opposes Nkrumah on Arab policy, 50; preventive detention act (PDA), 54; intelligence office first established, 59; aid to liberation movements, 66-67; growth of diplomatic network and embassies, 105-06; writing Constitution of, 1960, 111-12; impact of Congo crisis, 117; 1961 power struggle, 162-63, 167; foreign investment, 163; 1961 strike, 182, 184-85; 1962 domestic political developments, 194-97; refugees in Togo, 234; domestic policy in, effect on foreign investment, 258; "7-year plan," 272; UN voting, 289-90; 1963-64 domestic politics, 290; plebiscite, 291-92; strategic location, 429. *See also* domestic politics

Ghana-Congo Union, 123, 125-26, 140

Ghana-Guinea Union, 67-73; and African Group, 41; declaration of, 57; reactions in Ghana to, 69-70; "Conakry Declaration," 72; begins to fail, 75-77; currency zone, 76-77; ideological impact of, 77; attitudes to, in West, 94

Ghana-Guinea-Mali Union, formation, 150-52, 160; disagreements on Congo, 151, 154; attitude of diplomats toward, 152; 1st quarterly meeting, 202; "Union of African States" declared, 203; possibility of expansion, 204; Bamako meeting, 207; Ghana's views of, 1962, 260; effect of Kulungugu, 268; dissolution, 329

Gizenga, Antoine, 127, 152

Gold Coast: federal vs. unitary issue, 5; Committee on Defence and External Affairs, 18, 19

Grunitzky, Nicholas, 81; opposes Olympio, 81; becomes pres. of Togo, 313

Guevara, Che, visit to Accra, 407

Guinea: independence, 41; relations with France, 71; ideological impact on Ghana, 72, 108; and Ghana-Congo Union, 125; and Lumumba, 135; aid to Congo, 137; relations with Soviet Union, 185, 199; and Monrovia Group, 199; becomes less radical, 199; loans from Ghana, 202-03; supports Ghana in OAU, 342, 351

Hammarskjold, Dag, 130-44 passim; helps Togo, 85-86; Soviet transport planes in Congo crisis, 132; compares Congo crisis to Lebanese, 136; and possibility of Ghanaian troop withdrawal, 153; "preventive diplomacy," 158-59

Harlley, John, 291

Harriman, Averell, 292; 1964 mission to Ghana, 303

Harriman, Leslie, 239, 242

Herter, Christian, 166

Heymann, Charles, 267

High Command, Joint African, 156, 201, 237, 337-40, 354; discussion of, 49, 58; proposed by Gen. Alexander, 137; Nkrumah formally proposes, 149-50; and Casablanca Group, 208, 218-19; 1963-64, 337; Ghanaian campaign for, 337-40

Hoskyns, Catherine, 138, 143, 158; on Kasavubu-Lumumba reconciliation, 142

Houphouet-Boigny, Dr. Félix, 244-45, 268, 431; early attitude toward independence, 12; bet with Nkrumah, 12-13;

Nye, Joseph, 333
Nyerere, Julius, 31, 338, 391, 416; and
Ghana's relations with Israel, 46; and
Commonwealth, 172; opposes Nkrumah
on E. African federation, 331; reaction
to Nkrumah's Cairo speech, 352-53, 436-
37
Nylander, C. T., 254

Obote, Milton, 386; supports Nkrumah,
322, 324, 331
O'Brien, Conor Cruise, 395
Odinga, Oginga, 331n
Okoh, Enoch, 153, 199, 288, 294
Olympio, Sylvanus, 81-87; testifies at UN,
10; VRP, 192; discussions with Touré,
229-30; attitude toward Nkrumah, 230;
Nkrumah's attempts to overthrow, 232-
33; refuses to go to Accra, 236-37;
encourages Ghana's refugees, 309; anti-
Ghana diplomacy, 309; murder of, 311
Organisation des Nations Unies au Congo
(ONUC), see United Nations
Organisation of African Unity (OAU),
16, 322-56 passim; IAS precedents, 38;
Addis Ababa summit, preparation for,
318-20; provisional secretariat, 323-27;
Dakar foreign ministers conf., 325-27;
liberation committee, 327-29; used
against Ghana, 336; defence commission, 337; 1964 Dar-es-Salaam extraordinary conf., 338; 1964 Lagos conf.,
340-43; "executive committee," 342;
"diplomatic basis," 343; Cairo summit
conf., 350-56; Ghana's financial contribution to, 354; 1964 special Congo
session, 357; Accra chosen for summit,
358; commissions, 359; question of
Accra conf., 1965, 376-81; 1965 Lagos
conf., 377-82; Accra conf., countries
not in attendance, 384; 1965 Accra
summit conf., 385; 1965 extraordinary
conf., Addis, 393. See also Liberation
Committee
Organisation of African Unity (OAU)
Charter, Ghana's response, 10, 321;
Nkrumah's signing, 320-23
Organisation Commun d'Afrique et Malgache (OCAM), 369-72; Nouakshott
conf., 369; Ghana's diplomacy against,
371-72; campaign against Nkrumah,
375; Abidjan conf., 1965, 377
"The Osagyefo," see Nkrumah
Osman, Aden Abdulla, visit to Ghana,
252
Otoo, Eric, 425; Congo coordinating
com., 124

Otu, Michael, 124

Padmore, George, 20, 39; organizes Manchester conf., 6; continental vs. regional
links, 8; presses socialism in Ghana,
14; criticized by duBois, 14n; attitude
toward USSR, 22-23; accepts Ghana's
position, 29; visits Cairo, 33; appoints
Indian for IAS, 34; dislike of Nasser,
47; opposes UAR at AAPC, 51; and
AAPC, 58-66, 90; and regionalism, 60;
opposes France, 87; death of, 106-07;
and Congo, 119
PAFMESCA, 331
Paga Agreement, 205-07, 248-49; failure
of, 207; effect on Niger, 246; renegotiated in Tenkodogo, 248; effect of
Kulungugu on, 268
Paintsil, Sylvester, 64, 65
Pakistan: relations with Ghana, 280-83
Palestine: IAS debate on, 37
pan-African Conferences. See Manchester
Conference; Independent African States,
Conferences of; All-African Peoples
Conference; Sanniquellie Conference;
"Positive Action" Conference; Organisation of African Unity
pan-Africanism, background of, xvii, 5-6;
role of Arab states, 8; regionalism vs.
continentalism, 7-9, 60-61, 109, 329-33,
419-21; need for administrative machinery, 37-39, 93-94, 109; economic vs.
political priorities, 90, 207, 211, 349,
356, 382, 436; importance of state sovereignty works against Nkrumah's plans,
210, 212, 431; "continental union government" (CUG), 317, 347, 358, 361,
386; strategy for CUG, 336; CUG discussed at OAU meetings, 322, 341-43,
350-56, 385, 430; "finest moment of,"
323; "African Unity" compared to Arab
unity, 429; importance of Nigeria toward, 80, 243-44
pan-Africanism—Nkrumah's views on, 7-
9; re-names movement, 58; 1965 concessions, 65; clashes with Tubman, 73-
75; intensifies the programme, 199; and
preservation of state sovereignty, 210;
pre-Addis 1963 formulations, 308, 316-
17, 319; intellectual confusion on, 419-
21
Peron, Juan, 434-35
Poku, Bediaku, 51n, 162, 249n, 332; and
Israel, 285
Poland: 102; nature of ties with Ghana,
277

459